The Teen Reader's Advisor

RoseMary Honnold

Neal-Schuman Publishers, Inc.

New York   London

Published by Neal-Schuman Publishers, Inc.
100 William St., Suite 2004
New York, NY 10038

Copyright © 2006 Neal-Schuman Publishers

Printed and bound in the United States of America.

The paper used in this publication meets the minimum requirements of American National Standard for Information Sciences – Permanence of Paper for Printed Library Materials, ANSI Z39.48-1992.

Library of Congress Cataloging-in-Publication Data

Honnold, RoseMary, 1954-
    The teen reader's advisor / by RoseMary Honnold.
        p. cm. — (Teens @ the library series)
    Includes bibliographical references and indexes.
    ISBN 1-55570-551-0 (alk. paper)
  1. Teenagers—Books and reading—United States. 2. Young adults' libraries—Book lists. 3. Young adult literature—Bibliography. 4. Libraries and teenagers. I. Title. II. Series.
  Z1037.H75 2006
  028.5'5—dc22

                                             2006012640

I dedicate *The Teen Reader's Advisor* to all librarians who serve teens, for taking on the challenging and rewarding work of connecting teens and books.

CONTENTS

Part II: The Subject and Genre Booklists: A to Z

SERIES EDITOR'S FOREWORD

Do you ever experience a state I call "RA brain freeze"?

I have read and worked extensively in the area of young adult literature for my entire professional career, which now spans nearly thirty years—first as a reading teacher and for the last two decades as a junior high school librarian. Because of this, the teachers in my school think of me as being "the book guy."

And certainly, one of the things I enjoy most about my job is trying to help each student find the right book to read at the right time. Sometimes students come with their teacher as a class, and then I can spend the entire period—or day—helping one student after another find a great book to check out. More often there may be a handful of readers who drift in and out of the library during a class period, several of whom might ask me for help in finding a book they want, a book they can't find, or—here's the fun part—a book I know we've got but that they don't know exists! They may say something very general, such as, "I need an exciting book to read," or something more specific, such as, "I like to read mysteries" or "the last good book I read was . . . " or "do you have something like . . . " and it's up to me to come up with some recommendations that will, I hope, be just what they want. And then there are the teachers—and students—who enjoy challenging me by coming up with pretty specific requests, such as (true example!), "I want a science fiction book about a guy with lots of action, some made-up monsters, and fighting, and a little romance."

What I hate is when that brain freeze strikes. I know I've read a book that is just what the student wants, just what's needed, but I can't quite remember what it is. Sure, I can go to the catalog and try searching by various key words and probably come up with something useful. But from now on I'm also going to have *The Teen Reader's Advisor* on the counter, ready to unfreeze my brain when it refuses to connect. Respected and experienced YA Services Coordinator RoseMary Honnold provides an introduction to the hows, whys, and wherefores of teen reader's advisory in the first five chapters, advice that will certainly be helpful to anyone new to teen services or with little or no professional training in it. But it will be equally useful to those of us who spend our lives in these teen trenches by reminding us of the guiding principles that we may overlook while caught up in day-to-day routine. Personally, I have had no trouble finding important ideas in each chapter that I want to discuss and reinforce with my staff, ideas that direct all of us toward providing improved service to our teen readers. And you won't want to miss Chapter 4, a summary of the most important awards given for young adult titles, which can help you keep up on the best new books each publishing year.

But beyond that, the best news for most readers of this outstanding new book will be Chapters 6 through 23, where Honnold has organized lists of recommended books for teens by genre. Every person who provides reader advisory service to teens will want to refer to these incredible lists! The number of entries and the diverse reading interests they reflect is large; the sub-genres listed in each chapter are so numerous as to be almost daunting. And then, to have lists of ten recommended books within each of these sub-genres, each annotated to give you an idea of it's appeal for specific kinds of readers, is simply quite remarkable. Read *The Teen Reader Advisor*, examine the lists, peruse the annotations, and I think you'll agree with me that this is a monumental work that is nevertheless reader-friendly and practical, with just the kind and amount of information about each book that you'll need and use to provide exemplary reader's advisory to your teen customers.

Oh, and the book I recommended for that science-fiction-adventure-romance reader? Robert Heinlein's *Glory Road*.

What would *you* recommend?

Joel Shoemaker
Teens@the Library Series Editor

PREFACE

The truism that every reader has his or her book and every book its reader is easier said than done for librarians serving teens. Even when young adults are forthcoming about their reading interests, the range of materials they find compelling can be daunting. So many factors influence their choices—parents, the media, school, friends, and so on—that untangling the forces at play for a given reader at a given time is often a formidable task.

Complicating matters is the complex world of YA literature, constituted as it is by a dizzying array of highly diverse characters, titles, series, and genres. In an ideal world, librarians would be able to read every book they are called upon to recommend, but the simple fact is that there is never enough time. None of us have the freedom to read every graphic novel, fantasy series, historical fiction, or vampire classic, let alone the countless other genres, sub-genres, and sub-sub-genres that populate YA shelves.

I developed *The Teen Reader's Advisor* to help librarians make sense of the complexity, confusion, and difficulty inherent in serving teen reading interests and understanding teen literature. This resource brings together some of the most frequent topics requested by members of this audience and offers multiple titles to recommend. You can use this guide as a ready reference, a collection development tool, or as a source for building your personal knowledge of teen literature.

How to Use this Book

Part I, "YA RA Suggestions For Success," contains five chapters that describe the qualities of an effective practitioner, providing tools you can use to engage in this work with confidence. Chapter 1, "Practice a 'YA Attitude' Toward Teens," offers ten tips for making yourself available to teen readers. Chapter 2, "Develop Useful Teen Reader's Advisory Practices," offers the best ideas for making books available to readers. Chapter 3, "Explore the Young Adult Literature Scene," investigates current trends, core authors, school connections, and more. Chapter 4, "Key Book Honors for YA Literature," lists some of the highest awards in YA literature and the criteria required to win them.

Chapter 5, "Recommended YA RA Resources," outlines the key techniques and resources an effective reader's advisor should employ to build skills and knowledge.

Finally, Part II, "The Subject and Genre Booklists: A to Z," features more than 1900 individual annotated book titles, organized so you can easily locate the ones you need. These titles are broken down into eighteen chapters focused on broad genres or themes. Each chapter contains seven to fifteen lists of narrower sub-genres or topics, and each of which contains multiple titles. Given that these lists span more than 180 subjects, you are sure to find numerous texts to meet the needs of any reader.

For example, Chapter 9, "Fantasy," is divided into a dozen sections of narrower topics, ranging from dragons to gaming to magic realism to wizards; these are designed to help you pinpoint specific needs. Chapter 16 is a multicultural collection arranged by setting the characters' ethnicity, so if readers require a book about Africa to help fulfill a school assignment, you will find a list of titles at your fingertips under "Africa as a Setting." On the other hand, if you need a list of titles with African American characters to create a display for Black History Month, there is another section to help you. Similar formulations are employed throughout all of the chapters in Part II, offering practical access to a remarkably varied array of materials. The resultant range and multitiered organization should make it easy to find texts that will match any reader interest, however specific the request or vague the query.

If you want to dive in and start using this guide for RA, I recommend that you first scan the chapter headings in Part II of the table of contents. These will give you a sense of the range of alphabetically arranged subjects and genres covered. When you find an appealing subject or genre, read over the following list of topics to determine which comes closest to your interest, and turn to that page. Each section includes at least ten annotated book titles to review and recommend.

Later, if you want to pinpoint a specific title or author, there are also extensive author and title indexes at the end of the book.

The annotations for every title in every list offers specific clues to help you determine whether a given book is right for a particular circumstance or reader. All entries provide a short plot summary along with details of the narrative's setting and the sex and age of the main character, crucial information for library patrons hoping to find stories with which they can identify; other points of interest are also noted. The letters CC accompanying a title indicate that it is included in *A Core Collection for Young Adults* by Patrick Jones, Patricia Taylor, and Kristen Edwards. Potentially objectionable language, sexual content, or violence that might limit the audience to mature readers is indicated when applicable, as are awards won by exceptional works. Titles that are particularly interesting to reluctant readers are marked as such.

I developed this book to be a reliable and practical resource to help you assist young library patrons. Although no guidebook can match a personal relationship with the reader or firsthand knowledge of the recommended book, it can enhance the advisory experience. Young adult readers are a diverse group, and *The Teen Reader's Advisor* embraces the challenge to serve this ever-changing community. I hope it will serve as a powerful new tool, whether you are a novice or experienced YA librarians, helping you to advise skillfully, competently, and, most importantly—with a sense of enthusiasm and joy.

ACKNOWLEDGMENTS

Writing a book is a solitary activity, but it is by no means accomplished alone. This kind of book could not be written without all the work done by the many authors, reviewers, and librarians before me. To them I give a huge, appreciative thank you.

The folks at Neal-Schuman Publishers, as always, were terrific. Charles Harmon suggested this book idea to me as I finished *More Teen Programs That Work*. My editor, Michael Kelley, knew how to cajole, flatter, and nudge me to the finish line. The Teens @ the Library series editor, Joel Shoemaker, gave me constant encouragement. Joel even offered a drink one time when the task became a bit overwhelming!

Thank you to Mary K. Chelton and Mary Arnold. As I brainstormed the book proposal, their input on what they would like to see in a Teen Reader's Advisory was very helpful.

A Core Collection for Young Adults by Patrick Jones, Patricia Taylor, and Kirsten Edwards gave me a great place to start when deciding what books to include in the lists.

And special thanks to my husband, Mike. During a peak stretch of the writing process, he decided if he couldn't beat 'em, he would join 'em, and he put together the useful author/title indexes at the end of the book.

PART I

YA RA SUGGESTIONS FOR SUCCESS

CHAPTER 1

PRACTICE A "YA ATTITUDE" TOWARD TEENS

Successful young adult librarians will tell you that *attitude* is everything when working with teens. While the skills and knowledge that make a librarian a good reader's advisor for adults will also be valuable when working with teen patrons, a receptive, friendly attitude toward teens will help you meet the unique reading and developmental needs of young adults.

As young adult librarians, our goal is to connect teens with the informational and entertainment materials they want and need. To do this, we must get to know our audience and learn about their wants and needs, and to do that, we must be able to communicate with them effectively. While there is a lot said about teens and *their* attitudes, at least they have the excuse that they are still in the process of forming them! It takes understanding on our part as adults to build mutual trust and rapport with teens.

There are constant changes in the interests of teens, which are reflected in the new, cutting-edge young adult literature. Walking the tightrope between teens' natural curiosity and their often more conservative parents, teachers, and community keeps working with teens a challenge. A unique aspect of serving young adults is becoming familiar with a field of literature that is in the midst of a great evolution. As reader's advisors, we also need to learn how to think and talk what exactly is it that determines what teens will like in a book . . . what is its appeal?

This chapter addresses the librarian and the attitude that will help him or her connect with teens and how to talk to them about books.

> Serve YA Patrons with Commitment and Enthusiasm
> Cultivate a Nonjudgmental Attitude
> Develop a Respectful Attitude
> Offer Steady Accessibility
> Know the Library's YA Books and Materials
> Read YA Literature
> Remember Your Teen Emotions and Experiences
> Understand Today's Teen Trends
> Learn How to Understand and Discuss a Book's Appeal
> Hone Your Skills with Reader's Advisory Tools

SERVE YA PATRONS WITH COMMITMENT AND ENTHUSIASM

Libraries need teens. Teens are valuable patrons, current and future supporters of the library, and future community leaders and patrons. Teens force libraries to step into the future and adapt to new technologies and formats faster than ever before. They bring a level of excitement and activity to the library. Teens need libraries not only to find answers but also to get a sense of community. In a teen-friendly library, teens can find information as well as a place to build many of their developmental assets. To provide a teen-friendly space, create a welcoming atmosphere with an area that allows for teens' needs to be social and relaxed—where they can talk and visit and work on posters or homework projects together without disturbing other patrons. Plan opportunities for teens to build the 40 developmental assets by providing the information they seek and activities they need through interesting programs. Become involved in the programs yourself to better connect with the teen patrons. While library reference and homework help service has often been replaced by the Internet in homes, fiction readers' advisory for teens is a service area in which public librarians have plenty of room to grow. Continue the process started by parents, teachers, and children's librarians to nurture lifelong readers and library supporters. Over the course of a year a teen's reading interests may vary greatly. During the school year, teens are fulfilling reading requirements. During the summer months, they have time to read for fun.

CULTIVATE A NONJUDGMENTAL ATTITUDE

Teens with nose rings, black eyeliner, purple hair, tattoos, and with belly buttons and more showing, come into the library looking for information, entertainment, and friends. Next year there will be new fashions to shock adults. Ironically, it is not our impressions of the teen but the teen's first impressions of the librarian that will make the library a teen-friendly place or push the teen away. Once a teen gets brave enough to approach us to ask for help, how do we respond? Too often we hear sad stories from teens about frowning, unhelpful librarians prejudging them with suspicious looks, and treating them like juvenile delinquents because of appearances or being in groups of more than two at a time.

Learn to respond to requests and questions from teens without making value judgments, assumptions, or embarrassing or ridiculing comments and inquiries. Teens come to the library for information and recreation, and they will resent being embarrassed or treated like children; they will often find ways to retaliate to save face with their friends. Teens are sometimes reluctant to ask for help because they fear they will look stupid if they can't make us understand want they want because they don't know library lingo.

Focus on the teen you are helping by making eye contact, smiling, and listening to what the teen is saying. If the teen is with a parent and the parent is doing all the talking, ask the teen for clarification, using open-ended questions when possible to encourage the teen to take an active role in selecting reading material. Take a moment to introduce yourself and ask the teen's name.

Sometimes teens do not want to ask anyone for help to find books on sensitive subjects. Teens have many questions about their lives and the world, and the library is a safe place to find answers. You can make possibly sensitive or embarrassing material more easily accessible for browsing in the library with displays and booklists on tough topics.

DEVELOP A RESPECTFUL ATTITUDE

Encourage the library staff to show a basic respect for fellow human beings in their developmental stages by modeling that behavior yourself. Value teen questions with the same weight as adult questions, acknowledging that their reading interests have the same value and importance, and possibly even more value, since they are building their view of the world through what they read, experience, and how people interact with them. Younger teens are moving into a new area of the library with a different atmosphere and different level of service than they knew in the children's room. They may need guidance and assistance until they learn the ropes. A welcoming, respectful, friendly attitude will help them feel comfortable. We want teens to learn that libraries add value to their lives.

A recent news story told of a shopping mall that adopted a policy for teens to be accompanied by a parent or guardian during evening hours. Rather than pulling aside the troublemakers and correcting them, the mall authorities punished the entire teen shopper population, since many teens consider shopping with their parents instead of shopping and hanging with their friends a punishment. Unfortunately, this is often the reception teens receive from the adult retail world, in spite of their enormous spending power. Teens in your library can tell you comparable stories; unfortunately, they expect a similar reception in the library, so they are naturally wary of librarians.

Librarians are modeling adult behavior to teens, who are our future adults. It is helpful to keep this in mind and refuse to be drawn into a power struggle that one of you will feel the need to win. Be polite and respectful toward teen patrons, and most often, the respect will be returned to you. A sense of humor when relating to teens is helpful. Humor can put things into perspective and help a teen and librarian connect. However, teens fear being ridiculed or laughed at, so humor that hurts won't endear you to your young patrons.

OFFER STEADY ACCESSIBILITY

Work on the floor in the library where teens hang out after school. Create an e-mail address for them to write to you on the library Web site. Be sure your name tag says what you want the teens to call you. Put your name on newsletters or bookmarks, and on the Web site. Always be accessible to teens on library turf. When you see a teen staring at rows of books, ask if he or she would like help finding a particular book or just want to browse. When a group of teens are just hanging around, stop by and say hi, invite them to an upcoming program, ask if they've seen the new CDs you just got in. Wave and smile at teens walking by when you are working at the reference desk, greeting them by name. Get out from behind the desk and spend some time in the YA area, where you can chat with your teen readers. Try not to appear to be checking up on them or looking for excuses to throw them out (which is what they often expect from adults). Straightening books on the shelf, pulling a few titles for a display, or hanging photos from the last teen program while greeting the teens is more comfortable. The message to send to the teens is that you are there to help them, and they are welcome, safe, and expected in the library. Personal contact will pave the way for them to come to you when they need help finding information in the future.

KNOW THE LIBRARY'S YA BOOKS AND MATERIALS

Browse the YA collection and the new book shelf each morning to see what's available that day. Read blurbs of new books. Read reviews even if you aren't doing the ordering so you know what titles are important and creating a buzz in the field. Become familiar with the reader's advisory tools discussed in this book. Learn what is available in YA literature by reading catalogs and journals, and by attending conference sessions about new titles in YA literature. Attend ALA and ALAN conferences when you can and take advantage of any opportunities you have to listen to YA authors and editors at state or regional conferences and workshops. Join discussion lists that talk about new young adult titles, such as YALSA-BK or adbooks, to hear about forthcoming titles and opinions of other young adult librarians and authors.

READ YA LITERATURE

Read a variety of young adult titles in various genres and formats. Reading is the first and best way to learn a book's appeal. Try a CD or tape in the car for the titles you can't make yourself sit and read. Read for the appeal of the book. How does it read to you? While you read it, think of teens you know who might enjoy the book. Think of similar titles you have read, similar characters in other books, familiar plots. Does the plot model a classic title? It is helpful to keep a reading list with a few notes so you can recall the main characters and plot lines. You can create a reading journal on your computer or purchase one at a bookstore.

REMEMBER YOUR TEEN EMOTIONS AND EXPERIENCES

The questions you had and decisions you once had to make as a teenager—about identity, education, family, friendship, dating, romance, sex, sports, and social issues—are still the concern's of today's teens. Novels with characters dealing with these same topics can guide and teach young readers in an entertaining, nonthreatening way without being preachy or didactic. The main characters often find ways to change their circumstances against the odds, which can be inspiring and informative to teen readers. There are many young adult titles listed in this book that feature teens facing life issues.

UNDERSTAND TODAY'S TEEN TRENDS

Pop culture affects the reading interests of all ages, but this is particularly so for teens. Activities such as gaming, trends like the popularity of anime films and reality TV shows, even a local popular sport in the community can bring teens into the library looking for reading material. Current events and social issues in the news as well as local events will rouse the curiosity of teens who need to understand how

SIGN UP FOR DISCUSSION LISTS TO LEARN THE LATEST
NEWS ABOUT YOUNG ADULT LITERATURE.

Adbooks—Discuss young adult authors and books
Moderator: Krista Fiabane, a seventh-grade English teacher at Julius West
    Middle School in Rockville, Maryland
http://groups.yahoo.com/group/adbooks/
Post message: adbooks@yahoogroups.com
Subscribe: adbookssubscribe@yahoogroups.com
Unsubscribe: adbooksunsubscribe@yahoogroups.com

Booktalking—discuss booktalks and improve booktalking skills
Moderator: Dr. Joni Richards Bodart
http://groups.yahoo.com/group/booktalking/
Post message: booktalking@yahoogroups.com
Subscribe: booktalkingsubscribe@yahoogroups.com
Unsubscribe: booktalkingunsubscribe@yahoogroups.com

*Graphic Novels in Libraries—librarians share reviews and resources for collection
development of graphic or comic novels*
Moderator: Steve Miller
www.topica.com/lists/GNLIB-L/
www.angelfire.com/comics/gnlib/
Post message: GNLIB-L@topica.com
Subscribe: GNLIB-L-subscribe@topica.com
Unsubscribe: GNLIB-L-unsubscribe@topica.com

*PUBYAC PUBlic libraries, Young Adults, and Children—discuss children and
young adult services in public libraries*
List moderator: Shannon VanHemert
www.pallasinc.com/pubyac/
Post message: pubyac@prairienet.org
Subscribe: listproc@prairienet.org Message: subscribe pubyac
Unsubscribe: listproc@prairienet.org Message: unsubscribe pubyac

YALSA-BK—Discuss young adult books and issues about young adult reading
Subscribe: listproc@ala.org Message: Subscribe YALSA-bk first name last name
Unsubscribe: listproc@ala.org Message: Unsubscribe YALSA-bk

these events could affect their lives; they need to figure out how to fit them into their big picture of the world. Popular television shows and movies will generate an interest in novelizations and biographies about the actors. Browse teen magazines and ask the teens you know about the current trends. Teen pop culture may not appeal to you as an adult, but a teen advisory group can be very helpful in keeping you informed of current trends.

LEARN HOW TO UNDERSTAND AND DISCUSS A BOOK'S APPEAL

Appeal is what a reader likes about a book: how the book affects the reader. Usually it is more than just the topic; it is the pace, the characters, the setting, the time period, and/or the place. It is a combination of all the things that make a book a good read. The sex and age of the characters may be important to a teen reader, and teens often want to read about characters who are a little older than they are.

What is the mood of the book? What kind of book is the teen in the mood for? When readers are busy or under stress, they often want safety, reassurance, and confirmation. They will reread old favorites or read new books by trusted authors or choose a favorite series. When life is less stressful, they can afford to take more risks. They may want to be amazed by something unpredictable and might pick books on sheer impulse from a display, or through random selection of an author's name.

Practice talking about a book's appeal with teens in your Teen Advisory Group or in your discussion groups. When teens talk about what they are reading, ask questions that lead them to talk about a book's appeal and you will be teaching them how to talk effectively to their friends about books.

HONE YOUR SKILLS WITH READER'S ADVISORY TOOLS

Get to know the RA tools available to you in your library. Learn what each offers. Borrow some of the suggested RA tools in this book from other libraries to see if they meet your needs. All the resources listed are librarian favorites for different reasons and uses. Create your own RA tools . . . a reader's corner with RA resources or a reader's advisory notebook. A notebook or Web site with the title and author of the books you read with a few key words will help you remember the essence of the books. You might like to rate them and build recommended reading lists of your own. Use the lists in this book to get you started!

CHAPTER 2

DEVELOP USEFUL TEEN READER'S ADVISORY PRACTICES

Thankfully, reference librarians do not have to rely on their own remembered knowledge to answer reference questions. Their expertise lies in knowing where to look for answers: how to find correct information in the resources available to them. When librarians act as reader's advisors, too often they try to rely on their own knowledge, their memory of books they have read themselves. However, there are reference tools and techniques to help librarians be more effective and more confident as reader's advisors, too.

This chapter is a quick-start how-to-do-it on reader's advisory for teens. Any library serving teens can benefit from implementing the ideas in this chapter, even though some practices, such as inviting young adult authors to speak, may only fit into larger library budgets or be special occasion events. Even author visits can be managed with careful planning and/or partnering with schools or nearby libraries.

A variety of ideas is offered here because the teen audience is varied, and different ideas will work at different times for different teens. Each of the ten practices discussed here will evolve as you begin using them to match teens and books. You will personalize and customize the service to the teens in your library as you become comfortable using these practices. Several of the ideas help teens learn how to look for books independently. Independence is empowering, and teens will feel a greater sense of satisfaction when they learn to use the library's resources confidently on their own.

Read YA Books to Recognize Patron Appeal
Create a "Reader's Corner"
Market the Collection in YA Area
Booktalk YA Books
Present Independent Programs and Contests
Promote Books Using the Internet
Launch and Maintain a Teen Book Discussion Group
Develop a Comprehensive Reader's Advisory Interview
Learn to Do Reader's Advisory on the Run
Teach Teens How to Utilize the Catalog and Online RA Tools

READ YA BOOKS TO RECOGNIZE PATRON APPEAL

Read a young adult book not only for its subject matter, but for its appeal. Even a quick read of the blurb, covers, and first chapter can give you a feel for the pace, character, plot, and setting—the main elements of appeal. Record important elements in a notebook as you read; your notes will help you remember the book and think about teens who might like to read it.

While you read, consider some of these questions:

1. What is the book's best feature?
2. What is the age of the main character?
3. Is there one point of view? Or multiple points of view?
4. Is the plot character-driven or action-driven?
5. Do the characters change psychologically, as in a coming-of-age novel?
6. What is the frame of the story: the time period, the setting?
7. Is it a fast-paced, compelling page-turner or does the story develop slowly and have lots of description?
8. Does it have lots of dialogs, short sentences and paragraphs, and white space, making it appealing to reluctant readers or someone wanting a quick read?
9. What elements limit its appeal? Is there explicit sex, rough language, or violence that limits it to a mature reader? Does it have an annoying voice or a strong political or social position? Are social or moral issues addressed? Does the ending wrap up the story? Or does the book leave you hanging, wondering what to think, or waiting for a sequel?
10. Do other titles come to mind with similar appeal? Are there similar authors or titles? What other authors and titles fit in the same genre with similar appeal? What are the similarities and differences in the books within the genre?

Any or all of these elements can be important in determining a book's appeal, which determines how it makes the reader feel. That feeling is what the reader is looking for when he or she asks for similar books. Keeping these questions in mind as you begin to read or browse a book will help you talk about books to patrons. When you bring these elements of appeal to teen readers' attention, they learn how to better describe the kinds of books they enjoy.

CREATE A "READER'S CORNER"

A reader's corner can be anything from a pamphlet rack on a wall or a shelf in the YA room to a roomy seating area with shelving and display areas and a computer with Internet access, bookmarked with reader's advisory resources and databases. The reader's corner is most helpful if located near the fiction collection. Use this space to display your booklists, reader's advisory books, bookmarks with annotations or read alike lists, bestselling teen books, prize winners, annotated bulletin board postings, featured book displays, and shelf talkers. Create a display of sure hits: local popular titles and favorite authors. Start a list binder to collect booklists printed from this book or created from other sources. Leave the binder open on a tabletop, ready for browsing. Create appropriate displays on school reading assignments, current event topics, and seasonal reading programs; these spawn requests for fiction on specific topics. Even if you don't have a separate YA area, you can promote the collection you have with a reader's corner with just a few of these tools, using the space you have. Check out the recommended reader's advisory tools in the next chapter.

MARKET THE COLLECTION IN YA AREA

Think of a grocery store when marketing books and use some of the same tactics to attract attention to your products. Good signage will help teens easily find the young adult collection and determine where the fiction and nonfiction collections are, and will point out special materials, such as music and graphic novels. Use shelf talkers to announce new titles or small collections on a table, windowsill, or a cleared shelf. Shelf talkers are inexpensive; they can be purchased from a library supply company, such as Demco, or be as simple as a tent card printed on your computer. You can turn accompanying titles face-out for a display that's easy to change frequently.

The third edition of *Connecting Young Adults and Libraries* by Jones, Gorman, and Suellentrop reported that in a survey of Hennepin County Library teens, 38 percent of teens said displays were the way to go to promote reading. Themed displays, created from booklists such as those in this book, will connect teens to more titles with the same topic or theme. Read alike lists are most helpful if they are placed near the relevant titles. Slip bookmarks labeled "Amazon Bestseller" or "Award Winner" or "Recommended in *Seventeen* Magazine" into selected titles; they will catch a reader's eye if printed on bright paper in cool fonts. End caps get attention, so use the ends of your shelf rows by installing slat walls, shelving, or bulletin boards, whichever is most affordable, so you can use this eye-catching space. Casual displays look more accessible, and since the main idea is to invite patrons to pick up a book, don't worry about making elaborate showcases on every horizontal surface. The covers of the books should be the focus.

Keep these tips from *Connecting Young Adults and Libraries* in mind when making posters, bulletin boards, and signs to feature collections that will attract teens:

1. use humor;
2. be honest/realistic;
3. be clear;
4. be original;
5. don't try to be too cool;
6. don't use sex to sell;
7. make it attention-grabbing;
8. don't be preachy;
9. don't talk down to teens;
10. and, adding my own tip here . . . change your displays frequently

When they are organized alphabetically by author, it isn't easy for teens to find books they want, so try shelving paperbacks by genre; use genre labels so they can find their favorite kinds of books independently. Many series have several different authors, so shelving a whole series together will help their readers. We keep a library organized so that we can find books, but if it is done in a way that patrons can't find what they want without being a librarian, we've defeated our main purpose . . . connecting books and readers. Be a little flexible in how you arrange your collection, and choose user-friendly tools to locate the items in it.

Keep the young adult collection weeded. While a worn paperback cover indicates a well-loved book, if you can't read the title on the spine or the pages are golden and crumbly, it just means it is old. Covers with teens wearing the last decade's hair and clothing styles need to be pulled or replaced with updated editions if the titles are still relevant. If the book is in great shape and it is old, then it is a dud and should go anyway. The cover art should depict the age of the main character accurately. If there are several editions available, take a look at the cover art at Amazon.com before choosing which one to buy. Well-weeded shelves that have empty space to display a book face-out on a book easel at the end will look more inviting to browse than a shelf crammed with old books. The space makes it easier to locate titles, and easier to remove and replace the books when browsing. Local junior high and senior high schools may be very happy to take your discards, or you can sell them to raise money for teen programs.

Resources for Displays

1.   Skaggs, Gayle. 1999. *On Display: 25 Themes to Promote Reading.* Jefferson, NC: McFarland.

BOOKTALK YA BOOKS

Learn to talk about books in front of a classroom or a TAG meeting. Several books and Web sites listed in the following section offer booktalks, so you don't have to write your own. However, creating short commercials for favorite titles is fun and a good activity to do with teen patrons. Teach them to "sell" a book, rather than do a book report. Tell them why they just can't NOT read this book!

Reader's theater is a fun and entertaining way to present an audience participation booktalk. Use an interesting passage of dialog from the book, asking teens to read the different characters' parts, or ask them to read sketches of the main characters in first-person narrative. You can do an RT booktalk with a minimum of preparation if you color-code the characters and their lines and number the characters' speaking parts, so they are read in order. To give the readers insight into the characters, include notes in italics at the top of their scripts regarding mood or situation, and give them a moment to prepare. This activity is fun in a classroom, a book discussion, or a teen advisory meeting. No costumes or props are required, but a single important prop that is integral to the story will capture the audience's attention. In this version of reader's theater, the object is to spark interest in the book, not tell the entire story.

Remember you aren't the only person booktalking the YA collection. Teens ask each other and tell their friends about what they are reading. Give them the means to spread the word about their favorite books with "Tell a Friend About This Book!" bookmarks they can fill out. Create the bookmarks with spaces for the author and the title and why the reader liked the book. Print a statement on the bottom: "Find it at the [name of your library]!" and slip these bookmarks into new books and every book in a display. The teens can give them to friends or leave them at a designated place in the YA room to post on a bulletin board.

Resources for Booktalking
and Reader's Theater

1. Bodart, Joni Richards. 2002. *Radical Reads: 101 YA Novels on the Edge*. Lanham, MD: Scarecrow Press.
   Dr. Bodart is working on the second edition of this terrific resource for booktalks on the edgier books of recent years. The topical index was an inspiration for lists in *The Teen Reader's Advisor*.
2. Bromann, Jennifer. 2001. *Booktalking That Works* and (2005) *More Booktalking That Works*. New York: Neal-Schuman.
   This handy guide with how tos, dos and don'ts, and resources for booktalkers, has fifty booktalks, and the follow-up edition offers two hundred more talks!
3. Gillespie, John T., and Corrine J. Naden. 2003. *Teenplots: a Booktalk Guide to Use with Readers Ages 12–18*. Westport, CT: Libraries Unlimited.
   One hundred titles are organized by theme. Each title includes author and bibliographic information, character description, plot summary, theme, and critical comments.
4. Schall, Lucy. *Booktalks and More: Motivating Teens to Read*. Westport, CT: Libraries Unlimited, 2003.
   Features more than one hundred booktalks for young adult titles published between 1997 and 2001; the author includes related articles and nonfiction titles helpful to teachers and librarians.
5. Brodart, Joni. "The Booktalker." Available: www.thebooktalker.com
   Dr. Brodart has written lots of books about booktalking for all ages and this is her Web site. She features new booktalks here each month and has many booktalks archived. This site is a favorite among YA librarians and teachers.
6. Keane, Nancy. "Booktalks: Quick and Simple." Available: http://nancykeane.com/booktalks/ya.htm
   These booktalks are exactly as the title of the Web site says, quick and simple. School librarian Nancy Keane's booktalks are handy for a quick peek at titles you haven't had a chance to read yet. Check out the link to the Booktalking Tips, with collected tips from many experienced booktalkers on a discussion list.
7. Random House Children's Books. "Librarians @ Random: Booktalks." Available: www.randomhouse.com/teachers/librarians/booktalks.html
   Featured monthly booktalks are short and sweet, with links to more information about the Random House authors and the authors' other titles.
8. YALSA. "Booktalking." Available: www.ala.org/ala/yalsa/profdev/booktalking.htm
   YALSA's site for booktalking lists print and online resources for learning to booktalk.
9. Barchers, Suzanne I., and Jennifer L. Kroll. 2002. *Classic Reader's Theater for Young Adults*. Greenwood Village, CO: Teacher Ideas Press.
10. Sheppard, Aaron. "Tips on Scripting." Available: www.aaronshep.com/rt/Tips1.html

Aaron Shepard has an RT Web site with many prepared scripts that are useful to present to children; however, his tips on this page can help you create your own scripts for teens.

PRESENT INDEPENDENT PROGRAMS AND CONTESTS

When creating contests and games, use book titles, covers, main characters, authors, worlds—anything that will make a teen need to pick up and look at a book in a display or explore the catalog to find the answer. Try featuring a matching game with photos of birthday authors each month with a few of their titles and you have an easy bulletin board independent program and display planned for a year. The teens can match the authors' photos with titles of their books to win a small prize. Another easy idea is matching first lines of popular novels with the titles or matching fantasy worlds with authors. In the process of finding the answers, readers may find them-selves wanting to finish reading the story.

Resources for Independent Programs

1. Honnold, RoseMary. 2003. *101+ Teen Programs That Work.* New York: Neal-Schuman.
2. Honnold, RoseMary. 2005. *More Teen Programs That Work.* New York: Neal-Schuman. Both of my programming books have ideas for independent programs that feature books. Independent programs are easy, fast, and cheap, but they are also fun and attract teens to books and make attractive displays.

PROMOTE BOOKS USING THE INTERNET

Think of Internet technology as a way to promote books, not as something in competition with them. Write new book annotations for the teen Web site, create electronic newsletters, and build e-mail lists to communicate with your teen readers. Invite TAB members to send in book reviews to post in online publications to lead other teens to good books. Add links on the teen's page to reader's advisory sites suggested in this book. Create a message board on the teen's page where teens can post questions or opinions about books, following the model for customer feedback set by Amazon.com. Add links to the homepages of favorite authors.

Some libraries sponsor online book chats, even inviting an author to join in, which may have more appeal than a teen book discussion group in your library. Avid teen readers can fill out a reader profile card similar to what homebound service librarians use for their patrons. The cards list reading preferences, such as favorite authors, genres, and formats. You can then send reading recommendations via e-mail when new titles come in that a teen might like. The Internet will also reach teens who are not going to come in and talk to you on their own.

Annotate genre lists, themed lists, read alike lists, and recommended lists for your teen's page, and add graphics of book covers. Write booktalks and post them in a blog for teens. In either case, link the title and image to the catalog listing, to easily place holds.

BookLetters is a *BookPage* product that libraries can use to beef up the reader's advisory part of a Web site. Their software makes it easy to generate lists of books, movies, and music linked directly to your catalog. BookLetters also publishes newsletters and lists that can be e-mailed to subscriber lists regularly and event calendars for your programs. Take a look at www.bookletters.com/.

LAUNCH AND MAINTAIN A TEEN BOOK DISCUSSION GROUP

Hooking teens with book discussion groups can be tricky. Since reading for school takes priority, one more reading assignment may not sound appealing to busy teens. Some of the more successful groups are specialized, attracting teens who have a particular hobby or reading interest. Junior high or middle school girls and their mothers have found shared book discussions to be a special together time just when communication can begin to get strained. Other groups focus on special interests, such as fantasy and role-playing or graphic novels, mixing books with game and drawing activities. It will make a big difference in your success if you share the special interest with your teens.

Another approach is having everyone bring in and talk about a favorite title in a different genre each month. For example, while Harry Potter is still popular, teens may like to talk about other fantasy titles they have enjoyed. Listen to your teens, be flexible, and be willing to experiment with different genres of reading material and different ages of teens to find what combination will work with the teens who visit your library. Coshocton Public Library offers "Teens Talk Books," a group that meets monthly to talk about favorite books, current reads, and new books over pizza and sodas.

Virtual book discussion groups have the advantage of being accessible to all of your teen patrons at any time. An electronic discussion list can be initiated, where readers comment on the assigned books. The librarian begins by posting chosen titles with descriptions, and discussion can begin on the first of each month. Details on how Baltimore County Public Library's Virtual Book Discussion Group works can be found at www.bcplonline.org/centers/library/bookclub.html.

Book discussion kits are helpful for teachers, home-schooling groups, and independent book clubs. Kits can circulate within a whole library system or a consortium to share the expense. A sample kit might include:

- multiple paperback copies of the same title;
- author biographical information and photo;
- reviews;
- discussion questions; and
- helpful hints on facilitating a group discussion.

Resources for Book Discussion Groups

1. Dickerson, Constance. 2004. *Teen Book Discussion Groups at the Library.* New York: Neal-Schuman.
2. Dodson, Shireen. 1997. *The Mother-Daughter Book Club: How Ten Busy Mothers and Daughters Came Together to Talk, Laugh and Learn Through Their Love of Reading.* New York: Harper Perennial.

3. Teenreads.com. "Book Clubs and Reading Guides." Available: www.teenreads.com/clubs/index.asp

DEVELOP A COMPREHENSIVE READER'S ADVISORY INTERVIEW

Perhaps a better term for "interview" is reader's advisory conversation. In a reference interview, the librarian is the expert, asking questions to refine the patron's question so he or she can be led to the most helpful resource that will provide the correct answers. Then the patron leaves the library satisfied. A reader's advisory interview needs to be led by the reader, offering information so that the librarian, acting as an advisor or guide, can suggest titles. But only the reader will know if the results are correct, at a later date!

The object of the reader's advisory interview is to encourage readers to talk about the books they have enjoyed. Be approachable and responsive when a teen comes to you with questions about what to read. Teens unfamiliar with the library are often accompanied by a parent, and the parent will do the talking for the teen who is meanwhile looking at the floor or checking out who else is in the library. Reroute the conversation by asking the teen to clarify what the parent has requested or ask for more details. When talking to teens one on one, or creating an online form for reader's advisory, take your time. Don't assume that what teens or parents ask for initially is what they ultimately want, because they may not yet know the labels to describe what they want. You may try asking open-ended questions as you would for adults, but offering options may better help a teen to begin to articulate what he or she likes to read. One of our missions as teen readers' advisors is teaching teen readers how to talk about books, not using library speak, but using words they already know.

Asking few of the following questions can help move along the conversation so you can make good suggestions:

1. Is this an assignment? What are the teacher's requirements?
2. What was the last good book you read?
3. Who was the author? Did you like the writing style?
4. Do you want something like this or different?
5. Do you care if the main character is a guy or a girl?
6. How about the age of the main character? (Teens usually want to read about teens slightly older than themselves in realistic fiction. Age is not as much a factor in fantasy and science fiction.)
7. Do you prefer an urban or rural setting? Contemporary or historical?
8. How much time reading and how much difficulty do you want? Do you like to read a lot or do you have a book report due tomorrow?
9. Do you prefer a paperback or hardback or audio?
10. If you're not a reader, what are your favorite movies or television programs?

Consider the pacing, characterization, storyline, and frame of what they have read as they describe the books they like. Pay as much attention to any dislikes the teen reveals. Get a feel for the teen's mood and the mood of the book he or she is looking for. When a reader wants to feel safe, a favorite series, topic, character, or author can be comforting. In a more adventuresome, experimental mood, teen readers may want to try something new or edgier. Realize that this afternoon's mood may not match tonight's reading mood!

Consult reader's advisory tools if needed, or if one would be of particular interest to the reader. Avid readers may be thrilled to find there is a Web site or a book that focuses on their favorite genre. Show the teen how to use the resource as you use it.

Take teens to the YA room and pull a few titles off the shelves as you make suggestions so they can see the covers and learn where to find the authors if they decide they do like the books you suggest. Open the book to the blurb or look on the back to demonstrate how to learn about a book quickly. Point out other titles in a series or by the same author. Explain genre labels if the teen is interested in a particular genre. It's nice to know there are several more books waiting after you've found a good one you really like. Rather than trying to recommend a book that is "good for you," simply suggest books the teen may enjoy. There's no need to oversell a book, as pushing a title can turn a teen off. Offer a few suggestions and let the teen choose. Choosing one's own reading material is a step toward independence.

Follow up after teens have browsed through your suggestions. Did they find what they want? Human interaction with you will determine teens' satisfaction, even if they don't find the exact right book the first time. A receptive, open, helpful attitude will help teens open up and talk with you about the books they would like to read the next time they come in. If you are successful, the patrons will come back for more recommendations.

LEARN TO DO READER'S ADVISORY ON THE RUN

Unfortunately, there is not always enough time to take teen patrons to the shelves and talk about books. Most libraries don't have a dedicated teen reader's advisory desk; many still do not have a young adult librarian! When we are wearing other hats or stationed at the reference desk and answering the phone, we can still give teen readers some direction until we are able to help them. Make an effort not to overlook a teen's request; make a note, if needed, so you can help after you finish with your current work. To get them started on their own, direct teens to the reader's corner you've created where they can browse the booklists you've printed from this book and placed in a binder. Point out any new books or featured topic displays.

The tools that help you when you are busy are also helpful to your coworkers who do not read young adult literature. Or if you get put on the spot because you haven't read very much in a requested genre or if you just can't remember a title, you can consult these resources yourself. Share one of the reader's advisory books at each staff or reference meeting and point out how the resource will help them meet the needs of their teen patrons.

Make a note of the requests you find hard to fill, do a little research, and consider creating displays or booklists featuring those kinds of books. What a pleasant surprise for the teen the next time he or she is in the library and finds a whole list of books featuring the very thing asked for!

TEACH TEENS HOW TO UTILIZE THE
CATALOG AND ONLINE RA TOOLS

Teaching information literacy includes teaching teens how to find what they want to read on their own. Teens need to learn the following skills to become independent lifelong readers:

- learn how to describe the books they like to read;
- learn how to use tools to find more books like the ones they like to read;
- learn how to locate the books they want to read on the shelves;
- learn how to evaluate the book from the cover, blurbs, and browsing to determine if they might like the book;
- learn how to determine if it is a book they should read based on content; and
- learn to have a responsible and ethical reaction to what they read in the book.

When you can, take the time to show a teen how to search the library's catalog. You can also offer computer lab programs to teens that feature the library's catalog and teen Web pages. Offer your services to local schools to come and demonstrate the catalog and library's Web site. Create scavenger hunts to play at lock-ins that make using the catalog a part of the game. Show the links to Web sites with teen reviews on the teen's page of your library's Web site. Walk teen's through the steps you are taking to find the books they want, explaining the resources and methods that teens could learn to use on their own. All these methods help teens build developmental assets, including independence and confidence in their skills in the library. They will be much more likely to continue to use the library because they know how.

CHAPTER 3

EXPLORE THE YOUNG ADULT LITERATURE SCENE

This chapter provides an overview of some of the current trends in young adult literature, first by defining the audience and the scope of the literature, then discussing core authors, teen authors, and other areas of interest to school and public librarians.

> "The achievement of great YA literature is that it extends and applies the spare language, the focused story, the sharply etched conflicts of younger books to the multilayered, vexing, often ambiguous situations of the dawning adult world."—Marc Aronson, *Exploding the Myths: The Truth about Teenagers and Reading*

Characteristics
Trends
School Reading Assignments
Core Young Adult Authors
Teen Authors
Most Challenged Young Adult Authors

CHARACTERISTICS

To define young adult literature, we might begin by defining the audience. What is meant by the term "young adult"? Even in library circles there is confusion and disagreement about the age range we are discussing. Some use the term synonymously with adolescent or teenager, while others may include preteens and middle schoolers as young as ten. Others include patrons in their early twenties. YALSA has defined the age group termed "young adults" as ages 12 to 19, the age range coinciding with junior high and high school. Many libraries are changing labels so the materials designated for this age group are called teen collections, and young adult librarians are becoming teen librarians or teen services specialists. These terms are at least clearer to our patrons for defining the group we are trying to serve.

"Adolescence"—the period between childhood and adulthood—is a relatively recent development. Until the nineteenth century, children lived and worked with their parents and then married in their teen years. They could then work and support themselves and provide for their families. With the development of the printing press, compulsory education, and industrialization, children didn't need to enter the work force at such a young age. More education became necessary, and a longer dependent period for the younger generation evolved to allow time for education. Now, with college education required for more and more careers, the dependent period of adolescence can extend into a person's mid-twenties. Only then is a person ready to have a career, be self-supporting, and to start a family, the traditional passage into adulthood. The task of separating from family and developing a sense of one's own identity is now prolonged over a decade.

What we are going to define as young adult literature had a much later beginning. Children's literature first appeared in the seventeenth century and for the next three hundred years, books were written for children or adults. The beginning point for a separate body of literature to be published for and about teens was in 1967 with the publication of *The Outsiders* by S.E. Hinton, who was a teen herself. From that point young adult literature included books written for and about teens, and publishers marketed them for teens. While teens enjoy reading about characters like themselves, many teens also enjoy books with younger or older characters. We find our teen readers in the adult sections of the library reading Stephen King and "chick lit," and in the children's room enjoying Lemony Snicket adventures. And there are many adult librarians who enjoy reading books marketed to teens!

Any definition of young adult literature will have lots of exceptions. If we say the main character of the novel is a teen, we also take a look at the early Harry Potter books and *Hitchhiker's Guide to the Galaxy,* Brian Jacque's Redwall series, and many fantasy series, and then have to say, well, not always. If we say the reader is a teen, then we have to include many children's and adult books that teens read that aren't found in our YA collections. Publishers help us out by telling us which market they are aiming for, and that is the guide most libraries and award committees follow. If the publisher says it is young adult literature, then that's what we'll call it. But realize there are many adult and children's books that your teens will enjoy, too. Some of the titles listed in this book include books marketed to younger and older audiences, but teens like to read them.

TRENDS

Young adult fiction has changed a great deal since the mid-twentieth century. Then, adults believed youths should read stories with characters coming of age and setting an example by modeling acceptable middle-class behavior. The trend then turned to more realistic fiction that addressed life and its problems. Problem novels brought to readers characters more often from lower-class families; they dealt with the difficult issues poverty often brings. The language became more realistic, and included dialects, profanity, and poor grammar when it fit the characters and settings.

These more realistic good and bad characters needed realistic situations in which to flex their strengths and weaknesses. Family, school, friends, social situations, health and body issues, and sex are common themes and settings for realistic young adult literature. The key for the novel to work is that the teen character's problem needs to be believable to the reader. Good realistic fiction will leave the reader with something to think about, and perhaps give some insight into a new situation.

Common characteristics of realistic YA fiction include some of the following elements.

- The author writes from the point of view of an adolescent, usually either in the first person or a young third person, about the passage from childhood to adulthood. The first-person point of view makes readers feel that they are the character's confidant(e), that they know the character and have insight to the character's motives. Third person gives insight into more of the characters.
- Teen readers want to see the characters as independent from adults. The protagonists solve their problems without the help of their parents, so parents are often absent or inadequate, which presents opportunities for the protagonists to prove themselves.
- Young adult fiction is fast-paced, usually plot-driven. The story needs to start immediately, with powerful images and action that moves along to keep the reader turning pages. Long descriptive passages are rarely found in young adult titles.
- Young adult literature must include a variety of genres and subjects. All teens are not alike, and their reading interests are not alike. Some teen readers will go through periods of reading only one genre for pleasure for several years.
- The characters need to be from many different ethnic and cultural groups. This trend reflects the change in our society, which has become more multicultural. A peer group is important as teens strive to achieve independence, the main task of adolescence. Teens may explore different groups and different roles within the group through the characters in a novel. Fiction extends that peer group, so a reader may explore new roles vicariously and safely through fiction.
- Characters need a healthy optimism and the ability to accomplish things and solve their problems, thereby becoming worthy role models. As they "come of age," they lose the innocence of childhood and gain maturity.
- Teens are dealing with many intense emotions. Characters dealing with emotions important to teens can help the reader understand, accept, and assimilate his or her own normal feelings.
- Young adult literature incorporates the developmental tasks teens need to achieve: acquiring a mature social role; achieving a masculine or feminine sex role; accepting body changes and one's physique; achieving emotional independence from parents; preparing for sex, marriage, and parenthood; selecting and preparing for an occupation; developing a personal ideology and ethical standards; assuming membership in the community; and, ultimately, achieving a unique identity.

Some trends in young adult literature are due to the constant changes in technology. New writing styles are popular, such as e-mail or IM format novels. Authors also include technology in their novels, with teens text-messaging each other and using cell phones to communicate. Technology has changed how teens read as well. Books on CD and ebooks make the novels more available and accessible to readers on the go.

Other recent trends are multiple points of view, where every chapter of a book introduces another point of view about one incident, like *Give a Boy a Gun* by Todd Strasser. Each "chapter" is an interview or news story telling about one event, a school shooting. By using two points of view, an author shows us both sides of a relationship, as in *Things Change* by Patrick Jones. Johanna and Paul tell both sides of their relationship, which becomes progressively abusive, so while we may dislike a character's behavior, we can have some understanding of the character's situation and motivations.

Some authors are using edgier language and edgier situations, showing the sadder, more sordid side of life that their characters find themselves in. Teens caught in abusive or neglectful families, crime or gangs, drugs or alcohol are given a voice to tell their stories. Some of their stories don't have the happy ending we might expect . . . another realistic punch. Even in novels that are not so gritty, the situations need to be relevant to how teens are living, and the characters need to feel real. Each young generation tries to show they are different from their parents, and want their own stories to reflect the unique challenges of their own generation.

More adult fiction authors are turning to young adult fiction, recognizing a ready and willing audience. With more freedom of expression, accomplished authors are enjoying the challenge of writing for a demanding and particular audience.

Humor and fantasy have important roles amid all the seriousness of everyday life, and this is reflected in today's YA literature. The same novel may be humorous and deal with serious issues at the same time. *The Earth, My Butt, and Other Big Round Things* by Carolyn Mackler is such a book. Her protagonist, Virginia, is fifteen years old, overweight, and an outsider at home and school; her brother is accused of date rape. Her sense of humor makes her likable and more realistic, and more able to cope. Fantasy novels provide escapism into other worlds but the characters may be dealing with many of the same developmental issues teens face.

What value does YA literature offer to teens? Many times teens can find answers to their questions about life in their reading. Young adult literature often appeals to those at the younger end of the teen years, who are first discovering the real world and comparing it to the ideal world they want to live in. They are discovering themselves, finding their roles, how they fit in the world, how to connect with others. Identity seeking is a developmental task teens must accomplish, answering the Who am I? What do I want? Where do I belong? questions. Fiction provides a safe place for teens to examine their values, feelings, and ideals through another teen's experiences in real and imaginary worlds. The novels that adults may consider "edgier" have protagonists that change their situations, situations the readers may find themselves or their friends in.

Teens also read for entertainment and excitement. Through adventurous characters, teens can experience places and events that may not be possible or desirable. As Patrick Jones tells us, "What people read helps to define them." This means teens will see qualities they admire and qualities they will reject in the characters and the characters' experiences and incorporate them in their own identities. A teen can identify with a sympathetic main character and gain an empathy and understanding for others in similar situations. A quality young adult book does this without being didactic.

Quality books have well developed characters, an interesting setting and plot, a crisis, and a satisfying conclusion—or at least a good cliffhanger to lead us on to the next title in a series. However, quality and popularity do not always go hand in hand.

VOYA magazine's book reviews rate the quality of writing and the popularity on a scale of one to five. Teen readers may overlook some element of the story that isn't well developed or forgive a few stray story lines if they really like the author or the main character is fun and cool. Most awards are for literary merit, but YALSA recognizes the importance of popular reading by producing lists of Popular Paperbacks.

SCHOOL READING ASSIGNMENTS

The schools in your area may have reading lists for each English class or use Accelerated Reader lists. Collect copies of the lists and keep them in a notebook or file, with the names of the schools and teachers on the lists. Many students or their parents will come to the library with only one or two titles in mind and not have the list with them as a backup if those two titles are out. Whether you consider Accelerated Reader a friend or foe, students will be looking for those titles to fulfill assignments if your local schools use them. Some libraries put AR labels on the spines of the books, but if you have several schools to serve, you may have several different lists and labeling becomes a monumental task. It is helpful to note AR (Accelerated Reader) or HS RL (High School Reading List) on the inside covers of titles for your own convenience when weeding the collection, so older titles don't get pulled while they are still needed. The reading history of many of your teens may be limited to books assigned at school. When teens have a choice, help them choose a book that not only meets the teacher's criteria, but also one that may turn the teen on to reading for pleasure.

Reader's advisory tools like this book can help you steer teachers toward newer fiction for their students. The classics are important, but many new books get passed over because they are not on a list to fulfill an assignment. Add English teachers and school media specialists to your e-mail list so they can receive updates on reviews you post to your blog. Or send them copies of your handouts and newsletters that have annotated lists on relevant topics.

CORE YOUNG ADULT AUTHORS

There are *many* good young adult authors and many good young adult titles. If you are in the position to create a new collection or introduce someone to young adult literature, don't miss these authors and one of their sure bet titles:

Anderson, Laurie Halse. *Speak.* New York: Farrar, Straus and Giroux, 1999.
Bauer, Joan. *Hope Was Here.* New York: Putnam Publishing Group, 2000.
Block, Francesa Lia. *Weetzie Bat.* New York: Harper & Row, 1989.
Blume, Judy. *Forever.* Scarsdale, N.Y.: Bradbury Press, 1975.
Cooney, Caroline. *The Face on the Milk Carton.* New York: Bantam Books, 1990.
Cormier, Robert. *The Chocolate War.* New York: Pantheon Books, 1974.
Crutcher, Chris. *Whale Talk.* New York: Greenwillow Books, 2001.
Dessen, Sarah. *Dreamland.* New York: Puffin Books, 2000.
Duncan, Lois. *Killing Mr. Griffin.* Boston: Little, Brown, 1978.

Flake, Sharon G. *The Skin I'm In.* New York: Jump at the Sun/Hyperion Books for Children, 1998.

Flinn, Alex. *Breaking Point.* New York: HarperTempest, 2002.

Garden, Nancy. *Annie on My Mind.* New York: Farrar, Straus, Giroux, 1982.

Giles, Gail. *Shattering Glass.* Brookfield, Ct.: Roaring Brook Press, 2002.

Hinton, S. E. *The Outsiders.* New York, Viking Press, 1967.

Kerr, M.E. *Dinky Hocker Shoots Smack!* New York: Harper & Row, 1972.

Klause, Annette Curtis. *The Silver Kiss.* New York: Delacorte Press, 1990.

Le Guin, Ursula K. *Earthsea.* London: Gollancz, 1977.

L'Engle, Madeleine. *A Wrinkle in Time.* New York: Ariel Books, 1962.

Lipsyte, Robert. *The Contender.* New York:Harper & Row, 1967.

McCaffrey, Anne. *Dragonflight.* New York: Ballantine Books, 1988.

Myers, Walter Dean. *Monster.* New York, N.Y.: HarperCollins Publishers, 1999.

Paulsen, Gary. *Hatchet.* New York, N.Y.: Viking Penguin, 1987.

Peck, Richard. *Are You in the House Alone?* New York: Viking Press, 1976.

Voigt, Cynthia. *Dicey's Song.* New York: Atheneum, 1982.

Zindel, Paul. *The Pigman.* New York: Harper & Row, 1968.

TEEN AUTHORS

Here is a list of authors whose first fiction books were published when they were teens. Teen authors are an inspiration for other teens who want to write. Create a display of their books that also includes nonfiction books about writing and a handout with publishers and Internet sites where teens can get published for Teen Read Week. This is also a good way to publicize a writing workshop.

Atwater-Rhodes, Amelia (14 years old) *In The Forests of the Night* 1999, *Demon in My View* 2000, *Shattered Mirror* 2001, *Midnight Predator* 2002, The Kiesha'ra series 2003, 2004, 2005

Carmody, Isbelle (15 years old) *Obernewtyn* 1999, *Farseekers* 2001, *Ashling* 2003

Daly, Maureen (17 years old) *Seventeenth Summer* 1942

Farley, Walter (15 years old) *Black Stallion* 1941

Franklin, Miles (16 years old) *My Brilliant Career* 1901

Fuller, Kimberly (16 years old) *Home* 1998

Geile, Robert (18 years old) *On Our Way: A Collection of Short Stories by Young American Filmmakers* 2004

Hinton, S. E. (16 years old) *Outsiders* 1967

Korman, Gordan (16 years old) *This Can't Be Happening at McDonald Hall* 1978

Lebert, Benjamin (16 years old) *Crazy* 2000

Libby, Megan McNeil (16 years old) *Postcards from France* 1998

Paolini, Chrisopher (18 years old) *Eragon* 2003, *Eldest* 2005

Pilkey, Dav (19 years old) *World War Won* 1987

Shelley, Mary (19 years old) *Frankenstein* 1816

MOST CHALLENGED YOUNG ADULT AUTHORS

Facing a situation in which a book is challenged is unnerving to a librarian. The American Library Association offers support by sponsoring Banned Books Week and publishing *Hit List for Young Adults,* which lists the most frequently challenged titles. The ALA's Web site at www.ala.org/bbooks has supportive information and a plan of action in the event one of the books in your collection is challenged.

The most frequently challenged young adult authors from 1990 to 2004 are listed as follows:

Alvin Schwartz (YA)
Judy Blume (YA)
Robert Cormier (YA)
J. K. Rowling (YA)
Katherine Paterson (YA)
Stephen King (popular with teens)
R. L. Stine (YA)
John Steinbeck (in teen collections)
Phyllis Reynolds Naylor (YA)

Of the top ten challenged books in 2004, the following were young adult titles or often included in young adult collections.

The Chocolate War by Robert Cormier, for sexual content, offensive language, religious viewpoint, being unsuited to age group, and violence.
Fallen Angels by Walter Dean Myers, for racism, offensive language, and violence.
The Perks of Being a Wallflower by Stephen Chbosky, for homosexuality, sexual content, and offensive language.
What My Mother Doesn't Know by Sonya Sones, for sexual content and offensive language.
I Know Why the Caged Bird Sings by Maya Angelou, for racism, homosexuality, sexual content, offensive language, and being unsuited to age group.
Of Mice and Men by John Steinbeck, for racism, offensive language, and violence.

CHAPTER 4

KEY BOOK HONORS
FOR YA LITERATURE

Teen book awards bring attention to young adult literature and encourage the selected authors to keep writing. The awards also put quality books in the hands of many more teens, as librarians and teachers rush to provide what the judges have chosen as the best. While a few titles land on more than one list, many of the prizes go to different titles, since the criteria are different for each award. These awards recognize quality as determined by professional librarians, teachers, and publishers serving on committees.

Quality as defined by the award winners isn't the only criterion for librarians to use when purchasing YA literature. Teens may seek an escapist fanciful read now and then, but they also deserve and appreciate quality literature. Several of the awards assure that the bar for quality young adult literature is set high, and authors will strive to reach it. Other lists are compiled with popularity and reluctant readers in mind. The awards listed here are presented to books on any subject and for any genre. A short history of each award and the criteria for winning each are presented here to give an informative overview of the awards discussed at conferences and on discussion lists.

The winning titles are good choices for the YA collection, but remember to consider your knowledge of your community or school and your target audience when purchasing books. There are resources listed in each section if you want to learn even more about each award or want to become involved in the selection process. Genre-specific awards are discussed later in the relevant chapters in Part II. The awards and lists discussed in this chapter include:

The Alex Awards
The Mildred L. Batchelder Award
The Margaret A. Edwards Award
The National Book Awards
The John Newbery Award
Popular Paperbacks for Young Adults
The Printz Award
Teens Top Ten
Top Ten Best Books for Young Adults
Top Ten Quick Picks for Reluctant Readers
Young Adult Canadian Book Award

THE ALEX AWARDS

The Alex Awards honor the top ten adult books appealing to teenagers published during a calendar year. Margaret Alexander Edwards, who was called "Alex" by her friends, was a young adult specialist for many years at the Enoch Pratt Library in Baltimore. Her work is described in her book *Fair Garden and the Swarm of Beasts*. Over the years she has served as an inspiration to librarians who serve young adults.

The Alex Awards were first given annually beginning in 1998. The titles were selected by the YALSA Adult Books for Young Adults Task Force from books published in the previous year, and the award was funded by the Margaret Alexander Edwards Trust. With the approval of the Trust, the task force appointed to develop and implement the project named the awards the Alex Awards after Edwards. The task force decided to select a top ten list annually rather than a single title or a long list because of the popularity of the concept and because it parallels the top ten titles selected by the Best Books for Young Adults and Quick Picks for Reluctant Young Adult Readers committees. The task force wanted to make diversity a priority in the lists. The Alex Awards are announced annually in conjunction with National Library Week. In 2002, the Alex Awards were approved as an official ALA award, and the task force was superseded by the Alex Awards Committee. The major sponsor of the Alex Awards continues to be the Margaret Alexander Edwards Trust. *Booklist* is also a sponsor.

To qualify for consideration, a book must meet certain requirements:

- Published in the calendar year prior to the announcement.
- Must come from a publisher's adult list.
- Works of joint authorship and editorship are eligible.
- Books published in another country in English or in the United States in translation are eligible.
- Books are selected from genres that have special appeal to young adults.
- Are well written and very readable.

The Alex Awards Committee consists of nine YALSA members, including the chair, plus a consultant from *Booklist*. Committee members are selected by the YALSA vice-president/president-elect in the fall. Members serve a two-year term, with the possibility of reappointment for another two-year term. One of the members is designated to serve as the chair.

The chair accepts nominations throughout the year from committee members and librarians in the field. A nomination form is available on the YALSA Web site; it asks for bibliographic information and a brief explanation of why the title is deserving of an Alex Award. Nominated titles are not announced. The committee meets to discuss and vote on the titles at the midwinter and annual meetings, and a majority vote determines the winners.

The final annotated list is included in the annual edition of ALA's *Guide to Best Reading* and in the April issue of *Booklist*, as close as possible to the dates selected for that year's National Library Week. The list is also made available on the YALSA Web site. The Alex Awards are presented at a program at the ALA annual conference. The author of each book selected receives a medal that has been designed by the Margaret Alexander Edwards Trust for the Alex Awards.

Further Reading about the Alex Awards

American Library Association. "Alex Awards." Available: www.ala.org/yalsa/booklists/alex Accessed: November 2005.

THE MILDRED L. BATCHELDER AWARD

The Mildred L. Batchelder Award goes to an outstanding children's book (published for children up to age 14) that was originally published in a foreign language in a foreign country and translated into English for the United States. The Association for Library Service to Children gives the award to encourage American publishers to seek out superior children's books abroad and to promote communication among the peoples of the world. This award honors Mildred L. Batchelder, a former executive director of the Association for Library Service to Children, a believer in the importance of good books for children in translation from all parts of the world. She began her career working at the Omaha Public Library in Nebraska, then served as a children's librarian at St. Cloud State Teachers College in Minnesota, and later as librarian of Haven Elementary School in Evanston, Illinois. Batchelder was a member of ALA for thirty years, working as an ambassador to the world on behalf of children and books, encouraging and promoting the translation of the world's best children's literature. Her life's work was "to eliminate barriers to understanding between people of different cultures, races, nations, and languages." She served as an executive director for ALSC, and the award was established in her honor in 1966.

Until 1979, there was a two-year lapse between the publication date and the award date. That year two awards were given, for 1978 and 1979, for books published in the preceding year. Honor books were selected beginning in 1994. If the committee is of the opinion that no book of a particular year is worthy of the award, none is given. The award is decided on and announced at the midwinter meeting of ALA, and the winning publisher receives a citation and commemorative plaque. The presentation used to be made on April 2, International Children's Book Day, but is now given at the ALA annual conference held each summer.

Qualities that are evaluated for the award include:

- The text as the focus of attention.
- The translation, which must be true to the substance, flavor, style, and viewpoint of the original author, as well as the style of the original language, as much as possible, so the reader can sense that the book came from another country.
- Folk literature is not eligible.
- Quality may depend on the type of book being considered, but includes evaluations on interpretation of theme, accuracy and clarity of information, plot development, how characters are represented, and appropriateness of the style.
- Potential appeal to a children's audience.

29

- Overall design of the book.
- Retention of any original artwork.

A title can be submitted to the chair of the Batchelder Award Committee, comprised of the chair and four committee members. Each member serves one year.

Further Reading about the Mildred L. Batchelder Award

Association for Library Service to Children. "Batchelder Award." Available: www.ala.org/alsc/batch.html Accessed: November 2005.

THE MARGARET A. EDWARDS AWARD

The Margaret A. Edwards Award, established in 1988, honors an author's lifetime achievement in writing books for young adults that have been popular over a period of time. Formerly called The School Library Journal Young Adult Author Award, selected and administered by the American Library Association's Young Adult Services division, the title was changed to The Margaret A. Edwards Award in 1990. The annual award is administered by YALSA and sponsored by *School Library Journal* magazine.

Edwards, the author of *Fair Garden and Swarm of Beasts*, has been the inspiration for many young adult librarians. She reached out to young adults in her Baltimore suburb and talked to them about books. She read voraciously and charged her employees to do the same. She booktalked in area high schools in the 1930s and even took books out to the neighborhoods in a horse-drawn wagon to reach teens who couldn't come to the library. She advocated for teens and reading before publishers began targeting the young adult audience.

The annual award in her honor recognizes an author's work in helping adolescents understand themselves, understand the world in which they live, and their relationship with others and with society. The books must have been accepted by young adults as authentic and been in print at least five years, so that many teens have had the opportunity to read them. Nominations for the award are submitted by both young adult librarians and teenagers.

To be considered for the award:

- The author must be living at the time of the nomination. In the case of coauthors, one must be living.
- The book or books honored must have been published in the United States no less than five years prior to nomination.
- The book or books must be in print at the time of the nomination.
- Selection criteria include literary quality, popularity with young adults, and how well the books satisfy the curiosity of young adults and help them develop a philosophy of life.
- If an author continues to write books of interest and appeal to young adults, then he or she may receive the award more than once as warranted, as long as it is not more frequently than every six years.

- The titles must be written specifically for young adults or adult books which continue to be requested and read by young adults

A committee of five, including the chair, is responsible for the final selection of the recipient of the award. Two members of the committee are appointed by the YALSA vice-president and three members are elected from names placed on the YALSA ballot. Each year, librarians and young adults can send the committee input about their preferences for the award winner by June 1.

Winners are announced at the ALA midwinter meeting, usually in January; they receive $2,000.00 along with a citation at the annual conference the following summer. *School Library Journal* is the award's donor and funds the award and administrative costs. The award is presented to the winning author at a luncheon during the ALA annual conference. The author is required to attend the event to accept the award and make a short acceptance speech.

Further Reading about the Margaret A. Edwards Award

Young Adult Library Services Association. "Margaret A. Edwards Award." Available: www.ala.org/ala/yalsa/booklistsawards/margaretaedwards/margaretedwards.htm Accessed: November 2005.

THE NATIONAL BOOK AWARDS

The National Book Awards have been presented annually by the National Book Foundation since 1950 for the best fiction, nonfiction, and poetry; they were created to bring attention to exceptional books and to increase the popularity of reading. In 1996, the Young People's Literature Award was added. The winners, selected by five-member, independent judging panels for each genre, receive a $10,000 cash award and a crystal sculpture.

Publishers can submit titles by contacting the Foundation (see Web site following) for entry forms; a copy of the book, with accompanying form, must be mailed in by June 15. There is a $100 entry fee for each eligible title submitted. Four panels of five judges each for the fiction, nonfiction, poetry, and young people's literature categories, each including a chairperson, are chosen by the National Book Foundation. In October, the Foundation announces a finalist short-list of the five outstanding books submitted in each category. One winner in each category receives $10,000 for the best book from the short-lists. The remaining short-list authors receive prizes of $1,000 each.

To be eligible for the award:

- Full-length books of fiction, general nonfiction, collections of short stories, and collections of essays by one author, collected and selected poems by one author, and eBooks published only in electronic form.
- All books must be published in the United States.
- Judging will be based on literary merit only.
- Authors must be U.S. citizens.

- Books scheduled for publication between December 1 and November 30 of the previous year.
- Author must be living.
- Self-published books and eBooks are eligible, provided that the author/publisher also publishes titles by other authors.

The following are not eligible:
- An English translation of a book originally written in another language.
- Anthologies containing work written by multiple authors.
- Collections and/or retellings of folk tales, myths, and fairy tales.
- A reprint of a book published in a previous award year.

The publisher must agree to contribute $1,000 toward a promotion campaign if the book becomes a short-listed finalist and must inform authors of nominated books; they must be present at the National Book Awards Ceremony and at related events in New York City prior to the ceremony at the publisher's expense.

Further Reading about the National Book Awards

National Book Foundation. "National Book Awards" Available: www.nationalbook.org/ Accessed: November 2005.

THE JOHN NEWBERY AWARD

The John Newbery Award has the honor of being the first children's book award in the world. Frederic G. Melcher proposed the award to the American Library Association meeting of the children's librarians' section in June 1921 and suggested that it be named for the eighteenth-century English bookseller John Newbery. The idea was enthusiastically accepted by the children's librarians, and Melcher's official proposal was approved by the ALA Executive Board in 1922. The purpose of the Newbery Medal has remained the same as was originally stated by Melcher: "To encourage original creative work in the field of books for children. To emphasize to the public that contributions to the literature for children deserve similar recognition to poetry, plays, or novels. To give those librarians, who make it their life work to serve children's reading interests, an opportunity to encourage good writing in this field."

The Newbery Medal is awarded annually by the American Library Association for the most distinguished American children's book (for children up to age 14) published the previous year. The award committees can, and usually do, cite other books as worthy of attention. Such books were referred to as Newbery or Caldecott "runners-up" before 1971, when the term was changed to "honor books." The new terminology was made retroactive, so that all former runners-up are now referred to as Newbery Honor Books.

The award-winning authors must be citizens or residents of the United States, and the book must be published originally in the United States. The elements the committee examines in nominated titles include:

- interpretation of the theme or concept;
- presentation of information including accuracy, clarity, and organization;
- development of a plot;
- delineation of characters;
- delineation of setting; and
- appropriateness of style.

A book can be nominated for the award by sending a copy to the chairperson of the award committee. The Newbery Award committee currently consists of fifteen members. Seven members are elected annually from a slate of no fewer than fourteen candidates, a chairperson is elected annually from a slate of two candidates, and seven members are appointed by the vice-president. The award winners are announced at the annual ALA midwinter meeting and the winners are invited to speak at the ALA annual conference in the following summer. Since the Newbery and Printz cover some of the same books, many librarians believe the Newbery age level should be lowered. For now, YA librarians will need to check out the Newbery winners for important titles to include in their collections.

Further Reading about the Newbery Award

Association for Library Service to Children. "The Newbery Medal." Available: www.ala.org/alsc/newbery.html Accessed: November 2005.
Bostrum, Kathleen Long. 2003. *Winning Authors: Profiles of the Newbery Medalists.* Englewood, Colo.: Libraries Unlimited.
Hegel, Claudette. 2000. *Newbery and Caldecott Trivia and More for Every Day of the Year.* Englewood, Colo.: Libraries Unlimited.

POPULAR PAPERBACKS FOR YOUNG ADULTS

The Popular Paperbacks List is compiled to encourage young adults to read for pleasure. The themed or genre lists are selected by committee annually. The committee consists of fifteen members, who are appointed by the YALSA vice-president/president-elect for two-year terms starting immediately after the conclusion of one midwinter meeting and ending at the conclusion of midwinter two years later. Each committee determines the number of lists, up to five; it creates and selects its own topics to ensure the inclusion of timely topics, currently fashionable subjects, and fads, and includes popular genres, topics, or themes. Each list has at least ten and no more than twenty-five recommended paperback titles.
To be eligible for the list:

- Titles must be in print and available in paperback.
- Both young adult and adult titles may be considered.
- Popularity is more important than literary quality.
- Both fiction and nonfiction may be considered.
- Copyright dates are not a consideration.
- A book which has appeared on a previous Popular Paperbacks list can be selected after five years have passed since it last appeared on the list.

- Nominations from authors or publishers of their own titles are not eligible for the list.

After the topics have been selected, committee members begin reading and evaluating titles. Members submit nominations (including the author, title, publisher, year of publication, price, and a brief annotation specifying those qualities the member finds noteworthy) to the chair by May 1. The chair compiles the nominations onto a ballot for the committee by May 15. Completed ballots must be returned to the chair no later than June 1. Only titles receiving "yes" votes from a majority of committee members will remain on the list for discussion meetings at the annual conference. At the final meeting a vote is taken and titles not receiving a majority vote are eliminated from the working list.

During the months following the annual meetings to November 1, committee members read and evaluate the remaining titles. Additional nominations must be submitted to the chair no later than November 1. Another ballot is sent to the committee, and the vote is tallied so the resulting list can be discussed at three meetings at midwinter. The nominated titles are posted on the YALSA-BK discussion list periodically.

Comments from observers are welcome at the midwinter meetings. A final list (or lists) is assembled on a ballot at the conclusion of the third meeting. The committee determines its own voting procedures (most require a two-thirds majority for their final vote).

After the list titles have been selected, the committee writes brief annotations to appeal to young adults aged 12 to 18. The final list of selected titles is announced in a press release by the ALA Public Information Office the morning following the committee's last meeting. The press release is posted on YALSA-L. The list is also available on the YALSA Web site and appears in the ALA publication *ALA's Guide to Best Reading*.

Further Reading about Popular Paperbacks for Young Adults

Young Adult Library Services Association. "Popular Paperbacks for Young Adults"
    Available: www.ala.org/yalsa/booklists/poppaper Accessed: November 2005.

THE PRINTZ AWARD

The king of the teen book awards is The Michael L. Printz Award, established in 2000, sponsored by *Booklist*, and awarded by the Young Adult Library Services Association. The award is given to the young adult title published in the previous calendar year that exemplifies excellence in young adult literature. An honor award may be given to up to four more titles.

Michael L. Printz was a school librarian at Topeka West High School in Kansas and worked as a marketing consultant for Econo-Clad Books. Mike was active in YALSA and served on the Best Books for Young Adults Committee and the Margaret A. Edwards Award Committee. Mike was serving his second term of duty on the YALSA's Best Books for Young Adults committee when he became seriously ill and died. His devotion to books and to teens inspired the creation of an award that honors literary excellence in teen literature. The Best Young Adult Book Award Feasibility Task Force (Michael Cart, Hazel Rochman, David Gale, Linda Waddle, and Joel Shoemaker) laid the groundwork for the award that was approved by the YALSA board in January 1999.

The winning title is selected by a committee, which changes from year to year. Currently five of the committee members are appointed by the YALSA administration and four are elected by the YALSA membership, and all members serve two-year terms. Readers can nominate titles for the Printz Award online at the Web site listed below. The award may be given posthumously, providing the other criteria are met. If no title is deemed sufficiently meritorious, no award will be given that year.

To be considered for the Printz Award:

- The nominated titles must be intended for the young adult audience, ages 12–18, by the publisher.
- Titles can be published inside or outside the United States.
- Nominations are open to fiction and nonfiction, graphic novels, anthologies, books with multiple authors, and books in other languages.

The main criterion of the award is literary excellence, which can be a subjective and often fairly controversial judgment. Popularity and the message of the book are not crucial elements for winning this award. Interesting discussions usually follow the announcement of the winner, with many librarians elated with the committee's choices, and many disappointed that their favorite titles were not chosen. The Printz committee aims to award titles that appeal to the best readers rather than the average reader, in the hopes of bringing these excellent books to a wider audience. According to Marc Aronson in *Exploding the Myths: The Truth about Teenagers and Reading*, literary excellence does not mean the book offers moral instruction, values or role models, but recognizes "an author's ability to go deeper, higher, or further—more insightful, more lyrical, more challenging, more revealing, funnier, more inspiring, more thought-provoking—than most." While popularity gives readers what they want, literary excellence will challenge readers to think for themselves and invite them to change.

Depending on the book, one or more of these criteria will be examined:

- story;
- voice;
- style;
- setting;
- accuracy;
- characters;
- theme;
- illustration; and
- design.

Committee members may nominate an unlimited number of titles up to December 1. Librarians and teens may also nominate titles with the cosignature of a committee member. Publishers, authors, or editors may not nominate their own titles.

Each nomination includes the following information: author, title, publisher, price, ISBN, and an annotation specifying those qualities that justify the title for consideration. Nominated titles are discussed at midwinter and annual conference meetings.

The winners are announced at the press conference on Monday of the midwinter meeting. Immediately after the press conference, the Best Books for Young Adults Committee is informed of the winning and honor book titles, bibliographic information, and draft annotations, for automatic inclusion on the final Best Books list.

The award winners are informed with a call and announced at the annual American Library Association midwinter meeting, and the authors are invited to speak at the ALA annual conference the following summer. YA librarians attending the annual conference will get a real treat if they attend the Printz Award Program and Reception to hear these talented authors speak about their writing experiences and inspirations.

Further Reading about the Printz Award

Aronson, Marc. 2001. "Calling All Ye Printz and Printzesses." *Exploding the Myths: The Truth About Teenagers and Reading.* Pp. 109–122. Lanham, Md.: Scarecrow Press.

Bankston, John. 2003. *Michael L. Printz and the Story of the Michael L. Printz Award* (Great Achiever Awards). Bear, DE: Mitchell Lane Publishers.

Young Adult Library Services Association. "The Michael L. Printz Award for Excellence in Young Adult Literature." Available: www.ala.org/yalsa/printz November 2005.

TEENS TOP TEN

Teen readers across the country vote for the annual Teens' Top Ten list sponsored by YALSA. The vote takes place during Teen Read Week in October and gives teens a voice to choose the best new young adult books. YALSA's Young Adult Galley Project provides advance copies of young adult books to teen book discussion groups in schools and libraries, who then create a list of nominations. Teens across the country then cast ballots online for their three favorites during Teen Read Week, creating the Teens' Top Ten booklist of the best new books for young adults.

Further Reading about the Teens Top Ten

American Library Association. "Teens' TopTen Books." Available: www.ala.org/ala/yalsa/teenreading/teenstopten/teenstopten.htm Accessed: February 2006.

TOP TEN BEST BOOKS FOR YOUNG ADULTS

The Top Ten Best Books for Young Adults is selected from the BBYA list of fiction and nonfiction titles published in the past sixteen months that are recommended by the BBYA committee for ages 12–18. The annual list includes fiction and nonfiction titles and is announced at the ALA midwinter meeting.

The BBYA Committee and chair are appointed by the vice-president/president-elect of YALSA for a one-year term renewable for a two-year consecutive term.

Members will be appointed on a staggered basis so that the ideal committee will have five new members appointed each year. Members are expected to attend all committee meetings and read widely from books eligible for nomination. Reappointment is based upon participation. There are fifteen committee members. The editor of the "Books for Youth" section of *Booklist* is a nonvoting member of the committee and serves as an advisor. As of 2002, the Printz Award titles are automatically included in the BBYA list.

The committee considers and votes on books published within their assigned calendar year, January 1 to December 31, in addition to those published between September 1 and December 31 of the previous year. Only committee members may nominate titles published the last four months (September to December) of the previous year. Nominations may be accepted from the field with a second from a BBYA committee member up to November 1 of that calendar year. The nominating form is available at the YALSA Web site below. Publishers cannot nominate their own titles.

To be considered for the BBYA:

- Titles should incorporate acceptable literary quality and effectiveness of presentation.
- Fiction should have characterization and dialog that is believable within the context of the novel or story.
- Nonfiction should have an appealing format and a readable text.

Final selections are made at the midwinter meeting during an intensive series of meetings. After comments from observers and discussion by committee members, a vote is taken to determine if a title should be included on the final list. Publishers can not comment. After observer comments, the chair will provide each book's nominator with the first opportunity to address that title if he or she so desires. Teens who participate at midwinter must have read ten of the titles. They tell how they feel about a book.

A book must receive a minimum of nine "yes" votes to be placed on the final list. Only members attending the midwinter meeting will be allowed to vote, and only on books they have read. After the final discussion and selection, titles are then anno-tated by the committee, to be completed at the last meeting of the committee. The list is prepared for the use of young adults themselves, and annotations will be written to attract the YA reader.

From the Best Books for Young Adults list, the committee selects the Top Ten to showcase the quality and diversity of literature being published for teens.

Further Reading about the Top Ten Best Books for Young Adults

Campbell, Patty. "Blood on the Table: Looking at Best Booking." *The Horn Book Magazine.* May/June 2002, pp. 275–280.
Young Adult Library Services Association. "Best Books for Young Adults." Available: www.ala.org/yalsa/booklists/bbya Accessed: November 2005.

TOP TEN QUICK PICKS FOR RELUCTANT READERS

The Top Ten Quick Picks for Reluctant Readers is compiled annually by an eleven-member committee from the Quick Picks for Reluctant Readers list. The committee selects outstanding titles that will appeal to reluctant teen readers for recreational reading. Reluctant readers are considered those teenagers who, for whatever reason, choose not to read. These titles are provided to stimulate their interest in doing so. The list is not intended for teenagers with reading disabilities, though some of the selected titles may be appropriate for those teens.

The committee consists of eleven members who are appointed by the vice-president of YALSA on a staggered basis for a balance of old and new members. The members serve a one-year term that is renewable for a second year based on participation. The editor of the Books for Youth section of *Booklist* serves as a consultant.

Anyone can nominate a title on a form from the ALSA Web site up to sixty days before the midwinter meeting. Nominations from the field must have a second vote from a committee member. The nominated titles are posted monthly on the YALSA-BK discussion list with the final list of nominations posted on November 1.

To be eligible for the list:

- A book must have a copyright date during the current calendar year or have been published from July to December of the previous calendar year to be considered for the list.
- A book originally published outside the United States will be considered according to its U.S. publication year.
- Any book which was voted on at the midwinter meeting is not eligible for nomination the following year.
- All titles should have appeal as self-selected leisure reading for young adults.
- Books should be evaluated by subject, cover art, readability, format, and style.

The final decisions are made at the midwinter meeting. The committee meets several times to discuss and vote on titles and observers are welcome to comment. Committee members can vote only on nominated books they have read. The final list includes books receiving six or more "yes" votes. Publishers are requested to refrain from promoting their own books.

From this list, the Top Ten are selected. The lists are announced during a press release the morning following the committee's last meeting and posted on the YALSA-L discussion list, on the YALSA Web site and published in ALA's *Guide to Best Reading* and in a spring issue of *Booklist*.

Further Reading about the Top Ten Quick Picks for Reluctant Readers

Young Adult Library Services Association. "Quick Picks for Reluctant Young Adult Readers." Available: www.ala.org/yalsa/booklists/quickpicks Accessed November 2005.

Young Adult Canadian Book Award

The Canadian Library Association Young Adult Services Interest Group announces the Young Adult Book Award at the annual CLA meeting. The award was established in 1980 by the Young Adult Caucus of the Saskatchewan Library Association to recognize the author of an outstanding English language Canadian book for young adults. The award is presented at the book awards banquet at he annual Canadian Library Association conference. The winner receives a leatherbound book with the title, author, and award seal embossed on the cover in gold. The award seal was designed by a young adult from Regina.

To qualify for the award, the book:

- must be creative literature: a novel, short stories, a play, or poetry;
- must be published in Canada during the previous year;
- must appeal to young adults between the ages of 13 and 18; and
- must be written by a Canadian citizen or landed immigrant.

Further Reading about the Young Adult
Canadian Book Award

Canadian Library Association. "Young Adult Canadian Book Award." Available: www.cla.ca/awards/yac.htm Accessed: November 2005.

CHAPTER 5

RECOMMENDED YA RA RESOURCES

Choosing the Right Resource
Print Resources
Review Journals
Electronic Resources
Booklists Online
Readers as Resources

CHOOSING THE RIGHT RESOURCE

The library catalog is the handiest resource to turn to for nonfiction reference searches, but until recently, fiction entries have rarely included subject headings. Newer print resources, and now Internet resources, have helped to provide some of this information by compiling topical lists of titles. Requests for titles to add to a topical list are one of the most popular uses of the YALSA-BK electronic discussion list.

Reading a novel is clearly the best way to get to know it so that you can discuss it and recommend it to readers. If you have enjoyed a book, your enthusiasm while talking about it will increase its appeal to your listeners. However, not too many of us can claim to have read the hundreds of new novels for young adults that publishers release each year. Even if you had the time, there would always be some kinds of books you just couldn't make yourself read. However, with good reader's advisory resources, you can still be knowledgeable about many more books than you can read.

To help match teens and books, several bibliographies and books about booktalking and collection development are discussed in this chapter. Most have a general scope, but many more genre-specific resources appear with the relevant booklists in Part II. It is important to establish a collection of good reader's advisory tools and make them accessible to teens, teachers, parents, and librarians who don't regularly work with teens. Use them yourself when you are unfamiliar with a genre or want to lead teens to resources they can learn to use on their own. These resources can serve as the backbone for your reader's corner. Ten important things to look for when choosing resources are:

Indexes
Plot Summaries

Characteristics of Authors
Best and Representative Titles of Authors
Point of View
Genre
Similar Titles
Recommended Audience
Appeal
Indicates Internal or External Journeys

Indexes

Author, title, and subject indexes are all helpful at different times when searching for information in a reader's advisory resource. Indexes always make a book more accessible, and if you need a quick reference for a reader's advisory, indexes are indispensable. An author index will help you find more titles by the same author, and a title index will help you turn directly to the title entry in the resource, where you can find information about a particular book. A subject index is helpful for finding lists of fiction titles about particular topics of interests to teens. Genre indexes are helpful when searching for more popular titles and authors in a particular genre. The lists and indexes in *The Teen Reader's Advisor* can be used for collection development, for creating title lists for bookmarks and flyers, collecting titles for building displays, and pulling collections together for teachers. They can be most helpful when helping a teen reader find a book.

Plot Summaries

A plot summary is a brief description of what happens in the book. Some books have familiar plots, as noted in the lists of repeated plots later in this book. A classic plot can take us through a whole new adventure in a different setting even though we may know what the ending will be. Knowing what will happen in a story is important to teen readers, and therefore many YA novels are plot-driven, which makes them quick reads. When describing the plot, an accessible resource needs to use language that suits the teen audience. A reader's advisory resource is built into young adult books by publishers, whose blurbs on jackets and back covers offer introductions to characters and plots in language that's friendly to teens. Be aware that library bindings usually do not include these reader-friendly tools.

Characteristics of Authors

A helpful resource will tell something about how an author writes. The style, language, sentence structure, and whether there is a little or a lot of dialog will affect the appeal of a book. In recent years, several authors—Sonya Sones is a popular example—have written verse novels. While verse novels can touch on any subject matter, the format of these books by their various authors is similar: The author tells his or her story using short lines with lots of white space. Other authors might have a lyrical style that includes magical realism (often said of David Almond's work), while authors like Chris Crutcher and Alex Flinn use realistic language and situations. Authors sometimes like to try different styles to reach more of the teen audience, but many build a fan base by using a consistent and comfortably predictable writing style. Since several authors write for both the adult and young adult audiences, we can't assume that all their titles are appropriate for teens, even when the author is very popular with teens—for example, Meg Cabot.

Best and Representative Titles of Authors

Everything an author writes may not satisfy a teen reader—even if it's a work by the teen's favorite author. When recommending a new author to a reader, it's best to choose a popular title or an award winner. When a title is recommended in several RA resources, it is because it has satisfied a lot of readers and reviewers; it is probably worth introducing to your teen patrons. The reader can then make a decision if the author is right for him or her. The titles included in *The Teen Reader's Advisor* are award winners by popular authors, often from *The Core Collection*, or recommended by YA librarians, and/or have received good reviews.

Point of View

A teen reader can be very particular about the speaker in a story. A first-person point of view—one that tells everything from the main character's point of view—can give us insight into that character's motives, yet the other characters may not be fully revealed. First person is pretty common in YA literature, since it feels more like you are the main character's confidant(e). First person offers more insight into the motivations of the character. Authors may opt to use first person for more than one character by alternating voices with each chapter, so the reader gets insight into the thoughts of several characters. Some readers do object to the "I did this and then this happened to me" flavor of a first-person story. An omnipotent third-person point of view can give us more insight into several characters and show us what is happening to them before they are brought together in the story. Reader's will sometimes find out that the narrator is not reliable. At some point in the story, readers are given a clue that perhaps they haven't heard the whole story. Gale Giles' *Dead Girls Don't Write Letters* is one such title.

Genre

The genre, or type of book, is often one of the first things a teen reader looks for when choosing a book. Popular genres for teens include romance, historical fiction, science fiction, fantasy, realistic fiction, horror, and inspirational stories. Within those genres are sub-genres, such as the "problem novel" that became popular in the 1980s and same-sex romance, which is popular now. Classifying fiction into genres is a start, but other elements that determine appeal are also at work in a novel, so a reader may like Star Wars science fiction and turn away from Roswell High or a Star Trek series. A romance reader may prefer historical or contemporary romances, or only those with happy endings. A fantasy reader may love dragons and knights, but not care for elves, dwarves, or fairies. Genre lists are helpful to guide readers and advisors toward a group of books, but you can't assume that a reader who likes a specific genre will like everything in that genre. Within the chapters that focus on genre lists in this book, each list focuses on one aspect of the genre.

Similar Titles

Read alike lists are a good guide for readers but can be a little more difficult to compile. "If you liked this book (or author), then you might like this one . . . " Besides covering a similar topic, read alike titles may have similar main characters, a similar style of writing, or a similar plot. Read alike lists are only suggestions; they are subjective, as are most reader's advisory lists, so every reader or librarian may not agree about every title on a read alike list! Lists of this type include the King Arthur stories in Chapter 9, Fantasy, and the lists in Repeated Plots and Recycled Characters, Chapter 8.

Recommended Audience

Resources that list a recommended audience for a title are helpful for collection development and reader's advisory. The recommended age or grade level helps you determine if the book is appropriate for the audience you want to serve. Since teens mature at different rates and have different issues at different ages, and sometimes are worried about appearing to read under their grade level, our library groups all young adult books for grades 7 through 12 in the same collection. Other libraries prefer to divide the collection into two parts, one for younger teens and one for older teens. Physical division of the collection is a matter of philosophy and finding what works for your community. Knowing a book's targeted audience can help you guide a reader to an appropriate selection once you've determined the reading level and interest level of the teen. This book uses grade levels recommended by reviewers and publishers. If no grade level has been specified, the term "YA" is used. If the book is an adult title with young adult appeal, the term used is "YA/A."

Appeal

Pace, characterization, story line, and frame are the real nuts and bolts of what determines a good read. If the book is a page-turner, if the characters are quirky, if the story line follows a classic plot like *Romeo and Juliet,* if the story takes place in a large contemporary city or in the country—any variation and combination of these elements will attract and satisfy different readers. A reader's advisory tool needs to address appeal factors to be useful, so you can define exactly what makes a book a good read to a certain kind of reader.

Indicates Internal or External Journeys

Generally speaking, girls enjoy books that have internal journeys. That is, books about changes within a character, such as a coming-of-age experience, and the characters' interaction with one another, such as friendships and romances. Reading about feelings and relationships with parents, siblings, friends, and lovers appeals to girls more often than boys. Boys usually enjoy books that have external journeys and tell the reader something about the real world around them or explore an imaginary world. Because of this natural interest, boys are often drawn to nonfiction, but they may also enjoy science fiction because of technology and space exploration, fantasy because of quests into other worlds, and adventures because of exploration of the earthly world. Some books in these genres may also include relationship and coming-of-age stories, but those aspects generally aren't the major attraction to boys.

Following is a list of ten useful print reader's advisory resources. These are good additions to your own reference shelf but may be even more useful in a reader's corner area that is accessible to all librarians and patrons. If your library has staff or reader's advisory meetings, take a couple of these books to each meeting and describe the highlights of each title with your coworkers.

> *Teen Genreflecting : A Guide to Reading Interests*
> *A Core Collection for Young Adults*
> *What Do Children and Young Adults Read Next?*
> *Radical Reads: 101 YA Novels on the Edge*
> *The World's Best Thin Books*
> *Best Books for Middle and Junior High Readers*
> *Popular Series Reading for Middle School and Teen Readers*
> *High/Low Handbook*
> *100 More Popular Young Adult Authors*
> *Teen Reading Connections*

Herald, Diana Tixier. 2003. *Teen Genreflecting: A Guide to Reading Interests.* Second edition. Westport, CT.: Libraries Unlimited.

Librarians love *Teen Genreflecting* for the way its groups suggested titles into genre lists. This second edition includes genre and theme lists of more than 1500 titles, most of which were published in the last decade. The text includes brief summaries of each title, and there are author, title, and subject indexes. The appendices include reader's advisory resources and tips for building a teen fiction collection.

Jones, Patrick, Patricia Taylor, and Kirsten Edwards. 2003. *A Core Collection for Young Adults.* New York: Neal-Schuman.

This core collection includes more than 700 annotated fiction titles and favorites lists compiled by many veteran young adult librarians. An accompanying CD is convenient to use for collection development.

Ansell, Janis, and Pam Spencer Holley. 2004. *What Do Children and Young Adults Read Next? A Reader's Guide to Fiction for Children and Young Adults.* Volume 6. Detroit, MI: Thomson Gale.

What Do Children and Young Adults Read Next?: A Reader's Guide to Fiction for Children and Young Adults has been combined with the children's titles in this newest edition. Title listings include subject, recommended ages, time period, locale, summary, awards, other books by the author, and other books the reader might like. The many indexes, including character descriptions and country settings, make it a valuable tool for reader's advisory. The book's imposing size (over 1000 pages) limits its use to librarians.

Bodart, Joni Richards. 2002. *Radical Reads: 101 YA Novels on the Edge*. Lanham, MD: Scarecrow.

This book provides booktalks, plot summaries, subject lists, and more for 101 edgier titles. A new edition is in the works at this writing.

Bodart, Joni Richards. 2000. *The World's Best Thin Books*. Lanham, MD: Scarecrow Trade.

An almost universal trait of teens is procrastination, so YA librarians often encounter desperate students and parents looking for a skinny book to read by tomorrow! This book has a good list of titles you may want to include in your collection.

Gillespie, John T., and Catherine Barr. 2004. *Best Books for Middle and Junior High Readers, Grades 6–9*. Westport, CT: Libraries Unlimited.

More than 1400 titles are arranged by theme with plot summaries. Title copyrights are from 1999 to 2003, with some earlier classics included.

Gillespie, John T., and Catherine Barr. 2004. *Best Books for High School Readers, Grades 9–12*. Westport, CT: Libraries Unlimited.

More than 1200 titles, also arranged by theme with plot summaries. Title copyrights are from 1999 to 2003.

Thomas, Rebecca L., and Catherine Barr. 2004. *Popular Series Reading for Middle School and Teen Readers: A Reading and Selection Guide*. Westport, CT: Libraries Unlimited.

This is a guide to more than 800 series for teens; it includes Accelerated Reader notations.

Libretto, Ellen V., and Catherine Barr. 2002. *High/Low Handbook: Best Books and Web Sites for Reluctant Teen Readers*. Fourth edition. Westport, CT: Libraries Unlimited

Many titles and Web sites that reluctant readers will like are listed here in subject categories. Many titles are from smaller publishers.

Drew, Bernard A. 2002. *100 More Popular Young Adult Authors: Biographical Sketches and Bibliographies*. Libraries Unlimited.

A companion to *100 Most Popular Young Adult Authors*, this volume has 100 more biographical sketches and provides bibliographies of each author's titles.

Reynolds, Tom K. 2005. *Teen Reading Connections*. New York: Neal-Schuman

Includes tips and suggestions for more effective booktalks, teen spaces, book displays, promotion, discussion groups, school programs, and use of technology.

REVIEW JOURNALS

Review journals are indispensable to librarians for selecting books, but they are also helpful for reader's advisory. Some reviewers will compare titles to others, recommend age groups, and discuss other elements of appeal. Librarians, writers, editors,

and teens are solicited for their opinions on the newest titles in young adult literature. *VOYA* also adds a popularity rating and teen reviews, which give us a good hint
if the book might do well with teens at our library. Here is a list of review journals
popular with young adult librarians, with Web site URLs where you can find current
subscription information:

VOYA Voice of Youth Advocates
School Library Journal
YALS Young Adult Library Services
Teacher Librarian
Horn Book
Kirkus Reviews
ALAN Review
Booklist
Kliatt
Library Media Connection

VOYA Voice of Youth Advocates

VOYA Voice of Youth Advocates. 6 issues per year. The magazine for young adult
librarians has recently taken on a new look, but still contains valuable reviews rating
YA titles by quality and popularity, 1–5. Articles focusing on genre titles or graphic
formats can increase your knowledge about these areas. The Web site can be found at
www.VOYA.com.

School Library Journal

School Library Journal. Monthly, August to May. The magazine and Web site both
provide news, features, reviews, and columns about children's and young adult
materials. The Web site—www.schoollibraryjournal.com/—offers online access to
reviews with a subscription. The database is searchable using several criteria, including grade level (goes to grades 9 and up).

YALS Young Adult Library Services

Young Adult Library Services. YALSA. 4 issues per year. Articles from YA librarians in
the field about all aspects of YA service. Subscription is free to YALSA members.

Teacher Librarian

Teacher Librarian. 5 issues per year. This professional development magazine for
school librarians has articles, reviews, and commentary and criticism on management
and programming issues. The Web site is www.teacherlibrarian.com.

Horn Book Magazine

Horn Book Magazine. 6 issues per year. *Horn Book* has extensive book reviews,
choosing the best of what is published for children and young adults. The Web site is
www.hbook.com/publications/magazine/.

Kirkus Reviews

Kirkus Reviews. 24 issues per year. Kirkus publishes nearly 5,000 reviews per year. Either a print or an online subscription gives you access to 500 prepublication book reviews every month. Web site is www.kirkusreviews.com/kirkusreviews/index.jsp.

ALAN Review

The Assembly for Literature for Adolescents publishes the *ALAN Review* three times each year (fall, winter, and spring). The journal contains articles on teaching YA literature, interviews with authors, reports on publishing trends, current research on YA literature, a section of reviews of new books, and ALAN membership news. An electronic archive of past issues is available at http://scholar.lib.vt.edu/ejournals/ALAN/alan-review.html.

Booklist

Booklist. 22 issues per year. *Booklist* offers author interviews and reviews of print and nonprint materials for small and medium-size public libraries and school libraries. The Web site is http://archive.ala.org/booklist/.

Kliatt

Kliatt. 6 issues per year. *Kliatt* has critical in-depth reviews of selected paperbacks, hardcover fiction, audio books, and educational software programs for junior high, high school, and public libraries.

Library Media Connection

Library Media Connection. 7 issues per year. LMC has information, tips, and ideas for library service and collaborations with book and technology reviews. The Web site is www.linworth.com/lmc.html

ELECTRONIC RESOURCES

The computer is a great tool for librarians and readers. Web sites, databases, and discussion lists provide resources that can be updated quickly and frequently. Ten electronic resources helpful for reader's advisory are:

Novelist
YALSA-BK Discussion List
Best Books for Young Adults
Quick Picks for Reluctant Young Readers
Popular Paperbacks for Young Adults
Best of the Best
Reading Rants
Adbooks Discussion List
Genrefluent
Favorite Teenage Angst Books

Novelist

Novelist is an online database by subscription. Novelist keeps adding new features and is a valuable readers advisory resource for both librarians and readers. Helpful for finding read alike titles and authors. Be sure to show teen readers how to use this database. Available: http://connection.epnet.com/content/

YALSA-BK Discussion List

YALSA-BK is a book discussion e-mail list hosted by YALSA. You are invited to discuss YA literature with other YA librarians. Learn what's up and coming, what's hot and what's not, and the newest book challenges around the country. Available: http;//lists.ala.org/wws/info/yalsa-bk

Best Books for Young Adults

BBYA is an annual list selected by fifteen YALSA committee members plus an administrative assistant and a consultant from the staff of *Booklist*. The titles are adult and teenage books significant for young adults selected from the year's publications. The lists are available at www.ala.org/yalsa/booklists/bbya.

Quick Picks for Reluctant Young Readers

A YALSA committee of eleven plus one administrative assistant and one consultant from the staff of *Booklist* prepares an annual annotated list of recommended books appropriate for reluctant young adult readers. The list can be viewed at www.ala.org/ala/yalsa/booklistsawards/quickpicks/quickpicksreluctant.htm.

Popular Paperbacks for Young Adults

A YALSA committee of fifteen, plus an administrative assistant if requested, prepares one to five annotated list(s) of approximately twenty-five recommended paperback titles, selected from popular reading/genre themes or topics. Available: http://www.ala.org/ala/yalsa/booklistsawards/popularpaperback/popularpaperbacks.htm

Best of the Best

The Young Adult Library Services Association periodically selects the best books for young adults from the past decade. At the preconference of the ALA annual conference, participants choose 100 titles from YALSA's Best Books for Young Adults, Alex, and Printz awards lists.

Reading Rants

Jennifer Hubert, a middle school librarian in Manhattan, maintains the Reading Rants book review site just for teens. Her booklists have hip titles, and the reviews are written to be teen-friendly. Reading Rants is updated every two months and is available at http://tln.lib.mi.us/~amutch/jen/.

Adbooks Discussion List

Adbooks is a busy book discussion list for librarians and readers of adolescent fiction. The discussion focuses on two titles each month but may venture on to other titles. The Web site is www.adbooks.org/.

Genrefluent

Diana Tixier Herald, the author of *Teen Genreflecting,* hosts her book review Web site at www.genrefluent.com/index.html.

Favorite Teenage Angst Books

The Grouchy Café presents Favorite Teenage Angst Books at www.grouchy.com/angst/. Cathy Young, consultant, editor, and reviewer, posts reviews for teen readers. Author interviews and a message board for teens rounds out the site.

BOOKLISTS ONLINE

Many public libraries offer their own topical booklists of suggested titles at their Web sites. You might start with one of their lists, add new titles or your favorites, and create reader's advisory lists for own your library's Web site. The Virtual YA Index lists "Public Libraries with Young Adult Web Pages" at http://yahelp.suffolk.lib.ny.us/virtual.html. This is a useful site for browsing teen pages of many libraries. Check out how they are offering readers advisory services for teens and borrow their best ideas to build your own site. Search for libraries that publish teen booklists and reviews, add links to their sites, then show them to your teen patrons to provide models for creating their own review page.

Berkeley Public Library

Teen Services. "Booklists." Available: http://berkeleypubliclibrary.org/teen/booklist.html. Accessed: March 2006.

Boston Public Library

"Booklists for Teens: Teen Lounge." Available: www.bpl.org/teens/booklists/index.htm. Accessed: March 2006.

Carnegie Library of Pittsburgh

"Teens: Staff Suggestions" Available: www.clpgh.org/teens/read/teenlists.html. Accessed: March 2006.

Fresno County Public Library

"Recommended Reads: Fiction." Available: www.fresnolibrary.org/teen/bn/fiction.html. Accessed: March 2006.

Hennepin County Public Library

"TeenLinks: Read On." Available: www.hclib.org/teens/read.cfm. Accessed: March 2006.

Kalamazoo Public Library

"Teen: Reading Rocks." Available: www.kpl.gov/teen/ReadingRocks.aspx. Accessed: March 2006.

King County Library System

"Teen Zone: Booklists." Available: www.kcls.org/teens/Accessed: March 2006.

Mid-Continent Public Library

"Teen Reading Lists." Available: www.mcpl.lib.mo.us/readers/lists/teen/. March 2006.

New York Public Library

"TeenLink: More Books." http://teenlink.nypl.org/MoreBooks.cfm Available: March 2006.

Pasadena Public Library

"Teen Scene: Read All About It." Available: www.ci.pasadena.ca.us/libraryteens/read.asp. Accessed: March 2006.

Plymouth District Library

"Teen Zone: PDL Teen Booklists." Available: http://plymouthlibrary.org/yabibs.htm. Accessed: March 2006.

Santa Clara County Public Library

"Books & Authors for Teens." Available: www.santaclaracountylib.org/teen/biblcent.html. Accessed: March 2006.

Springfield City Library

"Recommended Reading Lists: Booklists for Teens." Available: www.springfieldlibrary.org/reading/booklist.html. Accessed: March 2006.

READERS AS RESOURCES

Feedback from teen readers is listed last in this chapter but not because it is the least important reader's advisory resource. Our readers are not always thought of as helpful resources, but there are several fun and easy ways to encourage teens to share what they read with you and other teen readers. A display of books with a sign that says "Our Teen Advisory Board Recommends . . . " or "Coshocton Public Library Teens

Suggest . . . " will not only attract teen readers, but encourage teens to share what they read. Here is a list of Web sites that offer book reviews written by teens:

Amazon Online
Smart Girl
Miss Thang Reads
Barnes and Noble Online
Y Read
Teenreads
Review and React

Amazon Online

"The world's largest online bookstore" offers many features that are valuable to librarians and readers, and now libraries are beginning to adopt some of their practices. Customer reviews and "Listmania" give readers several ways to interact with other readers and share their reading interests. Available: www.amazon.com

Smart Girl

The University of Michigan hosts SmartGirl at www.smartgirl.com. SmartGirl invites teen reviews on books, movies, Web sites, magazines and more. SmartGirl sponsors a reading survey each year during Teen Read Week.

Miss Thang Reads

Here is an example of a live journal site where teens are invited to comment on the posts. Miss Thang (Hannah) writes a review of what she is reading, and teens can leave comments about the books. Check it out at www.livejournal.com/users/missthang_reads.

Barnes and Noble Online

Barnes and Noble is another commercial book site that welcomes customer reviews. The site is www.barnesandnoble.com.

Y Read

Y Read at www.yread.org/intro.html is hosted by the Cleveland Public Library. The site features a new title each month and invites readers to post their thoughts on the book on a message board.

Teenreads

The Book Report Network hosts Teenreads at www.teenreads.com. The site provides information and features about favorite authors, books, series, and characters, and a place where teens can talk about their favorite books and find hip new titles.

Review and React

This site was developed for a high school library in Minnesota for students to write reviews and react to posted reviews. Take a look at www.reviewandreact.com.

PART II

THE SUBJECT AND GENRE BOOKLISTS: A TO Z

CHAPTER 6

ADVENTURE

Facing adversity while trying to survive or accomplish a quest is an exciting adventure theme. The adventure begins when our likable protagonists face the threatening forces of nature, or human or animal opponents. The teen heroes in contemporary YA adventures test their limits. Sometimes they make impulsive decisions, but they always triumph in the end. The adventure, while exciting, dramatic, and action-packed, is merely the background for the growth and changes that inevitably occur in the characters. Romance, history, and fantasy may accompany the reader on an adventure.

Classic Adventure
On the Water
Pirates/Swashbucklers
Runaways
Survival
Traveling Teens
Unexpected Heroes
Resources: Additional Titles

CLASSIC ADVENTURE

Alexander, Lloyd. **Westmark.**
Dutton, 1981.
Series: Westmark Trilogy: **Kestrel; The Beggar Queen.**
Setting: Renaissance kingdom.
Main Character: Male, Theo, young boy, a printer's apprentice.

Theo flees criminal charges with his companions—a charlatan, a dwarf, and an urchin girl—and wanders about the kingdom of Westmark. Awards: CC; BBYA. Grades: 6–9.

George, Jean Craighead. **Julie of the Wolves.**
HarperCollins, 1972.
Sequels: **Julie; Julie's Wolf Pack.**
Setting: Alaska.
Main Character: Female Eskimo, Julie, 13 years old.

Julie runs away from an arranged marriage, hoping to find her pen pal in San Francisco. She becomes lost in the Alaskan tundra and is adopted by a wolf pack. In *Julie*, she returns to the Alaskan community, and then comes back to study the wolves as an adult in *Julie's Wolf Pack*. Julie is torn between her native Eskimo ways and the modern white culture. Awards: Newbery. Grades: 7–8.

George, Jean Craighead. *My Side of the Mountain.*
Dutton, 1959.
Sequels: *On the Far Side of the Mountain; Frightful's Mountain.*
Setting: Catskills Mountains.
Main Character: Male, Sam Gribley, young boy.

Sam lives alone in the mountains for a year, making a home in a hollowed out tree and befriending the animals. Sam's sister Alice joins him in the second book and *Frightful's Mountain* is from his falcon friend's perspective. Awards: CC; Newbery Honor. Grades: 7–8.

London, Jack. *Call of the Wild.*
Scholastic Paperbacks, 2001.
Setting: Yukon Territory, 1896.
Main Character: Buck, a dog.

As the Gold Rush boomed in the Klondike, a black market developed for large dogs to be used for beasts of burden. Buck is stolen and taken to work in the gold fields where he struggles for survival and his place among the huskies and half breeds. Originally published in 1903, the story is told from Buck's point of view. Awards: CC. Grades: 6–12.

Montgomery, Lucy Maud. *Anne of Green Gables.*
Children's Classics, 1998.
Sequels: *Anne of the Island; Anne of Avonlea; Anne of Windy Poplars; Anne's House of Dreams; Anne of Ingleside; Rainbow Valley; Rilla of Ingelside.*
Setting: Avonlea, Prince Edward Island, Canada, late nineteenth century.
Main Character: Female orphan, Anne Shirley, 11 years old.

Anne is sent to live on a farm on Prince Edward Island with Marilla and Matthew, who were expecting a boy. Anne's plucky spirit wins them over and attracts friends and trouble. The first book of the series covers Anne's first five years in Avonlea. Originally published in 1908. Awards: CC. Grades: 6–10.

Stevenson, Robert Louis. *Kidnapped.*
Atheneum, 2004.
Setting: Scotland, the sea, Eighteenth century.
Main Character: Male, David Balfour, 17 years old.

After the death of his father, David sets out through the highlands of Scotland to meet his Uncle Ebenezer and claim his inheritance. He encounters murder, adventure on the high seas, and betrayal when he is kidnapped and carried off to the Carolinas. Originally published in 1886. Grades: 5–9.

Stevenson, Robert Louis. *Treasure Island.*
Signet Classics, 1998.
Setting: The sea.
Main Character: Male, Jim Hawkins, early teens, a cabin boy.

Jim finds an old pirate map showing a small island marked with a red cross; he knows that a fortune in gold lies waiting for him. Aboard a ship named the *Hispaniola,* Jim sails toward Treasure Island. He learns that the one-legged man who signed on as ship's cook is really the famous pirate Long John Silver. Originally published in 1883. Grades: 7–12.

Twain, Mark. *The Adventures of Tom Sawyer.*
Gramercy, 2002.
Sequel: *Adventures of Huckleberry Finn* (CC).
Setting: Missouri, Mississippi River.
Main Characters: Male, Tom Sawyer; Male, Huckleberry Finn; both young teens.

Tom's adventures are an exploration of childhood and the many adventures it brings through imagination and the reality of witnessing a murder. In Huck's adventures, Huck escapes "sivilization" with runaway slave Jim. Action and adventure keep the reader engaged, but the dialects, while adding authenticity, can be difficult for some readers. Originally published in 1894. Grades: 6–12.

Verne, Jules. *Around the World in Eighty Days.*
Modern Library, 2003.
Setting: London, England, 1872.
Main Character: Male, Phileas Fogg, adult male.

Phileas tries to win a bet that he can travel around the world in eighty days. He is tracked by bounty hunter Detective Fix, who is sure he is on the trail of a notorious bank robber. A classic action adventure recently made into a second movie version. Originally published in 1872. Awards: CC. Grades: 7–12.

Verne, Jules. *Twenty Thousand Leagues under the Sea.*
Tor Classics, 1995.
Setting: The sea, 1866.
Main Characters: French Male, Professor Arronax, and two companions, adult males.

The three companions investigate reports of a sea monster and become prisoners in Captain Nemo's submarine, the *Nautilus.* This science fiction sea adventure is even more fascinating when the reader realizes that Verne's vision of the *Nautilus* was written before submarines existed. Originally published in 1870. Awards: CC. Grades: 7–12.

ON THE WATER

Carter, Alden. *Between a Rock and a Hard Place.*
Scholastic Trade, 1995.
Setting: Minnesota wilderness.
Main Characters: Males, Mark, 15 years old and his diabetic cousin, Randy, also 15 years old.

Mark and Randy begin a canoe trip that becomes a fight for survival when a bear takes their food and they lose their canoe and supplies in the rapids. This survival tale will appeal to Gary Paulsen readers. Awards: CC. Grades: 7–10.

Fama, Elizabeth. *Overboard.*
Cricket Books, 2002.
Setting: Off the coast of Sumatra.
Main Characters: Female, Emily, 14 years old and Isman, an Islamic Indonesian boy younger than Emily.

Emily survives a ferry accident with Isman, a boy she meets in the water. They draw comfort from each other, as Isman's Islamic faith gives Emily strength but also frustrates her. The story was inspired by a real ferry accident off the coast of Sumatra. Grades: 5–8.

Hobbs, Will. *Downriver.*
Atheneum, 1991.
Setting: Colorado River through the Grand Canyon.
Main Character: Female, Jessie, 15 years old

In an action-packed and suspenseful tale with well-developed characters, eight problem teens sent to a camp steal supplies to raft the Colorado River. Awards: CC. Grades: 6–12.

Hobbs, Will. *Wild Man Island.*
HarperCollins, 2002.
Setting: Admiralty Island, Alaska, contemporary.
Main Character: Male, Andy Galloway, 14 years old.

Andy leaves his kayaking group to visit the site of his archeologist father's death. Stranded by a storm, he encounters the island inhabitants and searches for traces of prehistoric immigrants to America. Archeology, survival, and suspense keep the reader engaged, as Andy discovers what his father was trying to find. Grades: 5–9.

Martel, Yann. *Life of Pi.*
Harvest Books, 2003.
Setting: India, Pacific Ocean.
Main Character: Male, Pi Patel, 16 years old.

The son of an Indian zookeeper, Pi is shipwrecked when his family packs up to move to Canada. Stranded on a lifeboat with a wounded zebra, a spotted hyena, a seasick orangutan, and a 450-pound Bengal tiger named Richard Parker, Pi survives for 227 days. A fascinating survival story with a thought-provoking twist at the end. Grades: 9–12.

McKernan, Victoria. *Shackleton's Stowaway.*
Knopf Books for Young Readers, 2005.
Setting: Antarctica, 1914.
Main Character: Male, Perce Blackbarow, 18 years old.

Perce stowed away on the *Endurance* to accompany Shackleton to the Antarctic, but the ship is crushed in the ice and sinks. An authentic accounting of the

Shackleton expedition from the young stowaway's point of view, in a diary format. Grades: 6–9.

O'Dell, Scott. *Island of the Blue Dolphins.*
Houghton Mifflin, 1990.
Setting: Deserted island off the coast of California.
Main Character: Female, Karana, 12 years old.
   When her tribe is evacuated from their home island, Karana jumps ship when she realizes her little brother was left behind. After he is killed, she survives alone on an island for eighteen years. A Native American survival story based on a true story. Awards: Newbery. Grades: 5–8.

Salisbury, Graham. *Lord of the Deep.*
Delacorte Books for Young Readers, 2001.
Setting: Hawaii.
Main Character: Male, Mikey Donovan, 13 years old.
   Mikey is the new deckhand on his stepfather's charter fishing boat, learning deep-sea fishing secrets from a master. Thrilling sports fishing scenes. Grades: 5–12.

Taylor, Theodore. *Rogue Wave and other Red-Blooded Sea Stories.*
Harcourt Children's Books, 1996.
   Eight short stories about survival on the seas appealing to reluctant readers. Grades: 7–12.

Zindel, Paul. *Reef of Death.*
Hyperion, 1998.
Setting: Great Barrier Reef, Australia.
Main Character: Male, PC McPhee, 17 years old.
   PC helps a beautiful Aboriginal girl find her family's treasure in this page-turner fantasy with a treasure hunt, an evil scientist, and a monster. Grades: 6–9.

PIRATES/SWASHBUCKLERS

Avi. *The True Confessions of Charlotte Doyle.*
Scholastic, 1990.
Setting: Sea journey from England to Rhode Island in 1832.
Main Character: Female, Charlotte Doyle, 13 years old.
   Charlotte is the only passenger on a ship when the crew launches a mutiny against the murderous captain. Awards: CC; Newbery Honor. Grades: 6–9.

Dumas, Alexandre. *The Three Musketeers.*
Borgo Press, 2002.
Sequels: *Twenty Years After; The Man in the Iron Mask.*
Setting: Paris, France.
Main Character: Male, D'Artagnan, adult male.
   D'Artagnan arrives in Paris hoping to enlist with the King's Musketeers. He is challenged to three duels in his first afternoon in the city by men who turn out to be

Porthos, Aramis, and Athos—the Three Musketeers. Twists of fate have D'Artagnan battling for them against the evil Cardinal Richelieu's guards, demonstrating his worth with a sword. Political intrigue and language may challenge younger readers. Awards: CC. Grades: 8–12.

Ferris, Jean. *Into the Wind.*
Flare, 1996.
Series: American Dreams: *Song of the Sea; Weather the Storm.*
Setting: 1814.
Main Character: Female, Rosie, 17 years old.
　　Rosie's father is killed in a barroom brawl, and she is rescued by a dashing ship's captain, Raider, in this romantic historical adventure trilogy. Grades: 9–12.

Hawkins, Karen. *Catherine and the Pirate.*
Avon, 2002.
Series: Avon True Romance: *Amelia and the Outlaw; Tess and the High-lander; Emily and the Scot; Samantha and the Cowboy; Josephine and the Soldier.*
Setting: Voyage from Boston to Savannah.
Main Character: Female, Catherine Markham, 17 years old.
　　Catherine falls in love with the pirate that escorts her on the voyage in this historical romance. Grades: YA.

Lawrence, Iain. *The Wreckers.*
Yearling, 1999.
Sequels: High Seas Trilogy: *The Smugglers; The Buccaneers.*
Setting: Coast of Cornwall, England.
Main Character: Male, John Spencer, 14 years old.
　　John and his father are shipwrecked, and it turns out to be no accident. Mary, a 13-year-old girl, helps John find his father and stop the wreckers who are luring ships into the rocky shore. An exciting page-turner historical adventure, like *Treasure Island* and *Kidnapped.* Awards: CC. Grades: 7–9.

McCaughrean, Geraldine. *The Pirate's Son.*
Scholastic, 1999.
Setting: Voyage from England to Madagascar, eighteenth century.
Main Characters: Male, Nathan Gull, 14 years old; Tamo, the pirate's son; Nathan's little sister, Maud.
　　Nathan and Maud are left penniless and accompany Tamo to his homeland of Madagascar, where they encounter cutthroats. Dramatic events and descriptions and an exciting ship chase are told through shifting points of view. Grades: 7–12.

Meyer, Louis A. *Bloody Jack: Being an Account of the Curious Adventures of Mary "Jacky" Faber, Ship's Boy.*
Harcourt Children's Books, 2002.
Sequels: Bloody Jack Adventures: *Curse of the Blue Tattoo: Being an Account of the Misadventures of Jacky Faber, Midshipman and Fine Lady;*

Under the Jolly Roger: Being an Account of the Further Nautical Adventures of Jacky Faber.
Setting: London, 1797.
Main Character: Female orphan, Mary, 13 years old.
Mary disguises herself as a boy to get on a British warship set for the high seas.
Grades: 7–12.

Oppel, Kenneth. ***Airborne.***
Eos, 2004.
Sequel: ***Skybreaker.***
Setting: Airship.
Main Characters: Male, Matt, 15 years old and Kate, a passenger, teenager.
Matt, a cabin boy, and Kate, a passenger on the airship *Aurora*, team up to look for mysterious winged creatures, encountering thieving pirates in a fantasy adventure. Awards: Printz Honor. Grades: 6–10.

Rees, Celia. ***Pirates!***
Bloomsbury USA Children's Books, 2003.
Setting: Jamaica, 1722.
Main Characters: Female, Nancy Kington and slave friend, Minerva Sharpe; both 16 years old.
Nancy escapes an arranged marriage to become a pirate with Minerva in search of treasure. Exciting swashbuckling action and a page-turner showdown with the evil Brazilian Nancy was to marry. Grades: 6–9.

Thompson, Julian F. ***Terry and the Pirates.***
Atheneum, 2000.
Setting: Island in the Bermuda Triangle.
Main Character: Female, Terry Talley, 16 years old.
Terry stows away on a yacht, encounters another runaway, and is shipwrecked in the Bermuda Triangle with pirates looking for treasure. Outrageous and farfetched, but a funny and lighthearted romp. Grades: 9–12.

RUNAWAYS

Almond, David. ***Heaven Eyes.***
Delacorte, 2001.
Setting: England.
Main Characters: Orphans Erin Law, January Carr, and Mouse Gullane; all middle school age.
Erin, January, and Mouse escape an orphanage on a raft and float into another world, where they meet a strange old man and a girl with webbed fingers.
Awards: CC; Carnegie Medal. Grades: 6–9.

Crutcher, Chris. ***The Crazy Horse Electric Game.***
Greenwillow, 1987.
Setting: Montana, California.

Main Character: Male, Willie Weaver, 17 years old.

Willie, a star pitcher, leads his team against the powerful squad from Crazy Horse Electric for the Eastern Montana American Legion baseball championship. When Willie suffers a head injury in a water skiing accident, he is unable to accept the loss of his athletic prowess, the pity of others, and his parents' troubled marriage. Willie runs away and ends up in the inner city of Oakland, California. Willie's story has a lot going on: the crib death of his sister, divorce, drugs, sexual feelings, gang violence, mental handicaps, physical handicaps, prostitution, child beating, and more. Awards: CC. Grades: 8–12.

Farmer, Nancy. *A Girl Named Disaster.*
Orchard, 1996.
Setting: Mozambique, Africa, 1981.
Main Character: Female, Nhamo, 11 years old.

Nhamo runs away to Zimbabwe to escape from an arranged marriage. Recommend to readers who liked *Island of the Dolphins* and *Julie of the Wolves.* Awards: CC; Newbery Honor; National Book Award. Grades: 6–9.

Gilstrap, John. *Nathan's Run.*
HarperCollins, 1996.
Setting: Virginia, 1990s.
Main Character: Male, Nathan, 12 years old.

Nathan, an orphan, is locked up in a juvenile detention center after stealing a car belonging to his no-good guardian. He escapes after killing a guard in self-defense, then eludes the police with limited street smarts and dumb luck. While holed up in a vacant house, he tunes into a call-in radio show on which he is the topic of discussion. After hearing a number of adults condemn his behavior, he calls the show and tells his side of the story. One officer investigates Nathan's side of the story, and it's a race between the good cop and a contract killer to see who finds the boy first. A page-turner for older readers due to violence and gore. Awards: CC. Grades: 9–12.

Kidd, Sue Monk. *The Secret Life of Bees.*
Viking, 2002.
Setting: South Carolina, 1960s.
Main Character: Female, Lily Owen, 14 years old.

Lily imagines a blissful infancy when she was loved and nurtured by her mother, Deborah, whom, according to the family story, Lily accidentally shot and killed. All Lily has left of Deborah is an image of a Black Madonna, with the words "Tiburon, South Carolina" scrawled on the back. When Lily's beloved African American nanny, Rosaleen, manages to insult a group of angry white men on her way to register to vote and has to skip town, Lily takes the opportunity to go with her, fleeing to the only place she can think of, Tiburon, South Carolina, determined to find out more about her dead mother. Grades: 9–12.

Hobbs, Will. *The Maze.*
HarperCollins, 1998.
Setting: Canyonlands National Park, Utah.
Main Character: Male, Rick, 14 years old.
Rick is in and out of foster homes, then runs away from a juvenile correctional facility and ends up lost in a wilderness and found by a scientist who teaches him to hang-glide. Awards: CC. Grades: 6–9.

Mac, Carrie. *Charmed.*
Orca Soundings, 2004.
Setting: Canada.
Main Character: Female, Isabelle "Izzy" McAfferty, 15 years old.
Izzy 's mom is often away, cooking in northern logging camps, and Izzy is left with mom's boyfriend, Rob the Slob. Cody Dillon, a high school dropout, is the object of her affection, and he seduces Izzy emotionally and sexually. When Lizzie runs away to live with him, she ends up in the world of prostitution. Quick realistic read with reluctant reader appeal. Grades: 8–12.

Paulsen, Gary. *The Beet Fields: Memories of a Sixteenth Summer.*
Delacorte Books for Young Readers, 2000.
Setting: North Dakota.
Main Character: Male, "the boy," 16 years old.
Fleeing his mother's confusing drunken advances, the boy runs away and finds work in the beet fields of North Dakota. During the summer, the boy learns about life and people and his own ability to work and survive. With sensual scenes and gritty language, this is a powerful novel that will speak to boys. Grades: 9–12.

Pearsall, Shelley. *Trouble Don't Last.*
Knopf Books for Young Readers, 2002.
Setting: Kentucky, 1859.
Main Character: Male slave, Samuel, 11 years old.
Samuel, an impulsive boy who seems prone to trouble, and Harrison, an elderly slave, attempt to escape their Kentucky master to Canada via the Underground Railroad. Faith, luck, and perseverance see the man and boy safely into Canada, where a new journey of self-discovery and self-healing begins. Suspenseful. Awards: Scott O'Dell. Grades: 5–8.

Stoehr, Shelly. *Weird on the Outside.*
Delacorte Books for Young Readers, 1995.
Setting: New York City.
Main Character: Female, Tracey Bascombe, 17 years old.
Tracey runs away to New York City in hopes of living anonymously, away from her neglectful father and pill-popping mother. Alone in the huge city, without real skills, Tracey turns to stripping in order to survive. Tracey describes her life in painful, lurid detail, resulting in a powerful, cautionary tale for mature teens. Grades: 9–12.

SURVIVAL

Burks, Brian. **Walks Alone.**
Harcourt Children's Books, 1998.
Setting: New Mexico Territory in 1879.
Main Character: Female, Walks Alone, 15 years old.
     Walks Alone struggles to survive after her Apache village is massacred. Similar to Gary Paulsen's survival stories. Grades: 5–9.

Golding, William. **Lord of the Flies.**
Berkley, 1959.
Setting: A deserted island.
Main Characters: Male, Ralph; Male, Piggy; Male, Jack; all around 12 years old.
     A group of English schoolboys survive a plane wreck on a deserted island. Ralph initially keeps some order, but the boys are soon divided when some of them decide they would rather play and hunt than keep the signal fire burning. A study of the beast inside man, this is also an exciting classic tale of survival. Grades: 10–12.

Hobbs, Will. **Far North.**
Morrow, 1996.
Setting: Northwest Territory in winter.
Main Characters: Male, Gabe; Male, Raymond; both 15 years old.
     Gabe and Raymond are stranded in the wilderness with Raven, a Dene elder, after a plane crash. Raven teaches them to hunt and other Indian survival skills they will need as they face blizzards, starvation, injuries, bears, and—eventually—Raven's death. Dene Indian culture and the wilderness landscape add interest and depth to this exciting adventure. Awards: CC. Grades: 6–9.

King, Stephen. **The Girl Who Loved Tom Gordon.**
Scribner's, 1999.
Setting: Appalachian Trail, Maine.
Main Character: Female, Trisha McFarland, 9 years old.
     After her parents divorce, Trisha is lost in the woods on a hiking trip with her bickering mother and brother. With only her Walkman for company, Trisha tries to find her way back, but reality and hallucination begin to blur. King pulls the reader into the woods with Tricia to experience the confusion and fear of being lost. Awards: CC. Grades: 9–12.

Marsden, John. **Tomorrow, When the War Began.**
Scholastic, 2006.
Series: Tomorrow: **Burning for Revenge; The Other Side of Dawn; The Night is for Hunting; Dead of Night; A Killing Frost; Darkness Be My Friend.**
Setting: Australia.
Main Characters: Female, Ellie, and six of her teenage friends.
     Ellie and friends return from a camping trip to find everyone taken prisoner; a war has begun. The friends work together to survive, then fight back. A fast-paced

survival adventure, the reader is left wanting to know what will happen and will most likely pick up more of the series. Awards: CC. Grades: 7–10.

Mikaelsen, Ben. *Touching Spirit Bear.*
HarperCollins, 2001.
Setting: Alaskan island.
Main Character: Male, Cole Matthews, 15 years old.
    Angry Cole agrees to accept the sentence given to him by Native American Circle Justice. He is sent to a remote Alaskan island, where he encounters Spirit Bear. Awards: CC. Grades: 6–9.

O'Brien, Robert C. *Z for Zachariah.*
Collier, 1987.
Setting: Burden Valley.
Main Character: Female, Ann Burden, 16 years old.
    Ann believes she is the lone survivor of a nuclear accident, until Mr. Loomis finds her in a valley. He swims in the creek that has been contaminated and gets radiation sickness. Ann cares for him, and when he gets better, he becomes controlling and violent. Awards: CC. Grades: 7–10.

Paulsen, Gary. *Hatchet.*
Atheneum, 1987.
Sequels: *The River; Brian's Winter; Brian's Return.*
Setting: Canadian wilderness.
Main Character: Male, Brian, 13 years old.
    After a plane crash, Brian spends 54 days in the wilderness with a hatchet that his mother gave him. A cliffhanger in every chapter. Awards: CC; Newbery Honor. Grades: 6–9.

Sweeney, Joyce. *Free Fall.*
Delacorte, 1996.
Setting: Ocala National Forest, Florida.
Main Character: Male, Neil, 17 years old.
    When two brothers and their friends are trapped in a cave in a Florida forest, they reveal hidden truths to each other. Readers will enjoy the suspense and learning caving and survival skills. Grades: 7–10.

Zindel, Paul. *Raptor.*
Hyperion, 1998.
Setting: Utah.
Main Characters: Male, Zack; Female, a Ute Indian; both teenagers.
    Zack and a friend are trapped in a cave with a Utah raptor in this gory page-turner.
Grades: 6 and up.

TRAVELING TEENS

Allende, Isabel. *City of the Beasts.*
Rayo, 2002.
Sequel: *Kingdom of the Golden Dragon.*
Setting: Amazon rain forest.
Main Characters: Male, Alexander Cold, 15 years old; Female, Nadia Sanos, 12 years old.

    While his mother is in Texas for chemotherapy treatment, Alex is spending the summer with his emotionally distant grandmother, who has been hired to find and write an article on the "Beast" that has been terrorizing the jungle. There are dangers such as the terrifying humanoid Beast that kills with huge claws, anacondas, natives with poison dart arrows, and an untrustworthy member of the expedition. A fast-paced page-turner. The story is a struggle between good and evil, filled with surprises and adventure. Grades: 6–10.

Avi. *Crispin: The Cross of Lead.*
Hyperion, 2002.
Setting: Fourteenth-century England.
Main Character: Male orphan, Crispin, 13 years old.

    Crispin, accused of theft and a murder he didn't commit, journeys across the English countryside. Action-packed page-turner, historical mystery, and empathetic characters. Awards: Newbery. Grades: 6–9.

Bauer, Joan. *Rules of the Road.*
Putnam, 1998.
Sequel: *Best Foot Forward.*
Setting: Illinois to Texas.
Main Character: Female, Jenna, 16 years old.

    Jenna isn't much good in school and didn't get the good looks in her family, but she can sure sell shoes. She gains confidence as she chauffeurs her boss from Chicago to Texas, and saves the day when Mrs. Madeleine Gladstone suddenly dies and her sleazy son tries to take over the company. A humorous and touching story with a likable heroine. Awards: CC. Grades: 7–10.

Brashares, Ann. *The Sisterhood of the Traveling Pants.*
Delacorte Books for Young Readers, 2001.
Sequels: *The Second Summer of the Sisterhood; Girls in Pants: The Third Summer of the Sisterhood.*
Setting: Washington, D.C.; Greece; Mexico, 2000s.
Main Characters: Females, Lena, Bridget, Carmen, Tibby, all 15 years old.

    A pair of jeans from a thrift shop bond four friends together over a first summer spent apart. Grades: 7–12.

Creech, Sharon. *The Wanderer.*
HarperTrophy, 2002.
Setting: On a sailboat, the Wanderer, from Connecticut to England.

Main Characters: Female, Sophie, 13 years old; Male, Cody, teenager.

Sophie and her cousin Cody tell of their journey across the Atlantic in a sailboat, the *Wanderer,* in a journal. Humor. Awards: CC. Grades: 6–9.

Dygard, Thomas J. *River Danger.*
HarperCollins, 1998.
Setting: Buffalo River, Arkansas.
Main Character: Male, Eric, 18 years old; Male, Robbie, 11 years old.

Brothers Eric and Robbie go on a canoe trip, and Robbie rescues Eric from a car-theft ring. Fast-paced action and danger. Grades: 5–9.

Ellis, Deborah. *Parvana's Journey.*
Groundwood Books, 2003.
Prequel: *The Breadwinner.*
Setting: Afghanistan.
Main Character: Female, Parvana, 12 years old.

When Parvana's father dies, she disguises herself as a boy to search through war-torn Afghanistan for her siblings, who had disappeared during a Taliban takeover. Parvana comes across a baby, the only survivor in a bombed village, and takes him along. Taking shelter in a small cave, she discovers an angry one-legged boy who is starved for both food and human companionship. The three continue Parvana's search, stopping on the edge of a minefield where an 8-year-old lives with a near comatose grandmother. When their home is destroyed, the four children join a long line of refugees, arriving finally at a camp. Grades: 7–10.

Farmer, Nancy. *Sea of Trolls.*
Atheneum, 2004.
Setting: Norway, 793 A.D.
Main Characters: Male, Jack, 11 years old; Female, Lucy, little sister.

Jack can feel everything at once which makes him vulnerable to The Life Force. When Jack and Lucy are captured by Vikings, they are taken to King Ivar the Boneless and undertake a quest to the home of the trolls. Grades: 5–9.

Fleischman, Paul. *Mind's Eye.*
Henry Holt, 1999.
Setting: A convalescent home in contemporary North Dakota.
Main Characters: Female, Courtney, 16 years old; Female, Elva, 88 years old.

Courtney, a paraplegic, struggles to accept her body's condition and Elva, a former schoolteacher, encourages her to transcend her physical limitations. Elva uses a 1910 *Baedeker's Italy* to lure Courtney into joining her on an imaginary grand tour of Italy. After Elva's death, Courtney persuades her new roommate to join in the fantasy excursion. The script format works for reading alone or presentation as a play. Awards: CC. Grades: 7–12.

Johnson, Maureen. *13 Little Blue Envelopes.*
HarperCollins, 2005.
Setting: London; Edinburgh; Rome; Paris, 2000s.

Main Characters: Female, Ginny, 17 years old; Male, Keith, a young starving artist.

The rules are that she has to open one little envelope at a time, in order. Inside little blue envelope 1 are $1,000 and instructions to buy a plane ticket. In envelope 2 are directions to a specific London flat. The note in envelope 3 tells Ginny to find a starving artist. Because of envelope 4, Ginny and her artist friend, Keith, go to Scotland together, with somewhat disastrous, but romantic results. Adventures in Rome and Paris await in envelopes 6 and 8. Grades: 8–10.

Voight, Cynthia. *Jackaroo.*
Atheneum, 1985.
Series: Kingdom Cycle: *On Fortune's Wheel; Wings of a Falcon.*
Setting: Distant time and far off place.
Main Character: Female, Gwyn, 16 years old.

Gwyn, an innkeeper's daughter, finds a costume of Jackaroo, a Robin Hood-like character, and decides to use Jackaroo's disguise to help those less fortunate. She then follows a quest to find the secret behind the legend of Jackaroo. A historical romance with mystery. Awards: CC. Grades: 7 and up.

UNEXPECTED HEROES

Cooney, Caroline B. *Flight 116 is Down.*
Sagebrush, 1999.
Setting: The Landseth property.
Main Character: Female, Heidi Landseth, 16 years old.

Wealthy Heidi gets a chance to prove herself in the confusion of an emergency situation when a 747 crashes in the woods behind her house. Awards: CC. Grades: 7–10.

Hill, Donna. *Shipwreck Season.*
Clarion Books, 1998.
Setting: Cape Cod, Massachusetts, seacoast, 1880.
Main Character: Male, Daniel, 16 years old.

Daniel is forced to work in a lifesaving station with his uncle and encounters challenges and danger. Grades: 5–8.

Horowitz, Anthony. *Stormbreaker.*
Scholastic, 2000.
Series: Alex Rider: *Point Blank; Skeleton Key; Eagle Strike.*
Setting: London, England, 2000s.
Main Character: Male, Alex Rider, 14 years old.

When his uncle is mysteriously killed, the government wants Alex to take over his uncle's job as a spy. Teen spy story with humor, cliffhangers, and computer crime. A cleaner take on James Bond. Grades: 7–10.

Howe, Norma. *The Adventures of the Blue Avenger.*
Henry Holt, 1999.

Sequels: *Blue Avenger Cracks the Code; Blue Avenger and the Theory of Everything.*
Setting: Oakland, California.
Main Character: Male, David Schumaker, 16 years old.
David is trying to cope with his father's death by changing the world as the Blue Avenger, in entertaining and funny adventures. Grades: 7–12.

Major, Kevin, and David Blackwood. *Ann and Seamus.*
Groundwood Books, 2004.
Setting: Newfoundland, 1828.
Main Character: Female, Ann Harvey, 17 years old.
Ann and her father and brother rescue 163 passengers of the *Despatch*. Written in free verse, the story is based on a true event. Grades: 7–12.

Pattison, Darcy. *The Wayfinder.*
Greenwillow, 2000.
Setting: Heartland.
Main Character: Male, Winchal Eldras, 11 years old.
Winchal must brave the dangers of the Rift to reach the healing Well of Life, when a plague comes to the Heartland in this fast-paced fantasy quest. Grades: 5–9.

Sachar, Louis. *Holes.*
Farrar, Straus & Giroux, 1998.
Setting: Camp Green Lake, Texas.
Main Character: Male, Stanley Yelnats IV, 15 years old.
Stanley is sent to a correctional camp in the desert and has to dig holes because the warden is looking for something. Two story lines come together with quirky characters and an ambiguous ending. Made into a movie. Awards: CC; Newbery. Grades: 6–12.

Smith, Roland. *Cryptid Hunters.*
Hyperion, 2005.
Setting: Congo.
Main Characters: Marty and Grace, twins, 13 years old.
When their parents disappear, Marty and Grace are taken in by their Uncle Travis, who searches the world for mythical creatures. The twins parachute from an airplane into the middle of the Congo, where a surviving dinosaur may still exist. Once the twins hit the jungle, things get exciting, with narrow escapes and ruthless villains. Grades: 5–8.

Stone, Jeff. *Tiger.*
Random House, 2005.
Series: Five Ancestors: *Monkey; Snake* (others forthcoming).
Setting: China, seventeenth-century.
Main Character: Male, Fu (Tiger), 12 years old.
Five orphans are being raised as foster brothers and Buddhist monks. Grandmaster has given the boys animal names and has trained each of them in a martial-arts

style related to his animal's strengths. When the temple is attacked, the orphans hide and escape. Fu is determined to reclaim the valuable ancient training scrolls that have been taken from the temple. A page-turner, employing slapstick humor from time to time, appealing to readers who love computer games and Japanese anime. Grades: 6–9.

Voight, Cynthia. *Homecoming.*
Atheneum, 1981.
Series: Tillerman: *Dicey's Song* (Newbery); *A Solitary Blue.*
Setting: Bridgeport, Connecticut.
Main Characters: Female, Dicey Tillerman, 13 years old, and her siblings.

The Tillerman children have been abandoned by their mother. They have to find their way to Great-aunt Cilla's house in Bridgeport, which may be their only hope of staying together as a family. When they get to Bridgeport, they learn that Great-aunt Cilla has died. Awards: CC. Grades: 7–10.

RESOURCES: ADDITIONAL TITLES

Libretto, Ellen V., and Catherine Barr. 2002. *High/Low Handbook: Best Books and Web Sites for Reluctant Teen Readers.* Fourth edition. Westport, CT: Libraries Unlimited.

CHAPTER 7

THE ARTS

Among the lists in this chapter you will find movies based on books teens will like. The movies can be shown at the library if you have a license to show copyrighted films. You might display the videos and DVDs with the novels under a banner that says "Read the Book, See the Movie," or create a program by the same title and invite the teens to read the book first, then gather together to watch the movie. Follow up with a discussion or a vote on which they liked best. Just for fun, there is a Web site included that has lists of movies with librarians as characters! The chapter continues with lists of books with teen characters involved in the creative or performing arts. These titles can be suggested to teens who are involved in the arts or displayed with complementary nonfiction titles.

> Books to Movies
> Librarians in Movies
> Music, Song, and Dance
> Painting and Graffiti
> Photography and Filmmaking
> Theater and Plays
> Writing

BOOKS TO MOVIES

10 Things I Hate About You (1999).
Based on: ***The Taming of the Shrew*** by William Shakespeare.
Genre: Comedy, Romance.

   Pretty and popular, Bianca Stratford has never had a date and can't have one until her older sister does. Her ill-tempered sister Kat's acerbic wit is matched only by her determination to alienate any guy who might be interested in her. Desperate Bianca and her hopeful boyfriend hatch a convoluted scheme to match Kat with a sullen young man with a mysterious past.
Rating: PG-13 for crude sex-related humor and dialog, alcohol and drug-related scenes, all involving teens.

Clueless (1996).
Based on: ***Emma*** by Jane Austen.

Genre: Comedy, Romance.

Cher is a high school student and must survive the ups and downs of adolescent life in Beverly Hills. Her demeanor seems superficial, but it hides her wit, charm, and intelligence, which help her deal with relationships, friends, family, school, and the all-important teenage social life.

Rating: PG-13 for sex-related dialog and some teen use of alcohol and drugs.

Confessions of a Teenage Drama Queen (2004).

Based on: *Confessions of a Teenage Drama Queen* by Dyan Sheldon.

Genre: Comedy.

Mary "Lola" Steppe is out of place in the suburban sprawl of Dellwood, New Jersey, after her mother divorces and leaves the trendy life of New York City. Lola sets her sights on the lead in the school play while fantasizing about her favorite rock group and how her life is supposed to be. When her favorite rock group schedules their final farewell concert in New York City, Lola pulls out all the stops to make it to the concert and meet the lead singer.

Rating: PG for mild thematic elements and strong language.

Ella Enchanted (2004).

Based on: *Ella Enchanted* by Gail Carson Levine.

Genre: Comedy, Fantasy, Romance, Adventure.

Ella was given a gift of obedience by a fairy named Lucinda, and she must obey anyone who tells her to do anything. When her mother passes away, Ella is left in the care of her thoughtless and greedy father who remarries a loathsome woman with two treacherous daughters. This modern-day Cinderella features fairies, ogres, and elves, and a hero in the guise of Prince Charmont, whom Ella falls in love with. Ella must depend on herself and her intelligence instead of a fairy godmother to get her through her troubles, then find Lucinda in order for her "curse" to be broken.

Rating: PG for some crude humor and language.

Freaky Friday (2003).

Based on: *Freaky Friday* by Mary Rodgers.

Genre: Comedy, Drama, Fantasy.

Overworked Dr. Tess Coleman and her 15-year-old daughter, Anna, are not getting along. At dinner in a Chinese restaurant, their disagreements reach a fevered pitch. Two identical fortune cookies cause a little magic, and the next morning, Tess and Anna find themselves inside the wrong bodies, walking a mile in each other's shoes. They gain newfound respect for each other's point of view. Tess's wedding is coming on Saturday, and they have to find a way to switch back fast.

Rating: PG for mild thematic elements and some language.

Harry Potter and the Sorcerer's Stone (2001).

Based on: *Harry Potter and the Sorcerer's Stone* by J.K. Rowling.

Sequels: *Harry Potter and the Chamber of Secrets; Harry Potter and the Prisoner of Azkaban; Harry Potter and the Goblet of Fire; Harry Potter and the Order of the Phoenix; Harry Potter and the Half-Blood Prince.*

Genre: Adventure, Fantasy.

Harry is rescued from the neglect of his aunt and uncle and fulfills his destiny at the Hogwarts School of Witchcraft and Wizardry.
Rating: PG for some scary moments and mild strong language.

Holes (2003).
Based on: *Holes* by Louis Sachar.
Genre: Adventure, Comedy, Drama, Mystery.

Stanley Yelnats is sent to a brutal desert detention camp where he joins the job of digging holes because the warden is looking for something.
Rating: PG for violence, mild strong language, and some thematic elements.

How to Deal (2003).
Based on: *Someone Like You* and *That Summer* by Sarah Dessen.
Genre: Comedy, Drama, Romance.

Halley is disillusioned with love after seeing the many dysfunctional relationships around her: her parents are divorced and her father has a new young girlfriend she doesn't care for too much; her mother is always alone; and her sister is so overwhelmed by her upcoming wedding that she barely leaves the house. The shallowness of all the girls and guys at her school convinces Halley that finding true love is impossible. A tragic accident leads her to meeting Macon, and suddenly Halley finds that true love can occur under unusual circumstances.
Rating: PG-13 for sexual content, drug material, explicit language, and some thematic elements.

I, Robot (2004).
Based on: *I, Robot* by Isaac Asimov.
Genre: Action, Science Fiction, Thriller.

In 2035 A.D., robots are common assistants and workers for their dependent human owners. The Three Laws of Robotics prevents robots from harming humans. A Chicago detective investigates the murder of Dr. Alfred Lanning, who worked at U.S. Robotics and a robot, Sonny, is implicated.
Rating: PG-13 for intense stylized action and some brief partial nudity.

The Lord of the Rings: The Fellowship of the Ring (2001).
Based on: The Lord of the Rings Trilogy: *The Fellowship of the Ring* by J. R. R. Tolkien.
Sequels: *The Lord of the Rings: The Two Towers; The Lord of the Rings: The Return of the King.*
Genre: Action, Adventure, Fantasy.

An ancient lost Ring has been found, and has been given to a Hobbit named Frodo. Gandalf discovers the Ring is the One Ring of the Dark Lord Sauron. Frodo must make an epic quest to the Cracks of Doom in order to destroy the Ring. He is joined by the Fellowship: Gandalf, Legolas the elf, Gimli the Dwarf, Aragorn, and Boromir and his three Hobbit friends, Merry, Pippin, and Samwise. Their quest to destroy the One Ring is the only hope for the end of the Dark Lord's reign.
Rating: PG-13 for epic battle sequences and some scary images.

The Mighty (1998).
Based on: **Freak the Mighty** by Rodman Philbrick.
Genre: Action, Drama, Comedy.

Kevin, afflicted with a rare physical disability that prevents him from living a normal childhood, is an extremely intelligent boy who lives in the world of his imagination. Max is an overweight boy who suffers from a learning disability and has failed the seventh grade several times. Kevin is assigned to tutor Max in his reading skills, and a great friendship begins. These two friends find they share many painful realities of being outcasts and of being abandoned by their fathers early in life.
Rating: PG-13 for elements of violence and peril.

The Outsiders (1983).
Based on: **The Outsiders** by S. E. Hinton.
Genre: Crime, Drama.

Two rival gangs, the Greasers and the Socs, continually fight against each other over their "turf." When two greasers, Johnny and Ponyboy, are assaulted by Socs, Johnny kills one of the attackers and the tension builds between the gangs.
Rating: PG-13 for violence, teen drinking and smoking, and some sexual references.

The Princess Bride (1987).
Based on: **The Princess Bride: S. Morgenstern's Classic Tale of True Love and High Adventure** by William Goldman.
Genre: Adventure, Comedy, Fantasy, Romance.

A kindly grandfather sits down with his grandson and reads him a bedtime tale of love and adventure. The beautiful Buttercup is kidnapped and held against her will in order to marry the odious Prince Humperdinck, and Westley attempts to save her. On the way, Westley meets an accomplished swordsman and a huge, super-strong giant, both of whom become his companions in his quest.
Rating: PG.

The Princess Diaries (2001).
Based on: **The Princess Diaries** by Meg Cabot.
Sequels: **The Princess Diaries 2** (2004).
Genre: Comedy.

Mia is 15 years old. Socially awkward but very bright, she discovers that she is the princess of a small European country because of the recent death of her long-absent father, who, unknown to her, was the crown prince of Genovia. She must make a choice between continuing the life of a San Francisco teen or stepping up to the throne. While Mia makes up her mind, she takes princess lessons from her grandmother.
Rating: G.

Sisterhood of the Traveling Pants (2005).
Based on: **Sisterhood of the Traveling Pants** by Ann Brashares.
Genre: Adventure, Comedy, Drama.

Four best friends pass around a pair of secondhand jeans that fits each of their bodies perfectly, so they can stay connected with one another as their lives start off in different directions.

Rating: PG for thematic elements, some sensuality, and language.

___

Speak (2004).
Based on: *Speak* by Laurie Halse Anderson.
Genre: Drama.

Melinda was raped at a high school party and hasn't told anyone what happened. Struggling with school, friends, and family, she tells the dark tale of her experience, and why she has chosen not to speak to anyone about it.
Rating: PG-13 for mature thematic material.

___

Tuck Everlasting (2002).
Based on: *Tuck Everlasting* by Natalie Babbitt.
Genre: Drama, Romance, Fantasy.

Winnie meets and falls in love with Jesse Tuck, who is part of the immortal Tuck family. The secret of their immortality is a spring that is actually a fountain of youth. Winnie must choose between being immortal and being with Jesse or following the circle of life and dying someday.
Rating: PG for some violence.

___

A Walk to Remember (2002).
Based on: *A Walk to Remember* by Nicholas Sparks.
Genre: Drama, Romance.

Serious and conservative, Jamie is far from cool and doesn't care. Landon hangs with the in-crowd, breezing through school on looks and bravado with no plans, no future, and no faith in himself. When a prank goes terribly wrong, landing a kid in the hospital, Landon is assigned to tutor on the weekends and participate in the Drama Club's spring play as community service. Over his head with both assignments, Landon asks Jamie for help. Landon falls in love with Jamie who possesses a passion for life he never imagined possible.
Rating: PG for thematic elements, language, and some sensual material.

___

War of the Worlds (2005).
Based on: *War of the Worlds* by H. G. Wells.
Genre: Action, Adventure, Science Fiction, Thriller

Ray Ferrier is a working-class man living in New Jersey. He's estranged from his family, his life isn't in order, and he's too caught up with himself. His small-town life is shaken violently by the arrival of aliens, who have come to destroy Earth. As the aliens plow through the country in a wave of mass destruction and violence, Ray must come to the defense of his children.
Rating: PG-13 for disturbing images and frightening sequences of sci-fi violence.

___

Where the Heart Is (2000).
Based on: *Where the Heart Is* by Billie Letts.
Genre: Drama, Romance.

Pregnant 17-year-old Novalee Nation is abandoned by her boyfriend, Willie Jack, at a Wal-Mart in Sequoyah, Oklahoma. Novalee has no job, no skills, and only $5.55 in

her pocket, so she secretly lives in the Wal-Mart until her daughter, Americus, is born six weeks later. Novalee decides to raise her daughter and rebuild her life in Sequoyah, with the help of eccentric but kind strangers.
Rating: PG-13 for intense thematic material, language, and sexual content.

LIBRARIANS IN MOVIES

Schmidt, Steven J. "Film Librarian." Available: www.filmlibrarian.info/.
This site lists Steven's top ten picks for depictions of librarians in the movies. Another browse-by-title list offers movies with librarian characters since the early twentieth century. While all of the Top Ten are not rated for teens to view, the list is interesting to their librarians!

MUSIC, SONG, AND DANCE

Block, Francesca Lia. **Cherokee Bat and the Goat Guys.**
HarperCollins, 1992.
Series: Weetzie Bat: **Witch Baby; Missing Angel Juan; Baby Be-Bop.**
Setting: California.
Main Character: Female, Cherokee Bat, teen.
 Cherokee Bat and almost-sister Witch Baby are left behind when their parents go to South America to make a film. Witch Baby stops eating and starts withdrawing into herself and Cherokee has to save her. Nothing seems to work until Angel Juan, Witch Baby's special childhood friend, returns from Mexico. With another friend on guitar, the four start a band, the Goat Guys, and only with the help of mystical powers does it become a hit, but success has a price. Grades: 8–12.

Brooks, Bruce. **Midnight Hour Encores.**
Harper & Row, 1986.
Setting: Cross-country trip in a VW bus.
Main Character: Female, Sib, 16 years old.
 Self-assured Sib is a cellist and musical prodigy and is traveling cross country with her father, Taxi, to meet her mother, who abandoned her as a baby. Taxi wants Sib to understand the spirit that captured her mother and him during the late 1960s: they travel in a 20-year-old VW bus, Taxi sings and speaks of that era at every opportunity, and he takes Sib to meet some of his old acquaintances on the way. Sib's mother turns out to be a wealthy real-estate agent with expensive tastes and no interest in music, quite comfortable in the upper class. Awards: CC. Grades: 9–12.

Cohn, Rachel. **Pop Princess.**
Simon & Schuster, 2004.
Setting: Cape Cod, Massachusetts.
Main Character: Female, Wonder Blake, 15 years old.
 Wonder isn't popular, and she works at a Dairy Queen until she is discovered by her sister's agent. Her first release is a hit, and she catapults to fame, finding it is no bed of roses. A pop fantasy with "American Idol" and VH1's "Behind the Music" fan appeal. Grades: 8–12.

Dent, Grace. *LBD: It's a Girl Thing.*
Putnam, 2003.
Sequel: *LBD: Live & Fabulous.*
Setting: England.
Main Characters: Females, Ronnie, Fleur, and Claudette; all 14 years old

    The three LBDs (Les Bambinos Dangereuses), Ronnie, Fleur, and Claudette, want to attend the Astlebury Music Festival but are forbidden to go, so they devise a plan to stage their own music festival as part of the school's summer garden party. The appealing characters are well drawn with their typical teenage foibles, and the plot, which moves at a steady pace, is a nice mix of humor and seriousness. Fans of *Angus, Thongs, and Full Frontal Snogging* and *Sisterhood of the Traveling Pants* will like this book. Grades: 7–10.

Henry, Chad. *DogBreath Victorious.*
Holiday House, 1999.
Setting: Seattle, Washington.
Main Character: Male, Tim Threlfall, teen.

    Tim leads an alternative rock band called DogBreath and is dreaming of stardom. When Dirt Club owner Lewd Fingers announces a "Battle of the Bands," with a recording contract audition as grand prize, Tim is determined to win. In the meantime, his mother forms her own band, The Angry Housewives, behind his back. The Housewives strike a nerve with the teen crowd with their epic song "Eat Your $%@@!!!*&& Cornflakes," and they win the contest. A good choice for reluctant readers. Grades: 6–10.

McCaffrey, Anne. *Crystal Singer.*
Bantam, 1980.
Sequels: *Killashandra; Crystal Line.*
Setting: Ballybran, a planet.
Main Character: Female, Killashandra Ree, young adult.

    Killashandra fails her final exam in music school and is left without prospects after ten years of training. Then she signs on as a crystal singer on the planet Ballybran for the mysterious Heptite Guild. Science fiction, romance, danger, and a strong female protagonist will appeal to many teen girls. Awards: CC. Grades: 9–12.

McNamee, Graham. *Hate You.*
Delacorte Books for Young Readers, 1999.
Setting: Hospital, 1990s.
Main Character: Female, Alice, 17 years old.

    Alice writes the songs she cannot sing because her father choked her during a fight between her parents and permanently damaged her vocal cords. It is only after she finds the courage to sing her songs out loud and realizes the power of her unique voice to give meaning to her dark poetry that she is able confront her father just days before his death. Alice takes ownership of her voice, her art, and her life. Edgy plot, haunting lyrics, and short chapters appeal to reluctant readers. Awards: CC; Grades: 8–12.

Malkin, Nina. *6X: The Uncensored Confessions.*
Scholastic, 2005.
Sequel: *Loud, Fast, & Out of Control.*
Setting: On the road with the band, present day.
Main Characters: Female, Kendell; Female, Wynn; Female, Stella; Male, A/B; all teenagers.

Sweet, trusting Kendall sings like an angel—and is about to discover her devilish side—while rich, spoiled Wynn can't keep a beat to save her life. No-nonsense Stella is all confidence, attitude, style, and smarts, but her relationship with the band's manager might reveal her to be more vulnerable than she thinks. A/B is a bit of a dork, but he's got real talent. The band members tell about their rise to stardom, the glamour of being in a band, and the darker picture of rock star life. Grades: 7 and up.

Manning, Sarra. *Guitar Girl.*
Dutton Children's Books, 2004.
Setting: England and USA.
Main Character: Female, Molly, 17 years old.

Molly enjoyed writing songs and playing music with her friends, Jane and Tara, never planning to reach pop stardom. When they start a rock band called The Hormones, T and Dean maneuver their way into the group. Suddenly famous, Molly takes off on tour with the band. Despite Dean and Molly's frequent confrontations, they fall in love, until she learns that his motivation for the relationship hasn't been totally honest. Grades: 8–12.

Nelson, Blake. *Rock Star Superstar.*
Viking, 2004.
Setting: 2000s.
Main Character: Male, Pete, 16 years old.

When Pete, a talented bass player, moves from playing in the high school jazz band to playing in a popular rock group, he finds the experience exhilarating, even as his new fame jeopardizes his relationship with new girlfriend Margaret. A tender, funny, and believable novel about music and relationships that takes a down-to-earth view of the road to stardom, including the hard work and disappointment. Grades: 9–12.

Powell, Randy. *Tribute to Another Dead Rock Star.*
Farrar, Straus & Giroux, 1999.
Setting: Seattle.
Main Character: Male, Grady Grennan, 15 years old.

Grady is invited to speak at a tribute to his dead rock star mother in Seattle, while staying with his father and his new family. Awards: CC. Grades: 8–11.

Shaw, Tucker. *Confessions of a Backup Dancer.*
Simon Pulse, 2004.
Setting: Los Angeles, California.
Main Character: Female, Kelly Kimball, 17 years old.

Kelly is a talented dancer. When her best friend convinces her to attempt a Los

Angeles audition, Kelly ultimately finds herself on a summer tour as a backup with pop princess Darcy Barnes, who soon views Kelly as her new best friend.

The story is told through Kelly's entries into personal diary software, interspersed with instant messages and e-mails. Grades: 8–12.

Triana, Gaby. *Backstage Pass.*
HarperCollins, 2004.
Setting: Miami, Florida.
Main Character: Female, Desert McGraw, 16 years old.

Desert's father is aging rock star Flesh. When she starts a new school in Miami, she tries to make real friends and avoid her father's fans, who have always tried to use her. She meets Becca and Liam, and through the school year friendships grow. Desert begins to write her own songs and discovers her own gifts, coming to rely on herself to solve her problems. Grades: 9–11.

Tucker, Lisa. *The Song Reader.*
Downtown Press, 2003.
Setting: Tainer, Missouri, 1981.
Main Character: Female, Leeann Norris, 12 years old.

After her mother is killed in a car crash, Mary Beth, 23, takes on the care of her younger sister, Leann, in the absence of their father. She supports the two of them, and eventually a hyperactive foster child with learning problems, by waitressing and "song reading," a skill she developed to help people uncover their problems by charting the songs running through their heads. Mary Beth breaks down when one of her clients attempts suicide and is sent off to a mental hospital. Leeann slowly puts the family together again. An attempted date rape and Leeann's first loving sexual encounter are sensitively handled, and there is a hopeful resolution. Grades: YA/A.

Williams-Garcia, Rita. *Blue Tights.*
Puffin, 1996.
Setting: Urban, 1990s.
Main Character: Female, Joyce Collins, 15 years old.

Joyce rebuffs the advances of an older man, struggles for acceptance with snobbish peers, mourns an unrequited love, and aspires for a ballet career denied to her lonely mother. By accident, she intrudes on a practice session of African dancers, and after joining the group, Joyce finds that her spirit, style, and abilities are unleashed in this dance form, which reveals her talents.
Awards: CC. Grades: 9–12.

PAINTING AND GRAFFITI

Anderson, Laurie Halse. *Speak.*
Farrar, Straus & Giroux, 1999.
Setting: Merryweather High School, 1990s.
Main Character: Female, Melinda Sordino, teen.

Everyone, even her closest friend, is angry at Melinda for calling the police to break up the big end-of-the-summer party. Melinda can't speak of what happened to make her call; she was raped at that party by an upperclassman, who is still taunting her at school. Her grades plummet, and she withdraws into herself to the point that she's barely speaking. Her only refuge is her art class, where she learns to find ways to express some of her feelings. When the boy tries again, Melinda finds her voice. Awards: CC. Grades: 8–12.

Balliett, Blue. *Chasing Vermeer.*
Scholastic, 2004.
Setting: Chicago, Illinois.
Main Characters: Female, Petra Andalee; Male, Calder Pillay; both 11 years old.

Petra and Calder are determined to solve the mystery of a missing painting, Vermeer's *A Lady Writing*, which disappeared on its way to an exhibition at the Art Institute of Chicago. They pool their unusual talents to solve the crime. Lots of plot twists, red herrings, black-and-white illustrations, puzzles, codes, letters, number and wordplay, a bit of danger, a vivid sense of place, and a wealth of quirky characters. Grades: 5–8.

Butcher, Kristin. *Zee's Way.*
Orca Book Publishers, 2004.
Setting: Hardware store.
Main Character: Male, Zee, teenager.

Zee and his friends look like bad news. Danny has blue hair, Horace has none, Benny's lip is pierced, Mike likes leather and studs, and they all like tattoos. Zee is a painter and decides to fight the way he and his friends are treated by spray-painting graffiti on the hardware store wall. Each time he does, Mr. Feniuk just paints over it again, until Zee decides to paint a closed door that's a work of art. When Zee gets caught, Feniuk makes him a deal: cover up the graffiti and paint the rest of the picture, and he won't tell Zee's dad what he's been up to. Gangs and graffiti will attract reluctant readers, and a message is delivered as Zee and the shopkeeper begin to understand and respect each other. Grades: YA.

Coburn, Jake. *Prep.*
Dutton, 2003.
Setting: Four days in New York City, 2000s.
Main Character: Male, Nick, teen.

A onetime tag-artist, Nick tries to figure out who he really is while coming to terms with the death of a friend amid the violence of wealthy prep school hoods. With too much money, too little family, and too few morals, these young men beat and cut one another for fun, territory, or girls, and to gain reputation, power, and control. Reveals the darker side of growing up rich, including drugs, easy sex, and drinking. Brief sentences and often-raw gang slang. Grades: 9–12.

Johnson, Angela. *The First Part Last.*
Simon & Schuster, 2003.
Setting: New York City.

Main Character: Male, Bobby, 16 years old.

Bobby struggles to balance parenting his infant daughter, school, and friends. Alternate chapters go back to the story of Bobby's relationship with his girlfriend, Nia, and how parents and friends reacted to the news of her pregnancy. Flashbacks lead to the revelation in the final chapters that Nia is in an irreversible coma caused by eclampsia. Bobby snaps from the pressure of trying to raise his daughter and spray-paints a picture on a brick wall, getting arrested for vandalism. Awards: Printz. Grades: 8–12.

Peck, Richard. *Unfinished Portrait of Jessica.*
Delacorte, 1991.
Setting: Acapulco, Mexico.
Main Character: Female, Jessica, 14 years old.

Jessica idolizes her handsome, photographer father, and is devastated by her parents' divorce. Blaming her mother entirely, she hides in her room, until a holiday visit with her father in Mexico forces her to see the situation more clearly. Jessica quickly discovers that her father's boyishness is really immaturity, and that his easy charm often disguises his lack of responsibility. She finds that her mother's career as a writer is not as boring as she imagines, and that her mother is the parent upon whom she can rely. In Acapulco, Jessica and her father stay with his uncle, Lucius Pirie, a famous artist. Awards: CC. Grades: 7–10.

PHOTOGRAPHY AND FILMMAKING

Bauer, Joan. *Thwonk.*
Puffin, 2005.
Setting: 1990s.
Main Character: Female, A.J. McCreary, 17 years old.

A. J., photographer extraordinaire, lovelorn, and invisible to school hunk Peter Terris, is unable to capture a fitting cover shot for the school paper's special Valentine's Day edition. She stumbles upon a stuffed cupid, who comes to life and offers her one of three choices: artistic, academic, or romantic assistance. In spite of the cupid's protests against romantic assistance, and his admitted failure in teen love, A. J. follows her heart. After Peter is smitten and her date for the King of Hearts dance is secure, she finds his devotion and attention embarrassing, and he is boring. Grades: 7–10.

Block, Francesca Lia. *Violet & Claire.*
HarperCollins, 1999.
Setting: Los Angeles, California.
Main Character: Female, Violet, 17 years old; Female, Claire, teen.

Violet has a passion for the movies and writing screenplays. Claire is a poet with gauze wings sewn on her shirt. They become friends as they chase their dreams through dangerously beautiful Los Angeles. Alternating points of view. Awards: CC. Grades: 9–12.

Castellucci, Cecil. *Boy Proof.*
Candlewick, 2005.
Setting: Los Angeles, California.
Main Character: Female, Victoria Denton, 16 years old.
Victoria hides behind the identity of a favorite movie character, until an interesting new boy arrives at school and helps her realize that there is more to life than just the movies. Grades: 8–12.

Johnson, Angela. *Toning the Sweep.*
Scholastic, 1994.
Setting: Desert home.
Main Character: Female, Emily, 14 years old.
Emily's grandmother is terminally ill with cancer. Emily and her mother arrive to pack her up and take her back to Cleveland. Emily videotapes her grandmother's friends so she can take her memories with her. African American characters. Awards: CC; Coretta Scott King Honor. Grades: 7–12.

Meyer, Carolyn. *The Luck of Texas McCoy.*
Atheneum, 1984.
Setting: Western ranch.
Main Character: Female, Texas, 16 years old.
Texas sells some acreage to a movie company as a location for Western films to keep the ranch left to her by her grandfather. She gets involved with a young actor. Grades: 7–9.

Nelson, Theresa. *Ruby Electric.*
Atheneum, 2003.
Setting: California.
Main Character: Female, Ruby Miller, 12 years old.
Ruby, a movie buff and aspiring screenwriter, tries to resolve the mysteries surrounding her little brother's stuffed woolly mammoth and their father's five-year absence. Grades: 5–8.

THEATER AND PLAYS

Bennett, Cherie and Jeff Gottensfeld. *A Heart Divided.*
Delacorte, 2004.
Setting: Redford, Tennessee.
Main Character: Female, Kate Pride, 16 years old.
When her parents decide to move from New Jersey to Tennessee, Kate gives up her friends and her spot in a prestigious playwriting workshop. Racial tensions abound in Redford, and Kate decides to write a play about the opposition after the town's act of flying the Confederate flag. When she meets Jack Redford, a Romeo-and-Juliet-type romance begins. Grades: 8 and up.

Cirrone, Dorian. *Dancing in Red Shoes Will Kill You.*
HarperCollins, 2005.
Setting: Florida Arts High School.
Main Character: Female, Kayla, 16 years old.

Kayla, a talented ballet dancer, is the sort of funny, generous person anyone would love to have for a best friend. But her breasts are so large that they interfere with the visual composition of the performances and limit the roles she is chosen for in school productions. After *Cinderella* tryouts, when Kayla is selected to play one of the ugly stepsisters instead of the coveted starring role, a dance teacher suggests that she consider breast-reduction surgery. Almost immediately, the students polarize into two camps: those who would "Save the Hooters" (boys) vs. those who would "Reduce the Rack" (mainly girls). Grades: 7–10.

Cooper, Susan. *King of Shadows.*
Margaret K. McElderry, 1999.
Setting: London, England, 1500s.
Main Character: Male, Nat Field, teen.

An orphan, Nat, is chosen as part of an American theater group to perform at the new Globe Theatre in London. Nat's big role will be Puck in "A Midsummer Night's Dream." When he is put to bed with a high fever, he wakes up in Elizabethan England, 400 years in the past. He has switched places with Nathan Field, who is being treated for bubonic plague in the present. Nat becomes William Shakespeare's protégé. Grades: 5–8.

Danzinger, Paula. *This Place Has No Atmosphere.*
Delacorte, 1986.
Setting: The moon, 2057.
Main Characters: Female, Aurora, 15 years old; Male, Hal, 16 years old.

Aurora's family has been invited to inhabit a colony on the moon, but Aurora is devastated by the thought of leaving her boyfriend and a school where she feels important. At the low point of her depression, she suggests to Hal that they produce a play and involve all the kids in the tiny moon colony. Eventually Aurora's parents become more involved with her. She finds she actually likes little kids, and she listens when a teacher tells her that we are "not always the center" but rather a "part of the Universe." Grades: 6–9.

Fleischman, Paul. *Breakout.*
Cricket/Marcato, 2003.
Setting: California.
Main Character: Female, Del, 17 years old.

Running away from her latest foster home, Del begins her new life trapped in traffic on the Santa Monica freeway. Del whiles away her time cleaning her new car, watching the people around her, wandering off in search of food and a bathroom, and finally participating in an impromptu talent show, gathering the experiences that will fuel her successful later life as Elena Franco, playwright and performance artist.

Scenes from Elena's monologues written eight years later are presented in italics throughout. Grades: 10 and up.

Garden, Nancy. ***Good Moon Rising.***
Farrar Straus & Giroux, 1996.
Setting: 1990s.
Main Characters: Female, Jan; Female, Kerry; both 17 years old.

Jan is back from summer stock and hoping for the role of Elizabeth in the school production of *The Crucible.* A new student named Kerry gets the part, and Jan's larger-than-life mentor, Mrs. Nicholson, assigns Jan to be stage manager instead. When Mrs. Nicholson falls ill, Jan becomes the stand-in director and coaches Kerry. Eventually, the two realize that they are sexually attracted to each other. Other cast members notice, too. Grades: 8 and up.

Karr, Kathleen. ***Gilbert and Sullivan Set Me Free.***
Hyperion, 2003.
Setting: Sherborn Prison for Women, Massachusetts, 1900s.
Main Character: Female, Libby Dodge, 16 years old.

Mrs. Wilkinson, the chaplain, insisted on bringing music inside the prison walls. Libby's life is deeply affected by her involvement in the production of *Pirates of Penzance*, and she is granted a full music scholarship. Grades: 5–7.

Koja, Kathe. ***Talk.***
Frances Foster, 2005.
Setting: 2000s.
Main Characters: Male, Kit Webster; Female, Lindsey Walsh; Male, Blake Tudor; young adults.

Kit auditions for a controversial school play and discovers his talent for acting. He struggles with coming out, and both he and his costar face crises in their view of themselves and in their close relationships. Told from two points of view. Grades: 8 and up.

Korman, Gordon. ***No More Dead Dogs.***
Hyperion, 2000.
Setting: 1990s.
Main Character: Male, Wallace Wallace, 13 years old.

Tired of stories where the dogs always die, Wallace expresses his true views of his English teacher's favorite book, *Old Shep, My Pal.* Wallace earns a detention that takes him off the football team and puts him in the auditorium, where his English teacher is directing a theatrical version of *Old Shep, My Pal.* Wallace makes a few suggestions to punch up the production, turning it into a rock musical where the dog lives, to the delight of his classmates. Grades: 5–7.

Mackler, Carolyn. ***Vegan Virgin Valentine.***
Candlewick, 2004.
Setting: Present day.

Main Character: Female, Mara Valentine, 17 years old.

Mara's drive stems from the belief that she is her parents' "only hope." Her 35-year-old sister has achieved nothing but having a daughter, V, who is only a year younger than Mara and appears to be a "nicotine-addicted nympho." Mara is competing with her ex-boyfriend for class valedictorian; she has been accepted early decision to Yale and has alienated most of her friends with her rigid, single-minded attitudes. Her life is thrown into chaos when V comes to live with the family. Grades: 8 and up.

Myers, Walter Dean. *Monster.*
HarperCollins, 1999.
Setting: Harlem.
Main Character: Male, Steve Harmon, 16 years old.

Steve is accused of serving as a lookout for a robbery of a Harlem drugstore. The owner was shot and killed, and now Steve is in prison awaiting trial for murder. Steve, an amateur filmmaker, recounts his experiences in the form of a movie screenplay. Interspersed within the script are diary entries in which the teen describes the nightmarish conditions of his confinement. Awards: CC; Printz, Coretta Scott King Honor. Grades: 7–10.

Sheldon, Dyan. *Confessions of a Teenage Drama Queen.*
Candlewick, 1999.
Setting: New Jersey.
Main Character: Female, Mary Elizabeth Cep, 16 years old.

When she and her family move to New Jersey, Mary Elizabeth, who plans to be an actress someday, changes her name to Lola and begins a campaign to enrich the "humdrum" lives of suburbanites. Lola's new classmates are not quite ready to receive her guidance, as they are too busy worshipping their reigning "drama queen," snooty Carla Santini. Carla and Lola compete to be Number 1. Carla is armed with sophistication, beauty, confidence, and an entourage of admirers. Lola, on the other hand, has an overactive imagination, the lead role in the school play, and one loyal friend, Ella. Awards: CC. Grades: 7 and up.

Weatherly, Lee. *Child X.*
David Fickling, 2002.
Setting: Great Britain.
Main Character: Female, Jules, 13 years old.

Jules' father has suddenly walked out after a fight with her mother. In between landing the role of Lyra in a theatrical production of Philip Pullman's *Northern Lights* and having troubles with her best friend at school, Jules learns that shortly before Jules's parents' wedding, her mother had had a one-night stand, resulting in Jules's conception, and her father has only just found out. He sues for damages, and the case appears in the paper, with Jules's identity masked as "Child X." When a newspaper reporter interviews Jules about her role as Lyra, she reveals that she is Child X. Soon Jules is at the center of a media circus, and it gets worse when she flips on a TV talk show just in time to watch a guest inform viewers that Jules's natural father is, in fact, her uncle. British. Grades: 4–9.

Weston, Martha. *Act I, Act II, Act Normal.*
Roaring Brook, 2003.
Setting: Hope Springs Middle School.
Main Character: Male, Topher, 13 years old.

Each year the eighth-graders write plays and one is selected for production. Topher believes wholeheartedly that his friend Kip's mystery, *The Sweet Tooth of Death*, will be picked and that he will get the lead. Instead, *Rumpelstiltskin—The Musical* wins. Kip convinces Topher to audition, and he's cast as Rumpelstiltskin. Give it to fans of Gordon Korman's *No More Dead Dogs* or Avi's *Romeo & Juliet—Together (and Alive!) at Last* Grades: 5–8.

WRITING

Cabot, Meg. *The Princess Diaries.*
HarperCollins, 2000.
Series: The Princess Diaries: *Princess in the Spotlight; Princess in Love; Princess in Waiting; Princess in Pink; Princess in Training; Princess Present; Project Princess.*
Setting: Albert Einstein High, Manhattan, New York, 2000s.
Main Character: Female, Mia Thermopolis, 14 years old.

Raised in a Greenwich Village loft by her artist mother, Mia is shocked to learn from her father that she is Princess Amelia Mignonette Grimaldi Thermopolis Renaldo, the heir apparent to Genovia, the tiny European kingdom he rules. Her paternal grandmother comes to town to mold Mia into a proper royal. Made into two movies. Awards: CC. Grades: 7 and up.

Goldstein, Lisa. *Dark Cities Underground.*
Tor, 1999.
Setting: California, 1990s.
Main Characters: Female, Ruth Berry; Male, Jeremy "Jerry" Jones; both 50+ years old.

Ruth, a journalist, is writing a biography of E.A. Jones, the author of *The Adventures of Jeremy in Neverwas*, a series of children's books based on stories that Jones's son Jeremy told her about the imaginary Land of Neverwas. Mysterious Barnaby Sattermole insists that Neverwas is a real alternate world, and he wants Jerry to show him the entrance, underground in the World Below. As Ruth and Jerry investigate, they uncover links between the plot of the Neverwas series and Egyptian myths. Ruth begins to wonder if many of the best-known children's books might actually be based on places and events in Neverwas. Sattermole kidnaps Ruth's daughter, Gilly, and Ruth and Jerry enter the World Below to find the Eye of Horus, the key to Neverwas. Awards: CC. Grades: YA/A.

Ives, David. *Scrib.*
HarperCollins, 2005.
Setting: The West, 1863.
Main Character: Male, Scrib, 16 years old.

Scrib travels around the West making his living writing and delivering letters, an occupation that leads to him nearly getting killed, being jailed as a criminal, joining up with the notorious villain Crazy James Kincaid, and delivering a letter from President Abraham Lincoln to a Paiute Indian. Humor for the fans of the movie *O Brother, Where Art Thou?* and Terry Prachett's **The Wee Free Men.** Grades: 6–9.

Koja, Kathe. **Straydog.**
Farrar, Straus & Giroux, 2002.
Setting: High school.
Main Character: Female, Rachel, teenager.

　　Rachel wears her anger on her sleeve: anger at her parents, at her classmates, and at the world. She takes solace in her writing and in her volunteer job at an animal shelter, where she feels an instant kinship with a feral collie. She devises plans to save the dog. Grades: 7 and up.

Major, Kevin. **Dear Bruce Springsteen.**
Delacorte, 1987.
Setting: 1980s.
Main Character: Male, Terry Blanchard, 14 years old.

　　Terry's father has left home; his mother wants a divorce and is seeing another man; and Terry can't talk with girls comfortably. He decides to write about his problems in letters to his musical hero, Bruce Springsteen, even though he knows that they won't be answered. The novel consists entirely of Terry's letters, relating changes in his life over six months. Grades: 6–10.

Shamsie, Kamila. **Broken Verses.**
Harvest, 2005.
Setting: Karachi, Pakistan, 2000s.
Main Character: Female, Aasmaani Inqalab, 31 years old.

　　Growing up in Pakistan, Aasmaani was no stranger to government corruption and intrigue. Her mother, an outspoken activist, and her mother's lover, a poet known for his criticism of bureaucracy, had a pattern of disappearing into exile when the government drew too close and reappearing months or years later. When Aasmaani was a teen, the poet was beaten to death, and her mother vanished shortly afterward. Aasmaani begins receiving coded messages that suggest that the poet's death was staged by the government, and she is drawn into a web of intrigue in which her own life may be in danger. Grades: YA/A.

CHAPTER 8

FAMILIES

Families are the luck of the draw. Sometimes we are lucky and have loving relatives who support and care for us through all our challenges, and sometimes we struggle to get by in spite of our families. Families are an important element in all the following titles, because of either the strengths or the weaknesses of the relationships. The lists in this chapter reflect several of the family situations in which teens find themselves.

> Absent Parents
> Abusive/Dysfunctional Families
> Adoption
> Fathers
> Grandparents
> Mothers
> Divorce
> Orphans
> Siblings
> Teen Fathers
> Teen Mothers

ABSENT PARENTS

Bauer, Joan. *Hope Was Here.*
Putnam, 2000.
Setting: Rural Mulhoney, Wisconsin.
Main Character: Female, Hope Yancey, 16 years old.

Hope lives with her aunt, a diner cook, after her mother disappears. When she moves with Hope to work in the Welcome Stairways diner, they become involved with the diner owner's political campaign to become mayor, in spite of his leukemia. An engaging, warm, and friendly story, as wholesome as the food Hope's aunt serves up in the diner. Awards: CC; Newbery Honor. Grades: 7–12.

Creech, Sharon *Walk Two Moons.*
HarperTrophy, 1994.

Setting: Kentucky to Idaho road trip.
Main Character: Female, Salamanca Tree Hiddle, 13 years old.

A story within a story. After Sal's mother leaves home, Sal and her father move to Kentucky, where she meets a new friend, Phoebe. Sal and her grandparents take a car trip retracing her mother's route, and along the way, Sal tells them the story of Phoebe, whose mother also left. Due to Sal's initial confusion, denial, and then anger, the reader is not aware that her mother has died. Native American characters. Awards: CC; Newbery Medal. Grades: 6–9.

Earls, Nick. *48 Shades of Brown.*
Penguin, 1999.
Setting: Australia.
Main Character: Male, Dan, 16 years old.

While his parents are in Geneva, Dan spends his last year of high school living with his 22-year-old bass-playing aunt, Jacq, and her beautiful friend, Naomi, whose active love life is audible through the wall between their bedrooms. Awards: VOYA Perfect Ten. Grades: 9–12.

Johnson, Angela. *Heaven.*
Simon & Schuster, 1998.
Setting: Heaven, Ohio.
Main Character: Female, Marley, 14 years old.

Marley's seemingly perfect life in the small town of Heaven is disrupted when she discovers that her father and mother are not her real parents. Her mysterious Uncle Jack turns out to be her real, very absent father. Marley is angry at her parents for not telling her the truth, for not being perfect, and she questions what's real yet wonders if it really matters as much as the love she feels for her family. African American characters. Awards: CC; Coretta Scott King. Grades: 7–10.

Koller, Jackie French. *A Place to Call Home.*
Aladdin, 1997.
Setting: Connecticut.
Main Character: Female, Anna, 15 years old.

Mama's gone again, but this time she doesn't come back, and Anna discovers her old yellow car submerged in the lake. Anna, the black child of a white mother and unknown father, loves her two white siblings passionately, though she can't forget she's different while she struggles to make a home for them. A fast-paced, compelling read, with a memorable and feisty heroine and satisfying social values. Awards: CC. Grades: 7–10.

Slade, Arthur G. *Tribes.*
Wendy Lamb Books, 2002.
Setting: Saskatoon, Canada.
Main Character: Male, Percy, 17 years old.

Percy tells us that his anthropologist father died three years ago, and in his grief he takes on an anthropologist's point of view of his classmates, classifying them into tribes, without becoming a part of one. Percy is an original character, who has created an unusual way to cope with the loss of his father and a good friend. Grades: 7–12.

Voigt, Cynthia. *Homecoming.*
Atheneum, 1981.
Series: Tillerman: *Dicey's Song* (Newbery); *Seventeen against the Dealer.*
Setting: Connecticut.
Main Character: Female, Dicey Tillerman, 13 years old.

The Tillerman children have been abandoned by their mother. They have to find their way to Great-aunt Cilla's house in Bridgeport, which may be their only hope of staying together as a family. When they get to Bridgeport, they learn that Great-aunt Cilla has died. Awards: CC. Grades: YA.

ABUSIVE/DYSFUNCTIONAL FAMILIES

Goobie, Beth. *Something Girl.*
Orca Soundings, 2005.
Sequel: *Sticks and Stones.*
Setting: Present day.
Main Character: Female, Sophie, 15 years old.

Sophie believes she is a "stupid, no good, nothing girl," because her father, an upstanding figure in the community, needs to smack and kick her. Dreading both her dad's retaliation and the stigma of a group home, Sophie guards the secret of her abuse, until her former babysitting charge, 12-year-old Jujube, intervenes when Sophie ends up in the hospital. Orca Soundings covers and short, relevant stories attract the reluctant reader. Grades: 5–8.

Block, Francesca Lia. *I Was a Teenage Fairy.*
Joanna Cotler, 1998.
Setting: Los Angeles, California.
Main Characters: Female, Barbie; 16 year old model; Mab, a fairy.

Barbie, a teen model, copes with her overbearing stage mother, a pedophile photographer, and a dark secret while listening to the honest, crabby commentary of her pinky-size, opinionated fairy friend, Mab. A rich mix of classical and pop-culture allusions and magical realism, as well as Mab's outrageous observations, make this problem novel more of a romantic comedy. Language and situations suit mature teens. Grades: 9–12.

Coman, Carolyn. *What Jamie Saw.*
Front Street, 1995.
Setting: Trailer park.
Main Character: Male, Jamie, 9 years old.

Jamie wakes up to see his stepfather try to throw his baby sister against the wall. His mother catches her and flees with her two children to try to put their lives back together with the help of a battered wives support group. Jamie's love of magic and illusion helps see him through the hard times, and a teacher plays a supportive role for Jamie. While Jamie is a young narrator, the domestic violence images make this a book for teens who like *A Child Called It.* Awards: CC; Newbery Honor. Grades: 5–12.

Draper, Sharon M. *Forged by Fire.*
Atheneum, 1997.
Series: Hazelwood High Trilogy: *Tears of a Tiger; Darkness Before Dawn.*
Setting: Inner city.
Main Character: Male, Gerald Nickelby, 13 years old, a minor character from *Tears of a Tiger.*

Gerald, burned, battered and neglected, is taken from his mother and sent to live with his Aunt Queen. When Aunt Queen dies, Gerald is sent back home to meet Angel, his 4 1/2-year-old half sister, who is sexually abused by her father. Her father is sent to prison, but when released, he returns to the family and attempts to molest Angel again. African American characters. Awards: CC. Grades: 5–12.

Frank, E. R. *America.*
Atheneum, 2002.
Setting: New York, 2000s.
Main Character: Male, America, 15 years old.

Multiracial and abused, America is lost in the foster care system for eleven years, until he tries to end his own life. Through painful and agonizing therapy with Dr. B. and after years of institutionalization, America begins to feel a glimmer of hope for his future. The raw authentic language and situations will resonate with many readers and appall others. This is a realistic portrayal of some teens' experiences with abusive families and a system that often falls short of saving them. Awards: CC. Grades: 9–12.

Hawes, Louise. *Waiting for Christopher.*
Candlewick, 2002.
Setting: Florida.
Main Character: Female, Feena Harvey, 14 years old.

Feena's memory of her baby brother who died of SIDS inspires her to rescue an abused toddler and hide him from his mother. Feena and a friend manage to secretly care for the toddler for three weeks and then agree to return him if his mother doesn't call the police. Feena is mourning several losses: not only her little brother but her father, who left the family, and her mother's retreat into alcohol and soap operas. Grades: 7–9.

Holeman, Linda. *Mercy's Birds.*
Tundra Books, 1998.
Setting: 1990s.
Main Character: Female, Mercy Donnelly, 15 years old.

Mercy lives with her depressed, alcoholic, suicidal mother and her Aunt Moo, who has a boyfriend who has made sexual advances toward Mercy. Loneliness and depression threaten to absorb Mercy too. Poverty, alcoholism, suicide, and depression are all heavy issues dealt with realistically. Grades: 8–12.

Klass, David. *You Don't Know Me.*
Frances Foster, 2001.
Setting: High school.
Main Character: Male, John, 14 years old.

John creates alternative realities in his mind to deal with abuse from his mother's boyfriend. He has a crush on the beautiful but shallow Gloria, but slowly discovers that down-to-earth Violet is right for him. John is quirky, making his narrative funny and unique, yet sometimes difficult. Awards: CC. Grades: 7–12.

Konigsburg, E. L. *Silent to the Bone.*
Atheneum, 2000.
Setting: Clarion County Juvenile Behavioral Center.
Main Character: Male, Connor, 13 years old.

Connor's best friend, Branwell Zamborska, loses his power of speech when he is accused of shaking and dropping his baby sister. Connor believes Branwell is innocent and is determined to prove it by finding out why he became silent and what really happened to the baby. A suspenseful and insightful novel that reads like a mystery, with clues revealed throughout. Awards: CC. Grades: YA.

Lamb, Wally. *She's Come Undone.*
Pocket Books, 1992.
Setting: 1950s–1990s.
Main Character: Female, Dolores Price, 4 to 40 years old.

Dolores struggles with the pain of abuse by trying to fill it with food. Her parents' divorce when she was 4 years old sends her on a long emotional journey to try to regain a sense of normalcy. Amazingly, Dolores's voice is right on, although written by a male author. Awards: CC. Grades: 9–12.

Mackler, Carolyn. *The Earth, My Butt, and Other Big Round Things.*
Candlewick, 2003.
Setting: Manhattan.
Main Character: Female, Virginia Shreves, 15 years old.

Virginia's mother expects perfection from her children but Virginia's figure isn't cooperating, while her older sister escapes to the Peace Corps and her brother is accused of date rape. Awards: Printz Honor. Grades: 7–10.

McNamee, Graham. *Hate You.*
Delacorte, 1999.
Setting: Hospital.
Main Character: Female, Alice, 17 years old.

Alice hates her father for damaging her voice as a child, when he choked her for stepping into a brutal fight between her parents. After years of no contact, Alice learns her father is dying of cancer and she goes to confront him with her pain and damaged voice, but is prevented by the shock of his appearance. When she gains courage to sing her songs with her unique voice, Alice takes back her life. Haunting lyrics, an edgy plot, and short chapters will appeal to reluctant readers. Awards: CC. Grades: 8–12.

Randle, Kristen D. *Only Alien on the Planet.*
Scholastic, 1994.
Setting: East Coast.
Main Character: Female, Ginny, 15 years old.

Ginny feels like an outsider in her new school after moving to the East Coast from California. Then she meets Smitty, who never speaks or allows anyone to touch him. Ginny and a new circle of friends attempt to communicate with Smitty and bring him into the human race again. Awards: CC. Grades: 8–12.

Williams, Lori Aurelia. *When Kambia Elaine Flew in from Neptune.*
Simon & Schuster, 2000.
Setting: Houston, Texas.
Main Character: Female, Shayla, 12 years old.

Shayla, a self-possessed, verbally precocious teen aspiring to be a writer, is intrigued by the wild stories told by her neighbor, Kambia Elaine. An engrossing and disturbing novel that would be suitable for mother-daughter book groups. African American characters. Awards: CC. Grades: 8–12.

Woodson, Jacqueline. *I Hadn't Meant to Tell You This.*
Laurel Leaf, 1995.
Setting: Athens, Ohio
Main Character: Female, Marie, 13 years old.

After Marie's mother deserts their family, Marie befriends "white trash" Lena, becoming Lena's confidante about sexual abuse from her father. When Lena and her sister run away, Marie has her friend's disappearance to cope with, too. A haunting story that is hopeful and inspiring, despite the sad themes. African American characters. Awards: CC; Coretta Scott King Honor. Grades: 7–12.

ADOPTION

Alvarez, Julia. *Finding Miracles.*
Knopf, 2004.
Setting: Central America.
Main Character: Female, Milly Kaufman, 15 years old.

Milly hid her adoption from her friends, until Pablo, a new student at her school, inspires her to search for her birth family in his native country. Captured between cultures and languages, Milly's journey has a satisfying resolution. Grades: 6–9.

Bauer, Cat. *Harley Like a Person.*
Winslow Press, 2000.
Setting: New Jersey.
Main Character: Female, Harley, 14 years old.

Harley is sure her verbally abusive father can't be her natural parent. The search for her true identity alienates her best friend, hooks her up with the drug crowd, and drags her grades down. Awards: CC. Grades: 7–12.

Blacker, Terence. *The Angel Factory.*
Simon & Schuster, 2002.
Setting: Future.
Main Character: Male, Thomas, 12 years old.

Thomas discovers two secrets: he is adopted and his too perfect family is part of an other-worldly organization on a mission to save the world from destruction. Readers who like *The Giver* or *House of the Scorpion* find this science fiction novel thought-provoking. Grades: 6–9.

Carlson, Melody. *Just Ask: Diary of a Teenage Girl.*
Multnomah, 2005.
Series: Kim's Diaries: *Book 1.*
Setting: Present day.
Main Character: Female, Kim Peterson, 16 years old.

Kim loses her driving privileges and has to earn them back by writing a teen advice column for the newspaper for which her father is managing editor. Kim is a Korean American adopted by Caucasian Americans. Part of a Christian series for teen girls, several characters' diaries are featured. Grades: 10–12.

Crutcher, Chris. *Whale Talk.*
Greenwillow, 2001.
Setting: Cutter High School.
Main Character: Male, T. J. Jones, 18 years old.

Multiracial and adopted, T.J. is a natural athlete but steers away from organized sports. During his senior year, his favorite teacher, Mr. Simet, convinces him to form a school swim team. By choosing the school outcasts for his team, the Cutter All Night Mermen, T.J. gets revenge on the jock establishment. His team's dedication to swimming and each other helps them overcome many obstacles. Awards: CC; BBYA. Grades: 8–12.

Hite, Sid. *The King of Slippery Falls.*
Scholastic, 2004.
Setting: Slippery Falls, Idaho.
Main Character: Male, Lewis Hinton, 16 years old.

When his sixteenth birthday approaches Lewis pursues an elusive giant white trout in the river near his home and he receives a letter from his birth mother telling him he is descended from French royalty. His adoptive parents support his search for his heritage. Offbeat and likable characters make this an entertaining read. Grades: 6–8.

Johnson, Angela. *Heaven.*
Simon & Schuster, 1998.
Setting: Heaven, Ohio.
Main Character: Female, Marley, 14 years old.

When her family receives a letter from Alabama requesting a replacement for Marley's baptismal record, she discovers she is adopted. The parents she has known her whole life are not her real parents, launching Marley's journey toward revelation of what family really means. Awards: CC. Grades: 6–9.

Fathers

Caletti, Deb. *Queen of Everything.*
Simon Pulse, 2002.
Setting: Pacific Northwest island.
Main Character: Female, Jordan, 17 years old.
  Jordan's biggest problem until now was dealing with her hippy-dippy mom. She preferred the company of her calm, measured father, who never embarrassed her in front of her friends. Jordan is stunned when her nice, divorced dad starts acting like a lovelorn teenager over one of their pretty, but married neighbors, Gayle D'Angelo. Jordan tries everything, from directly confronting her dad to dating local thug Kale Kramer, to gain her father's attention. When Gayle's husband goes missing and the police name Jordan's dad as a suspect, Jordan's life rapidly spins out of control. Grades: 8 and up.

Cormier, Robert. *In the Middle of the Night.*
Delacorte, 1995.
Setting: 1970s, 1990s.
Main Character: Male, Denny, 16 years old.
  A deadly accident in a theater where Denny's father worked as a teen still haunts their family twenty-five years later. Vengeance and obsession of the victims' relatives draw Denny into a dangerous game of cat and mouse. Intricate, suspenseful plot, with complex characters and a surprise ending. Awards: CC; Grades: 7–12.

Hamilton, Virginia. *Plain City.*
Point Signature, 1993.
Setting: Plain City.
Main Character: Female, Buhlaire-Marie Sims, 12 years old.
  Buhlaire is determined to find and communicate with her dad when she discovers that her mother and relatives lied about her father dying in Vietnam. When her father rescues her during a January blizzard, he leads her to a highway underpass, his space among the homeless of Plain City. African American characters. Awards: CC. Grades: 7–12.

Myers, Walter Dean. *Somewhere in the Darkness.*
Apple, 1997.
Setting: New York to Arkansas.
Main Character: Male, Jimmy Little, 14 years old.
  Jailed for his involvement in an armed robbery and falsely accused of killing a man, Crab escapes from prison to convince his son Jimmy of his innocence. Crab whisks Jimmy away from the stability of a home life with his devoted grandmother, but is unable to break free of a lifestyle of stealing and moving on that leaves little room for security. For Jimmy, the flicker of hope that he and his father might work things out becomes a realization that love is built on trust, concern, and honesty. African American characters. Awards: CC; Newbery Honor. Grades: 7–10.

Philbrick, W. Rodman. *Young Man and the Sea.*

Blue Sky, 2004.
Setting: Coastal Maine.
Main Character: Male, Skiff Beaman, 12 years old.

After his mother dies and his father withdraws, Skiff decides that he will earn money to take care of himself and his father. He undertakes a dangerous trip out on the ocean in a ten-foot plywood boat with a harpoon to catch a huge bluefin tuna. A take off on Hemingway's *Old Man and the Sea,* with adventure, suspense, and a triumphant ending. Grades: 5–8.

Salisbury, Graham. *Lord of the Deep.*
Delacorte, 2001.
Setting: Hawaii.
Main Character: Male, Mikey Donovan, 13 years old.

Mikey has put his stepfather on a high pedestal while learning the charter ocean fishing trade from him. Mikey's faith in his stepdad falters when he sees him make difficult decisions. Exciting scenes of deep-sea fishing are described vividly. Grades: 5–8.

Sones, Sonya. *One of Those Hideous Books Where the Mother Dies.*
Simon & Schuster, 2004.
Setting: Los Angeles, California.
Main Character: Female, Ruby Milliken, 15 years old.

When her mother dies, Ruby leaves everyone she knows in Boston to live with her movie star father in Los Angeles; she doesn't even know him. Turning her grief into anger toward her father, Ruby shows contempt for everything, until there is an earthquake. A sometimes humorous verse novel with a satisfying ending. Grades: 7–10.

Watt, Alan. *Diamond Dogs.*
Little, Brown, 2000.
Setting: Outside Las Vegas, Nevada.
Main Character: Male, Neil Garvin, 17 years old.

Neil, abandoned by his mother when he was 3, blames his abusive father, the local sheriff, for driving her away. Good-looking, popular, and the quarterback of the high school football team, Neil is as cruel to his peers as his father is to him. One night after heavy drinking, he accidentally kills a classmate with his car. His father covers up for him in a twisted attempt at love. Dark, psychological suspense and a powerful conclusion. Awards: CC. Grades: 7 and up.

Wells, Ken. *Meely LaBauve.*
Random House, 2000.
Setting: Louisiana Bayou, 1960s.
Main Character: Male, Meely LaBauve, 15 years old.

Meely's mother died in childbirth eight years ago and his alligator-hunting father spends much of his time drinking or hiding from the law. Meely is arrested and tried for assault and battery and attempted murder, while facing racism and bullying. An exciting Huck Finn–type adventure, Cajun-style. Grades: 7–12.

GRANDPARENTS

Holt, Kimberley Willis. *My Louisiana Sky.*
Holt, 1998.
Setting: Saitter, Louisiana, 1957.
Main Character: Female, Tiger Ann, 12 years old.
    When her bossy grandmother dies in the butter bean patch, Tiger Ann must choose whether to stay and care for her mentally slow parents and face the cold shoulder from the girls at school or move to Baton Rouge with her wealthy aunt. Made into a movie with the same title. Grades: 6–8.

Johnson, Angela. *Toning the Sweep.*
Scholastic, 1994.
Setting: California desert.
Main Character: Female, Emily, 14 years old.
    Grandmother Ola has cancer and Emily and her mother arrive to take her home with them to Cleveland, Ohio. Emily videotapes her grandmother's friends and relatives to take her memories with her. An inspirational look at three generations bonding and coping with grief and hardship. African American characters. Awards: CC; Coretta Scott King. Grades: 7–12.

Monthei, Betty. *Looking for Normal.*
HarperCollins, 2005.
Setting: Washington, D.C.
Main Character: Female, Annie, 12 years old.
    When Annie's father kills her mother and commits suicide, she and her brother try to cope with their own grief, made more difficult by their grandmother's drinking and grandfather's increased absences. A tough story that gives a peek at the people behind headline stories. Grades: 6–8.

Mosher, Richard. *Zazoo.*
Clarion, 2001.
Setting: France.
Main Character: Female, Zazoo, 13 years old.
    Zazoo, a Vietnamese orphan, lives with her adoptive grandfather in France. Grand-Pierre is considered a hero in France's resistance to the Nazi invasion, but at 78 he is slowing down, and Zazoo is caring for him more and more, seeking to understand her grandfather's trauma and loss. Awards: CC; Notable Books for a Global Society. Grades: 6–10.

Newbery, Linda. *Sisterland.*
David Fickling, 2004.
Setting: Britain, Germany, Middle East.
Main Character: Female, Hilly, 16 years old.
    Grandmother Heidigran becomes ill with Alzheimer's disease and comes to live with Hilly's family. Heidigran has a secret that turns her family upside down and makes Hilly question her identity: she was a Jewish child who came to England in the

Kindertransports from Nazi Germany. Alternating points of view between Hilly and Heidigran. Grades: 8–12.

Peck, Richard. *Long Way From Chicago.*
Dial, 1998.
Sequel: *A Year Down Yonder.*
Setting: Wabash, Illinois, 1930s Depression era.
Main Characters: Male, Joey Dowdel, older brother; Female, Mary Alice Dowdel, 7 years old.

Joey and Mary Alice make their annual trip to visit Grandma Dowdel, their eccentric and entertaining grandmother. Each chapter is written by Joey as an adult, as short stories of memories at grandma's house. Awards: CC; Newbery Honor. Grades: 4–8.

MOTHERS

Caletti, Deb. *Honey, Baby, Sweetheart.*
Simon & Schuster, 2004.
Setting: Nine Miles Falls, 2000s.
Main Character: Female, Ruby McQueen, 16 years old.

In the summer of her junior year, Ruby falls in love with Travis and gets sucked into criminal activity with him. Ruby's mother, a librarian with a broken heart, pulls Ruby away from Travis and takes her to a senior citizen book group she leads. The senior "Casserole Queens" deliver inspiring messages, encouraging the mother and daughter to insist on a true love. Grades: 7–12.

Curtis, Christopher Paul. *Bucking the Sarge.*
Wendy Lamb, 2004.
Setting: Flint, Michigan.
Main Character: Male, Luther T. Farrell, 15 years old.

Luther works for the Sarge, his slumlord, loan shark mother. Luther has greater aspirations than following in his mother's footsteps and manages to go against his tough mom to do what is right. Humorous with fast-paced action and wonderful characters. African American characters. Awards: VOYA Perfect Ten. Grades: 8–12.

Weeks, Sarah. *So B. It: A Novel.*
Laura Geringer, 2004.
Setting: Reno, Nevada, to New York.
Main Character: Female, Heidi, 12 years old.

Heidi's mentally disabled mom knows twenty-three words and can tell Heidi nothing of her past. One of her words, "soof," and the discovery of long-lost photos leads Heidi on a quest across the country to find the truth about her family. Grades: 6–9.

DIVORCE

Bauer, Joan. **Stand Tall.**
Putnam, 2002.
Setting: 2000s.
Main Character: Male, Tree, 12 years old.
Tree, six foot three inches tall, finds strength to cope with his parents' recent divorce by helping his grandfather, a Vietnam vet and recent amputee, and by focusing on his friendship with Sophie, a new girl at school. Grades: 6–9.

Caseley, Judith. **Losing Louisa.**
Farrar, Straus & Giroux, 1999.
Setting: 1990s.
Main Character: Female, Lacey, 16 years old.
Lacey worries about the effect of her parents' divorce on her family, especially her mother. Her older sister's sexual activity, which has led to a pregnancy, puts a strain on their relationship. Grades: 8–12.

Cooney, Caroline B. **Tune in Any Time.**
Delacorte, 1999.
Setting: Small town.
Main Character: Female, Sophie Olivette, 16 years old.
When Sophie's father suddenly decides to divorce her mother and marry Sophie's older sister's college roommate, Sophie feels like she is trapped in an endless soap opera. The humor of the over-the-top chaos caused by Sophie's parents is tempered by Sophie's pain and outrage. Grades: 7–12.

Dessen, Sarah. **That Summer.**
Viking, 2006.
Setting: Suburb.
Main Character: Female, Haven, 15 years old.
Haven's parents divorce, her sister gets married, and she is too tall, all of which makes her feel out of place in her changing world. Haven's sense of humor helps her cope. Awards: CC. Grades: 7–9.

Deuker, Carl. **Night Hoops.**
Houghton Mifflin, 2000.
Setting: Basketball court.
Main Character: Male, Nick Abbott, 16 years old.
While trying to prove that he is good enough to play on his high school's varsity basketball team, Nick must also deal with his parents' divorce and the erratic behavior of a troubled classmate who lives across the street. Suspenseful page-turner for basketball fans. Grades: 8–10.

Peters, Julie Ann. **Define "Normal."**
Little, Brown, 2000.
Setting: Middle school.

Main Character: Female, Antonia, 16 years old.

When she agrees to meet with Jasmine as a peer counselor at their middle school, Antonia never dreams that this girl with the black lipstick and pierced eyebrow will become a good friend and help her deal with the serious problems she faces at home. Antonia and Jazz learn to look beyond the outside to find common feelings and frustrations on the inside. Awards: CC. Grades: 7–10.

Thomas, Rob. *Rats Saw God.*
Simon & Schuster, 1996.
Setting: California.
Main Character: Male, Steve York, 18 years old.

Steve agrees to complete a 100-page writing assignment so he can graduate. The assignment helps him sort out his relationship with his famous astronaut father and the events that changed him from promising student to troubled teen. Steve has a funny intelligent voice as he reflects over the last four years. Awards: CC. Grades: 9–12.

ORPHANS

Childress, Alice. *Rainbow Jordan: She's Too Brave to Be a Child, Too Scared to Be a Woman.*
Avon Flare, 1982.
Setting: 1980s.
Main Character: Female, Rainbow Jordan, 14 years old.

Rainbow's mother, her foster guardian, and Rainbow comment on the state of things as she prepares to return to a foster home for yet another stay. African American characters. Awards: CC. Grades: 6–12.

De La Peña, Matt. *Ball Don't Lie.*
Delacorte, 2005.
Setting: Los Angeles, California.
Main Character: Male, Sticky, 17 years old.

Sticky is a foster kid with nowhere to call home but the street, and an outer shell so tough that no one will take him in. He's a white boy living and playing in a world where he doesn't seem to belong, but basketball may be his ticket out. Grades: YA.

Hartinger, Brent. *The Last Chance Texaco.*
HarperTempest, 2004.
Setting: Group home.
Main Character: Female, Lucy Pitt, 15 years old.

Lucy's last chance is to make it at Kindle House, a group home where the dedicated counselors try to connect with the kids. If she makes any mistakes, she'll be sent to the prisonlike facility known as Eat-Their-Young Island. With a little romance and a little mystery, this is a realistic portrayal of teens caught in the foster care system. Grades: 7–10.

Hobbs, Will. *The Maze.*
HarperCollins, 1998.
Setting: Canyonlands National Park, Utah.
Main Character: Male, Rick, 14 years old.

Rick is in and out of foster homes. When he runs away from a juvenile correctional facility, he ends up lost in a wilderness and is found by a scientist who teaches
him to hang-glide. Awards: CC. Grades: 6–9.

Horowitz, Anthony. *Raven's Gate.*
Scholastic, 2005.
Series: Gatekeepers: *Evil Star.*
Setting: Lesser Malling, England.
Main Character: Male, Matt, 14 years old.

As punishment for being present during an assault, Matt must choose between
life with Mrs. Deverill in a remote Yorkshire village or jail. Lesser Malling is much
worse than jail, because strange and dangerous things occur there. Raven's Gate,
an ancient portal to the world of evil, is about to be opened, and Matt is to be the
blood sacrifice. The thrills and horror in a real-world setting and vivid descriptions
with characters to care about will have readers looking for more in the series. Grades:
5–8.

Lundgren, Mary Beth. *Love, Sara.*
Henry Holt, 2001.
Setting: Foster homes.
Main Character: Female, Sara, 16 years old.

Sara reveals her feelings about living in several foster homes and being sexually
abused by her father in e-mails, diary entries, and fiction stories; she is sometimes an
unreliable narrator. Fast-paced. Grades: 7–12.

Nolan, Han. *Born Blue.*
Harcourt, 2001.
Setting: Contemporary.
Main Character: Female, Janie, 16 years old.

Janie was 4 years old when she was placed in foster care because she nearly
drowned due to her mother's neglect. Janie's dearest friend is a fellow foster child,
Harmon, an African American. When Harmon is adopted into a loving, well-to-do
family, she is heartsick. Janie's mother comes to visit and this time sells Janie to a
couple in exchange for drugs. Janie changes her name to Leshaya and grows into a
wild young woman, destroying every healthy relationship she has. Awards: CC.
Grades: 8–12.

Shaw, Susan. *The Boy from the Basement.*
Dutton, 2004.
Setting: Basement, hospital.
Main Character: Male, Charlie, 12 years old.

Imprisoned in the basement for many years by his violent father, Charlie is sure
he's being punished because he is bad, and when he escapes and is placed in a loving

foster home, it takes him a long time to feel safe in the strange world outside. Charlie's therapy sessions reveal how isolated and removed from the world he has been. Grades: 6–9.

Wolfson, Jill. *What I Call Life.*
Henry Holt, 2005.
Setting: 2000s
Main Character: Female, Cal, 11 years old.

When her unstable mother has a psychotic episode, Cal is placed in a group home run by an elderly woman called the Knitting Lady. Her new roommates are four girls, all in different stages of denial about their own situations. The girls learn to knit, and the Knitting Lady tells stories about two girls from long ago: one who was abandoned at an orphanage by her own mother and another who was sent West on an orphan train. Grades: 5–8.

SIBLINGS

Abbott, Hailey. *The Bridesmaid.*
Delacorte, 2005.
Setting: Massachusetts, 2000s.
Main Character: Female, Abby Beaumont, 15 years old.

Abby knows weddings make ordinary women turn into "Bridezillas." Her parents own a catering hall, and she and her older sister Carol have helped with these events all their lives. When Carol plans to marry, her family turns into the worst of customers, bickering over nearly every detail. Grades: 7–10.

Choldenko, Gennifer. *Al Capone Does My Shirts.*
Putnam, 2004.
Setting: Alcatraz Island, California, 1935.
Main Character: Male, Moose, 12 years old.

Moose's father is an electrician at Alcatraz, where the notorious Al Capone is incarcerated. Moose takes care of his autistic sister and gets in a bit of trouble with the warden's daughter. Awards: Newbery Honor. Grades: 6–8.

Freymann-Weyr, Garret. *My Heartbeat.*
Houghton Mifflin, 2002.
Setting: New York City.
Main Character: Female, Ellen, 14 years old.

Ellen idolizes her brother Link and his best friend James, seniors at a private high school, where some girls assume that Link and James are a couple. James tells Ellen he has slept with men, but that he is also attracted to women, and Ellen has her first sexual experience with him. Ellen desperately wants to understand her brother, and realizes that her parents do not know him the way they think they do. Awards: Printz Honor. Grades: 9–12.

Giles, Gail. *Dead Girls Don't Write Letters.*
Roaring Brook, 2003.

Setting: 2005.
Main Character: Female, Sunny, 14 years old.

Sunny's older sister, Jazz, has been presumed dead for several months, but then Sunny receives a letter from her explaining that she was away working in a repertory theater when her apartment burned to the ground. When Jazz, or Not-Jazz as Sunny calls her, returns home, Sunny and her father soon realize that the young woman is indeed not Jazz, even though she knows a great deal about their family history and secrets. An ambiguous ending suggests Sunny is not a reliable narrator. Grades: 9–12.

Griffin, Adele. *The Other Shepards.*
Hyperion, 1998.
Setting: New York City.
Main Character: Female, Geneva Shepard, 13 years old.

Geneva and her older sister, Holland, have lived their lives in the shadow of the memory of their three siblings who were killed in a car accident twenty years earlier. Geneva suffers from nearly debilitating psychological difficulties. Then one day, an artist arrives to paint a mural in their home and becomes part therapist, part friend, and part angel. Awards: CC. Grades: 8–12.

Hinton, S. E. *Rumble Fish.*
Delacorte, 1975.
Setting: 1960s–1970s.
Main Character: Male, Rusty James, 14 years old.

Rusty James idolizes his older brother, Motorcycle Boy, the coolest, toughest guy in the neighborhood and wants to be just like him. Awards: CC. Grades: YA.

Mazer, Norma Fox. *When She Was Good.*
Scholastic, 1997.
Setting: 1990s.
Main Character: Female, Em Thurkill, 17 years old.

When Em's mother died and her father remarried, Em and her sister moved out on their own. Now her abusive, manipulative older sister Pamela has died and Em is on her own, but she is still haunted by her abuse. Awards: CC. Grades: 8–12.

Paterson, Katherine. *Jacob Have I Loved.*
Crowell, 1980.
Setting: Rass Island, Chesapeake Bay, Maryland, 1940s.
Main Character: Female, Sarah Louise "Wheeze" Bradshaw, 13 years old.

Wheeze has always been in the shadow of her perfect twin sister, Caroline. As children, Caroline was feminine and pretty, while Wheeze was a tomboy. Only when Wheeze moves away does she find happiness being herself. Twins sibling rivalry like the biblical Jacob and Esau, where Jacob was the favored twin. Awards: CC; Newbery. Grades: 5 and up.

Paulsen, Gary. *Hermanas/Sisters.*
Harcourt, 1994.
Setting: Houston, Texas.

Main Characters: Female, Rosa; Female, Traci; both 14 years old.

Rosa is an illegal alien, and a prostitute, but she has dreams and aspirations. Traci is the privileged child of controlling, wealthy parents. When Rosa and Traci meet by chance in a mall, Traci recognizes a kinship with Rosa that is quickly denied and buried by her mother. Each girl's story is told in alternating chapters. Awards: CC. Grades: 8–12.

Picoult, Jodi. *My Sister's Keeper.*
Pocket, 2004.
Setting: 2000s.
Main Character: Female, Anna, 13 years old.

Anna was genetically engineered to be a perfect match for her cancer-ridden, older sister Kate. Anna has donated platelets, blood, her umbilical cord, and bone marrow, and is being considered as a kidney donor in an attempt to save her 16-year-old sister. Anna has hired a lawyer to represent her in a medical emancipation suit to allow her to have control over her own body. The thought-provoking story is told from multiple points of view. Grades: YA/A.

Sones, Sonya. *Stop Pretending: What Happened When My Big Sister Went Crazy.*
HarperCollins, 1999.
Setting: Contemporary.
Main Character: Female, Cookie, 12 years old.

Cookie tells of her family's crisis when her 19-year-old sister was hospitalized due to manic depression. A verse novel based on the journals Sones wrote at the age of 13, when her 19-year-old sister was hospitalized due to manic depression. Awards: CC. Grades: 6–9.

Staples, Suzanne Fisher. *Shabanu: Daughter of the Wind.*
Knopf, 1989.
Series: Border Trilogy: *Haveli; Shiva's Fire.*
Setting: Pakistan.
Main Character: Female, Shabanu, 11 years old.

Shabanu and her sister, Phulan, live among the camel-dealing nomads in modern Pakistan, where a daughter abides by her father's decisions and a wife obeys her husband's wishes. Phulan and Shabanu's weddings are already planned. When the sisters are threatened with rape by a powerful local landowner, they escape but humiliate him. In revenge, he kills Phulan's betrothed and threatens to cut off the family's water supply. As one condition for restoring peace, Shabanu must marry the landlord's older brother. Awards: CC; Newbery Honor. Grades: 7–12.

Zeises, Lara M. *Contents under Pressure.*
Delacorte, 2004.
Setting: Delaware.
Main Character: Female, Lucy Doyle, 14 years old.

Lucy's freshman year isn't going as expected. Her friends leave her behind when they discover boys and her perfect brother moves back home from college with his pregnant girlfriend in tow. Lucy meets Tobin and suddenly there is a lot more to think about, like dating and sex. Grades: 7–10.

TEEN FATHERS

Bechard, Margaret. *Hanging on to Max.*
Roaring Brook, 2002.
Setting: Alternative school, 2000s.
Main Character: Male, Sam, 17 years old.
    Sam ends up taking care of his baby, Max, when the baby's teenaged mom decides she can't raise him. Attending an alternative high school that provides day care, Sam juggles homework and parenting duties with little support from anyone. A tearjerker. Grades: 7–12.

Horniman, Joanne. *Mahalia.*
Knopf, 2003.
Setting: New South Wales.
Main Character: Male, Matt, 17 years old.
    Baby Mahalia's parents, Matt and Emmy, drop out of school and try to provide a home for her, but Emmy can't cope and leaves when the baby is five months old. Matt moves back to his hometown into a rental house inhabited by a 22-year-old music student. Matt struggles to cope with the loss of Emmy and the stresses of taking care of a baby with the help of friends. Grades: 8–12.

Johnson, Angela. *First Part Last.*
Simon & Schuster, 2003.
Setting: New York City.
Main Character: Male, Bobby, 16 years old.
    Bobby struggles to balance parenting, school, and friends who don't comprehend his new role as a parent. Alternating chapters that flash back to the story of Bobby's relationship with his girlfriend, Nia, lead to the revelation in the final chapters that Nia is in an irreversible coma caused by eclampsia. Teens who enjoyed Margaret Bechard's *Hanging on to Max* will love this book too. Awards: Printz; Coretta Scott King Honor. Grades: 8 and up.

Klein, Norma. *No More Saturday Nights.*
Knopf, 1988.
Setting: New York City.
Main Character: Male, Tim Weber, 18 years old.
    Tim escapes small-town life in Massachusetts when he is accepted at Columbia. When a casual relationship with a high-school classmate results in an unwanted pregnancy, Tim decides to go to court to win custody of baby Mason. Tim and Mason share an apartment in the city with three females. Tim attempts to balance dirty diapers, day care, dating, and studying. Grades: 10–12.

Reynolds, Marilyn. *Too Soon for Jeff.*
Morning Glory, 1994.

Series: True-To-Life Series from Hamilton High: *Telling; Baby Help; Beyond Dreams; If You Loved Me; The Plum Tree War; Love Rules.*
Setting: Southern California.
Main Character: Male, Jeff Browning, 18 years old.

Jeff and his girlfriend, Christy, have been together for a year, and Jeff has just decided that he needs more independence and time to spend with his friends. When Christy reveals that she is pregnant, Jeff is outraged and insists on an abortion. Christy has the baby, hoping Jeff will stay with her. Jeff finally takes responsibility for his son and learns to balance college life with fatherhood. Grades: 8–12.

TEEN MOTHERS

Arnoldi, Katherine. *The Amazing True Story of a Teenage Single Mom.*
Hyperion, 1998.
Setting: 1990s.
Main Character: Female, Katherine Arnoldi, teenager.

Black-and-white cartoon panels feature Arnoldi recounting her years from the birth of her daughter through her attempts to earn their keep in a Latex factory, her disastrous relationship with an abusive man, and her eventual success in getting her education back on track and discovering her earning abilities as an illustrator.
Awards: CC. Grades: YA.

Eyerly, Jeannette. *Someone to Love Me.*
Lippincott Williams & Wilkins, 1987.
Setting: 1980s.
Main Character: Female, Patrice Latta, 15 years old.

Patrice is flattered by the attention of Lance, whose friends made a bet that he would have sex with her. Lance gets engaged to his real girlfriend, while Patrice is left dealing with pregnancy and motherhood. A tearjerker. Grades: 8 and up.

Ferris, Jean. *Looking for Home.*
Farrar, Straus & Giroux, 1989.
Setting: 1980s.
Main Character: Female, Daphne, 17 years old.

In spite of Daphne's abusive father, a cowed mother, and unhappy younger brothers, she dreams of a loving family and a happy home. A prom night spent with Scott leaves her pregnant, and fear of her father's reaction pushes her into hopping a bus to a different city. She begins waitressing and plans to put the baby up for adoption. Surrounded by new friends, Daphne becomes independent and secure, and decides to keep the baby. Grades: 7–12.

McDonald, Janet. *Spellbound.*
Farrar, Straus & Giroux, 2001.
Sequel: *Chill Wind* (John Steptoe).
Setting: New York City.
Main Character: Female, Raven, 16 years old.

Raven, a once promising student, has been derailed by the birth of a baby conceived during a first sexual encounter with a guy who was a stranger to her when they met at a party. When Raven's older sister hears about a college prep and scholarship program, she goads Raven into studying for the spelling bee, in spite of the baby, a fast-food job, her best friend's loud mocking, and the reemergence of the baby's father into her life. Raven decides to learn to spell so that she can compete and win. African American characters Awards: CC. Grades: 7–10.

Porter, Connie. *Imani All Mine.*
Houghton Mifflin, 1999.
Setting: Buffalo, New York.
Main Character: Female, Tasha, 15 years old.

Tasha is the mother of Imani, conceived as the result of a rape. Tasha's mother is distant and has an alcoholic boyfriend. Daily occurrences include gunfire and encounters with crack dealers. Imani is killed, the victim of gang violence, and Tasha chooses to become pregnant again. The story is entirely in dialect with no quotation marks, which sometimes creates confusion. Awards: CC. Grades: YA.

Reynolds, Marilyn. *Detour for Emmy.*
Morning Glory, 1993.
Setting: Southern California.
Main Character: Female, Emmy, 16 years old.

Emmy's carefree days and dreams of college end when she becomes pregnant. The hardship, tedium, and responsibility of parenting and the pain of deferred dreams present strong messages to sexually active teens. Grades: 8–12.

Sparks, Beatrice. *Annie's Baby: The Diary of Anonymous, a Pregnant Teenager.*
Avon, 1998.
Setting: 1990s.
Main Character: Female, Annie, 14 years old.

Annie's diary traces her victimization and impregnation by Danny, her manipulative and sadistic 16-year-old boyfriend. With the support of her exceptionally tolerant mother, patient teachers, and a nonjudgmental therapist, Annie changes from a self-deprecating romantic to a more level-headed realist, who painfully, learns to put her baby's needs before her own. Presents a strong antiabortion message and valuable information about sex, pregnancy, and birth control, as well as a love quiz to help girls assess their relationships. Awards: CC. Grades: 7–12.

Williams-Garcia, Rita. *Like Sisters on the Homefront.*
Perfection Learning Prebound, 1996.
Setting: Georgia.
Main Character: Female, Gayle, 14 years old.

Life is hard for a teen mother, especially when she lives in a bad neighborhood. Gayle has two brothers, a sister, and no father. When Gayle found she was six weeks pregnant with her second child, her mother took her to a clinic to get an abortion. Gayle moves to her uncle's farm, and she turns her life around. African American characters. Awards: CC. Grades: 7 and up.

CHAPTER 9

FANTASY

According to *Connecting Young Adults and Libraries*, 10 percent of teen readers prefer fantasy and science fiction. Readers who like fantasy enjoy the journeys and challenges the characters meet while exploring imaginary worlds with magical, mythical, and supernatural elements. The protagonists are clearly good guys and have strong moral character; they choose to do the right thing. The noble-hearted hero fights against evil and defends the good, as he struggles to accomplish a quest. Many fantasy anthologies are also available, either exploring a specific topic, such as dragons, featuring the year's best, or featuring short story collections from favorite authors, such as *Legends: Short Novels by the Masters of Modern Fantasy* by Robert Silverberg. The collections provide readers with introductions to new authors, often leading them to a new series.

Fantasy Awards
Classic Fantasy
Dragons
Fairies/Trolls/Elves
Gaming
King Arthur
Magic
Magical Realism
Unicorns
Talking Animals
Urban Fantasy
Wizards
Resources: Additional Titles

FANTASY AWARDS

The Mythopoeic Society organizes a Mythcon each summer and presents awards in four categories, one of which includes a fantasy award for children's literature. This award can go to titles from picture books to young adult in the tradition of *The Hobbit* or *The Chronicles of Narnia*.

The World Fantasy Convention is an annual meeting of 850 fantasy enthusiasts. Five judges appointed by the administration of the WFC select the winning titles for the World Fantasy Awards from a ballot comprised of five titles published in the preceding year in each of the following areas: life achievement; novel; novella (10,001 to 40,000 words); short story (under 10,000 words); anthology (multiple author—original or reprint—single or multiple editors); collection (single author—original or reprint—single or multiple editors); artist; special award professional; special award nonprofessional. The winners are announced at the convention in November. Read more about the awards at www.mythsoc.org/ and www.worldfantasy.org/.

CLASSIC FANTASY

Adams, Richard. **Watership Down.**
Rex Collings, 1972.
Setting: English countryside, 1970s.
Main Character: Male, Hazel, a rabbit.
　　A warren of Berkshire rabbits search for a safe haven after fleeing the destruction of their home by a land developer. This rabbit world is complete with its own culture, folk history, mythos, and rabbitese language. Awards: CC. Grades: 7–12.

Cooper, Susan. **Over Sea, Under Stone.**
Harcourt, 1966.
Series: The Dark is Rising: **The Dark is Rising; Greenwitch; The Grey King; Silver on the Tree.**
Setting: Cornwall, England.
Main Characters: Male, Simon Drew, older brother; Female, Jane Drew, middle child; Male, Barney Drew, younger brother.
　　Simon, Jane, and Barney find an old map in a hidden room while summering at the Grey House in Cornwall. Along with their Great-uncle Merry, they become embroiled in a web of intrigue that surrounds an Arthurian legend. Grades: 5–7.

Goldman, William. **Princess Bride: S. Morgenstern's Classic Tale of True Love and High Adventure.**
Ballantine, 1998.
Setting: Florin, Guilder.
Main Characters: Male, Westley, young man; Female, Buttercup, young woman.
　　The most beautiful girl in the world marries the most handsome prince of all time but he isn't the man she dreamed he would be, in a fairy-tale love story with beasts, bad guys and good guys, pirates, and sorcerers. Made into a movie. Awards: CC. Grades: 9–12.

LeGuin, Ursula. **A Wizard of Earthsea.**
Spectra, 1984.
Series: The Earthsea Cycle: **The Tombs of Atuan, The Farthest Shore, Tehanu, Tales from Earthsea, The Other Wind** (World Fantasy Award).
Setting: Earthsea 1032.
Main Character: Male, Sparrowhawk, young adult.
　　A reckless, awkward boy becomes a wizard's apprentice after the wizard reveals the boy's true name: Sparrowhawk. Great challenges await Sparrowhawk, including an

almost deadly battle with a sinister creature, a monster that may be his own shadow. Earthsea is often compared to Tolkien's **Middle Earth** or Lewis's **Narnia.** Awards: CC. Grades: 6–9.

L'Engle, Madeleine. *A Wrinkle in Time.*
Farrar, Straus & Giroux, 1962.
Sequels: The Time Quintet: *A Wind in the Door; A Swiftly Tilting Planet; Many Waters; An Acceptable Time.*
Setting: Outer space.
Main Characters: Female, Meg Murray, 13 years old; Male, Charles Wallace Murray, 5 years old; Male, Calvin O'Keefe, older teen.

Everyone in town thinks Meg is volatile and dull-witted and that her younger brother Charles Wallace is dumb. People are also saying that their father has run off and left their brilliant scientist mother. Meg, Charles Wallace, and new friend Calvin embark on a perilous quest through space to find their father via "tesseracts," the wrinkles in time. Awards: CC; Newbery. Grades: 5–7.

Lewis, C. S. *The Lion, the Witch and the Wardrobe.*
HarperCollins, 1994.
Series: The Chronicles of Narnia: *The Magician's Nephew; The Horse and His Boy; Prince Caspian; The Voyage of the Dawn Treader; The Silver Chair; The Last Battle.*
Setting: England, Narnia.
Main Characters: Male, Peter Pevensie; Female, Susan Pevensie; Male, Edmund Pevensie; Female, Lucy Pevensie.

Lucy looks into the wardrobe and discovers Narnia and the faun. She and her siblings assist Aslan, the golden lion, to rid Narnia of the White Witch, who has cursed the land with eternal winter. A Christian fantasy. Movie version released in the winter of 2005. Grades: 5 and up.

Orwell, George. *Animal Farm.*
Harcourt Brace, 1946.
Setting: Manor Farm.
Main Characters: Pigs and other farm animals.

In a satire on communism, the downtrodden beasts of Manor Farm oust their drunken human master and take over management of the land. Everyone willingly works overtime, productivity soars, and for one brief, glorious season, every belly is full. The pigs, self-appointed leaders by virtue of their intelligence, succumb to the temptations of privilege and power, and the common animals are once again left hungry and exhausted, no better off than in the days when humans ran the farm. Awards: CC. Grades: YA.

Tolkien, J. R. R. *The Hobbit, or There and Back Again.*
Houghton Mifflin, 1999.
Sequels: Lord of the Rings: *Fellowship of the Ring; The Two Towers; The Return of the King.*
Setting: Middle Earth. 2941 of the Third Age.

Main Character: Male, Bilbo Baggins, 51 years old.

Bilbo is rousted from his cozy home and sent on a quest by the wizard Gandalf to the Lonely Mountains with a troop of rowdy dwarves. His nephew, Frodo, inherits the responsibility of The Ring in the *Lord of the Rings* trilogy that follows. Originally published in 1937, Tolkien is the father of fantasy, and his **Middle Earth** is by which all other fantasy is measured. Awards: CC. Grades: YA.

DRAGONS

Davis, Bryan, *Raising Dragons.*
CLW Communications/AMG, 2004.
Series: Dragons in Our Midst Chronicles: *The Candlestone.*
Setting: Present day.
Main Character: Male, Billy Bannister, junior high.

When Billy, who is called Dragon Breath because of his extraordinarily scorching breath, accidentally sets off the bathroom fire systems at school he realizes he can't conceal his problem any longer. His parents tell him the family heritage: his dad is a former dragon who has been living in human form for hundreds of years. A Christian fantasy. Grades: YA.

Dugald Steer. *Dragonology: The Complete Book of Dragons.*
Templar Pub, 2003.

"The proper study of the dragonologist or student of dragon lore" is a faux reproduction of an 1896 work by English dragonologist, Ernest Drake. The book covers dragon habitats; physiology; behavior; and finding, tracking, taming, and flying them. Appendixes provide advice on setting up a dragonology lab, useful spells and charms, and a history of dragonologists and dragon slayers. The foldouts, insets, maps, ads, advice, and full-color illustrations on antique-looking paper will appeal to dragon lovers of all ages. Grades: 7–12.

Funke, Cornelia Caroline. *Dragon Rider.*
Scholastic, 2004.
Setting: Firedrake's Valley.
Main Characters: Male, Firedrake, a "young" dragon; Male, "a boy;" Sorrel, a Brownie; Twigleg; Nettlebrand.

Firedrake, who uses moonlight to fly, goes on a quest to find the legendary valley known as the Rim of Heaven, the ancient ancestral home of dragons; he is accompanied by a brownie and an orphan boy. Grades: 5 and up.

McCaffrey, Anne. *Dragonflight.*
Ballantine, 1968.
Series: Dragonriders of Pern: *Dragonquest; The White Dragon.*
Setting: Pern, a planet.
Main Character: Female, Lessa, young woman.

Thread has not fallen for over 400 Turns, and only one Weyr remains. The general population, as well as the various Lords, has begun to doubt that Thread will ever return, and they grow weary and resentful of supporting the dragonfolk. Even the dragonriders have become lax and less vigilant. Meanwhile, the last queen dragon lies dying as her last clutch of eggs (containing one final queen egg) prepares to hatch. Grades: YA/A.

McCaffrey, Anne. *Dragonsong.*
Atheneum, 1976.
Series: Harper Hall Trilogy: *Dragonsinger; Dragondrums.*
Setting: Pern, a planet.
Main Character: Female, Menolly, 14 years old.
 Menolly loved music and wanted to be a Harper, though her father would not allow it, as it was a disgrace for a woman even to think of such a thing. When he forbade Menolly to even sing for fear her ambition would become known, she had no choice but to run away. She meets a group of fire lizards who bring new adventure, challenge, and direction to her life. Awards: CC. Grades: YA/A.

Ohkami, Mineko. *Dragon Knights #1.*
TokyoPop, 2002.
Series: Dragon Knights 1–22.
Setting: Dragon Castle.
Main Characters: Male, Rath: Male, Rune; Male, Thatz; Female, Cesia; Female, Kitchel; Female, Tintlet.
 Rath, Rune, and Thatz become the Dragon Knights of Fire, Water, and Earth, and scour a mystic landscape for fortune, love, and honor. They face a man-eating witch and a one-eyed monster in their swashbuckling adventures, when they aren't fighting among themselves. Manga. Grades: 8–12.

Paolini, Christopher. *Eragon.*
Paolini International, 2003.
Series: Inheritance Trilogy: *Eldest;* (forthcoming title).
Setting: Alagaesia.
Main Characters: Male, Eragon, 15 years old; Female, Saphira, a dragon.
 Eragon, a young farm boy, finds a blue stone in a mystical mountain place. Before he can trade it for food for his family, it hatches a beautiful sapphire-blue dragon, a race thought to be extinct. Eragon bonds with the dragon and discovers that he is the last of the Dragon Riders. Eragon and Saphira set out to find their role, growing in magic power as they endure perilous travels and sudden battles, dire wounds, capture, and escape. Teen author. Grades: 7–12.

Wrede, Patricia. *Dealing with Dragons.*
Jane Yolen, 1990.
Series: Enchanted Forest Chronicles: *Searching for Dragons; Calling on Dragons; Talking to Dragons.*
Setting: Linderwall, Enchanted Forest.
Main Characters: Female, Cimorene, teenager; Female, Kazul, a dragon.
 Princess Cimorene is a strong-willed teenager who resents the dull, prissy life of a princess. She leaves home to avoid marrying a dim-witted prince and becomes the willing captive of Kazul, a cranky but good-hearted dragon. The combination of

medieval fairy-tale themes and modern teenage sarcasm will appeal to readers of many ages. Grades: 5–9.

Yolen, Jane. ***Dragon's Blood.***
Magic Carpet, 1996.
Series: Pit Dragon Chronicles: ***Heart's Blood; A Sending of Dragons.***
Setting: Austar IV.
Main Character: Male, Jakkin, 15 years old.
   Jakkin, a bond boy who works as a Keeper in a dragon nursery, steals a dragon hatchling and secretly trains it to be a fighting pit dragon, in hopes of winning his freedom. Grades: YA.

Yolen, Jane. ***Here There Be Dragons.***
Harcourt, 1993.
   Poems, short stories, and pencil drawings tell tales of heroic battles, romance, fantasy, science fiction, occasional blood and guts, and a story of Chinese origin—all about dragons. Yolen adds personal anecdotes to introduce each selection. Illustrated by David Wilgus. Awards: CC. Grades: 5–9.

Zahn, Timothy. ***Dragon and Thief.***
Tor, 2003.
Series: Dragonback: ***Dragon and Soldier; Dragon and Slave.***
Setting: Spaceship.
Main Character: Male, Jack Morgan, 14 years old.
   Orphaned, Jack is on the run after being framed for a crime he didn't commit. He is hiding out on a remote, uninhabited planet in his dead uncle's spaceship, where the computer program, Virge, is a virtual version of his uncle. Another spaceship crashes after a fierce battle, and the only survivor is Draycos, a dragonlike being who cannot live apart from a symbiotic relationship with a humanoid host. Jack and Draycos team up to clear Jack. Grades: YA.

FAIRIES/TROLLS/ELVES

Black, Holly. ***Tithe: A Modern Fairy Tale.***
Simon & Schuster, 2002.
Sequel: ***Valiant: A Modern Tale of Faerie.***
Setting: New Jersey.
Main Character: Female, Kaye Fierch, 16 years old.
   Kaye never imagined she was one of the green-skinned fairies she has interacted with since she was little. When Kaye's alcoholic rock-singer mother's boyfriend tries to kill her, mother and daughter quickly move back to grandma's on the New Jersey Shore where Kaye grew up, an event rigged by the Faerie world. Grades: 9 and up.

Brooks, Terry. ***Sword Of Shannara.***
Ballantine, 1978.
Sequels: ***The Elfstones of Shannara; The Wishsong of Shannara.***
Setting: Shady Vale.

Main Character: Male, Shea Ohmsford, Half-elven.

Living in peaceful Shady Vale, Shea knew little of the troubles that plagued the rest of the world. Then the giant, forbidding druid Allanon revealed that the Warlock Lord was plotting to destroy the world. The sole weapon against his Power of Darkness is the Sword of Shannara, which could only be used by a true heir of Shannara, Shea. Awards: CC. Grades: 7–12.

Colfer, Erin. *Artemis Fowl.*
Miramax, 2001.
Sequels: *The Arctic Incident; The Eternity Code.*
Setting: England, twenty-first century.
Main Character: Male, Artemis Fowl, 12 years old.

Artemis is the most ingenious criminal mastermind in history. He hatches a cunning plot to divest the fairyfolk of their pot of gold by kidnapping one of them and waiting for the ransom to arrive. He doesn't count on the appearance of the extra small, pointy-eared Captain Holly Short of the LEPrecon (Lower Elements Police Reconnaisance) Unit, and her senior officer, Commander Root, an elf who will stop at nothing to get her back. Colfer describes *Artemis Fowl* as "*Die Hard* with fairies." Grades: 6–12.

Datlow, Ellen, and Terri Windling, editors. *The Faery Reel: Tales from the Twilight Realm.*
Viking, 2004.

Short stories and poems about fairies from all over the world by Steven Berman, Holly Black, Emma Bull, Bill Congreve, Charles de Lint, A.M. Dellamonica, Jeffrey Ford, Gregory Frost, Nan Fry, Neil Gaiman, Bruce Glassco, Hiromi Goto, Nona Kiriki Hoffman, Tanith Lee, Kelly Link, Gregory Maguire, Patricia A. McKillip, Delia Sherman, Ellen Steiber, and Katherine Vaz. Grades: 9–12.

Farmer, Nancy. *Sea of Trolls.*
Gardners, 2004.
Setting: Medieval Norway, 793 A.D.
Main Character: Male, Jack, 11 years old.

Jack's never been much good at anything, until the Bard of his medieval village makes him an apprentice. Then he and his little sister are kidnapped and taken to the court of King Ivar the Boneless and his half-troll queen, Frith. When one of Jack's amateur spells causes the evil queen's beautiful hair to fall out, he is sent on a dangerous quest across the Sea of Trolls to make things right, or his sister will be sacrificed to Frith's patron goddess, Freya. Grades: 7–9.

Gaiman, Neil. *Stardust.*
Spike, 1998.
Setting: Wall, England, Faerie Land, nineteenth century.
Main Character: Male, Tristran Thorn, 17 years old.

Tristran falls in love with Victoria Forester, and to win her affection, he vows to bring to her the fallen star that they see one night. The star has fallen in Faerie, where a star is not a ball of flaming gas, but a living, breathing woman. Tristran finds her but has a hard time holding on to her. The sons of the Lord of Stormhold also seek the star, for he who finds her can take his father's throne. Awards: CC. Grades: YA.

Pratchett, Terry. *Wee Free Men.*
HarperCollins, 2003.
Sequels: *A Hat Full of Sky; Colour of Magic* (CC), plus over 20 more Discworld titles.
Setting: Discworld.
Main Character: Female, Tiffany Aching, 9 years old.
　　Tiffany, a powerful witch, takes care of her irritating brother, makes good cheese on her father's farm, and knows how to keep secrets. When monsters from Fairyland invade her world and kidnap her brother for the Fairy Queen, Tiffany, armed only with courage, clear-sightedness, a manual of sheep diseases, and an iron frying pan, goes off to find him. The alcohol-swilling, sheep-stealing Wee Free Men are Tiffany's allies, and she becomes their temporary leader as they help her search for the Fairy Queen. Hitchhiker fans will enjoy the Discworld spoofs. Awards: Mythopoeic. Grades: 7–12.

Shetterly, Will. *Elsewhere.*
Harcourt, 1991.
Series: Borderland: *Nevernever.*
Setting: Borderland.
Main Character: Male, Ron Starbuck, 14 years old.
　　Elsewhere is a bookstore in Bordertown, where humans and elves coexist. Ron gets a job there after he runs away to look for his brother, who has committed suicide. Awards: CC. Grades: 9–12.

GAMING

Anderson, M. T. *Game of Sunken Places.*
Scholastic, 2004.
Setting: Vermont.
Main Characters: Male, Brian Thatz; Male, Gregory Buchanan; both 13 years old.
　　When Brian and Gregory stay with weird Uncle Max and cousin Prudence at his mansion in rural Vermont, they discover an old-fashioned board game called The Game. As players they are drawn into a mysterious adventure and must deal with attitudinal trolls and warring kingdoms. Grades: 5–9.

Anthony, Piers. *Killobyte.*
Putnam, 1993.
Setting: 1990s.
Main Characters: Male, Walter Toland, adult; Female, Baal Curran, teenager.
　　Paraplegic ex-policeman Walter and diabetic teen Baal discover the virtual reality computer game known as Killobyte. They revel in their temporary ability to escape their handicaps, until a malicious hacker turns a friendly game into a deadly race against time. Grades: YA/A.

Fredericks, Mariah. *Head Games.*
Atheneum, 2004.
Setting: New York City.
Main Character: Female, Judith, 15 years old.

Since she was attacked last year walking home, Judith only feels safe role-playing as a male online. After Irgan, her Internet enemy, forfeits the right to kill her off, Judith drops out of the Game and becomes determined to learn his identity. She discovers the player is Jonathan, who lives in her building. They become close, and Jonathan helps Judith overcome her fears through a real-life game. Grades: 7–12.

Lain, T. H. *The Savage Caves.*
Wizards of the Coast, 2002.
Series: Dungeons and Dragons: *Return of the Damned; Plaque of Ice; The Bloody Eye.*
Setting: Caves.
Main Character: Male, Regdar, young warrior.

The first book in a series featuring characters from the D&D role-playing games. Grades: YA.

Lubar, David. *Wizards of the Game.*
Philomel Books, 2003.
Setting: Contemporary.
Main Character: Male, Mercer Dickensen, 13 years old.

Mercer's passion is the fantasy role-playing game Wizards of the Warrior World. When he is asked to help with a fund-raiser to benefit a homeless shelter, he suggests bringing a gaming convention to his school, causing controversy with fundamentalist Christians in the community. During his visit to the shelter, he meets four genuine wizards who are trapped on Earth and want his help in returning to their own world. Grades: 5–8.

Raskin, Ellen. *The Westing Game.*
Dutton, 2003.
Setting: Sunset Towers.
Main Characters: Sixteen heirs of Samuel W. Westing.

The mysterious death of the eccentric millionaire Samuel W. Westing brings together sixteen heirs; one is his murderer. The heirs must uncover the circumstances of his death before they can claim their inheritance. They could become millionaires, depending on how they play the tricky and dangerous Westing game, which involves blizzards, burglaries, and bombings. Awards: Newbery. Grades: 4 and up.

Sleator, William. *Interstellar Pig.*
Dutton, 1984.
Sequel: *Parasite Pig.*
Setting: Seaside.
Main Character: Male, Barney, young teenager.

Barney's boring seaside vacation suddenly becomes more interesting when he meets three exotic neighbors, who are addicted to a game they call "Interstellar Pig."

In the game, rival aliens wage war over an item that allowed their planet to survive and all other planets to die. Barney slowly realizes they are looking for something just like their characters in the game, and losing could mean the end of mankind. Awards: CC. Grades: 7–12.

Vande Velde, Vivian. *Heir Apparent.*
Harcourt, 2002.
Setting: Medieval cyber-kingdom.
Main Character: Female, Giannine Bellisario, 14 years old.
    While playing Heir Apparent, a total immersion virtual-reality game of kings and intrigue, Giannine learns that demonstrators have damaged the equipment to which she is connected, and she must win the game quickly or be brain-damaged. Fantasy and science fiction appeal. Grades: 6–9.

Vande Velde, Vivian. *User Unfriendly.*
Harcourt, 1991.
Setting: Virtual world.
Main Character: Male, Arvin Rizalli, 14 years old.
    Arvin, his mother, and his friends enter a computer-controlled role-playing game that simulates a magical world, even though the computer program is a pirated one containing unpredictable errors. The seven players encounter giant rats, trolls, werewolves, swordplay, and general mayhem, usually accompanied by death and destruction. Grades: 6–10.

Werlin, Nancy. *Locked Inside.*
Delacorte, 2000.
Setting: Basement.
Main Character: Female, Marnie Skyedottir, 16 years old.
    Marnie is addicted to the computer game Paliopolis, where as Sorceress Llewellyne she competes with the clever but pesky Elf, escaping from labyrinths and dungeons and evading the blind Rubble-Eater. The game is safe to Marnie, unlike her real life, where she is flunking out at her exclusive boarding school, her famous mother, Skye, is dead, and her guardian, Max, refuses to let her have the millions she will inherit at 21. A crazed chemistry teacher, believing that she, too, is Skye's daughter, imprisons Marnie and Elf in a windowless basement, with only a blanket, a half-empty bottle of seltzer, and a sand bucket, and the Elf has a gunshot wound in his leg. Grades: 7–12.

KING ARTHUR

Bradley, Marion Zimmer. *Mists of Avalon.*
Ballantine, 1982.
Series: Avalon: *The Forest House; Forests of Avalon; Lady of Avalon; Priestess of Avalon; Ancestors of Avalon* (prequel).
Setting: Britannia, Camelot, Avalon, seventh century.
Main Characters: Female, Morgaine/Morgan Le Fay; Female, Gwenhwyfar/Guinevere; Female, Viviane, adult.

The King Arthur legend told from the point of view of the women behind the throne. Christianity vs. Faery and God vs. Goddess are dominant themes. Awards: CC. Grades: YA/A.

Crossley-Holland, Kevin. *The Seeing Stone.*
Arthur A. Levine, 2001.
Series: Arthur Trilogy: *At the Crossing Places; King of the Middle March.*
Setting: Welsh marshes, twelfth century.
Main Character: Male, Arthur, 13 years old.
 Merlin gives young Arthur a magical seeing stone, where Arthur sees visions of another Arthur, the once and future king. Told in diary entries. Grades: 7 and up.

McCaffrey, Anne. *Black Horses for the King.*
Harcourt Brace, 1996.
Setting: Britannia, fifth century.
Main Characters: Male, Galwyn Varianus, teenager; Male, Artos, adult.
 Galwyn is gifted at languages and handling horses. He escapes from his tyrannical uncle and joins Lord Artos, later known as King Arthur, to help secure and care for the Libyan horses that Artos hopes to use in battle against the Saxons. Horse lovers and historical fiction lovers will enjoy the detail. Awards: CC. Grades: 6–9.

Morris, Gerald. *Squire's Tale.*
Houghton Mifflin, 1998.
Series: Squire's Tales: *The Squire, His Knight, and His Lady; The Savage Damsel and the Dwarf; Parsifal's Page; The Ballad of Sir Dinadan; The Princess, the Crone, and the Dung-Cart Knight.*
Setting: Camelot, sixth century.
Main Characters: Male, Terence, 14 years old; Male, Gawain of Orkney, young adult.
 Terence leaves his forest home to become the squire of the young Gawain of Orkney. Terence accompanies Gawain on a long quest to prove Gawain's worth as a knight, and eventually learns an important secret about his own true identity. Awards: CC. Grades: 5–9.

Paterson, Katherine. *Parzival: The Quest of the Grail Knight.*
Lodestar, 1998.
Setting: Camelot.
Main Character: Male, Parzival, teenager.
 Parzival, the Grail Knight, unaware of his noble birth, stumbles through one adventure after another in his fast-paced quest for the Holy Grail. Grades: 5 and up.

Stewart, Mary. *The Crystal Cave.*
Morrow, 1970.
Series: The Arthurian Saga: *The Hollow Hills; The Last Enchantment; The Wicked Day.*
Setting: Britain, fifth century.
Main Character: Male, Merlin, childhood to adult.
 Merlin leads a perilous childhood, haunted by portents and visions. Destiny has

great plans for this bastard son of a Welsh princess, taking him from prophesying before the High King Vortigern to the crowning of Uther Pendragon and the conception of Arthur, the once and future king. Awards: Mythopoeic. Grades: YA/A.

White, T. H. *The Once and Future King.*
Putnam, 1958.
Series: *The Sword in the Stone; The Queen of Air and Darkness; The Ill-Made Knight; The Candle in the Wind; The Book of Merlyn.*
Setting: England.
Main Character: Male, King Arthur.

The series is a retelling of the Arthurian legend, from Arthur's birth to the end of his reign, and is based largely on Sir Thomas Malory's *Le Morte D'arthur.* After White's death, a conclusion to *The Once and Future King* was found among his papers and published as *The Book of Merlyn.* Awards: CC. Grades: 9–12.

Yolen, Jane. *Passager.*
Harcourt, 1996.
Series: Merlin Trilogy: *Hobby; Merlin.*
Setting: Medieval Britain.
Main Character: Male, Merlin, 8 years old.

Merlin lives alone in the forest until a falconer takes him in. When he is introduced to the falcons, Merlin is given back his own true name. Thin book size will appeal to reluctant readers. Grades: 5–8.

Yolen, Jane. *Sword of the Rightful King: A Novel of King Arthur.*
Harcourt, 2003.
Setting: Britannia, sixth century.
Main Characters: Male, Arthur, 22 years old; Male, Merlinnus, elderly; Female, Morgause, adult; Male, Gawen, teen; Male, Gawaine, young.

Merlinnus the magician devises a way for King Arthur to prove himself the rightful king of England by pulling a sword from a stone. Trouble arises when someone else removes the sword first. A secret creates a surprise ending that departs from traditional Arthurian legend. Grades: 6–9.

MAGIC

Anthony, Piers. *A Spell for Chameleon.*
Del Rey, 1987.
Series: Xanth: many titles.
Setting: Xanth.
Main Character: Male, Bink, adult.

Bink is without magical powers in a world ruled entirely by magic. If he doesn't discover his own magical talent soon, he will be forever banished from North Village. According to the Good Magician Humphrey, the charts said that Bink was as powerful as the King or even the Evil Magician Trent. Humorous fantasy series known for outrageous word puns and bizarre characters. Awards: CC. Grades: 6–12.

Bernstein, Nina. *Magic by the Book.*
Farrar, Straus & Giroux, 2005.
Setting: New York City, twentieth century.
Main Characters: Female, Anne, 11 years old; Female, Emily, younger sister; Male, Will
Thornton, 6 years old.

    After returning from a trip to the library, Anne and her younger brother and
sister discover a magic book that sends them on adventures in which they meet Robin
Hood, giant bugs, and a dark, sinister man from *War and Peace.* Illustrated by Boris
Kulikov.
Readers are also "read into the book" in *Inkheart.* Grades: 5–8.

Brooks, Terry. *Magic Kingdom for Sale—Sold!*
Del Rey, 1986.
Series: Magic Kingdom of Landover: *The Black Unicorn; Wizard at Large; The
Tangle Box; Witches' Brew.*
Setting: Chicago, Magic Kingdom of Landover, 1980s.
Main Characters: Male, Ben Holiday, adult; Male, Meeks, a wizard, adult; Female,
Willow, a sprite.

    Ben purchases Landover, complete with fairy folk and wizardry, for a million
dollars. The ad didn't mention the kingdom was falling into ruin. Awards: CC. Grades:
7–12.

Bujold Lois McMaster. *The Curse Of Chalion.*
Eos, 2001.
Series: Chalion: *Paladin of Souls.*
Setting: Medieval Cardegoss.
Main Characters: Male, Castillar Lupe dy Cazaril, middle aged; Female, Iselle, 19 years old.

    Cazaril is chosen to tutor Iselle, the princess of Chalion, and her lady-in-waiting,
Bertriz. To rescue Iselle, and to save Chalion, Cazaril must play matchmaker between
Iselle and the prince of another realm, fight off assassins, lift an old curse, and risk
everything. Awards: CC; World Fantasy. Grades: 10–12.

Card, Orson Scott. *Seventh Son.*
Tor Fantasy, 1993.
Series: Tales of Alvin Maker: *Red Prophet; Prentice Alvin; Alvin Journeyman;
Heartfire; Crystal City.*
Setting: Northwest Territory, late eighteenth century.
Main Character: Male, Alvin Miller, Jr., 6 years old.

    Alvin, seventh son of a seventh son, is heir to great powers that he must learn to
use and control. It becomes apparent that Alvin is the focus of gathering forces of
good and evil preparing for battle. Awards: CC. Grades: YA.

Dickinson, Peter. *Ropemaker.*
Delacorte, 2001.
Setting: Valley to the Empire.
Main Characters: Female, Tilja Urlasdaughter, teenager; Female, Meena, grandmother;
Male, Tahl Ortahlson, teenager; Male, Alnor, grandfather.

Tilja comes from a magical family but is disappointed to find she has inherited no magic of her own. Now the magical protection of her home is breaking down, Tilja, her grandmother Meena, Tahl, and his grandfather Alnor set out on a quest to find the Ropemaker, whose magic is mightier than any in the Empire. Awards: CC; Printz Honor; Mythopoeic. Grades: 7–10.

Eddings, David. *Pawn of Prophecy.*
Del Rey, 1986.
Series: The Belgariad: *Queen of Sorcery; Magician's Gambit; Castle of Wizardry; Enchanters' End Game.*
Series: Malloreon: *Guardians of the West; King of the Murgos; Demon Lord of Karanda; Sorceress of Dashiva; Seeress of Kell.*
Setting: Sendaria.
Main Characters: Male, Garion, 14 years old; Male, Belgarath, "ancient," a sorcerer; Female, Polgara, a sorceress, does not age.

The evil god Torak drove men and Gods to war, but Belgarath the Sorcerer led men to reclaim the Orb, for Riva to protect the men of the West. Garion did not believe the stories. Brought up on a quiet farm by his Aunt Pol, he doesn't know his destiny. Belgarath and Polgara take him on a journey to find a stolen priceless artifact. Awards: CC. Grades: 6–10.

Ende, Michael. *Neverending Story.*
Dutton, 1997.
Setting: Fantastica.
Main Character: Male, Bastian Balthazar Bux, young boy.

Bastian steals a book, and when he brings it home to read, he is amazed to discover that he has become a character with a mission. He must go to Fantasia and give the Childlike Empress a new name. On his journey, he learns about friendship, trust, and love. To find his way home, he must find the true meaning of why he wants to go home. His journey lasted months in Fantastica but only a day on Earth. Awards: CC. Grades: 6–12.

Funke, Cornelia. *Inkheart.*
Chicken House/Scholastic, 2003.
Sequels: *Inkspell.*
Setting: Italy.
Main Characters: Female, Meggie, 12 years old; Male, Mo, adult; Male, Capricorn, adult; Male, Dustfinger, adult.

Mo has an amazing ability to read characters out of books, bringing them to real life. Unfortunately, when Meggie was a baby, Mo accidentally read her mother into *Inkheart,* reading Capricorn and Dustfinger out. Meggie doesn't know of his power—only that he refuses to read aloud to her. Now Capricorn wants to find Mo and make him read a monster out of *Inkheart* to conquer all of his enemies. He captures Meggie to use her for bait. Grades: 5–10.

Jones, Diana Wynne. *Howl's Moving Castle.*
Eos, 2001.
Setting: Howl's castle.

Main Character: Female, Sophie Hatter, young woman.

The oldest of three sisters, Sophie resigns herself to making hats for a living. Angry at the competition, the Witch of the Waste turns her into an old woman. Sophie seeks refuge in the wizard Howl's moving castle, becomes the cleaning lady, and falls in love. Awards: CC. Grades: 6 and up.

Jordan, Sherryl. ***Secret Sacrament.***
HarperCollins, 2001.
Setting: Navoran Empire.
Main Character: Male, Gabriel, 7 years old.

Gabriel learns the healing arts and becomes involved in the treacherous politics of the Navoran Empire. He cannot prevent the bloodshed, but eventually he paves the way for a more positive future by making a tragic personal sacrifice. Awards: CC. Grades: 7 and up.

Jordan, Robert. ***Eye of the World.***
Tor Fantasy, 1990.
Series: Wheel of Time: ***The Great Hunt; The Dragon Reborn; The Shadow Rising; The Fires of Heaven; Lord of Chaos; A Crown of Swords; The Path of Daggers; Winter's Heart; Crossroads of Twilight.***
Setting: Edmond's Field.
Main Characters: Male, Rand al'Thor; Female, Lady Moiraine; both young adults.

The Dark Lord, imprisoned by the Creator at the beginning of the world, is seeking those who will help bring about the apocalypse that will free him. He sends his agents to the village of Edmond's Field to find Rand, Perrin, and Mat. The Aes Sedai is also looking for them, because they believe they will determine the fate of the world. Awards: CC. Grades: 10–12.

LeGuin, Ursula. ***Gifts.***
Harcourt, 2004.
Setting: Uplands.
Main Characters: Female, Gry, teenager; Male, Orrec, 16 years old.

The people of the Uplands have unusual powers that can be dangerous. Gry can communicate with animals. Orrec can unmake living things, but his gift is uncontrollable because his mother is a Lowlander. He is blindfolded to protect the ones he loves. Grades: 7 and up.

McKillip, Patricia A. ***Tower at Stony Wood.***
Ace, 2001.
Setting: Skye, Yves, Ysse, Stony Wood.
Main Characters: Male, Cyan Dag; Female, Lady Gwynne of Sky; Male, Thayne, Female, Melanthos; all young adults.

Cyan Dag, knight of Gloinmere, is sworn to serve King Regis Aurum of Yves. Idra, Bard of Skye, reveals that the King's new bride, Lady Gwynne, is an impostor and the true Lady Gwynne is trapped in an enchanted tower in Skye. Cyan rides west to free Lady Gwynne and becomes tangled with the lives of Thayne and Melanthos, and in the mysterious motives of Idra. Awards: CC. Grades: 7–10.

McKinley, Robin. *The Blue Sword.*
Greenwillow, 1982.
Sequel: *Hero and the Crown.*
Setting: Damar.
Main Character: Female, Harry Crewe, teenager.

Harry is an orphan who comes to live in Damar, the desert country shared by the Homelanders and the secretive, magical Hillfolk. Her life is quiet and ordinary—until the night she is kidnapped by Corlath, the Hillfolk King, who takes her deep into the desert. Harry is to be trained in the arts of war until she is a match for any of his men. Awards: CC. Grades: 6–12.

Nimmo, Jenny. *Midnight for Charlie Bone.*
Orchard, 2003.
Series: The Children of the Red King: *Charlie Bone and the Invisible Boy; Charlie Bone and the Time Twister; Charlie Bone and the Castle Of Mirrors.*
Setting: Bloor's Academy, England, 2000s.
Main Character: Male, Charlie Bone, 10 years old.

Charlie discovers he can hear the thoughts and voices of people in photographs. One conversation sets him on a search for a girl who has been missing for years. His sinister relatives and the Bloors try to stop him. Awards: VOYA Perfect Ten. Grades: 7 and up.

Nix, Garth. *Sabriel.*
Eos, 1997.
Series: The Abhorsen Trilogy: *Lirael; Abhorsen; Across the Wall: A Tale of the Abhorsen and Other Stories.*
Setting: Old Kingdom.
Main Characters: Female, Sabriel, 18 years old; Male, Kerrigor, adult; Male, Touchstone, young adult; Male, Mogget, cat.

Sabriel and her father are necromancers, fighting the dead who seek to return to life. While Sabriel is away at Wyverly College, where magic does not work, her father is trapped in Death, and she must journey into the Old Kingdom to find him. Awards: CC. Grades: 7 and up.

Pierce, Tamora. *Sandry's Book.*
Scholastic, 1999.
Series: Circle of Magic: *Tris's Book; Daja's Book; Briar's Book.*
Series: Circle Opens: *Magic Steps; Street Magic; Cold Fire; Shatterglass.*
Setting: Winding Circle Temple.
Main Characters: Daja, Briar, Tris, Sandry; all children.

The mage (wizard) Niko brings the misfits Daja, Briar Moss, Tris, and Sandry to Winding Circle Temple for training in crafts and magic, where they form the Magic Circle.
Awards: CC. Grades: 6–10.

Pierce, Tamora. *Alanna: The First Adventure.*
Knopf, 1989.

Series: Song of the Lioness: *In the Hand of the Goddess; The Woman Who Rides Like a Man; Lioness Rampant.*
Series: The Immortals: *Wild Magic; Wolf-Speaker; Emperor Mage; The Realms of the Gods.*
Series: Protector of the Small: *First Test; Page; Squire; Lady Knight.*
Series: Daughter of the Lioness: *Trickster's Choice; Tricksters.*
Setting: Tortall.
Main Character: Female, Alanna, 11 years old.
   Alanna switches places with her twin brother, Thom, and disguises herself as a boy to become a royal page so she can become a knight. Awards: CC. Grades: 6–8.

Pullman, Philip. *The Golden Compass.*
Knopf, 1996.
Series: His Dark Materials Trilogy: *The Subtle Knife; The Amber Spyglass.*
Setting: Oxford, England, Arctic Region, twentieth century.
Main Character: Female, Lyra Belacqua, 14 years old.
   Lyra is a young precocious orphan growing up within the precincts of Oxford University. People there each have a personal dæmon, the manifestation of their soul in animal form, and science, theology, and magic are closely allied. Lyra's carefree existence changes forever when she and her dæmon, Pantalaimon, first prevent an assassination attempt against her uncle and then overhear a secret discussion about a mysterious entity known as Dust. Awards: CC; World Fantasy. Grades: 6–12.

Stroud, Jonathan. *The Amulet of Samarkand.*
Hyperion, 2003.
Series: Bartimaeus Trilogy: *The Golem's Eye* (forthcoming title).
Setting: London, twenty-first century, alternate world.
Main Characters: Male, Nathaniel, 12 years old; Male, Bartimaeus, a genie; Male, Simon Lovelace, magician.
   Nathaniel, a magician's apprentice, summons up Bartimaeus and instructs him to steal the Amulet of Samarkand from the powerful magician Simon Lovelace. Awards: VOYA Perfect Ten. Grades: 6 and up.

MAGICAL REALISM

Almond, David. *Kit's Wilderness.*
Delacorte, 2000.
Setting: Stoneygate, England.
Main Characters: Male, Christopher "Kit" Watson; Male, John Askew; both 13 years old.
   Kit goes to live with his grandfather in the decaying coal mining town of Stoneygate, and finds both the old man and the town haunted by ghosts of the past. Awards: CC; Printz. Grades: 6–9.

Almond, David. *Heaven Eyes.*
Delacorte, 2001.
Setting: Black Middens, England.
Main Characters: Female, Erin Law; Male, January Carr; Male, Mouse Gullane; Female, Heaven Eyes; all children.

Runaways from their orphanage, Erin, January, and Mouse float on a raft down into another world of abandoned warehouses and factories, meeting a strange girl with webbed fingers and little memory of her past, and her grandfather. Awards: CC. Grades: 6–9.

Almond, David. *Skellig.*
Delacorte, 1999.
Setting: England, twentieth century.
Main Characters: Male, Michael; Female, Mina; both 10 years old.
   Michael, upset about his baby sister's illness and the chaos of moving into a dilapidated old house, retreats to the garage where he finds Skellig, a mysterious stranger who is something like a bird and something like an angel. He meets Mina, the girl next door, whose precious blackbird chicks and tawny owls are in her secret attic. Awards: CC; Printz Honor; Carnegie. Grades: 5 and up.

Gaiman, Neil. *American Gods.*
Morrow, 2001.
Setting: United States road trip.
Main Characters: Male, Shadow Moon, 32 years old; Male, Mr. Wednesday, adult.
   A convict called Shadow is flung into the midst of a supernatural fray of gods such as Odin, Anansi, Loki One-Eye, Thor, and a multitude of other ancient divinities as they struggle for survival in an America beset by trends, fads, and constant upheaval. Awards: CC; Hugo; Nebula; World Fantasy. Grades: YA/A.

Jones, Diana Wynne. *Fire and Hemlock.*
Greenwillow, 1984.
Setting: England, 1980s.
Main Character: Female, Polly, 19 years old.
   Polly has two sets of memories. The stranger memories begin nine years ago, when she was 10 and gate-crashed an odd funeral in the mansion near her grandmother's house. She's just beginning to recall the sometimes marvelous, sometimes frightening adventures she embarked on with cellist Tom Lynn. Then she did something terrible, but she can't remember. Awards: CC. Grades: YA.

Murphy, Rita. *Night Flying.*
Delacorte, 2000.
Setting: Vermont.
Main Character: Female, Georgia Hansen, 16 years old.
   Consumed with grief, Georgia Hansen's great-great-great grandmother leaned into the air and discovered her gift of flight that she eventually passed down to all of her female descendants. The time for her solo flight on her 16th birthday approaches, and Georgia begins to question the course of her life and her relationships with the other women in her unusual family. Awards: CC. Grades: 5–9.

O'Brien, Tim. *Going After Cacciato.*
Doubleday, 1978.
Setting: Vietnam to Paris.

Main Character: Male, Paul Berlin, young man.

Private Cacciato deserts his post in Vietnam, intent on walking 8,000 miles to Paris for the peace talks. The remaining members of his squad are sent after him; they chase him into the mountains, corner him on a small grassy hill, and surround the hill. They wait through the night and at dawn they move in. After that the men find themselves following an elusive trail of chocolate M&Ms through the jungles of Indochina, across India, Iran, Greece, and Yugoslavia to the streets of Paris. Awards: CC. Grades: YA/A.

Sherwood, Ben. *Man Who Ate the 747.*
Bantam, 2000.
Setting: Superior, Nebraska, twentieth century.
Main Characters: Male, J. J. Smith; Male, Wally Chubb.

J.J. Smith, keeper of the records for the Book of Records, receives an anonymous tip from Superior about Wally Chubb, who is on a mission to prove his love for Willa Wyatt. His plan is to consume an entire Boeing 747, ground into grit. J.J. records his progress for the Book and falls in love with Willa. Awards: CC. Grades: YA/A.

TALKING ANIMALS

Clement-Davies, David. *Fire Bringer.*
Dutton, 2000.
Setting: Scotland, Middle Ages.
Main Character: Male, Rannoch, a deer.

The Lore of the Herla foretells the coming of one deer that will restore the traditional ways of life to the herd. Rannoch seems destined to fulfill this prophecy. The Herla talk and have a mythology, but they are deer through and through. They search for food, the stags fight for their harems, and protection of the young is one of the highest priorities. Grades: 6 and up.

Clement-Davies, David. *The Sight.*
Dutton, 2002.
Setting: Transylvania, Middle Ages.
Main Character: Female, Larka, a white wolf.

Larka's pack sets out on a perilous journey to prevent their enemy, Morgra, from calling upon a Man Varg, which will give her the power to control all animals. Young Larka has the Sight, a form of esp, and her pack is torn apart as Morgra attempts to capture her. Roman mythology, Christianlike theology, and supernatural horror all lead the Varg toward their destinies. Grades: 7 and up.

Collins, Suzanne. *Gregor the Overlander.*
Scholastic, 2003.
Series: The Underland Chronicles: *Gregor and the Prophecy of Bane.*
Setting: The Underland, New York City, 21st century.
Main Character: Male, Gregor, 11 years old.

Gregor and his sister are pulled into an underground world where their father is a prisoner of the rats. They trigger an epic battle involving men, bats, rats, cockroaches, and spiders. Gregor may be the "overlander" destined to save the humans from the warlike rodents. Grades: 7–9

Duane, Diane. *The Book of Night with Moon.*
Warner Books, 1997.
Setting: Grand Central Station, New York City.
Main Characters: Female, Rhiow; Female, Saash; Male, Urruah, Male, Arhua.

When worldgates in the subway system malfunction and threaten our world with an invasion of Downside's monsters, four feline musketeers, Rhiow, Saash, Urruah, and Arhu, enter the Downside to find the renegade wizard responsible for the mayhem. Grades: YA/A.

Hunter, Erin. *Into the Wild.*
HarperCollins, 2003.
Series: Warriors: *Fire and Ice; Forest of Secrets; Rising Storm; A Dangerous Path; The Darkest Hour.*
Setting: Forest.
Main Character: Male, Rusty aka Firepaw, a cat.

For generations, four clans of wild cats have shared the forest. When their warrior code is threatened by mysterious deaths, a house cat named Rusty may turn out to be the bravest warrior of all. Grades: 5 and up.

Jacques, Brian. *Redwall.*
Philomel Books, 1986.
Series: Redwall: *Mossflower; Mattimeo; Mariel of Redwall; Salamandastron; Martin the Warrior; The Bellmaker; Outcast of Redwall; The Pearls of Lutra; The Long Patrol; Marlfox; The Legend of Luke; Lord Brocktree; Taggerung; Triss.*
Setting: Redwall Abbey.
Main Character: Male, Matthias, a mouse.

The peaceful life of ancient Redwall Abbey is shattered by the arrival of the evil rat Cluny and his villainous hordes. Matthias, a young mouse, determines to find the legendary sword of Martin the Warrior which, he is convinced, will help Redwall's inhabitants destroy the enemy. Grades: 6 and up.

King, Gabriel. *The Wild Road.*
Ballantine, 1997.
Sequels: *The Golden Cat.*
Setting: London and Cornwall.
Main Character: Male, Tag, a cat.

In the spiritual tradition of cats, The Wild Road is a dimension containing the memories of all animals that have gone before. An evil sorcerer has tortured cats for many lifetimes in a quest to harness the power of the Wild Road and now, as a modern scientist, he is on the verge of succeeding. Descriptions of felines suffering in human hands are graphic and horrible, but true to life. Grades: YA.

McKillip, Patricia A. *Forgotten Beasts of Eld.*
Magic Carpet Books, 1996.
Setting: Eld Mountain.
Main Character: Female, Sybel.

Raised on Eld with only her father's magical menagerie for company, Sybel, a beautiful young sorceress, is drawn into the human world with all its sorrows and delights when a baby comes into her care. Awards: CC; World Fantasy. Grades: YA.

Pierce, Meredith Ann. *Treasure at the Heart of the Tanglewood.*
Viking, 2001.
Setting: Tanglewood Forest.
Main Character: Female, Hannah.

Hannah, a healer with unusual powers, leaves the wizard she has always served and, along with a magpie, a badger, and three fox pups, begins a journey which uncovers the truth about her real nature. Grades: 8–10.

Pierce, Meredith Ann. *The Woman Who Loved Reindeer.*
Little, Brown, 1985.
Setting: Far North.
Main Characters: Female, Caribou; Male, Reindeer.

Caribou is a wisewoman who was brought the infant Reindeer to raise. From early on he shows signs of being more than human and is a trangl, one who can take the form of deer or mortal. When the deer part of his nature calls him to run with the wild herds, Caribou grieves and rejoices when the man side compels his return as her lover. Awards: CC. Grades: 8–12.

Randall, David. *Clovermead: In the Shadow of the Bear.*
Margaret K. McElderry Books, 2004.
Setting: icy north.
Main Character: Female, Clovermead Wickward, 12 years old.

Clovermead wears a bear tooth necklace, a relic of the bear-priests of Ursus. She learns that her father has stolen a gem from a nearby kingdom and they set out to right the wrong. They are attacked by bears and Clovermead discovers her ability to communicate with them. The necklace begins to speak to her, turning her into a creature, with bloodlust and fangs and fur. Grades: 7 and up.

UNICORNS

Coville, Bruce. *Glory of Unicorns.*
Scholastic, 2000.

Thirteen short stories show unicorns that are sometimes splendid, sometimes ugly, sometimes dangerous, and sometimes glorious in far-reaching times and places, from the fantastical world of Luster and the mystical land of ancient China to modern-day America. Each story has a full page black-and-white drawing. Grades: 4–8.

Lee, Tanith. *Black Unicorn.*
Maxwell Macmillan International, 1991.

Series: Unicorn: *Gold Unicorn; Red Unicorn.*
Setting: Fortress, desert.
Main Character: Female, Tanaquil, 16 years old.
 With her talent for mending things, Tanaquil reconstructs a unicorn which, when brought to life, lures her away from her desert fortress home and her sorceress mother to find a city by the sea and the way to a perfect world. Awards: CC. Grades: YA.

Pierce, Meredith Ann. *Birth of the Firebringer.*
Scholastic, 1985.
Series: Firebringer Trilogy: *Dark Moon; Son of Summer Stars.*
Setting: Hallow Hills.
Main Character: Male, Aljan, a unicorn.
 Aljan, the hothead son of Korr, the prince of the unicorns, goes on a pilgrimage with Dagg and Tek against gryphons, sly pans, wyverns, pards, and renegade unicorns. Grades: 6–9.

URBAN FANTASY

Bull, Emma. *War for the Oaks.*
Ace, 1987.
Setting: Minneapolis, Minnesota, 1980s.
Main Character: Female, Eddi McCandry.
 Eddi sings rock and roll but her boyfriend just dumped her, her band just broke up, and life could hardly be worse. Walking home through downtown Minneapolis on a dark night, she finds herself drafted into an invisible war between the faerie folk. Grades: YA/A.

De Lint, Charles. *Dreams Underfoot: The Newford Collection.*
Tor Books, 1997.
Series: Newford: *Memory and Dream; The Ivor and the Horn: A Newford Collection; Trader (CC); Someplace to Be Flying; Moonlight and Vines: A Newford Collection; Forests of the Heart; The Onion Girl; Tapping the Dream Tree: A Newford Collection; Spirits in the Wires.*
Setting: Newford, Alternate Worlds.
Main Character: Male, Max Trader, adult.
 Ghosts, spirits of place, goblins, and conjure men all make appearances in the city of Newford where seeing magic allows it to exist. Awards: CC. Grades: YA/A.

De Lint, Charles. *Jack of Kinrowan.*
Tor, 1995.
Setting: Ottawa, Ontario, 1980s.
Main Character: Female, Jacky Rowan.
 Jacky was a young woman who led an uneventful urban life until a brush with magic gave her the Sight. Soon she became a pivotal player in the magical war between two factions of Faerie. Jackie has a wizard to face and a giant to slay and if she fails, the music, the dreams and the magic of Faerie World will be lost forever. Grades: YA/A.

De Lint, Charles. **Waifs and Strays.**
Viking, 2002.
    Fifteen dark fantasy short stories with female main characters, including a vampire, an elf, and even humans. Grades: 8 and up.

Gilman, Laura Anne. **Staying Dead.**
Luna, 2004.
Series: Wren Valere: **Curse the Dark.**
Setting: New York City.
Main Characters: Female, Wren Valere; Male, Sergei Didier.
    Wren is a Retriever, a mage (wizard) who specializes in finding things gone missing when people don't want the police involved. In this case she has to track down a deadly ghost released when a cornerstone with a spell of protection was stolen from the Fronts building. Grades: YA/A.

WIZARDS

Duane, Diane. **So You Want to Be a Wizard.**
Harcourt, 1996.
Series: Young Wizards: **Deep Wizardry; High Wizardry; A Wizard Abroad; The Wizard's Dilemma; A Wizard Alone; The Wizard's Holiday; Wizards at War.**
Setting: New York.
Main Characters: Female, Juanita "Nita" Callahan, 13 years old; Male, Christopher "Kit" Rodriguez, 13 years old.
    Nita, tormented by a gang of bullies because she won't fight back, finds refuge in the library. She finds the book, *So You Want to Be a Wizard*, and within days, she and her friend Kit are wizards. Awards: CC. Grades: 5–8.

McKillip, Patricia A. **Ombria in Shadow.**
Ace Books, 2002.
Setting: Ombria.
Main Character: Female, Domina Pearl, aka "The Black Pearl."
    The Prince of Ombria lies dying, his heir too young to rule, and already his sinister great-aunt Domina Pearl is seizing power. Beneath the streets of Ombria lies a second, shadow Ombria, a buried city inhabited not only by ghosts, but by a powerful, mysterious sorceress and her creation, a girl sculpted from wax. Awards: CC; Mythopoeic Fantasy; World Fantasy; Nebula. Grades: YA/A.

McKillip, Patricia A. **Riddle-Master of Hed.**
Atheneum, 1976.
Series: Riddlemaster Trilogy: **Heir of Sea and Fire; Harpist in the Wind.**
Setting: Hed.
Main Character: Male, Morgan, young man.
    Long ago, the wizards had vanished from the world, and all knowledge was left hidden in riddles. Morgon proved himself a master of such riddles when he staked his life to win a crown from the dead Lord of Aum. Now ancient evil forces are threaten-

ing him and the greatest of unsolved riddles—the nature of the three stars on his forehead that seemed to drive him toward his ultimate destiny. Awards: CC; World Fantasy Grades: YA.

Rowling, J. K. *Harry Potter and the Sorcerer's Stone.*
A. A. Levine Books, 1998.
Series: Harry Potter Series: *Harry Potter and the Chamber of Secrets; Harry Potter and the Prisoner of Azkaban; Harry Potter and the Goblet of Fire; Harry Potter and the Order of the Phoenix; Harry Potter and the Half-Blood Prince.*
Setting: Hogwart's School of Witchcraft and Wizardry, England.
Main Character: Male, Harry Potter, 11 years old.

Harry has endured ten miserable years with his aunt and uncle, when he receives a mysterious letter inviting him to attend the Hogwarts School for Witchcraft and Wizardry. Awards: CC. Grades: YA.

Silverberg, Robert. *Lord Valentine's Castle.*
Harper & Row, 1980.
Series: Majipoor Cycle: *The Mountains of Majipoor; Majipoor Chronicles; Valentine Pontifex.*
Setting: Majipoor, a planet.
Main Character: Male, Valentine, adult.

Valentine travels the planet Majipoor with a group of eccentric performers on a quest to discover who Valentine is to help him lay claim to the rewards of birth that await him. Awards: CC. Grades: YA/A.

Stasheff, Christopher. *A Wizard in Mind: The First Chronicle of Magnus D'Armand, Rogue Wizard.*
Tor Books, 1995.
Series: Chronicles of the Rogue Wizard: *A Wizard in Bedlam; A Wizard in War; A Wizard in Peace; A Wizard in Chaos; A Wizard in Midgard; A Wizard and a Warlord; A Wizard in the Way; A Wizard in a Feud.*
Setting: Petrarch, a planet like Renaissance Italy.
Main Character: Male, Magnus d'Armand, aka Gar Pike.

Magnus is rebelling against his famous warlock father, Rod Gallowglass, attempting to prove himself twice the hero. However, Magnus has inherited not only his father's awesome psychic gifts, but his uncanny knack for getting into trouble as well. Magnus travels to the island of Pirogia on the planet Petrarch, to lead a revolution and befriends Gianni Braccalese, the son of a leading merchant. Grades: YA/A.

Wrede, Patricia C. *Mairelon the Magician.*
Tom Doherty Associates, 1991.
Sequel: *Magician's Ward.*
Setting: London.
Main Character: Female, Kim, 16 years old.

Kim is surviving the streets of some London in never-never land by disguising herself as a boy and working at the least objectionable and illegal tasks offered to her.

She knows that her age is bringing her masquerade to an end, so when Mairelon offers a job and a destination, she takes the opportunity. Awards: CC. Grades: YA.

Wrede, Patricia C. and Caroline Stevermer. ***Sorcery and Cecelia or the Enchanted Pot: Being the Correspondence of Two Young Ladies of Quality Regarding Various Magical Scandals in London and the Country.*** Harcourt, 2003.
Sequel: ***The Grand Tour.***
Setting: London, Essex, 1817.
Main Characters: Female, Cecelia "Cecy"; Female, Katherine "Kate", teens.

Cousins Cecy and Kate write letters to keep each other informed of their magical exploits, beginning with the witch who tried to poison Kate at Sir Hilary's induction into the Royal College of Wizards. Poison, charms, and spells are so much fun until the girls are confronted by evil wizards. Awards: VOYA perfect ten. Grades: 7–12.

RESOURCES: ADDTIONAL TITLES

Hirschfelder, Arlene, and Yvonne Beamer. 1999. ***Fluent in Fantasy: A Guide to Reading Interests.*** Westport, Conn. Libraries Unlimited.
Kunzel, Bonnie and Suzanne Manczuk. 2001. ***First Contact: A Reader's Selection of Science Fiction and Fantasy.*** Lanham, MD. Scarecrow.
Lynn, Ruth Nadelman. 2004. ***Fantasy Literature for Children and Young Adults: A Comprehensive Guide 5th ed.*** Westport Conn. Libraries Unlimited.
Mediavilla, Cindy. 1999. ***Arthurian Fiction: An Annotated Bibliography.*** Lanham, MD. Scarecrow.
Wadham, Tim, and Rachel L. Wadham. 1999. ***Bringing Fantasy Alive for Children and Young Adults.*** Worthington, OH. Linworth.

CHAPTER 10

FORMAT AS CONTENT

Many novelists tell their stories in a variety of forms to a receptive young adult audience. Journals, letters, e-mails, IMs, scripts, verse, news stories, and pictures have all given a fresh flavor to today's young adult literature, reflecting the way technology and the media have influenced the ways teens communicate. Other helpful lists in this chapter of books categorized by format include short classic novels—always useful for those last-minute book reports—short story collections, and picture books that teens will like.

    Diary/Journal Novels—Boy Journalist
    Diary/Journal Novels—Girl Journalist
    E-mail/Snail Mail Novels
    Graphic Novels—Fantasy and Science Fiction
    Graphic Novels—Manga Series
    Graphic Novels—Superhero Series
    Graphic Novels—Too Good to Miss
    Mixed Documents
    Points of View: Multiple, Alternating, Second Person
    Picture Books Teens Will Like
    Short Classics Under 200 Pages
    Short Novels Under 150 Pages
    Short Story Collections
    Verse Novels
    Resources: Additional Titles

DIARY/JOURNAL NOVELS— BOY JOURNALIST

Black, Jonah. *The Black Book: Diary of a Teenage Stud, Vol. I: Girls, Girls, Girls.*
Avon, 2001.
Series: The Black Book: Diary of a Teenage Stud: *Stop, Don't Stop; Run, Jonah, Run; Faster, Faster, Faster.*
Setting: Pompano Beach, Florida.

Main Character: Male, Jonah Black, 16 years old.

Jonah's diary reveals his difficulty in separating his fantasy life with the real world. He writes about his steamy encounters with the beautiful and probably made-up Sophie, and also documents some cold, hard facts about his real life. He reveals hints about his unexplained expulsion from boarding school and why he has retreated into a fantasy world. Darkly humorous and quirky, this complex diary will appeal to Douglas Adams and Daniel Pinkwater readers. Grades: 9–12.

Chbosky, Stephen. *The Perks of Being a Wallflower.*
MTV, 1999.
Setting: 1991.
Main Character: Male, Charlie, 15 years old.

In a series of letters to an unnamed friend, Charlie reveals the angst of his sophomore year and the suicide of his pal Michael. Awards: CC. Grades: 7–12.

Flinn, Alex. *Breathing Underwater.*
HarperCollins, 2001.
Setting: Key Biscayne, Florida.
Main Character: Male, Nick, 16 years old.

Nick tells how his violent behavior toward his girlfriend Caitlin earned him a restraining order and a weekly visit to an anger management class, where he was assigned to keep a journal. Awards: CC. Grades: 8–12.

Koller, Jackie French. *The Falcon.*
Atheneum, 1998.
Setting: 1990s.
Main Character: Male, Luke Carver, 17 years old.

Luke's English teacher wants him to write a little each day to prepare for writing a college essay. Once he gets going he doesn't mind writing, and he's pretty good at it, too. Luke's descriptions of his recent "screw-ups" flow fast and furiously from his pen, but he can't face the loss of his eye. Awards: CC. Grades: 9–12.

Lubar, David. *Sleeping Freshman Never Lie.*
Dutton, 2005.
Setting: Pennsylvania.
Main Character: Male, Scott Hudson, 14 years old.

Scott's journal is advice for his mother's unborn baby. As a freshman who is small, lost, laden with homework, and sure his gym teacher is trying to kill him, his advice is comical, bordering on absurd, but his introspective musings reflect his growth through the nine months of school and pregnancy. Grades: 7–10.

Runyon, Brent. *Burn Journals.*
Knopf, 2004.
Setting: Virginia.
Main Character: Male, Brent Runyan, 14 years old.

Brent drenches his bathrobe with gasoline and sets himself on fire. The burns cover 85 percent of his body and require six months of painful skin grafts. His journals tell of his struggles to heal body and mind. Grades: 8–12.

Sparks, Beatrice. *Jay's Journal.*
Times Books, 1978.
Setting: Pleasant Grove.
Main Character: Male, Jay, 16 years old.
    Jay's journal reveals his growing involvement with drug abuse and the occult before his suicide. Awards: CC. Grades: YA.

Townsend, Sue. *The Secret Diary of Adrian Mole, Aged 13³/₄: The Growing Pains of Adrian Mole.*
HarperTempest, 2003.
Series: Adrian Mole Diaries: *Adrian Mole: The Cappuccino Years; Adrian Mole: the Lost Years; Adrian Mole and the Weapons of Mass Destruction; True Confessions of Adrian Albert Mole.*
Setting: Great Britain.
Main Character: Male, Adrian Mole, 13³/4 years old.
    Adrian Mole excruciatingly details every morsel of his turbulent angst-filled adolescence. Mixed in with humorous daily reports are heartrending passages about his parents' chaotic marriage. Awards: CC. Grades: YA.

DIARY/JOURNAL NOVELS—
GIRL JOURNALIST

Easton, Kelly. *Life History of a Star.*
Margaret K. McElderry, 2001.
Setting: California, 1973.
Main Character: Female, Kristen Folger, 14 years old.
    Kristen uses her journal as a buffer against a world gone crazy. It's what Kristin doesn't write about that bothers her the most, and that's her brother who lives upstairs—or rather, the howling, drooling ghost who used to be her brother David before he came back from Vietnam. Awards: CC. Grades: 7–12.

Grimes, Nikki. *Jazmin's Notebook.*
Dial Books, 1998.
Setting: Harlem, 1960s.
Main Character: Female, Jazmin Shelby, 14 years old.
    Jazmin fills her notebook with glimpses of her life, neighborhood, family, and dreams. When their alcoholic mother is institutionalized, her older sister rescues Jazmin from a series of foster homes and makeshift living arrangements. Awards: Coretta Scott King Honor. Grades: 6–10.

Haddix, Margaret Peterson. *Don't You Dare Read This, Mrs. Dunphrey.*
Simon & Schuster, 1996.
Setting: Contemporary.

Main Character: Female, Tish Bonner, 16 years old.

Mrs. Dunphrey only looks at the completed writing and doesn't read the sensitive contents of Tish's journal. Her father is abusive and mostly absent; her mother is depressed and at her lowest point, penniless and starving. Tish shoplifts from a grocery store to feed herself and her brother, Matthew, and then faces being evicted from her home. Mrs. Dunphrey writes brief comments to express her concern. Tish finally turns over her entire journal to Mrs. Dunphrey in hopes of getting help. Awards: CC. Grades: 7–12.

Juby, Susan. *Alice, I Think.*
HarperTempest, 2003.
Setting: Smithers, Bristish Columbia.
Main Character: Female, Alice, 15 years old.

Alice has been home-schooled by her hippie mom and indifferent dad, leaving her with what her therapist calls "a shocking poverty of age-appropriate, real-life experience." Now Alice agrees to go to the public high school. Her journal is full of observations of what passes for normal teenage behavior. Grades: 7–12.

Marsden, John. *So Much to Tell You.*
Joy St. Books, 1989.
Setting: Australia.
Main Character: Female, Marina, 14 years old.

Marina lives at a boarding school and has not spoken since being facially disfigured by acid intended for her unfaithful mother. An English teacher makes diary writing a class assignment; the diary becomes Marina's voice. Marina nurses a great bitterness toward the world and she rejects the overtures of her dorm mates. Awards: CC. Grades: 7–9.

McCafferty, Megan. *Sloppy Firsts.*
Three Rivers, 2001.
Sequel: *Second Helpings: A Novel.*
Setting: Pineville, New Jersey, 2000s.
Main Character: Female, Jessica Darling, 16 years old.

Jessica shows us a year in her life when her best friend, Hope, has moved away. Her ex-boyfriend, Scotty, still follows her around like a puppy dog, even though they dated three years ago and only for eleven days. And the dreg of society, Marcus "Krispy Kreme" Flutie, has chosen Jessica to bear the brunt of his mental games. For mature readers. Awards: CC. Grades: 9–12.

Rennison, Louise. *Angus, Thongs, and Full Frontal Snogging: Confessions of Georgia Nicolson.*
HarperCollins, 2000.
Sequels: *On the Bright Side, I'm Now the Girlfriend of a Sex God: Further Confessions of Georgia Nicolson; Knocked Out by My Nunga-Nungas: Further, Further Confessions of Georgia Nicolson; Dancing in My Nuddy-Pants: Even Further Confessions of Georgia Nicolson; Away Laughing on a Fast Camel: Even More Confessions of Georgia Nicolson;*

***Then He Ate My Boy Entrancers: More Mad, Marvy Confessions of
Georgia Nicolson.***
Setting: England.
Main Character: Female, Georgia Nicolson, 14 years old.
  With embarrassing parents, a 3-year-old sister who leaves wet diapers at the
foot of her bed, and Angus, an insane cat who is prone to leg-shredding "call of the
wild" episodes, Georgia also struggles with the important issues like boys and
plucking eyebrows. Awards: CC; Printz Honor. Grades: 7–12.

Smith, Dodie. *I Capture the Castle.*
Wyatt Book, 1998.
Setting: Castle, England.
Main Character: Female, Cassandra Mortmain, 17 years old.
  Cassandra wants to become a writer, but times are lean since her author father
has writer's block. Her family is barely scraping by in a crumbling English castle they
leased when times were good. Cassandra gets hold of a journal and begins her writing
career by refusing to face the facts. Romantic isolation comes to an end, both for the
family and for Cassandra's heart, when the wealthy, adventurous Cotton family takes
over the nearby estate. Originally published in 1948. Awards: CC. Grades: 10–12.

Sparks, Beatrice. *Go Ask Alice.*
Simon Pulse, 1998.
Setting: 1970s.
Main Character: Female, Anonymous, 15 years old.
  "Anonymous" chronicles the torture and hell of an addicted teen. Her mood
swings madly between optimism and despair. A new friend spikes her drink with
LSD, beginning her frightening journey into darkness. Awards: CC. Grades: 7–12.

Stratton, Allan. *Leslie's Journal.*
Annick, 2000.
Setting: High school.
Main Character: Female, Leslie, sophomore, 15 years old.
  Leslie keeps a journal for an English assignment, and Ms. Graham has promised
not to read it. So Leslie writes honestly about her single mom she can't talk to, her
father who moved in with his girlfriend, and Jason, a rich older boyfriend who gets
her drunk, rapes her, and takes Polaroid pictures of her. A new English teacher reads
the diary and brings it to the attention of the principal, who takes Jason's side. Leslie
fears for her life and runs away. For mature readers. Awards: CC. Grades: 8–12.

E-MAIL/SNAIL MAIL NOVELS

Danziger, Paula, and Ann Martin. *P. S. Longer Letter Later.*
Scholastic, 1998.
Sequel: *Snail Mail No More* (e-mail).
Setting: Ohio.
Main Characters: Female, Tara*Starr; Female, Elizabeth; both 12 years old.
  Two best friends stay in contact through letters after one moves to another

state. Elizabeth is the shy quiet one and Tara streaks her hair purple. Their letters record the chaotic changes that have been happening in their lives. Grades: 5–8.

Marsden, John. *Letters from the Inside.*
Pan MacMillan, 1992.
Setting: Australia.
Main Characters: Females, Mandy; Tracey; both 16 years old.

Mandy answers Tracey's ad in a magazine, and the girls become pen pals. Their early letters are innocuous, but then there are hints that Tracey is hiding something. She reveals that she is in a maximum security unit of a correctional institution for an unspeakable crime and scared of the brutal truths of young women living together behind bars. Mandy's life seems nearly perfect in comparison. Her complaints about her brother's violent outbursts are easy to ignore, until Mandy's letters stop. For mature readers. Awards: CC. Grades: 8–12.

Myracle, Lauren. *TTYL.*
Harry N. Abrams, 2004.
Setting: Internet.
Main Characters: Female, Angela; Female, Zoe; Female, Madigan; all 15 years old.

A novel of instant messages sent among three high school sophomores, lifelong best friends—boy-crazy Angela, quiet Zoe, and hot-headed Madigan—about dating, new friends, and getting drunk; they give each other advice. Each of the friends has her own unique style and voice. Page layout resembles a computer screen. Grades: 8–12.

Peterson, P. J., and Ivy Ruckman. *Rob&Sara.com.*
Delacorte, 2004.
Setting: Internet chat room.
Main Characters: Male, Rob; Female, Sara; both 16 years old.

Rob's chat-room critique of Sara's poem marks the beginning of their relationship, which develops through e-mails over the course of a school year. With each letter, the teens build trust and reveal more of the intimate details of their lives. Then Shannon, a student at Rob's alternative school, e-mails Sara to say that Rob is actually Alex, a boy who is suffering from multiple personality disorder and is suicidal. Grades: 7–11.

Rosen, Michael. *ChaseR: A Novel in E-mails.*
Candlewick, 2002.
Setting: Pickerington, Ohio.
Main Character: Male, Chase Riley, 14 years old.

Chase has recently moved from Columbus, Ohio, to a farmhouse sixty miles away, and experiences the culture shock of country life. His funny and compassionate e-mails to friends and his sister in college reveal his efforts to understand his new friends and neighbors. Chase invents emoticon smileys for all his friends, which add humor and design to the pages. Grades: 6–9.

Wittlinger, Ellen. *Heart on My Sleeve.*
Simon & Schuster, 2004.

Setting: Connecticut.
Main Characters: Female, Chloe, 18 years old; Male, Julian, 17 years old.
    Chloe and Julian meet during a college visit and create sparks with one another. When they go home an online romance develops, with e-mails, and instant messages, then pen-and-paper letters and postcards. There's just one problem: Chloe already has a boyfriend. Grades: 9–12.

GRAPHIC NOVELS—FANTASY
AND SCIENCE FICTION

Golden, Christopher. *Buffy the Vampire Slayer: The Origin.*
Dark Horse Comics, 1999.
Setting: Sunnydale, California.
Main Character: Female, Buffy Anne Summers, teenager.
    Valley Girl Buffy is chosen by fate to be a vampire slayer under the guidance of the Watcher. She has superhuman strength, agility, and endurance to fight demons and vampires. Grades: 10–12.

Kesel, Barbara. *Meridian, Flying Solo.*
CrossGen Comics, 2002.
Sequels: *Going to Ground; Taking the Skies; Coming Home.*
Setting: Meridian.
Main Character: Female, Sephie, 15 years old.
    Sephie is the daughter of the Minister of Meridian, one of many islands floating above the world of Demetria. When her father dies, both she and her uncle Ilahn, minister of Cadador, are granted a mysterious mark of power. The power-hungry Ilahn attempts to manipulate Sephie and control Meridian, but the people of Meridian have secrets Ilahn is unaware of, and Sephie has not only emerging powers, but a mind of her own. Grades: 7 and up.

Pini, Wendy and Richard Pini. *Elfquest.*
DC Comics, 1978.
Series: The Grand Quest 1–14.
Setting: World of Two Moons.
    After humans burn their forest home, a tribe of elves set out to find others of their own kind. The elves are brave, loyal, and persistent, and the elf tribes learn not only to coexist but also to benefit from each other's strengths. Appeals to girls and *Lord of the Ring* readers. Grades: 7–10.

Smith, Jeff. *Bone.*
Cartoon Books, 1991–2004.
Series: *Out from Boneville; The Great Cow Race; Eyes of the Storm; The Dragonslayer; Rock Jaw: Master of the Eastern Border; Old Man's Cave; Ghost Circles; Treasure Hunters; Crown of Horns.*
Setting: Boneville, a mysterious valley.
Main Characters: Fone Bone, Phoney Bone, Smiley Bone.

Three cousins—good-hearted Fone, avaricious Phoney, and dimwitted Smiley, are driven out of Boneville and end up in an unknown mysterious valley, where they find adventure and many strange creatures. Awards: CC. Grades: 6–12.

Multiple Authors. *Star Wars.*
Dark Horse Comics, 1991–present.
Setting: A long time ago in a faraway galaxy.
Main Character: Male, Darth Vader.
The Jedi defend the Republic from the evil forces of the Dark Side. Many series by various authors and artists are in print with, different time lines that fit around, between, and beside the films. The *Star Wars* fans will want even more *Star Wars*. Grades: 7–12.

Tolkien, J. R. R. *The Hobbit.*
Del Rey, 2001.
Setting: Middle Earth.
Main Character: Male, Bilbo Baggins, 51 years old.
A comics version of the classic J.R.R. Tolkien novel. Bilbo is rousted from his cozy home and sent on a quest by the wizard Gandalf to the Lonely Mountains with a troop of rowdy dwarves. His nephew, Frodo, inherits the responsibility of The Ring in the *Lord of the Rings* trilogy that follows. Illustrated by Peter Sis. Grades: YA.

GRAPHIC NOVELS—MANGA SERIES

Akino, Matsuri. *Pet Shop of Horrors, Vol. 1.*
TokyoPop, 2003.
Series: Pet Shop of Horrors Vols. 1–10.
Setting: Chinatown.
Main Character: Male, Count D, adult.
Count D operates a pet shop in Chinatown, but the pets aren't ordinary pets. He provides rare and exotic species not recorded in reference books, and his clientele is from high society. There are three terms to the contract if you purchase one of the pets, and if even one of the terms is broken, the pet shop isn't responsible for the consequences. Leon, a young detective, is investigating several mysterious deaths that have one thing in common: all the victims are Count D's customers. Grades: YA.

Fujishima, Kosuke. *Oh My Goddess.*
Dark Horse, 2005.
Series: Oh My Goddess Vols. 1–24
Setting: Earth.
Main Characters: Male, Keiichi Morisato, college student; Female, Belldandy, appears to be 21.
Keiichi accidentally dials the phone number for the Relief Goddess Office and receives a visit from Belldandy, a lovely goddess who grants him one wish. He wishes for a goddess like her to stay with him always, and she surprises him by announcing that she herself will stay to live with him. Grades: YA.

Otomo, Katsuhiro. *Akira #1.*
Dark Horse Comics, 2001.
Series: Akira #1–6.
Setting: Future Neo-Tokyo, Japan.
Main Character: Male, Akira, appears 6 years old with face of an old man.
    Akira, a child psychic, caused World War III, destroying Tokyo. Grades: 9–12.

Sakai, Stan. *Usagi Yojimbo.*
Fantagraphics, 1987.
Series: Usagi Yojimbo #1–19.
Setting: Japan, seventeenth century.
Main Character: Male rabbit, Miyamoto Usagi.
    Miyamoto is a rabbit Samurai bodyguard wandering feudal Japan, righting wrongs. Grades: 7–10.

Tezuka, Osamu. *Astro Boy.*
Dark Horse Comics, 2002.
Series: Astro Boy Volumes 1–10.
Setting: Future.
Main Character: Male robot, Astro.
    In the future, androids coexist with humans. Astro is a little robot boy created by Dr. Tenma to replace his son, who died in an accident. When Dr. Tenma realizes that the robot boy will never grow up, he casts him out. Astro is then discovered by Professor Ochanomizu, who sees great potential in him. He names him "Astro" and trains and teaches him, and Astro becomes involved in many adventures. The most famous Japanese manga character. Grades: YA

Takahashi, Rumiko. *Ranma 1/2.*
Viz Media, 1993.
Series: Ranma 1/2 #1–34.
Setting: Japan.
Main Character: Male, Ranma Saotome, 16 years old.
    A magic curse causes Ranma to turn into a girl every time he is splashed with cold water; hot water reverses the effect. The curse complicates the engagement his father had arranged. Awards: CC. Grades: 8–12.

Toriyama, Akira. *Dragon Ball; Dragon Ball Z.*
Viz Media, 2000.
Series: Dragon Ball 42 volumes.
Setting: Earth.
Main Character: Male, Son Goku.
    Son Goku is a monkey-tailed boy. The series follows his whole life, as he becomes the strongest martial artist in the universe. Seven Dragon Balls are magical spheres scattered throughout the world. When brought together, Shenlong the dragon is summoned to grant one wish. Grades: YA

Takahashi, Kazucki. *Yu-Gi-Oh!*
VIZ Media, 2003.
Series: Yu-Gi-Oh! #1–7.
Setting: Japan.
Main Character: Male, Yugi Mutou, 15 years old.

Yugi was given the pieces of the millennium puzzle. When he assembles the puzzle, he is infused with the spirit of a five-thousand-year-old Egyptian pharaoh. One chamber in Yugi's mind is his, but when he is under stress or playing a game, the other chamber, belonging to the pharaoh, takes over, and he becomes Yu-Gi-Oh. Grades: YA.

Takahashi, Rumiko. *Inu Yasha.*
VIZ Media, 2003.
Series: *Inu Yasha #1–24.*
Setting: Tokyo, Japan.
Main Character: Female, Kagome Higurashi, 13 years old.

Kagome is pulled into an old well at her family's Shinto shrine by a mysterious force, and a demon claims she has the Jewel of the Four Souls and tries to take it. Kagome fights back and climbs out of the well into feudal Japan, where she is recognized as the reincarnation of the priestess Kikyo, who had sealed Inu Yasha, the half-human dog demon, to a tree with magic arrows. Grades: YA.

Ueda, Miwa. *Peach Girl.*
Tokyopop, 2000.
Series: Peach Girl #1–10.
Setting: Japan.
Main Character: Female, Momo Adachi, teenager.

Momo tans very easily and has light-colored hair, both uncommon in Japan, and is looked down upon by her classmates as a "playgirl." She's loved her friend Toji for a long time, but hasn't told him so, and she's being pursued by Kiley, a boy she doesn't like. Grades: YA.

Various artists. *Mobile Suit Gundam Wing.*
TokyoPop, 2000.
Series: Mobile Suit Gundam Wing #1–15.
Setting: After Colony, 195.
Main Characters: Male, Heero Yuy, 5 years old; Male, Duo Maxwell, 15 years old; Male, Trowa Barton; Male, Quatre Raberba Winner, 15 years old; Male, Chang Wufei, 15 years old.

Scientists from the space colonies have trained five boys and outfitted them with super-strong mobile suits and send them to Earth. Grades: YA.

GRAPHIC NOVELS—SUPERHEROES SERIES

Multiple Authors. *Captain America.*
Marvel Comics, 1941–present.
Setting: United States.

Main Character: Male, Captain America, aka Steve Rogers.

Loyal to the American Dream, Captain America sometimes finds himself at odds with the U.S. government. He possesses no superhuman powers, but has been conditioned and treated with a Super Soldier formula. Grades: YA.

Multiple Authors. *Batman.*
DC Comics, 1939–present.
Related Series: The Dark Knight, Robin, Batgirl, Catwoman.
Setting: Gotham City.
Main Character: Male, Batman, aka Bruce Wayne.

Bruce Wayne, billionaire industrialist, playboy, and philanthropist, fights crime in a bat cowl and cape, and has lots of cool equipment to help him. His ward, Dick Grayson, joins him as Robin. He is sometimes called the Caped Crusader and the Dark Knight. His parents were murdered when he was a child, which causes him periods of dark angst. Awards: CC. Grades: 7–12.

Multiple Authors. *Daredevil.*
Marvel Comics, 1946–present.
Setting: New York City.
Main Character: Male, Daredevil, aka Matthew Murdock.

Blinded in an accident, Daredevil's other senses developed to superhuman strength. Attorney by day, crime fighter by night, in a cool red suit and with sonar sense. Awards: CC. Grades: 10–12.

Multiple Authors. **Fantastic Four.**
Marvel Comics, 1961–present.
Setting: New York City.
Main Characters: Male, Mister Fantastic; Female, Invisible Woman; Male, Human Torch; Male, The Thing.

After an experimental rocket passes through a storm of cosmic rays, the ship crashes back on Earth and the four occupants find themselves transformed, with bizarre new abilities. Mister Fantastic is stretchy, Invisible Woman can be invisible and project force fields, Human Torch can control fire and project flames, and The Thing looks like orange rocks with incredible strength. Luckily, they use their power to protect humanity. The characters were named after the Greek four elements: earth, fire, wind, and water. Grades: YA.

Multiple Authors. **Hellboy.**
Dark Horse Comics, 1993–present.
Setting: Earth.
Main Character: Male, Hellboy.

A red-skinned demon with tail and horns, Hellboy was summoned and appeared in a fireball in a church in England. Raised in America, Hellboy became an agent for the Bureau of Paranormal Research and Defense. Awards: CC. Grades: 10–12.

Multiple Authors. **Incredible Hulk.**
Marvel Comics, 1962–present.
Setting: United States.

Main Character: Male, Incredible Hulk, aka Robert Bruce Banner.

Dr. Banner is a genius in nuclear physics. As a result of exposure to gamma radiation, he becomes a superhumanly strong green creature with regenerative powers and little self-control. Grades: YA.

Multiple Authors. **JLA/Justice League of America.**
DC Comics, 1960–present.
Setting: Happy Harbor.
Main Characters: Original Roster: Superman, Batman, Wonder Woman, Flash, Green Lantern, Aquaman, and Martian Manhunter. Current Roster: Aquaman, Black Canary, Green Arrow, Green Lantern, and Manitou Dawn.
Working from Secret Sanctuary, the Justice League works as a superhero team against crime. Awards: CC. Grades: 6–12.

Multiple Authors. **Spider-Man.**
Marvel Comics, 1962–present.
Related Series: Spider-Girl.
Setting: Queens, New York.
Main Character: Spider-Man, aka Peter Benjamin Parker.

Peter was bitten by a spider and developed a spidey sense and the ability to cast webs and climb walls. Awards: CC. Grades: 6–12.

Multiple Authors. **Superman.**
DC Comics, 1938–present.
Setting: Metropolis.
Main Character: Male, Superman, aka Clark Kent.

Superman was shipped to Earth as an infant when his home planet blew up. He now leads a double life as Clark Kent, mild-mannered reporter, and as Superman, a super-strong hero. Awards: CC. Grades: 7–12.

Multiple Authors. **Wonder Woman.**
DC Comics, 1941–present.
Setting: Paradise Island.
Main Character: Female, Wonder Woman, aka Princess Diana.

The first female superhero and still the most famous, she can fly, is super-strong and fast, with enhanced senses. Bulletproof bracelets and a golden lasso help her fight the bad guys. Awards: CC. Grades: 7–12.

Multiple Authors. **X-Men.**
Marvel Comics, 1963–present.
Setting: X-Mansion.
Main Characters: Cyclops, Emma Frost, Shadowcat, Colossus, Beast, Wolverine, Storm, Nightcrawler, Marvel Girl III, Bishop, Psylocke, X–23, Havok, Polaris, Iceman, Rogue, Gambit.

All these characters are mutants who experienced a sudden leap in evolution, which gives them superhuman traits that develop during puberty. They attend a special academy where they are trained to protect themselves and the world from Magneto. Grades: YA.

GRAPHIC NOVELS—TOO GOOD TO MISS

Busiek, Kurt, and Brent Anderson. **Astro City: Life in the Big City.**
Wildstorm, 1999.
Series: Astro City 1–6.
Setting: Astro City.
Main Character: Multiple main characters.
   Superheroes have existed in Astro City since the nineteenth century. The series shows the superheroes, villains, and other people reacting to their world.
Awards: CC. Grades: 7–12.

Clowes, Daniel. **Ghost World.**
Fantagraphic, 2001.
Setting: Los Angeles, California.
Main Characters: Female, Enid Coleslaw; Female, Rebecca; Male, Seymour; all 18 years old.
   Examines the lives of two recent high school graduates, Enid and Rebecca, friends on the verge of leading separate lives. For mature readers. Awards: CC. Grades: 10–12.

Eisner, Will. **A Contract with God.**
DC Comics, 2001.
Setting: Bronx Tenement, 1930s.
   A semiautobiographical collection of four stories about immigrant and first-generation experiences. Awards: CC. Grades: 8–12.

Kudo, Kazuya. **Mai, the Psychic Girl.**
Viz Media, 1995.
Setting: Japan.
Main Character: Female, Mai Kuju, 14 years old.
   Mai has great psychic powers and is being pursued by the Wisdom Alliance, which secretly controls the world. Brief nudity. Awards: CC. Grades: 7–12.

Moore, Terry. **Strangers in Paradise.**
Abstract Studio, 2005.
Series: Strangers in Paradise 1–3.
Setting: Contemporary.
Main Characters: Female, Francince Peters; Female, Katina "Katchoo" Choovanski; Male, David Qin.
   Francine and Katchoo are best friends, but Katchoo is in love with Francine. Their friend David is in love with Katchoo. Meanwhile, the Big Six organization looms in the background, infiltrating the political system. Awards: CC. Grades: 10–12.

Satrapi, Marjane. **Persepolis I: The Story of a Childhood.**
Pantheon, 2004.
Sequel: **Persepolis II.**
Setting: Iran.
Main Character: Female, Marji Satrapi, 14 years old.
    Describes the childhood of the author in Iran during the overthrow of the Shah and the war between Iran and Iraq. Grades: YA/A.

Spiegelman, Art. **Maus a Survivor's Tale: My Father Bleeds History.**
Pantheon, 1986.
Sequel: **Maus II.**
Setting: Poland, WWII.
Main Character: Male, Vladek Spiegelman; Female, Anna Spiegelman.
    Based on interviews with his father, Spiegelman tells the Holocaust experience in a graphic novel. The Jews are mice, the Germans cats, the Poles pigs, the French frogs, and the Americans dogs. Awards: CC; Pulitzer. Grades: YA.

Talbot, Bryan. **Tale of One Bad Rat.**
Dark Horse, 1995.
Setting: Great Britain.
Main Character: Female, Helen Potter, teenager.
    Helen runs away to the countryside to escape sexual abuse from her father; she takes responsibility for her recovery. The characters she meets are inspired by the works of Beatrix Potter. Awards: CC. Grades: 10–12.

Thompson, Craig. **Blankets.**
TopShelf Productions, 2003.
Setting: Wisconsin.
Main Character: Male, Craig Thompson.
    The memoir of the author's life from childhood through his teen years and into adulthood. Grades: YA.

Waid, Mark, and Alex Ross. **Kingdom Come.**
DC Universe, 1997.
Setting: Metropolis.
Main Character: Male, Norman McCay, adult.
    In the near future, Superman abandons his battle for truth and justice, and many other superheroes withdraw. Norman, a minister, is suffering a crisis of faith and is asked to pass judgment on the approaching superhero apocalypse by the Spectre. Awards: CC. Grades: 7–12.

MIXED DOCUMENTS

Avi. **Nothing But the Truth: a Documentary Novel.**
Scholastic, 1991.
Setting: High school.
Main Character: Male, Philip Malloy, 14 years old.

Philip is unable to participate on the track team because of his failing grade in English. Convinced the teacher, Margaret Narwin, dislikes him, he concocts a scheme to get transferred from her homeroom: instead of standing "at respectful, silent attention" during the national anthem, Philip hums. His parents take his side, ignore the fact that he is breaking a school rule, and concentrate on issues of patriotism. The conflict escalates, and the national news media become involved. Told through conversations, diary entries, letters, school memos, newspaper articles, transcripts. Awards: Newbery Honor. Grades: 6–9.

Cormier, Robert. **I Am the Cheese.**
Knopf, 1977.
Setting: New England.
Main Character: Male, Adam Farmer, 14 years old.

Adam discovers his whole life has been fiction and trusts no one. As he searches for who he really is, he uncovers a missing father, government corruption, and espionage. A psychological thriller told in tape transcripts, with a shocking conclusion. Awards: CC. Grades: YA.

Meyer, Adam. *The Last Domino.*
Putnam, 2005.
Setting: High school.
Main Characters: Male, Travis Ellroy; Male, Daniel; both 16 years old.

Travis' depression and anger about his older brother's suicide is funneled into increasingly violent behavior by manipulative Daniel, until a final deadly shooting spree that begins in his home and ends at school. Police interviews and journal entries; for mature readers. Grades: 10–12.

Moriarty, Jaclyn. *Feeling Sorry for Celia: A Novel.*
St. Martin's Griffin, 2000.
Setting: Sydney, Australia, 1990s.
Main Character: Female, Elizabeth Clarry, 15 years old.

Elizabeth's pen pal letters tell about her absentee father, who just moved back to Australia from Canada for a year and now wants to spend "quality time" with her. She's getting anonymous love notes from a boy. Worst of all, her best friend has run away and joined the circus. #1 bestseller in Australia. Grades: 7–12.

Myers, Walter Dean. *Monster.*
Amistad, 1999.
Setting: Harlem.
Main Character: Male, Steve Harmon, 16 years old.

Steve is accused of serving as a lookout for a robbery of a drugstore. The owner was shot and killed, and now Steve is in prison awaiting trial for murder. From prison, he tells about his case and his incarceration in the form of a movie screenplay. Diary entries are interspersed among the scenes. Awards: CC; Printz; Coretta Scott King Honor; National Book Award. Grades: 7–12.

Myers, Walter Dean. *Shooter.*
Amistad, 2004.
Setting: Harrison County High School.
Main Characters: Male, Len; Male, Cameron Porter, 17 years old; Female, Carla; teenagers.
    Len brought his Kalashnikov rifle, his AR–18, and his Ruger pistol to school, where he shot and killed football jock Brad Williams, and then himself. Interviews with Cameron and Carla by the Harrison County School Safety Committee, newspaper reports, a police report, Len's handwritten "die-ary" of his deranged thoughts, and finally, a grim medical examiner's report give different perspectives to the story. Grades: 7–12.

Hrdlitschka, Shelly. *Dancing Naked: A Novel.*
Turtleback, 2002.
Setting: Contemporary.
Main Character: Female, Kia, 16 years old.
    Kia's life changes forever when she learns she is pregnant. Kia's journal, her e-mails to Justin, and third-person prose take readers through her pregnancy, week by week. Kia struggles with the decision of whether to keep the baby or to choose loving parents who can give the infant the life it deserves. Grades: 8–12.

Yolen, Jane, and Bruce Coville. *Armageddon Summer.*
Harcourt, 1998.
Setting: Massachusetts, 2000.
Main Characters: Male, Jed, 16 years old; Female, Marina, 14 years old.
    Reverend Raymond Beelson is gathering 144 Believers atop Mount Weeupcut in Massachusetts to camp out, pray, and await Armageddon. He predicts that his faithful flock will be saved as the rest of the world is set ablaze in fire and brimstone on July 27, 2000. Jed and Marina have come to the compound with their families. Two points of view, excerpts from sermons, FBI files, camp schedules, and e-mails. Grades: 7–10.

POINTS OF VIEW: MULTIPLE, ALTERNATING, SECOND PERSON

Jenkins, A.M. *Damage.*
HarperCollins, 2001.
Setting: Parkersville.
Main Character: Male, Austin Reid, 17 years old.
    Austin is depressed and suicidal but afraid to tell anyone he needs help. He refers to himself in the second-person voice, illustrating how disconnected and distant he feels. Awards: CC. Grades: 7–12.

Jones, Patrick. *Things Change.*
Walker Books, 2004.
Setting: Michigan.
Main Characters: Female, Johanna, 16 years old; Male, Paul, 17 years old.
    Johanna is a straight-A student, ecstatic when the boy she adores returns her affections. They date, he hits her, she leaves him, he promises to change, she takes him

back. Paul struggles with his feelings about his father. Chapters alternate between Johanna's and Paul's points of view. Grades: 8–12.

Lynch, Chris. *Freewill.*
HarperCollins, 2001.
Setting: Vocational high school.
Main Character: Male, Will, 17 years old.
    Will is disconnected from reality due to the deaths of his parents, which may have been a murder-suicide. The narrator is another voice in Will's mind. When there are two more possible suicides, Will begins to sink into oblivion. Awards: CC; Printz Honor. Grades: 8–12.

Lynch, Chris. *Gypsy Davey.*
HarperCollins, 2004.
Setting: United States, 1990s.
Main Characters: Male, Davey, 1 to 12 years old; Female, Jo, 17 years old.
    Davey is neglected and deprived. His drunken mother leaves him in his sister's care, and he later becomes the caretaker of his sister's new baby. Told in first and third person, for mature readers. Awards: CC. Grades: 7–10.

Strasser, Todd. *How I Changed My Life.*
Simon & Schuster, 1995.
Setting: High school.
Main Characters: Female, Bovita Vine, senior; Male, Kyle, 17 years old.
    Kyle, injured football jock, gets the lead in the school play, and his girlfriend, Chloe, is the star. Bo is the stage manager, and the scene is set for a love triangle. Told in alternating points of view, and ends with a twist. Awards: CC. Grades: 7–12.

Strasser, Todd. *Thief of Dreams.*
Putnam, 2003.
Setting: Contemporary.
Main Character: Male, Martin Hunter, 13 years old.
    Martin's parents are off on another business trip over the holidays, and Martin is left in the care of an au pair and his Uncle Lawrence, who, it seems, is robbing the neighborhood. Told in second person. Grades: 6–8.

Thomas, Rob. *Slave Day.*
Simon & Schuster, 1997.
Setting: Texas.
Main Character: Male, Keene Davenport, 17 years old.
    Keene protests the annual Slave Day fund-raiser at his high school. Eight points of view. Awards: CC. Grades: 8–10.

Van Draanen, Wendelin. *Flipped.*
Knopf, 2001.
Setting: Junior high school.
Main Characters: Female, Juli Baker; Male, Bryce Loski, 13 years old.

Since second grade, Juli has been smitten with Bryce, but Bryce thought the tree-sitting, chicken-raising Juli was weird. But in eighth grade, Bryce suddenly thinks Juli is pretty interesting, while Juli thinks Bryce's baby blue eyes are as empty as the rest of him seems to be. Alternating points of view. Grades: 6–9.

Wittlinger, Ellen. *Long Night of Leo and Bree.*
Simon & Schuster, 2002.
Setting: Contemporary.
Main Characters: Male, Leo; Female, Bree; both 18 years old.

On the anniversary of his sister's murder, Leo is consumed with anger and despair. He drives around and abducts Bree at knifepoint and holds her as a hostage in his building's basement. They begin talking to each other, and by morning Bree has decided not to turn him in. Alternating points of view. Awards: CC. Grades: 8–12.

Wolff, Virginia Euwer. *Bat 6.*
Scholastic, 1998.
Setting: Oregon, May 28, 1949.
Main Characters: Female, Shazam; Female, Aki, 11 years old.

The members of two rival girls baseball teams begin the traditional annual game between them, but are interrupted when Shazam violently attacks Aki, a Japanese American. Twenty-one points of view. Awards: CC. Grades: 5–8.

PICTURE BOOKS TEENS WILL LIKE

Anno, Mitsumasa. *Anno's Journey.*
Philomel, 1981.

The author records his journey through northern Europe, drawing his impressions of the land, the people at work and play, and their art, architecture, folklore, and fairy tales. Another title: *Topsy Turvies.*

Breathed, Berke. *Red Ranger Came Calling.*
Little, Brown, 1997.

Red is spending Christmas with his aunt and discovers that Santa Claus lives nearby.

Bunting, Eve. *Fly Away Home.*
Clarion, 1993.

A homeless boy who lives in an airport with his father, moving from terminal to terminal and trying not to be noticed, is given hope when he sees a trapped bird find its freedom. More titles: *Sunshine Home; Smoky Night; Wall; Doll Baby.*

Cole, Babette. *Prince Cinders.*
Putnam, 1997.

A fairy grants small, skinny, spotty Prince Cinders a change in appearance (accidentally, a hairy ape) and the chance to go to the Palace Disco. Another title: *Princess Smartypants.*

Hamilton, Virginia. ***Drylongso.***
Harcourt, 1997.
Lindy and her family rescue Drylongso from a dust storm, and its presence gives them hope for water.

Larson, Gary. ***There's a Hair in My Dirt: A Worm's Story.***
HarperCollins, 1999.
    When a young earthworm laments being a worm, his father tells him a story about his role in the environment. Awards: CC.

Myers, Walter Dean, and Christopher Myers. ***Harlem.***
Scholastic, 1997.
    A group of people settle in Harlem, hoping to improve their lots in life, only to discover that racism could still keep them from achieving success. Another title: ***Blues Journey.*** Awards: CC; Caldecott; VOYA Top Ten.

Paterson, Katherine. ***King's Equal.***
HarperTrophy, 1996.
    In order to wear the crown of the kingdom, an arrogant young prince must find an equal in his bride. Instead, he finds someone far better than he.

Scieszka, Jon. ***The Stinky Cheese Man and Other Fairly Stupid Tales.***
Viking, 1992.
    Jack retells traditional fairy tales with sarcasm and an irreverent reconstruction. Another title: ***Baloney.*** Awards: CC; Caldecott Honor.

Van Allsburg, Chris. ***Wretched Stone.***
Houghton Mifflin, 1991.
    A strange glowing stone picked up on a sea voyage captivates a ship's crew and transforms them into apes. Awards: CC.

Wiesner, David. ***Free Fall.***
HarperTrophy, 1991.
    A boy falls asleep looking at an atlas and floats through a wordless surreal dream, where swans turn into leaves and fortress walls become dragons. More Titles: ***Tuesday; The Three Pigs.*** Awards: Caldecott Honor.

Short Classics Under 200 Pages

Bradbury, Ray. ***Fahrenheit 451.***
Simon & Schuster, 2003.
Setting: Earth.
Main Character: Male, Guy Montag, adult.
    Guy Montag is a book-burning fireman. His wife spends all day with her television "family," imploring Montag to work harder so that they can afford a fourth TV wall. When Clarisse, a young girl next door who is thrilled by the ideas in books, disappears mysteriously, Montag is moved to make some changes, and he starts

hiding books in his home. His wife turns him in, and he must burn his secret cache of books. After fleeing to avoid arrest, Montag winds up joining an outlaw band of scholars who keep the contents of books in their heads. Originally published in 1953. Awards: CC. Grades: YA/A.

Crane, Stephen. *Red Badge of Courage.*
Tor Books, 1990.
Setting: Civil War.
Main Character: Male, Henry Fleming, teenager.

Against his mother's wishes, Henry enlists in the Union army. The reality of battle comes soon enough when he witnesses the death of his friend Jim Conklin. Torn between wanting to run away and wanting to earn his red badge of courage, he receives a head wound in a scuffle and lies to his regiment, but then has an opportunity to test his true courage. Originally published in 1895. Awards: CC. Grades: 8–12.

Fitzgerald, F. Scott. *The Great Gatsby.*
Scribner's, 1996.
Setting: Long Island, New York, 1910–1920s.
Main Character: Male, Jay Gatsby, adult.

Self-made millionaire Jay loves Daisy, but when he serves overseas, Daisy marries Tom Buchanan. Originally published in 1925. Awards: CC. Grades: 9–12.

Kafka, Franz. *Metamorphosis and Other Stories.*
Bantam, 1972.
Setting: Gregor's bedroom.
Main Character: Male, Gregor Samsa, adult.

Gregor, a traveling salesman, wakes up one morning and discovers he has been transformed overnight into a giant beetle. Originally published in 1915. Awards: CC. Grades: 10–12.

Knowles, John. *A Separate Peace.*
Scribner's, 1996.
Setting: Devon, New Hampshire, 1940s.
Main Characters: Male, Gene Forrester; Male, Phineas "Finny"; both teenagers.

Gene and Finny are roommates at the Devon prep school the summer before WWII. Their friendship draws out both the best and worst characteristics of each boy and leads ultimately to violence, a confession, and the betrayal of trust. Originally published in 1960. Awards: CC. Grades: 9–12.

Orwell, George. *Animal Farm.*
Harcourt Brace, 1946.
Setting: Manor Farm.

In this satire on Communism, the downtrodden beasts of Manor Farm oust their drunken human master and take over management of the land. Everyone willingly works overtime, productivity soars, and for one brief, glorious season, every belly is full. Too soon, the pigs, self-appointed leaders by virtue of their intelligence, succumb to the temptations of privilege and power, and the common animals are once again left hungry and exhausted, no better off than in the days when humans ran the farm. Awards: CC. Grades: 7–12.

Richter, Conrad. *The Light in the Forest.*
Vintage, 2004.
Setting: Midwest, 1764.
Main Character: Male, John Camera Butler, 15 years old.
John was captured by the Delaware Indians when he was four years old and renamed True Son. Now, eleven years later, he is forced to return to his white parents but longs for the freedom of his Indian life. Originally published in 1953. Grades: 4–8.

Wells, H.G. *The Invisible Man.*
Signet, 2002.
Setting: Iping, England, 1890s.
Main Character: Male, Griffin.
Griffin, an obscure scientist, has discovered how to make himself invisible. He arrives in town with dark glasses, gloves, and his head wrapped in bandages. He can't find a way to become visible again and goes murderously insane. Originally published in 1897. Grades: YA/A.

Wells, H. G. *War of the Worlds.*
Aerie, 2005.
Setting: Southeastern England.
Main Character: Male, anonymous narrator.
Martians invade Earth with huge machines armed with heat rays, and no weapons can stop them. Originally published in 1898. Grades: YA/A.

Wharton, Edith. *Ethan Frome.*
Signet, 2000.
Setting: Berkshire Hills, Massachusetts.
Main Character: Male, Ethan Frome.
Ethan's life is nearly unbearable, working his unproductive farm and living with his difficult, suspicious, and hypochondriac wife, Zeena. Zeena's vivacious cousin enters their household as a "hired girl," and Ethan becomes obsessed with her and with the possibilities for happiness she comes to represent. Originally published in 1938. Grades: YA/A.

SHORT NOVELS UNDER 150 PAGES

Adoff, Jaime. *Names Will Never Hurt Me.*
Dutton, 2004.
Setting: High school.
Main Characters: Male, Ryan; Male, Kurt; Male, Floater; Female, Tisha, teenagers.
On the first anniversary of the shooting death of Jake Stiles at their school, four students narrate the events and attempt to make sense of it. 150 pages; multiple points of view. Grades: 6–10.

Brooks, Bruce. *Vanishing.*
HarperTempest, 2000.
Setting: Hospital.
Main Character: Female, Alice, 11 years old.
   Alice is in the hospital for bronchitis but extends her stay with a hunger strike so she won't have to go home to her alcoholic mother. Meanwhile, her roommate Rex, a cancer patient, is trying to hang on to life. 112 pages. Grades: 5 and up.

Cushman, Karen. *The Midwife's Apprentice.*
Clarion, 1995.
Setting: Medieval England.
Main Characters: Female, Alyce, aka "Beetle," girl; Female, Jane Sharp, adult.
   A nameless, homeless girl is taken in by a temperamental midwife, Jane. She names herself Alyce and learns how to deliver babies. 128 pages. Awards: CC; Newbery. Grades: 7 and up.

Fleischman, Paul. *Bull Run.*
HarperCollins, 1993.
Setting: Civil War.
   Readers gain insight into the first battle of the Civil War and into the nature of war through the alternating viewpoints of sixteen characters. 112 pages. Awards: CC. Grades: 5 and up.

Hoffman, Alice. *Aquamarine.*
Scholastic, 2001.
Setting: Capri Beach Club.
Main Characters: Mermaid Female, Aquamarine; Female, Hailey; Female, Claire; both 12 years old.
   A love-struck mermaid named Aquamarine supplies adventure and insights to Hailey and Claire, lifelong friends who are spending their last summer together before one of them moves away. 112 pages. Grades: 4–8.

Johnson, Angela. *Toning the Sweep.*
Scholastic, 1994.
Setting: California desert.
Main Character: Female, Emily, 14 years old.
   Grandmother Ola has cancer, and Emily and her mother arrive to take her home with them to Cleveland, Ohio. Emily videotapes her grandmother's friends and relatives to take her memories with her. African American characters. 103 pages. Awards: CC; Coretta Scott King Honor. Grades: 7–12.

Paulsen, Gary. *Nightjohn.*
Doubleday, 1993.
Sequels: *Sarny, A Life Remembered.*
Setting: 1850s.
Main Character: Female, Sarny, 12 years old.
   Sarny exposes the abuse (routine beatings, bondage, dog attacks, forced "breed-ing") suffered by her people on the Waller plantation. Nightjohn, a new slave who has

given up his freedom to educate slaves, inspires Sarny to learn to read and write and continue her studies. Well researched and written in dialect, a graphic depiction of slavery. 96 pages. Awards: CC. Grades: 7–10.

Trueman, Terry. **Stuck in Neutral.**
HarperTempest, 2001.
Sequel: **Cruise Control.**
Setting: Seattle, Washington.
Main Character: Male, Shawn McDaniel, 14 years old.
   Shawn has had cerebral palsy since birth and is unable to communicate or show affection or any other emotion. Yet, he is happy to be alive and has a rich full life inside his head. He suspects his father wants to kill him because he thinks Shawn is suffering. Shawn has no way to tell him otherwise. 128 pages. Awards: CC; Printz Honor. Grades: 6–10.

Woodson, Jacqueline. **Behind You.**
Putnam, 2004.
Setting: New York City.
Main Character: Male, Jeremiah, 15 years old.
   After Jeremiah is mistakenly shot by the police, the people who love him struggle to cope with their loss as they recall his life and death, unaware that Miah is watching over them. 118 pages. Grades: 7–12.

Woodson, Jacqueline. **Miracle's Boys.**
Putnam, 2000.
Setting: Harlem, 2000s.
Main Character: Male, Lafayette, 12 years old.
   Lafayette's close relationship with his older brother, Charlie, changes after Charlie is released from a detention home and blames Lafayette for the death of their mother. African American characters. 133 pages. Awards: CC; Coretta Scott King Honor. Grades. 5 and up.

SHORT STORY COLLECTIONS

Avi. **What Do Fish Have to Do With Anything? and Other Stories.**
Candlewick, 1997.
   Stories of teens choosing their fate and using their eyes and minds over accepting conventional adult wisdom. Awards: CC. Grades: 4–8.

Bauer, Marion Dane. **Am I Blue? Coming Out from the Silence.**
HarperCollins, 1994.
   Eighteen short stories exploring the various meanings of gay/lesbian identity in the lives of teenagers, by Bruce Coville, M.E. Kerr, Francesca Lia Block, Jacqueline Woodson, Gregory Maguire, Ellen Howard, James Cross Giblin, Nancy Garden, C.S. Adler, Leslea Newman, Lois Lowry, Jane Yolen, Jonathan London, Cristina Salat, William Sleator. Awards: CC. Grades: 7–12.

Duncan, Lois. *Trapped: Cages of Mind and Body.*
Simon & Schuster, 1998.

Thirteen stories on the theme of containment; the characters are all physically, socially, or emotionally trapped. By Lois Lowry, Rob Thomas, Francesca Lia Block, David Skinner, Marc Talbert, Lois Duncan, Walter Dean Myers, Gregory Maguire, Joan Bauer, Rita Williams-Garcia, Gary Crew, Gillian Rubenstein. Awards: CC. Grades: 7 and up.

Flake, Sharon G. *Who Am I Without Him? Short Stories About Girls and the Boys in Their Lives.*
Jump At The Sun, 2004.

Ten stories, written in the vernacular of urban African American teens, tell of urban teen girls coming of age. Some are funny and uplifting, while others are disturbing and sad. Awards: Coretta Scott King Honor. Grades: 7–12.

Frank, E. R. *Life is Funny.*
DK Children, 2000.
Setting: Brooklyn, New York.

Stories about eleven loosely connected Brooklyn students over a seven-year period. The characters deal with physically abusive, drug-addicted, or absent parents, an unwanted pregnancy, or a friend's suicide, but each tale is tempered by humor. Gritty language. Awards: CC. Grades: 7–12.

Gallo, Don, editor. *On the Fringe.*
Dial, 2001.
More short story collections by the author: *No Easy Answers* (CC); *Sixteen; Connections; Visions; Short Circuits; Within Reach; Destinations; Time Capsule; First Crossing: Stories About Teen Immigrants.*

Inspired by the events at Columbine High School, speculations about teens who could react so powerfully and violently. By Jack Gantos, Chris Crutcher, Ron Koertge, Graham Salisbury, Nancy Werlin, Francess Lin Lantz, Angela Johnson, M. E. Kerr, Will Weaver, Alden R. Carter, and Joan Bauer. Awards: CC. Grades: 7 and up.

Howe, James, editor. *13: Thirteen Stories that Capture the Agony and Ecstasy of Being Thirteen.*
Atheneum, 2003.

Stories by Ann Martin, Bruce Coville, Todd Strasser, Rachel Vail, Stephen Roos, Ron Koertge, James Howe Meg Cabot, Alex Sanchez, Ellen Wittlinger, and Lori Aurelia Williams. Grades: 6–9.

McCafferty, Megan, editor. *Sixteen: Stories about that Sweet and Bitter Birthday.*
Three Rivers, 2004.

Stories by Sonya Sones, Jacqueline Woodson, Steve Almond, Sarah Dessen, Ned Vizzini, Emma Forrest, Carolyn Mackler, and Megan McCafferty. Grades: YA/A.

Singer, Marilyn, editor. *Stay True: Short Stories for Strong Girls.*
Scholastic, 1999.
   Short stories about teenage girls finding strength within themselves and bringing it forth for the whole world to see. By M.E. Kerr, Rita Williams-Garcia, Norma Fox Mazer, Marian Flandrick Bray, Andrea Davis Pinkney, Peni R. Griffin, and C. Drew Lamm. Awards: CC. Grades: 7 and up.

Sleater, William. *Oddballs.*
Sagebrush, 1999.
   Ten bizarre and humorous semiautobiographical stories about the author's parents and siblings. Awards: CC. Grades: 6–9.

Thomas, Rob. *Doing Time: Notes from the Undergrad.*
Simon & Schuster, 1997.
   Ten teens look at their attitudes and motivations about doing community service. Teachers may find this useful to stimulate classroom discussion. Awards: CC. Grades: 8 and up.

Wittlinger, Ellen. *What's in a Name.*
Simon & Schuster, 2000.
   While the debate goes on about which name is best for the town, Scrub Harbor or Folly Bay, ten teens engage in personal journeys of self-discovery. Awards: CC. Grades: 7 and up.

VERSE NOVELS

Corrigan, Eireann. *You Remind Me of You: A Poetry Memoir.*
Push, 2002.
Setting: 2000s.
Main Character: Female, Corrigan, teenager.
   Corrigan, an anorexic, recounts her teen years with an eating disorder in a series of poems. Her high school boyfriend, Daniel, shoots himself between the eyes only to have the bullet ricochet out of an eye socket, leaving him alive and, eventually, able to function. Corrigan is with another boyfriend, Ben, when the suicide attempt takes place, but she rushes to Daniel's bedside, aids in his slow recovery, and realizes she wants to recover, too. Awards: CC. Grades: 9–12.

Frost, Helen. *Keesha's House.*
Farrar, Straus & Giroux, 2003.
Setting: Joe's house, 2000s.
Main Character: Female, Keesha, 14 years old.
   The house is really Joe's, left to him by his aunt, who took him in when he was 12 years old. Now he helps other kids, including Keesha, whose mother has died and whose father gets drunk and mean. Keesha tells her friends who need help about the house. The poems tell the circumstances that brings the teens to the house, in sestinas and sonnets. Awards: Printz Honor. Grades: 9–12.

Grimes, Nikki. *Bronx Masquerade.*
Dial, 2002.
Setting: Bronx, New York.

Open Mike Friday is everyone's favorite day in Mr. Ward's English class. Eighteen of his multicultural high school students reveal the poets, painters, readers, and dreamers that exist within each of them. Awards: CC; Coretta Scott King Honor. Grades: 7–12.

Herrera, Juan Felipe. *CrashBoomLove: A Novel in Verse.*
University of New Mexico Press, 1999.
Setting: Fowlerville, California.
Main Character: Male, Cesar Garcia, 16 years old.

Cesar doesn't fit in at his new school or at home with his broken family. He wants to crash into everything and gets involved in petty crimes, some violence, and drugs, but he is always searching for something more. Awards: CC. Grades: 8 and up.

Hesse, Karen. *Out of the Dust.*
Scholastic, 1997.
Another verse novel by the author: *Witness* (CC).
Setting: Oklahoma dust bowl.
Main Character: Female, Billie Jo, 14 years old.

In her poetry journal, Billie Jo reveals the grim domestic realities of living during the years of constant dust storms. She finds the courage to face the death of her mother after a hideous accident that also leaves her piano-playing hands in pain and permanently scarred. Her father is decaying with grief and skin cancer before her very eyes, and she decides to flee the homestead and jump a train West. Awards: CC; Newbery. Grades: 5 and up.

Koertge, Ron. *The Brimstone Journals.*
Candlewick, 2001.
Another verse novel by the author: *Shakespeare Bats Cleanup.*
Setting: Branston High School.
Main Character: Male, Boyd, 17 years old.

Fifteen seniors at Branston (nicknamed "Brimstone") High School reveal their struggles in poems, while Boyd plans a shooting spree to get back at everyone on his list who has ever hurt him. Awards: CC. Grades: 9–12.

Sones, Sonya. *One of Those Hideous Books Where the Mother Dies.*
Simon & Schuster, 2004.
More verse novels by the author: *Stop Pretending: What Happened When My Big Sister Went Crazy* (CC), *What My Mother Doesn't Know* (CC).
Setting: California.
Main Character: Female, Ruby Milliken, 15 years old.

After Ruby's mother dies, she moves from Boston to California to live with her estranged movie-star father. E-mails to her best friend, her boyfriend, and her mother "in heaven," with outpourings of her innermost thoughts, display her personality, unhappiness, and feelings of isolation, loss, and grief. Grades: 7–10.

Wild, Margaret. *Jinx.*
Walker, 2004.
Setting: Australia.
Main Character: Female, Jen, teenager.

When Jen's boyfriend commits suicide, she is lonely, sad, bewildered, and rebellious; she starts drinking and having casual sex. Then she meets Ben, but when he dies, a classmate calls her Jinx, and Jen decides the name fits her. Grades: 9–12.

Wolff, Virginia Euwer. *Make Lemonade.*
Henry Holt, 1993.
Another verse novel by the author: *True Believer* (CC, Printz Honor).
Setting: New York City.
Main Character: Female, LaVaughn, 14 years old.

LaVaughn tries to earn the money she needs to make college a reality by taking on a job babysitting for Jolly's, an abused, 17-year-old single parent who lives in squalor with her two children. LaVaughn's steady support helps Jolly to bootstrap herself into better times, and Jolly, in turn, helps LaVaughn to clarify her own values. Awards: CC. Grades: 7–12.

Woodson, Jacqueline. *Locomotion.*
Grosset & Dunlap, 2003.
Setting: 2000s.
Main Character: Male, Lonnie Collins "Locomotion" Motion, 11 years old.

Lonnie writes about the fire that killed his parents, his sister's adoption, and life in foster care in poetry. His writing leads to discoveries about poetry as a form, from haiku to sonnets to the epistle poems he writes to his father and to God. Awards: Coretta Scott King Honor. Grades: 5 and up.

RESOURCES: ADDITIONAL TITLES

Benedict, Susan, and Lenore Carlisle, editors. 1992. *Beyond Words: Picture Books for Older Readers and Writers.* Portsmouth, NH: Heinemann, 1992.

Goldsmith, Francisa. 2005. *Graphic Novels Now: Building, Managing, and Marketing a Dynamic Collection.* Chicago, Il: American Library Association.

Lyga, Allysin A. W., with Barry Lyga. 2004. *Graphic Novels in Your Media Center: a Definitive Guide.* Westport, Conn.: Libraries Unlimited.

Miller, Steve. 2005. *Developing and Promoting Graphic Novel Collections.* New York: Neal-Schuman.

Nichols, C. Allen. 2004. *Thinking Outside the Book: Alternatives for Today's Teen Library Collections.* Westport, Conn. Libraries Unlimited.

CHAPTER 11

HISTORY: PREHISTORY TO 1899

Historical novels are good stories and also a fascinating way to learn about how people lived long ago. Some titles are set around significant historical events and real characters, while others are more of the author's imagination at work, extrapolating from a hint of a real person or event and suggesting how people lived and thought in different times. The teen characters face many of the same challenges as modern-day teens trying to understand and find their place in the world.

Historical Fiction Award
Prehistoric to 475 A.D.
Middle Ages/476–1499
The Renaissance/1500–1700
Colonial America
Salem Witch Trials
Pioneer/Frontier Life
Great Britian/1600–1899
Revolutionary War
Pre Civil War
Civil War
Post Civil War
Resources: Additional Titles

HISTORICAL FICTION AWARD

Established by Scott O'Dell, the first Scott O'Dell Historical Award was given in 1984. It is given annually to a title published in English for children or young adults by a U.S. publisher and set in the New World (North, Central, or South America); the book must have been published in the previous year. The Scott O'Dell Foundation sponsors the award, and the winner is decided by an advisory committee. For further reading about the Scott O'Dell Historical Fiction Award, go to www.scottodell.com/sosoaward.html.

PREHISTORIC TO 475 A.D.

Bradshaw, Gillian. *The Beacon at Alexandria.*
Ticknor & Fields, 1986.
Series: Hera: *Her Own Terms; Lady of the Reeds; Call the Darkness Light; Reich Angel; Great Maria.*
Setting: Rome, Alexandria, 371 A.D.
Main Character: Female, Charis, young woman.

Charis flees to Alexandria when she is betrothed by her father to the hated Roman governor Festinus. She studies medicine and becomes a famous healer and doctor for the Roman army until captured by the Goths. The political, social, and intellectual climate of the fourth century and attitudes toward women and medicine are excellently described. Grades: 9–12.

Carter, Dorothy Sharp. *His Majesty, Queen Hatshepsut.*
Lippincott, 1987.
Setting: Ancient Egypt.
Main Character: Female, Hatshepsut, teen through adult.

A fictionalized account of the life of Hatshepsut, a princess who declared herself king and ruled for more than twenty years. Grades: 5–12.

Denzel, Justin F. *Land of the Thundering Herds.*
Philomel, 1993.
Setting: Prehistory.
Main Character: Prehistoric animals.

The adventures and daily routine of a young lion, stallion, condor, herd of mammoths, and other prehistoric animals sharing grassland. The animals are given names, thoughts, and motivations. Readers will not sympathize with the prehistoric people, who are introduced late to the scene, especially the ones that use "pointed sticks." Grades: 6–10.

Dickinson, Peter. *A Bone from a Dry Sea.*
Delacorte, 1993.
Setting: Prehistoric/modern Africa.
Main Characters: Female, Vinny; Female, Li; teenagers.

Li, an intelligent female member of a prehistoric tribe, becomes instrumental in advancing the lot of her people, and Vinny, the daughter of a paleontologist, is visiting her father on a dig in Africa when important fossil remains are discovered. In parallel stories told in alternating chapters, modern anthropologists investigate the site, finding a fragment of a dolphin's scapula with a hole that could only have been drilled by a not-quite-human hand. Grades: 7–12.

Galloway, Priscilla. *The Courtesan's Daughter.*
Delacorte, 2002.
Setting: Ancient Athens.
Main Characters: Female, Phano, 14 years old; Male, Theo, 30 years old.

Phano and Theo are in love and want to marry. A family enemy spreads rumors to ruin the marriage plans. Based on an actual court case. The social structure of Ancient Athens is well researched. Grades: 7–10.

Geras, Adele. *Troy.*
Harcourt, 2001.
Sequel: *Ithaka.*
Setting: Troy, Ancient Greece, Trojan War.
Main Characters: Female, Marpessa; Female, Xanthe; Male, Alastor, 17 years old.
 The great battles of the Trojan War are seen at a distance from the walls of the city, where the townsfolk gather to sit each day and cheer the action like spectators at an archaic football game. The complicated love affairs and bloody battles are given a stir by the bored gods and goddesses. The Trojan Horse, Helen, Paris, Achilles, Hector, and all the gods make cameo appearances, and there is a great battle scene at the end. Grades: 7–12.

Hoover, Helen M. *The Dawn Palace: The Story of Medea.*
Dutton, 1988.
Setting: Ancient Greece.
Main Character: Female, Medea, 13 years old.
 Trained in supernatural knowledge, Medea finds herself in a unique position to help when Jason comes to her father's kingdom in search of the Golden Fleece. Medea loves Jason from the moment she sets eyes on him; but he later dismisses his sacred oath to her and divorces her. Medea's changes in fortune parallel the demise of matriarchal rule and the victory of male-dominated religions over the worship of the Great Mother Goddess. Grades: 6–12.

Jordan, Sherryl. *Wolf Woman.*
Houghton Mifflin, 1994.
Setting: Prehistory.
Main Character: Female, Tanith, 16 years old.
 When she was 3 years old Tanith was found living with a wolf pack by hunters. The chieftain, Ahearn, took her back to his village to become an adopted daughter for his wife, Nolwynn. After Nolwynn's death, Tanith seeks out her wolf family for solace and kinship. Tanith is torn between her feelings for Gibran, a neighboring village's chieftain's son, and the harmonious kinship offered by the wolves. Awards: CC. Grades: 6–10.

McGraw, Eloise Jarvis. *The Golden Goblet.*
Peter Smith, 1988.
Setting: Ancient Egypt.
Main Character: Male, Ranofer, a young boy.
 In this exciting, suspenseful mystery, Ranofer struggles to thwart the thefts of his evil half-brother, Gebu, so he can become a master goldsmith like their father. Awards: Newbery Honor. Grades: 5–8.

Miklowitz, Gloria D. *Masada: The Last Fortress.*
Wm. B. Eerdmans, 1998.
Setting: Masada, 72 C.E.
Main Characters: Male, Simon, 19 years old; Male, Flavius Silva.
 The siege of Masada is told through the first-person narrations of Simon, the

son of Jewish leader Eleazar, and Flavius Silva, commander in chief of the Roman Tenth Legion. Through Simon, readers experience life at Masada. Flavius Silva's account details the life in the Roman camp and finally the hollow conquest. Grades: 5 and up.

THE MIDDLE AGES/476–1499

Barrett, Tracy. **Anna of Byzantium.**
Delacorte, 1999.
Setting: Byzantium, eleventh century.
Main Character: Female, Anna Comnena, 17 years old.
  Princess Anna, designated as a child to inherit the throne, was educated to be a ruler. She learned from her mother and grandmother to manipulate the intrigues and factions of the court, and when she is displaced as heir by her brother, she schemes without success to assassinate him and regain her position. Grades: 6–10.

Bradford, Karleen. **There Will Be Wolves.**
Lodestar (Dutton), 1996.
Setting: Crusades, 1096.
Main Character: Female, Ursula, young girl.
  Ursula, condemned as a witch because of her knowledge of healing, escapes being burned to death when she joins her father and many others who follow Peter the Hermit on the first Crusade, from Cologne to Jerusalem. Grades: 6–8.

Cadnum, Michael. **Book of the Lion.**
Viking, 2000.
Setting: England, Third Crusade, twelfth century.
Main Character: Male, Edmund, 17 years old.
  Edmund travels to the Holy Land as squire to a knight crusader on his way to join the forces of Richard Lionheart. Grades: 7 and up.

Cushman, Karen. **Catherine, Called Birdy.**
Clarion, 1994.
Setting: England, 1290.
Main Character: Female, Lady Catherine, aka Birdy, 14 years old.
  Birdy, the daughter of an English country knight, keeps a journal in which she records the events of her life, particularly her longing for adventures beyond the usual role of women and her efforts to avoid being married off. Awards: CC; Newbery Honor. Grades: 6–9.

Cushman, Karen. **The Midwife's Apprentice.**
Clarion, 1995.
Setting: Medieval England.
Main Character: Female, Alyce, aka Beetle, 12 or 13 years old.
  Alyce, a homeless orphan, is taken in by Jane Sharp, a sharp-tempered midwife, and in spite of obstacles and hardship, eventually gains the three things she most wants: a full belly, a contented heart, and a place in this world. Awards: CC; Newbery. Grades: 6–9.

Garden, Nancy. *Dove and Sword: A Novel of Joan of Arc.*
Farrar, Straus & Giroux, 1995.
Setting: France, 1455.
Main Character: Female, Joan of Arc, 17 years old.

Gabrielle is visited by Pierre d' Arc, a brother of Joan of Arc. They reminisce about their childhood together in Domremy and Joan's subsequent trial and burning at the stake at Rouen, twenty-four years before. Grades: 7 and up.

Grant, K. M. *The Blood Red Horse.*
Walker, 2005.
Sequels: de Granville Trilogy: *Green Jasper* and forthcoming title.
Setting: Third Crusade, twelfth century.
Main Characters: Male, Gavin de Granville, older brother; Male, William de Granville, 13 years old.

A Christian and a Muslim tell their two points of view during a battle of the Crusades. A special horse named Hosanna changes the lives of two brothers, Gavin and William, and those around them, as they fight with King Richard I against Saladin's armies during the Third Crusade. Grades: 5–9.

Hunter, Mollie. *The King's Swift Rider: A Novel on Robert the Bruce Scotland.*
HarperTrophy, 2000.
Setting: 1306–1329.
Main Character: Male, Martin, 16 years old.

Unwilling to fight but feeling a sense of duty, Martin joins Scotland's rebel army as a swift rider and master of espionage for Robert the Bruce. Grades: 7 and up.

Hunter, Mollie. *The Stronghold.*
Harper & Row, 1974.
Setting: Scotland, 1057.
Main Character: Male, Coll, young man.

Crippled in a Roman raid on his native island, Coll spends many years planning an impregnable defense, but has to overcome many obstacles before he is given a chance to put it to the test. Grades: YA.

Jinks, Catherine. *Pagan's Crusade.*
Candlewick, 2003.
Sequels: *Pagan in Exile, Pagan's Vows.*
Setting: Jerusalem, Third Crusade, twelfth century.
Main Character: Male, Pagan Kidrouck, 16 years old.

Orphaned Pagan is assigned to work for Lord Roland, a Templar knight, as Saladin's armies close in on the Holy City. Well researched. Awards: VOYA Perfect Ten. Grades: 7 and up.

McCaffery, Anne. *Black Horses for the King.*
Harcourt Brace, 1996.
Setting: Britannia, fifth century.

Main Character: Male, Galwyn Varianus, teenager.

Galwyn, son of a Roman Celt, escapes from his tyrannical uncle and joins Lord Artos, later known as King Arthur. Using his talent with languages and way with horses, he helps secure and care for the Libyan horses that Artos hopes to use in battle against the Saxons. Awards: CC. Grades: 7–10.

McCaughrean, Geraldine. *Kite Rider.*
HarperCollins, 2002.
Setting: China, thirteenth century.
Main Character: Male, Haoyou, 12 years old.

After trying to save his widowed mother from a horrendous second marriage, Haoyou has life-changing adventures when he takes to the sky as a circus kite rider and ends up meeting the great Mongol ruler Kublai Khan. Grades: 5–9.

Temple, Frances. *The Ramsay Scallop.*
Orchard, 1994.
Setting: England, thirteenth century.
Main Character: Female, Elenor, 14 years old.

Elenor and her betrothed, Lord Thomas, are sent on a memorable pilgrimage to far-off Spain. Awards: CC. Grades: 7 and up.

Tingle, Rebecca. *The Edge on the Sword.*
Putnam, 2001.
Setting: Britain, ninth century.
Main Character: Female, Aethelflaed, 15 years old.

Aethelflaed, the daughter of King Alfred of West Saxony, weds the Mercian King Ethelred out of family loyalty, and embarks on a journey to become one of the most well-respected and loved women in early British history, Queen Aethelflaed of Mercia. Grades: 6–10.

Wein, Elizabeth E. *A Coalition of Lions.*
Viking, 2003.
Trilogy: *The Winter Prince; Sunbird.*
Setting: Askum (Ethiopia), sixth century.
Main Character: Female, Princess Goewin, young woman.

After the deaths of Artos, High King of Britain, and his sons, his daughter, Princess Goewin, journeys to Aksum to meet Constantine, her intended husband, but finds the country in political turmoil. Grades: 7 and up.

Wilson, Diane L. *I Rode a Horse of Milk White Jade.*
Scholastic, 1998.
Setting: Mongolia, 1339.
Main Character: Female, Oyuna, elderly woman talking about her young days.

Oyuna tells her granddaughter the story of how love for her horse enabled her to win a race and bring good luck to her family. Grades: 6–10.

Yolen, Jane, and Robert J. Harris. *Girl in a Cage.*
Philomel, 2002.

Setting: England, 1306.
Main Character: Female, Princess Marjorie, 13 years old.

As English armies invade Scotland, Princess Marjorie, daughter of the newly crowned Scottish king, Robert the Bruce, is captured by England's King Edward Longshanks and held in a cage on public display. Grades: 6–10.

THE RENAISSANCE/1500–1700

Brooks, Geraldine. *Year of Wonders: A Novel of the Plague.*
Viking, 2001.
Setting: Eyam, Derbyshire, England, 1665–1666.
Main Character: Female, Anna Firth, 18 years old.

As bubonic plague sweeps through England, Anna and other residents of her small mountain village quarantine themselves in an attempt to escape the deadly virus. Grades: YA/A.

Burgess, Melvin. *Burning Issy.*
Simon & Schuster, 1994.
Setting: England, 1600s.
Main Character: Female, Issy, 12 years old.

Issy is accused of being a witch and struggles with the belief that she actually does have strange powers. Grades: 5–8.

Chevalier, Tracy. *Girl with a Pearl Earring.*
Dutton, 1999.
Setting: Delft, Netherlands, 1664.
Main Character: Female, Griet, 16 years old.

Griet, a servant in the house of Dutch painter Vermeer, is the fictional subject of his famous painting "Girl with a Pearl Earring." The household is turned upside down when everyone questions whether Griet is more than a model to Vermeer. Grades: YA/A.

Haugaard, Erik Christian. *The Samurai's Tale.*
Houghton Mifflin, 1984.
Setting: Japan, sixteenth century.
Main Character: Male, Taro, begins when he is 5 years old.

Orphaned Taro is taken in by a general serving the great warlord Takeda Shingen. He grows up to become a samurai fighting for the enemies of his dead family. Grades: YA

Hooper, Mary. *At the Sign of the Sugared Plum.*
Bloomsbury, 2003.
Setting: London, England, 1665.
Main Character: Female, Hannah, teen.

Hannah arrives in London to help her sister run her sweetmeats shop just as the bubonic plague is taking hold of the city. At first it seems far away in the poorer sections, but gradually creeps closer to Hannah and Sarah. Grades: 5–8.

Horowitz, Anthony. *Devil and His Boy.*
Philomel, 2000.
Setting: England, 1593.
Main Character: Male, Tom Falconer, 13 years old.
    As Tom travels through the English countryside to London, he falls in with a troupe of actors whose production "The Devil and His Boy" is a ruse to overthrow Queen Elizabeth. Awards: CC. Grades: 5–7.

Luhrman, Winifred Bruce. *Only Brave Tomorrows.*
Houghton Mifflin, 1989.
Setting: Massachusetts, 1675.
Main Character: Female, Faith, 15 years old.
    Faith comes from England to the colony of Massachusetts, where the Indian uprising known as King Philip's War threatens to destroy everything she holds dear. Grades: 5–9.

Meyer, Carolyn. *Mary, Bloody Mary.*
Harcourt Brace, 1999.
Setting: England, 1500s.
Main Character: Female, Mary Tudor, teenager.
    Mary Tudor, who reigned briefly as Queen of England, tells the story of her troubled childhood as daughter of King Henry VIII. Grades: 6 and up.

Napoli, Donna Jo. *Daughter of Venice.*
Wendy Lamb, 2002.
Setting: Venice, 1592.
Main Character: Female, Donata, 14 years old.
    Donata isn't allowed to go to school or explore the piazzas and canals of her city, all because she is a girl, so she dresses up as a boy to seek out adventure. Grades: 5 and up.

O'Dell, Scott. *The Hawk That Dare Not Hunt by Day.*
Houghton Mifflin, 1975.
Setting: Pre-Colonial America.
Main Character: Male, Tom Barton, young man.
    Amid political turmoil and threats of plague, Tom accepts the risks of helping William Tyndale publish and smuggle into England the Bible he has translated into English. Grades: 7–9.

Torrey, Michele. *To the Edge of the World.*
Knopf, 2003.
Setting: Spain, the sea, 1519.
Main Character: Male, Mateo Macias, 14 years old.
    Mateo's parents have just been killed by bubonic plague. Orphaned and penniless, he joins the crew of the famous explorer Magellan and embarks on a dangerous and exciting voyage to find a route to the Spice Islands. Grades: 5–8.

COLONIAL AMERICA

Anderson, Laurie Halse. *Fever 1793.*
Simon & Schuster, 2000.
Setting: Philadelphia, Pennsylvania, 1793.
Main Character: Female, Mattie Cook, 16 years old.
    Yellow fever is sweeping through Philadelphia and in the mayhem, Mattie must locate her missing mother and try to outlast the wildly infectious disease. Each chapter begins with an authentic diary entry. Awards: CC. Grades: 6–9.

Levitin, Sonia. *Roanoke: A Novel of the Lost Colony.*
Atheneum, 1973.
Setting: Roanoke Colony, Virginia,
Main Character: Male, William Wythers, 16 years old.
    William is anxious to try life in the New World, and when he falls in love with a Native American, Telana, life looks promising in Roanoke. William works to establish a peaceful relationship between the whites and the Indians who hate them. When John White arrives with supplies from England, everyone in the settlement has disappeared. Grades: 7 and up.

Speare, Elizabeth George. *The Sign of the Beaver.*
Houghton Mifflin, 1983.
Setting: Maine, 1700s.
Main Character: Male, Matt, 13 years old.
    Left alone to guard the family's wilderness home, Matt is hard-pressed to survive until two Indians, Attean and his grandfather, teach him their skills. In return, Matt teaches Attean to read. Awards: CC; Newbery; Scott O'Dell. Grades: 5–8.

SALEM WITCH TRIALS

Lasky, Kathryn. *Beyond the Burning Time.*
Blue Sky, 1994.
Setting: Salem, Massachuestts, 1691.
Main Character: Female, Mary Chase, 12 years old.
    When accusations of witchcraft surface in her village, Mary fights to save her mother from execution. Grades: 5–9.

Petry, Ann. *Tituba of Salem Village.*
Crowell, 1964.
Setting: Salem, Massachusetts.
Main Character: Female, Tituba, young woman.
    Tituba is taken from her home in Barbados to be a slave in Salem, and is suspected of witchcraft. Grades: YA.

Rees, Celia. *Witch Child.*
Candlewick, 2001.
Sequel: *Sorceress.*
Setting: Salem, Massachuestts, 1659.

Main Character: Female, Mary Newbury, 14 years old.

Mary keeps a journal of her voyage from England to the New World, and her experiences living as a self-confessed witch in a community of Puritans near Salem, Massachusetts. Awards: CC. Grades: 7–10.

Rinaldi, Ann. *A Break with Charity: A Story about the Salem Witch Trials.*
Harcourt Brace, 1992.
Setting: Salem, Massachuestts, 1706.
Main Character: Female, Susanna English, 14 years old.

While waiting for a church meeting, Susanna, the daughter of a wealthy Salem merchant, recalls the malice, fear, and accusations of witchcraft that tore her village apart in 1692. Grades: 6–10.

Speare, Elizabeth George. *The Witch of Blackbird Pond.*
Houghton Mifflin, 1958.
Setting: Connecticut, 1687.
Main Character: Female, Kit Taylor, 16 years old.

Kit's family moves from sunny Barbados to Puritan Connecticut. Her headstrong ways and friendship with Quaker Hannah Tupper draws suspicion from the community that she might be a witch. Awards: Newbery. Grades: 5–8.

PIONEER/FRONTIER LIFE

Cather, Willa. *O Pioneers!*
Penguin, 1994.
Setting: Hanover, Nebraska.
Main Character: Female, Alexandra Bergson, young woman.

A Swedish immigrant, Alexandra's determination and love of the land yield a productive farm in the harsh open plains. Grades: YA/A.

Conrad, Pam. *Prairie Songs.*
HarperCollins, 1985.
Setting: Nebraska.
Main Character: Female, Louisa, young girl.

Louisa's life on the prairie in a loving pioneer family is altered by the arrival of a new doctor and his beautiful, tragically frail wife. Awards: CC. Grades: 6–12.

Coville, Bruce. *Fortune's Journey.*
BridgeWater, 1995.
Setting: The West, 1853.
Main Character: Female, Jenny, 16 years old.

Jenny faces many challenges on an overland journey to California with the acting company she inherited from her father. Grades: 5–7.

Cushman, Karen. *The Ballad of Lucy Whipple.*
Clarion Books, 1996.
Setting: Lucky Diggins, California, 1849–1850.
Main Character: Female, California Morning Whipple, aka Lucy, 12 years old.

California Morning Whipple, who renames herself Lucy, finds her escape in books when her mother moves the family from Massachusetts to a rough California gold-mining town. Grades: 5–8.

Fleischman, Paul. *The Borning Room.*
HarperCollins, 1991.
Setting: Ohio, 1918.
Main Character: Female, Georgina, elderly woman telling the story of her life.
    Lying at the end of her life in the room where she was born in 1851, Georgina remembers what it was like to grow up on the Ohio frontier. Grades: 6–10.

Garland, Sherry. *The Last Rainmaker.*
Harcourt Brace, 1997.
Setting: The West.
Main Character: Female, Caroline Long, 13 years old.
    When her grandmother dies, Caroline lives with her cruel Aunt Oriona. Her father arrives, but he plans to let Aunt Oriona adopt her. So Caroline runs away to join Shawnee Sam's Wild West Extravaganza, in the hope of learning more about her mother, a performer who died in childbirth, and whose Indian heritage has been kept a secret from Caroline. Grades: 5–8.

Gregory, Kristiana. *Across the Wide and Lonesome Prairie: The Oregon Trail Diary of Hattie Campbell, 1847.*
Live Oak Media, 2005.
Series: Dear America, over 40 titles.
Setting: North America, 1847.
Main Character: Female, Hattie, 13 years old.
    Hattie chronicles her family's arduous journey from Missouri to Oregon on the Oregon Trail. Grades: 4–8.

Holtze, Sollace. *A Circle Unbroken.*
Clarion, 1988.
Setting: Missouri, 1845.
Main Character: Female, Rachel, 17 years old.
    Captured by a roving band of Sioux Indians and brought up as the chief's daughter, Rachel is recaptured by her white family and finds it difficult to adjust; she longs to return to the tribe. Grades: 6–9.

Levitin, Sonia. *The No-Return Trail.*
Harcourt Brace, 1978.
Setting: 1841.
Main Character: Female, Nancy Kelsey, 17 years old.
    A fictionalized account of the 1841 Bidwell-Bartleson expedition, which included Nancy, the first American woman to journey from Missouri to California. Grades: YA.

Murphy, Jim. *West to a Land of Plenty: The Diary of Teresa Angelino Viscardi.*

Scholastic, 1998.
Series: Dear America, over 40 titles.
Setting: 1883.
Main Character: Female, Teresa Viscardi, 14 years old.

While traveling with her Italian American family (including a meddlesome little sister) and other immigrant pioneers to a utopian community in Idaho, Teresa keeps a diary of her experiences along the way. Grades: 4–8.

Rinaldi, Ann. *The Second Bend in the River.*
Scholastic, 1997.
Setting: Ohio Territory, 1798.
Main Character: Female, Rebecca Galloway, 7 years old through teen years.

Rebecca, a young settler in the Ohio territory, meets the Shawnee called Tecumseh. She develops a deep friendship with him that later leads to a proposal of marriage. Grades: 5–9.

GREAT BRITAIN/1600–1899

Hausman, Gerald. *Escape from Botany Bay: The True Story of Mary Bryant.*
Orchard, 2003.
Setting: Australia, 1791.
Main Character: Female, Mary, 19 years old.

Mary is sent from her England home to Botany Bay, Australia, as a prison sentence for stealing a lady's bonnet. Conditions on the ship and in the penal colony are atrocious, which prompts Mary to lead a group of prisoners in an escape back to England. Grades: 7 and up.

Laker, Rosalind. *Circle of Pearls.*
Doubleday, 1990.
Setting: England, 1600s.
Main Character: Female, Julia Pallister, young woman.

Julia, daughter in a Cavalier family, is charged with keeping the only remaining Elizabethan gown and the family estate safe in Puritan England. Julia is in love with a family friend, Christopher Wren, whose career grows from astronomer to architect. The novel continues through the Restoration, the plague, and the Great Fire. Lifestyles of the rich and the lower class are described in detail. Grades: YA.

O'Dell, Scott. *My Name is Not Angelica.*
Houghton Mifflin, 1989.
Setting: St. John, 1733–1734.
Main Character: Female, Raisha, 16 years old.

Raisha, a Senegalese girl, is betrothed to Konje, the young king of her tribe. They are betrayed by a rival ruler, sold to slavers, and taken to the Danish Virgin Islands. Konje escapes and Raisha later joins him as both the cruel punishments and revolution grow. The rebel slaves are trapped by a troop of French soldiers from nearby Martinique and throw themselves from the cliffs into the sea, all except Raisha who chooses to save the life of her unborn child. Grades: 6–8.

Pullman, Philip. *The Ruby in the Smoke.*
Knopf, 1988.
Sequels: *The Shadow in the North, The Tiger in the Well.*
Setting: 1880s, Victorian England.
Main Character: Female, Sally Lockheart, 16 years old.
   Sally investigates her father's mysterious death. Awards: CC; Grades: 7–12.

REVOLUTIONARY WAR

Avi. *The Fighting Ground.*
Lippincott, 1984.
Setting: Revolutionary War.
Main Character: Male, Jonathan, 13 years old.
   Jonathan goes off to fight in the Revolutionary War and discovers that the real war is being fought within himself. Awards: Scott O'Dell. Grades: 4 and up.

Beatty, John Louis, and Patricia Beatty. *Who Comes to King's Mountain?*
Morrow, 1975.
Setting: 1780, South Carolina.
Main Character: Male, Alec, teenager.
   Young Scottish Alec, whose own family is divided between Loyalist and rebel, must decide which side he will follow. Grades: 7–9.

Collier, James Lincoln, and Christopher Collier. *My Brother Sam Is Dead.*
Four Winds Press, 1974.
Setting: Redding, Connecticut, Revolutionary War.
Main Character: Male, Tim Meeker, 11 years old.
   Tim has always looked up to his brother Sam, who is now part of the American Revolution. His father has always been loyal to the king. Tim must decide where his loyalties lie. Grades: YA.

Collier, James Lincoln, and Christopher. *War Comes to Willy Freeman.*
Delacorte, 1983.
Setting: Connecticut, Revolutionary War.
Main Character: Female, Willy Freeman, 13 years old.
   Willy, a free black girl, is caught up in the horror of the Revolutionary War and the danger of being returned to slavery, when her patriot father is killed by the British and her mother disappears. Grades: YA.

Deford, Deborah H. *Enemy Among Them.*
Houghton Mifflin, 1987.
Setting: Revolutionary War, 1776.
Main Characters: Male, Christian Monitor, young man; Female, Margaret Volpert, young woman.
   Christian, a wounded Hessian soldier is taken to the home of the Volperts, a German American family from Pennsylvania. While there, he becomes friendly with Margaret and her brother, John. Christian begins to question his loyalty to the Loyalists, and Margaret waits for him, hoping he will survive the war. Grades: 6–8.

Fast, Howard. *April Morning.*
Crown Publishers, 1961.
Setting: Lexington and Concord, Massachusetts, April 19, 1775.
Main Character: Male, Adam Cooper, 15 years old.

Adam stands next to his father to confront the British soldiers marching out of Boston. Adam witnesses his father fall on the village green, and he nervously responds by shooting at the marching British. Awards: CC. Grades: 6–12.

Forbes, Esther. *Johnny Tremain.*
Houghton Mifflin, 1943.
Setting: Boston, Massachusetts, 1773.
Main Character: Male, Johnny Tremain, teenager.

After injuring his hand, Johnny, a young apprentice silversmith in Boston, becomes a messenger for the Sons of Liberty in the days before the American Revolution. Grades: 5 and up.

Gregory, Kristiana. *The Winter of Red Snow: The Revolutionary War Diary of Abigail Jane Stewart.*
Scholastic, 1996.
Setting: Valley Forge, Pennsylvania, 1777–1778.
Main Character: Female, Abby Stewart, 11 years old.

Abby's family lives near the encampment. She records in her diary her varying emotions toward the soldiers—curiosity, pity, anger, revulsion, enthusiasm. Her daily chores (especially cooking and laundry), amusements, trials, worries, and family interactions are integrated into the story. Grades: 5–8.

O'Dell, Scott. *Sarah Bishop.*
Houghton Mifflin, 1980.
Setting: Long Island, New York Colony.
Main Character: Female, Sarah Bishop, 15 years old.

Sarah struggles to begin a new life for herself in the wilderness after the deaths of her father and brother, who had taken opposite sides in the War for Independence. Grades: YA.

Rinaldi, Ann. *Time Enough for Drums.*
Laurel Leaf, 2000.
Setting: Trenton, New Jersey.
Main Character: Female, Jemima Emerson, teenager.

Jemima's family is on the side of freedom and independence, while her tutor, John Reid, is a Tory loyal to Britain. Though John is at first a thorn in her side, Jemima falls in love with him. Grades: 6–9.

PRE CIVIL WAR

Beatty, Patricia. *Who Comes with Cannons?*
Morrow, 1992.
Setting: North Carolina, 1861.

Main Character: Female, Truth, 12 years old.

Truth, a Quaker girl from Indiana, is staying with relatives who run a North Carolina station of the Underground Railroad. Her world is changed by the beginning of the Civil War. Grades: 4–8.

Berry, James. *Ajeemah and His Son.*
HarperCollins Publishers, 1991.
Setting: Jamaica, 1807.
Main Characters: Male, Ajeemah; Male, Atu, 18 years old.

At the height of the slave trade, Ajeemah and his son, Atu, are snatched by slave traders from their home in Africa while en route to deliver a dowry to Atu's bride-to-be. Ajeemah and Atu are then taken to Jamaica and sold to neighboring plantations never to see one another again. Grades: 5 and up.

Cooper, J. California. *Family: A Novel.*
Doubleday, 1991.
Setting: The South, pre-Civil War.
Main Character: Female, Clora, young woman's spirit.

Clora describes the life she and her mother share, her mother's suicide, her own unsuccessful attempt to kill her children, and the successful taking of her own life to escape mistreatment by her masters. After her death, Clora follows her children's lives in spirit form. The treatment of the slaves is heart-wrenching. Grades: YA.

Fox, Paula. *Slave Dancer: A Novel.*
Bradbury, 1973.
Setting: Slave ship.
Main Character: Male, Jessie Bollier, 13 years old.

Kidnapped by the crew of an Africa-bound boat, Jessie discovers to his horror that he is on a slave ship and that his job is to play his fife for the exercise periods of the human cargo. Awards: Newbery. Grades: 5 and up.

Houston, Gloria. *Bright Freedom's Song: A Story of the Underground Railroad.*
Harcourt Brace, 1998.
Setting: North Carolina.
Main Character: Female, Bright Cameron, 15 years old.

In the years before the Civil War, Bright discovers that her parents are providing a safe house for the Underground Railroad. She helps to save a runaway slave named Marcus. Grades: 5–8.

Lasky, Kathryn. *True North: A Novel of the Underground Railroad.*
Scholastic, 1996.
Setting: Virginia, 1858.
Main Characters: Female, Lacy Bradford, teenager; Female, Afrika, 14 years old.

Lucy, a Boston socialite, and Afrika, a runaway slave from Virginia, meet and begin a treacherous journey to the Canadian border via the Underground Railroad. Awards: CC. Grades: 6–9.

Lester, Julius. *Day of Tears.*
Hyperion, 2005.
Setting: Georgia, 1859.
Main Character: Female, Emma, 12 years old.
  The largest slave auction in U.S. history took place in 1859 on Pierce Butler's plantation, to settle gambling debts. Emma, a house slave who cared for the master's daughters, was promised she would never be sold. On the last day of the auction, she is sold to a woman from Kentucky. In Kentucky, Emma marries and runs away to gain her freedom in Canada. Told in monologs, dialogs, and memories. The liberal use of the word "nigger," will be jarring to modern-day readers. Awards: Coretta Scott King. Grades: 6–12.

Lyons, Mary E. *Letters from a Slave Girl: The Story of Harriet Jacobs.*
Scribner's, 1992.
Setting: North Carolina, 1842.
Main Character: Female, Harriet Jacobs.
  A fictionalized version of the life of Harriet Jacobs, told in the form of letters that she might have written during her slavery in North Carolina and as she prepared for escape to the North. Grades: 5–9.

Lyons, Mary E. *The Poison Place: A Novel.*
Atheneum, 1997.
Setting: Philadelphia, Pennsylvania.
Main Character: Male, Moses Williams, young man.
  A former slave named Moses reminisces about his famous owner, Charles Willson Peale, and the intrigue surrounding Peale's son's suspicious death. Grades: 5–8.

Paterson, Katherine. *Jip, His Story.*
Hamish Hamilton, 1997.
Setting: Vermont, 1855.
Main Character: Male, Jip West.
  Abandoned as an infant, Jip accepts his grim fate, living on a poor farm, until he becomes caretaker of a lunatic brought to the farm. The boy's growing friendship with the mysterious, moody man called Put coincides with Jip's discovery that his mother was a runaway slave. Then Jip's biological father, the master of a Southern plantation, arrives to retrieve his "property." Awards: Scott O'Dell. Grades: 5–9.

Paterson, Katherine. *Lyddie.*
Penguin, 1991.
Setting: Lowell, Massachusetts, 1840s.
Main Character: Female, Lyddie Worthen, 13 years old.
  Lyddie stares down a bear on her family's debt-ridden farm in the Vermont mountains, spends a year as a servant girl at an inn, and works for months under grueling conditions as a factory worker. An encounter with a runaway slave brings out her generosity and starts her wondering about slavery and inequality. Awards: CC. Grades: 5–9.

Paulsen, Gary. **Nightjohn.**
Doubleday, 1993.
Sequels: **Sarny, A Life Remembered.**
Setting: 1850s.
Main Character: Female, Sarny, 12 years old.

Sarny exposes the abuse (routine beatings, bondage, dog attacks, forced "breed-ing") suffered by her people on the Waller plantation. Nightjohn, a new slave who has given up his freedom to educate slaves, inspires Sarny to learn to read and write and continue her studies. Written in dialect, a well-researched, graphic depiction of slavery. Awards: CC. Grades: 7–10.

Pearsall, Shelley. **Trouble Don't Last.**
Knopf, 2002.
Setting: 1859.
Main Character: Male, Samuel, 11 years old.

Samuel is awakened by 70-year-old Harrison, who has decided they should flee their tyrannical Kentucky master. Harrison is mindful of the dangers and wary of trusting even the strangers who might offer help. Samuel, an impulsive boy who seems prone to trouble, is grudgingly accustomed to his life of servitude and reluctant to leave it. Days of hiding and nights of stealthy movement take them farther away from their former lives and safely into Canada. Awards: Scott O'Dell; Grades: 5–8.

Rabin, Staton. **Betsy and the Emperor.**
Margaret K. McElderry, 2004.
Setting: St. Helena.
Main Character: Female, Betsy Balcombe, 14 years old.

Betsy returned to her remote island home of St. Helena from boarding school in London to play host to Napoleon Bonaparte, who is exiled on the forbidding island after his capture at Waterloo. Betsy strikes up a friendship with "Boney" that sur-prises both of them. An author's note fills in some of the details about the real Betsy Balcombe. Grades: 5–9.

Rinaldi, Ann. **Mine Eyes Have Seen.**
Scholastic, 1997.
Setting: Maryland, 1859.
Main Character: Female, Annie, 15 years old.

Annie travels to the Maryland farm where her father, radical abolitionist John Brown, is secretly assembling his provisional army prior to their raid on the U.S. arsenal at nearby Harpers Ferry. Grades: 7 and up.

Rinaldi, Ann. **Wolf by the Ears.**
Scholastic, 1991.
Setting: 1820.
Main Character: Female, Harriet Hemings, 19 years old.

Harriet, possibly the daughter of Thomas Jefferson and his slave Sally Hemings, struggles with the decision whether to claim her freedom away from the security and comfort of Monticello, or to stay and remain a slave. She decides to move to Washing-ton, D. C., and to pass as white. Awards: CC. Grades: 7–12.

CIVIL WAR

Beatty, Patricia. *Charley Skedaddle.*
Morrow, 1987.
Setting: Civil War.
Main Character: Male, Charlie Quinn, 12 years old.
 A Bowery Boy from New York City joins the Union Army as a drummer, deserts during a battle in Virginia, and encounters a hostile old mountain woman.
Awards: Scott O'Dell. Grades: 5–8.

Beatty, Patricia. *Jayhawker.*
Morrow, 1991.
Setting: Kansas, Civil War.
Main Character: Male, Elija "Lije" Tulley, 13 years old.
 Farm boy Lije Tulley becomes a Jayhawker, an abolitionist raider freeing slaves from the neighboring state of Missouri, and then goes undercover there as a spy.
Grades: 5–8.

Calvert, Patricia. *Bigger.*
Maxwell Macmillan International, c1994.
Setting: Civil War.
Main Character: Male, Tyler, 12 years old.
 When his father disappears near the Mexican border at the end of the Civil War, Tyler decides to go after him. Along the journey he finds a strange dog which he names Bigger. Grades: 4–8.

Clapp, Patricia. *The Tamarack Tree: A Novel of the Siege of Vicksburg.*
Lothrop, Lee & Shepard, 1986.
Setting: Vicksburg, Mississippi, 1863.
Main Character: Female, Rosemary Leigh, 18 years old.
 When Rosemary joins her brother in Vicksburg, her loyalties are divided and all her resources are tested as she and her friends experience the terrible physical and emotional hardships of the forty-seven-day siege. Grades: 6–9.

Collier, James. *With Every Drop of Blood.*
Delacorte, 1994.
Setting: Virginia, Civil War.
Main Character: Male, Johnny, 14 years old.
 Johnny promises his dying father that he'll stay on the farm with his mother and younger sisters, but he convinces his mother to let him join a wagon train carrying food to Confederate soldiers. He is then captured by a black Union soldier.
Grades: 6–9.

Crane, Stephen. *Red Badge of Courage.*
Tor Books, 1990.
Setting: Civil War.
Main Character: Male, Henry Fleming, young man.
 Against his mother's wishes, Henry enlists in the Union army. The reality of battle comes soon enough, when he witnesses the death of his friend Jim Conklin.

Torn between wanting to run away and wanting to earn his red badge of courage, he receives a head wound in a scuffle and lies to his regiment, but then has an opportunity to test his true courage. Awards: CC. Grades: 8–12.

Fleischman, Paul. *Bull Run.*
HarperCollins, 1993.
Setting: Battle of Bull Run, 1861.
Main Character: Multiple characters.
    Northerners, Southerners, generals, couriers, dreaming boys, and worried sisters—sixteen characters in all—describe the glory, the horror, the thrill, and the disillusionment of the first battle of the Civil War. Awards: CC; Scott O'Dell. Grades: 6–12.

Forrester, Sandra. *Sound the Jubilee.*
Lodestar, 1995.
Sequel: *My Home is Over Jordan.*
Setting: Civil War, 1862.
Main Character: Female, Maddie, 11 years old.
    Maddie and her family are owned by the McCarthas, who retreat from their plantation to a summer home in Nag's Head. Now in the path of the invading Yankee army, Maddie's family escapes to Roanoke Island. Grades: 6–9.

Hansen, Joyce. *Which Way Freedom?*
Walker, 1986.
Setting: Tennessee, Civil War.
Main Character: Male, Obi, young man.
    Obi escapes from slavery during the Civil War, joins a black Union regiment, and soon becomes involved in the bloody fighting at Fort Pillow, Tennessee. Grades: 6–9.

Hunt, Irene. *Across Five Aprils.*
Follett, 1964.
Setting: 1861.
Main Character: Male, Jethro Creighton, 9 years old.
    Jethro comes of age during the turbulent years of the Civil War. Grades: 4–8.

Mitchell, Margaret. *Gone with the Wind.*
Macmillan, 1939.
Setting: Atlanta, Georgia.
Main Characters: Scarlett O'Hara, 16 years old-to adult; Rhett Butler, adult; Ashley Wilkes, adult; Melanie Wilkes, 17 years old-to adult.
    A love story set against the Civil War and Reconstruction. Made into a movie. Awards: CC. Grades: 10–12.

Nixon, Joan Lowery. *A Family Apart.*
Laurel Leaf, 1995.
Series: Orphan Train: *A Dangerous Promise; Caught in the Act; A Place to Belong.*
Setting: St. Joseph, Missouri, 1856.
Main Character: Female, Frances Mary Kelly, 13 years old.

When widowed Mrs. Kelly can no longer care for her six children, she sends them West on the Orphan Train, to be adopted by farm families. Frances disguises herself as a boy to be able to stay with her youngest brother, Petey. She is adopted by a family that works for the Underground Railroad. Grades: 4–8.

O'Dell, Scott. *Sing Down the Moon.*
Houghton Mifflin, 1970.
Setting: Cannon de Chelly, 1864.
Main Character: Female, Bright Morning, 14 years old.
   Bright Morning recounts the events of 1864, when her Navajo tribe was forced to march to Fort Sumner as prisoners of the Spanish slave traders. Awards: Newbery Honor. Grades: 5 and up.

Paulsen, Gary. *Soldier's Heart: A Novel of the Civil War.*
Delacorte, 1998.
Setting: Civil War, 1861.
Main Character: Male, Charley Goddard, 15 years old.
   Charley leaves his Minnesota farm to enlist in the Union army in 1861. An almost festive train ride to the South soon gives way to the harrowing realities of war. After four major battles, he is badly wounded at Gettysburg. A final chapter shows him at 21, joyless, hopeless, and contemplating suicide. Paulsen's introduction explains that having a "soldier's heart" is the Civil War equivalent of shell shock and post-traumatic stress disorder. Awards: CC. Grades: 7–10.

Peck, Richard. *River Between Us.*
Dial, 2003.
Setting: 1916/1861, Illinois.
Main Characters: Male, Howard Leland Hutchings; Female, Tilly Pruitt; both 15 years old.
   Opening in 1916, the story begins with Howard's recollections of a trip to his father's home. There he meets the four people who raised his father and the time shifts to fifty years ago, with his grandmother Tilly at the age of 15, telling the story of two mysterious ladies who came to stay in their home. Tilly's twin Noah, falls in love with one of them, who is a quadroon. Awards: Scott O'Dell. Grades: 7 and up.

Reeder, Carolyn. *Across the Lines.*
Atheneum, 1997.
Setting: Petersburg, May 1864 to May 1865.
Main Characters: Male, Edward, 12 years old; Male, Simon, 13 years old.
   Edward, the son of a white plantation owner, and his black house servant and friend, Simon, witness the siege of Petersburg during the Civil War. Grades: 5–9.

Reeder, Carolyn. *Shades of Gray.*
Collier Macmillan (London), 1989.
Setting: 1865.
Main Character: Male, Will, 12 years old.
   Will, having lost all his immediate family, reluctantly leaves his city home to live in the Virginia countryside with his aunt and the uncle he considers a "traitor" because he refused to take part in the war. Awards: Scott O'Dell. Grades: 4–7.

Rinaldi, Ann. *In My Father's House.*
Scholastic, 1993.
Setting: Civil War.
Main Character: Female, Osceola McLean, 7 years old.

The McLean family entertained Confederates at their Manassas home just before the battle of Bull Run and also hosted the peace negotiations at Appomattox, where they had moved to escape the war. Oscie is at odds with her stepfather's progressive stance toward slavery and his profiteering. A sweeping, romantic, and dramatic overview of the war. Includes a bibliography and a chronology. Grades: 7–10.

Rinaldi, Ann. *Last Silk Dress.*
Holiday House, 1988.
Setting: Richmond, Virginia, Civil War.
Main Character: Female, Susan Chilmark, 14 years old.

Susan and her best friend, Connie, collect silk dresses from the ladies of Richmond to make a balloon to spy on the Yankees. Susan's views on the war change when she discovers family secrets and realizes how adultery and slavery have all but destroyed her family. Awards. CC. Grades: 7 and up.

Post Civil War

Burks, Brian. *Soldier Boy.*
Harcourt Brace, 1997.
Setting: 1870s.
Main Character: Male, Johnny McBane, teenager.

When prizefighter Johnny's life is threatened, he flees Chicago and joins the U.S. Cavalry, even though he is underage. Johnny has never ridden a horse or fired a rifle, yet he proves himself during an unduly severe training period. Ultimately assigned to serve under the legendary Lieutenant Colonel George Armstrong Custer, Johnny harbors mixed emotions about the army's Indian policy and the impending confrontation with the Sioux at Little Big Horn. Grades: 6–9.

Lawrence, Iain. *Convicts.*
Delacorte, 2005.
Setting: London, nineteenth century.
Main Character: Male, Tom Tin, 14 years old.

After his father is sent to debtor's prison, Tom's fortune takes twists and turns. He finds a valuable diamond, only to lose it again; stumbles across the corpse of a boy who could pass as his twin; and is then mistaken for the deceased boy and dragged off to serve a seven-year term on the *Lachesis,* a prison ship for boys. There he goes through near starvation, torture, bondage, and bullying. An exciting page-turner adventure for reluctant readers. Grades: 5–8.

Taylor, Mildred. *The Land.*
Dial, 2001.
Series: The Well: *David's Story; Mississippi Bridge; Song of the Trees; The Friendship; Roll of Thunder, Hear My Cry* (CC; Newbery Medal); *Let the Circle Be Unbroken; Road to Memphis.*

Setting: Post Civil War.

Main Character: Male, Paul Edward Logan, 14 years old.

Paul Edward, the son of a slave and her white master, is caught between two worlds: colored folks and white folks. He is treated well by his half-brothers and father, but doesn't receive the same privileges as his white siblings. He is initially tormented by a black boy, Mitchell Thomas, who works for his father. Paul Edward and Mitchell become best friends and run away to pursue their dreams. The sequels follow the Logan descendents in their struggles for dignity against poverty and racism. Awards: Coretta Scott King; Scott O'Dell. Grades: 7–10.

RESOURCES: ADDITIONAL TITLES

Barnhouse, Rebecca. 2004. *The Middle Ages in Literature for Youth: A Guide and Resource Book.* Lanham, MD: Scarecrow Press.

Lowe, Joy L. and Kathryn I. Matthew. 2003. *Colonial America in Literature for Youth: A Guide and Resource Book.* Lanham, MD. Scarecrow Press.

Stephens, Elaine C., and Jean E. Brown. 1998. *Learning About . . . the Civil War: Literature and Other Resources for Young People.* North Haven, Conn.: Linnet Professional Publications.

CHAPTER 12

HISTORY: 1900 TO PRESENT

Many new young adult historical fiction titles have been published in recent years, providing the gritty realism and authenticity of contemporary realistic fiction. The titles in this chapter cover each decade of the twentieth century.

    1900–WWI
    Great Depression/Pre WWII
    Holocaust
    WWII
    1950s/Post WWII
    1960s/Civil Rights Movement
    1970s/Vietnam War
    1980s–1990s
    Resources: Additional Titles

1900–WWI

Bagdasarian, Adam. **Forgotten Fire.**
DK Children, 2000.
Setting: Turkey, 1915.
Main Character: Male, Vahan Kendarian, 12 years old.

Vahan lives a sheltered life as the son of a wealthy and respected Armenian man until the triumvirate of Turkish leaders—Enver Pasha, Talaat Bey, and Djemal Pasha—begins the systematic massacre of nearly three-quarters of the Armenian population of Turkey, including 1.5 million men, women, and children. Vahan witnesses the deaths of his family members and is suddenly an orphan on the run. Vivid brutality; parental guidance strongly suggested for younger readers. Grades: 9–12.

Crew, Linda. **Brides of Eden: A True Story Imagined.**
HarperCollins, 2001.
Setting: 1903.
Main Character: Female, Eva Mae Hurt, 16 years old.

Eva Mae is active in the Salvation Army. When handsome Franz Edmund Creffield sets up his own ministry, Eva Mae and other girls become obsessed with him and his teachings. Soon Creffield "issues a directive" that his followers throw their finery into bonfires and don strange-looking smock dresses. He takes them on an island retreat, and announces that one girl will be chosen to be the "mother of the Second Christ." Based on real events and characters and illustrated with black-and-white photos of key sites. Grades: 8–12.

Donnelly, Jennifer. *A Northern Light.*
Harcourt, 2003.
Setting: Adirondack Mountains, New York, 1906.
Main Character: Female, Mattie Gokey, 16 years old.
    Mattie, a talented writer, promised her dying mother that she would always take care of her father and younger siblings, so she is stuck on a farm, living in near poverty, even though she has been accepted at Barnard College. She promises to marry handsome Royal Loomis, even though he doesn't appear to love her. Mattie works at an Adirondack summer resort and has promised a guest, Grace Brown, to burn two bundles of letters. Before Mattie can comply, Grace's body is found in the lake, and Chester Gillette, the young man who was with her, disappears, presumed drowned. But Grace was killed by Chester because she was poor and pregnant, and he hoped to make his fortune by marrying a rich, society girl. Grace's story is told in Theodore Dreiser's *An American Tragedy.* Awards: Printz; Carnegie. Grades: 8–12.

Laker, Rosalind. *Orchids and Diamonds.*
Doubleday, 1995.
Setting: Paris, France, 1907, to WWI Venice.
Main Character: Female, Juliette Cladel, young woman.
    Juliette meets the suave Russian count Nikolai Karasvin in Paris and is immediately captivated by his charm and good looks. When Nikolai returns to Russia due to the rising unrest there, Juliette marries Italian designer Marco Romanelli and returns with him to Venice, always hoping that one day she will be reunited with Nikolai. The tragedy of World War I and its effect on both Juliette and the city of Venice is woven into the love story. Grades: YA.

Morpurgo, Michael. *Private Peaceful.*
Scholastic, 2004.
Setting: France, WWI.
Main Character: Male, Thomas Peaceful, 15 years old.
    Thomas lies about his age to become a soldier and is now at the front in France with his older brother, Charlie. He stands a lonely nighttime vigil, reflecting on his past for reasons that are not explained until the book's end. Finally, he describes how Charlie disobeyed a direct order to stay with him after he was wounded in action, fully aware of this decision's dire consequences. Grades: 7–12.

Namioka, Lensey. *Ties that Bind, Ties that Break.*
Delacorte, 1999.
Setting: China, 1911.
Main Character: Female, Tao Ailin, 12 years old.
    Ailin, the third daughter in a wealthy upper-class family, resists having her feet bound, and her progressive father gives in to her. The family her parents have arranged for her to marry into breaks off the engagement. Ailin's father sends her to a

missionary school, where she learns English and other subjects her grandmother dismisses as useless. When her father dies, the new head of the family, Ailin's volatile uncle, stops Ailin's education and offers her the only three choices suitable for a woman with unbound feet: becoming a nun, a concubine, or a farmer's wife. Ailin chooses to create her own destiny. Grades: 7–10.

Nixon, Jean Lowery. *Land of Hope.*
Delacorte, 1994.
Series: Ellis Island: *Land of Promise, Land of Dreams.*
Setting: New York City, 1902.
Main Character: Female, Rebekah Levinsky, 15 years old.
    Rebekah, a Jewish immigrant, almost abandons her dream of getting an education when she is forced to work in a sweatshop. Grades: 5 and up.

Remarque, Erich Maria. *All Quiet on the Western Front.*
Little, Brown, 1929.
Setting: WWI.
Main Character: Male, Paul Baumer, 19 years old.
    Paul enlists with his classmates in the German army of World War I. Youthful and enthusiastic, they become soldiers. When these young men are confronted with trench warfare and dying in hellish agony, Paul is irrevocably changed. Awards: CC. Grades: YA.

Rostkowski, Margaret I. *After the Dancing Days.*
HarperCollins, 1986.
Setting: Kansas, post WWI.
Main Character: Female, Annie, 13 years old.
    When her father, a doctor, begins to work in the veterans hospital, and her grandfather reads to a blind vet there, Annie has the opportunity to visit and make friends with two soldiers. Awards: CC. Grades: 6–9.

Schmidt, Gary D. *Lizzie Bright and the Buckminster Boy.*
Clarion, 2004.
Setting: Phippsburg, Maine, 1911.
Main Character: Male, Turner Buckminster, 13 years old.
    Friendless and feeling the burden of being the new preacher's son, Turner is miserable in his new home until he meets Lizzie Bright Griffin, the first African American he has ever met. Lizzie lives on Malaga Island, which the racist town elders decide to destroy to establish a tourist trade. Awards: Printz Honor. Grades: 6–9.

Sinclair, Upton. *The Jungle.*
Bantam, 1981.
Setting: Chicago, Illinois, 1905.
Main Character: Male, Jurgis Rudkos, young man.
    Jurgis and his family are Lithuanian immigrants eking out a living in Chicago, underpaid and cheated at every turn. An exposé of Chicago's gory meat-packing industry and Sinclair's most pointed social and political commentary. Originally published in 1906. Awards: CC; Grades: YA/A.

Smith, Betty. *A Tree Grows in Brooklyn.*
HarperPerennial, 2005.
Setting: Brooklyn, New York, 1900.
Main Character: Female, Francie Nolan, 11 years old.

Francie, avid reader, penny-candy connoisseur, and adroit observer of human nature, grows up with a sweet, tragic father, a severely realistic mother, an aunt who gives her love too freely to men, and a brother who will always be the favored child. Francie learns early the meaning of hunger and the value of a penny. Like the Tree of Heaven that grows out of cement or through cellar gratings, resourceful Francie struggles against all odds to survive and thrive. Originally published in 1943. Grades: 5–12.

Great Depression/Pre WWII

Choldenko, Gennifer. *Al Capone Does My Shirts.*
Putnam Juvenile, 2004.
Setting: Alcatraz Island, California, 1935.
Main Character: Male, Moose Flanagan, 12 years old.

Moose and his family move to Alcatraz Island when his father gets a job in the prison where noted criminals Al Capone and Machine Gun Kelly were housed. Moose is given almost complete responsibility for his autistic older sister, while trying to cope in a new school, yearning over the warden's daughter, and living in an isolated and strange place. Awards: Newbery Honor. Grades: 6–8.

Hesse, Karen. *Out of the Dust.*
Scholastic, 1997.
Setting: Oklahoma, 1934–1935.
Main Character: Female, Billie Jo, 15 years old.

Billie Jo tells of her life in Oklahoma during the Dust Bowl years of the Depression. Her mother dies after a gruesome accident caused by her father's leaving a bucket of kerosene near the stove, and Billie Jo sustains injuries that seem to bring to a halt her dreams of playing the piano. Her grief is compounded by her taciturn father, who went on a drinking binge while Billie Jo's mother, not yet dead, begged for water. Told in dated free verse entries that span the winter of 1934 to the winter of 1935. Awards: CC; Newbery; Scott O'Dell. Grades: 9–12.

Peck, Richard. *A Long Way from Chicago.*
Dial, 1998.
Sequel: *A Year Down Yonder.*
Setting: Illinois, 1930s.
Main Characters: Male, Joe Dowdel, older brother; Female, Mary Alice Dowdel, 7 years old.

Joe and Mary Alice make their annual August trek to visit their eccentric grandmother, who lives in a sleepy Illinois town somewhere between Chicago and St. Louis. Grandma Dowdel never ceases to amaze her grandchildren, as she uses her wit and ability to tell whoppers to get the best of manipulative people or those who put on airs. Awards: CC. Grades: 4–8.

Porter, Tracey. *Treasures in the Dust.*
HarperCollins, 1997.
Setting: Oklahoma, 1930s.
Main Characters: Female, Annie; Female, Violet; both 11 years old.

Annie and Violet are friends who alternate in telling their families' stories about living in rural Oklahoma during the drought and Great Depression. Annie is more grounded and accepting of the dust that has drifted through her life since infancy, while Violet is imaginative, story-crazy, and "always looking to fly away." They tell of the everyday events of Dust Bowl life. Grades: 4–8.

Puzo, Mario. *The Godfather.*
Putnam, 1969.
Setting: New York City, 1940s.
Main Character: Male, Don Vito Corleone, adult.

Corleone, the head of the Mafia family in New York City, struggles to maintain control as he resists pressure to bring narcotics into the city. For mature readers. Awards: CC. Grades: 10–12.

Raymond, Patrick. *Daniel and Esther.*
M. K. McElderry, 1989.
Setting: Devon, England, 1936.
Main Character: Male, Daniel, 13 years old.

While attending Dartington Hall, a progressive school in England, Daniel meets Esther, who, as the next three years go by, becomes the focus of his life. As the war approaches, Daniel is sent to America and Esther to Vienna. A story for music lovers. Grades: 7–9.

Steinbeck, John. *The Grapes of Wrath.*
Penguin, 2000.
Setting: Western United States, Depression era.
Main Character: Joad family members.

A chronicle of the Joad family, once Oklahoma farmers, then migrant workers, and their journey west to California, where they hope to find work. Struggling to maintain their human dignity. Originally published in 1939. Awards: CC; Pulitzer Prize. Grades: 9–12.

Uhlman, Fred. *Reunion.*
Farrar, Straus & Giroux, 1997.
Setting: Germany, 1932.
Main Character: Male, Hans Schwartz, teenager.

Hans is Jewish, the son of a doctor who believes that the rise of the Nazis is "a temporary illness. . . . " Hans's friend, the young Count Konradin von Hohenfels, has a mother who keeps a portrait of Hitler on her dresser. The two boys share their most private thoughts on trips to the countryside in southwest Germany; they discuss poetry and the past and present of their country, and argue the existence of a benevolent God. Soon the outside world alters their friendship forever. Grades: YA/A.

HOLOCAUST

Bat-Ami, Miriam. *Two Suns in the Sky.*
Open Court, 1999.
Setting: Oswego, New York.
Main Characters: Female, Chris Cook, 15 years old; Male, Adam Bornstein, 15 years old.
    Chris is fascinated by the exotic strangers living in the grim refugee camp so close by. She and her friends sneak into the camp, where she meets Adam, a Yugoslavian Jew. The two fall passionately in love, in spite of differences of language and religion and the angry resistance of Chris's father. Their distinct voices alternate in telling the story of their ill-fated attraction. Awards: Scott O'Dell. Grades: 6–10.

Bennett, Cherie, and Jeff Gottesfeld. *Anne Frank and Me.*
Putnam, 2001.
Setting: Occupied Paris,1940s/2000s.
Main Character: Female, Nicole Burns, teenager.
    Nicole believes the Holocaust is ancient history and doesn't understand why she needs to study it. When touring an Anne Frank exhibit with her class, a shot rings out and a sudden pain pierces Nicole. Nicole regains consciousness in wartime France, living the destiny of a Jewish teen. Time travel. Grades: 7–9.

Bitton-Jackson, Livia. *I Have Lived a Thousand Years.*
Simon Pulse, 1999.
Setting: WWII Work Camps.
Main Character: Female, Elli Friedmann, 13 years old.
    Elli and her mother manage to survive and stay together, comforting each other as they are taken to various camps. Awards: CC. Grades: 7–12.

Chotjewitz, David. *Daniel Half Human and the Good Nazi.*
Atheneum/Richard Jackson Books, 2004.
Setting: Hamburg, Germany, 1930s.
Main Character: Male, Daniel, 13 years old.
    Daniel is a Hitler Youth member, until he discovers his mother is Jewish and is thrown out of his school; he is now considered half human. As tension and racism increase, his best friends begin to pull away. Awards: Notable Books for a Global Society; Batchelder Honor. Grades: 7 and up.

Dahlberg, Maurine F. *Play to the Angel.*
Puffin, 2002.
Setting: Vienna, Austria, 1938.
Main Character: Female, Greta Radky, 12 years old.
    Greta loves playing the piano, and her new teacher is Herr Hummel, who has had to flee the Nazis. When Hitler annexes Austria, Greta helps her teacher to escape. Grades: 5–8.

Denenberg, Barry. *One Eye Laughing, the Other Weeping: The Diary of Julie Weiss.*
Scholastic, 2000.

Series: Dear America, over 40 titles in the series.
Setting: Vienna, Austria, 1938.
Main Character: Female, Julie Weiss, 11 years old.

Julie adores her rich and successful father, but is ambivalent toward her superficial mother. Step by step, Julie, her Jewish family, and their friends suffer from the violent persecution inflicted on them by the Nazis. Her mother commits suicide. Her father sends Julie to her mother's sister in America, where she starts a new life. Grades: 5–9.

Isaacs, Anne. *Torn Thread.*
Blue Sky, 2002.
Setting: Czechoslovakia.
Main Characters: Female, Eva, 12 years old; Female, Rachel, 14 years old.

Eva and Rachel are sisters who survive two years in a labor camp, working twelve hours a day spinning yarn for blankets and uniforms for Nazi soldiers. When the Soviet soldiers rescue them, they start a new life in Canada. Grades: 6–8.

Jung, Reinhardt. *Dreaming in Black and White.*
Dial, 2003.
Setting: Germany, 2000s/1930s.
Main Character: Male, Hannes Keller, teenager.

Hannes lives in modern Germany and has speech and walking disabilities. He has waking dreams about 1930s Germany and the persecution of persons with disabilities, who were often taken to psychiatric institutions and killed. When he dreams his father has betrayed him and signed papers to have him taken by the Nazis, Hannes's relationship with his father is changed in the present. Translated from German. Grades: 6–8.

Keneally, Thomas. *Schindler's List.*
Simon & Schuster, 1994.
Setting: Germany.
Main Character: Male, Oskar Schindler, adult.

Schindler was an influential German industrialist with high-level connections in Nazi Germany. He used his position to save more than one thousand Polish Jews. The book is based on interviews with many of those helped by Schindler. Awards: CC; Booker Prize. Grades: 10–12.

Kositsky, Lynne. *Thought of High Windows.*
Kids Can, 2004.
Setting: France.
Main Character: Female, Esther, 15 years old.

Esther was taken from Germany by the Red Cross, to find refuge in Belgium and then France. When France surrenders to the Nazis, refugees are in great danger. Esther becomes part of the Jewish Underground, where she is teased because of her traditional ways and being overweight. Flying out of high windows seems like her only escape. For mature readers. Grades: 8 and up.

Levitin, Sonia. **Room in the Heart.**
Puffin, 2005.
Setting: Denmark.
Main Characters: Female, Julie Weinstein, 15 years old; Male, Niels Nelson, 15 years old.

Life for Julie's Jewish family becomes more and more restrictive until martial law is finally declared and her family escapes to Sweden. Niels, Julie's best friend's brother, is angry about what is happening and joins the resistance. Told in alternating points of view. Grades: 7 and up.

Lowry, Lois. **Number the Stars.**
Houghton Mifflin, 1984.
Setting: Denmark, 1943.
Main Character: Female, Annemarie Johansen, 10 years old.

The story of the Danish resistance and of the Danish people who helped rescue almost the entire Jewish population of Denmark as seen through Annemarie's eyes. Awards: Newbery. Grades: 5–9.

Matas, Carol. **Daniel's Story.**
Scholastic, 1993.
Setting: Labor camps.
Main Character: Male, Daniel, 14 years old.

Daniel is swept from a comfortable life in Frankfort to a Polish ghetto, then to Auschwitz and Buchenwald, losing most of his family along the way. He records the atrocities he encounters with a smuggled camera. Grades: 6–9.

Mazer, Norma Fox. **Good Night, Maman.**
Harcourt, 1999.
Setting: Paris, 1940.
Main Character: Female, Karin Levi, 12 years old.

Karin's world is torn apart when the German army occupies Paris. Karin, her older brother, Marc, and their *maman* must flee to seek safety, but Maman falls ill and is unable to travel, forcing Karin and Marc to leave her behind. When Marc manages to obtain two coveted places aboard a ship bound for America, the distance between them grows even greater. Grades: 5–9.

Newbery, Linda. **Sisterland.**
David Fickling, 2004.
Setting: England, present day.
Main Characters: Female, Hilly, 16 years old; Female, Zoe, 15 years old.

Hilly and her sister, Zoe, prepare for their HeidiGran to move in with them. Suffering from Alzheimer's disease, HeidiGran begins to share bits of her past she had always kept secret. She had been transported to England in the Kindertransports of Jewish children from Nazi Germany. Grades: 8 and up.

Orgel, Doris. **The Devil in Vienna.**
Puffin, 1988.
Setting: Vienna, Austria, 1938.
Main Characters: Female, Inge; Female, Lieselotte; both 13 years old.

Through her diary entries, Inge, a Jew, recounts the difficulties of maintaining her close friendship with Lieselotte, a Hitler Youth. Based partly on the author's own experiences. Grades: 5–9.

Orlev, Uri. *The Man from the Other Side.*
Puffin, 1995.
Setting: Warsaw, Poland, 1943.
Main Character: Male, Marek, 14 years old.
Marek has extremely negative feelings about Jews, until his Catholic mother informs him that his father was a Jew and had been killed in prison because he was a Communist. Based on a true story. Grades: 9–12.

Orlev, Uri. *Run, Boy, Run.*
Houghton Mifflin/Walter Lorraine, 2003.
Setting: Polish ghetto.
Main Character: Male, Surlick, 8 years old.
Surlick, an illiterate ghetto survivor, escaped into the Polish countryside, stealing, foraging, begging, working. He hides his circumcision and invents a Catholic identity; he forgets his real name, his family, and the street where he lived. But he is later discovered to be Jewish and loses his right arm because a Polish doctor refuses to operate on a Jew. He survives, and immigrates to Israel. Some sexual situations. Awards: Batchelder Honor. Grades: 5–7.

Pausewang, Gudrun, and Patricia Crampton. *Final Journey.*
Puffin, 1998.
Setting: Germany.
Main Character: Female, Alice Dubsky, 11 years old.
Alice spent two years hiding in a basement, protected from the knowledge of the Nazi persecution of the Jews. Now, crammed with nearly fifty people in the hot, stinking darkness of a train car, she faces the fact that they are prisoners being taken to a camp. At Auschwitz, the commander sends some to the right; Alice goes to the left, together with the other children, the old, the disabled, and the newborn baby, to strip for the "showers." Grades: 8–12.

Pressler, Mirjam. *Malka.*
Puffin, 2005.
Setting: Hungary, WWII.
Main Character: Female, Malka, 7 years old.
Dr. Hannah Mai and her two daughters escape German-occupied Poland to Hungary. Malka becomes ill, so Hannah leaves her with a family promising to bring her to Hungary, as soon as she is well. Fearing the Germans, the family turns her out on her own, and Malka is passed along from one family to another, each fearing the Germans. Finally, Malka lives alone in a coal cellar, scrounging for food and remembering to drink liquids as the lady doctor had said was so important. Her mother finally decides to leave her older daughter in Hungary and make the dangerous trip back into Poland to rescue Malka. Grades: 6–10.

Spiegelman, Art. *Maus: A Survivor's Tale: My Father Bleeds History.*
Pantheon, 1986.
Sequel: *Maus II.*
Setting: Poland.
Main Characters: Male, Vladek Spiegelman; Female, Anna Spiegelman; all adult mice.

Based on interviews with his father, Spiegelman tells the Holocaust experience of his parents in a graphic novel. The Jews are mice, the Germans cats, the Poles pigs, the French frogs, and the Americans dogs. Awards: CC; Pulitzer Prize. Grades: YA.

Spinelli, Jerry. *Milkweed.*
Knopf, 2003.
Setting: Warsaw, Poland, 1939.
Main Character: Male, boy without a name.

A young boy doesn't know if he's a Jew or a Gypsy; he has never known family or community. He lives by stealing; his name may be "Stopthief." He lives in the ghetto, where the daily atrocities he witnesses, the hanging bodies, massacres, shootings, roundups, and transports, are the only reality he knows. He finds shelter with a gang of street kids, where one fierce older boy protects him, invents an identity for him, and teaches him survival skills. Grades: 6 and up.

Yolen, Jane. *The Devil's Arithmetic.*
Puffin, 1990.
Setting: Poland, 1940s/contemporary.
Main Character: Female, Hannah, 12 years old.

Hannah is tired of remembering the Holocaust, and is embarrassed by her grandfather, who rants and raves at the mention of the Nazis. During a Passover Seder, Hannah opens the door to welcome the prophet Elijah and is transported to a village in Poland in the 1940s, where everyone thinks that she is Chaya, who has just recovered from a serious illness. She is captured by the Nazis and taken to a death camp, where she is befriended by a young girl named Rivka. Time travel. Awards: CC. Grades: 4–8.

WWII

Boulle, Pierre. *Bridge Over the River Kwai.*
Amereon, 1988.
Setting: Japan, WWII, 1942.
Main Character: Male, Colonel Nicholson, adult.

Colonel Nicholson and his men are in a Japanese prison camp, where they are ordered to build a bridge over the six-hundred-foot wide Kwai River. Grades: YA/A.

Bruchac, Joseph. *Code Talker: A Novel About the Navajo Marines of World War Two.*
Dial, 2005.
Setting: WWII.
Main Character: Male, Ned Begay, a grandfather telling of when he was a young man.

In the measured tones of a Native American storyteller, a Navajo grandfather tells his grandchildren about his World War II experiences. Ned starts with his early schooling at an Anglo boarding school, where the Navajo language is forbidden, and continues through his Marine career as a "code talker," explaining his long silence until "de-classified" in 1969. Begay's lifelong journey honors the Navajos and other Native Americans in the military, fostering respect for their culture. Grades: 5 and up.

Choi, Sook Nyul. *Year of Impossible Goodbyes.*
Yearling, 1993.
Setting: North Korea, WWII.
Main Character: Female, Sookan, 10 years old.
　　While her resistance-fighter father hides in Manchuria and her older brothers toil in Japanese labor camps, Sookan and her family run a sock factory for the war effort, with the dream that the fighting will soon cease. Sookan watches her people become increasingly angry and humiliated when forced to renounce their native ways. The war's end brings a new type of domination from the Russian Communists. Sookan and her brother must escape across the 38th Parallel after their mother has been detained at a Russian checkpoint. Grades: 5–9.

Greene, Bette. *Summer of My German Soldier.*
Puffin, 1999.
Setting: Arkansas, WWII.
Main Character: Female, Patty Bergen, 12 years old.
　　Patty's hometown becomes the site of a camp housing German prisoners during World War II. Although she's Jewish, she begins to see a prison escapee, Anton, not as a Nazi, but as a lonely, frightened young man who understands and appreciates her in a way her parents never will. Awards: CC. Grades: 6–12.

Huth, Angela. *Land Girls: A Spirited Novel of Love and Friendship.*
St. Martin's Griffin, 1998.
Setting: England, WWII.
Main Characters: Female, Ag Marlowe; Female, Prue Lumley; Female, Stella Sherwood; young women.
　　As the war rages in the background, three young city women learn about love and themselves on an English farm. Serving in the Women's Land Army of replacements for farmhands gone to war are Ag, a studious Cambridge undergraduate; Prue, a sexy, working-class hairdresser; and the dreamily romantic Stella. For a year, the three share an attic dormitory at the Lawrence farm in Dorset and do the hard outdoor farm work. Grades: YA/A.

Lawrence, Iain. *B for Buster.*
Delacorte, 2004.
Setting: Europe, WWII.
Main Character: Male, Kak, 16 years old.
　　Kak lies about his age to enlist in the Canadian Air Force, where he works as a wireless operator, flying night bombing raids over Germany, from a base in Yorkshire on an antiquated Halifax bomber named *B for Buster*. His eagerness and idealism slowly turns to disillusionment and horror, as he experiences the grim realities of battle and death. Grades: 7–12.

Mazer, Harry. *A Boy at War: A Novel of Pearl Harbor.*
Simon & Schuster, 2005.
Sequels: *A Boy No More; Heroes Don't Run: A Novel of the Pacific War.*
Setting: Pearl Harbor, WWII.
Main Character: Male, Adam Pelko, 14 years old.

Adam witnesses the Pearl Harbor attack with his friends. Mistaken for an enlisted man, Adam is ordered to help rescue survivors and proves himself a hero. Grades: 7–10.

Mazer, Harry. *The Last Mission.*
Laurel Leaf, 1981.
Setting: Europe, WWII.
Main Character: Male, Jack Raab, 15 years old.

Jack uses a false ID to join the U.S. air force and flies twenty-four bombing missions over Europe. During the last one, he is shot down, taken prisoner, and sent to a German POW camp. Grades: 7–10.

Napoli, Donna Jo. *Stones in Water.*
Puffin, 1999.
Setting: WWII.
Main Character: Male, Roberto, 11 years old.

Sneaking into the cinema to see an American Western during World War II has grave consequences for Roberto, a Venetian middle-school student, his brother, and two friends. The young boys are trapped by German soldiers and transported by train out of Italy as cheap forced labor. Separated from his older brother, timid Roberto relies on his quick-thinking friend, Samuele, but both realize the necessity of hiding Samuele's Jewish identity from their captors and fellow prisoners. Grades: 4–9.

Reuter, Bjarne. *The Boys from St. Petri.*
Puffin, 1996.
Setting: Denmark, WWII.
Main Characters: Male, Lars; Male, Gunnar; Male, Otto, teenagers.

Lars and Gunnar, sons of the local minister, form the core of a small band of Danish high school boys who meet secretly in the loft of St. Petri church and plan petty acts of resistance against the occupying troops. When Otto is recruited into the organization, the level of sabotage escalates. The boys raid an airfield building to steal explosives and plot to destroy a German arms train. The train is destroyed, the boys are caught, and all but Otto are arrested. Grades: 8 and up.

Rylant, Cynthia. *I Had Seen Castles.*
Harcourt, 2004.
Setting: Pittsburgh, WWII.
Main Character: Male, John Dante, 17 years old.

Told when John is 67 and living in Toronto, this is the story of his eagerness to join a war cause in his youth. Grades: 7 and up.

Salisbury, Graham. *Under the Blood Red Sun.*
Dell, 1995.

Setting: Oahu, Hawaii, WWII.

Main Character: Male, Tomi Nakaji, 13 years old.

Tomi and his best friend, Billy, witness the bombing of Pearl Harbor. Tomi's father, a poor fisherman, and later his grandfather are arrested, and his father's fishing partner is killed. Tomi assumes responsibility for the family honor and *katama*, or samurai sword. Racial/ethnic tension escalates following the Japanese attack, and Tomi's mother loses her job as a housekeeper. Billy disappears for a while, though he returns as a loyal and helpful friend. Awards: CC; Scott O'Dell. Grades: 6–8.

Taylor, Theodore. *The Bomb.*

HarperTrophy, 1997.

Setting: Bikini Atoll, WWII.

Main Character: Male, Sorry Rinamu, 14 years old.

Sorry lives on Bikini Atoll. Shortly after the Americans liberate his island home, they decide to use it as a site for atomic testing, with the promise that people could return to their island in two years. Sorry's uncle Abram argues that it would never again be safe to inhabit, but the islanders agree to the plan. When Abram dies suddenly, Sorry vows to fulfill his uncle's intention to stop the tests and is joined by several others. A serious misjudgment leads the young man and his companions to be blown up during the test. Awards: Scott O'Dell. Grades: 6–10.

Taylor, Theodore. *The Cay.*

Delacorte, 1987.

Setting: Curaçao, West Indies, WWII.

Main Character: Male, Phillip, 11 years old.

Philip's mother wanted to return to the safety of Virginia but their ship is sunk by the Germans, and Phillip and his mother end up on separate life rafts. After being hit on the head with a beam from the sinking ship, Phillip awakens to find himself alone with Timothy, an old black ship hand, and Stew Cat, the ship's tomcat. The three survive on a raft for several days, during which time Phillip loses his eyesight due to the head injury. They eventually come ashore on a small unpopulated island. Phillip must learn to deal with his blindness and overcome his dislike for Timothy. Grades: 5–8.

Thesman, Jean. *Molly Donnelly.*

Houghton Mifflin, 1993.

Setting: Seattle, WWII.

Main Character: Female, Molly Donnelly, 12 years old.

Molly's world is turned topsy-turvy when war is declared. There are nightly blackouts and long lines to buy strictly rationed goods; strangers flood into Seattle to work in the newly opened factories; her best friend (a Japanese girl) is deported to an internment camp; and a beloved cousin dies. Most of the household duties fall to Molly when her mother goes to work in a factory. Her optimistic and thoughtful Uncle Charlie and her own reserves of strength see her through. Grades: 7–10.

Watkins, Yoko Kawashima. *So Far From the Bamboo Grove.*

Peter Smith, 1995.

Sequel: *My Brother, My Sister, and I.*

Setting: North Korea, WWII.

Main Character: Female, Yoko Kawashima, 11 years old.

A true account that is filled with violence and death, yet is also a story of family love and life. Yoko had led a peaceful and secure life as the daughter of a Japanese government official stationed in North Korea. Abruptly, she, her older sister, Ko, and their mother flee the vengeance-seeking North Korean Communists and eventually make their way to war-ravaged Japan. All their Japanese relatives are dead, and their mother dies. Yoko and Ko create a home to await the return of their brother. Points of view alternates between the sisters and the brother. Grades: 6 and up.

Westall, Robert. *Time of Fire.*

Scholastic, 1997.

Setting: England, WWII.

Main Character: Male, Sonny, young boy.

Sonny has memorized all the planes on the aircraft recognition chart. His mother is killed in a bombing raid doing an errand he forgot to do, and he is now overwhelmed by guilt. He tells his father what kind of plane it was that killed his mother. Sonny and his father grapple with feelings of vengeance. Grades: 6–9.

Wulffson, Don. *Soldier X.*

Puffin, 2003.

Setting: Russia, WWII.

Main Character: Male, Erik Brandt, 16 years old.

Erik is forced to fight for the German army, and because of his knowledge of the Russian language, he is sent to the Russian front with only a few weeks of basic training and instructions to kill or be killed. After the first battle, Erik makes a life-altering decision to take the uniform of a dead Russian soldier and pretend to be Russian for most of his remaining time as a soldier, surviving serious wounds and finding the love of his life while he recuperates in a war hospital. There he pretends to have amnesia as "Soldier X." Based on a true story. Grades: 8 and up.

1950s/POST WWII

Bee, Clair. *Touchdown Pass.*

Broadman & Holman, 1998.

Series: Chip Hilton Sports: over 24 titles.

Setting: Valley Falls.

Main Character: Male, Chip Hilton, 16 years old.

Former coach Clair Bee wrote twenty-four volumes of sports stories set in the 40s, 50s, and 60s. Chip Hilton and his friends play baseball, basketball, and football. Grades: 5–8.

Cormier, Robert. *Heroes.*

Laurel Leaf, 2000.

Setting: Hometown.

Main Character: Male, Francis Cassavant, 18 years old.

Although he can still see and hear, a grenade has blown away Francis's nose, ears, teeth, and cheeks, leaving him faceless. Hiding his wounds with bandages and a white silk scarf, Francis welcomes the anonymity his mutilation brings him. He has returned to his hometown with a secret mission: a plot for revenge against his enemy, Larry LaSalle. Awards: RR. Grades: 8–11.

Cormier, Robert. *Tunes for Bears to Dance To.*
Laurel Leaf, 1994.
Setting: 1950s, post WWII.
Main Character: Male, Henry Levine, 14 years old.

Henry is lucky to be employed. Since his brother's recent death, his father is paralyzed by depression and his mother works long hours to support the family. Unfortunately, Henry's boss is a bigoted, abusive individual, whose hatred of others is so consuming that he intentionally sets out to corrupt the boy's goodness. He forces Henry to commit an ugly, violent act, betraying a friendship with an elderly neighbor who has lost his home and family to the Nazis. As part of his rehabilitative therapy, Mr. Levine lovingly carves his vanished village and its population out of wood. Grades: 6–9.

Wolff, Virginia Euwer. *Bat 6.*
Scholastic, 1998.
Setting: Oregon, May 28, 1949.
Main Characters: Female, Shazam; Female, Aki, 11 years old.

The members of two rival girls' baseball teams begin the traditional annual game between them, but are interrupted when Shazam violently attacks Aki, a Japanese American. Told from twenty-one points of view. Awards: Book Hook; CC; RR. Grades: 5–8.

1960s/CIVIL RIGHTS MOVEMENT

Almond, David. *Fire-Eaters.*
Delacorte, 2004.
Setting: Great Britain, 1962.
Main Character: Male, Bobby Burns, 12 years old.

Bobby and his mom take a day trip to Newcastle, where Bobby encounters an odd little man, Mr. McNulty. He is his own wandering sideshow; he pierces his cheeks with a dagger, escapes from shackles, and breathes fire in exchange for coins. Bobby enrolls at the prestigious Sacred Heart School with his new, upper-crust neighbor, Daniel, and both quickly suffer at the hands of Mr. Todd, a masochistic teacher. Daniel plots revenge while Bobby worries that his father's increasingly frail health might prove fatal. Overhanging everything is the Cuban missile crisis and possible nuclear war. Grades: 7 and up.

Alvarez, Julia. *Before We Were Free.*
Laurel Leaf, 2004.
Setting: Dominican Republic, 1960–1961.
Main Character: Female, Anita, 12 years old.

Anita's cousins, the Garcia girls, abruptly leave for the United States with their parents; Anita's immediate family members are now the only ones occupying the extended family's compound. Anita's parents protect her from the criminal and even murderous ways of her country's ruler and also from knowledge of their involvement in a planned coup. Her crush on the American boy next door is at first as important as knowing that the maid is almost certainly working for the secret police and spying on them. When the revolution fails, Anita's father and uncle are immediately arrested, and she and her mother go underground, living in secret in their friends' bedroom closet. Awards: Pura Belpré. Grades: 7 and up.

Curtis, Christopher Paul. *The Watsons Go to Birmingham—1963.*
Delacorte, 1995.
Setting: Alabama, 1963.
Main Character: Male, Kenny Watson, 9 years old.

The Watsons leave Flint, Michigan, to visit relatives in Birmingham, Alabama, just in time for the historical church bombing. Awards: CC; Newbery; Coretta Scott King. Grades: 6–10.

Davis, Ossie. *Just Like Martin.*
Puffin, 1995.
Setting: 1963.
Main Character: Male, Isaac Stone, 14 years old.

Isaac admires Martin Luther King, Jr. and wants to go to the civil rights march in Washington, D.C. Since his mother has just died, his father is worried that something will happen to him. His father is also bitter from the Korean War and disagrees with King's nonviolent methods. Grades: 7–9.

Gaines, Ernest J. *The Autobiography of Miss Jane Pittman.*
Bantam, 1982.
Setting: Louisiana, 1960s.
Main Character: Female, Miss Jane Pittman, 110 years old.

Miss Jane was a child at the end of the Civil War, and now, at 110 years old, she has lived to see the flowering of the civil rights movement. She has seen it all and relates her recollections in tape-recorded conversations. Awards: CC. Grades: 7–12.

King, Stephen. *Hearts in Atlantis.*
Pocket, 2000.
Setting: 1960s.

A collection of five stories about kids in the 1960s, with the Vietnam War in the background. Awards: CC. Grades: 9–12.

Krisher, Trudy. *Spite Fences.*
Laurel Leaf, 1996.
Setting: Kinship, Georgia, 1960.
Main Character: Female, Maggie Pugh, 13 years old.

Maggie has lived in Kinship all her life. The poor live on the west side of town and the rich live at the north end. White folks use one bathroom at Byer's Drugs and colored folks use another, until the summer of 1960, when Maggie's younger sister triumphs in the Hayes County Little Miss Contest and Maggie gets her first camera, a tool that becomes a way for her to find independence and a different kind of truth. Civil Rights. Awards: CC. Grades: 7–10.

1970s/Vietnam War

Crist-Evans, Craig. *Amaryllis.*
Candlewick, 2003.
Setting: Singer Island, Florida, 1967.
Main Characters: Male, Frank Staples, 18 years old; Male, Jimmy Staples, younger teen brother.

Frank enlists to escape the war at home with his alcoholic father. He becomes a heroin addict after being wounded and is soon missing in action. His younger brother, Jimmy, blames their father. Grades: 9 and up.

Eisner, Will. *Last Day in Vietnam.*
Dark Horse, 2000.
Setting: Vietnam.

Six short stories about the feelings soldiers have during wartime, presented as sepia-toned graphic novels. Grades: YA/A.

McDaniel, Lurlene. *When Happily Ever After Ends.*
Laurel Leaf, 1992.
Setting: Horse ranch.
Main Character: Female, Shannon Campbell, 15 years old.

Shannon and her mother try to make sense of her Vietnam vet father's violent suicide. Grades: YA.

Myers, Walter Dean. *Fallen Angels.*
Scholastic, 1988.
Setting: Vietnam, late 1960s.
Main Character: Male, Perry, 18 years old.

A Harlem teen who volunteers when he doesn't get into college, Perry questions why he and the United States are in Vietnam, and why black troops get the most dangerous assignments. For mature readers. Awards: CC; Coretta Scott King. Grades: 8–12.

O'Brien, Tim. *The Things They Carried.*
Broadway, 1998.
Setting: Canada.
Main Character: Male, Tim, young man.

Twenty-two short works about Vietnam soldiers and their lives after the war, for mature readers. Awards: CC. Grades: 10–12.

Paulsen, Gary. *The Beet Fields: Memories of a Sixteenth Summer.*
Laurel Leaf, 2002.
Setting: North Dakota, 1955.
Main Character: Male, "The Boy," 16 years old.

"The boy," as he is called, wakes up to find his drunk mother in his bed and realizes that tonight "something [is] different, wrong, about her need for him." He runs away and lands a backbreaking job on a beet farm in North Dakota, where his wages are cancelled out by the farmer's charges for the use of his hoe, for the tumbledown lodgings, and for the only food available, sandwiches made of week-old bread that cost a dollar apiece. Eventually the boy starts working for a carnival, where he learns carny scams and is initiated into sex by the carnival stripper, Ruby. Awards: CC. Grades: 9–12.

Paulsen, Gary. **The Car.**
Harcourt, 1994.
Setting: Cleveland, Ohio.
Main Character: Male, Terry Anders, 14 years old.

Terry's parents abandon him, and Terry builds the car kit his dad left behind. He decides to drive it west to Oregon to find his uncle. He meets up with two Vietnam vets, who travel with him. Grades: 7 and up.

Soto, Gary. **Jesse.**
Scholastic, 1996.
Setting: Fresno, California, 1968.
Main Character: Male, Jesse, 17 years old.

Mexican American Jesse works as a field laborer to pay his way at the community college while the threat of the Vietnam draft hangs over his head. Awards: CC. Grades: 8–10.

Talbert, Marc. **The Purple Heart.**
Backinprint.com, 2000.
Setting: Midwest.
Main Character: Male, Luke Canvin, elementary age.

Luke treasures the Purple Heart awarded his father, and yet he is afraid to ask the brooding man how he earned it. His sensitive, pregnant mother encourages him to be patient with his father, who must accept his injury, find a new career, and cope with critics of the war. He eventually learns the traumatic but unglorious details of his father's injury, and his romantic illusions about the Purple Heart are replaced by a realistic understanding of courage. Grades: 5–8.

1980s–1990s

Antle, Nancy. **Lost in the War.**
Puffin, 2000.
Setting: 1982.
Main Character: Female, Lisa Grey, 12 years old.

Lisa describes her life with her mother, who is haunted and depressed by memories of her tour of duty as a nurse in Vietnam and by the experiences of her soldier husband, who was killed there. When Lisa's history teacher assigns a project on Vietnam, Lisa rebels, tired of the war that has plagued her family. Grades: 5–8.

Kubert, Joe. **Fax from Sarajevo: A Story of Survival.**
Sagebrush, 1998.
Setting: Sarajevo, Bosnia and Herzegovina U.C., 1992.
Main Character: Male, Ervin Rustemagic, adult.

The Rustemagic family survives the deadly siege of their homeland, and over the next $2^1/_2$ years Ervin Rustemagic sends sporadic faxes to his American friend and client, Joe Kubert. The graphic portion of the book is followed by a condensed version of each chapter, with photos of the actual people and places depicted in the narrative. The package was put together by the Rustemagic's American friend and fellow comic artist, Joe Kubert. Grades: YA.

Mason, Bobbie Ann. *In Country.*
HarperPerennial, 2005.
Setting: Hopewell, Kentucky, 1980s.
Main Character: Female, Sam, 17 years old.

Sam examines the effects the Vietnam War has had on her life. She lost a father she never knew and is now living with Uncle Emmett, who seems to be suffering from the effects of Agent Orange. She also sees the war's effects on the other vets in her community. Awards: CC. Grades: YA.

Mead, Alice. *Adem's Cross.*
Laurel Leaf, 1998.
Setting: Kosovo,Yugoslavia, 1990s.
Main Character: Male, Adem, 14 years old.

Adem, an Albanian, tries to survive despite the random violence and cruelty of the Serbians. Adem goes to a school without chairs, books, or heat, where the school's annual first day tradition is getting tear gassed and beating up the principal. Personal freedom is an even more valuable commodity than nonexistent gasoline. Adem's beloved older sister attempts to make a stand and is cut down by Serbian bullets, and Adem is consumed by guilt that he might have prevented her death. After Adem is mutilated by Serbian soldiers, he escapes, aided by a Serb and a gypsy, who is killed during the flight. Grades: 5–8.

Sacco, Joe, and Christopher Hitchens. *Safe Area Gorazde: The War in Eastern Bosnia 1992–1995.*
Fantagraphics, 2002.
Setting: Bosnia, 1992–1995.
Main Character: Male, Joe Sacco, adult.

In this graphic novel, Sacco alternates between detailing his own visits to Gorazde, giving a straightforward history of the war, and letting his friends and interviewees recount their own terrible experiences. Grades: YA/A

RESOURCES: ADDITIONAL TITLES

Adamson, Lynda G. 1999. *American Historical Fiction: An Annotated Guide to Novels for Adults and Young Adults.* Phoenix, AZ: Oryx Press.
Berg, Rebecca L. 2004. *The Great Depression in Literature for Youth: A Geographical Study of Families and Young Lives: A Guide and Resource Book.* Lanham, MD: Scarecrow Press.
Overstreet, Deborah Wilson. 1998. *Unencumbered by History: The Vietnam Experience in Young Adult Fiction.* Lanham, MD: Scarecrow Press.

Sullivan, Edward T. 1999. *The Holocaust in Literature for Youth: A Guide and Resource Book.* Lanham, MD: Scarecrow Press.
Wee, Patricia Hachten, and Robert James Wee. 2004. *World War II in Literature for Youth: A Guide and Resource Book.* Lanham, MD: Scarecrow Press.

CHAPTER 13

HORROR

According to *Connecting Young Adults and Libraries*, the horror genre is the most popular one with teen readers. The essential element in horror is a monster, which may be in the form of a beast, a serial killer, a disease, or even a mental state. In horror stories, readers experience fear in a controlled setting, which may help them deal with real fears or may be a fix for a thrill seeker. Some say that the reason teens are so addicted to horror stories is because disgusting monsters, ghouls, and tentacled amphibians psychologically and creatively personify teens' innermost angst. Usually suspenseful, a good horror story will keep the reader turning pages.

Classic Horror
Dead Narrators
Demons and Possession
Ghosts
Gruesome
Monsters
Occult and Supernatural
Scary Stories
Vampires
Werewolves
Witches
Resources: Additional Titles

Classic Horror

Bradbury, Ray. ***Something Wicked This Way Comes.***
Avon, 1998.
Setting: Green Town, Illinois.
Main Characters: Male, James Nightshade; Male, William Halloway; both 13 years old.
    William and James save the souls of their small midwestern town (and their own) when a "dark carnival" arrives one autumn midnight. Grades: YA/A.

Endore, Guy. ***The Werewolf of Paris.***
Carol Publishing, 1992.
Setting: France, nineteenth century.

Main Character: Male, Bertrand Caillet, adult.

Werewolf Bertrand Caillet travels around seeking to calm the beast within. A sympathetic character, Bertrand's acts seem mild in comparison to the atrocities going on around him. Originally published in 1933, this book has influenced generations of horror and science fiction authors who came after it. Grades: YA/A.

Hawthorne, Nathaniel. *Twice Told Tales.*
Modern Library, 2001.
Setting: New England.

Thirty-nine short stories reflecting Hawthorne's moral insight and his lifelong interest in the history of Puritan New England. Originally published in 1837. Grades: YA/A.

Jackson, Shirley. *The Haunting of Hill House.*
Amereon, 1959.
Setting: New England.
Main Character: Female, Eleanor Vance, 32 years old.

Eleanor has always been a loner, bitterly resentful of the eleven years she lost while nursing her dying mother. Eleanor has always sensed that something *big* would happen to her, and one day she receives an unusual invitation from Dr. John Montague, a man fascinated by "supernatural manifestations." He organizes a ghost watch, inviting Eleanor, his assistant, Theodora, and Luke, a well-to-do aristocrat. They meet at Hill House, a foreboding structure of towers, buttresses, Gothic spires, gargoyles, strange angles, and rooms within rooms. Grades: YA/A.

Jackson, Shirley. *The Lottery, and Other Stories.*
Farrar, Straus & Giroux, 2005.
Setting: A village.
Main Character: Female, Tessie Hutchison, adult.

Tessie lives in a happy, healthy small town that holds an annual lottery, but the object of the lottery is to lose, not win. As the winner of this year's lottery, Tessie is stoned to death by her friends and relatives. Grades: YA/A.

Poe, Edgar Allan. *Tales of Mystery and Imagination.*
Usborne, 2004.

Locked doors, bricked-up alcoves, and premature burial close in on Poe's narrators as they, like their victims, are cut off from light, air, and human society in forty-six tales. Originally published in 1845. Grades: 6 and up.

Shelley, Mary Wollstonecraft. *Frankenstein.*
Bantam Classics, 1984.
Setting: Europe.
Main Character: Male, Dr. Victor Frankenstein, adult.

Dr. Frankenstein is an ambitious, brilliant scientist who wants to play God by creating a human life. When his creation comes to life, it turns out to be a monster, terrifying its creator. Yet, the monster is fully human—sad and then enraged by the hatred and rejection he receives. Originally published in 1818. Grades: 9 and up.

Stevenson, Robert Lewis. ***The Strange Case of Dr. Jekyll and Mr. Hyde.***
Signet, 1997.
Setting: London.
Main Character: Male, Dr. Jekyll, adult.

Dr. Jekyll invents a poison that changes a person into his alter ego. The battle between man's good nature and his dark side is played out in the character of Dr. Jekyll, whose monster is himself, Mr. Hyde. Originally published in 1886. Awards: CC. Grades: 7–12.

Stoker, Bram. ***Dracula.***
Signet, 1997.
Setting: Transylvania, late nineteenth century.
Main Characters: Male, Jonathan Harker; Male, Count Dracula, adult.

Harker, a business agent from London, visits Transylvania, where he meets Count Dracula to discuss his transition to London. Harker becomes Dracula's victim and is unable to tell his fiancé, Mina, that Dracula is a vampire. Dracula and Harker, now a damaged man who eats insects, come to London. It is up to the God-fearing Van Helsing to destroy Dracula by stabbing him with a stake through his heart while he sleeps in his daytime coffin. Originally published in 1897. Grades: 7 and up.

Wells, H.G. ***The Invisible Man.***
Signet Classics, 2002.
Setting: Iping, England, 1890s.
Main Character: Male, Griffin, adult.

Griffin, an obscure scientist, has discovered how to make himself invisible. He arrives in town with dark glasses, gloves, and his head wrapped in bandages. He can't find a way to become visible again and goes murderously insane. Originally published in 1897. Grades: YA/A.

DEAD NARRATORS

Crutcher, Chris. ***The Sledding Hill.***
Greenwillow, 2005.
Setting: Idaho.
Main Character: Male, Billy Bartholomew, 14 years old.

A dead narrator and an author who writes himself into the story gives this novel about censorship an interesting twist. After he dies and is found by his best friend, Eddie, Billy tries to help Eddie deal with his recent losses, supporting him when one of Chris Crutcher's books is challenged at school. A statement against censorship with no profanity, sex, drugs, alcohol, or violence. Grades: 7 and up.

Griffin, Adele. ***Where I Want to Be.***
Putnam, 2005.
Setting: Rhode Island.
Main Characters: Female, Jane; Female, Lily, teenagers.

Mentally ill, Jane is envious of her popular normal sister, Lily. When Jane is killed in an accident, their story continues in alternating chapters, as they try to make peace with one another. Grades: 7 and up.

Sebold, Alice. *The Lovely Bones.*
Little, Brown, 2002.
Setting: 1973.
Main Character: Female, Susie Salmon, 14 years old.

Susie was lured to a hideaway by a neighbor, Mr. Harvey, then raped and murdered. Susie learns to accept her death and watches over her family in their grief. Grades: YA/A.

Sleator, William. *Rewind.*
Dutton, 1999.
Setting: 1990s.
Main Character: Male, Peter, 11 years old.

Peter gets three chances to go back in time and avoid his death, but he is not sure what needs to be changed to do so. Peter is adopted. Grades: 5–8.

Soto, Gary. *The Afterlife.*
Harcourt, 2003.
Setting: Fresno, California.
Main Character: Male, Chuy, 17 years old.

The book begins with Chuy being knifed in a restroom; he then dies. Now Chuy is able to accomplish a few things that he wasn't able to do in life. He saves a life, punishes a thug, falls in love, and recognizes how much he is loved by family and friends. A glossary in the back helps with the Mexican Spanish words. Grades: 6 and up.

Whitcomb, Laura. *A Certain Slant of Light.*
Graphia, 2005.
Setting: High school.
Main Character: Female, Helen, teenage.

Helen died 130 years ago but didn't go to heaven. Her spirit attaches to human hosts and has been undetected until now, with her current English teacher host, Mr. Brown. James is another ghost who has inhabited the body of a student in the class. James and Helen fall in love, and he teaches Helen how to get a body of her own. She moves to the body of Jenny, a teen girl whose spirit has left her body. For mature readers. Grades: 9 and up.

Zevin, Gabrielle. *Elsewhere.*
Farrar, Straus, & Giroux, 2005.
Setting: Elsewhere.
Main Character: Female, Liz Hall, 15 years old.

Liz is looking forward to all life has to offer when she is killed in a hit-and-run accident. Struggling to understand what has happened to her and all she has lost, she can't accept her new existence in Elsewhere. The reader witnesses her passages backward in time, to when she can journey down the river to be reborn. Comforting to grieving readers. Grades: 7–10.

DEMONS AND POSSESSION

King, Stephen. *Christine.*
Signet, 1983.
Setting: Pittsburgh, Pennsylvania.
Main Character: Male, Arnie Cunningham, teenager.
   Arnie gets a car—a 1958 red and white Plymouth Fury, his beloved Christine. But he doesn't know the car is possessed; it is alive and obsessed with Arnie. Anyone that comes between Arnie and Christine ends up dead. Awards: CC. Grades: 9–12.

Koja, Kathy. *Blue Mirror.*
Farrar, Straus, & Giroux, 2004.
Setting: Blue Mirror coffeehouse.
Main Character: Female, Maggy, 16 years old.
   Maggy, a gifted artist, keeps a sketchbook called "The Blue Mirror" that shares its name with the coffeehouse where she regularly nurses a cappuccino for hours and draws what she sees. Tourists, bicycle cops, and especially the homeless kids or "skwatters" are her regular subjects. Maggy meets an attractive skwatter, Cole, who takes a keen interest in her. Mags forgets about her disastrous home life and feels as if she has finally met someone who understands her, but Cole is no Prince Charming. Grades: 9 and up.

Westall, Robert. *Demons and Shadows: The Ghostly Best Stories of Robert Westall.*
Farrar, Straus & Giroux, 1993.
   British short stories about vampires, corpses, shape-shifting cats, and hauntings. Grades: 9 and up.

Wooding, Chris. *Haunting of Alaizabel Cray.*
Orchard, 2004.
Setting: Alternate Victorian England.
Main Character: Male, Thaniel, 17 years old.
   Hot on the trail of a vampire-like "Cradlejack" wych-hunter, Thaniel stumbles upon beautiful Alaizabel Cray, who unknowingly has been possessed by an "old wych" named Thatch. Determined to rescue Alaizabel, Thaniel slashes and burns his way through a nightmarish city crawling with enough ghastly human and supernatural villains to stock a wax museum. Grades: 7 and up.

GHOSTS

Card, Orson Scott. *Homebody.*
HarperCollins, 2000.
Setting: North Carolina, 1990s.
Main Character: Male, Don Lark, adult.
   Don enjoys fixing up the old Bellamy Mansion and the lives associated with the tragedies that occurred there. He encounters danger and true love. Awards: CC. Grades: 7–12.

De Lint, Charles. *The Blue Girl.*
Viking, 2004.
Setting: Redding High School.
Main Characters: Male, Adrian, a teen ghost; Female, Imogene Yeck, 17 years old.

On her first day of school in a new town, Imogene meets Maxine, and the two become friends despite their polar opposite personalities; Imogene is bold and brash, while Maxine is mousy and quiet. Imogene notices a pale boy watching her and learns the story of Ghost, Adrian, another outcast who was harassed by bullies, died under mysterious circumstances a few years earlier, and now haunts the school. His only companions are a handful of amoral fairies. Adrian and Imogene alternate as narrators. Grades: 9–12.

Hahn, Mary Downing. *Look for Me by Moonlight.*
Clarion, 1995.
Setting: Maine.
Main Character: Female, Cynda, 16 years old.

Cynda moves in with her estranged father and his much younger wife at the isolated Maine inn by the ocean that they run; the inn is haunted by the ghost of a young woman murdered there some sixty years ago. Soon after Cynda's arrival, handsome, sophisticated Victor Morthanos checks in for a monthlong stay. Cynda's half-brother, Todd, hates him on sight, but Cynda quickly falls in love and feels Victor alone understands and appreciates her. By the time Cynda figures out that Victor is a vampire and the murderer of the ghostly girl, she is nearly a ghost herself. Grades: 7 and up.

Hamilton, Virginia. *Sweet Whispers, Brother Rush.*
Philomel, 1982.
Setting: 1980s.
Main Characters: Female, Teresa "Tree," 15 years old; Male, Dabney, 17 years old.

Tree, resentful of her working mother who leaves her in charge of Dab, her retarded brother, encounters the ghost of Brother Rush her dead uncle. She knows she must follow him through the magic mirror to find out the truth. Awards: CC. Newbery Honor; Grades: 7–12.

Hoffman, Nina Kiriki. *A Stir of Bones.*
Viking, 2003.
Sequels: *A Red Heart of Memories; Past the Size of Dreaming.*
Setting: Haunted house.
Main Character: Female, Susan Backstrom, 12 years old.

Susan is a prisoner of her abusive father, who beats his wife whenever he disapproves of his daughter's behavior. At the library, Susan overhears a group of kids talking about entering a haunted house, and she convinces them to let her go with them. She discovers that the house has a life of its own and forms a close bond with it and with Nathan, the ghost of a boy who committed suicide in it. She decides to kill herself to be with Nathan and the house forever, and it is up to her new friends to stop her. Grades: 7 and up.

Morrison, Toni. *Beloved.*
Knopf, 1987.
Setting: Ohio, 1870s.
Main Character: Female, Sethe, adult.

Sethe wants peace for her family after the Civil War but finds her new home haunted by a troubled spirit she wants to believe is the spirit of her dead baby, Beloved. For mature readers. Awards: CC; Pulitzer Prize. Grades: 10–12.

Naylor, Phyllis Reynolds. *Jade Green: A Ghost Story.*
Atheneum, 2000.
Setting: South Carolina.
Main Character: Female, Judith Sparrow, 15 years old.

Judith lives with her uncle in a house haunted by the ghost of a young woman. Recently orphaned, Judith wonders if her one small transgression is causing the mysterious happenings. Grades: 6–8.

Rosenbloom, Eileen. *Stuck Down.*
Llewellyn, 2005.
Setting: Nirvanaville.
Main Character: Male, Kevin, 17 years old.

Kevin fights with his father, storms off, and dies in a skiing accident. He's happily spending his afterlife with his girlfriend in Nirvanaville, when he volunteers to take a letter from his girlfriend to her mother on Earth. He flies there on a motorcycle, but gets arrested, and his father is the prosecuting attorney. Kevin finally convinces his father he is his dead son, and they reconcile. Kevin goes back to Nirvanaville knowing he will be with his family again someday. Grades: 6–10.

Wallace, Rich. *Restless: A Ghost's Story.*
Viking, 2003.
Setting: Sturbridge, Pennsylvania.
Main Character: Male, Herbie, 17 years old.

Athletic Herbie is running through the town cemetery when he meets Eamon Connolly, the ghost of a distant relative, and Frank, the ghost of his older brother. Grades: 8 and up.

Yolen Jane and David Wilgus. *Here There Be Ghosts.*
Harcourt, 1998.

Short stories, poems, and pencil drawings about likable ghosts with endearing personalities. Grades: 6–9.

GRUESOME

Alten, Steve. *Meg: A Novel of Deep Terror.*
Tsunami, 2005.
Sequels: *The Trench; Meg: Primal Waters.*
Setting: California.
Main Character: Male, Jonas Taylor, 45 years old.

Carcharodon megalodon, a prehistoric ancestor of the shark, survived in the abyss, trapped in place by seven miles of frigid ocean water. Paleontologist Jonas Taylor watches helplessly as the "Meg" that destroys his friend's capsule is then ripped to shreds by its mate, who then migrates to the surface. The female Meg is pregnant and hungry and far too large to be contained. Taylor and other scientists try to corral the beast, while idiotic tourists and news crews flock to the scene to watch. Grades: YA/A.

Barker, Clive. *Thief of Always.*
HarperCollins, 1997.
Setting: Holiday House.
Main Character: Male, Harvey Swick, 10 years old.

Mr. Hood's Holiday House has stood for a thousand years, welcoming countless children to its miracles: a blissful round of treats and seasons, where every childhood can be satisfied . . . for a price. Bored, Harvey enters the house, mindless of the consequences. Awards: CC. Grades: 6–9.

Cormier, Robert. *Tenderness.*
Delacorte, 1997.
Setting: Massachusetts.
Main Characters: Male, Eric Poole, 18 years old; Female, Lori, 15 years old.

Lori has a crush on Eric, who was recently released from a juvenile correctional facility for murdering his mother and stepfather. Eric believes Lori is a witness to his undiscovered murders. For mature readers. Awards: CC; VOYA Perfect Ten. Grades: 9–12.

Fleischman, Paul. *Fate Totally Worse Than Death.*
Candlewick, 1995.
Setting: Cliffside High.
Main Characters: Female, Danielle; Female, Tiffany; Female, Brooke; all teenagers.

In this spoof of teen horror novels, rich and cliquish Danielle, Tiffany, and Brooke send outsider Charity Chase off a cliff to her death. Now Helga, an exchange student from Norway, seems to be Charity's avenging ghost, and the three girls are suffering all the signs of old age. Grades: 7 and up.

Gaiman, Neil. *Coraline.*
HarperCollins, 2002.
Setting: England.
Main Character: Female, Coraline, young girl.

Coraline's parents are preoccupied, and that leaves plenty of time for Coraline to explore the big old house she lives in and the gardens around it. She's counted all the windows and doors, and it is the fourteenth door that is sometimes blocked with bricks that opens to another universe. Caroline steps through, and at first the mirrored world and family seem much more interesting. Her other parents have button eyes and are determined to keep Coraline on their side of the door. Awards: Hugo; Nebula. Grades: 5 and up.

King, Stephen. *It.*
Signet, 1987.

Setting: Derry, Maine, 1958.
Main Character: Seven teens.

It fed on children, hunting them, preying on them, and devouring them. It could shape itself in any way It liked, but always appeared as a clown. The seven friends all had one thing in common: they had all escaped It at some point. In that summer, they learned about It, confronted It, and killed It . . . or so they thought. Twenty-eight years later, they are all called back to Derry when a boy is thrown off a bridge by a clown with balloons. Awards: CC. Grades: 9–12.

King, Stephen. *The Shining.*
Doubleday, 1990.
Setting: Overlook Hotel.
Main Character: Male, Jack Torrance, adult.

Jack takes his family to the Overlook Hotel for the winter so he can finish his new novel. It seems like the perfect place, until the resident evil ghost torments Jack with his alcoholism, taunts Wendy to try to save her family, and makes little Danny the center of its vicious desires. Awards: CC. Grades: 9–12.

Morgan, Nicola. *Fleshmarket.*
Delacorte, 2004.
Setting: Edinburgh, Scotland, early 1822.
Main Character: Male, Robbie Anderson, 14 years old.

Robbie is only 8 years old when his mother dies at the hands of Dr. Knox, a savage surgeon with an interest in human anatomy. His father disappears when Robbie is 14 and he is left to care for his sister, Essie. Robbie gets involved with two shady characters who provide fresh bodies for Dr. Knox, and he begins to realize people are being murdered for his experiments. Grades: 8 and up.

Napoli, Donna Jo. *Breath.*
Atheneum, 2003.
Setting: Hamelin, 1284.
Main Character: Male, Salz, 12 years old.

There are torrential rains, animals are sick and dying, and the people are suffering from a variety of maladies. It could be the infestation of rats, and Salz hopes the Piper can help them in this retelling of the Pied Piper of Hamelin. Grades: 8 and up.

Nix, Garth. *Sabriel.*
HarperCollins, 1996.
Sequels: *Lireal; The Abhorsen.*
Setting: Old Kingdom.
Main Character: Female, Sabriel, 18 years old.

Sabriel's father, the Abhorsen, contacts her after his death. She leaves her school in the real world to return to her magical homeland to save him and her world, bridging the boundary between life and death. Awards: CC. Grades: 7–10.

Westerfeld, Scott. *Peeps.*
Penguin/Razorbill, 2005.

Setting: Manhattan, New York City.
Main Character: Male, Cal, college freshman, 18 years old.

"Peeps" are maniacal cannibals that cause illness. Cal was lucky: he contracted the sexually transmitted disease during a one-night stand, but it never developed into its full-blown form. Now he works for an underground bureau in Manhattan that tracks down peeps. Apart from cravings for rare meat and enforced celibacy, life is okay, until a hip, cute journalism student intensifies Cal's yearnings for companionship. Peeps appear to have an evolutionary purpose. Grades: 9–12.

Zindel, Paul. *Rats.*
Hyperion, 1999.
Setting: Manhattan, New York City.
Main Character: Female, Sarah, 15 years old.

Rats from Staten Island invade Manhattan, until Sarah comes to the rescue with a plan to hypnotize the rats. Plenty of gross-out scenes. Awards: CC. Grades: 6–9.

MONSTERS

Koontz, Dean. *Watchers.*
Berkley, 1987.
Setting: California.
Main Character: Male, Travis Cornell, adult.

Two very different creatures, the result of DNA research, escape from a top-secret laboratory and roam the land. One is divinely inspiring, engendering love and caring. The other is a hellish nightmare that leaves unspeakable slaughter in its wake. Awards: CC. Grades: 8–12.

Plum-Ucci, Carol. *The She.*
Harcourt, 2003.
Setting: New Jersey.
Main Character: Male, Evan Barrett, 17 years old.

Evan unknowingly ingests the LSD put into his drink as a prank, and the whole horrible evening his parents disappeared in the ocean unfolds again: the violent storm, the frantic mayday call from his parents that came through on the family's ship-to-shore radio, the hopelessness of knowing that there was nothing he or his older brother, Emmett, could do. Now Evan must discover once and for all what really happened to his parents. Was it the shrieking, ship-eating sea hag known as The She, who lies in wait for victims off the Jersey Shore? Grades: 9 and up.

Zindel, Paul. *Doom Stone.*
Hyperion, 1996.
Setting: Stonehenge, England.
Main Character: Male, Jackson, 15 years old.

While driving past Stonehenge on his way to visit his anthropologist aunt, Jackson sees a creature mauling a young man. Aunt Sarah is leading a team of scientists and military personnel to investigate a series of mutilations in the area. Awards: CC. Grades: 7–10.

Zindel, Paul. **Loch.**
Hyperion, 2005.
Setting: Lake Alban, Vermont.
Main Character: Male, Luke "Loch" Perkins, 15 years old.

Loch and his younger sister, Zaidee, join their oceanographer father on an expedition searching for enormous prehistoric creatures sighted in Lake Alban. Their ruthless leader, Cavenger, would just as soon annihilate as preserve the Plesiosaurs, water beasts thought to be extinct for over 10 million years. Luke, Zaidee, and Cavenger's daughter befriend Wee Beastie, an infant Plesiosaur, and help it and its family escape to safety. Grades: 6–9.

Zindel, Paul. **Reef of Death.**
HarperCollins, 1998.
Setting: Australia.
Main Character: Male, P. C. McPhee, teenager.

P.C. McPhee hops a plane to Australia to help his crazy uncle solve an offshore mystery. Adventure, villains, and the biggest, nastiest, man-eating fish on earth await him Down Under, in a fast-paced thriller. Grades: 5–9.

OCCULT AND SUPERNATURAL

Anderson, M. T. **The Game of Sunken Places.**
Scholastic, 2004.
Setting: Vermont.
Main Characters: Male, Brian Thatz; Male, Gregory Buchanan; both 13 years old.

Brian and Gregory accept a cryptic invitation to visit Gregory's weird Uncle Max and cousin Prudence in Vermont. Uncle Max takes them to his creepy old manor house. Once there, he burns the boys' luggage and everything in it, forcing them into the Victorian heavy tweed knickerbockers and starched shirt collars he prefers. Then a game begins that subjects the boys to every fiend Anderson can imagine, from bridge trolls and ogres to nefarious man-monsters in billowing cloaks. Grades: 5–9.

Bray, Libba. **A Great and Terrible Beauty.**
Delacorte, 2003.
Sequel: **Rebel Angels.**
Setting: Victorian England.
Main Character: Female, Gemma Doyle, 16 years old.

In India, Gemma has a vision and witnesses her mother's death. After her mother dies, Gemma is sent to boarding school in England, where she still has visions. She learns to enter the magical realm and discovers the Order, an ancient group of women who maintained the realms. Her mother is there to instruct her in what she must now do. Grades: 9 and up.

Carmody, Isobelle. **The Gathering.**
Puffin, 1996.
Setting: Cheshunt, Australia.
Main Character: Male, Nathaniel, 15 years old.

Nathaniel moves to a new model neighborhood, but soon senses something is very wrong. Nathaniel joins a group of misfits at school in a struggle against the evil that is seeking to control the community. Grades: 7–10.

Duncan, Lois. *Stranger with My Face.*
Dell, 1990.
Setting: 1980s.
Main Character: Female, Laurie, 17 years old.
　　Laurie senses she is being spied on and impersonated, and she discovers a stranger with her face who is her twin. Awards: CC. Grades: 6–8.

Duncan, Lois. *Third Eye.*
Bantam Doubleday Dell, 1991.
Setting: New Mexico.
Main Character: Female, Karen Connor, high school senior, 17 years old.
　　For the first time in her life, Karen is part of the popular crowd at school. When one of the neighborhood children disappears, Karen worries that her psychic powers will make her seem different from other people. Awards: CC. Grades: 6–8.

Feist, Raymond. *Faerie Tale.*
Bantam, 1989.
Setting: Upstate New York.
Main Characters: Female, Gloria Hastings, adult; Male, Philip Hastings, adult; three Hastings children, teenage daughter; twin 8 year old boys.
　　The Hastings' new house is the battlefield for an upcoming war among fairies and other Irish mythological creatures. Awards: CC. Grades: 8–12.

King, Stephen. *Carrie.*
Random House, 2001.
Setting: Maine.
Main Character: Female, Carrie White, teenager.
　　Carrie is the victim of vicious schoolmates and a mother who is a religious fanatic. Carrie exacts her revenge when she discovers her telekinetic powers. Awards: CC. Grades: 9–12.

Sedgwick, Marcus. *Book of Dead Days.*
Wendy Lamb, 2004.
Setting: Christmas to New Year's.
Main Character: Male, Boy, teenager.
　　Boy belongs to Valerian, a magician whose pact with the devil is coming due. Boy follows Valerian's mysterious and dangerous instructions to save his life. Grades: 6–9.

Shusterman, Neal. *Full Tilt.*
Simon & Schuster, 2003.
Setting: Six Flags Amusement Park.
Main Character: Male, Blake, 16 years old.
　　Blake, a straight-arrow, Ivy league college-bound kid, is at a carnival with Quinn, his thrill-seeking brother and two friends. A beautiful girl invites Blake to another

carnival in a remote part of town; the carnival only admits invited guests. Later Quinn is found at home in a comatose state, with Blake's invitation by his side. Blake and his friends go in search of the mysterious carnival and discover that the price of admission is one's soul. To save Quinn, Blake must survive seven different carnival rides before dawn, each one a terrifying reflection of one of his deepest fears. Grades: 6–10.

Sleator, William. *The Boy Who Couldn't Die.*
Harry N. Abrams, 2004.
Setting: New York, Adirondacks, Caribbean.
Main Character: Male, Ken Protchard, 16 years old.

After his best friend dies in a plane crash, Ken keeps thinking of a folktale about a monster that hid his soul, ensuring eternal life. Determined to avoid death himself, Ken finds a woman who removes his soul from his body. At first he is pleased; he gains physical invulnerability and a respite from his misery. But the woman is a zombie master, and he has become a modern-day monster, partially under her control. Fast-paced and suspenseful, this book will appeal to reluctant and avid readers alike. Grades: 7–9.

Sleator, William. *Others See Us.*
Puffin, 1995.
Setting: Seaside.
Main Character: Male, Jared, 16 years old.

Jared's bike brakes give out, and he ends up in an industrial waste pit. The toxic substance gives him telepathic powers. He can now see his cousin is a murderous psychopath, and Granny, who also has telepathic powers, might be one, too. Awards: CC. Grades: 6–9.

Snyder, Zilpha Keatley. *Unseen.*
Delacorte, 2004.
Setting: Present day.
Main Character: Female, Xandra Hobson, 12 years old.

Xandra likes to embark on imaginary adventures involving magic to escape from her genius family. One day in the woods, she encounters real magic when she rescues a bird from some hunters; the feather it leaves behind is the key to the unseen world. A classmate, Belinda and her grandfather attempt to explain the mystical world of the unseen to Xandra. Grades: 5–8.

Stine, R. L. *Nightmare Hour: Time for Terror.*
HarperCollins, 1999.

Ten scary short stories with cliffhangers, realistic dialog, and illustrations. Awards: CC. Grades: 6–7.

SCARY STORIES

Card, Orson Scott. *Maps in the Mirror.*
Orb, 2004.

Forty-six short works in one volume for Card fans. Horror, fantasy, science fiction, philosophy, and Mormon life are framed by introductions and afterwords by the author. Grades: YA/A.

Duncan, Lois, editor. *Night Terrors: Stories of Shadow and Substance.*
Simon & Schuster, 1996.
    Scary short stories by Joan Aiken, Alane Ferguson, Madge Harrah, Annette Curtis Klause, Chris Lynch, Harry Mazer, Norma Fox Mazer, Joan Lowery Nixon, Richard Peck, Theodore Taylor, and Patricia Windsor. Awards: CC. Grades: 6–10.

King, Stephen. *Night Shift.*
Signet, 1976.
    Scary short stories, some of which were later developed into novels and movies. Awards: CC. Grades: 9–12.

Noyes, Deborah, editor. *Gothic! Ten Original Dark Tales.*
Candlewick, 2004.
    Scary short stories by Joan Aiken, Vivian Vande Velde, M.T. Anderson, Neil Gaiman, Caitlin R. Kiernan, Barry Yourgrau, Janni Lee Simner, Gregory Maguire, Celia Rees, and Garth Nix. Grades: 7–12.

Vande Velde, Vivian. *Being Dead.*
Magic Carpet, 2003.
    Seven short stories featuring ghosts, cemeteries, suicides, murders, and other death themes with teen characters. Grades: 7 and up.

VAMPIRES

Anderson, M. T. *Thirsty.*
Candlewick, 2003.
Setting: Massachusetts.
Main Character: Male, Chris, teenager.
    In addition to the usual adolescent hormonal churnings, Chris is also becoming a vampire. He has more and more difficulty keeping his blood lust hidden, and sexy vampire Lolli challenges him to come out of the coffin to fulfill his destiny. Grades: 7 and up.

Atwater-Rhodes, Amelia. *In the Forests of the Night.*
Bantam Doubleday, 1999.
Sequels: *Demon in My View; Midnight Predator.*
Setting: New York City, 1984.
Main Character: Female, Riska, 300—appears 17 years old.
    Riska was bitten by a vampire in 1684 and turned into one of the undead. Three hundred years later, she haunts New York City. By a teen author. Awards: CC. Grades: 7–10.

Cary, Kate. *Bloodline.*
Razorbill, 2005.
Setting: Transylvania, Romania.

Main Character: Female, Mary Seward, young woman.

Mary recognizes the patient who has just been brought into the Purfleet sanatorium as Lt. John Shaw, who lives in the mansion near the hospital with his sister, Lily. Hoping to help him, Mary reads his diary, written in France during the Great War. The diary describes John's encounters with Captain Quincey Harker, a brave and bloodthirsty leader. When Lily meets Captain Harker, they fall in love, and he takes her home to Dracula's Castle in Romania to be married and fulfill the family's destiny. Lily must decide to live forever as a vampire or to end it all. Grades: 7 and up.

Hautman, Pete. *Sweetblood.*
Simon & Schuster, 2003.
Setting: Internet chat room.
Main Character: Female, Lucy Szabo, 16 years old.

Lucy has been a diabetic since she was 6, and now she has developed a theory that links vampirism with diabetic ketoacidosis. When she explains her theory in a creative writing paper, her teacher, counselor, and parents become concerned and take steps to find help for her. Her computer is removed from her room, and she is unable to frequent the Transylvanian chat room, so Lucy decides that perhaps real-life adventures are in order. With a new friend, she ventures into the world of tarot cards and goth, meeting Draco, a real vampire in the flesh, while allowing her diabetes to spiral out of control. Grades: 9 and up.

Hill, William. *Vampire Hunters.*
Otter Creek Press, 1998.
Setting: Texas.
Main Character: Male, Scooter Keyshawn, 15 years old.

Scooter wants to join the Graveyard Armadillos and has to get a picture of the reclusive albino filmmaker Marcus Chandler to prove if he is a vampire or not. Since teens are turning up dead, it's up to Scooter and friends to clear the innocent and trap the real vampires. Appeals to reluctant readers. Grades: 7–12.

King, Stephen. *Salem's Lot.*
Pocket, 2000.
Setting: Jerusalem's Lot, Maine.
Main Character: Male, Ben Mears, adult.

Ben has come back to The Lot to write about the creepy old Marsten house on the hill. He discovers shape-shifting vampires are sucking the blood of the inhabitants of Jerusalem's Lot. Awards: CC. Grades: 9–12.

Klause, Annette Curtis. *The Silver Kiss.*
Dell, 1992.
Setting: 1980s.
Main Character: Female, Zoe, 17 years old.

Zoe's mother is dying of cancer, and she feels alone and scared. Then she meets and falls in love with Simon, who knows a lot about death; he is a vampire. A few erotic scenes. Appeals to reluctant readers. Awards: CC. Grades: 8–12.

Maxwell, Katie. *Got Fangs?*
Dorchester Smooch, 2005.
Setting: Europe.
Main Characters: Female, Fran, teenager; Male, Benedikt, a vampire, 312 years old.
    Fran is tagging along with her mother, who is a witch, in a traveling psychic fair. Fran can read people if she touches them, something her mother thinks she should use at the faire but which makes Fran uncomfortable. Then a sexy motorcycle rider named Benedikt shows up who is also a very old vampire. He tells Fran that she is his beloved and only she can lift his curse. Add a mystery of who is robbing the faire, a very special horse, and Fran's fight for her life against demons. Grades: YA.

Pierce, Meredith Ann. *The Darkangel.*
St. Martin's, 1998.
Sequels: Darkangel Trilogy: *A Gathering of Gargoyles, The Pearl of the Soul of the World.*
Setting: Avarra.
Main Character: Female, Ariel, adult.
    Ariel attempts to save her mistress, Eoduin, the dark angel, and her twelve other brides before the White Witch's power is cemented forever. Awards: CC; Grades: 8–10.

Rice, Anne. *Interview with the Vampire.*
Ballantine, 1991.
Series: The Vampire Chronicles: *The Vampire Lestat, Queen of the Damned, The Body Thief.*
Setting: Louisiana/Paris.
Main Character: Male, Louis.
    Louis, a reluctant vampire, tells his story to a reporter. Lush, complex, and absorbing for mature readers. Awards: CC. Grades: 10–12.

Schreiber, Ellen. *Vampire Kisses.*
Katherine Tegen, 2003.
Sequel: *Vampire Kisses 2: Kissing Coffins.*
Setting: Dullsville.
Main Character: Female, Raven, 16 years old.
    Goth girl Raven is fascinated with Alexander who has moved into the old town mansion. She is sure he is a vampire. A humorous vampire love story without the gore. Grades: 7 and up.

Shan, Darren. *A Living Nightmare.*
Little, Brown, 2002.
Series: Cirque du Freak: *The Vampire's Assistant; Tunnels of Blood; Vampire Mountain; Trials of Death; The Vampire Prince; Hunters of the Dusk; Allies of the Night; Killers of the Dawn; The Lake of Souls.*
Setting: England, 2000s.
Main Character: Male, Darren Shan, 12 years old.
    Darren and his buddy Steve find a flier for "Cirque Du Freak," a traveling freak show promising performances by the snake-boy, the wolf-man, and Larten Crepsley and his giant spider, Madame Octa. They sneak out and discover the show is real, and

Darren decides to steal the trained spider. Fast-paced, with short chapters and reluctant reader appeal. Grades: 5 and up.

Stine, R.L. ***Dangerous Girls.***
HarperCollins, 2003.
Sequel: ***Taste of the Night.***
Setting: Camp Blue Moon, 2000s.
Main Characters: Female, Destiny Weller; Female, Livvy Weller; both 16 years old.

Twins Destiny and Livvy are completing their summer jobs as camp counselors. Their mother committed suicide only months before, and they found the camp a healing environment. One of the other counselors, a mysterious and very handsome young man with an Italian accent, Renz, is the cause of much tragedy and distress for the twins in upcoming weeks. Renz had drawn each teen away, revealed his true identity, and then sucked her blood. Grades: 7 and up.

Vande Velde, Vivian. ***Companions of the Night.***
Jane Yolen, 1995.
Setting: Brockport, New York.
Main Character: Female, Kerry Nowicki, 16 years old.

Kerry helps a sexy young man escape from a gang attacking him, but it turns out the guy is a vampire. A romance for mature readers. Awards: CC. Grades: 7–10.

West, Terry M. ***The Turning.***
Scholastic, 1997.
Series: Confessions of a Teenage Vampire: ***Zombie Saturday Night.***
Setting: Lemanchard.
Main Character: Female, Lily.

Lily is an outcast; the bullies pick on her, and she doesn't fit in with the in crowd. She befriends the founder of the town, Phillip Lemacchard II. Then she discovers his secret: he's a 400-year-old vampire. A graphic novel. Grades: YA.

WEREWOLVES

Armstrong, Kelley. ***Bitten.***
Plume, 2002.
Series: Women of the Underworld: ***Stolen; Industrial Magic; Haunted; Dime Store Magic.***
Setting: Toronto, Ontario/Upstate New York.
Main Character: Female, Elena Michaels, 30 years old.

The only female werewolf in existence, Elena, was bitten by her werewolf fiancé and learned to live within the pack. Still struggling after ten years to accept her identity, and feeling anger toward her former lover and creator, she leaves the pack to live a relatively normal life with a nice normal guy in Toronto. Before long she is called back to help discover and destroy some dangerous nonpack werewolves, called mutts, which are torturing and killing humans. Grades: YA.

Cole, Stephen. ***The Wereling: Wounded.***
Razorbill/Penguin, 2005.

Sequels: *Prey; Resurrection.*
Setting: 2000s.
Main Characters: Male, Tom Anderson, 16 years old; Female, Kate Folan, 17 years old.
   Tom has a run-in with a bear and is nursed back to health by Marcie Folan. He feels strange, with heightened senses, and he discovers the Folans are turning him into a mate for their werewolf daughter, Kate. Grades: 9–12.

Jennings, Patrick. *The Wolving Time.*
Scholastic, 2003.
Setting: France, sixteenth century.
Main Character: Male, Lazlo Emberek, 13 years old.
   Lazlo herds sheep for his family. When a wolf appears, he whistles for his mother, who comes running and turns into a wolf. Lazlo discovers Muno, the orphaned witch girl, has witnessed his mother's change, and he is worried she won't keep the secret. Grades: 5–8.

Klause, Annette Curtis. *Blood and Chocolate.*
Delacorte, 1997.
Setting: Maryland.
Main Character: Female, Vivian, 18 years old.
   Vivian is a werewolf who leads a double life. At school she is madly in love with Aiden, but can never show him her true self. At home with her pack, she is involved in rivalries and fights for her life. Awards: CC. Grades: 9–12.

Lackey, Mercedes. *The Fire Rose.*
Baen, 1996.
Setting: San Francisco, 1905.
Main Character: Female, Rose Hawkins, young adult.
   After her father dies and leaves her penniless, Rose becomes a governess in a household with no children. She is hired to read books for a reclusive alchemist, Jason Cameron, who is a magician caught in a werewolf spell. Grades: YA/A.

WITCHES

Atwater-Rhodes, Amelia. *Hawksong.*
Random House, 2004.
Series: The Kiesha'ra: *Snakecharm; Falcondance.*
Setting: Shape-shifter world.
Main Character: Female, Danica Shardae, young adult.
   Danica is an avian shape-shifter and the princess of her people, who have been at war with the serpiente. Zane Cobriana is a prince among the serpiente. In a Romeo and Juliet theme, Danica and Zane are determined to stop the war and agree to marry, but the mediating parties are so offended by the plan they leave. Grades: 7–10.

Furlong, Monica. *Juniper.*
Random House, 1992.
Sequel: *Wise Child.*
Setting: Medieval.

Main Character: Female, Nonnoc, young girl.

Euny, the healer, teaches Ninnoc, the indulged daughter of King Mark, the Craft of the Wise. Ninnoc returns home from her lessons and sees her father's kingdom is under her evil aunt's enchantment. She must use her new powers to save herself and her cousin Gamal. Awards: CC. Grades: 6–12.

Rees, Celia. **Witch Child.**
Candlewick, 2001.
Setting: Salem, Massachusetts, 1659.
Main Character: Female, Mary Newbury, 14 years old.

Mary is a witch who saw her grandmother burned at the stake; she sails to colonial America to escape a similar fate. She must hide her powers from the "normals" to avoid persecution. Awards: CC. Grades: 7–10.

Thesman, Jean. **Other Ones.**
Viking, 1999.
Setting: High school.
Main Character: Female, Bridget, 15 years old.

Bridget can't decide whether to embrace her fate as a family witch or just be normal. Awards: CC. Grades: 6–9.

Vande Velde, Vivian. **Magic Can Be Murder.**
Harcourt, 2000.
Setting: Medieval.
Main Character: Female, Nola, 17 years old.

Nola and her mother are witches, and Nola is magically disguised as a house servant to avoid being discovered and killed. When she falls in love with the chief investigator and tries to help him solve a murder, a comedy of errors ensues. Awards: CC. Grades: 7–10.

RESOURCES: ADDITIONAL TITLES

Altner, Patricia. 1998. **Vampire Readings: An Annotated Bibliography.** Lanham, MD: Scarecrow Press.

Barron, Neil. 1999. **Fantasy and Horror: A Critical and Historical Guide to Literature, Illustration, Film, TV, Radio, Internet.** Lanham, MD: Scarecrow Press.

Fonseca, Anthony J., and June Michele Pulliam. 2002. **Hooked on Horror: A Guide to Reading Interests in Horror Fiction.** Westport, CT: Libraries Unlimited.

Jones, Patrick. 1998. **What's So Scary About R. L. Stine?** Lanham, MD: Scarecrow Press.

Spratford, Becky Siegel, and Tammy Hennigh Clausen. 2004. **The Honor Readers' Advisory: The Librarians Guide to Vampires, Killer Tomatoes, and Haunted Houses.** Chicago, IL: American Library Association.

CHAPTER 14

LOVE, SEX, AND ROMANCE

In the classic romance, two people meet, fall in love, have a conflict or obstacle to overcome, and then live happily ever after. In real life, relationships aren't so predictable! Young adult novels help teens cope with the confusion and searching they go through when discovering their own sexuality and what a loving relationship means for them. Then there is the dance of finding the right partner for that relationship. The lists in this chapter reflect the complicated puzzles of love gone right and love gone wrong.

> Classic Love, Sex, and Romance
> Bisexual/Transgendered/Questioning Teens
> Dating/Crush
> Dating Violence/Rape
> First Love
> Gay Guys
> Lesbian Girls
> Unplanned Pregnancy/Abortion
> Resources: Additional Titles

CLASSIC LOVE, SEX, AND ROMANCE

Austen, Jane. ***Pride and Prejudice.***
Bantam, 1983.
Setting: Longbourn, England, early nineteenth century.
Main Characters: Female, Elizabeth Bennet; Male, Mr. Darcy; all adults.

Elizabeth's wit and humor and Mr. Darcy's eloquent dodging and parrying puts off the inevitable romance waiting to bring them together. Originally published in 1813; perfect for hopeless romantics. Awards: CC. Grades: 7–12.

Bronte, Charlotte. ***Jane Eyre.***
Puffin, 1995.
Setting: Thornfield, northern England, early nineteenth century.
Main Characters: Female, Jane Eyre; Male, Mr. Rochester, adults.

Jane is an unhappy orphan who becomes a governess at Mr. Rochester's Thornfield. Jane marries Mr. Rochester, only to be faced with a shocking revelation on her wedding day. A gothic romance originally published in 1847. Awards: CC. Grades: 7–12.

Bronte, Emily. ***Wuthering Heights.***
Bantam, 1983.
Setting: Yorkshire moors, 1770s.
Main Characters: Female, Catherine Earnshaw; Male, Heathcliff, adults.
    Catherine, the precocious daughter of the house, and Heathcliff, the ruggedly handsome, uncultured foundling her father brings home, quickly become attached to each other. As they grow older, their companionship turns into obsession. Family, class, and fate work cruelly against them, as do their own jealous and volatile natures, and much of their lives are spent in revenge and frustration. Originally published in 1847. Awards: CC. Grades: 8–12.

---

du Maurier, Daphne. ***Rebecca.***
Doubleday, 1948.
Setting: Manderley, Cornwall, England 1930s.
Main Characters: Female, Mrs. De Winter; Male, Maxim DeWinter; Female, Mrs. Danvers; adults.
    Manderley is filled with memories of the first Mrs. DeWinter, the elegant and flamboyant Rebecca. The young, timid second Mrs. DeWinter is greeted by the housekeeper, Mrs. Danvers, with sullen hostility. The new Mrs. DeWinter slowly grows and asserts herself, surviving the wicked deceptions of Mrs. Danvers and the silent deceits of her husband, Maxim, to emerge triumphant, in a surprise ending. Originally published in 1938. Grades: YA/A.

Mitchell, Margaret. ***Gone with the Wind.***
Scribner's, 1936.
Setting: Atlanta, Georgia, Civil War.
Main Characters: Female, Scarlett O'Hara; Male, Rhett Butler, adults.
    A romantic love story set against the Civil War, originally published in 1936. Made into a movie. Awards: CC; Pulitzer Prize. Grades: 10–12.

Orczy, Baroness. ***The Scarlet Pimpernel.***
1st World Library, 2004.
Setting: France, 1792.
Main Character: Male, the Scarlet Pimpernel, adult.
    The Pimpernel is a British fop who daringly spirits condemned innocents out of France during the Reign of Terror after the French Revolution. Originally published in 1905. Grades: YA/A.

Rostand, Edmund. ***Cyrano de Bergerac.***
Applause, 2000.
Setting: France.
Main Characters: Male, Cyrano de Bergerac; Female, Roxane, adults.
    Cyrano is in love with his extraordinarily beautiful cousin Roxane. Embarrassed by his large nose, Cyrano refuses to tell Roxane of his love and, instead, helps Christian, who also loves her, profess his feelings for her. Roxane falls in love with Cyrano's

poetry and letters but believes they are from Christian. Originally published in 1897.
Grades: YA/A.

Chbosky, Steve. *The Perks of Being a Wallflower.*
Pocket Books, 1999.
Setting: Pennsylvania, 1991.
Main Character: Male, Charlie, high school freshman, 14 years old.

Charlie—shy, introspective, and intelligent—is a wallflower. The reader learns about Charlie through the letters he writes to an unnamed someone about his friends, a crush, his sexuality, experimenting with drugs, family tensions, and his best friend's recent suicide. Charlie mostly manages to avoid the depression he feels creeping up on him with the help of a teacher and his two friends, seniors Samantha and Patrick. Awards: CC. Grades: 9–12.

De Oliveira, Eddie. *Lucky.*
Scholastic, 2004.
Setting: Surrey, England.
Main Characters: Male, Sam Smith; Male, Toby; both 19 years old.

Sam enjoys hanging out with his friends, Brenda and Pod, and is passionate about playing on the local football team. He meets Toby, another football player, who is gay; and Toby introduces Sam to the gay Soho nightlife. Sam wonders if he might also be gay, especially after he notices mysterious and attractive "Him," a young stranger who occasionally shows up at football games. Eventually Sam comes to realize he is attracted to both boys and girls. British slang. Grades: 9 and up.

Freymann-Weyr, Garret. *My Heartbeat.*
Puffin, 2003.
Setting: New York City, 2000s.
Main Character: Female, Ellen, 14 years old.

Ellen idolizes her brother, Link, and his best friend, James, who are seniors in a private Manhattan high school, where some girls assume that Link and James are a couple. Ellen asks them and things begin to unravel: Link avoids James, starts dating Polly, and drops out of a special college math program to pursue his interest in music. James tells Ellen he has slept with men, but that he is also attracted to women. Ellen has her first sexual experience with James, which is his first with a female. Ellen wants to understand her brother, and realizes that their parents do not know him the way they think they do. Awards: Printz Honor. Grades: 9 and up.

Koja, Kathe. *Talk.*
Frances Foster Books, 2005.
Setting: 2000s.
Main Characters: Male, Kit Webster; Female, Lindsey Walsh; Male, Blake Tudor; teenagers.

Kit auditions for a controversial school play and discovers his talent for acting. He struggles with coming out, and both he and his costar face crises in their view of themselves and in their close relationships. Told from two points of view. Grades: 8 and up.

Manning, Sarra. ***Pretty Things.***
Dutton, 2005.
Setting: North London, England.
Main Characters: Female, Brie; Male, Charlie; Male, Walker; Female, Daisy; teenagers.

Members of a summer drama group that will be performing *The Taming of the Shrew* create their own drama, in a complicated romantic rectangle. Brie invites Charlie, her gay best friend, to sleep over in her bed. Charlie falls for Walker, a straight teen. Walker leads Charlie on, but his heart belongs to Daisy, a lesbian. Daisy discovers she is attracted to and enjoys sex with Walker as much as with her girlfriend, Claire. Charlie decides that even though he is really, truly gay, he still loves Brie enough as his best friend to want to have sex with her, though she does not reciprocate. Daisy finds Brie pitiful and annoying, but she forces an intense kiss on her, just to show her what it's like to be kissed by another girl. Brie knows she is straight, but the boy she likes is sexually demanding, and she thwarts his ultimate attempt to rape her. For mature readers. Grades: 9–12.

Matthews, Andrew. ***The Flip Side.***
Laurel Leaf, 2005.
Setting: England.
Main Characters: Male, Robert Hunt; Female, Milena; both 15 years old.

Robert is asked to do as was done in Shakespeare's time and play the female role of Rosalind in *As You Like It*, opposite his classmate Milena as Orlando. Rob discovers that he likes dressing up as a woman, and, more importantly, he likes who he is as Rosalind: stronger and more confident than when he's just Rob. Milena is also confused, and the two become instant confidants. Then, Rob's best friend reveals that he is gay. Another classmate throws a cross-dressing party, and it suddenly seems that many kids are fascinated by gender-bending. Rob concludes that he is not gay, and that what he feels for Milena is "the real thing." Grades: 8–10.

Peters, Julie Anne. ***Luna: A Novel.***
Little, Brown, 2004.
Setting: Present day.
Main Characters: Female, Regan, 15 years old; Male, Liam, aka Luna, 17 years old.

Regan has always been there for her transgendered brother, Liam, sacrificing her needs for his, but when he announces that he is ready to "transition" into Luna permanently, Regan is not sure she can handle the consequences. Liam realizes that in order for his sister to be free, he, too, must free himself to become the woman who lives inside him. Grades: 9–12.

DATING/CRUSH

Bradley, Alex. ***24 Girls in 7 Days.***
Dutton, 2005.
Setting: 2000s.

Main Character: Male, Jack Grammar, 17 years old.

When the love of his life rejects Jack's invitation to the senior prom, his friends propose that he put a personal ad in the school's online newspaper, soliciting a date. Jack agrees to go along with the plan, but it is hard to avoid the young ladies who descend on him without warning, as he tries to speed-date 24 girls in 7 days. Meanwhile, a mysterious online pen pal gives him dating advice. Grades: 7–12.

Castellucci, Cecil. *Boy Proof.*
Candlewick, 2005.
Setting: Melrose Prep School, Los Angeles, California, 2000s.
Main Character: Female, Victoria, 16 years old.

Victoria considers herself boy-proof—too smart and tough to be appealing to guys. She has renamed herself Egg and wears an all-white cloak. Victoria spends Tuesdays after school happily sculpting movie monsters with her father, a special-effects guru, and squabbles with her actor mother and debates with the Science Fiction and Fantasy Club. Then Max Carter arrives, and he is the first person to see past her aggressive exterior. Soon her grades are falling, and she starts to think about Max in exciting and disturbing ways. Grades: 8–12.

Conford, Ellen. *Crush.*
HarperCollins, 1998.
Setting: High school, 1990s.

Ten stories about couples all getting ready for the upcoming Valentine's Day dance. Awards: CC. Grades: 6–9.

Dessen, Sarah. *This Lullaby.*
Viking, 2002.
Setting: 2000s.
Main Character: Female, Remy, 18 years old.

Remy is cynical about love, including her romance-writer mother's betrothal to a car dealer and her brother's infatuation with self-improvement guru Jennifer Anne. Then rocker Dexter "crashes" into her life, and her resolve to remain unattached cracks. Quirky characters, and the end has a twist. Grades: 7–12.

Heynen, Jim. *Cosmos Coyote and William the Nice.*
Holt, 2000.
Setting: Iowa farm.
Main Character: Male, Cosmos De Haag, 17 years old.

Cosmos spends his senior year away from home, living with relatives in a religious farming community in Iowa after he was threatened with six months in "juvie." He leaves behind his rock band, the OughtaBs, and his girlfriend, Salal, for wide-open spaces, cow dung, and Dutch Center Christian Academy. To fit in, he swaps his rebellious persona of Cosmos Coyote for that of William the Nice and meets beautiful and devout Cherlyn Van Dyke, who seems bent on saving him. When a string of thefts occur, all fingers point to Cosmos. A Christian romance. Grades: 9 and up.

Kindl, Patrice. *Owl in Love.*
Graphia, 2004.

Setting: New York City.
Main Character: Female, Owl, 14 years old.

Owl is a wereowl, a trait that runs in her family. She spends her nights in a tree near the object of her crush, her science teacher, Mr. Lindstrom. When she spots a boy hanging around the same place, her interests shift. Awards: CC. Grades: 5 and up.

Standiford, Natalie. ***The Dating Game.***
Little, Brown, 2005.
Setting: California, 2000s.
Main Characters: Female, Madison; Female, Holly; Female, Lina; both 15 years old.

Buddies Madison, Holly, and Lina all become the talk of their high school when they start their own Web site, giving advice on romance and setting up those in need with dates. The teens eventually come to the conclusion that the guys they were originally interested in are not necessarily right for them. Grades: 8 and up.

Wilson, Jacqueline. ***Girls in Love.***
Laurel Leaf, 2002.
Series: Girls Quartet: ***Girls Under Pressure; Girls Out Late; Girls in Tears.***
Setting: Great Britain.
Main Characters: Female, Ellie Allard, 14 years old; Female, Magda, 14 years old; Female, Nadine, freshman teen; Male, Dan, 12 years old.

Ellie is fed up with her weight, her teachers, her family, and herself. Ellie's friends are Nadine and Magda, and nerdy Dan. She feels jealous after hearing about Nadine's new older boyfriend and Magda's summer flirtations, so she pretends that Dan is her boyfriend. When Dan expresses romantic feelings in letters to her, it becomes obvious that she won't be able to keep it up forever. British atmosphere, like *Bridget Jones' Diary*. Grades: 7–10.

Zeises, Lara M. ***Contents Under Pressure.***
Delacorte, 2004.
Setting: Delaware.
Main Character: Female, Lucy Doyle, 14 years old.

Lucy's friends leave her behind when they discover boys. Then her older brother, Jack, moves back home from college with his girlfriend, Hannah, in tow. Lucy can't stand Hannah, and Jack is mysteriously distant. When she runs into junior Tobin Scacheri, she is swept off her feet, and Hannah helps her sort out first boyfriend questions. Lucy then finds out that Hannah is pregnant. Grades: 7–10.

DATING VIOLENCE/RAPE/INCEST

Anderson, Laurie Halse. ***Speak.***
Farrar, Straus & Giroux, 1999.
Setting: High school.
Main Character: Female, Melinda Sordino, 14 years old.

Melinda can't tell anybody why she broke up an end-of-summer party by calling the cops, and now nobody at school will talk to her. So she becomes a silent observer of people's lies and hypocrisies, while she lives in fear of the boy who raped her at the party. Only through her work in art class, and with the support of the compassionate art teacher, does she begin to reach out to others and eventually find her voice. Awards: CC. Grades: 7–10.

Andrews, V. C. *Flowers in the Attic.*
Pocket, 1990.
Sequels: *Petals in the Wind; If There Be Thorns; Seeds of Yesterday.*
Setting: Virginia.
Main Characters: Male, Chris Dollanganger; Female, Cathy Dollanganger; both teens; Female, Carrie Dollanganger; Male, Cory Dollanganger; young children.

The Dollangangers were a happy family until the day their father died in a horrible accident, which left them all penniless. Out of desperation, their mother decides to move them back to her wealthy parents' mansion, where dark family secrets make the children unwelcome guests. The children are locked in a room in a wing that has been unused for years. Carrie and Cory look to their older siblings for parental love, and Chris and Cathy turn to each other in romantic love. For mature readers. Awards: CC. Grades: YA/A.

Block, Francesca Lia. *Wasteland.*
Joanna Cotler, 2003.
Setting: Los Angeles, California.
Main Characters: Female, Marina; Male, Lex; teens.

Marina and her brother Lex are in love and are sexually attracted to each other. They consummate their love, and as a result, Lex commits suicide. Marina later learns that her brother was adopted. Narrative switches from first to third person and includes portions of Lex's journal. For mature readers. Grades: 9–12.

Caletti, Deb. *Honey, Baby, Sweetheart.*
Simon & Schuster, 2004.
Setting: Nine Miles Falls, 2000s.
Main Characters: Female, Ruby McQueen, 16 years old; Female, Ann McQueen, adult.

During the summer of her junior year, shy, quiet Ruby falls in love with the rich boy down the block. After their first motorcycle ride, Travis gives her a beautiful gold chain, and she wears it everywhere. Only later, while on a date with him, does she learn where he got the gift—he breaks into houses and steals jewelry. By spending time with the Casserole Queens (her librarian mother's senior citizen book group) and listening to their life stories, Ruby and her mother Ann finally discover the role models that they've been lacking. Grades: 9 and up.

Clarke, Kathryn Ann. *The Breakable Vow.*
Avon, 2004.
Setting: Texas.
Main Character: Female, Annie, 18 years old.

Annie is in love with Kevin. He has a temper, but that doesn't concern her because she knows that he cares deeply for her. Then Annie becomes pregnant and refuses to accept Kevin's offer of money for an abortion; she has a baby girl. After a rushed marriage, Kevin's abuse ebbs and flows; his threats and her fear that he will take baby Mary from her keep Annie in the marriage. It takes a final, violent event to prove to Annie that she has to break free. Grades: 9 and up.

Cole, Brock. *Facts Speak for Themselves.*
Front Street, 1997.
Setting: Police station.
Main Character: Female, Linda, 13 years old.

Linda has just come to the police station after witnessing the murder of a married man with whom she's been having an affair. Linda argues that she wasn't raped. She tries to tell the story straight, to let the facts speak for themselves. Awards: CC. Grades: 7 and up.

Dessen, Sarah. *Dreamland.*
Viking, 2000.
Setting: Contemporary.
Main Character: Female, Caitlin.

Caitlin felt she could be anybody, not just the second-rate shadow of her older sister, Cass. But now she is drowning in the vacuum Cass left behind when she turned her back on her family's expectations by running off with her boyfriend. Caitlin wanders in a dreamland of drugs and a nightmare of her boyfriend's Rogerson's sudden fits, lost in her search for herself. All around her are women who care—best friends, mother, sister, mentor, but shame keeps her from confiding in any of them. Awards: CC. Grades: 9 and up.

Draper, Sharon. *Darkness Before Dawn.*
Atheneum, 2001.
Setting: Hazelwood.
Main Character: Female, Keisha, high school senior.

Keisha's senior year of high school is quite an ordeal. Her ex-boyfriend recently committed suicide; a good friend is killed in a car crash; and she is attracted to the new track coach, the principal's college-age son. When he begins to make advances, Keisha decides that she is mature enough to date this older man. Jonathan, however, turns out to be more than a smooth talker, and he attempts to rape her after a romantic date. Awards: CC. Grades: 9–12.

Flake, Sharon. *Who Am I Without Him?: Short Stories About Girls and the Boys in Their Lives.*
Jump At The Sun, 2004.

Ten short stories written in the vernacular of urban African American teens. Some are funny and uplifting; others, disturbing and sad. In "So I Ain't No Good Girl," a teen wants to be with a good-looking popular boy, so much so that she tolerates his disrespect and abuse. Awards: Coretta Scott King Honor. Grades: 7 and up.

Flinn, Alex. *Breathing Underwater.*
HarperCollins, 2001.
Setting: Miami, Florida.
Main Character: Male, Nick Andreas, 16 years old.

Nick ends up in court, facing a restraining order by his girlfriend, Caitlin. He is sentenced to six months of counseling and to write 500 words per week in a journal, explaining what happened from the day he met Caitlin to the present. Awards: CC. Grades: 8 and up.

Jones, Patrick. *Things Change.*
Walker Books, 2004.
Setting: Michigan.
Main Characters: Female, Johanna, 16 years old; Male, Paul, 18 years old.
 Johanna is a straight-A student, ecstatic when the boy she adores returns her affections. They date, he hits her, she leaves him; he promises to change, she takes him back. Paul struggles with his feelings about his father. Chapters alternate between Johanna's and Paul's points of view. Grades: 8–12.

Lackey, Mercedes. *Magic's Pawn.*
DAW, 1989.
Series: Last Herald Mage Trilogy: *Magic's Promise; Magic's Price.*
Setting: Valdemar.
Main Character: Male, Vanyel, teen.
 Due to his father's intense disapproval and neglect, Vanyel is sent away to live with his Aunt Savil, a Herald Mage of Valdemar. The heralds of Valdemar protect the people; they bond to magical horses as companions with amazing abilities. Vanyel falls in love with his aunt's protégé, but their relationship has to be kept hidden from Vanyel's father, as both are boys. Tragedy strikes, and results in Vanyel becoming the most powerful Herald Mage ever in the history of Valdemar. Vanyel is raped by non-homosexual men. Grades: YA/A.

Miklowitz, Gloria. *Past Forgiving.*
Simon & Schuster, 1995.
Setting: High school.
Main Characters: Female, Alex, 15 years old; Male, Cliff, 18 years old.
 Cliff, graduating from high school, enchants Alex with love and praise. Then he demeans her, with stinging barbs at the things she loves best. He envies anyone who enjoys any of her time or attention. His jealous outbursts begin to turn violent, but she accepts his apologies and promises of reform. As Cliff's behavior escalates, Alex withholds her affections, until he hears her out. Cliff refuses to listen and rapes her, an act clearly about rage and power, not about sex. Awards: CC. Grades: 8–10.

Plummer, Louise. *A Dance for Three.*
Laurel Leaf, 2001.
Setting: Contemporary.
Main Character: Female, Hannah Ziebarth, 15 years old.
 Hannah is pregnant. When she tells her rich, good-looking boyfriend, Milo, he slugs her. Her beloved father has died suddenly in a freak accident, and her mother has retreated into agoraphobia and needs her care. Hannah hides in Milo's car and overhears him having sex with his old girlfriend. A psychotic break lands her in a mental hospital for juveniles, and she begins the long process of putting the pieces of her life back together with the help of a compassionate young therapist. Grades: 9 and up.

Schraff, Anne. *Someone to Love Me.*
Townsend, 2001.
Series: Bluford High: *Lost and Found; Secrets in the Shadows; The Gun; The Bully; Matter of Trust.*
Setting: Bluford High School.
Main Character: Female, Cindy Gibson, 14 years old.

Cindy's mother is always gone and her mother's boyfriend is always telling Cindy she is ugly. Cindy suspects he is selling drugs in their home, and she tries to tell her mother, but her mother never believes her. Then she meets Bobby Wallace, an older, handsome, young man. Bobby is bad news. He hits Cindy and leads her into the world of drugs. Grades: YA.

Sparks, Beatrice. *It Happened to Nancy.*
Avon, 1994.
Setting: South Carolina.
Main Character: Female, Nancy, 14 years old.

Nancy, an asthmatic, meets 18-year-old Collin, a gentle, caring young man who appears to be the answer to her dreams until he rapes her and leaves her HIV-infected. Nancy declines rapidly as the result of her weakened immune system yet leads a full, happy life because of the loving support of both friends and family. Written in a diary format with educational information at the end of the book. Awards: CC. Grades: 7–12.

Stratton, Allan. *Leslie's Journal.*
Annick, 2000.
Setting: Contemporary.
Main Character: Female, Leslie, 15 years old.

Leslie keeps a journal for an English assignment. She is completely honest, since her teacher, Ms. Graham, has promised never to read it and keeps it in a locked cabinet. Leslie has a single mom whom she loves but can't communicate with; a dad who recently moved in with his girlfriend; and wild older boyfriend, Jason, with whom she is totally obsessed. Jason gets her drunk, rapes her, and takes Polaroid pictures of her. His behavior is abusive, and when Leslie tries to break up with him, he stalks and threatens her. A new English teacher reads her diary and brings it to the attention of the principal, who takes Jason's side. Leslie fears for her life and runs away. For mature readers. Awards: CC. Grades: 8 and up.

Tashjian, Janet. *Fault Line.*
Henry Holt, 2003.
Setting: Contemporary.
Main Character: Female, Becky, teenager.

Both sides of dating abuse are presented as Becky, a teenage comedienne, is drawn into an abusive relationship with her boyfriend, Kip. Their insecurities and Kip's possessiveness and anger develop slowly, and Kip tells of his pain and frustration when he loses control. Grades: 7 and up.

Williams-Garcia, Rita. *Every Time a Rainbow Dies.*
Amistad, 2001.
Setting: Brooklyn, New York.

Main Character: Male, Thulani, 16 years old.

Thulani came to Brooklyn from Jamaica with his mother and brother. His mother returned to their homeland to die four years ago, and Thulani spends a lot of time on the rooftop of his building, tending his doves. One day he hears screams, rescues a rape victim, and takes her home. He follows her around and falls in love with her. For mature readers. Awards: CC. Grades: 9 and up.

FIRST LOVE

Berry, Liz. *China Garden.*
HarperTempest, 1999.
Setting: England.
Main Character: Female, Clare Meredith, 17 years old.

Clare, waiting to hear the results of her school exams, goes with her widowed mother to Ravensmere, an ancient English estate, where she's attracted to a handsome biker. Clare makes friends and enemies; sees visions; learns of past Ravensmere women and of her previously unknown connection to the area; and rethinks her plans for the future. Awards: CC. Grades: 9 and up.

Block, Francesca Lia. *Dangerous Angels: The Weetzie Bat Books.*
HarperTrophy, 1998.
Setting: Hollywood, California.
Main Character: Female, Weetzie Bat, teenager.

All the Weetzie Bat books are collected here in one volume: *Weetzie Bat; Witch Baby; Cherokee Bat and the Goat Guys; Missing Angel Juan; Baby Be-Bop.* Quirky characters, including Weetzie, her Secret Agent Lover Man, Dirk, Duck, Cherokee, Witch Baby, friends, and family, all loving and caring for one another. Magical realism with fairy-tale qualities. Awards: CC. Grades: YA.

Block, Francesca Lia. *Echo.*
Joanna Cotler, 2001.
Setting: Los Angeles, California.
Main Character: Female, Echo, teenager.

In interconnected short stories, Echo, who believes that "the only things I know how to do well are shoplift, kiss, and dance," feels excluded from her parents' perfect love for each other. She sets out alone to try to fill the void inside. Echo meets a broken angel, iron-pumping vampires, and the fairy daughter of a rock star. Echo finally finds her own true "love-boy" when she learns to look for love within instead of through food, sex, or doomed relationships. Awards: CC. Grades: 8 and up.

Block, Francesca Lia. *Girl Goddess #9: Nine Stories.*
HarperTrophy, 1998.

A collection of short stories about love—straight, gay, familial, and otherworldly—that show the reader that all girls are goddesses. Awards: CC. Grades: 7 and up.

Blume, Judy. *Forever.*
Atheneum/Richard Jackson, 2002.

Setting: New Year's Eve through summer.

Main Characters: Female, Katherine; Male, Michael; both teenagers.

Katherine loves Michael so much she's willing to lose her virginity to him; and it gets hard to imagine living without him; their love seems strong and true enough to last forever. When they are separated for the summer, Katherine begins to have feelings for another guy. The first "going all the way" YA book. Awards: CC. Grades: YA.

Cart, Michael. *Love and Sex: Ten Stories of Truth for Teens.*
Simon & Schuster, 2001.

Ten short stories take a look at the first overwhelming feelings of passion: the yearning, aching, sweaty miseries, and ecstasies of young love by Joan Bauer, Michael Lowenthal, Garth Nix, Sonya Sones, Laurie Halse Anderson, Emma Donoghue, Louise Hawes, Chris Lynch, Shelley Stoehr, and Angela Johnson. Awards: CC. Grades: 9 and up.

Earls, Nick. *After Summer.*
Graphia, 2005.
Setting: Australia.
Main Character: Male, Alex Delaney, 18 years old.

Alex is waiting to hear if he's been accepted to Queensland University. When he meets a girl at the beach, he is diverted from his worries. He spends every moment with her, and soon, Alex's problem isn't whether or not he's accepted to the university, but if he can leave the girl with whom he's fallen in love. Grades: 9 and up.

Garfinkle, Debra. *Storky: How I Lost My Nickname and Won the Girl.*
Putnam, 2005.
Setting: California.
Main Character: Male, Mike Pomerantz, 14 years old.

Mike, dubbed "Storky" due to his height/weight proportions, contends with his parents' divorce and a disinterested, midlife-crisis father. He began keeping a journal in the hopes that Gina, whom he has known for years and has fallen in love with, would view him as the "sensitive" type and fall madly in love with him. Grades: 9–12.

Krovatin, Christopher. *Heavy Metal and You.*
Push, 2005.
Setting: New York City.
Main Character: Male, Sam, young teenager.

Sam attends an expensive all-boys prep school in New York City, and he and his buddies often cut classes to smoke and get wasted. He is also intelligent, with encyclopedic knowledge of both heavy-metal music and classical literature. Sam begins to date straight-edge Melissa, who doesn't like the fact that he drinks and does drugs. Melissa is more important to him than he ever thought possible, but pleasing her means completely changing who he is. Includes raw language, with sexual talk and innuendo. Grades: 11 and up.

McNeal, Laura and Tom McNeal. *Crooked.*
Laurel Leaf, 2002.

Setting: New York City.
Main Characters: Female, Clara Wilson; Male, Amos MacKenzie; both 14 years old.

Clara has a crooked nose, a best friend who deserts her, and parents who argue all the time. Then her mother accepts a job in Spain, leaving Clara feeling abandoned and resentful. Amos MacKenzie has parents who embarrass him and keep secrets from him. He is attacked by the town bad boys, Charles and Eddie Tripp, then becomes lost and confused when his father unexpectedly dies. His relationship with Clara is his only consolation. Told from the alternating viewpoints of the two main characters. Grades: 6–10.

Plummer, Louise. *Unlikely Romance of Kate Bjorkman.*
Laurel Leaf, 1997.
Setting: 1990s.
Main Character: Female, Kate Bjorkman, 17 years old.

Kate narrates her tale of teen romance as a spoof of torrid bodice rippers. A six-foot-tall heroine with glasses as thick as Coke bottles and an I.Q. off the charts proves that true love awaits even the gawkiest, most socially inept teen. Written in chapters that alternate novel segments with Kate's revision notes. Grades: 7–10.

Schindler, Nina. *An Order of Amelie, Hold the Fries.*
Annick, 2004.
Setting: Canada.
Main Characters: Male, Tim, 18 years old; Female, Amelie, 19 years old.

Tim sees the girl of his dreams while walking down the street. When she drops a paper, he picks it up and writes a letter to the name and address on it, but it isn't the address of the girl he saw. Tim begins a letter-writing exchange with Amelie, and eventually he falls madly in love with her. Amelie is at first annoyed, but after his dogged pursuit, her feelings for him begin to grow, and she is faced with the dilemma of choosing between her long-term boyfriend and Tim. Letters, text messages, take-out menus, postcards, black-and-white photos, collages, and graphics tell the story. Grades: 7 and up.

Spinelli, Jerry. *Stargirl.*
Knopf, 2000.
Setting: Mica, Arizona.
Main Characters: Male, Leo Borlock, 16 years old; Female, Stargirl Caraway, 15 years old.

Stargirl wears pioneer dresses and kimonos to school, strums a ukulele in the cafeteria, laughs when there are no jokes, and dances when there is no music. The student body is helpless to resist Stargirl's wide-eyed charm, pure-spirited friendliness, and penchant for celebrating the achievements of others; she is even recruited as a cheerleader. Popularity is fickle, but Stargirl seems impervious to the shunning, while Leo Borlock, who is in love with Stargirl, is not made of such strong stuff. Awards: CC. Grades: 5–9.

Young, Cathy, editor. *One Hot Second: Stories about Desire.*
Knopf, 2002.

Eleven stories about teens and their cravings. Some are humorous, some haunting. Authors include Sarah Dessen, Victor Martinez, Jacqueline Woodson,

THE TEEN READER'S ADVISOR

Jennifer Armstrong, Norma Fox Mazer, Rich Wallace, Ellen Wittlinger, Nancy Garden, Rachel Vail, Emma Donoghue, and Angela Johnson. Grades: 7 and up.

Young, Karen Romano. *The Beetle and Me—A Love Story.*
Greenwillow, 1999.
Setting: 1990s.
Main Character: Female, Daisy Pandolfi, turning 16 years old.
　　Daisy wants to restore her father's abandoned 1957 Volkswagen and claim it as her own before her sixteenth birthday. She is interested in a new boy in town, but her beautiful cousin captures his attention. Daisy focuses on the car, but it seems an impossible goal. While working backstage during a school play, Daisy is surprised by a kiss delivered by a fellow stage-crew member, Billy, who drives a neat Thunderbird, but she's grossed out. Grades: 6–10.

Gay Guys

Bauer, Marion Dane, editor. *Am I Blue? Coming Out from the Silence.*
HarperCollins, 1994.
　　Original short stories depicting both gay teens and teens living with gay parents, friends, and teachers, with subjects ranging from first love to coming out, self-discovery to homophobia, delivering a message of tolerance and acceptance. Includes stories by C.S. Adler, Bauer, Francesca Lia Block, Bruce Coville, Nancy Garden, James Cross Giblin, Ellen Howard, M.E. Kerr, Jonathan London, Lois Lowry, Gregory Maguire, Leslea Newman, Cristina Salat, William Sleator, Jacqueline Woodson, and Jane Yolen. Awards: CC. Grades: 7 and up.

Cart, Michael. *My Father's Scar.*
St. Martin's Griffin, 1998.
Setting: Homophobic community.
Main Character: Male, Andy Logan, college freshman, 18 years old.
　　Andy recalls his childhood and teen years, when he was isolated from both family and peers by his weight, his intellect, and his love for books. He discovers running and conquers the weight problem, but Andy can't go public about his homosexuality; he knows he'll never please his bullying, alcoholic father. Awards: CC. Grades: 7 and up.

Ferris, Jean. *Eight Seconds.*
Harcourt, 2000.
Setting: Rodeo school.
Main Character: Male, John Ritchie, 17 years old.
　　Between his junior and senior years in high school, John and his best friend spend a week at rodeo school. He is intensely interested in Kit and learns that Kit is gay. They meet from time to time during the summer, and by summer's end, John realizes that he is gay as well. Grades: 9 and up.

Fox, Paula. *Eagle Kite.*
Orchard, 1995.
Setting: Seaside cottage.

Main Character: Male, Liam, freshman, 14 years old.

Liam learns that his father is dying of AIDS. Suddenly, his comfortable family is in pieces, and his father has gone to live in a seashore cottage two hours from the family's city apartment. Liam remembers having seen his father embrace a young man years before. Liam and his parents wrestle with truths that encompass not just disappointment and betrayal, but intense love. Awards: CC. Grades: 8–12.

Hartinger, Brent. *Geography Club.*
HarperTempest, 2003.
Setting: Goodkind High School, 2000s.
Main Character: Male, Russel Middlebrook, 15 years old.

Russel and his gay friends set up the Geography Club to have a place to discuss their lives in openness and honesty. Peer pressure takes its toll, but the club becomes the Goodkind High School Gay-Straight-Bisexual Alliance. Occasional profanity. Grades: 7–12.

Howe, James. *The Misfits.*
Atheneum, 2001.
Setting: Paintbrush Falls Middle School.
Main Characters: Male, Bobby Goodspeed; Female, Addie; Male, Skeezie; Male, Joe, all 12 years old.

Four outcast friends form the Gang of Five and decide to run for student council on a platform promising to end name calling. One of the friends is comfortable being gay. Awards: CC. Grades: 5–9.

Jenkins, A. M. *Breaking Boxes.*
Delacorte, 1997.
Setting: 1990s.
Main Character: Male, Charlie Calmont, 16 years old.

Charlie is a loner, but he gets by with his older brother, Trent, since both of their parents are gone. Charlie gets suspended for fighting with guys at school who care more about the kind of shoes he wears than who Charlie is on the inside. He then befriends Chase, one of the guys who tried to beat him up. Explicit language and sex. Awards: CC. Grades: 9 and up.

Kerr, M. E. *"Hello," I Lied.*
HarperCollins, 1997.
Setting: 1990s.
Main Character: Male, Lang Penner, 17 years old.

Lang is a happily adjusted gay teen who is engaged in a loving relationship with Alex, a 20-year-old actor. Then Lang becomes emotionally involved with Huguette, the French daughter of a famous deceased rock star. Grades: 7 and up.

Koertge, Ron. *The Arizona Kid.*
Joy Street, 1988.
Setting: Arizona.
Main Character: Male, Billy, 16 years old.

Billy thinks he's too short, too pale, too wimpy, and too tentative to make a place for himself in a world that is taller, tanner, and classier. When he spends a summer in Arizona living with his uncle and working with racehorses, he finds a wonderful girl who thinks he's terrific and a job that he discovers he's really good at. Billy's Uncle Wes is gay, and Billy's father has sent him to a man whose own battle with life has given him a strength to guide and help a nephew in need of a little strength himself. Grades: 9 up.

Levithan, David. **Boy Meets Boy.**
Knopf, 2003.
Setting: Contemporary.
Main Character: Male, Paul, sophomore, 15 years old.
    Paul has both gay and straight friends and they all hang out together at terrific bookstores and concerts, advising one another on the sometimes troubled progress of their romances. A gay utopia with quirky characters. Grades: 7 and up.

Levithan, David. **The Realm of Possibility.**
Knopf, 2004.
Setting: High school.
    Twenty teens take turns pouring out their hearts in free verse, each chapter presenting four points of view that weave together to form a view of the school community. Grades: 9 and up.

Malloy, Brian. **The Year of Ice.**
St. Martin's Griffin, 2003.
Setting: Minneapolis, Minnesota, 1978.
Main Characters: Male, Kevin Doyle, 17 years old; Male, Patrick Doyle, 40+ years old.
    Kevin is head over heels in love with classmate Jon Thompson, who is oblivious to Kevin's interest. He learns that the accident that killed his mother two years before was most likely an act of suicide. Kevin's knowledge leads him to a showdown with his father. Awards: Alex. Grades: YA/A.

Saenz, Benjamin Alire. **Sammy and Juliana in Hollywood.**
Cinco Puntas Pr., 2004.
Setting: Late 1960s, Las Cruces, New Mexico, in a Mexican American barrio.
Main Character: Male, Sammy Santos, 17 years old.
    Sammy comes to grips with the death of his first love, Juliana, and the demands and needs of his friends, family, and neighbors. Among Sammy's friends are two boys who meet first with violence and then banishment from the community when they are caught together in a romantic moment. Expletives appear throughout, as do large helpings of Spanish. Grades: 9 and up.

Sanchez, Alex. **Rainbow Boys.**
Simon Pulse, 2003.
Setting: Walt Whitman High School.
Main Characters: Male, Nelson Glassman; Male, Kyle Meeks; Male, Jason; all 17 years old.
    Nelson, openly gay, is secretly in love with his best friend Kyle. Kyle is secretly in love with Jason, a popular jock who has a popular girlfriend but who can't stop dreaming of sex with boys. When Jason, trying to sort out his confusion, shows up at

a Rainbow Youth meeting, he is greeted by both "Nelly" and Kyle, who are as shocked to see him as he is to be seen. Awards: CC. Grades: 9 and up.

Steinhofel, Andreas. *The Center of the World.*
Delacorte, 2003.
Setting: Germany.
Main Characters: Male, Phil; Female, Dianne; both 17 years old.

Phil and Dianne, brother and sister, live at Visible, a decrepit Gothic mansion in a tiny, provincial German town. Their mother, Glass, is unwed, promiscuous, and self-involved, and she doesn't care what anyone thinks of her or her children. Dianne is withdrawn and secretive, and communicates better with animals than with people. Unapologetically gay, Phil is too passive to approach gorgeous Nicholas, so he's thrilled when the other boy takes the lead. They meet often for wordless sex, but Phil craves intimacy. When he includes his feisty friend, Katja, in their encounters, jealousy and betrayal ensue. Grades: 9 and up.

Summer, Jane, editor. *Not the Only One: Gay and Lesbian Fiction for Teens.*
Alyson. 2004.

Twenty short stories with elemental coming-of-age themes, such as leaving home, falling in love, and confronting secrets. Includes stories by Angela Brown, Bonnie Shimko, Pam McArthur, Michael Thomas Ford, Claire McNab, Malka Drucker, Laurel Winter, Judith P. Stelboum, Christina Chiu, Brian Sloan, Judd Powell, Jane Summer, Nan Prener, Lesléa Newman, Gregory Maguire, Donna Allegra, Brent Hartinger, Melanie Braverman, William Moses, Stephen Greco. Grades: 7–12.

Taylor, William, *The Blue Lawn.*
Alyson, 1999.
Setting: New Zealand.
Main Character: Male, David Mason, 15 years old.

From the moment David sees Theo Meyer, the new guy who smokes, drinks, and drives fast, David is drawn to him. David soon becomes a regular at Theo's house, where he meets the boy's grandmother, Gretel, a Holocaust survivor. As David and Theo's friendship grows, both teens are aware of its sexual energy. When Gretel discovers the teens together, she separates them, and their friendship is suspended. Originally published in New Zealand. Grades: 9 and up.

Wersba, Barbara. *Whistle Me Home.*
Henry Holt, 1997.
Setting: Sag Harbor, Long Island, New York.
Main Character: Female, Noli, 17 years old.

Noli fell in love with TJ and he seemed to fall in love with her, but then she discovered that he was gay. TJ tries to tell Noli that he loves her, which he does in his own way. Noli screams, "Do not use that word to me! You dirty faggot," and then wonders what she's done. Awards: CC. Grades: 9 and up.

Wieler, Diana. *Bad Boy.*
Groundwood, 1997.
Setting: Canada.

Main Character: Male, A.J. Brandiosa, 16 years old.

A.J. and his best friend, Tulsa Brown, are selected for the high school ice hockey team. A. J. becomes an "enforcer," someone whose main job is to make cheap, violent hits against opposing players. Then he discovers that Tulsa is gay and his secret crush on Tulsa's sister becomes public just as his friendship with Tulsa deteriorates. His father then brings home a female friend who is closer in age to A.J. Fast-paced hockey action. Grades: 8–12.

Wittlinger, Ellen. **What's in a Name?**
Simon & Schuster, 2000.
Setting: Scrub Harbor.

The ongoing debate about which name is best for the town, Scrub Harbor or Folly Bay, is the catalyst for a group of ten teens to find out who they really are. One boy faces the fact that he is gay and chooses to "come out" via a poem published in the school literary magazine, while his football-star jock older brother is forced to deal with being linked to his brother. Each chapter is narrated by one of the teens. Awards: CC. Grades: 7 and up.

Yates, Bart. **Leave Myself Behind.**
Kensington, 2003.
Setting: New Hampshire.
Main Character: Male, Noah York, 17 years old.

After his father dies, Noah, a closeted gay teenager, relocates with his mother to a small New Hampshire town. The crumbling house they try to renovate reveals dark secrets in its walls. Letters, poems, and journal entries reconstruct a history of pain and violence. Rape and other physical violence, alcoholism, and incest are described in brutal detail that may leave some readers uncomfortable. Awards: Alex. Grades: YA/A.

LESBIAN GIRLS

Boock, Paula. **Dare, Truth, or Promise.**
Houghton Mifflin, 1999.
Setting: New Zealand.
Main Characters: Female, Louie Angelo; Female, Willa; both 17 years old.

Louie is the talented daughter of wealthy and cultured parents, and Willa is a strong-minded redhead who lives over the pub. They meet working at Burger Giant, and are soon frantically in love. Louie's mother banishes Willa after discovering them in an embrace, and Willa is threatened by hostile anonymous notes. In confusion and pain, they avoid each other. With the support of her mother, Willa gains the strength to wait it out, but a psychologist tells Louie that her feelings are a passing phase. Grades: 11 and up.

Donoghue, Emma. **Kissing the Witch: Old Tales in New Skins.**
HarperTrophy, 1999.

Thirteen retellings of fairy tales with a feminist and lesbian point of view. Awards: CC. Grades: 7 and up.

Gantos, Jack. **Desire Lines.**
Farrar, Straus & Giroux, 1997.

Setting: Florida.
Main Character: Male, Walker, teenager.

Walker is openly disdainful of Christian zealots who cruise around his high school in a panel truck with speakers mounted on top, broadcasting their judgment of homosexuals and other "sinners." Angry at being rebuffed, Preacher Boy queer-baits Walker, who's actually straight. For a while Walker resists the temptation to reveal two girls from school who use his favorite pond for romantic trysts. When he finally outs them, the lovers try to commit suicide together, and one of them dies. Awards: CC. Grades: 8 and up.

Garden, Nancy. **Annie on My Mind.**
Farrar, Straus & Giroux, 1992.
Setting: New York City.
Main Characters: Female, Liza, teenager; Female, Annie, teenager.

In the first lesbian romance with a happy ending, Liza and Annie fall in love with each other in a bittersweet love story. Awards: CC; Margaret Edwards. Grades: 9 and up.

Garden, Nancy. **Good Moon Rising.**
Farrar, Straus & Giroux, 1996.
Setting: High school.
Main Character: Female, Jan, senior, 17 years old.

Jan is back from summer stock and hoping for the role of Elizabeth in the school production of *The Crucible.* Kerry gets the part, and Mrs. Nicholson assigns Jan to be stage manager instead. Jan becomes the stand-in director and coaches Kerry when Mrs. Nicholson falls ill. The two soon realize that they are sexually attracted to each other, and other cast members notice, too. Grades: 8 and up.

Garden, Nancy. **The Year They Burned the Books.**
Farrar, Straus & Giroux, 1999.
Setting: New England.
Main Character: Female, Jamie Crawford, 17 years old.

Jamie is the editor in chief of her small New England high school's paper. She is fairly sure she is gay, and when Tessa Gillespie, a new girl from Boston, shows up wearing a red cape and a star-shaped stud in her nose, Jamie starts falling in love. Fundamentalist Mrs. Buel, a "stealth candidate" during her campaign for a seat on the school committee, leads the committee to set aside the new sex education curriculum and stages a book burning on Halloween. The liberal faculty adviser to the school paper is put on leave, and Jamie is forbidden to write on controversial subjects in her editorials. Jamie and her staff publish an underground paper. Grades: 7 and up.

Johnson, Maureen. **The Bermudez Triangle.**
Razorbill, 2005.
Setting: Stanford University/ Saratoga Springs, New York.
Main Character: Female, Nina, 17 years old.

During the summer before their senior year in high school, Nina is separated from her friends Avery and Mel and attends a workshop at Stanford. Nina falls head over heels for Steve, who has grown up in a commune on the West Coast. Upon her return to New York, she senses that Mel and Avery are keeping secrets, and soon discovers that they have become lovers. Grades: 9 and up.

Kerr, M. E. *Deliver Us from Evie.*
HarperTrophy, 1995.
Setting: Missouri.
Main Character: Female, Evie Burrman, 17 years old.

A skilled mechanic and farmer on her family's Missouri spread, Evie is warding off the assumption that she'll marry Cord Whittle and help Dad keep the farm going. Evie is falling in love, not with Cord, but with the daughter of the man who holds the mortgage on their farm. Told by Evie's brother, Parr. Awards: CC. Grades: 9 and up.

Myracle, Lauren. *Kissing Kate.*
Puffin, 2004.
Setting: High school.
Main Character: Female, Lissa, 16 years old.

Lissa kisses Kate, her best friend since seventh grade, after they get drunk at a party. Since then, Kate has been cold to her, and Lissa is hurt and confused; she wants to talk about it. Grades: 9 and up.

Peters, Julie Anne. *Far from Xanadu.*
Megan Tingley, 2005.
Setting: Coalton, Kansas.
Main Character: Female, Mike (Mary-Elizabeth) Szabo, 16 years old.

Mike's alcoholic father committed suicide, her obese mother has given up on life, and her no-good brother has driven the family plumbing business into the ground. Then Mike falls deeply in love with straight bad-girl Xanadu, who has been sent to live with her aunt and uncle after getting into serious trouble dealing drugs. Grades: 10 and up.

Peters, Julie Ann. *Keeping You a Secret.*
Megan Tingley, 2003.
Setting: High school.
Main Character: Female, Holland Jaeger, 17 years old.

Holland goes steady with a good-looking boy and contemplates attending an Ivy League college in the fall. When she meets out-and-proud lesbian Cece Goddard, her life changes. Soon the two begin an affair that eventually leads to a committed relationship. Holland loses old friends, encounters vicious discrimination, and is thrown out of the house by her hysterical mother. Grades: 9 and up.

Ryan, Sara. *Empress of the World.*
Viking, 2001.
Setting: Summer school, 1990s
Main Character: Female, Nicola, teenager.

Nicola goes away to a summer program for gifted students, expecting to explore her interest in archaeology while also continuing her artwork. On the very first day, she is attracted to another girl, but she refuses to be labeled as a lesbian because she thinks she's also attracted to boys. Awards: CC. Grades: 9 and up.

Watts, Julia. *Finding H.F.: A Novel.*
Alyson, 2001.

Setting: Morgan, Kentucky.
Main Characters: Female, Heavenly Faith Simms, 16 years old; Male, Bo, 16 years old.

Abandoned by her mother and raised by her loving but religious grandmother, H.F. has never felt like she belonged anywhere. After she finds her mother's address in a drawer, H.F. and her gay best friend, Bo, head south to Florida in Bo's scrap-heap Escort. Their journey awakens both teens to the realization that there is a life waiting for them that is very different from what they have known when they find a loving gay community. Grades: YA/A.

Wittlinger, Ellen. *Hard Love.*
Simon & Schuster, 1999.
Setting: Boston, Massachusetts, 1990s.
Main Characters: Male, John Galardi, 16 years old; Female, Marisol Guzman, teenager.

John and Marisol share a love of 'zines, each having created their own as a medium for expressing themselves. John falls in love with Marisol, and Marisol loves John, but not the same way. Marisol is a lesbian and has no idea how to let John down gently without losing her new best friend. Awards: CC; Printz Honor. Grades: 7 and up.

Woodson, Jacqueline. *From the Notebooks of Melanin Sun.*
Scholastic, 1995.
Setting: Brooklyn, New York.
Main Character: Male, Melanin Sun, 14 years old.

Melanin has a lot to say—not out loud, but in the notebooks he keeps. His mother, a law student who sometimes acts more like a best friend, tells him she's in love with a woman, and a white one, at that. Excerpts from his notebook are alternated with first-person descriptions. Grades: 7–11.

Woodson, Jacqueline. *The House You Pass on the Way.*
Puffin, 2003.
Setting: The South.
Main Character: Female, Staggerlee Canan, 14 years old.

Staggerlee is shunned by her peers because her mother is white. She also has a secret from sixth grade, when she kissed another girl. Rejected by that friend, Staggerlee has no one to talk to about her sexual feelings until her adopted cousin, Trout, visits for the summer, and both wonder if they are gay. Grades: 6–9.

UNPLANNED PREGNANCY/ABORTION

Calvert, Patricia. *Stranger You and I.*
Scribner's, 1987.
Setting: 1980s.
Main Character: Male, Hughie McBride, 17 years old.

Sandwiched in age between twin sisters and a "surprise" younger brother, Hughie feels invisible. Zee, his childhood friend and confidante, announces that she is pregnant by Jordie, boyfriend of Melissa, on whom Hughie has a crush. Hughie sees Zee through her pregnancy and his mom through a midlife crisis. Grades: 7–10.

Cole, Sheila. *What Kind of Love? The Diary of a Pregnant Teenager.*
Lothrop, Lee & Shepard Books, c1995.
Setting: 1990s.
Main Character: Female, Valerie Larch, 15 years old.

   Valerie is pregnant. By the time she visits Planned Parenthood, an abortion is
not an easy option. Both sets of parents are against her marrying Peter, who is sent to
live with his father in Santa Barbara. This is a six-month excerpt from Valerie's diary,
reflecting her thoughts and feelings about her pregnancy. Grades: 8 and up.

Dessen, Sarah. *Someone Like You.*
Viking, 1998.
Setting: 1990s.
Main Characters: Female, Halley; Female, Scarlett, 16 years old.

   Halley and Scarlett have been best friends since grade school. Growing up like
sisters, they've shared everything except a bedroom, until boys step into their lives.
Scarlett's romance the summer before her junior year has serious consequences, when
her boyfriend Michael dies in a motorcycle accident and she's left carrying his child.
Halley's close relationship with her psychologist mother is fractured as the girl's
friendship with secretive, irresponsible Macon Faulkner deepens into romance.
Awards: CC. Grades: 7 and up.

Doherty, Berlie. *Dear Nobody.*
HarperTrophy, 1994.
Setting: England, 1990s.
Main Characters: Female, Helen, teen; Male, Chris, 18 years old.

   Helen and Chris face the consequences of one night's unprotected passion that
changes the course of their lives forever. Chris wants to get married, and Helen's
mother wants her to have an abortion, as teen parenthood changes college plans.
Helen tells her feelings to the baby in letters addressed to Dear Nobody. At the
abortion clinic, Helen can't go through with it, and comes home to have and keep her
baby. Awards: CC; Carnegie. Grades: 7–10.

Feinberg, Anna. *Borrowed Light.*
Laurel Leaf, 2002.
Setting: Australia.
Main Character: Female, Callisto May, 16 years old.

   When Callisto May discovers she's pregnant, her surfer boyfriend wants no part
of fatherhood. Her dysfunctional family is unavailable. Her "spiritualist" mother is
distant to her children. Her father deals in African art and barely acknowledges his
family, even when he is at home. Even her grandmother, a world-renowned astronomer and Callisto's intellectual mentor, is unavailable. Callisto considers an abortion.
Grades: 9 and up.

Hobbs, Valerie. *Get It While It's Hot: Or Not.*
HarperTrophy, 1998.
Setting: 1990s.
Main Characters: Female, Megan, junior; Female, Kit, 16 years old.

   Kit announces her pregnancy and toxemia to her three best friends, and they work out a rotation plan of caring for her, since her mother is rarely home. Megan, an aspiring journalist, explores attitudes about birth control, abortion, teen pregnancy, parenting, and STDs for the school newspaper. A wealthy yuppie couple offer material comforts in exchange for the baby, until the teen father is diagnosed as HIV-positive. School authorities squelch Megan's article. Kit's emergency delivery motivates everyone into action, including her mother, who plans to sell her bar and open a baby clothing store. Grades: 7–10.

Hrdlitschka, Shelley. *Dancing Naked: A Novel.*
Orca, 2001.
Setting: Canada.
Main Character: Female, Kia, 16 years old.
　　Kia is pregnant. She must confront not only her own fears but also the feelings of her parents and her friends from her church youth group. Her boyfriend wants her to have an abortion, but she doesn't want to end a life. She struggles with the decision of whether to keep the baby or to choose loving parents who can give the infant a life it deserves. Awards: CC. Grades: 8–12.

Kaye, Geraldine. *Someone Else's Baby.*
Hyperion, 1992.
Setting: 1990s.
Main Character: Female, Terry, 17 years old.
　　Terry got pregnant by an unknown assailant while in a drunken daze at a party. Her journal chronicles her indecision about keeping the baby or giving it up. Her feelings toward her unborn child change from indifference to love. Grades: 9 and up.

Pennebaker, Ruth. *Don't Think Twice.*
Henry Holt, 2001.
Setting: 1967.
Main Character: Female, Anne Harper, 17 years old.
　　Anne is forced to enter a home for pregnant teens by her parents. The woman in charge, Mrs. Landing, insists that Anne attend group meetings. The teen girls express anger, resentment, loneliness, confusion, longing, and love as they face the hard facts of life and try to learn from one another's experiences. Awards: CC. Grades: 7 and up.

Rodowsky, Colby. *Lucy Peale.*
Farrar, Straus & Giroux, 1994.
Setting: Maryland.
Main Character: Female, Lucy Peale, 17 years old.
　　Lucy is pregnant by a boy who raped her when he saw her handing out her father's religious pamphlets in Ocean City, Maryland. Now she is cruelly rejected by her preacher father and taken in by Jake, who has dropped out of college in order to write. Lucy gets a job and shares the rent; the two become close friends who talk, help each other, and fall in love, planning to marry and raise the baby together. Grades: 7 and up.

Williams-Garcia, Rita. *Like Sisters on the Homefront.*
Lodestar, 1995.

Setting: Chicago, Illinois, 1930s.
Main Character: Female, Gayle, 14 years old.

Gayle is sent south to live with relatives she doesn't know and doesn't particularly like when she becomes pregnant for a second time. Sullen and angry, she
gradually gets to know her great-grandmother, her aunt and uncle, and her cousin,
and discovers the importance of family and friendship. Awards: CC; Coretta Scott
King Honor; Notable Books for a Global Society. Grades: 7–10.

Woodson, Jacqueline. **The Dear One.**
Dell, 1993.
Setting: New York City suburb.
Main Character: Female, Feni, 12 years old.

Feni has to adjust to sharing her room with pregnant 15-year-old Rebecca, who
has come from Harlem to stay. Feni is determined to dislike Rebecca, until she realizes
that her toughness is just a facade that hides a strong, nurturing young woman.
When Rebecca's baby is born and she prepares to leave, Feni faces losing her new
friend. African American characters. Grades: 7–12.

RESOURCES: ADDITIONAL TITLES

Bouricius, Ann. 2000. **The Romance Reader's Advisory: The Librarian's
    Guide to Love in the Stacks.** Chicago, IL American Library Association.
Carpan, Carolyn. 2004. **Rocked by Romance: A Guide to Teen Romance
    Fiction.** Westport, CT: Libraries Unlimited.
Cart, Michael, and Christine A. Jenkins. 2005. **Gay and Lesbian Fiction for
    Young Adults.** Lanham, MD: Scarecrow Press.
Day, Frances Ann. 2000. **Lesbian and Gay Voices: An Annotated Bibliogra-
    phy and Guide to Literature for Children and Young Adults.**
    Westport, CT: Greenwood Press.

CHAPTER 15

MENTAL ILLNESS AND PHYSICAL DISABILITY

"Issues" or "problem novels," whatever you want to call them, deal with the situations teens face in real life. Why would a teen want to read about these topics, which are anything but pretty? The teen characters in novels actually expand a teen's peer group, so a teen reader can learn vicariously about teens, whether like themselves or like their friends, who are learning to cope in less than perfect circumstances. The emotions involved are safer to experience vicariously, as well. Many readers have . . . enjoyed? . . . sobbing over a particularly tragic situation or character, and then cheering when he or she comes through it all a stronger person.

Alcohol Abuse/Addiction—Parents
Alcohol Abuse/Addiction—Teens
Anger
Autism
Body Image/Eating Disorders
Drug Abuse/Addiction
Female Circumcision
Mental Illness
Physical Disabilities
Physical Illness—AIDS
Physical Illness—Cancer
Physical Illness—Miscellaneous

ALCOHOL ABUSE/ADDICTION—PARENTS

Brooks, Kevin. *Martyn Pig.*
Push, 2003.
Setting: England.
Main Character: Male, Martyn Pig, 15 years old.

Martyn's mother left years ago, and his father is an abusive alcoholic. When Martyn yells at his drunken father, who is coming at his son with his fist raised, his father stumbles, falls, hits his head on the fireplace wall, and dies. Martyn decides not to notify the police, and with the help of his friend Alex, he sews his father and some rocks into a sleeping bag and pitches him into a quarry. There are gripping plot twists and turns, and the bleakness is tempered by some tongue-in-cheek zany humor. Grades: 8 and up.

Carter, Alden R. *Up Country.*
Puffin Books, 2004.
Setting: Milwaukee and Blind River, 1980s.
Main Character: Male, Carl, 16 years old.

Carl knows he's playing with fire every time he fixes up a stolen car stereo to resell. He needs the money to get away from his boozing mom and her endless parade of men. One night his mother is arrested, and Carl is sent to live with an aunt in a small town, where Carl is faced with a decision: run away and stick with The Plan, or come up with a new one. Grades: 8 and up.

Covington, Dennis. *Lasso the Moon.*
Bantam Doubleday Dell, 1996.
Setting: St. Simon Island, Georgia.
Main Character: Female, April, 17 years old.

April is curious about her father's new patient, Fernando, an illegal alien from El Salvador, and soon her curiosity turns to fascination, then love for the young man, who has a frightening past. When Immigration and Naturalization Service officials begin snooping around and threatening her father for helping Fernando, she discovers a whole new side to her father. Grades: 8 and up.

Dean, Carolee. *Comfort.*
Houghton Mifflin, 2002.
Setting: Comfort, Texas.
Main Character: Male, Kenny Roy Willson, 14 years old.

Kenny applies for a hardship driver's license because his mother needs Kenny to drive his father, soon to be released from the penitentiary, to AA meetings. His father had twenty-three DWI arrests before he robbed the liquor store. Kenny is a good kid, talented in band and football, and a gifted writer, but his mother plans for him to quit school at 16 and support her dream for her husband to become a country-and-western singer. Grades: 7–10.

Deaver, Julie Reece. *Chicago Blues.*
HarperCollins, 1995.
Setting: Chicago, Illinois.
Main Character: Female, Marnie, 11 years old.

Marnie is forced to move in with her 17-year-old sister, an art student, when alcoholism overwhelms their mother. The two girls learn to live together and depend on one another, but then Mom wants Marnie back when her drinking is under control. Grades: 6–9.

Fox, Paula. *The Moonlight Man.*
Aladdin, 2003.
Setting: Nova Scotia.
Main Character: Female, Catherine Ames, 15 years old.

Catherine vacations in a cottage in Nova Scotia with a father whom she barely knows, an alcoholic and a failed writer. Catherine is filled with denial, anger, fear, loneliness, exhaustion, disgust, pity, grief, and sympathy for her father's cycle of bingeing, blaming, unreasonable demands, apologies, reforms, and relapses. Grades: 6–10.

Koja, Kathe. *The Blue Mirror.*
Farrar, Straus & Giroux, 2004.
Setting: Blue Mirror coffeehouse.
Main Character: Female, Maggy, 16 years old.

Maggy, a gifted artist, keeps a sketchbook called "The Blue Mirror," which shares its name with the coffeehouse where she regularly sips a cappuccino for hours and draws what she sees. She meets Cole, an attractive "skwatter," who makes Maggy feel as if she has finally met someone who understands her. She soon learns that Cole is no Prince Charming, and she must find the strength to escape from his clutches. Her alcoholic mother spends the days passed out on the couch. Grades: 9 and up.

Hogan, Mary. *The Serious Kiss.*
HarperCollins, 2005.
Setting: San Fernando Valley, California.
Main Character: Female, Libby Madrigal, 14 years old.

Libby's family: older brother, Rif, smokes on the sly; little brother, Dirk, drools; her mom is loud, fat, and relentlessly cheerful; their ancient Chihuahua yips constantly and poops in front of boys Libby likes; and her dad is an abusive alcoholic, whose disease is tearing their family apart. Libby voices her despair and anger as her father's many failures force the family to move, to get counseling, and to begin the road back to some sort of functionality. Grades: 7–10.

Martinez, Victor. *Parrot in the Oven: Mi Vida.*
Joanna Cotler, 1996.
Setting: California barrio.
Main Character: Male, Manuel Hernandez, 14 years old.

Manny has compassion and love for the unstable people around him. He picks up his alcoholic and violent father from the local pool hall and withstands the ethnic slurs of white schoolmates. Manny begins to understand the sense of self that he derives from his role within this dysfunctional family. Awards: CC; National Book Award. Grades. 12 and up.

Moore, Peter. *Blind Sighted.*
Viking, 2002.
Setting: New Jersey.
Main Character: Male, Kirk Tobak, 16 years old.

Kirk is a brilliant, undersize underachiever. His uneventful life in small-town New Jersey includes playing parent to his alcoholic mother, blowing off school, and shelving books in the library he loves. Kirk is involuntarily hired to read to a blind woman. Just as life looks hopeful, his mother takes off to California. Grades: 9 and up.

Quarles, Heather. *A Door Near Here.*
Laurel Leaf, 2000.
Setting: Present day.
Main Character: Female, Katharine, 15 years old.

The mother of the four Donovan kids has taken to her bed with a bottle, stumbling out of her room only when in search of more vodka. Katharine tries to keep her brother and sisters clean and fed and in classes, but things are slipping out of her control. When a kindly teacher begins to ask questions, Katharine panics and lashes out with an accusation that could destroy this concerned man, but is met with an act of forgiveness. Awards: CC. Grades: 7 and up.

Saksena, Kate. *Hang On in There, Shelley.*
Bloomsbury USA, 2003.
Setting: South London.
Main Character: Female, Shelley Wright, 14 years old.
Shelley writes semimonthly letters to her idol, Ziggy, of the band Arctic 2000, in which she tells him her troubles. Her black father has left the family, and her white, unemployed mother, Liz, is plagued by alcoholic episodes during which she is sometimes abusive toward Shelley and her younger brother. Each chapter opens with lyrics from one of Ziggy's inspirational songs and ends with another of his encouraging postcards. Grades: 5–8.

Wilhelm, Doug. *Raising the Shades.*
Farrar, Straus & Giroux, 2001.
Setting: Present day.
Main Character: Male, Casey, 13 years old.
Casey has been taking care of his alcoholic father since his mother and sister moved out. When his aunt suggests an intervention, Casey begins to understand that his father's drinking problem is more than he can handle. Grades: 5 and up.

ALCOHOL ABUSE/ADDICTION—TEENS

Bunting, Eve. *A Sudden Silence.*
Fawcett, 1990.
Setting: California.
Main Character: Male, Jesse, teen.
Jesse's deaf younger brother, Bryan, was killed by a drunk hit-and-run driver. Ashamed of his attraction to Bryan's girlfriend, Chloe, Jesse works with her to search for the hit-and-run driver. Money is offered, posters are made, and people are questioned. Finding the drunken driver doesn't bring the expected redemption. Awards: CC. Grades: 9 and up.

Coburn, Jake. *LoveSick.*
Dutton, 2005.
Setting: Present day.
Main Characters: Male, Ted; Female: Erica; both 18 years old.
Ted is an alcoholic jock who lost his athletic scholarship after destroying his knee in a drunk-driving accident. Erica is a foul-mouthed, bulimic Park Avenue princess, whose wealthy father will do anything to cure her eating disorder, including bribing Ted to spy on Erica's eating habits by offering to replace his scholarship. Grades: 9–12.

Cormier, Robert. *We All Fall Down.*
Laurel Leaf, 1993.

Setting: Burnside, Wickburg.
Main Character: The Avenger.

Three teenage boys trash Karen Jerome's suburban home, beat her, and throw her down the stairs; now she lies in a coma. Her sister, Jane, unknowingly falls in love with one of the boys involved. An unseen witness, The Avenger, seeks revenge. Awards: CC. Grades: 8 and up.

Deaver, Julie Reece. *Say Goodnight, Gracie.*
HarperTrophy, 1989.
Setting: Chicago, Illinois.
Main Character: Female, Morgan, 17 years old.

Morgan and Jimmy have been inseparable friends since birth. When Jimmy is killed by a drunk driver, Morgan's pain seems unbearable. Morgan narrates the events leading up to the accident and following it. Awards: CC. Grades: 8–10.

Draper, Sharon M. *Tears of a Tiger.*
Atheneum, 1994.
Series: Hazelwood High Trilogy: *Forged by Fire; Darkness Before Dawn.*
Setting: Hazelwood High School.
Main Character: Male, Andy.

Andy, the drunk driver in an accident that killed his best friend, cannot bear his guilt or reach out for help. Counselors, coaches, friends, and family all fail him, as his disintegration builds to inevitable suicide. The story is told through English class assignments, including poetry; dialogs; police and newspaper reports; and letters. Awards: CC. Grades: 9 and up.

Fleischman, Paul. *Whirligig.*
Henry Holt, 1998.
Setting: Road trip.
Main Character: Male, Brent Bishop, 17 years old.

Brent suffers a very public rejection by the girl he's been lusting after. Drunk, furious from his humiliation, he tries to kill himself on the way home, but kills a lovely, talented, motivated high school senior instead. Brent's parents would like to minimize his sense of guilt and his punishment, but Brent is tormented. The court arranges a meeting with his victim's mother, who asks Brent to make four whirligigs that look like Lea and set them up in Washington, California, Florida, and Maine. Awards: CC. Grades: 7–12.

Keizer, Garret. *God of Beer.*
HarperCollins, 2002.
Setting: Vermont.
Main Character: Male, Kyle, 17 years old.

Kyle and his friends, "Quaker" Oats and Diana, form a social protest against drinking. During a party, newcomer Condor gets drunk and sober, Diana is killed while driving him home. Grades: 8 and up.

Leitch, Will. *Catch.*
Razorbill, 2005.

Setting: Mattoon, Illinois, 2000s.
Main Characters: Male, Tim Temples, 18 years old; Female, Helena, 22 years old.

During the summer between his high school graduation and leaving for state college, Tim works and drinks hard and watches his older brother, a former baseball star like their father, degenerate socially and physically for no obvious reason. Tim spends daytimes working in a food packaging plant, hauling boxes, and noticing that his old high school friends are quickly fading into the old men who staff the plant year-round. Tim realizes that he is different from most of his friends, most of his family, and most of the town. Grades: 10 and up.

McCormick, Patricia. *My Brother's Keeper.*
Hyperion, 2004.
Setting: 2000s.
Main Characters: Male, Toby Malone, 13 years old; Male, Jake Malone, older brother.

Toby's father has left the family and his mother is struggling to make ends meet. His older brother, Jake, is using drugs and alcohol, and his younger brother, Eli, is confused by all of the sudden changes. Toby cleans up after Jake when he is sick, hides bills from his mom, feeds Eli whatever he can find in the refrigerator, and signs his own permission slips for school. Then a policeman brings Eli home, injured from a bike accident, while another officer brings Jake home from a car accident involving drugs and alcohol. Grades: 7–10.

Murray, Jaye. *Bottled Up: A Novel.*
Dial, 2003.
Setting: Present day.
Main Character: Male, Pip, 16 years old.

Either Pip stops skipping classes and begins seeing a counselor after school or he's expelled. Pip is more afraid the principal might call his father, who he's been trying to avoid thinking about by getting high. Now he has to decide if he will be like his father or if he will invent his own future. Grades: 7 and up.

Sullivan, Mark J. II. *Jonah Sees Ghosts.*
Akashic, 2003.
Setting: 1990s.
Main Character: Male, Jonah Hart, 15 years old.

Jonah's alcoholic father died on his sixth birthday. At 15, Jonah has started to see ghosts everywhere. Neither he nor his mother has dealt with the loss of his father. Jonah retreats more into himself, until he finds himself escaping through his dreams. Grades: 9 and up.

Wersba, Barbara. *Whistle Me Home.*
Henry Holt, 1997.
Setting: Sag Harbor, Long Island, New York.
Main Character: Female, Noli, 17 years old.

Noli is insecure and has a drinking problem; she is startled that a boy as wonderful as T.J. could be attracted to her. T.J. wants a girl who is thin and boyish-looking, and when Noli finally figures out why, she is shocked and devastated. Awards: CC. Grades: 9–12.

Atkins, Catherine. *Alt Ed.*
Putnam, 2003.
Setting: Wayne High School.
Main Character: Female, Susan Callaway, sophomore, 15 years old.

    Susan is overweight and painfully self-conscious. She suspects her longtime nemesis, Kale Krasner, is behind the harassing phone calls she's been getting. She makes friends with a fellow outcast, gay Brendan Slater, and they vandalize Kale's pickup truck. They enter a new twelve-week, after-school group designed as an alternative to expulsion. The teens begin to talk in frank, argumentative, and sometimes rude discussions, but with the counselor's guidance, they gradually build respect and understanding for each other. Grades: 8 and up.

Davis, Terry. *If Rock and Roll Were a Machine.*
Eastern Washington University Press, 2003.
Setting: Present day.
Main Character: Male, Bert Bowden, 16 years old.

    Bert reveals his inner feelings, challenges, and relationships in poetic and powerful journal entries. From the purchase of his first motorcycle and the freedom it represents, to his job working at Shepard's garage and visits to his grandfather in a nursing home, Bert learns what it takes to make it in life and to like himself. Awards: CC. Grades: 9–12.

Flinn, Alexandra. *Breathing Underwater.*
HarperCollins, 2001.
Setting: Present day.
Main Character: Male, Nick, 16 years old.

    After beating his girlfriend, Caitlin, Nick is ordered by the court to attend Mario Ortega's family violence classes and write a journal to explain what happened in his relationship. Grades: 8 and up.

Lynch, Chris. *Who the Man.*
HarperCollins, 2002.
Setting: Present day.
Main Character: Male, Earl Pryor, 13 years old.

    Earl is bigger and physically more mature than the other kids in his school, and is egged on by his father to use violence to handle conflicts. Earl is suspended from school for a week for fighting, and he feels confused and angry. Grades: 5–8.

Mikaelsen, Ben. *Touching Spirit Bear.*
HarperCollins, 2001.
Setting: Alaska.
Main Character: Male, Cole Matthews, 15 years old.

    Cole is a violent teen offender convicted of viciously beating a classmate, Peter, causing him neurological and psychological problems. Cole chooses Circle Justice, an alternative sentencing program based on traditional Native American practices, which results in his being banished to a remote Alaskan Island, where he is left to survive for a year. Expecting to escape by swimming off the island, he instead encounters the Spirit Bear. Grades: 7 and up.

Ritter, John H. *Over the Wall.*
Philomel Books, 2000.
Setting: New York City.
Main Character: Male, Tyler Waltern, 13 years old.

Tyler spends the summer with his aunt, uncle, and cousins to play serious baseball while escaping his moody, troubled father, who has been a recluse since the accidental death of Tyler's sister nine years earlier. The boy's worst enemy is his own explosive temper and combative disposition. With the help of his coach and younger cousin, Tyler gains a level of self-awareness by unraveling some of the tangled stories in his family's past. Grades: 6–9.

Trueman, Terry. *Cruise Control.*
HarperTempest, 2004.
Prequel: *Stuck in Neutral.*
Setting: Seattle, Washington.
Main Character: Male, Paul McDaniel, 17 years old.

Paul is the older brother of Shawn, the disabled boy in *Stuck in Neutral.* Paul is a straight-A student and all-around athlete who disrespects his deserting father, who feels both love and shame for Shawn, and who exhibits violent tendencies on and off the basketball court. Grades: 7 and up.

AUTISM

Choldenko, Gennifer. *Al Capone Does My Shirts.*
Putnam, 2004.
Setting: Alcatraz Island, California, 1935.
Main Character: Male, Moose Flanagan, 12 years old.

Moose and his family move to Alcatraz Island when his father gets a job as an electrician at the prison, and his mother hopes to send his autistic older sister to a special school in San Francisco. When Natalie is rejected by the school, Moose is unable to play baseball because he must take care of her. Mob boss Al Capone is the prison's most infamous inmate. Awards: Newbery Honor. Grades: 6–8.

Haddon, Mark. *Curious Incident of the Dog in the Night Time.*
Doubleday, 2003.
Setting: England, 2000s.
Main Character: Male, Christopher Boone, 15 years old.

Christopher is overwhelmed by sensations and can only make sense of the chaos of stimuli by imposing arbitrary patterns. He relaxes by groaning and doing math problems in his head; he screams when he is touched. When his neighbor's poodle is killed and Christopher is falsely accused of the crime, he decides that he will model Sherlock Holmes and track down the killer. Grades: YA/A.

Ogaz, Nancy, and Patricia Shubeck. *Buster and the Amazing Daisy: Adventures with Asperger Syndrome.*

Jessica Kingsley, 2002.
Setting: Ocean Vista school, present day.
Main Character: Female, Daisy, teen.

Daisy has Asperger's syndrome, a mild form of autism. Daisy reacts explosively to surprises, noises, and things that don't match. She finds solace in the understanding of teachers and in spending time in a quiet area outside, training Buster, the classroom rabbit. Grades: 4–8.

Rodowsky, Colby. *Clay.*
Farrar, Straus & Giroux, 2001.
Setting: Present day.
Main Character: Female, Elsie "Clay" McPhee, 11 years old.

Elsie is home-schooled and warned by her mother never to leave their apartment. She takes care of Tommy, her 7-year-old autistic brother. Elsie defies her mother's rules and takes Tommy to meet new neighbors. The next day, her mother packs the family and moves, fearing discovery. The long car journey triggers Elsie to remember that they were abducted by their mother four years ago. Clay is the new middle name Elsie gives herself. Grades: 5–8.

BODY IMAGE/EATING DISORDERS

Bennett, Cherie. *Life in the Fat Lane.*
Laurel Leaf, 1999.
Setting: Nashville, Tennessee.
Main Character: Female, Lara Ardeche, 16 years old.

Lara is thin, beautiful, smart, popular and dating one of the cutest boys in school. Then she notices that she's gained a few pounds, and her weight keeps going up; soon Lara weighs over 200 pounds. She spends a week in a hospital on a controlled liquid diet, and the doctors and nutritionists can't understand why she becomes even heavier. Suddenly, she is no longer popular and is faced with ridicule from everyone around her. Awards: CC. Grades: 8 and up.

Brooks, Bruce. *Vanishing.*
Laura Geringer, 1999.
Setting: Hospital room.
Main Character: Female, Alice, 11 years old.

Alice is hospitalized for bronchitis because of her father's and grandmother's neglect. She goes on a hunger strike in order to avoid being released to her alcoholic mother and her hateful stepfather. Meanwhile, her roommate, Rex, a cancer patient, concentrates his energies on remaining earthbound. Grades: 5 and up.

Cirrone, Dorian. *Dancing in Red Shoes Will Kill You.*
HarperCollins, 2005.
Setting: Florida Arts High School.
Main Character: Female, Kayla, junior.

Kayla is a talented ballet dancer but she has a big problem that is limiting the roles she is chosen for in school productions: her breasts are so large that they interfere with the visual composition of the performances. After *Cinderella* tryouts, when Kayla is selected to play one of the ugly stepsisters instead of the coveted starring role, a dance teacher takes her aside to commiserate and suggests that she consider breast-reduction surgery. Almost immediately, the students form into two camps: those who would "Save the Hooters" (boys) vs. those who would "Reduce the Rack" (mainly girls). Grades: 7–10.

Crutcher, Chris. *Staying Fat for Sarah Byrnes.*
Greenwillow, 1993.
Setting: High school/Child and Adolescent Psychiatric Unit.
Main Characters: Male, Eric Calhoune, senior; Female, Sarah Byrnes, 17 years old.
    A social outcast in junior high, overweight Eric found a kindred spirit in Sarah Byrnes, whose face and hands were hideously disfigured in a childhood accident. Now a senior and slimmed down through competitive swimming, Eric is still devoted to her. When Sarah abruptly stops talking and is committed to a mental ward, Eric is compelled to take action to help her. He risks their friendship by breaking his vow of secrecy and enlisting others' aid. Awards: CC. Grades: 7 and up.

Dessen, Sarah. *Keeping the Moon.*
Viking, 1999.
Setting: Colby, North Carolina.
Main Character: Female, Colie, 15 years old.
    Because her aerobics-star mother is taking her famous weight-loss program to Europe, Colie spends the summer with her unusual Aunt Mira. Colie has dropped 45 pounds but hasn't shed her negative self-image. Colie feels hopeless, until she accepts a job in a restaurant, where two fellow waitresses share their beauty, boy, and life-management secrets with her. Awards: CC. Grades: 7 and up.

Grover, Lorie Ann. *On Pointe.*
Margaret K. McElderry, 2004.
Setting: Present day.
Main Character: Female, Clare, teen.
    Clare struggles with bulimia while working to become one of sixteen dancers chosen for the City Ballet Company. She feels she is a failure when she is told that she is too tall to join the company. She gradually realizes that her years of training were not wasted. Grades: 7–10.

Hall, Kiza F. *Perk!: The Story of a Teenager with Bulimia.*
Gurze, 1997.
Setting: 1990s.
Main Character: Female, Perk, 15 years old.
    Perk discovers that eating smothers the hurt, while vomiting quiets the voice in her head that screams, "You're fat!" Her baby sister almost drowns while Perk is throwing up instead of watching her. At the hospital, a doctor examines Perk. Her sunken eyes, skeletal frame, and blistered throat reveal her bulimia. Grades: 6–9.

Hanauer, Cathi. *My Sister's Bones.*
Delta, 1997.
Setting: West Berry, New Jersey.

Main Character: Female, Billie Weinstein, 16 years old.

Billie, a doctor's daughter, is the only Jewish girl in an all Italian neighborhood. Her schoolwork is only adequate in a family that expects straight A's, and she harbors an inappropriate crush on a local gas-station attendant named Dom. Her best friend Tiffany is the school hood. Billie secretly communicates with her older sister, Cassie, who's away at college and giving veiled hints of self-destructive episodes. Cassie comes home for Christmas weighing 95 pounds and she refuses to eat. Grades: YA.

Hautzig, Deborah. *Second Star to the Right.*
Puffin, 1999.
Setting: 1980s.
Main Character: Female, Leslie Hiller, 14 years old.

Leslie, a perfectionist, can't control the fear that she will somehow fail to be the perfect daughter, perfect student, and perfect friend. She decides to master the one thing over which she is certain she has complete domain: food. Even when it is apparent to everyone that her severe dieting has become a life-threatening habit, Leslie still can't stop. Awards: CC. Grades: 7–10.

Holt, Kimberly Willis. *When Zachary Beaver Came to Town.*
Henry Holt, 1999.
Setting: Antler, Texas.
Main Character: Male, Toby Wilson, 13 years old.

This summer Toby's heart has been broken by his mother, who left him and his father to become a country singer in Nashville. His crush, Scarlett Stalling, the town beauty, barely acknowledges Toby's existence. But when Zachary Beaver, "The World's Fattest Boy," comes to Antler as part of a traveling sideshow, Toby begins to realize that there just might be people who have it worse than him. Grades: 6–10.

Levenkron, Steven. *Best Little Girl in the World.*
Warner, 1989.
Setting: 1970s.
Main Character: Female, Kessie, 15 years old.

Kessie is five foot four and weighs ninety-eight pounds but she thinks she is overweight. Awards: CC. Grades: 7–12.

Lipsyte, Robert. *One Fat Summer.*
HarperTrophy, 1991.
Setting: Rumson Lake, summer.
Main Character: Male, Bobby Marks, 14 years old.

Bobby can't even button his jeans, reach over his belly or touch his toes. His parents can't stop fighting. His best friend, Joanie, goes home to New York City and won't tell him why. Dr. Kahn, a rich, stingy estate owner who hires him to manage an enormous lawn, is working him to death. And to top it off, a local bully won't stop torturing him. Awards: CC. Grades: 6–10.

Lynch, Chris. *Slot Machine.*
Peter Smith, 2003.
Setting: St. Paul's Seminary Retreat Center.

Main Character: Male, Elvin Bishop, 13 years old.

Elvin Bishop knows he's the "fat guy" whom everyone is going to pick on when he and his friends board the bus for the Catholic boys camp. He fails at sports before he finds his "slot," something that everyone must have according to the militaristic head priest. Elvin refuses to compromise himself just to be accepted by others. He and Mike find some happiness with the misfits in the scorned Arts Sectors, while Frank endures a brutal hazing to become one of the campus elite. Awards: CC. Grades: 7 and up.

Perez, Marlene. *Unexpected Development.*
Roaring Brook, 2004.
Setting: Pancake Palace.
Main Character: Female, Megan, 17 years old.

Megan's journal tells about her double D-size problem. She hides her figure in huge shirts, and she knows twenty words for breasts, which she can recite alphabetically. When the object of her daydreams breaks up with his girlfriend and asks her out, she finds it difficult to believe that he sees anything above her collarbone, but agrees to give the relationship a try. Grades: 9 and up.

Sparks, Beatrice. *Kim: Empty Inside: The Diary of an Anonymous Teenager.*
Avon, 2002.
Setting: Present day.
Main Character: Female, Kim, 17 years old.

Kim's downward spiral into anorexia is revealed in her diary. Her weight figures prominently in her wish to be accepted into the UCLA gymnastics program, and she blames food for most of the bad things that happen to her. Kim progresses from not eating to the use of laxatives. Awards: CC. Grades: 7–10.

Terris, Susan. *Nell's Quilt.*
Farrar, Straus and Giroux, 1996.
Setting: 1899.
Main Character: Female, Nell Edmonds, 18 years old.

Nell didn't plan to marry widower Anson Tanner, but her family perceives her as Nell the Good and Strong, who will pursue the dreams that will make everyone happy. So she agrees to marry him. Nell dreams of college and living in Boston. During her engagement, she begins working on a quilt from fabric scraps which she assumes are remnants of her suffragette grandmother's dresses. Nell extends the strict rules she imposes on her quilt-making to her eating habits, until she is consuming virtually nothing. Awards: CC. Grades: 10–12.

Tokio, Marnelle. *More Than You Can Chew.*
Tundra, 2003.
Setting: Silver Lake Hospital.
Main Character: Female, Marty, 17 years old.

Marty has always been a fighter; she played on the boys' football team at school and battled feelings of love and hate for her alcoholic mother while at home. Now she brings every ounce of her aggressive attitude to Silver Lake, where she is being treated for anorexia. Grades: 8 and up.

Williams-Garcia, Rita. **Blue Tights.**
Puffin, 1996.
Setting: 1980s.
Main Character: Female, Joyce Collins, 15 years old.

Joyce aspires to have a dancing career, which had been denied to her lonely mother. But her curvy physique excludes Joyce from her high school's classical ballet production of *Sleeping Beauty.* She accidentally intrudes on a practice session of African dancers. Joining the group, Joyce finds that her spirit, style, and abilities are at last unleashed in this dance form, which reveals her talents. Grades: 9–12.

Wilson, Jacqueline. **Girls Under Pressure.**
Delacorte, 2002.
Series: Girls Quartet: **Girls in Love; Girls in Tears; Girls Out Late.**
Setting: Great Britian.
Main Characters: Female, Ellie Allard; Female, Magda; Female, Nadine; Female, Zoe; all 14 years old.

Ellie's two best friends seem to be living life in the fast lane while she putters along the curb. Glamorous blond Magda has a thousand cute boys buzzing around her, and Goth girl Nadine has just been asked to take part in a national teen modeling contest. Ellie has massive panic attacks about her weight, so she decides to go on a diet. Instead of counting calories, Ellie just tries to stop eating altogether, and soon she's starving, miserable, and lying all the time to her friends and family. Grades: YA.

Whytock, Cherry. **My Cup Runneth Over: The Life of Angelica Cookson-Potts.**
Simon & Schuster, 2003.
Setting: Great Britain.
Main Character: Female, Angelica Cookson-Potts, 14 years old.

Angel wants to be a chef after high school. She is taller and heavier than all of her friends. Her used-to-be-a-model mother constantly reminds her to watch what she eats, and she can't get Adam, the love of her life, to notice her. Angel pokes fun at all that is wrong in her life. British humor and recipes. Grades: 7 and up.

DRUG ABUSE/ADDICTION

Block, Francesca Lia. **The Hanged Man.**
HarperTrophy, 1999.
Setting: Los Angeles, California.
Main Character: Female, Laurel, 17 years old.

Laurel lives just below the famous Hollywood sign. Her mind twisted and scarred from painful childhood experiences, Laurel becomes an addict and is driven toward reckless sex. When she finds the strength to confront her inner demons, she is able to reach out with love for others, and then love herself. For mature readers. Awards: CC. Grades: 10–12.

Burgess, Melvin. **Smack.**
Henry Holt, 1998.
Setting: Bristol, England.

Main Characters: Male, Tar; Female, Gemma; both teenagers.

Tar and Gemma are fed up with their parents. Tar's family is alcoholic and abusive, and Gemma feels her home life is cramped by too many restrictions. The couple runs away to Bristol in search of freedom, and finds it in a "squat," a vacant building occupied by two slightly older teens, who include Tar and Gemma in their heroin parties and adventures. Tar's personality changes dramatically over the course of the book, from sweet-natured, lonely boy to hard-edged, hit-seeking addict. Awards: CC; Carnegie. Grades: 8 and up.

Chbosky, Stephen. *The Perks of Being a Wallflower.*
MTV, 1999.
Setting: Pennsylvania, 1991.
Main Character: Male, Charlie, 15 years old.

Charlie writes letters to an unnamed "friend." The first letter reveals the suicide of Charlie's pal, Michael. Along with coping with his loss, Charlie has the usual adolescent problems, including sex, drugs, and bullies. Awards: CC. Grades: 9–12.

Childress, Alice. *A Hero Ain't Nothin' but a Sandwich.*
Putnam, 2000.
Setting: 1970s.
Main Character: Male, Benjie, 13 years old.

Benjie uses heroin, but he thinks he's not hooked. Woven into Benjie's ramblings are the thoughts of those he knows: his mother, stepfather, friends, the pusher, and teachers at his school. African American characters. Awards: CC. Grades: 7–12.

Going, K. L. *Fat Kid Rules the World.*
Grosset & Dunlap, 2003.
Setting: New York City.
Main Character: Male, Troy Billings, 17 years old.

Troy, a 296-pound teen, contemplates ending his life by jumping off a New York City subway platform. He is interrupted by Curt MacCrae, a legendary punk rock guitarist, drug addict, and sometime student at W. T. Watson High School. Curt connects with him, "saves his life," and convinces Troy to be the drummer in his band, even though he hasn't touched the drums since seventh grade. Awards: Printz Honor. Grades: 8 and up.

Grant, Cynthia D. *White Horse.*
Atheneum, 1998.
Setting: 1990s.
Main Character: Female, Raina, 16 years old.

Raina is pregnant and a victim of her drug-addicted mother's violent rages. Ms. Johnson is Raina's 40-something teacher who has a love-hate relationship with her job. Raina writes a journal that touches her teacher. Told in an alternating point of view of Raina and Ms. Johnson Grades: 7 and up.

Hinton, S. E. *That Was Then, This Is Now.*
Puffin, 1998.
Setting: 1970s.

Main Characters: Male, Mark; Male, Byron; both 16 years old.

Ever since Mark's parents died, he has been living with Bryon, and the friends are more like brothers. They've been inseparable until girls, gangs, and drugs begin to destroy their relationship. Grades: 7–10.

Hopkins, Ellen. *Crank.*
Simon Pulse, 2004.
Setting: 2000s.
Main Character: Female, Kristina Georgia Snow, 17 years old.

Kristina is introduced to crank on a visit to her wayward father and morphs into "Bree," her fearless, risk-taking alter ego. When Kristina goes home, things don't return to normal. Although she tries to reconnect with her mother and her former life as a good student, her drug use soon takes over. A page-turner written in free verse. Grades: 8 and up

James, Brian. *Pure Sunshine.*
Push, 2002.
Setting: Philadelphia, Pennsylvania.
Main Character: Male, Brendon, 16 years old.

Two days in the life of Brendon and two of his friends, spent on an LSD trip. Raw and gritty language, with no clear anti-drug message. Grades: 10 and up.

MacKall, Dandi Daley. *Kyra's Story.*
Thirsty Books, 2003.
Series: Degrees of Guilt: *Miranda's Story; Tyrone's Story.*
Setting: Mason, Iowa.
Main Character: Female, Kyra, 17 years old.

Kyra, stressed by her senior year, had begun taking prescription drugs, and her twin brother, Sammy, suffers the consequences. She and her friends all feel a measure of guilt for their role in Sammy's death. The trilogy is by three different authors giving three different points of view of the same incident. Grades: YA.

Mowry, Jess. *Babylon Boyz.*
Simon Pulse, 1999.
Setting: Oakland, California.
Main Characters: Male, Dante; Male, Pook; Male, Wyatt; all 14 years old.

Dante, Pook, and Wyatt don't have many choices in life. Dante might never be able to afford the operation that could fix his heart (damaged before birth by his mother's crack addiction). When they unexpectedly find a large package of pure cocaine, they have to decide if they should sell the drugs to get money for Dante's operation. Awards: CC. Grades: 8–10.

Myers, Walter Dean. *Beast.*
Scholastic, 2003.
Setting: Harlem, New York City.
Main Characters: Male, Anthony "Spoon" Witherspoon, 17 years old; Female, Gabi, teen.

Spoon leaves Harlem and his girl, Gabi, to spend his senior year at Wallingford

Academy, with the hope that he will get into an Ivy League college. While he adjusts to prep school life, Gabi's life comes undone. Her mother is dying, her younger brother may be running with a gang, and her blind grandfather has come to stay. When Spoon comes home for Christmas, Gabi is addicted to heroin. Awards: Notable Books for a Global Society. Grades: 8 and up.

Nolan, Han. *Born Blue.*
Harcourt, 2001.
Setting: 1990s.
Main Character: Female, Janie, 16 years old.

Janie was 4 years old when she was placed in foster care due to her mother's neglect. Janie's dearest friend is a fellow foster child, Harmon, an African American, who has a collection of blues tapes that he and Janie listen to over and over again. Janie has a magnificent voice that pours out beauty and pain. When Harmon is adopted, she is heartsick. Her mother comes to visit and this time sells Janie to a couple in exchange for drugs. Janie changes her name to Leshaya and grows into a wild young woman, destroying every healthy relationship she has. Awards: CC. Grades: 8–12.

Sparks, Beatrice. *Go Ask Alice.*
Simon Pulse, 1998.
Setting: 1960s.
Main Character: Female, anonymous teen, 15 years old.

This anonymous teen girl swings madly between optimism and despair. When one of her new friends spikes her drink with LSD, she begins a frightening journey into darkness. The drugs take the edge off her loneliness and self-hate, but they also turn her life into a nightmare of exalting highs and excruciating lows. Grades: 8 and up.

Toten, Teresa. *The Game.*
Red Deer, 2001.
Setting: Riverwood Clinic, 2000s.
Main Character: Female, Danielle Webster, 14 years old.

Danielle's father beats her violently whenever she fails to meet his high standards of success. Finally driven to attempt suicide, Dani winds up in Riverwood, a clinic for troubled youth. There she bonds with her roommate, Scratch, a self-mutilator, and Kevin, whose Fundamentalist parents' refusal to accept his homosexuality has also driven him to attempt suicide. Her new friends and a caring therapist help Dani confront the truth about her younger sister, Kelly, and the "game" with vodka and pills they had played at home. Grades: 7–12.

FEMALE CIRCUMCISION

Collins, Pat Lowery. *The Fattening Hut.*
Houghton Mifflin, 2003.
Setting: Tropical island.
Main Character: Female, Helen, 14 years old.

Helen has been promised to 30-year-old Esenu. She needs to gain weight to be a bride and is sent to the fattening hut. The isolation, loss of youthful freedom, and the terrible secret mutilation she must go through have taken away Helen's appetite. Her unmarried Aunt Margaret, who has long been an outcast of the tribe, has taught Helen to read and helps Helen to escape. Written in prose poetry. Grades: 9 and up.

Kessler, Cristina. **No Condition is Permanent.**
Philomel, 2000.
Setting: Sierra Leone, Africa.
Main Character: Female, Jodie, 14 years old.
 Her mother received a grant to study in Sierra Leone, so Jodie is living with snakes and scorpions and without electricity or indoor plumbing. She finds a soulmate in Khadi, a local girl who helps her see the beauty of the village and the culture. When Khadi comes of age and is inducted into the women's Secret Society which practices female circumcision, Jodie must decide whether or not to interfere. Grades: 5–9.

Walker, Alice. **Possessing the Secret of Joy.**
Harcourt, 1992.
Setting: Africa/ United States.
Main Character: Female, Tashi, young woman.
 Tashi, a character in **The Color Purple** and **The Temple of My Familiar**, marries Celie's son, Adam, and submits to female circumcision, partially out of loyalty to the threatened tribal customs of her people, the Olinka. As a result, she endures physical pain and long-lasting emotional trauma. Grades: YA/A.

Williams-Garcia, Rita. **No Laughter Here.**
Amistad, 2004.
Setting: Queens, New York.
Main Character: Female, Akilah, 10 years old.
 Akilah, an African American girl from Queens, can't wait for her best friend, Victoria, to come home from a visit to her grandmother in Nigeria. When Victoria returns home, she seems like a very different girl—quiet, reserved, and unhappy. Akilah tries to figure out what happened to her friend, and Victoria finally spills the truth: her family allowed a doctor to remove her clitoris so she would be a "clean and proper" Nigerian girl. Grades: 5–8.

MENTAL ILLNESS

Avi. **Blue Heron.**
HarperTrophy, 1993.
Setting: Massachusetts shore.
Main Character: Female, Maggie, 12 years old.
 Maggie has a loving mother, a terrific stepmother, and a father who is delighted to see her each summer. This year, there's an infant half-sister for Maggie to meet, and she senses that something isn't right. Her father's anger is barely under control; the relationship between him and his wife is rapidly deteriorating; and Maggie is too young to understand fully the troubles that are destroying them. Then she learns that her father is suffering from depression. His health is poor, he has lost his job, and hasn't told his wife. Awards: CC. Grades: 5–8.

Frank, E.R. *America.*
Atheneum/Richard Jackson, 2002.
Setting: New York City, 2000s.
Main Character: Male, America, 16 years old.

America trustingly left the safe haven of his foster home for a visit with his desperate, drug-addicted mother when he was 5 years old. He is lost within the system until almost eleven years later, when he tries to end his own life. The patient therapist Dr. B. must coax an embittered and damaged America to revisit all the dark alleys of that lonely suicide road in order to face down his fears. Grades: 8 and up.

Gantos, Jack. *Joey Pigza Swallowed the Key.*
Farrar, Straus & Giroux, 1998.
Sequels: *Joey Pigza Loses Control* (Newbery Honor); *What Would Joey Do?*
Setting: Elementary school.
Main Character: Male, Joey Pigza, 9 years old.

Joey was emotionally abused by his grandmother, and he has never met his dad. He can't get along in his elementary school classroom because of his mood swings and his "dud meds." Joey has attention deficit disorder, which is not being effectively controlled with his current medication. Joey's control of his own behavior slips as he tries to get a grip on his life and fails. Grades: 5 and up.

Harrar, George. *Not As Crazy As I Seem.*
Houghton Mifflin, 2003.
Setting: Boston, Massachusetts.
Main Character: Male, Devon Brown, 15 years old.

Devon has obsessive compulsive disorder. He has a fixation on the number four, an obsession about germs, and an intolerance of untidiness, all of which have afflicted him since his grandfather's death when he was 8. His family moves to the Boston area, and Devon must adjust to the Baker Academy and a new therapist. When Devon rips up the neatly buttoned shirts in his closet, his father comes in and wraps his arms around him. Devon confesses he feels responsible for his grandfather's death. Grades: 6–10.

Hesser, Terry Spencer. *Kissing Doorknobs.*
Laurel Leaf, 1999.
Setting: 1990s.
Main Character: Female, Tara Sullivan, 14 years old.

Tara's compulsive behaviors include counting every sidewalk crack between her house and school. If she is ever interrupted or loses her place, she must run back to the beginning and start over, or her mother's spinal health will be endangered. Obsessive prayer rituals and the need to touch the doorknob then kiss her fingers thirty-three times before leaving the house are further compulsions that threaten her relationships. Grades: 7 and up.

Jenkins, A.M. *Damage.*
HarperCollins, 2001.
Setting: Parkersville.
Main Character: Male, Austin Reid, 17 years old.

Austin, the star of the football team, is depressed and suicidal but afraid to tell anyone he needs help. He refers to himself in the second person voice, illustrating how disconnected and distant he feels. Awards: CC. Grades: 7–12.

Johnson, Angela. *Humming Whispers.*
Orchard, 1995.
Setting: 1990s.
Main Character: Female, Sophy, 14 years old.
Sophy reveals the impact of her 24-year-old sister Nicole's schizophrenia on Nicole and the lives of those who love her. When "the whispers" return, Nicole sometimes simply disappears; other times she is hospitalized. Sophy feels powerless to help her and has an unspoken fear that she will end up like her sister. Awards: CC. Grades: 7–10.

Leavitt, Melina. *Heck, Superhero.*
Front Street, 2003.
Setting: 2000s.
Main Character: Male, Heck, 13 years old.
Abandoned by his mentally ill mother, Heck searches for her for three days, trying to do the good deeds that he hopes will allow him to find her. Heck finds his mother in the hospital and reminds her that he is not a superhero but a boy who also needs help. Grades: 6–9.

Levenkron, Steven. *Luckiest Girl in the World: A Young Skater Battles Her Self-Destructive Impulses.*
Penguin, 1998.
Setting: 1990s.
Main Characters: Female, Katie Roskova, 15 years old; Male, Sandy Sherman, adult.
Katie is a figure skater and a private school scholarship student with no time for friends. In public, Katie wears a megawatt smile meant to fool everyone, but she sometimes "spaces out" and cuts herself, which seems to lower her stress. One day, after repeatedly banging her head into the wall following a difficult skating session, Katie is whisked away to the hospital and ordered into therapy with Sandy Sherman. Grades: 7–12.

McCormick, Patricia. *Cut.*
Front Street, 2000.
Setting: Sea Pines Psychiatric Hospital, 2000s.
Main Character: Female, Callie, 13 years old.
Callie is confined to a mental hospital and begins to understand she hurts herself because she feels responsible for her brother's illness. Grades: 7 and up.

Slade, Arthur. *Tribes.*
Wendy Lamb, 2002.
Setting: Saskatoon, Saskatchewan, Canada.
Main Character: Male, Percy Montmount, 17 years old.
Ever since the death of his famous anthropologist father three years ago and the suicide of his friend, Percy has blocked his grief by becoming an aloof observer of his

classmates' odd rituals instead of an active player. He names and describes the tribes of students in his school without including himself in any of them. Grades: 7 and up.

Sones, Sonya. *Stop Pretending: What Happened When My Big Sister Went Crazy.*
HarperTempest, 2001.
Setting: Author's childhood.
Main Character: Female, Cookie, 13 years old.

This book of poems is based on the journals Sones wrote at the age of 13, when her 19-year-old sister was hospitalized due to manic depression. She dreads having her friends learn of her sister's illness and wonders what she could have done to prevent the breakdown. Grades: 6–9.

Stoehr, Shelley. *Crosses.*
Writers Club Press, 2003.
Setting: Babylon, Long Island, New York.
Main Character: Female, Nancy, 15 years old.

Nancy deals with alcoholic, abusive parents by hurting herself and drinking. At school she meets Katie, and they become best friends; both are freshmen, both are punkers, and both are scarred from cutting to escape from the sordid reality and lack of control of their lives. Strong street language, sex, and violence. Grades: 9–12.

Trueman, Terry. *Inside Out.*
HarperTempest, 2003.
Setting: Spokane, Washington.
Main Character: Male, Zach, 16 years old.

Zach sits in the coffee shop, waiting for his mother to bring his antipsychotic medication so the voices won't start. But two young brothers about Zach's age walk into the coffee shop, pistols drawn, and announce, "This is a robbery." The tension builds, as Zach is now a hostage and is very much the wild card turning the story inside out. For mature readers. Grades: 9 and up.

Willey, Margaret. *Saving Lenny.*
Backinprint.com, 2002.
Setting: Isolated woodlands cottage.
Main Characters: Male, Lenny Stevens; Female, Jesse Davis; both 17 years old.

Jesse and Lenny, two overachieving high school seniors, fall in love and declare their independence from their parents' expectations. They set up housekeeping in an isolated woodlands cottage. Their life together starts well, but as winter approaches, Lenny's cyclical depression reappears. He loses his job and grows possessive of Jesse, until he traps her in the web of his own destructive illness. Jesse and her disapproving friend, Kay, tell the story in alternating chapters. Awards: CC. Grades: 10–12.

Wilson, Dawn. *Saint Jude.*
Tudor, 2001.
Setting: Ashville, North Carolina.
Main Character: Female, Taylor Drysdale, 18 years old.

Taylor suffers from bipolar disorder. During her senior year, she is admitted to

"Brick House," the outpatient program at St. Jude Hospital, where she meets other teens coping with mental illness. Grades: 6 and up.

PHYSICAL DISABILITIES

Clements, Andrew. *Things Not Seen.*
Philomel, 2002.
Setting: Chicago, Illinois, 2000s.
Main Character: Male, Bobby, 15 years old.

Bobby has turned invisible overnight. He breaks the news to his parents who, afraid of being hounded by the media, instruct him to keep his condition a secret. Bobby ventures out of the house and visits the library; he meets Alicia, a blind girl, to whom he confides his secret. His physicist father struggles to find a scientific explanation for and a solution to his son's condition. Bobby is determined to take control of the situation and of his own destiny. Magical realism. Grades: 5–9.

Greenberg, Joanne. *In This Sign.*
Owl Books, 1984.
Setting: 1980s.
Main Characters: Female, Janice; Male, Abel; all adults.

Janice and Abel leave their school for the deaf and get married; they have a hearing daughter. Their daughter becomes their link to the hearing world they don't understand and don't trust. Awards: CC. Grades: 10–12.

Jordan, Sherryl. *The Raging Quiet.*
Simon Pulse, 2000.
Setting: Seaside village, medieval times.
Main Character: Female, Marnie, 16 years old.

Marnie is taken to a seaside thatched cottage by her much older husband, whom she endures only to save her family from starvation. When he is killed in a fall, she feels more release than grief, in spite of the village rumors that she caused his death with a witch's curse. She befriends a "mad" boy called Raver, whose rages and yammerings look to villagers like the work of the devil. Marnie realizes that the boy is deaf, and his bursts of anger come from his inability to communicate. Awards: CC. Grades: 7–10.

LaFaye, A. *Worth.*
Simon & Schuster, 2004.
Setting: Nebraska, late nineteenth century.
Main Character: Male, Nathaniel, 11 years old.

Nathan's leg is crushed beneath a wagon when its team of horses, spooked by lightning, lurches out of control. His father brings home John Worth, a boy taken off the orphan train, to help take up the slack. Nathan now feels useless. Awards: Scott O'Dell. Grades: 5–8.

Shusterman, Neal. *The Schwa Was Here.*
Dutton, 2004.
Setting: Brooklyn, New York.

Main Character: Male, "Antsy" Bonano, 13 years old.

Antsy becomes an agent for Calvin Schwa by taking bets on what he can get away with by being able to fly almost entirely beneath the social radar. They accept a dare requiring "The Schwa" to enter the home of the legendary local eccentric, Crawley, to take a dog bowl belonging to any one of his fourteen Afghans. Crawley is a powerful restaurateur who also happens to be severely agoraphobic. He nabs Antsy and Calvin and orders them to return daily to walk his dogs, then to act as a companion for the man's blind granddaughter, Lexie. Grades: 7–10.

Voigt, Cynthia. *Izzy Willy Nilly.*
Atheneum, 2005.
Setting: 1980s.
Main Character: Female, Izzy, 15 years old.

Izzy's life had been colorful as a pretty, popular cheerleader, but grayness swallows her up after a car accident results in the amputation of her leg. Her girlfriends are too uncomfortable to be around her, but the void is filled by unattractive, blunt Rosamunde, who bounds into Izzy's life. Rosamunde's persistence helps Izzy over the hurdle of returning to school. Awards: CC. Grades: 6–9.

Wait, Lea. **Wintering Well.**
Margaret K. McElderry, 2004.
Setting: Maine, 1819.
Main Character: Female, Cassie, 11 years old.

Cassie's 12-year-old brother Will accidentally cuts himself with an ax, an injury that leads to the amputation of his leg. Will wonders what to do with his life, since his dream of being a farmer has been destroyed. Cassie nurses him back to health and also wonders what the future holds for her. Grades: 5–8.

PHYSICAL ILLNESS—AIDS

Flinn, Alex. *Fade to Black.*
Harper Tempest, 2005.
Setting: North Florida, 1990s.
Main Character: Male, Alex Crusan, 16 years old.

Alex, an HIV-positive Hispanic teen, is brutalized by an attacker wearing a high school letter jacket and all fingers point to Clinton Cole, a narrow-minded jock and jerk. Daria Bickell, a special-ed student with Down syndrome, is the only witness to the crime. Grades: 8 and up.

Hoffman, Alice. *At Risk.*
Berkley, 1998.
Setting: New England, 1990s.
Main Character: Female, Amanda, 11 years old.

Amanda, the star gymnast on her school team, has been diagnosed with AIDS, which she contracted from a blood transfusion for an appendectomy. Her family experiences disbelief, anger, sorrow, rejection by old friends, and trouble at school. As

Amanda's life dwindles away, the family struggles and begins to dissolve, but finally reconnects. Grades: YA/A.

Kerr, M. E. *Night Kites.*
HarperTrophy, 1987.
Setting: 1980s.
Main Character: Male, Erick Rudd, 17 years old.

Erick is delighted with his girlfriend, Dill, and his best friend, Jack. But then Jack falls for Nikki, an insecure fashion-plate who wants only what she can't have. Erick tries to steer Jack clear of such a troublemaker, so Nikki sets her sights on Erick next. Complicating Erick's guilt for seeing Nikki is finding out his older brother, Pete, is gay and dying of AIDS. Awards: CC. Grades: 7 and up.

Minchin, Adele. *The Beat Goes On.*
Simon & Schuster, 2004.
Setting: Manchester, England.
Main Character: Female, Leyla, 15 years old.

Leyla is an aspiring drummer who wishes for a "really good drama" to spice up her life. She gets far more than she bargained for when her cousin Emma, 16, is diagnosed with HIV. Leyla begins to spend her Saturdays giving drumming lessons at an HIV outreach center to support Emma. British, fast-paced, and will appeal to reluctant readers. Grades: 7 and up.

Nelson, Theresa. *Earthshine.*
Orchard, 1994.
Setting: Los Angeles, California.
Main Character: Female, Slim, 12 years old.

Slim's father, Mack, is dying of AIDS. Slim tells about herself, her father, and Larry, her father's lover and devoted companion, and their relationship with Isaiah, 11, and his loving mother. Awards: CC. Grades: 6–9.

Porte, Barbara Ann. *Something Terrible Happened.*
Orchard, 1994.
Setting: Tennessee.
Main Character: Female, Gillian, 10 years old.

Raised by her mother and grandmother to have a strong sense of her Caribbean roots, Gillian rarely thinks about her white father, who died when she was 3, killed by the drugs that followed him back from Vietnam. Her only contact with his family has been long-distance phone calls on holidays. When her mother is diagnosed with AIDS, Gillian is sent to Tennessee to live with her white uncle and his family. Grades: 5–8.

Stratton, Allan. *Chanda's Secret.*
Annick, 2004.
Setting: Africa.
Main Character: Female, Chanda, 16 years old.

Chanda remembers living with both parents. Her family's troubles began after her father was killed in the diamond mines. Her first stepfather abused her; the second died of a stroke; the third is a drunken philanderer with AIDS, a taboo topic in her village. Chanda's mother leaves to visit her family on the cattle post, and Chanda is forced to give up her dream of further education to care for her younger sister and brother. Slowly she begins to realize that her mother has AIDS, and that she might be infected herself. Awards: Printz Honor. Grades: 8 and up.

Physical Illness—Cancer

Cook, Karin. **What Girls Learn.**
Vintage, 1998.
Setting: Long Island, New York, 1990s.
Main Character: Female, Tilden, 12 years old.

Tilden's mother moves her and her sister to Long Island to be with her new beau, Nick. Her mother finds a lump in her breast and her health fails quickly, despite aggressive treatment. A tearjerker. Grades: YA.

Ferris, Jean. **Invincible Summer.**
HarperCollins, 1987.
Setting: Midwest hospital.
Main Character: Female, Robin Gregory, 17 years old.

Robin is a midwestern farm girl awaiting a battery of tests in the hospital when she meets Rick Winn. Rick, who is undergoing chemotherapy, distracts Robin from her anxiety through his warmth and humor. When Robin learns that she too has leukemia, Rick provides constant support, helping her cope with her fear and anger, and encouraging her when the treatments leave her moody, ugly, and debilitated. Grades: 9–12.

Hurwin, Davida Wills. **Time for Dancing.**
Puffin, 1997.
Setting: 1990s.
Main Character: Female, Juliana "Jules," 16 years old.

Dancers Jules and her best friend Samantha find their concerns about boyfriends and dance class seem trivial after Jules is diagnosed with histiocytic lymphoma, a deadly form of cancer. Alternating points of view. Grades: 7 and up.

McDaniel, Lurlene. **Don't Die, My Love.**
Laurel Leaf, 1995.
Setting: 1990s.
Main Characters: Female, Julie Ellis; Male, Luke Muldenhower; both 17 years old.

Julie and football star Luke had everything going for them: popularity, good grades, and love. Then Luke develops Hodgkin's lymphoma. Julie is determined to help him through his chemotherapy and get through this ordeal so their lives can return to normal. When masses are discovered in his chest and groin area, he begins radiation therapy. Their close relationship begins to deteriorate, as Luke pushes Julie away. Grades: 6–9.

McDaniel, Lurlene. **Till Death Do Us Part.**
Laurel Leaf, 1997.

Setting: Hospital.
Main Character: Female, April Lancaster, 18 years old.

April has a brain tumor which cannot be operated on. When she meets Mark Gianni, a 21-year-old with a passion for car racing, things change. Mark is handsome and charming, and has cystic fibrosis. Despite herself, April falls completely in love with him. April says yes when Mark asks her to marry him. Awards: CC. Grades: 6–8.

Pennebaker, Ruth. *Both Sides Now.*
Henry Holt, 2000.
Setting: Austin, Texas.
Main Character: Female, Liza, 15 years old.

Liza's carefully planned life is abruptly launched into a world without rules or meaning when her mother, Rebecca, gets breast cancer. Grades: 7–12.

PHYSICAL ILLNESS—MISCELLANEOUS

Camus, Albert. *The Plague.*
Vintage, 1991.
Setting: Oran, Algeria, 1940s.
Main Character: Male, Dr. Bernard R. Rieux, young adult.

A study of human life and its meaning in the face of the bubonic plague that sweeps through the city, taking a vast portion of the population with it. Grades: YA/A.

King, Stephen. *The Stand.*
Signet, 1991.
Setting: 1980s.
Main Character: Nick Andros, Nadine Cross, Larry Underwood, many others; all adults.

After the Superflu kills 90 percent of the world's population, the survivors follow instructions given to them in dreams to go west. The Good gather in Denver and the Bad in Las Vegas. Awards: CC. Grades: 9–12.

Koertge, Ron. *Stoner and Spaz.*
Candlewick, 2002.
Setting: Los Angeles, California, 2000s.
Main Characters: Female, Colleen Minou, teen; Male, Ben Bancroft, 16 years old.

Colleen is a hard-core stoner, and Ben is a movie-addicted preppie who suffers from cerebral palsy. Together, they form a most unlikely couple. For once, Ben is actually more interested in his real life than a movie. Colleen takes him clubbing, lights his first joint, and even challenges him to direct his own movie. Ben, in turn, dares her to stay straight, but Colleen still needs the drugs to "smooth out the edges." Grades: 8 and up.

Koertge, Ron. *Shakespeare Bats Cleanup.*
Candlewick, 2003.
Setting: Kevin's home.
Main Character: Male, Kevin Boland, 14 years old.

Kevin is an MVP first baseman whose whole life revolves around baseball. Diagnosed with mono, he is forced to stay at home for months to recuperate. Bored,

Kevin borrows his father's book of poetry and starts writing his own. At first, he imitates haiku and sonnets, but soon begins writing insightful verse, both funny and serious, in which he records his observations about life in junior high, romance, his dreams of baseball stardom, and his grief over the recent death of his mother. Grades: 6–9.

Newth, Mette. *Dark Light.*
Farrar, Straus & Giroux, 1998.
Setting: Bergen, Norway, nineteenth century.
Main Character: Female, Tora, 13 years old.

Tora tells about her childhood: about her mother, who concealed her leprosy and took her own life, and about her weak father. Her neighbor is her soulmate for life, and Marthe helps Tora survive in the leprosarium. Sunniva teaches her to read. Reading enlarges the girl's mental world, as her physical world contracts. Grades: 9 and up.

Truman, Terry. *Stuck in Neutral.*
HarperCollins, 2000.
Sequel: *Cruise Control.*
Setting: Seattle, Washington.
Main Character: Male, Shawn McDaniel, 14 years old.

Shawn can't talk or move to communicate, but he remembers everything and has beautiful visions during his seizures. He loves his life and is afraid his father wants to kill him because he believes Shawn is suffering. Awards: CC; Printz Honor. Grades: 6–9.

CHAPTER 16

MULTICULTURAL

Stories set in faraway places with characters from other cultures are exciting, exotic, and an interesting way to learn about the world. The reader can identify with the teen characters and learn about the culture, perhaps gaining an understanding of the perspective, traditions, and history of the culture through the experiences of the characters. Multicultural books also help immigrant teens understand their own cultural identity and heritage in a new setting, where they must cope with adjusting to a new way of life. Many of the titles will fill or complement school assignments, as well. For a sampling of multicultural short stories by popular young adult authors, try *Join In: Multiethnic Short Stories by Outstanding Writers for Young Adults*, edited by Don Gallo, or *Face Relations: 11 Stories About Seeing Beyond Color*, edited by Marilyn Singer. Multicultural stories are written in a wide variety of genres, as represented by the titles in the following lists.

Multicultural Awards
Africa as a Setting
African American Characters
Asia as a Setting
Asian American Characters
Australia/New Zealand as a Setting
Central America/Caribbean/Mexico/South America as a Setting
Europe as a Setting
Hispanic American Characters
Immigrants/Refugees as Characters
India as a Setting
Native American Characters
Southeast Asia as a Setting
Middle East as a Setting
Resources: Additional Titles

MULTICULTURAL AWARDS

The Coretta Scott King Award is given to authors and illustrators of African descent whose distinguished books promote an understanding and appreciation of the "American Dream." The award was first given in 1970 at a New Jersey Library Association dinner. The American Library Association recognized the award as an association award in 1982. Coretta Scott King Award books are chosen annually by a seven-member task force. The award commemorates the life and work of Dr. Martin Luther King, Jr., and honors his widow, Coretta Scott King, for her courage and determination in continuing the work for peace and world brotherhood. Winners of the Coretta Scott King Award receive a framed citation, an honorarium, and a set of the *Encyclopaedia Britannica* or the *World Book Encyclopedias*. Read more about the Coretta Scott King Award at www.ala.org/ala/emiert/corettascottkingbookawards/corettascott.htm.

The John Steptoe New Talent Award is an offshoot of the Coretta Scott King Award, was originally introduced as the Genesis Award. First awarded in 1995, the John Steptoe Award is given to a new African American author and illustrator at the beginning of his or her career for an outstanding book. The author award and the illustrator award may go to the same book or to two different books, and the winners cannot have more than three published works. An author selected to win the Coretta Scott King Award is not eligible, and an author or illustrator can only win this award once. The Coretta Scott King task force has the responsibility of selecting the winners each year, but has the option to not give the award. The award honors the work of John Steptoe, a noted African American children's books illustrator. Read more about the John Steptoe New Talent Award at www.ala.org/ala/emiert/corettascottkingbookawards/winnersa/newtalentawarda/newtalentaward.htm.

The Pura Belpré Award is presented to a Latino/Latina writer and illustrator whose work best portrays, affirms, and celebrates the Latino cultural experience in an outstanding work of literature for children and youth. Established in 1996, the award is cosponsored by the Association for Library Service to Children, a division of the American Library Association, and the National Association to Promote Library and Information Services to Latinos and the Spanish-Speaking, an ALA Affiliate. The award is named after Pura Belpré, the first Latina librarian from the New York Public Library who enriched the lives of Puerto Rican children in the U.S.A. through her pioneering work of preserving and disseminating Puerto Rican folklore. The award is given biennially in even numbered years. Read more about the Pura Belpré Award at www.ala.org/ala/alsc/awardsscholarships/literaryawds/belpremedal/belprmedal.htm.

The Children's Literature and Reading Special Interest Group of the International Reading Association established the Notable Books for a Global Society award list in 1996. To be eligible for the Notable Books for a Global Society selection, a book must have been published in the United States for the first time during the previous year. The book must meet one or more of the following criteria: portrays cultural accuracy and authenticity of characters in terms of (a) physical characteristics, (b) intellectual abilities and problem-solving capabilities, (c) leadership and cooperative dimensions, and (d) social and economic status; is rich in cultural details; honors and celebrates diversity as well as common bonds in humanity; provides in-depth treatment of cultural issues; includes characters within a cultural group or between two or more cultural groups who interact substantively and authentically; includes members of a "minority" group for a purpose other than filling a "quota." The book must also meet all of the following criteria: invites reflection, critical analysis, and response; demonstrates unique language or style; meets generally accepted criteria of quality for the genre in which it is written; has an appealing format; and is of enduring quality. Read more about the Notable Books for a Global Society Award at http://csulb.edu/org/childrens-lit/proj/nbgs/intro-nbgs.html.

Achebe, Chinua. *Things Fall Apart.*
Everyman's Library, 1995.
Setting: Nigeria.
Main Character: Male, Okonkwo, adult.
    Okonkwo is the tough and proud leader of an Igbo community; exiled for seven years when he accidentally kills a clansman. Traditional in his beliefs, Okonkwo is an old-order Nigerian and an outcast amid the British colonialism of his land and people. Awards: CC. Grades: 9–12.

Courtenay, Bryce. *The Power of One.*
Delacorte Books for Young Readers, 2005.
Setting: South Africa during apartheid.
Main Character: Male, Peekay, young man.
    Peekay, a white English-speaking boy, becomes a talented boxer and dreams of being welterweight champion of the world. He has the help of several mentors, including an Afrikaner, a German botanist and pianist, a mixed-race worker in the local jail, a brave librarian, and a Jewish teacher. Peekay not only wins the local boxing championship but helps desperate African chain-gang prisoners send letters home. Grades: 9–12.

Farmer, Nancy. *Ear, the Eye, and the Arm.*
Orchard, 1994.
Setting: Zimbawe, 2194.
Main Character: Male, Tendai, 13 years old.
    Tendai and his younger brother and sister, children of a military leader, leave their technologically overcontrolled home for adventure. They encounter mile-high buildings and other miracles of scientific advance, but also find fetid slums and toxic waste dumps. They are kidnapped, enslaved, accused of witchcraft, and pursued by mutant detectives. Awards: CC. Grades: 7–12.

Farmer, Nancy. *Girl Named Disaster.*
Orchard, 1996.
Setting: Mozambique, 1981.
Main Character: Female, Nhamo, 11 years old.
    Nhamo, a Shona girl whose life is filled with the traditions of her village people, flees a horrible marriage with only her grandmother's blessings, some gold nuggets, and her survival skills. What should have been a two-day boat trip across the border to her father's family in Zimbabwe spans an adventurous, humorous, and heart-wrenching year. Readers who enjoyed *Island of the Dolphins* and *Julie of the Wolves* will enjoy *Girl Named Disaster*. Awards: CC; Newbery Honor. Grades: 6–9.

Kessler, Cristina. *No Condition is Permanent.*
Philomel, 2000.
Setting: Sierra Leone.
Main Character: Female, Jodie, 14 years old.
    Jodie accompanies her anthropologist mother to live in Sierra Leone and

befriends a local girl, Khadi. When she discovers Khadi is about to be initiated into her tribe as a woman, and undergo female circumcision, Jodie tries to rescue her. Grades: 5–9.

Mankell, Henning. *Secrets in the Fire.*
Annick, 2003.
Sequel: *Playing with Fire.*
Setting: Mozambique, civil war, 1975–1992.
Main Character: Female, Sofia Alface, young girl.
   Sofia's village is attacked by ax-wielding bandits and her father is killed. Sophia, her mother, her sister, and her brother escape and travel by foot to a faraway village. Maria and Sofia are playing on a path when Sofia steps on a land mine. Maria dies and Sofia loses both legs. The book tells of Sophia's survival. Awards: Notable Books for a Global Society. Grades: 6–9.

Naidoo, Beverly. *Out of Bounds.*
HarperCollins, 2003.
Setting: South Africa, 1950 onward.
   Short stories personalize the political oppression and struggle of apartheid from the viewpoint of a child. Includes an introductory historical overview and endnotes about each decade, plus a foreword by Archbishop Tutu. Awards: Notable Books for a Global Society. Grades: 6–10.

Quintana, Anton. *The Baboon King.*
Walker, 1999.
Setting: Kenya.
Main Character: Male, Morengáru, young man.
   Morengru, a young man born of a Kikuyu mother and Masai father, lives alongside, but not part of, the Kikuyu, who are peaceful civilized farmers whom he views as earth-grubbers through the eyes of his Masai upbringing. After accidentally killing a Kikuyu tribesman, Morengru is exiled from the village. He falls in with a troop of baboons, and after a bloody fight with their leader, he becomes their new king. Grades: 8–12.

Stratton, Allan. *Chanda's Secrets.*
Annick, 2004.
Setting: South Africa.
Main Character: Female, Chanda, 16 years old.
   Chanda's life was good until her father was killed in the diamond mines. Her first stepfather abused her; the second died of a stroke; the third is a drunken philanderer infected with AIDS, the disease no one talks about. Chanda's mother leaves to visit her family on the cattle post, and Chanda is forced to care for her younger sister and brother. Chanda slowly realizes that her mother has AIDS and that she might be infected herself, but Chanda faces the disease head-on. Awards: Printz Honor; Notable Books for a Global Society. Grades: 8–12.

Zemser, Amy Bronwen. *Beyond the Mango Tree.*
Greenwillow, 1998.

Setting: Liberia.

Main Character: Female, Sarina, 12 years old.

Sarina, a white American, lives in Liberia with her diabetic, overly possessive mother. Her home life is unpredictably hostile and threatening. Sarina explores the world outside her home with a forbidden friend, Boima. Awards: Notable Books for a Global Society. Grades: 4–8.

AFRICAN AMERICAN CHARACTERS

Baldwin, James. *If Beale Street Could Talk.*
Dell, 1974.
Setting: New York, 1970s.
Main Character: Male, Fonny, 22 years old; Female, Tish, 19 years old.

Fonny and Tish are in love and expecting a baby. When Fonny is unjustly accused and arrested for rape, Tish is determined to free him. An emotional book of anger and pain and love. Awards: CC. Grades: 10–12.

Beatty, Paul. *White Boy Shuffle.*
Picador, 2001.
Setting: West Los Angeles, California, 1990s.
Main Character: Male, Gunnar Kaufman, third grade through college.

Gunnar earned his streetwise education in West Los Angeles. Gunnar is just trying to be Gunnar, an intelligent, sensitive young African American who survives great tribulations while sparing no one his enormous wit. A satire for mature readers. Awards: CC. Grades: 10–12.

Curtis, Christopher Paul. *Bud Not Buddy.*
Delacorte, 1999.
Setting: Michigan, Great Depression.
Main Character: Male, Bud, 10 years old.

Bud is fed up with the cruel treatment he has received at various foster homes, and after being locked up for the night in a shed with a swarm of angry hornets, he decides to run away. His goal: to reach the man he, on the flimsiest of evidence, believes to be his father, jazz musician Herman E. Calloway. Awards: CC; Newbery; Coretta Scott King. Grades: 6–8.

Draper, Sharon. *Tears of a Tiger.*
Atheneum, 1994.
Series: Hazelwood High Trilogy: *Forged by Fire* (CC; Coretta Scott King)*; Darkness Before Dawn.*
Setting: Hazelwood.
Main Character: Male, Andy, 17 years old.

Andy cannot bear the guilt of being the drunk driver in an accident that killed his best friend. His disintegration builds to inevitable suicide, as counselors, coaches, friends, and family all fail him. The story is told through English class assignments, including poetry; dialogs; police and newspaper reports; and letters. Awards: CC; Genesis (John Steptoe). Grades: 7–12.

Ellison, Ralph Waldo. *Invisible Man.*
Vintage, 1995.
Setting: Southern United States to Harlem, New York.
Main Character: A nameless young black man.

A young man journeys through the Deep South to the streets of Harlem, through frightening and enlightening events and experiences that range from tortured to macabre. As he moves through time, he learns about the black world, the white world, and a world of his own. Awards: CC; National Book Award. Grades: 10–12.

Flake, Sharon. *Who Am I Without Him?*
Jump at the Sun, 2004.

Ten short stories in the vernacular of urban African American teens, with universal themes and situations. Some are funny and uplifting; others, disturbing and sad, addressing issues many girls face in today's complex society. Awards: Coretta Scott King Honor. Grades: 7–12.

Flake, Sharon. *Money Hungry.*
Jump at the Sun, 2001.
Sequel: *Begging for Change.*
Setting: Urban, 2000s.
Main Character: Female, Raspberry Hill, 13 years old.

Ever since Raspberry's father got involved with drugs and she and her mother lived on the streets for a while, cash makes her feel safe. She sells clearance holiday candy and pencils, and she keeps her lunch money rather than eat. She hoards every dime she can gather and hides her cash in her room. When Raspberry's mother finds her stash, she thinks it's stolen and throws it out the window. Everything else— furniture, dishes, and clothing—is stolen from their apartment, and the teen and her mother are on the street again. Awards: CC; Coretta Scott King Honor. Grades: 6–12.

Gaines, Ernest J. *Autobiography of Miss Jane Pittman.*
Bantam, 1982.
Setting: Louisiana.
Main Character: Female, Miss Jane Pittman, 110 years old.

Miss Jane Pittman has been both a slave and a witness to the black militancy of the 1960s. Her story is told in transcripts of tape-recorded interviews. Awards: CC. Grades: 7–12.

Myers, Walter Dean. *145th Street: Short Stories.*
Delacorte, 2000.
Setting: Harlem, New York City.

Ten short stories create snapshots of a pulsing, vibrant community with diverse ethnic threads, told through the voices of witty, intelligent teens. Awards: CC. Grades: 7–10.

Sinclair, April. *Coffee Will Make You Black.*
Hyperion, 1993.
Setting: Chicago, Illinois, 1967.

Main Character: Female, Jean "Stevie" Stevenson, sixth-grade through teen years.

Stevie's father is a hospital janitor, her mother is a bank teller, and Grandma owns a popular South Side chicken stand. Stevie's dream is to be popular and cool, and her wish is granted when "all the way cool" Carla invites her to a party. Soon Stevie has had her first period, her first kiss, and is learning that cool is not always kind. Awards: CC. Grades: 10–12.

Thomas, Joyce Carol. *Marked By Fire.*
Avon Tempest, 1999.
Setting: Oklahoma.
Main Character: Female, Abyssinia Jackson, young woman.

Abyssinia, born in an Oklahoma cotton field in the wake of a tornado, is the pride and joy of her family, church, and community, until natural disasters and personal attacks threaten to break her spirit. But Mother Barker and her lessons in folk medicine help Abby survive through the Oklahoma tragedy. Awards: CC. Grades: 6–9.

Williams-Garcia, Rita. *Fast Talk on a Slow Track.*
Dutton, 1991.
Setting: New York City.
Main Character: Male, Denzel Watson, 18 years old.

Denzel, president and valedictorian of his class, graduates from high school with a 98 percent grade point average; he plans to enter Princeton in the fall. While at Princeton as part of a six-week minority candidate summer program, Denzel tries to wing it through his classes as he had done through high school, but it does not work. Denzel can't fail in his family's eyes. He returns home and decides he will attend the local college in the fall rather than Princeton, but lacks the courage to tell his parents. Awards: CC. Grades: 7–10.

ASIA AS A SETTING

Bass, L. G. *Outlaws of Moonshadow Marsh: Sign of the Qin.*
Hyperion, 2004.
Setting: Ancient China.
Main Character: Male, Prince Zong, young man.

Prince Zong, the mortal young Starlord chosen to save humankind from destruction, joins the twin outlaws, White Streak and Black Whirlwind, to fight the Lord of the Dead and his demon hordes. Fast-paced first of a trilogy, with Chinese mythological characters and wild action. Grades: 6 and up.

Chen, Da. *Wandering Warrior.*
Delacorte, 2003.
Setting: Ancient China.
Main Character: Male, Luka, 11 years old.

Although he lives as a wandering beggar, Luka learns that he bears the mark of a future emperor. Luka is trained in the ways of the kung fu wandering warriors by the wise monk, Atami. Grades: 6 and up.

Ellis, Deborah. *The Breadwinner.*
Groundwood, 2001.
Sequel: *Parvana's Journey* (Notable Book for a Global Society).
Setting: Afghanistan.
Main Character: Female, Parvana, 11 years old.

The Taliban have decreed that women must stay inside their homes, unless completely covered by a long, tentlike garment with a veil over the face. Girls can no longer go to school. Parvana accompanies father to the market, where he works as a letter writer and sells family possessions. After he is arrested and taken away, Parvana becomes the breadwinner, dressing as a boy and taking over her father's job. Grades: 5–8.

Hearn, Lian. *Across the Nightingale Floor.*
Riverhead, 2003.
Series: Tales of the Otori: *Grass for His Pillow; Brilliance of the Moon.*
Setting: Japan.
Main Character: Male, Otori Takeo, 16 years old; Female, Kaede Shirakawa, 15 years old.

Takeo is the only survivor of an attack on his village. He gives up speaking in his grief and acquires magical abilities. Grades: YA/A.

Hoobler, Dorothy and Thomas. *The Ghost in Tokaido Inn.*
Philomel, 1999.
Sequels: *The Demon in the Teahouse; In Darkness, Death.*
Setting: Japan, 1735.
Main Character: Male, Seikei, 14 years old.

Seikei wants to be a samurai but he is only a tea merchant's son. A priceless gem is stolen by a ghost at Tokaido Inn where he and his father are staying, and Seikei searches for clues to solve the mystery under Judge Ooka's guidance. Sherlock Holmes–style mysteries, set in Shogun Japan. Grades: 6–8.

Hosseini, Khaled. *The Kite Runner.*
Riverhead, 2003.
Setting: Kabul, Afghanistan/United States.
Main Characters: Male, Amir; Male, Hassan; both 12 years old.

Amir, the son of a wealthy businessman in Kabul, and Hassan, the son of Amir's father's servant, were inseparable friends as children. Amir and his father flee to America, but Amir is haunted that he left his friend behind. He returns to his war-torn native land after it comes under Taliban rule, only to learn Hassan has been enslaved by a former childhood bully, who has become a prominent Taliban official. Awards: Alex. Grades: YA/A.

Kim, Helen S. *The Long Season of Rain.*
Henry Holt, 1996.
Setting: Seoul, South Korea, 1969.
Main Character: Female, Junehee, 11 years old.

Junehee has a boy's name because her father wished for a son. An orphan boy comes to live with Junehee's family, offering her a special friendship before he finally leaves to live with a family who wants him. Junehee observes women's roles in her family and culture. Awards: CC. Grades: 7–10.

McCaughrean, Geraldine. *The Kite Rider.*
HarperCollins, 2002.
Setting: China, 1281.
Main Character: Male, Haoyou, 12 years old.
Haoyou becomes a circus kite rider and meets Kublai Khan just after China falls to the Mongols. Grades: 5–9.

Namioka, Lensey. *Den of the White Fox.*
Harcourt Brace, 1997.
Setting: Japan, sixteenth century.
Main Characters: Male, Matsuzo, young adult; Male, Zenta, older adult.
Freelance samurai Matsuzo and Zenta attempt to solve the mystery of the shadowy White Fox, and join him in resistance to a cruel occupying force. Grades: 7 and up.

Napoli, Donna J. *Bound.*
Atheneum, 2004.
Setting: China, Ming dynasty.
Main Character: Female, Xing Xing, 14 years old.
Xing Xing is left to the mercy of her stepmother after the death of her father. She finds comfort in a beautiful white carp in the pond that she believes is her mother's spirit. When her stepmother kills the fish, Xing Xing saves its bones, and while looking for a place to hide them, she discovers a beautiful gown and slippers that belonged to her mother. She wears them to a festival and loses one of the shoes, which is eventually bought by an unconventional prince in this Cinderella story. Grades: 5–9.

Park, Linda Sue. *A Single Shard.*
Clarion, 2001.
Setting: Ch'ulp'o, Korea, late twelfth century.
Main Character: Male, Tree-ear, 13 years old.
Tree-ear, an orphan, becomes an apprentice to a master potter of celadon ceramics. Awards: Newbery; Printz Honor; Notable Books for a Global Society. Grades: 5–8.

Park, Linda Sue. *When My Name Was Keoko.*
Clarion, 2002.
Setting: Korea, World War II.
Main Characters: Female, Sun-hee Kim, 10 years old; Male, Tae-yul Kim, 13 years old.
When Japan occupies Korea, Sun-hee and her brother, Tae-yul, describe the hardships their family faces, in alternating voices. Awards: Notable Books for a Global Society. Grades: 6–9.

Staples, Suzanne Fisher. *Shabanu: Daughter of the Wind.*
Knopf, 1991.
Sequel: *Haveli.*
Setting: Pakistan.
Main Character: Female, Shabanu, 13 years old.

Shabanu, the daughter of a nomad in the Cholistan Desert of present-day Pakistan, is pledged in marriage to an older man, whose money will bring prestige to the family. Now she must either accept the decision, as is the custom, or risk the consequences of defying her father's wishes. Awards: CC. Grades: 8–10.

Yumoto, Kazumi. *The Letters.*
Farrar, Straus & Giroux, 2002.
Setting: Japan.
Main Character: Female, Chiaki Hoshino, 25 years old.

Chiako returns to her childhood home for the funeral of the landlady who helped her cope with her father's death when she was 6 years old by promising to deliver letters to the dead when she passed. Grades: 9 and up.

ASIAN AMERICAN CHARACTERS

Balgassi, Haemi. *Tae's Sonata.*
Clarion, 1997.
Setting: United States.
Main Character: Female, Tae, 13 years old.

Korean American Tae tries to sort out her feelings when she is assigned a popular cute boy as a partner for a school report, which makes a clique of girls jealous. When her best friend starts hanging out with the clique, Tae has a falling-out with her. Grades: 5–8.

Carlson, Lori, editor. *American Eyes: New Asian-American Short Stories for Young Adults.*
Henry Holt, 1994.

Ten short stories reflect the conflicts Asian Americans face in balancing an ancient heritage and an unknown future. Includes stories by Katherine Min, Lois-Ann Yamanaka, Lan Samantha Chang, Ryan Oba, Marie G. Lee, Cynthia Kadohata, Mary F. Chen, Nguyen Duc Minh, Fae Myenne Ng, and Peter Bacho. Awards: CC. Grades: 7–12.

Crew, Linda. *Children of the River.*
Random House, 1994.
Setting: Oregon.
Main Character: Female, Sundara, 17 years old.

Cambodian American Sundara fled Cambodia with her aunt's family, leaving her own family behind. Now she's in Oregon, struggling to balance Khmer traditions with American ways. As a Khmer girl, she's not allowed to date or even be alone with a boy, and her marriage will be arranged. When handsome, popular Jonathan asks for help with a report on her native land, Jonathan is astounded that a girl in America can live like this, and he is deeply affected by Sundara's values and traditions. Grades: 7 and up.

Desai Hidier, Tanuja. *Born Confused.*
Push/Scholastic, 2002.
Setting: New Jersey, 2000s.

Main Character: Female, Dimple Lala, 17 years old.

Indian American Dimple, an aspiring photographer, struggles to balance two cultures at home and in the South Asian club scene without falling apart. She sees her hypnotically beautiful, blond, manipulative best friend, Gwyn, taking possession of both her heritage and the boy she likes. Grades: 9 and up.

Guterson, David. **Snow Falling on Cedars.**
Harcourt, 1994.
Setting: San Piedro, Washington, 1954.
Main Characters: Male, Kabuo Miyomoto, Japanese American; Female, Hatsue Miyomoto, Japanese American; Male, Ishmael Chambers; adults.

A local fisherman is found suspiciously drowned, and Kabuo Miyamoto is charged with his murder. San Piedro is haunted by the memories of a charmed love affair between a white boy and the Japanese girl who grew up to become Kabuo's wife, memories of land desired, paid for, and lost; memories of when an entire community of Japanese residents during World War II was sent into exile while the neighbors watched. For mature readers. Awards: CC. Grades: 10–12.

Lee, Marie G. **F Is for Fabuloso.**
Morrow, 1999.
Setting: Minnesota.
Main Character: Female, Jin-Ha, seventh-grader.

Korean American Jin-Ha's adjustment to American life is complicated by her mother's difficulty in learning to speak English. When she receives failing math grades, Jin-Ha tells her mother the F means fabuloso, and she seeks help from a classmate who becomes embarrassed by the rude remarks he has made about her. Grades: 6–8.

Lee, Marie G. **Finding My Voice.**
HarperCollins, 2001.
Setting: Minnesota.
Main Character: Female, Ellen Sung, 17 years old.

Pressured by her strict Korean immigrant parents to get into Harvard, high school senior Ellen tries to find some time for romance, friendship, and fun in her small Minnesota town. But the racism she encounters becomes impossible to ignore. Grades: 8 and up.

Lee, Marie G. **Necessary Roughness.**
HarperCollins, 1996.
Setting: Minnesota.
Main Character: Male, Chan Kim, 16 years old.

Korean American Chan moves from Los Angeles to a small town in Minnesota, where he must cope not only with racism on the football team but also with the tensions in his relationship with his father, who practices old world customs. He must then deal with the accidental death of his sister, Young. Awards: CC. Grades: 6–10.

Mochizuki, Ken. **Beacon Hill Boys.**
Scholastic, 2002.

Setting: Beacon Hill, Seattle, Washington, 1972
Main Character: Male, Dan Inagaki, junior, 16 years old.
Japanese American Dan's parents want him to conform and excel, but Dan earns a high profile by lobbying for the creation of a comparative American cultures class and for some books in the school library "to teach history from a different point of view." Grades: 8 and up.

Na, An. *A Step from Heaven.*
Speak, 2001.
Setting: Southern California, late twentieth century.
Main Character: Female, Young Ju, 4 through teen years.
After moving to California from Korea, Young Ju and her family find it difficult to adjust to a new language and culture. Awards: CC; Printz; Coretta Scott King; Notable Books for a Global Society. Grades: 8 and up.

Namioka, Lensey. *Ties That Bind, Ties That Break.*
Delacorte 1999.
Sequel: *An Ocean Apart, a World Away.*
Setting: Nanjing, China; United States, 1912–1928.
Main Character: Female, Tao Ailin, 5–21 years old.
Chinese American Ailin defies the traditions of upper-class Chinese society by refusing to have her feet bound. Her father arranges for her to attend a school run by American Protestant missionaries, but her plans to become a teacher are dashed when her father dies when she is 12 years old. Ailin finds a new home in the United States when she becomes the nanny for an American missionary couple. Grades: 7–10.

Tan, Amy. *The Joy Luck Club.*
Putnam, 1989.
Setting: San Fransisco, 1949/1989.
Main Character: Female, Jing-Mei, adult.
The Joy Luck Club—four Chinese American women drawn together by the shadow of their past—begin meeting to play mah jong, invest in stocks, eat dim sum, and "say" stories. Nearly forty years later, one of the members has died, and her daughter, Jing-Mei, has come to take her place. The other members ask Jing-Mei to tell her sisters, who were left at the side of a road in China, about her mother's life. Awards: CC. Grades: 10–12.

AUSTRALIA/NEW ZEALAND AS A SETTING

Disher, Garry. *The Divine Wind: A Love Story.*
A.A. Levine, 2002.
Setting: Broome, Australia, WW II.
Main Character: Male, Hart, adult flashbacks to 17 years old.
Hart waits for Misty, the Japanese Australian woman he loves, to return after the war. He describes their life together in Broome before the war. Awards: Australia YA Award. Grades: 9 and up.

Earls, Nick. *48 Shades of Brown.*
Graphia, 2004.

Setting: Brisbane, Australia, 2000s.
Main Character: Male, Dan, 16 years old.
While his parents are in Geneva, Dan spends his last year of high school living with his 22-year-old bass-playing Aunt Jacq and her beautiful friend, Naomi, whose active love life is audible through the wall between their bedrooms. Grades: 9 and up.

Ihimaera, Witi Tame. **Whale Rider.**
Harcourt, 2003.
Setting: Whangara, New Zealand.
Main Character: Female, Kahu, 8 years old.
As her beloved grandfather, chief of the Maori tribe of Whangara, struggles to lead in difficult times and to find a male successor, young Kahu is developing a mysterious relationship with whales, particularly the ancient bull whale whose legendary rider was her ancestor. Grades: 5–8.

Kotuku, Deborah. **Savage.**
Houghton Mifflin, 2002.
Setting: New Zealand.
Main Character: Female, Wim Thorpe, 17 years old.
Wim is trying to overcome her feelings of grief about her best friend's death. Wim becomes intensely involved with her work at the riding stable and her interest in nature study, almost to the exclusion of everything else. When required to care for her elderly great-aunt, she feels resentful and overwhelmed. A charismatic young man and his niece arrive from New Zealand to do research, and Wim learns about her Maori heritage. Grades: 7–10.

CENTRAL AMERICA/CARIBBEAN/MEXICO/ SOUTH AMERICA AS A SETTING

Abelove Joan. **Go and Come Back.**
Puffin, 2000.
Setting: Amazonian jungle, Peru
Main Character: Female, Alicia, teen.
Alicia, a young tribeswoman living in an Amazonian village in the Andes, tells about their life and customs to the two American women anthropologists who arrive to study the way of life of her people. Grades: 7 and up.

Alvarez, Julia. **Before We Were Free.**
Knopf, 2002.
Setting: Dominican Republic, 1960s.
Main Character: Female, Anita, 12 years old.
Anita learns that her family is involved in the underground movement to end the bloody rule of dictator General Trujillo. Awards: Pura Belpré. Grades: 6–10.

Cameron, Ann. **Colibri.**
Farrar, Straus, & Giroux, 2003.
Setting: Contemporary Guatemala.
Main Character: Female, Tzunun Chumil, 12 years old.

Tzunun, called Rosa Garcia by her "Uncle" Baltasar, travel together begging while he pretends to be blind. She believes he rescued her from abandonment when she was 4 and not until he dies does she find out he kidnapped her. Awards: Notable Books for a Global Society. Grades: 5–8.

Cofer, Judith Ortiz. *The Meaning of Consuelo.*
Farrar, Straus & Giroux, 2003.
Setting: Puerto Rico, 1950s.
Main Character: Female, Consuelo, young girl through 16 years old.

When book lover Consuelo notices a disturbing change in her little sister Mili, Consuelo must decide if she will rise to the occasion and fulfill the expectations of her family and culture or risk becoming an outsider. This is a funny and startling novel, with a strong Latina spirit. Awards: Americas Award. Grades: YA

Esquivel, Laura. *Like Water for Chocolate.*
Doubleday, 1992.
Setting: Mexico.
Main Character: Female, Tita De la Garza; Male, Pedro; both adults.

Tita is the youngest of three daughters born to Mama Elena, virago extraordinaire and owner of the de la Garza ranch. Tita falls in love with Pedro, but Mama Elena will not allow them to marry, since family tradition dictates that the youngest daughter remain at home to care for her mother. Instead, Mama Elena orchestrates the marriage of Pedro and her eldest daughter, Rosaura, and forces Tita to prepare the wedding dinner. Magical realism and recipes; for mature readers. Awards: CC. Grades: 10–12.

Mikaelsen, Ben. *Red Midnight.*
HarperCollins, 2002.
Setting: Guatemala
Main Character: Male, Santiago, 12 years old.

When guerrilla soldiers destroy Santiago's village, he and his sister set sail in a sea kayak their Uncle Ramos built while dreaming of his own escape. They head for the United States across hundreds of miles of open ocean. Awards: Notable Books for a Global Society. Grades: 5–9.

Temple, Frances. *Taste of Salt: A Story of Modern Haiti.*
Orchard, 1992.
Setting: Haiti.
Main Character: Male, Djo, 17 years old.

In the hospital after being beaten by Macoutes, Djo tells the story of his impoverished life to Jeremie who, like him, has been working with the social reformer Father Jean-Bertrand Aristide to fight repression in Haiti. Jeremie records Djo's story on tape, and when he is in a coma, she writes her own story. Grades: 8 and up.

Almond, David. *The Fire-Eaters.*
Delacorte, 2004.
Setting: England, 1962.
Main Character: Male, Bobby Burns, 12 years old.
   Bobby and his mother take a day trip to Newcastle, where Bobby meets Mr. McNutty, the fire-eater. Bobby's father is ill, and the Cuban missile crisis looms over them, but Bobby and his family find reasons to have hope for the future. Grades: 7 and up.

Bagdasarian, Adam *The Forgotten Fire.*
DK, 2000.
Setting: Turkey, 1915–1918.
Main Character: Male, Vahan Kenderian, 12 years old.
   Vahan survived the Armenian massacre that took his father, uncle, brothers, and other members of his family, one by one. He suffers hunger, destitution, beatings, and sexual abuse, and witnesses killings and rapes as he travels across Turkey to reach freedom in Constantinople. Grades: 8 and up.

Bawden, Nina. *The Real Plato Jones.*
Clarion, 1993.
Setting: Greece.
Main Character: Male, Plato Constantine Jones, 13 years old.
   While visiting Greece for his grandfather's funeral, Plato tries to come to terms with his mixed heritage as he finds out more about his two grandfathers: the Welsh one who was a World War II hero, and the Greek one, a supposed traitor. Grades: 6–9.

Chambers, Aidan. *Postcards from No Man's Land.*
Dutton, 2002.
Setting: The Netherlands, mid-1990s.
Main Characters: Male, Jacob, 17 years old; Female, Geetrui, older adult flashing back to young adult.
   Two stories are intertwined: one of Jack's visit to Amsterdam to represent his English grandmother at a ceremony commemorating the World War II Battle of Arnhem and the other about Geertrui, the nurse who took care of his grandfather during the war, and their love affair. Awards: Printz; Carnegie. Grades: 10 and up.

Friel, Maeve. *Charlie's Story.*
Peachtree, 1997.
Setting: Dublin, Ireland.
Main Character: Female, Charlotte Collins, 14 years old.
   Charlotte was abandoned by her mother in a subway when she was 4 years old. She is mercilessly bullied by her cruel classmates, and now Charlie is ready to give up on life. Grades: 6–10.

Magorian, Michelle. *Good Night, Mr. Tom.*
HarperCollins, 1981.

Setting: England, WWII.
Main Character: Male, Willie Beech, 8 years old.
Willie is an abused child of a single mother. When he is sent to live in the country as the war breaks out, he stays with Mr. Tom, an old man who shows Willie beauty, friendship, and affection. Then the telegram arrives from his mother for him to return to London. Mr. Tom doesn't hear from Willie, so he takes a train to London to find him. Awards: CC. Grades: 6–9.

Mead, Alice. **Adem's Cross.**
Laurel Leaf, 1998.
Setting: Kosovo, Yugoslavia, 1990s.
Main Character: Male, Adem, 14 years old.
Adem, an Albanian, tries to survive despite the random violence and cruelty of the Serbians. Adem goes to a school without chairs, books, or heat, where the school's annual first-day tradition is tear gas and beating up the principal. Adem's beloved older sister attempts to make a stand and is cut down by Serbian bullets, and Adem is consumed by guilt that he might have prevented her death. Grades: 5–8.

Mosher, Richard. **Zazoo.**
Clarion, 2001.
Setting: France.
Main Character: Female, Zazoo, 13 years old.
Zazoo, a Vietnamese orphan, lives with her adoptive grandfather in France. Her Grand-Pierre is considered a hero in France's resistance to the Nazi invasion, but at 78 he is slowing down, and Zazoo is caring for her grandfather more and more and seeking to understand his trauma and loss. Awards: CC; Notable Books for a Global Society. Grades: 6–10.

Rennison, Louise. **Angus, Thongs, and Full Frontal Snogging: Confessions of Georgia Nicolson.**
HarperCollins, 2000.
Sequels: **On the Bright Side, I'm Now the Girlfriend of a Sex God: Further Confessions of Georgia Nicolson; Knocked Out by My Nunga-Nungas: Further, Further Confessions of Georgia Nicolson; Dancing in My Nuddy-Pants: Even Further Confessions of Georgia Nicolson; Away Laughing on a Fast Camel: Even More Confessions of Georgia Nicolson; Then He Ate My Boy Entrancers: More Mad, Marvy Confessions of Georgia Nicolson.**
Setting: England.
Main Character: Female, Georgia Nicolson, 14 years old.
With embarrassing parents, a 3-year-old sister who leaves wet diapers at the foot of her bed, and Angus, an insane cat who is prone to leg-shredding "call of the wild" episodes, Georgia also struggles with the important issues like boys and plucking eyebrows. British slang and humor. Awards: CC; Printz Honor. Grades: 7–12.

Simoen, Jan. **What about Anna?**
Walker, 2002.
Setting: Belgium, 1999.

Main Character: Female, Anna, 16 years old.

Anna lost one brother to AIDS and the other is reported killed in Bosnia. Two years later, a letter arrives from a friend who offers evidence that her brother is still alive, but instructs Anna not to tell anyone. Grades: 7 and up.

HISPANIC AMERICAN CHARACTERS

Anaya, Rudolpho. *Bless Me, Ultima.*
Warner, 1994.
Series: New Mexico Trilogy: *Heart of Aztlan, Tortuga.*
Setting: New Mexico, 1940s.
Main Characters: Male, Antonio Marez, teen; Female, Ultima, older adult; Mexican Americans.

Antonio is torn between his father's cowboy side of the family who rides on the llano and his mother's village and farming relations. When Aunt Ultima, a healer, comes to live with the family, she teaches Antonio many things that will help carry him into adulthood. Awards: CC. Grades: YA/A.

Bertrand, Diane Gonzales. *Trino's Choice.*
Piñata, 1999.
Sequel: *Trino's Time.*
Setting: Texas.
Main Character: Male, Trino, 13 years old.

Living in a Texas trailer park with his working mother, three younger stepbrothers, and freeloading drunk of an uncle, Mexican American Trino hates his life. Frustrated, he is convinced by older rat-faced Rosca to hang out and maybe make some quick cash, which leads to tragedy. Grades: 6–9.

Canales, Viola. *The Tequila Worm.*
Delacorte, 2005.
Setting: Barrio McAllen, Texas, 2000s.
Main Character: Female, Sofia, 14 years old.

When Mexican American Sofia is singled out to receive a scholarship to boarding school, she longs to explore life beyond the barrio, even though it means leaving her family to navigate a strange world of rich, privileged kids. Grades: 7 and up.

Chambers, Veronica. *Marisol and Magdalena: The Sound of Our Sisterhood.*
Hyperion, 2001.
Setting: Panama.
Main Character: Female, Marisol, 13 years old.

Panamanian American Marisol spends a year with her grandmother in Panama, where she secretly searches for her real father, while missing her best friend Magdalena back home in Brooklyn. Grades: YA.

Cisneros, Sandra. *House on Mango Street.*
Vintage, 1991.
Setting: Chicago, Illinois.

Main Character: Female, Esperanza Cordero, teen.

Poems and stories about Mexican Americans living in the Hispanic quarter of Chicago. Awards: CC. Grades: 6–12.

Cofer, Judith Oritz. *An Island Like You: Stories of the Barrio.*
Orchard, 1995.
Setting: New Jersey.

Twelve stories about young people caught between their Puerto Rican heritage and their American surroundings. Awards: CC; Notable Books for a Global Society. Grades: 7–10.

Herrera, Juan Felipe. *CrashBoomLove: A Novel in Verse.*
University of New Mexico Press, 1999.
Setting: Fowlerville, California.
Main Character: Male, Cesar Garcia, 16 years old.

After his father leaves home, Cesar lives with his mother and struggles through the painful experiences of growing up as a Mexican American high school student. Awards: CC. Grades: 8 and up.

Jimenez, Francisco. *The Circuit: Stories from the Life of a Migrant Child.*
Houghton Mifflin, 1999.
Sequel: *Breaking Through* (Pura Belpré).
Setting: California.
Main Character: Male, Francisco, 14 years old.

After ten years, Mexican American Francisco is still working in the fields but fighting to improve his life and complete his education. Grades: 5–8.

Martinez, Floyd. *Spirits of the High Mesa.*
Piñata, 1997.
Setting: Northern New Mexico.
Main Character: Male, Flavio, teen.

Mexican American Flavio is torn between the lure of modern U.S. life and deep Hispanic cultural values held by El Grande, his mountainman grandfather. Awards: Pura Belpré. Grades: YA.

Martinez, Victor. *Parrot in the Oven: Mi Vida.*
HarperCollins, 1996.
Setting: California.
Main Character: Male, Manny, 14 years old.

Manny relates his coming-of-age experiences as a member of a poor Mexican American family, in which the alcoholic father only adds to everyone's struggle Awards: CC; Pura Belpré. Grades: 7–12.

Osa, Nancy. *Cuba 15.*
Delacorte, 2003.
Setting: Chicago, Illinois.
Main Character: Female, Violet Paz, 15 years old.

Cuban American Violet reluctantly prepares for her upcoming "quince," a

Spanish nickname for the celebration of a Hispanic girl's fifteenth birthday. Awards: Pura Belpré. Grades: 6–10.

Rice, David Talbot. *Crazy Loco.*
Puffin, 2003.
Setting: South Texas.
Main Character: Mexican Americans.
   A collection of nine short stories about Mexican American kids growing up in the Rio Grande Valley of southern Texas. Grades: 7–12.

Ryan, Pam Muñoz. *Esperanza Rising.*
Scholastic, 2000.
Setting: California, Great Depression.
Main Character: Female, Esperanza, 14 years old.
   Esperanza and her mother are forced to leave their life of wealth and privilege in Mexico to go work in the labor camps of Southern California, where they must adapt to the harsh circumstances facing Mexican farm workers. Awards: CC; Pura Belpré; Notable Books for a Global Society. Grades: 6–9.

Saldana, Rene Jr. *The Jumping Tree.*
Delacorte, 2001.
Setting: Nuevo Pietas, Texas.
Main Character: Male, Rey, 13 years old.
   Rey's Mexican American family, though poor, struggles and survives through their kind and honest efforts, religious beliefs, and hard work. His family maintains close contact with their Mexican relatives across the border. Grades: 5–9.

Soto, Gary. *Baseball in April and Other Stories.*
Harcourt, 2000.
Sequel: *Local News.*
Setting: Fresno, California.
Main Character: Mexican Americans.
   A collection of eleven short stories focusing on the everyday adventures of Hispanic young people growing up in Fresno, California. Awards: CC; Pura Belpré Honor. Grades: 5 and up.

Soto, Gary. *Buried Onions.*
Harcourt Brace, 1997.
Setting: Barrio, Fresno, California, 1990s.
Main Character: Male, Eddie, 19 years old.
   When Eddie's cousin is killed, his aunt pressures him to avenge his death. He drops out of City College and gets drawn into the violence he hates. Awards: CC. Grades: 9 and up.

Veciana-Suarez, Ana. *The Flight to Freedom.*
Orchard, 2002.
Setting: Miami, Florida, 1967.
Main Character: Female, Yara Garcia, 13 years old.

Yara and her family are forced to flee from Cuba to Miami, Florida, to live with relatives. Tension develops between her parents, as Mami grows more independent and Papi joins a militant anti-Castro organization. Grades: 6–9.

IMMIGRANTS/REFUGEES AS CHARACTERS

Banerjee, Anjali. *Maya Running.*
Wendy Lamb, 2005.
Setting: India to Manitoba, Canada, 1978.
Main Character: Female, Maya, 13 years old.
   Maya struggles with her ethnic East Indian identity, her infatuation with a classmate, and her beautiful Bengali cousin, Pinky, who comes for a visit bearing a powerful statue of the god Ganesh, the Hindu elephant boy. Grades: 6–8.

Danticat, Edwidge. *Behind the Mountains.*
Scholastic, 2003.
Setting: Haiti to Brooklyn, New York, 2000–2001.
Main Character: Female, Celiane Espérance, 13 years old.
   Celiane describes her life in Haiti and in Brooklyn. Grades: 5 and up.

De La Cruz, Melissa. *Fresh Off the Boat.*
HarperCollins, 2005.
Setting: Philippines to San Francisco, California.
Main Character: Female, Vicenza Arambullo, 14.
   In Manila, her family was wealthy, but now in America they struggle to make ends meet. On scholarship, Vicenza attends a private girls' school where as a Filipino American she is an outcast. Grades: 7–10.

Gallo, Donald. *First Crossing: Stories About Teen Immigrants.*
Candlewick, 2004.
   Short stories of recent Mexican, Venezuelan, Kazakh, Chinese, Romanian, Palestinian, Swedish, Korean, Haitian, and Cambodian immigrants reveal what it is like to face prejudice, language barriers, and homesickness along with common teenage feelings and needs. Stories are by Pam Muñoz Ryan, Dian Curtis Regan, Jean Davies Okimoto, Lensey Namioka, David Lubar, Elsa Marston, Alden R. Carter, Marie G. Lee, Rita Williams-Garcia, and Minfong Ho. Grades: 7 and up.

Giff, Patricia Reilly. *House of Tailors.*
Wendy Lamb, 2004.
Setting: Germany to Brooklyn, New York, 1871.
Main Character: Female, Dina, 13 years old.
   When Dina emigrates from Germany to America in 1871, her only wish is to return home as soon as she can. But as the months pass and she survives a multitude of hardships living with her uncle and his young wife and baby, she finds herself thinking of Brooklyn as her home. Grades: 5–8.

Guy, Rosa. *The Friends.*
Laurel Leaf, 1995.

Setting: Jamaica to Harlem, New York.
Main Character: Female, Phyllisia Cathy, 14 years old.

Rejected by her classmates because she "talks funny," Phyllisia Cathy, a West Indian girl, is forced to become friends with poor, frazzled Edith, the only one who will accept her. Originally published in 1973. West Indian American. Awards: CC. Grades: YA.

Hicyilmaz, Gaye. *Smiling for Strangers.*
Farrar, Straus & Giroux, 2000.
Setting: Yugoslavia to England, 1996.
Main Character: Female, Nina, 14 years old.

During the war, Nina flees from her village in Yugoslavia, armed only with some letters and a photograph, to search for an old friend of her mother's in England. Grades: 6–9.

Ho, Minfong. *The Stone Goddess.*
Orchard, 2003.
Setting: Cambodia to United States, 1979.
Main Character: Female, Nakri, 12 years old.

Nakri's beloved home in Cambodia is shattered when the nation's capital is overrun by government rebels. Her family is forced to flee, and she and her siblings end up in a children's labor camp, separated from everything they've ever known. At long last, Cambodia is liberated and Nakri's family sets out for America, a place to begin again. There, Nakri learns that she can leave Cambodia behind, but the memories will be a part of her forever. Grades: 6–10.

Lester, Julius. *Othello: A Novel.*
Scholastic, 1998.
Setting: Africa to Elizabethan England.
Main Characters: Male, Othello; Male, Iago; Female, Desdemona; adults.

Othello, Iago, and Iago's wife Desdemona share a three-way friendship that originated in their native Africa. Iago's envy of Othello and Desdemona drives him to plot to make Othello jealous. Othello's mistrust leads Desdemona to commit suicide. When her innocence is revealed, Othello kills himself. Shakespeare is quoted and paraphrased throughout. Awards: CC. Grades: 6–12.

Naidoo, Beverley. *The Other Side of Truth.*
HarperCollins, 2001.
Setting: Nigeria to London, mid-1990s.
Main Characters: Female, Sade Solaja, 13 years old; Male, Femi, 10 years old.

After their mother is shot and killed by assassins' bullets meant for their outspoken journalist father, Sade and Femi, abandoned in London, are unable to locate their uncle, a university professor who has been threatened and has gone into hiding. They are placed in a foster home until their father, who has illegally entered the country, contacts them from a detention center. Sade enacts a plan to tell "Mr. Seven O'Clock News" her father's story. Public attention and support follow, prompting his release. Grades: 5–8.

Shea, Pegi D. *Tangled Threads: A Hmong Girl's Story.*
Clarion, 2003.
Setting: Thailand to Providence, Rhode Island.
Main Character: Female, Mai Yang, 13 years old.

After ten years in a refugee camp in Thailand, Mai travels to Providence, Rhode Island, where her Americanized cousins introduce her to pizza, shopping, and beer, while her grandmother and new friends keep her connected to her Hmong heritage. Grades: 6–9.

Testa, Maria. *Something About America.*
Candlewick, 2005.
Setting: Kosovo to Maine.
Main Character: Female narrator, 13 years old.

The Serbian American narrator describes her life in America after having been horribly burned during the war in Kosovo. While she still carries the scars, she has assimilated into American culture much more than her parents. An act of racism inspires the entire town to stand up against prejudice. Poetic free verse inspired by actual events in Maine. Grades: 6–8.

Zephaniah, Benjamin. *Refugee Boy.*
Bloomsbury, 2001.
Setting: Africa to London, Eritrean-Ethiopian War, 1998.
Main Character: Male, Alem Kelo, 14 years old.

Alem adjusts to life as a foster child seeking asylum in London, while his Eritrean mother and Ethiopian father work for peace between their homelands in Africa. Grades: 6–9.

INDIA AS A SETTING

Alexander, Lloyd. *Iron Ring.*
Dutton, 1997.
Setting: India.
Main Character: Male, King Tamar, young man.

King Tamar, plays a losing game of chance with a mysterious stranger and the iron ring on his finger is a very real token that his life may be forfeited. A journey to the stranger's distant kingdom seems Tamar's only chance to discover the truth. Tamar and his companions, a brave and beautiful milkmaid, a cowardly eagle, and a wily monkey king who used to be a man face many adventures and diversions along the way. Awards: CC. Grades: 6–9.

Krishnaswami, Uma. *Naming Maya.*
Farrar, Straus & Giroux, 2004.
Setting: Chennai, India.
Main Character: Female, Maya, 12 years old.

New Jersey-born Maya goes to India with her mother to sell the family home in Chennai after her father's death. Maya feels responsible for her parents' separation due to their dispute over naming her. An old and loving housekeeper, Kamala Mami, returns to take care of Maya and her mother during their stay. Mami is in the early stages of dementia but shows that her memories remain even while everything else changes. Awards: Notable Books for a Global Society. Grades: 5–8.

Perkins, Mitali. *Monsoon Summer.*
Delacorte, 2004.
Setting: India.
Main Character: Female, Jazz, 15 years old.
Secretly in love with her best friend and business partner, Steve, Jazz must spend the summer away from him when her family goes to India to help set up a clinic. Grades: 6–9.

Staples, Suzanne. *Shiva's Fire.*
Farrar, Straus & Giroux, 2000.
Setting: India.
Main Character: Female, Parvati, 15 years old.
Parvati is both blessed and cursed with mysterious powers that confound her people. Wild animals flock to her; she is able to charm fish, birds, and even deadly cobras. Parvati's truly exceptional talent is her ability to dance like the Hindu god Shiva himself. The guru Pillai, a famous Indian dance teacher, hears of Parvati's talent and comes to offer her a position in his dance school in the large city of Madras. Grades: 7 and up.

Vijayaraghavan, Vineeta. *Motherland.*
Soho, 2002.
Setting: India.
Main Character: Female, Maya, 15 years old.
Maya was born in Southern India, and spent her first four years there with her grandmother; maternal uncle, Sanjay; and his wife, Reema. Maya often visits them in the summer, but this year she hopes to hang out at home with her friends in New York. When she gets into a little trouble, her parents send her back to India for summer vacation. She grows much closer to her grandmother, who helps her to understand why she feels alienated from her mother. Grades: YA/A.

Whelan, Gloria. *Homeless Bird.*
HarperCollins, 2000.
Setting: India.
Main Character: Female, Koly, 13 years old.
Koly feels apprehensive about leaving home to live in a distant village with her in-laws and husband, none of whom she has met. It is worse than she could have feared: the groom, Hari, is a sickly child, and his parents have wanted only a dowry in order to pay for a trip to Benares so Hari might bathe in the holy waters of the Ganges. Koly is soon widowed and abandoned in the holy city of Vrindavan by her cruel mother-in-law. She is saved from a dismal fate by her love of beauty, her talent for embroidery, and the philanthropy of others. Awards: CC; National Book Award; Notable Books for a Global Society. Grades: 6–9.

NATIVE AMERICAN CHARACTERS

Bruchac, Joseph. *Code Talker: A Novel About the Navajo Marines of World War Two.*
Dial, 2005.
Setting: WWII.
Main Character: Male, Ned Begay, old man.

In the measured tones of a Native American storyteller, a Navajo grandfather tells his grandchildren about his World War II experiences. Ned starts with his early schooling at an Anglo boarding school, where the Navajo language is forbidden, and continues through his Marine career as a "code talker," explaining his long silence until "de-classified" in 1969. Grades: 5 and up.

Fleischman, Paul. *Saturnalia.*
Harper & Row, 1990.
Setting: Boston, Massachusetts, 1681.
Main Character: Male, William, 14 years old.

William, a native American captured in a raid six years earlier, leads a productive and contented life as a printer's apprentice but is increasingly anxious to make some connection with his Narraganset past. Grades: 7 and up.

Hobbs, Will. *Bearstone.*
Atheneum, 1989.
Setting: Colorado.
Main Character: Male, Cloyd Atcitty, 14 years old.

Troubled, Cloyd, a Ute, goes to live with an elderly rancher, Walter Landis, on a remote ranch in Colorado. Cloyd finds a turquoise stone in a cave up high in the mountains; it's a carving of a bear. The Utes have a special relationship with bears, so this stone is a very special to Cloyd. Awards: CC. Grades: 7–10.

Hobbs, Will. *Ghost Canoe.*
HarperCollins, 1997.
Setting: Washington's Olympic peninsula, 1874.
Main Character: Male, Nathan, 14 years old.

With Lighthouse George, a Makah fisherman, Nathan paddles canoes on delivery runs to the damp, inhospitable island of Tatoosh, where his father is the lighthouse keeper. They also go on hunting expeditions for whales and seals. Curious about footprints found on a desolate beach near the shipwreck where all were supposedly lost, Nathan explores the peninsula and encounters a shadowy figure brandishing a knife in a dark cave, a nervous local trader burying a small metal box, and a burial "ghost" canoe mounted high among tree branches facing the sea. Awards: Edgars. Grades: 6–9.

Hudson, Jan. *Sweetgrass.*
Philomel, 1989.
Setting: Western Canada, nineteenth century.
Main Character: Female, Sweetgrass, 15 years old.

Living on the prairie, Sweetgrass saves her Blackfoot family from a smallpox epidemic and proves her maturity to her father. Grades: 5–10.

MacGregor, Rob. *Prophecy Rock.*
Simon & Schuster, 1995.
Setting: Northern Arizona.
Main Character: Male, Will Lansa, teen.
 Will's summer visit with his father, the Hopi tribal police chief, gives the teen the chance to explore his heritage, find romance, help solve two grisly murders, and derail a kidnapping. Will's adversary is a red-caped madman who believes himself to be Pahana, the legendary Hopi savior who will recover a sacred tablet he believes is necessary to bring about the Day of Purification for his people. Awards: Edgars. Grades: 7–10.

Mikaelsen, Ben. *Touching Spirit Bear.*
HarperCollins, 2001.
Setting: Alaskan island.
Main Character: Male, Cole Matthews, 15 years old.
 Angry Cole agrees to accept the sentence given to him by Native American Circle Justice and he is sent to a remote Alaskan Island, where he encounters Spirit Bear. Awards: CC; Grades: 6–9.

Power, Susan. *The Grass Dancer.*
Berkley, 1995.
Setting: Standing Rock Indian Reservation, North Dakota, 1864 to 1982.
 Interlocking chapter-long short stories about generations of Dakota Sioux and their lives on the reservation. Magical realism for mature readers. Awards: CC. Grades: 9–12.

SOUTHEAST ASIA AS A SETTING

Garland, Sherry. *Song of the Buffalo Boy.*
Harcourt, 1992.
Setting: Vietnam.
Main Character: Female, Loi, 17 years old.
 Loi grew up in Vietnam, insulted and hated. She works diligently for her uncle's family, is refused schooling, and is made to share her mother's shame. Only Khai, a buffalo herder, sees Loi as a person, and proclaims his love. Lewd, unsavory Officer Hiep also wants her, and her fearful family agrees to the marriage. Loi and Khai run away, but their plan goes awry, and Loi is left alone in Ho Chi Minh City. Armed with a photograph of her mother with an American soldier, she has a compelling desire to learn the truth of her birth. Awards: CC. Grades: 7–10.

Ho, Minfong. *The Stone Goddess.*
Orchard, 2003.
Setting: Cambodia, 1975.
Main Character: Female, Nakri, 12 years old.

After the Communists take over Cambodia and her family is torn from their city life, Nakri attempts to maintain her classical Cambodian dancing skills in the midst of her struggle to survive. Grades: 6–10.

Lewis, Richard. *Flame Tree.*
Simon & Schuster, 2004.
Setting: Indonesia, 2001.
Main Character: Male, Isaac, 12 years old.
Just before the September 11, 2001, terrorist attacks, an anti-American Muslim group gains power in Java, and Isaac, the son of American missionary doctors, is kidnapped by Islamic fanatics. Grades: 8 and up.

Yumoto, Kasumi. *The Spring Tone.*
Farrar, Straus & Giroux, 1999.
Setting: Vietnam.
Main Character: Female, Tomomi, 12 years old.
Plagued by headaches and nightmares, Tomomi tries to cope with her grandmother's death, her little brother's obsession with saving sick and abandoned cats, and her fear that she is becoming a monster. Grades: 7 and up.

MIDDLE EAST AS A SETTING

Banks, Lynne Reid. *One More River.*
Morrow, 1995.
Sequel: *Broken Bridge.*
Setting: Israel, 1967.
Main Character: Female, Lesley, 14 years old.
Spoiled and rich, Lesley moves with her family from Canada to an Israeli kibbutz to regain a sense of what it means to be Jewish. At home she was popular, successful at school, and trendily dressed, and now she has to start from scratch, including learning a new language, doing manual work, and sharing sleeping quarters with three others. And just across the river Jordan she can see the enemy. Grades: 6–9.

Laird, Elizabeth. *Kiss the Dust.*
Puffin, 1994.
Setting: Iraq and Iran, mid-1980s.
Main Character: Female, Tara, 13 years old.
Tara and her Kurdish refugee family are lucky. "Baba," secretly a power in the Kurdish military, still has money even after repeated searches, while "Daya" manages to smuggle her jewels. Escaping the police as they leave their luxurious home in a city in northern Iraq, they take a taxi to their primitive vacation house in the mountains. The bombs eventually drive the family over the border into Iran, to a refugee camp infested with bedbugs and assaulted by deafening prayers rasped from a loudspeaker. Eventually, Baba makes contact with relatives in Teheran, and passage to London is negotiated. Grades: 5 and up.

Levitin, Sonia. *The Singing Mountain.*
Simon & Schuster, 1998.

Setting: Israel.

Main Character: Male, Mitch Green, 17 years old.

During a summer trip to Israel, Mitch decides to stay and pursue a life of Jewish orthodoxy, instead of returning home to Southern California and attending UCLA. His family is sure he has been brainwashed. He maintains communication with his cousin Carlie, and Mitch and Carlie tell their stories in alternating chapters. Grades: 8 and up.

Nye, Naomi Shihab. *Habibi.*

Simon Pulse, 1999.

Setting: Israel.

Main Character: Female, Liyana Abboud, 14 years old.

Liyana's family moves from St. Louis to Israel, where her doctor father was born. Their new home is between Jerusalem and a Palestinian village, so they must face the tensions between the Jews and Palestinians. Awards: Notable Books for a Global Society. Grades: 5–9.

RESOURCES: ADDITIONAL TITLES

Darby, Mary Ann, and Miki Pryne. 2001. *Hearing All the Voices: Multicultural Books for Adolescents.* Lanham, MD: Scarecrow.

Day, Frances Ann. 1999. *Multicultural Voices in Contemporary Literature.* Updated and revised edition. Portsmouth, NH: Heinemann.

Givens, Archie, editor. 1998. *Strong Souls Singing: African American Books for Our Daughters and Sisters.* New York: W. W. Norton.

Molin, Paulette F. 2005. *American Indian Themes in Young Adult Literature.* Lanham, MD: Scarecrow Press.

Polette, Nancy. 2000. *Celebrating the Coretta Scott King Awards: 101 Ideas & Activities.* Fort Akkinson, WI: Alleyside Press.

Smith, Henrietta, editor. 1999. *The Coretta Scott King Awards Book 1970–1999.* Chicago, IL: American Library Association.

Richards, Phillip M., and Neil Schlager. 2000. *Best Literature By and About Blacks.* Detroit, MI: Gale Group.

Stephens, Claire Gatrell. 2000. *Coretta Scott King Award: Using Great Literature with Children and Young Adults.* Englewood, CO: Libraries Unlimited.

CHAPTER 17

MYSTERY AND SUSPENSE

Mysteries, where a crime has already been committed, provide a challenge to readers to solve the puzzle before the author reveals the answer. All the clues and suspects must be available to the reader in a mystery. Suspense gives a reader the thrill of impending danger, waiting for a crime to be committed and seeing if the protagonist will survive.

Mystery Awards
Classic Mystery
A Case of Murder
Disappearance/Kidnapping
Supernatural
Suspense
Teen Detectives
Wrongly Accused
Resources: Additional Titles

MYSTERY AWARDS

The Mystery Novel Writers of America give an annual award each April for the Best Young Adult Mystery Novel of the preceding year. The winners are given ceramic statuettes of Edgar Allan Poe, known as "Edgars," for outstanding contributions to mystery, crime, and suspense writing. Read more about the Edgars at www.mysterywriters.org/pages/awards/

CLASSIC MYSTERY

Chandler, Raymond. *The Big Sleep.*
Vintage, 1988.
Series: Philip Marlowe.
Setting: Los Angeles, California.
Main Character: Male, Philip Marlowe, adult.
    Detective Philip Marlowe attempts to protect the wealthy Sternwood family from blackmail by a sleazy Los Angeles porno promoter. He takes care of that matter

soon enough but eventually noses into the missing husband of the other daughter, the job everybody seems to think the General Sternwood really wanted solved. Originally published in 1939. Grades: YA/A.

Christie, Agatha. *And Then There Were None.*
Buccaneer, 2000.
Setting: Indian Island.
Main Character: Ten strangers.
   Ten strangers are invited to an island by the mysterious U.N. Owen. All are accused of murder and one by one, they begin to die, until there are none. Considered the best mystery novel ever written, it was also published as *Ten Little Indians.* Awards: CC. Grades: 8–12.

Doyle, Arthur Conan. *The Hound of the Baskervilles.*
Aladdin, 2000.
Sequel: *The Great Adventures of Sherlock Holmes.*
Setting: Dartmoor, Devonshire.
Main Character: Male, Sherlock Holmes, adult.
   Holmes and Watson investigate the haunted Baskerville family and the recent death of family head Sir Charles Baskerville, apparently from the hound of the legend. Originally published in 1902. Grades: 9 and up.

Hammett, Dashiell. *The Maltese Falcon.*
Vintage, 1989.
Setting: San Francisco, California.
Main Character: Male, Sam Spade, adult.
   Private eye Sam Spade's partner is murdered on a stakeout, and the cops blame Sam for the killing. A beautiful redhead with a heartbreaking story appears and disappears; grotesque villains demand a payoff he can't provide; and everyone wants a fabulously valuable gold statuette of a falcon, created as tribute for the Holy Roman Emperor Charles IV. Originally published in 1930. Grades: YA/A.

Le Carre, John. *The Spy Who Came in from the Cold.*
Walker, 2005.
Setting: London/ East Berlin, Cold War.
Main Character: Male, Alec Leamas, adult.
   Alec Leamas, a British agent in early Cold War Berlin, is ready to retire. Leamas is responsible for keeping the double agents under his care undercover and alive, but East Germans start killing them, so Alec gets called back to London by Control, his spymaster. Yet instead of giving Leamas the boot, Control gives him one last assignment: play the part of a disgraced agent deep in Communist territory to checkmate the bad-guy spies on the other side. Originally published in 1963. Grades: YA/A.

Lee, Harper. *To Kill a Mockingbird.*
Warner, 1988.
Setting: Maycomb, Alabama, Depression era.
Main Character: Female, Scout Finch, 8 years old.
   A young black man is arrested for raping a white woman, and his defense lawyer

is Atticus Finch. Atticus's daughter Scout tells the story of life in Maycomb and about the trial. Awards: CC. Pulitzer Prize. Grades: 8–12.

Leroux, Gaston. *The Phantom of the Opera.*
HarperPerennial, 1988.
Setting: Paris, France, nineteenth century.
Main Character: Male, Erik aka The Phantom of the Opera, adult.

Erik hides from the police by lurking in the bowels of the Paris Opera House. He seduces Christine by singing to her, and the police use his attraction to her to capture him. Originally published in 1911. Grades: YA/A.

Poe, Edgar Allan. *Tales of Mystery and Madness.*
Puffin, 1995.

Four novelettes, "The Gold Bug," "The Fall of the House of Usher," "The Tell-tale Heart," and "The Cask of Amontillado." Grades: 6 and up.

A CASE OF MURDER

Alphin, Elaine Marie. *Counterfeit Son.*
Harcourt, 2000.
Setting: Tennessee, twentieth century.
Main Character: Male, Cameron Miller, aka Neil Lacey, 14 years old.

When his serial killer father is killed by the police, Cameron adopts the identity of one of his father's victims, Neil Lacey. Fast-paced, with a clever twist. Awards: Edgars. Grades: 8–10.

Burke, Morgan. *Get It Started.*
Simon Pulse, 2005.
Sequels: The Party Room Trilogy: *After Hours; Last Call.*
Setting: Manhattan's Upper East Side, 2000s.
Main Character: Female, Kristen Sawyer, 17 years old.

Kristen and her friend Samantha frequent the Party Room to meet friends and drink, until Sam leaves with a stranger and is murdered. Affluent teens with cell phones, fake IDs, popular classmates, boyfriends, and a penchant for lying are the foundations of this series. Cliffhanger endings stir interest in the next book in the series. Grades: 7 and up.

Cooney, Caroline B. *The Terrorist.*
Scholastic, 1999.
Setting: London, England.
Main Character: Female, Laura Williams, 16 years old.

Laura searches for her brother Billy's killer, the person who handed him a bomb on the subway steps. A realistic view of terrorism with an ambiguous ending. Grades: 6–10.

Cormier, Robert. *The Rag and Bone Shop.*
Delacorte, 2001.
Setting: Monument, Massachusetts.

Main Character: Male, Jason, 12 years old.

Jason is accused of murdering his young neighbor. An investigator is sent to get a confession, whether it is the truth or not. Awards: CC. Grades: 7–12.

Flinn, Alex. ***Nothing to Lose.***
HarperTempest, 2004.
Setting: Miami, Florida.
Main Character: Male, Michael Daye, 16 years old.

Michael ran away with a traveling carnival to escape his unbearable home life a year ago, and when he returns to Miami, his mother is going on trial for the murder of his abusive stepfather. Alternating chapters tell the present story and what happened a year ago. Grades: 9–12.

Glenn, Mel. ***Foreign Exchange: A Mystery in Poems.***
HarperCollins, 1999.
Setting: Hudson Landing.
Main Character: Multiple.

A local student is murdered when a group of city teens spend a weekend in a rural town. Story told in verse. Grades: 6–10.

Guterson, David. ***Snow Falling on Cedars.***
Harcourt, 1994.
Setting: San Piedro, Washington, 1954.
Main Characters: Male, Kabuo Miyomoto; Female, Hatsue Miyomoto; Male, Ishmael Chambers; all adults.

A local fisherman is found suspiciously drowned, and Japanese American Kabuo Miyamoto is charged with his murder. San Piedro is haunted by the memories of a charmed love affair between a white boy and the Japanese girl who grew up to become Kabuo's wife, the memories of land desired, paid for, and lost, and the memory of what happened to its Japanese residents during World War II, when an entire community was sent into exile while its neighbors watched. For mature readers. Awards: CC. Grades: 10–12.

McDonald, Joyce. ***Swallowing Stones.***
Laurel Leaf, 1999.
Setting: Contemporary.
Main Character: Male, Michael MacKenzie, 17 years old.

On his birthday, Michael fired a rifle and accidentally killed a man working on his roof over a mile away. In alternating chapters, Michael and the dead man's 15-year-old daughter, Jenna, creep toward their inevitable confrontation. Awards: CC. Grades: 7 and up.

Nickerson, Sara. ***How to Disappear Completely and Never Be Found.***
HarperCollins, 2002.
Setting: Pacific Northwest.
Main Character: Female, Margaret, 12 years old.

Margaret finds three clues to help her unravel the mystery around her father's death: a key, a swimming medal, and a comic book. Some parts of the story are revealed in comic illustrations. Grades: 6–10.

Nixon, Joan Lowry. *The Name of the Game Was Murder.*
Laurel Leaf, 1994.
Setting: Catalina Island, California.
Main Character: Female, Samantha, 15 years old.
　　During a visit to her author great-uncle's fortresslike home on Catalina Island, Samantha becomes involved in the successful and self-centered author's manipulative game that leads to murder. Awards: Edgars. Grades: 7 and up.

Peretti, Frank. *Hangman's Curse.*
Tommy Nelson, 2001.
Series: Veritas Project: *Nightmare Academy.*
Setting: Baker High School.
Main Characters: Twins, Elijah and Elisha Springfield, 16 years old.
　　Elijah, Elisha, and their parents work undercover to seek the truth surrounding mysterious deaths and a legendary school ghost. Christian series about a family who aids the FBI. Grades: YA.

Pullman, Philip. *Ruby in the Smoke.*
Peter Smith, 2002.
Sequels: *The Shadow in the North; The Tiger in the Well; The Tin Princess.*
Setting: Victorian London, 1872.
Main Character: Female, Sally Lockheart, 16 years old.
　　Recently orphaned, Sally becomes involved in murder and adventure while searching for a legendary ruby that is rightfully hers. Awards: CC. Grades: 7–12.

Qualey, Marsha. *Close to a Killer.*
Laurel Leaf, 2000.
Setting: Dakota.
Main Character: Female, Barrie Dupre, 17 years old.
　　Barrie's mother is an ex-con who operates a beauty salon called Killer Looks. She and her employees become prime suspects when two people are murdered. Awards: CC. Grades: 7–10.

Roberts, Willo Davis. *Twisted Summer.*
Simon Pulse, 1998.
Setting: Crystal Lake, Michigan.
Main Character: Female, Cici Linden, 14 years old.
　　Cici searches for the real killer of a girl from Crystal Lake when her boyfriend's brother is convicted of the murder. Awards: Edgars. Grades: 6–9.

Springer, Nancy. *Toughing It.*
Harcourt, 1994.
Setting: 1990s.

Main Character: Male, Shawn "Tuff," 16 years old.

Shawn witnesses his older brother Dillon's murder and wants revenge. With the help of an older friend he thinks may be his father, Shawn gradually accepts his brother's death. Raw language. Awards: Edgars. Grades: 7–10.

Werlin, Nancy. **Black Mirror.**
Dial Books, 2001.
Setting: Boarding school.
Main Character: Female, Francis, 16 years old.

Francis suspects her bother Daniel's suicide was really a murder. She investigates a suspicious organization called Unity at her boarding school. Grades: 7–12.

DISAPPEARANCE/KIDNAPPING

Card, Orson Scott. **Lost Boys.**
HarperTorch, 1993.
Setting: Steuben, North Carolina.
Main Character: Fletcher family.

The Fletcher family moves to Steuben, which looks like the perfect place to raise a family, but boys keep disappearing. The names of the missing boys match the names of Stevie Fletcher's imaginary friends. It looks like Stevie is next on the list to disappear. For Stephen King fans and readers who like suspense mixed with the supernatural. Awards: CC. Grades. 9–12.

Cooney, Caroline B. **Face on the Milk Carton.**
Laurel Leaf, 1991.
Sequels: **Whatever Happened to Janie?; Voice on the Radio; What Janie Found.**
Setting: Connecticut, 1990s.
Main Character: Female, Jane Johnson, 15 years old.

Jane sees her face on a milk carton and questions her identity. She discovers she was kidnapped twelve years earlier and her real name is Jennie Spring. Awards: CC. Grades: 6–9.

Guy, Rosa. **Disappearance.**
Sagebrush, 1999.
Setting: Harlem, Brooklyn, New York.
Main Character: Male, Imamu Jones, teenager.

Imamu has been acquitted of murdering a grocery store owner and is placed in a foster home with the Aimsley family. When the Aimsley's youngest daughter disappears, Imamu is the prime suspect. Awards: CC. Grades: 6–12.

Oates, Joyce Carol. **Freaky Green Eyes.**
HarperTempest, 2003.
Setting: Northwest.
Main Character: Female, Franky, 15 years old.

Frankie tells of her alter ego, Freaky, and the events leading up to her mother's disappearance. Resembles the O.J. Simpson story. Haunting and fast-paced. Grades: 9–12.

Plum-Ucci, Carol. *The Body of Christopher Creed.*
Harcourt, 2000.
Setting: Steepleton.
Main Character: Male, Torey Adams, 16 years old.
   Torey wants to discover what happened to Christopher Creed, the weirdest kid in town, because everyone in town thinks Torey killed him. Awards: CC; Printz Honor. Grades: 7–10.

Sebestyen, Ouida. *Girl in a Box.*
Sagebrush, 1999.
Setting: Cement cell.
Main Character: Female, Jackie, teen.
   Jackie has been kidnapped and she has no idea why or by whom. She has a typewriter and a ream of paper, so she occupies her time writing stories, letters, and notes to herself. Awards: CC: Grades: 6–9.

Weatherly, Lee. *Missing Abby.*
David Fickling, 2004.
Setting: Southern England.
Main Character: Female, Emma, 13 years old.
   Emma and Abby used to be friends and shared an interest in Dungeons and Dragons. Then Emma is transferred to a new school, and to be more popular with new friends, she distanced herself from Abby and gamers. Now Abby has disappeared, and Emma joins the search. Grades: 6–9.

Werlin, Nancy. *Locked Inside.*
Delacorte, 2000.
Setting: Boarding school.
Main Character: Female, Marnie Skyedottir, 16 years old.
   Marnie is addicted to a computer game, Paliopolis, where she is the Sorceress Llewellyne, competing with the pesky Elf. Marnie is kidnapped from her exclusive boarding school by a crazed chemistry teacher, who locks her in a basement. Elf figures out who she is and tries to rescue her, and is trapped there, as well. Grades: YA.

Wynne-Jones, Tim. *The Boy in the Burning House.*
Farrar, Straus & Giroux, 2001.
Setting: Ladybank, Ontario.
Main Character: Male, Jim Hawkins, 14 years old.
   Jim's father disappeared two yeas ago in a small rural town. Now a mentally unbalanced girl, Ruth, claims her stepfather killed him. Awards: Edgars. Grades: 5–9.

Wynne-Jones, Tim. *A Thief in the House of Memory.*
Farrar, Straus & Giroux, 2005.
Setting: Ontario, 2000s.
Main Character: Male, Declan Steeple, 16 years old.

Dec's mother disappeared six years ago and now a dead man is found in their house. Dec tries to make sense of the fragmented memories he has of his mother. Grades: 7–10.

SUPERNATURAL

Bowler, Tim. **Storm Catchers.**
Margaret K. McElderry, 2003.
Setting: Cornwall, England.
Main Character: Male, Fin, teen.
    Fin tries to rescue his younger sister, Ella, who has been kidnapped by a huge teenage boy. Dark family secrets are revealed when Ella is found. A page-turner with strong language. Grades: 7–10.

Duncan, Lois. **Down a Dark Hall.**
Laurel Leaf, 1983.
Setting: Blackwood boarding school.
Main Character: Female, Kit, 14 years old.
    Kit is uneasy about the atmosphere of her new boarding school and slowly realizes why she and three other students were selected. Awards: CC. Grades: 6–8.

McDonald, Joyce. **Shades of Simon Gray.**
Delacorte, 2001.
Setting: Bellhaven, New Jersey.
Main Character: Male, Simon Gray, 16 years old.
    Simon lies in a coma from a car accident and his friends worry that a cheating ring they operate will be revealed. Simon meets the ghost of a man lynched 200 years ago while in his coma. Supernatural elements. Grades: 7–12.

Naylor, Phyllis Reynolds. **Jade Green: A Ghost Story.**
Atheneum, 2000.
Setting: South Carolina.
Main Character: Female, Judith Sparrow, 15 years old.
    While living with her uncle in a house haunted by the ghost of a young woman, recently orphaned Judith wonders if her one small transgression is causing the mysterious happenings. Grades: 6–8.

Nixon, Joan Lowery. **The Séance.**
Harcourt, 2004.
Setting: East Texas.
Main Character: Female, Lauren, teenager.
    Lauren is reluctant to be part of a séance and when the lights are turned off and only a candle flickers, she feels scared, as if something is watching her. Then Sara screams, and all the girls are frightened. When they turn the lights back on, Sara is missing. Her body is found, and then another girl from the group disappears. Awards: CC. Grades: 6–9.

Nixon, Joan Lowery. *Whispers from the Dead.*
Laurel Leaf, 1991.
Setting: Houston.
Main Character: Female, Sarah Darnell, 16 years old.

Sarah has a near-death experience. After moving to Houston, she receives messages about a murder committed in her house. Supernatural and compelling suspense. Awards: CC. Grades: 6–9.

Plum-Ucci, Carol. *The She.*
Harcourt, 2003.
Setting: New Jersey.
Main Character: Male, Evan Barrett, 17 years old.

Evan unknowingly ingests LSD put into his drink as a prank, and the whole horrible evening his parents disappeared in the ocean unfolds again: the violent storm, the frantic mayday that came through on the family's ship-to-shore radio, the hopelessness of knowing that there was nothing he or his older brother, Emmett, could do. Now Evan must confront his fear by discovering once and for all what really happened to his parents. Was it the shrieking, ship-eating sea hag known as The She who lies in wait for victims off the Jersey Shore? Grades: 9 and up.

Sleator, William. *The Boy Who Couldn't Die.*
Harry N. Abrams, 2004.
Setting: Manhattan, New York City.
Main Character: Male, Ken Pritchard, 16 years old.

When Ken's best friend dies in an accident, he makes a deal with a zombie master to remove his soul from his body so he wouldn't die. Fast-paced, suspenseful. Grades: 7–9.

Vande Velde, Vivian. *Never Trust a Dead Man.*
Laurel Leaf, 2001.
Setting: Medieval.
Main Character: Male, Selwyn, 17 years old.

Selwyn is wrongly convicted of a murder and is sealed in the victim's tomb as punishment. A witch helps him find the true murderer. Supernatural suspense and humor. Awards: CC; Edgars. Grades: 7–10.

Werlin, Nancy. *Killer's Cousin.*
Laurel Leaf, 2000.
Setting: Cambridge, Massachusetts.
Main Character: Male, David, 17 years old.

David accidentally killed his girlfriend and is sent to live with his aunt and uncle to finish his senior year, but his 11-year-old cousin, Lily, doesn't want him there. A ghost and multidimensional characters in this thrilling page-turner that fans of Lois Duncan and Joan Lowery Nixon will like. Awards: CC; Edgars. Grades: 7–10.

SUSPENSE

Avi. *Wolf Rider: A Tale of Terror.*
Simon Pulse, 1993.
Setting: 1990s.
Main Character: Male, Andy Zadinski, 15 years old.

Andy receives a call from a stranger who calls himself Zack. Zack confesses to murdering a woman named Nina Klemmer. Andy immediately calls the police, but they shrug it off as a crank call. Then Andy meets Nina, and she is just as Zack described her. Awards: CC. Grades: 6–12.

Bunting, Eve. *Someone is Hiding on Alcatraz Island.*
Berkley, 1994.
Setting: San Francisco, California.
Main Character: Male, Danny, 14 years old.

Danny angers the Outlaws, the school's toughest gang, when he beats up a mugger. Danny tires to escape to Alcatraz Island but ends up trapped there with the gang. Awards: CC. Grades: 7–10.

Cadnum, Michael. *Edge.*
Puffin, 1999.
Setting: California.
Main Character: Male, Zachary, teen.

Zachary, living with his divorced mother in California, finds violence gradually invading his life and making significant changes in his day-to-day existence. Awards: CC. Grades: 8–10.

Cooley, Beth. *Ostrich Eye.*
Delacorte, 2004.
Setting: Contemporary.
Main Character: Female, Ginger, 15 years old.

Ginger is mistakenly convinced that the new photographer in town who keeps showing up is her real father, and she allows her sister to ride off with him. Pedophilia is addressed without being explicit. Grades: 7–12.

Cormier, Robert. *Tenderness.*
Delacorte, 1997.
Setting: Massachusetts.
Main Characters: Male, Eric Poole, 18 years old; Female, Lori, 15 years old.

Lori has a crush on Eric, who was recently released from a juvenile correctional facility for murdering his mother and stepfather. Eric believes Lori is a witness to his undiscovered murders. For mature readers. Awards: CC; VOYA Perfect Ten. Grades: 9–12.

Duncan, Lois. *Summer of Fear.*
Laurel Leaf, 1977.
Setting: New Mexico.
Main Character: Female, Rachel, teen.

Soon after the arrival of cousin Julia, insidious occurrences begin that convince

Rachel that Julia is a witch and must be stopped before her total monstrous plan can be effected. Awards: CC. Grades: 7–12.

Grant, Vicki. **Dead-End Job.**
Orca Soundings, 2005.
Setting: Convenience store.
Main Characters: Female, Frances, young woman; Male, Devin, young man.
   Hoping to save money for art school, Frances works the late shift at a convenience store. Devin is a severely disturbed coworker who has an imaginary romance with Frances and begins stalking her. Appealing to reluctant readers. Grades: 7 and up.

Herman, John. **Deep Waters.**
Philomel, 1998.
Setting: Camp Winasaukee, present day.
Main Character: Male, Andy Schlesinger, 15 years old.
   Andy is still disturbed about a camp counselor's drowning two years ago. Bullying and peer pressure, with an ambiguous ending. Grades: 8–12.

Peck, Richard. **Are You in the House Alone?**
Puffin, 2000.
Setting: Late 1970s.
Main Character: Female, Gail, 16 years old.
   Gail receives obscene notes and phone calls and realizes she is being watched. She tells a friend and a counselor, who both think its just some boy trying to scare her. Gail is raped by someone she knows when she is babysitting. Since he is the son of a wealthy influential family, the police and prosecutor won't help her, and she has to face him again at school. Grades: 8 and up.

Plum-Ucci, Carol. **What Happened to Lani Garver?**
Harcourt, 2004.
Setting: Hackett Island.
Main Character: Female, Claire McKenzie, 16 years old.
   Claire's fears of her leukemia returning are comforted by her magical and mysterious androgynous friend, Lani, who is in peril from his homophobic classmates. Grades: 9 and up.

Zusak, Markus. **I Am the Messenger.**
Knopf, 2005.
Setting: Australia.
Main Character: Male, Ed Kennedy, 19 years old.
   Ed is drifting through life, driving a cab and playing cards with his mates. Then he stops a bank robbery one day and a mysterious stranger sends him playing cards as messages. Ed has to figure out the messages and so becomes an active participant in his own life. Raw language. Awards: Printz Honor; Australian Children's Book of the Year Award. Grades: 9 and up.

Teen Detectives

Bauer, Cat. *Harley Like a Person.*
Winslow, 2000.
Setting: New Jersey.
Main Character: Female, Harley, 14 years old.
    Harley is sure her verbally abusive father can't be her natural parent. The search for her true identity alienates her best friend, hooks her up with the drug crowd, and drags her grades down. Issues including identity, family, school, friendship, sex, drugs, and alcohol abuse, and love will ring true with teens. Awards: CC. Grades: 7–12.

Cooney, Caroline. *Burning Up.*
Laurel Leaf, 2001.
Setting: Connecticut.
Main Character: Female, Macey Clare, 15 years old.
    When a girl she had met at an inner-city church is murdered, Macey tries to discover the truth and the connection to the burning of a barn in 1959 and a black church in 1997. Awards: CC. Grades: 6–9.

Cooney, Caroline. *Fatality.*
Scholastic, 2001.
Setting: Angelica's summer home.
Main Character: Female, Rose Lymond, 15 years old.
    Rose spent a weekend at Angelica Lofft's magnificent summer home. She enjoyed the pool, the horses, and the expensive cars and living like a princess, if only for a weekend. But somebody ended up dead and now, four years later, the police have reopened the case, and they have the diary Rose kept all through that time. Rose will do almost anything to keep her secrets. Grades: YA.

Cormier, Robert. *I Am the Cheese.*
Laurel Leaf, 1991.
Setting: Vermont.
Main Character: Male, Adam Farmer, 14 years old.
    Adam discovers his whole life has been a fiction, and he trusts no one. He tries to figure out who he really is by assembling fragments of the story: a missing father, government corruption, espionage. Awards: CC. Grades: 6–12.

Golden, Christopher. *Body Bags.*
Sagebrush, 2001.
Series: Body of Evidence: *Thief of Hearts; Soul Survivor; Meets the Eye; Head Games; Skin Deep; Burning Bones Brain Trust; Last Breath; Throat Culture.*
Setting: Boston, Massachusetts, 1990s.
Main Character: Female, Jenna Blake, college freshman.
    Jenna starts college and gets a job in an autopsy lab as an administrative assistant to the medical examiner at Somerset Medical Center. Like *CSI*. Grades: YA.

Haddix, Margaret. ***Running Out of Time.***
Simon & Schuster, 1995.
Setting: Indiana, 1995
Main Character: Female, Jessie, 13 years old.

Jessie thinks the year is 1840, until diphtheria strikes in her town and she discovers her whole life is an experiment and tourist attraction. It's up to Jessie to escape the village to save the lives of the dying children. Similar plot to the film *The Village.* Grades: YA.

Haddon, Mark. ***Curious Incident of the Dog in the Night Time.***
Doubleday, 2003.
Setting: England.
Main Character: Male, Christopher John Francis Boone, 15 years old.

Christopher is overwhelmed by sensations and can only make sense of the chaos of stimuli by imposing arbitrary patterns. He relaxes by groaning and doing math problems in his head and screams when he is touched. When his neighbor's poodle is killed and Christopher is falsely accused of the crime, he decides that he will take a page from Sherlock Holmes and track down the killer. Grades: YA/A.

Hartinger, Brent. ***The Last Chance Texaco.***
HarperTempest, 2004.
Setting: Group home.
Main Character: Female, Lucy Pitt, 15 years old.

Lucy's last chance is to make it at Kindle House, a group home where the dedicated counselors try to connect with the kids. If she makes any mistakes, she'll be sent to the prisonlike facility known as Eat-Their-Young Island. With a little romance and a little mystery, this is a realistic portrayal of teens caught in the foster care system. Grades: 7–10.

Hiaasen, Carl. ***Hoot.***
Knopf, 2002.
Setting: Coconut Cove, Florida, 2000s.
Main Character: Male, Roy Eberhardt, 11 years old.

Roy's family has moved from Montana to Florida because of his dad's job. Through a strange homeless boy named Mullet Fingers, he learns about a nest of burrowing owls that will be destroyed by the construction of Mother Paula's Pancake House. Ray tries to save the owls. Quirky characters. Grades: 6–9.

Hiaasen, Carl. ***Flush.***
Random House, 2005.
Setting: Florida Keys, 2000s.
Main Character: Male, Noah Underwood, 14 years old.

Noah's dad is arrested for sinking the *Coral Queen*, a casino boat on a Florida key because he claims its owner, Dusty Muleman, has been illegally dumping raw sewage into the local waters. Noah and his sister Abbey begin trying to gather proof that will vindicate their father and put the casino out of business. Quirky characters. Grades: 5–8.

Hoobler, Dorothy & Thomas. *The Ghost in Tokaido Inn.*
Philomel, 1999.
Sequels: *The Demon in the Teahouse; In Darkness, Death.*
Setting: Japan, 1735.
Main Character: Male, Seikei, 14 years old.

Seikei wants to be a samurai, but he is only a tea merchant's son. A priceless gem is stolen by a ghost at Tokaido Inn where he and his father are staying, and Seikei searches for clues to solve the mystery under Judge Ooka's guidance. Sherlock Holmes–style mysteries in Shogun Japan. Grades: 6–8.

Ibbotson, Eva. *Star of Kazan.*
Dutton, 2004.
Setting: Vienna/Germany, nineteenth century.
Main Character: Female, Annika, 12 years old.

Abandoned as a baby, Annika is found and adopted by Ellie and Sigrid, the cook and housemaid for three professors. After Annika inherits a trunk of costume jewelry, a woman claiming to be her aristocratic mother arrives and takes her to live in a strangely decrepit mansion in Germany. Annika soon realizes that her new "family" has many nasty secrets. With the help of her friends, Annika escapes from a ghastly fate and faces the truth about her relatives. Grades: 5–8.

King, Laurie R. *The Game.*
Bantam, 2004.
Series: Mary Russell: *Locked Rooms; Justice Hall; O Jerusalem; The Moor; The Beekeeper's Apprentice.*
Setting: India, 1924.
Main Character: Female, Mary Russell, 24 years old.

Mary meets retired Sherlock Holmes as a teen and eventually marries him; they solve mysteries together. They search for Kim from Rudyard Kipling's novel in this mystery. Grades: YA/A.

Koontz, Dean. *Fear Nothing.*
Bantam, 1998.
Sequel: *Seize the Night* (CC).
Setting: Moonlight Bay, California, 1990s.
Main Character: Male, Christopher Snow, 28 years old.

While investigating the death of his mother who was a scientist, Chris Snow discovers she was engaged in secret experiments on a nearby military base. The experiments went wrong and produced monsters. They have come visiting and they are not friendly. Awards: CC. Grades: 8–12.

Madison, Bennett. *Lulu Dark Can See Through Walls.*
Penguin, 2005.
Setting: Halo City.
Main Character: Female, Lulu Dark, 16 years old.

Lulu loses her purse while at the Big Blonde club. She sets out to find it with her friends Charlie and Daisy, and becomes enmeshed in a wild case of identity theft and homicide. Grades: 9 and up.

Moloney, James. *Black Taxi.*
HarperCollins, 2005.
Setting: Prestwich, England, 2000s.
Main Character: Female, Rosie Sinclair, 18 years old.

When Rosie's grandfather is arrested and jailed for a crime, she inherits his Mercedes and the responsibilities the Merc entails: taxiing elderly citizens on errands. She even gets a cell phone, and her new vehicle helps catch the eye of sweet jock Todd and bad boy Chris. Soon she starts to get calls from a cranky and dangerous-sounding scoundrel who demands that she return The Ring. Rosie doesn't know what he's talking about but realizes that she'd better figure it out before anyone gets hurt. Rosie's friend Glenda is two years older and works as an exotic dancer in order to pay for her university schooling. Grades: 7 and up.

McNamee, Graham. *Acceleration.*
Wendy Lamb, 2003.
Setting: Toronto, Ontario.
Main Character: Male, Duncan, 17 years old.

Duncan is spending his summer cataloging lost junk in the Toronto Transit Commission's subterranean Lost and Found. He finds a brown leather journal that seems to be the personal history of a serial killer in the making. When local police take no interest, Duncan decides to use its clues to try to track down the potential killer himself. Awards: Edgars. Grades: 8–12.

Nixon, Joan Lowery. *Other Side of Dark.*
Laurel Leaf, 1987.
Setting: 1980s.
Main Character: Female, Stacey, 17 years old.

Stacey wakens from a four-year coma ready to identify the man who murdered her mother and injured her. Fast-paced with a clever premise and some humor. Awards: CC. Grades: 6–9.

Nixon, Joan Lowery. *Who Are You?*
Delacorte, 1999.
Setting: 1990s.
Main Character: Female, Kristi Evans, 16 years old.

Kristi, an aspiring artist, finds out that Mr. Merson, a stranger who has been shot, has kept a secret file on her entire life. Kristi investigates who this man is and why he has intruded on her privacy. When Kristi goes to see Mr. Merson in the hospital, she discovers he is a professional artist; he offers to help her pursue her own dream of being an artist. Grades: 5–9.

Qualey, Marsha. *Thin Ice.*
Sagebrush, 2001.
Setting: Wisconsin.
Main Character: Female, Arden, 17 years old.

Arden has been raised by her older brother, Scott, since their parents died when she was just 6 years old. When Scott is presumed drowned in a snowmobile accident,

Arden is convinced he's really run away. Readers don't find out the truth until Arden does. Awards: CC. Grades: 6–9.

Rose, Malcolm. *Framed!*
Kingfisher, 2005.
Series: Traces: *Lost Bullet; Roll Call.*
Setting: Boarding school, England, future.
Main Character: Male, Luke Harding, 16 years old.
　　Luke, a newly qualified forensic investigator, is called in on his first murder case when fellow student Crispin Addley is found with an arrow in his heart. Malc (Mobile Aid to Law and Crime), a robot whose technological capabilities include X-ray, lasers and scanners, and an enormous database that can cross-check facts within seconds, helps Luke throughout his investigation. Grades: 5–8.

Simmons, Michael Dahlie. *Finding Lubchenko.*
Penguin, 2005.
Setting: Paris, France.
Main Character: Male, Evan Macalister, 16 years old.
　　Evan hocks computer equipment from his dad's high-tech medical company on eBay. Then his dad is arrested for the murder of a colleague, and the evidence to clear him is on a laptop that Evan lifted from the victim's office just before he was killed. Now Evan must either turn the laptop over to the police and face the wrath of his father or solve the mystery himself. Evan chooses the latter, and, with his dad's credit card in tow, he and two friends travel first-class to Paris to find Lubchenko. A fast-paced, James Bond–like spy chase. Grades: 8 and up.

Stolarz, Laurie. *Blue is for Nightmares.*
Llewellyn, 2003.
Sequels: *White is for Magic; Red is for Remembrance; Silver is for Secrets.*
Setting: Hilcrest boarding school.
Main Character: Female, Stacey Brown, 16 years old.
　　Hereditary witch Stacey Brown has nightmares of her roommate, Drea, being murdered. She hopes that her magick will be enough to protect her, unlike the last person whose death Stacey dreamed. Grades: YA.

Van Draanen, Wendelin. *Sammy Keyes and the Hotel Thief.*
Knopf, 1998.
Series: Sammy Keyes: *Sammy Keyes and the Skeleton Man; Sammy Keyes and the Runaway Elf; Sammy Keyes and the Curse of Moustache Mary; Sammy Keyes and the Sisters of Mercy; Sammy Keyes and the Art of Deception; Sammy Keyes and the Hollywood Mummy; Sammy Keyes and the Search for Snake Eyes; Sammy Keyes and the Psycho Kitty Queen; Sammy Keyes and the Dead Giveaway.*
Setting: Senior citizens apartment.
Main Character: Female, Sammy Keyes, 13 years old.
　　Sammy lives illegally in a retirees' apartment building with her grandmother and sees a robbery across the street. Grades: 6–8.

Werlin, Nancy. **Double Helix.**
Dial, 2004.
Setting: Wyatt Transgenics Lab.
Main Character: Male, Eli Samuels, 18 years old.

Eli, whose mother is losing her long battle with Huntington's disease, is hired at the Wyatt Transgenics Lab. Eli's father is dead set against the job because of a secret he harbors concerning the lab's owner, Dr. Quincy Wyatt, and Eli's mother. Shortly after starting work, Eli meets Kayla Matheson, a beautiful girl who eerily reminds him of a photo of his mother when she was young. Slowly, Eli uncovers one secret after another about Dr. Wyatt's genetic-engineering experiments and their connection to his parents, Kayla, and himself. Grades: 8 and up.

WRONGLY ACCUSED

Cooney, Caroline B. **Wanted!**
Scholastic, 1997.
Setting: 1990s.
Main Character: Female, Alice, 15 years old.

Alice tries to prove her innocence while being pursued by the police and her father's killer. Grades: 6 and up.

Dowell, Frances O'Roark. **Dovey Coe.**
Atheneum, 2000.
Setting: Indian Creek, North Carolina, 1928.
Main Character: Female, Dovey Coe, 12 years old.

Dovey is charged with murdering Parnell, the meanest man around. Realistic dialect, with a fast-moving plot and unexpected ending. Awards: Edgars. Grades: 6–8.

Flinn, Alex. **Fade to Black.**
HarperTempest, 2005.
Setting: North Florida, 1990s.
Main Character: Male, Alex Crusan, 16 years old.

Alex, an HIV-positive, Hispanic teen, is brutalized by an attacker wearing a high school letter jacket. All fingers point to Clinton Cole, a narrow-minded jock and jerk. Daria Bickell, a special-ed student with Down syndrome, is the only witness to the crime. Grades: 8 and up.

Konigsburg, E. L. **Silent to the Bone.**
Atheneum, 2000.
Setting: Clarion County Juvenile Behavioral Center.
Main Character: Male, Connor, 13 years old.

Connor's best friend, Branwell Zamborska, loses his power of speech when he is accused of shaking and dropping his baby sister. Connor believes Branwell is innocent and is determined to prove it by finding out why he became silent and what really happened to the baby. A suspenseful and insightful novel that reads like a mystery, with clues revealed throughout. Awards: CC. Grades: YA.

Morgenroth, Kate. *Jude.*
Simon & Schuster, 2004.
Setting: Connecticut.
Main Character: Male, Jude, 15 years old.

Reeling from his drug-dealing father's murder, moving in with the wealthy mother he never knew, and transferring to a private school, Jude is tricked into pleading guilty to a crime he did not commit: a schoolmate's drug overdose. Older boys and reluctant readers will like the action. Grades: 8–12.

Myers, Walter Dean. *Monster.*
Amistad, 1999.
Setting: Harlem, New York City.
Main Character: Male, Steve Harmon, 16 years old.

Steve is accused of serving as a lookout for a robbery of a drugstore. The owner was shot and killed, and now Steve is in prison awaiting trial for murder. From prison, he tells about his case and his incarceration in the form of a movie screenplay. Diary entries are interspersed among the scenes. Awards: CC; Printz; Coretta Scott King; National Book Award. Grades: 7–12.

Sachar, Louis. *Holes.*
Farrar, Straus & Giroux, 1998.
Setting: Camp Green Lake, Texas.
Main Character: Male, Stanley Yelnats IV, teenager.

Stanley is sent to a correctional camp in the desert and has to dig holes because the warden is looking for something. Quirky characters and an ambiguous ending with two story lines that come together. Awards: CC; Newbery. Grades: 6–12.

RESOURCES: ADDITIONAL TITLES

Scottsdale, A. Z., John Charles, Joanna Morrison, and Candace Clark, editors. 2001. *The Mystery Reader's Advisory: Librarian's Clues to Murder and Mayhem.* Chicago, IL: American Library Association.

CHAPTER 18

REPEATED PLOTS AND RECYCLED CHARACTERS

Some stories are so good we like reading them over and over. The titles in this chapter have characters, themes, or settings from classic literature familiar to teens. Greek mythology, fairy tales, the Bible, and Shakespeare have provided the framework for many young adult titles.

Bible Stories Retold
Fairy Tales Retold
Greek Mythology
Shakespearean Themes—Romeo and Juliet
More Shakespearean Themes
Resources: Additional Titles

BIBLE STORIES RETOLD

Aidenoff, Elsie. **The Garden.**
HarperCollins, 2004.
Setting: Genesis, Old Testament, the Garden of Eden.
Main Characters: Female, Eve; The Serpent; Male, Adam; God.
  Eve and her mentor, the Serpent, explore the Garden and beyond, while Adam and an impatient God wait for the Creation to perform as designed. God is portrayed as an overbearing tyrant, while the Serpent is wise, lovely, and nurturing, teaching Eve about God and the world in a much different way than God is teaching Adam. Grades: 7–12.

Card, Orson Scott. **Sarah.**
Bookcraft, 2000.
Series: Women of Genesis: **Rebekah; Rachel and Leah.**
Setting: Genesis, Old Testament.
Main Character: Female, Sarah, adult.
  Sarah and Abraham had no children, so Sarah arranged for Hagar to have a baby with Abraham; his name was Ishmael. When Abraham was 99 and Sarah was 90, God told Abraham that Sarah would bear a son. Their son is Isaac. Ishmael mocked and taunted Isaac, so Sarah insisted that Hagar and Ishmael be sent from the camp. Grades: YA/A.

Diamant, Anita. *The Red Tent.*
St. Martin's, 2005.
Setting: Genesis, Old Testament, Mesopotamia, Canaan, Egypt.
Main Character: Female, Dinah.

This is the life of Dinah, the daughter of Leah and Jacob, from her birth and happy childhood in Mesopotamia through her years in Canaan and death in Egypt. When Dinah reaches puberty and enters the Red Tent (the place women visit to give birth or have their monthly periods), her mother and Jacob's three other wives initiate her into the religious and sexual practices of the tribe. Dinah later travels to Egypt, where she becomes a noted midwife. Grades: YA/A.

Douglas, Lloyd C. *The Robe.*
Mariner Books, 1999.
Setting: The Gospels, New Testament, Ancient Rome.
Main Character: Male, Marcellus.

A Roman soldier, Marcellus, wins Christ's robe as a gambling prize. He then sets forth on a quest to find the truth about the Nazarene's robe, which reaches to the very roots and heart of Christianity. Grades: YA/A.

George, Margaret. *Mary, Called Magdalene.*
Penguin, 2003.
Setting: The Gospels, New Testament, Palestine.
Main Character: Female, Mary Magdala.

Mary becomes one of Jesus' first believers and followers when he expels the demons that have ravaged her mind. She tells of the formation of Jesus' ragtag band of disciples and the crucifixion, and ends with her mission as the head of the Christian church in Ephesus, where she died at the age of 90. Grades: YA/A.

L'Engle, Madeleine. *Many Waters.*
Farrar, Straus & Giroux, 1986.
Prequels: The Time Quintet: *A Wrinkle in Time; A Wind in the Door; A Swiftly Tilting Planet; An Acceptable Time.*
Setting: Genesis, Old Testament.
Main Characters: Male, Dennys Murray; Female, Sandy Murray; twins 15 years old.

Dennys and Sandy accidentally get involved in their father's science experiment, involving tessering. They travel through space and time, ending up with Noah and his family as they build the ark. Grades: 6 and up.

Lester, Julius. *Pharaoh's Daughter: A Novel of Ancient Egypt.*
Silver Whistle, 2000.
Setting: Exodus, Old Testament, Ancient Egypt.
Main Characters: Female, Almah; Male, Mosis (Moses).

Meryetamun, the daughter of the Pharaoh, rescues infant Mosis and takes him to raise as her son. Mosis' sister Almah goes with them to live in the palace. The Pharaoh declares Almah to be his daughter because of her resemblance to his dead wife. Almah and Mosis are torn between the Egyptian and Hebrew cultures, trying to find their identity, loyalty, and religion. Grades: 7–10.

Levitin, Sonia. *Escape from Egypt.*
Little, Brown, 1994.
Setting: Exodus, Old Testament, Ancient Egypt.
Main Character: Male, Jesse.

When Moses comes to lead the Israelites to the Promised Land, Jesse, a Hebrew slave, is torn between Moses' demands and his love for Jennat. This is the story of the Exodus, including the plagues, the leaving, the crossing of the parted Red Sea, and the wandering in the wilderness, but seen through the eyes of Jesse's family. Grades: 6–9.

Maine, David. *The Preservationist.*
St. Martin's, 2004.
Setting: Genesis, Old Testament.
Main Character: Male, Noah.

Noah and his family build an ark as God directs, in preparation for the flood. All the many characters have distinct personalities and opinions about the project. Grades: YA/A.

Moore, Christopher. *Lamb: The Gospel According to Biff, Christ's Childhood Pal.*
HarperCollins Paperbacks, 2003.
Setting: The Gospels, New Testament, Asia.
Main Characters: Male, Levi bar Alpheus, aka Biff; Male, Joshua, aka Jesus.

Biff tells about the childhood and youth of his friend, Joshua, now known as Jesus. Joshua and Biff travel through the East and encounter Eastern philosophies as they seek what being the Messiah means. Grades: YA/A.

Myers, Walter Dean. *A Time to Love: Stories from the Old Testament.*
Scholastic, 2003.
Setting: Old Testament.

Six stories from the Hebrew scriptures tell the familiar tales of Samson, Joseph, Ruth, Abraham, Lot, and Moses from the viewpoints of secondary characters. Grades: 7 and up.

Napoli, Donna Jo. *Song of the Magdalene.*
Scholastic, 1996.
Setting: The Gospels, New Testament, Israel.
Main Character: Female, Mary Magdalene, "Miriam," 10 to 16 years old.

Miriam describes her life when she is deeply troubled by the occurrence of "fits," which come upon her seven times. Her closest relationship is with severely disabled Abraham. The two become lovers before he dies. Pregnant with his child, Miriam withdraws into herself but then is raped and loses the child. She hears of the great healer Joshua, or Jesus, and when she finds him; he cures her of the seven devils. Grades: 7 and up.

Provoost, Anne. *In the Shadow of the Ark.*
Arthur A. Levine, 2004.
Setting: Genesis, Old Testament.

Main Character: Female, Re Jana.

Re Jana is the daughter of a shipbuilder working on the ark. She meets Ham, a privileged son of the Great Builder (Noah) and they become lovers. Re Jana begins to realize who will be chosen to live on the ark and who will be left behind. Grades: 11 and up.

Rivers, Francine. **Unveiled.**
Tyndale House, 2000.
Series: The Lineage of Grace: **Unshamed; Unshaken; Unspoken; Unafraid.**
Setting: Genesis, Old Testament, Israel.
Main Character: Female, Tamar.

Tamar is sold as a child to be the bride of Judah's oldest son, Er. When Er dies, she is given Onan, one of Er's brothers, as husband, to beget a son in Er's memory. When Onan refuses her rights, he too falls dead. The third brother, Shelah, is deemed too young to be a husband, but when Judah promises Tamar a child when the boy grows up, she lives on hope for years. When she realizes that Judah has no intention of keeping his promise, she dresses as a temple prostitute and seduces him. After being threatened with death because of her disgraceful pregnancy, Tamar forces Judah to honor his promise. In return, she bears twin sons, Zerah and Perez, a forefather of Jesus. Grades: YA/A.

Twain, Mark. **The Diaries of Adam & Eve.**
Fair Oaks, 1998.
Setting: Genesis, Old Testament, Garden of Eden.
Main Characters: Male, Adam; Female, Eve.

Adam is a boring, conceited man who is annoyed by Eve and her curiosity about everything. Eve is wonderful; she names everything and has an abundance of scientific wonder of the world. Short, humorous diaries and an irreverent look at conventional religion. Grades: YA/A.

Fairy Tales Retold

Barry, Dave, and Ridley Peterson. **Peter and the Starcatchers.**
Hyperion, 2004.
Setting: *Never Land.*
Main Characters: Male, Peter; Female, Molly Aster; both 14 years old.

In a page-turner prequel to *Peter Pan*, Molly is an apprentice Starcatcher, a secret society formed to keep evildoers from obtaining "starstuff," the magic material that falls to earth and conveys happiness, power, increased intelligence, and the ability to fly. Peter, leader of a group of orphan boys being sent into slavery aboard the *Never Land*, helps Molly guard a trunk of stardust from Black Stache, a fearsome pirate who commands a villainous crew. Grades: 7–9.

Block, Francesca Lia. **Rose and the Beast: Fairy Tales Retold.**
HarperCollins, 2000.

Block revisits nine fairy tales with gritty, headline-grabbing issues, set in modern, magical landscapes, with endings with a twist. The darkness of the conflicts and subjects proves the strength of the magic of the power of love. Awards: CC. Grades: 7–12.

Cadnum, Michael. *In a Dark Wood.*
Scholastic, 1998.
Setting: Nottingham, England.
Main Character: Male, Geoffrey, Sheriff of Nottingham.

The King sends the Sheriff of Nottingham to capture the outlaw Robin Hood. The sheriff is much more concerned about his strained relationship with his wife; his affair with the Abbess; his anger at the mimicking Fool; his confusion over his feelings for his young squire, Hugh; and his desire to appear strong and courageous to the people he leads. Explicit sexual encounters, torture, and a hanging. Awards: CC. Grades: 9–12.

Card, Orson Scott. *Enchantment.*
Ballantine, 1984.
Setting: New York City, 1992/ Russia, 890.
Main Character: Male, Ivan Smetski, 10 years old to 20+ years old.

Ivan is drawn to a beautiful woman frozen in time in the middle of the primordial forest of Russia. More than a decade later, he returns to rescue and marry the princess. He has no skills useful in the ninth century, yet must find a way to defeat the witch Baba Yaga, who plans to take over Princess Katerina's kingdom. Ivan brings Katerina into the modern world to keep her from Yaga's clutches and the couple learns to understand each other, and their powers and weapons. When they return to the fairy-tale world, they are aided by Ivan's relatives, who turn out to be minor Russian deities and witches. A *Sleeping Beauty* story. Awards: CC. Grades: YA/A.

Dean, Pamela. *Tam Lin.*
Puffin, 2006.
Setting: Blackstock College, Minnesota, 1970s.
Main Character: Female, Janet Carter, 18 years old.

Janet, an English major, and her roommates, Christina and Molly, fall in with an eccentric group of classics students, who circle around Professor Medeous. Janet begins an affair with Nicholas Tooley, whose vast familiarity with Shakespeare and often distant approach to intimacy disturb her. When the affair ends, she takes up with the young man formerly attached to Christina and takes up a dangerous quest to save her lover. Based on the Scottish ballad. Awards: CC. Grades: YA/A.

Doman, Regina. *The Shadow of the Bear.*
Bethlehem, 2004.
Sequel: *Black as Night: A Fairy Tale Retold.*
Setting: New York City.
Main Characters: Female, Blanche; Female, Rose; both teens.

Blanche and Rose once lived in luxury in the country, but since the death of their father they live in New York City with their overworked mother. At their new school, they are generally ignored or abused, especially Blanche, who frequently has dizzy spells. When their mother brings home a homeless young man called "Bear," they are apprehensive, but soon they become close friends with him. A *Snow White and Rose Red* mystery. Grades: YA.

Ferris, Jean. ***Once Upon a Marigold.***
Harcourt, 2002.
Setting: Forest, castle.
Main Character: Male, Chris, 6–16 years old.

Chris runs away from home when he is 6 years old, determined to live on his own in the forest. Edric, a troll, finds him and gives him shelter, and Chris grows up with Edric and his dogs as his family, guided by an etiquette book found in the forest and Edric's own wisdom. As the boy grows, he continues an interest in inventing, and watches the princess in the castle across the river. She is headstrong but lonely, and when Chris contacts her by carrier pigeon (or p-mail), they become best friends. When he learns that her life is in danger, he must find a way to save her and the kingdom. A humorous *Cinderella* story, with quirky characters. Grades: 5–9.

Haddix, Margaret. ***Just Ella.***
Simon & Schuster, 1999.
Setting: Kingdom, castle.
Main Character: Female, Ella Brown, 15 years old.

Ella plans to live happily ever after when Prince Charming whisks her from her evil stepfamily. When she arrives at the castle, she discovers that the prince is a dull dud, needlepoint is now her most strenuous activity, and her ladies-in-waiting are abuzz with a concocted tale involving Ella, a fairy godmother and a pumpkin. When she refuses to marry the prince, she is thrown in the dungeon to be held there until the wedding day. A *Cinderella* story. Awards: CC. Grades: 7–12.

Hale, Shannon. ***Goose Girl.***
Bloomsbury, 2003.
Sequel: ***Enna Burning.***
Setting: Bayern.
Main Character: Female, Anidori-Kiladra Talianna Isilee, teenager.

Ani, Crown Princess of Kildenree, is able to speak to animals. When the king dies, the queen promises Ani in marriage to the prince of neighboring Bayern. Ani is sent with a retinue over the mountains to Bayern and is betrayed by her lady-in-waiting and most of her guards during the journey. Ani escapes, taking the name "Isi," and becomes a tender of geese, to survive until she can reveal her true identity and reclaim her crown. A *Goose Girl* story that is the first of a planned trilogy. Grades: 6–9.

Kindl, Patrice. ***Goose Chase.***
Houghton Mifflin, 2001.
Setting: Fairy-tale kingdom.
Main Character: Female, Alexandria Auroxa Fortunate, teenager.

After doing a good deed for an old hag, Alexandria is transformed. She is flawlessly lovely, she cries diamonds rather than tears, and combing her hair produces showers of gold dust. Her beauty and wealth attract unwanted attention from the evil

king of Gilboa and bumbling Prince Edmund of Dorloo. The geese fly Alexandria away
from the tower where her suitors have imprisoned her. Alexandria finally learns her
true identity and the identity of her geese when she dons crown jewels that had once
belonged to her own family. A humorous, fast-paced *Goose Girl* story. Grades: 7–12.

Levine, Gail Carson. ***Ella Enchanted.***
HarperCollins, 1997.
Setting: Kingdom.
Main Character: Female, Ella of Frell, 12 years old.
    Ella is cursed by a fairy named Lucinda who bestows on her the "gift" of
obedience. Anything anyone tells her to do, Ella must obey. When her mother dies,
she is left in the care of her avaricious father, a loathsome stepmother, and two
treacherous stepsisters. Ella sets out on a quest for freedom and self-discovery, trying
to track down Lucinda to undo the curse, fending off ogres, befriending elves, and
falling in love with a prince along the way. A *Cinderella* story. Awards: CC; Newbery
Honor. Grades: 5–8.

Lynn, Tracy. ***Snow.***
Simon Pulse, 2003.
Setting: Wales/London, England.
Main Character: Female, Jessica Kenigh, childhood–teenage years.
    Jessica grows up motherless on an isolated Welsh manor. Her stepmother, Anne,
a frustrated would-be scientist, becomes obsessed with having an heir and devises a
lethal fertility spell involving Jessica's heart. Escaping to London, Snow, nicknamed
for her pale appearance, takes up with "the Lonely Ones," a band of half-human, half-
animal outcasts. A fast-paced *Snow White* psychological thriller. Grades: 8 and up.

Marillier, Juliet. ***Daughter of the Forest.***
Tor, 2002.
Sequels: Sevenwaters Trilogy: ***Son of the Shadows; Child of the Prophecy.***
Setting: Ireland, England, tenth century.
Main Character: Female, Sorcha, teenager.
    Young Sorcha is the seventh child and only daughter of Irish Lord Colum of
Sevenwaters, a domain protected from invading Saxons and Britons by a dense forest,
where fey Deirdre, the Lady of the Forest, walks at night. Colum brings home a new
wife who casts a spell on Sorcha's brothers, turning them into swans. Only Sorcha,
hiding deep in the forest, can break the spell by painfully weaving shirts of starwort
nettle. A Celtic legend. Grades: YA/A.

McCaffrey, Anne. ***An Exchange of Gifts.***
Wildside, 1995.
Setting: Forest.
Main Character: Female, Meanne, teen.
    In a place where everyone is born with a special gift, Meanne is not allowed to
practice her gift of making plants grow and thrive, because it is so "unsuitable for a
princess of the Blood Royal to insert her royal hands in common dirt." Meanne runs
away to a deserted, run-down forest hunting lodge, where a boy named Wisp shows

up and joins forces with her. Wisp has a frightening gift that works a great change for Meanne yet bodes well for their future together. Illustrated by Pat Morrissey. Grades: YA.

McKinley, Robin. *Beauty: A Retelling of Beauty and the Beast.*
HarperCollins, 1993.
Setting: Beast's castle.
Main Character: Female, Beauty, 16 years old.

Beauty is thin and awkward; it is her two sisters who are the beautiful ones. But what Beauty lacks in looks, she makes up for in courage and honor. When her father comes home with the tale of an enchanted castle in the forest and the terrible promise he had to make to the Beast who lives there, Beauty knows she must go to the castle, a prisoner of her own free will. Beauty grows to love the Beast and through her love releases him from the spell which had turned him from a handsome prince into an ugly beast. Awards: CC. Grades: YA

McKinley, Robin. *Outlaws of Sherwood.*
Greenwillow, 1988.
Setting: Sherwood Forest, twelfth century.
Main Character: Male, Robin Hood, adult.

The backgrounds and motives of Robin's band of merry men are developed. Awards: CC. Grades: 9–12.

McKinley, Robin. *Rose Daughter.*
Ace, 1998.
Setting: Balladland, Rose Cottage.
Main Character: Female, Beauty, teenager.

The center of the Beast's palace, the glittering glass house that brings Beauty both comfort and delight in her strange new environment, is filled with leafless brown rose bushes. Grades: YA.

McKinley, Robin. *Spindle's End.*
Penguin Putnam, 2000.
Setting: Foggy Bottom.
Main Character: Female, Rosie, teenager.

Rosie wears trousers and talks to animals. Growing up in the village of Foggy Bottom and living with Aunt and Katriona, two fairies, Rosie has no idea that she is a princess or the future queen. She has been separated from her royal family, which hopes to protect her from the evil curse Pernicia cast on her on her name day. A *Sleeping Beauty* story. Awards: CC. Grades: 7–10.

Napoli, Donna Jo. *Beast.*
Simon Pulse, 2000.
Setting: Ancient Persia.
Main Character: Male, Prince Orasmyn, aka the Beast, young man.

Prince Orasmyn has been transformed by a curse into a lion and can only be redeemed by the love of a woman. The young prince struggles to learn how to survive as a beast while retaining his humanity in devotion to Islamic moral principles. Fleeing his father's hunting park, he travels as an animal across Asia to France, where he at last finds an abandoned chateau. There he plants a rose garden and prepares the castle for the woman he hopes will come to love him. Awards: CC. Grades: 7 and up.

Napoli, Donna Jo. *The Magic Circle.*
Puffin, 1995.
Setting: Enchanted forest.
Main Character: Female, Ugly One, adult.

Ugly One tells how, tricked by the devil's minions, she lost her gifts for healing and was forced to become a witch. Escaping from the stake where she was about to be burned, she ekes out a solitary existence in an enchanted forest until she takes in two wandering children named Hansel and Gretel. Awards: CC. Grades: 7 and up.

Napoli, Donna Jo. *Zel.*
Puffin, 1998.
Setting: Switzerland, mid-sixteenth century.
Main Character: Female, Zel, 13 years old.

Zel accompanies her mother on a rare trip from their remote cottage to the village. She meets Konrad, the son of the count, and he is charmed by her apparent simplicity and forthright manner. A desperate fear of Konrad's attentions drives her mother to imprison Zel in the tower. Isolated, Zel wavers between recognition of her mother's sacrifices and her own fury, and wanders into madness. A *Rapunzel* story. Grades: 9–12.

Pattou, Edith. *East.*
Harcourt, 2003.
Setting: Norway, France.
Main Character: Female, Nymah Rose, 15 years old.

There is an ancient belief that children inherit the qualities of the direction in which they are born. Nymah Rose, the last daughter of eight siblings born to a poor mapmaker and his superstitious wife, was a North-born baby. These babies are said to be wild, unpredictable, intelligent, and destined to break their mothers' hearts. To keep her close, Rose's mother lies and tells her she has been born of the obedient and pliable East. But destiny cannot be denied. One day, a great white bear comes to the mapmaker's door to claim Rose's birthright. A *Beauty and the Beast* story. Grades: 7–12.

Pratchett, Terry. *Amazing Maurice and His Educated Rodents.*
HarperTrophy, 2003.
Setting: Discworld.
Main Characters: Male cat, Maurice, 4 years old; Male rat, Darktan; Male human, Keith; Female human, Malicia.

Keith, Maurice the cat, and a troupe of rats arrive at the town of Bad Blintz. They have a nice racket going, where the rats pretend to infest a town and Keith poses as a piper to lead them away. But something is wrong with Bad Blintz; there are no native rats, yet the rat-catchers claim that there's an outright plague of them, producing rat-tails to prove it. With the help of Malicia, Keith, and Maurice begin to investigate why all the rats are gone, and what the rat-catchers are up to. A *Pied Piper* story. Awards: CC; Carnegie. Grades: 7 and up.

Pullman, Philip. *Clockwork.*
Scholastic, 1998.
Setting: Glockenheim, Germany.
Main Character: Male, Karl, young teen.

As the townspeople gather in the White Horse Tavern on the eve of the unveiling of a new figure for their great town clock, Karl, the clockmaker's apprentice, reveals to Fritz, a young storyteller, that he has not been able to construct the figure. A new clock figure is expected of all apprentices, and Karl is the first in hundreds of years to fail. Awards: CC. Grades: 6–7.

Tepper, Sheri. *Beauty.*
Spectra, 1992.
Setting: 1347.
Main Character: Female, Sleeping Beauty, 16 years old.

Beauty's diary from age 16 to 116. She narrowly escapes the curse set upon her at her christening. While her household falls into an enchanted sleep, she undertakes a journey across time to the modern world and beyond, into an imaginary universe, in search of her destiny. A *Sleeping Beauty* story. Awards: CC. Grades: YA.

Tomlinson, Theresa. *The Forestwife.*
Orchard, 1995.
Setting: England, 1100s.
Main Character: Female, Maid Marian, 15 years old.

Marian escapes from an arranged marriage to live with a community of forest folk, which includes a daring young outlaw named Robert. A *Robin Hood* story. Grades: 5–9.

Vande Velde, Vivian. *The Rumpelstiltskin Problem.*
Scholastic, 2002.
Setting: fairy tale castle.
Main Character: Rumpelstiltskin.

In six retellings of the Rumplestiltskin story, the author addresses questions about the original tale by changing elements in each story. Grades: 5–9.

Velde, Vivian Vande. *Tales from the Brothers Grimm and the Sisters Weird.*
Jane Yolen, 1995.

Thirteen twisted versions of familiar fairy tales. Grades: 4–8.

Viguie, Debbie. *Midnight Pearls.*
Simon Pulse, 2003.
Setting: Seaside.
Main Character: Female, Pearl, 17 years old.

Pearl is rescued from the sea during a storm and is taken in by a fisherman and his barren wife. Pearl lives a lonely life with only Prince James for a friend. When their boat capsizes, Pearl makes her way to shore, but James must be saved by Faye, a mermaid who instantly falls in love with him. Looking on from the waves is Kale, Faye's merman brother, who realizes that Pearl is actually Adriana, his betrothed who was kidnapped years before. After the Sea Witch becomes involved, Faye becomes a mute human charged to get a marriage proposal from James or die, and Kale becomes a blind human charged to attain the love of his beloved or meet the same fate. Grades: 6 and up.

Yolen, Jane. **Briar Rose.**
Tor, 2002.
Setting: Germany, Poland, 1940s, 1990s.
Main Character: Female, Rebecca Berlin, 20s.

Becca grew up hearing her grandmother Gemma tell an unusual and frightening version of the Sleeping Beauty legend. When Gemma dies, the fairy tale offers one of the very few clues she has to her grandmother's past. Rebecca follows the clues to Poland, the setting for the book's most engrossing scenes, where she meets its most interesting, best-developed characters. Awards: CC; Mythopoeic Fantasy. Grades: YA/A.

Yolen, Jane, and Adam Stemple. **Pay the Piper: A Rock and Roll Fairy Tale.**
Starscape, 2005.
Setting: 2000s.
Main Characters: Male, Gringas; Female, Callie, 14 years old.

Gringas, a banished prince of Faerie, forms a folk rock band to earn the gold and silver to buy off a curse cast when he murdered his brother. Gringras leads children into Faerie, where their souls power the land of the Ever Fair. He gets more than he can handle when he lures a group of trick-or-treaters that includes Callie's little brother. High school reporter Callie follows Gringras into Faerie and undoes the curse that compels him to steal away children. A Pied Piper story. Grades: 6–8.

GREEK MYTHOLOGY

Alexander, Lloyd. **The Arkadians.**
Dutton, 1995.
Setting: Arkadia.
Main Character: Male, Lucian, young man.

Lucian and his companions flee corrupt palace officials and roam the land, seeking adventure and purpose. Mythology: Narcissus, the Wooden Horse of Troy, Odysseus, Theseus, and the Minotaur. Grades: 5–8.

Cooney, Caroline B. **Goddess of Yesterday.**
Delacorte, 2002.
Setting: Greek island, pre–Trojan War.
Main Character: Female, Anaxandra, 6 through girlhood.

Anaxandra is taken from her home at a young age and survives by posing as two different princesses, before ending up as a servant to Helen and Paris as they make their way to Troy. Mythology: Helen of Troy. Grades: 5–8.

Fleischman, Paul. **Dateline: Troy.**
Candlewick, 1996.
Setting: Ancient Greece.
Main Characters: Male, Agamemnon; Male, Menelaus; Male, Achilles.

The retelling of the Trojan War is juxtaposed against collages of newspaper headlines of modern wars and political crises. Based on Homer's *The Iliad*. Grades: 6–9.

Geras, Adele. **Troy.**
Harcourt, 2001.
Sequel: **Ithaka.**
Setting: Troy, Ancient Greece, Trojan War, thirteenth century B.C.
Main Characters: Female, Marpessa; Female, Xanthe; Male, Alastor.
The great battles of the Trojan War are seen at a distance from the walls of the city, where the townsfolk gather to sit each day and cheer the action like spectators at an archaic football game. The complicated love affairs and bloody battles are given a stir by the bored gods and goddesses. The Trojan Horse, Helen, Paris, Achilles, Hector, and all the gods make cameo appearances, and there is a great battle scene at the end. Grades: 7–12.

Gibbons, Alan. **Shadow of the Minotaur.**
Orion, 2001.
Series: Legendeer Trilogy: **Vampyr Legion; Warriors of the Raven.**
Setting: Virtual reality.
Main Character: Male, Phoenix, 13 years old.
Phoenix is drawn into the virtual reality computer game of Greek mythology created by his father. Phoenix winds his way through the labyrinth to face the Minotaur. Grades: 7 and up.

Hall, Brian. **The Saskiad.**
Picador, 1997.
Setting: Ithaca, New York, Denmark, 1990s.
Main Character: Female, Saskia, 12 years old.
Saskia grows up on a 1960s-style commune run by her mother, Lauren; her father, Thomas, had abandoned the family many years earlier. Saskia dreams she is a cohort of Odysseus, a disciple of Marco Polo, and a friend of sixteenth-century astronomer Tycho Brahe. Saskia is thrilled when new student, Jane, becomes her friend; Jane is happy to play roles in Saskia's imaginary adventures and doesn't seem to mind that she's Saskia's sexual crush. Thomas invites Saskia to visit him in Denmark, and Saskia reunites with her father, taking Jane along. Thomas builds himself up in Saskia's eyes as a valiant activist, and he accepts Jane's sexual advances. Thomas returns home to reunite with Lauren, and Saskia learns some shocking truths about her father. She runs away to Manhattan. Mythology: Odysseus and Thomas, Lauren and Penelope. Grades: YA/A.

Kindl, Patrice. **Lost in the Labyrinth.**
Houghton Mifflin, 2002.
Setting: Ancient Greece.
Main Character: Female, Xenodice, 14 years old.
Despite his monstrous appearance, the Minotaur is gentle until provoked. His sister, Xenodice, loves him and tries to protect him from Theseus and the schemes of her own family. Xenodice attempts a midnight rescue of her brother and later helps

Daedalus and Icarus make their winged escape attempt. Mythology: Theseus and the Minotaur. Grades: 6–10.

McLaren, Clemence. *Aphrodite's Blessings: Love Stories from the Greek Myths.*
Atheneum, 2002.
Sequels: *Behind the Walls of Troy; Inside the Walls of Troy; Waiting for Odysseus.*
Setting: Ancient Greece.
Main Characters: Female, Atalanta; Female, Andromeda; Female, Psyche.
　　Three stories of the marriages of Atalanta, Andromeda, and Psyche. Grades: 7 and up.

Napoli, Donna Jo. *The Great God Pan.*
Wendy Lamb, 2003.
Setting: Ancient forest.
Main Character: Male, Pan, young man goat.
　　Pan frolics in the woods with maenads, playing his panpipes and creating panic. He meets Iphigenia and falls in love with her, but the curse placed upon him at birth, that he will never be loved, seems destined to come true. His life revolves around finding her again. He finds her just as she is about to be sacrificed by her own father. Pan devises a trick to save Iphigenia's life at the expense of his own. Fast-paced and intriguing. Grades: 8–10.

Napoli, Donna Jo. *Sirena.*
Scholastic, 2000.
Setting: Ancient Greece.
Main Character: Female, Sirena, 17 years old.
　　The Sirens' sweet, beckoning songs caused countless shipwrecks, but perhaps the Sirens were cursed. Ten Sirens are doomed to lead short mortal lives unless they can convince men to become their mates. After a shipwreck, Sirena tends to the wounds of a survivor, and they fall in love. Based on the myths of The Sirens, Mermaids, Aegean Sea. Grades: 7–10.

Riordan, Rick. *Percy Jackson and the Olympians: The Lightning Thief.*
Hyperion/Miramax, 2005.
Sequel: *Percy Jackson and the Olympians: The Sea of Monsters.*
Setting: New York City, 2000s.
Main Character: Male, Perseus Jackson, 12 years old.
　　Percy is the son of Poseidon and a mortal woman. As he discovers his heritage, he is sent to a boarding school for demigods. The gods are still very active in the twenty-first-century world and are about to go to war over a lost thunderbolt. Percy and sidekicks, Grover (a young satyr) and Annabeth (daughter of Athena), set out to retrieve it. Fast-paced, and told with humor. Grades: 5 to 9.

Spinner, Stephanie. *Quiver.*
Knopf, 2002.
Setting: Ancient Greece.

Main Character: Female, Atalanta.

Atalanta, a skilled archer and a runner, has dedicated her life to Artemis, the Goddess of the Hunt, and is as good as or better than many of her male counterparts. King Iasus, who abandoned her at birth, now demands her return so that she marry and produce a son, since he does not have an heir. Since Atalanta has vowed to remain chaste, she poses a challenge: she will only marry a man who can outrun her in a race; all others must die. Grades: 7–10.

Turner, Megan Whalen. *The Thief.*
Puffin, 1998.
Sequel: *The Queen of Attolia.*
Setting: Eddis.
Main Character: Male, Gen, young man.

Gen, an accomplished thief incarcerated for stealing the king's seal, is dragged from his cell by the king's magus, who is on a quest. The prize is Hamiathes's Gift, said to be a creation of the gods that confers the right of rule on the wearer. During the quest, the magus and Gen take turns telling the youngest member of their party myths about the Eddisian god of thieves. Awards: Newbery Honor. Grades: 6–12.

Voigt, Cynthia. *Orfe.*
Simon Pulse, 2002.
Setting: 2000s.
Main Characters: Female, Orfe; Male, Yuri; both teenagers then adults.

Orfe and Yuri are lovers. Orfe is a singer/songwriter of spellbinding power, Yuri is a recovering addict who succumbs to his weakness on the very day of their wedding. The narrator, Enny, begins Orfe's tale by recounting their school days. Based on The Three Graces. Grades: 7 and up.

SHAKESPEAREAN THEMES—ROMEO AND JULIET

Atwater-Rhodes, Amelia. *Hawksong.*
Random House, 2004.
Series: The Kiesha'ra: *Snakecharm; Falcondance.*
Setting: Shape-shifter world.
Main Character: Female, Danica Shardae, young woman (not human).

Danica is an avian shape-shifter and the princess of her people, who have been at war with the serpiente. Zane Cobriana is a prince among the serpiente. Danica and Zane are determined to stop the war, and they agree to marry, but the mediating parties are so offended by the plan, they leave. Grades: 7–10.

Avi. *Romeo and Juliet, Together (and Alive) At Last!*
HarperTrophy, 1988.
Setting: Junior high school, 1980s.
Main Characters: Male, Saltz; Female Anabell Stackpole, 13 years old.

Ed discovers that his best friend, Saltz, is nursing a secret love for Anabell Stackpoole, and he gets the rest of the other eighth-graders to produce their version of *Romeo and Juliet*. Saltz and Anabell get the leading roles in the rewritten play where Romeo & Juliet get together. Grades: 6–8.

Bennett, Cherie and Jeff Gottensfeld. ***A Heart Divided.***
Delacorte, 2004.
Setting: Redford, Tennessee.
Main Character: Female, Kate Pride, 16 years old.
   When her parents decide to move from New Jersey to Tennessee, Kate is unhappy about giving up her friends and her spot in a prestigious playwriting workshop. Racial tensions abound in Redford, and Kate learns quickly that she is a very northern girl in the middle of a very southern town. She writes a play about the town's act of flying the Confederate flag and the opposition that it causes. When she meets Jack Redford, a Romeo-and-Juliet-type romance begins. Grades: 8 and up.

Draper, Sharon. ***Romiette and Julio.***
Atheneum, 1999.
Setting: Cincinnati, Ohio.
Main Characters: Female, Romiette Capelle; Male, Julio Montague; both 16 years old.
   After falling in love on the Internet, African American Romiette and Latino Julio discover that they attend the same high school. They face their parents' prejudices and the threats of a local gang called The Family, whose members object to interracial dating. Awards: CC. Grades: 7–12.

Dai, Fan. ***Butterfly Lovers: A Tale of the Chinese Romeo and Juliet.***
Homa & Sekey, 2000.
Setting: China.
Main Characters: Female, Yingtai Zhu, young woman; Male, Shanbo Liang, young man.
   Yingtai, the only daughter of a prosperous family, despairs at the prospect of staying within the walls of her family's compound until she marries and goes off to live behind a new set of walls. She persuades her father to allow her to masquerade as a man and travel to Hangzhou to study with Master Zhou. On the way, she meets Shanbo Liang, and the two become friends and "sworn brothers." Yingtai falls in love with Shanbo, but she keeps up the pretense until she is called home and asks Mrs. Zhou to tell Shanbo after her departure. Shanbo wants to marry her once he learns the truth, but her parents have found her a groom. Grades: YA.

Howe, Norma. ***Blue Avenger Cracks the Code.***
HarperTempest, 2002.
Prequel: ***The Adventures of Blue Avenger.***
Setting: Venice, Italy.
Main Character: Male, David Schumacher, 16 years old.
   David is the self-made superhero Blue Avenger. He is on the hunt for the true author of Shakespeare's plays, William Shakespeare or the 17th Earl of Oxford, Edward De Vere. Blue heads to Venice, foils the dog-napping of his grammy's shih tzu, and discovers a way to secure the copyright of his friend Louie's stolen video game idea. As he saves the world bit by bit, Blue wonders how to win the trust and love of his friend and crush, Omaha Nebraska Brown. Grades: 7 and up.

Kerr, M. E. *Gentlehands.*
HarperTrophy, 1990.
Setting: Long Island, New York, summer.
Main Characters: Male, Buddy Boyle; Female, Sky Pennington; both 16 years old.
　　Buddy starts dating rich girl Skye and takes her to meet his wealthy but estranged grandfather. A writer at Skye's house suspects Buddy's grandfather is a former Nazi. Awards: CC. Grades: 7 and up.

Korman, Gordon. *Son of the Mob.*
Hyperion, 2002.
Setting: New York City, present day.
Main Character: Male, Vince Luca, 17 years old.
　　Vince refuses to become involved in the family "vending machine business." His father is a Mob boss, his older brother is their father's loser lackey, and his mother turns a deaf ear to everything, cooking up a steady storm in the kitchen. Things heat up when Vince dates and falls in love with the daughter of the FBI agent determined to bring down Vince's father. A page-turner, told with humor. Grades: 7 and up.

Pearson, Mary E. *Scribbler of Dreams.*
Harcourt, 2001.
Setting: California, present day.
Main Characters: Female, Kaitlin Malone; Male, Bram; both 17 years old.
　　Kaitlin and her well-to-do artist boyfriend, Bram have families with a tangled history. Borrowed diaries reveal to Kaitlin that the two families were related five generations back, when two sisters became estranged as the result of a marital infidelity. Now, Kaitlin's father is accused of killing Bram's father, perhaps accidentally, in a feud over rights to their neighboring properties. Kaitlin manages to win Bram over by concealing her identity. Grades: 7 and up.

Randle, Kristen D. *Breaking Rank.*
HarperCollins, 1999.
Setting: High school, 1990s.
Main Characters: Male, Thomas, aka Baby; Female, Casey Willardson; both 17 years old.
　　Baby is a member of a nontraditional gang called the Clan. The Clan disavows participation in school, doesn't believe in drugs or violence, and advocates self-education. The older members tutor younger apprentices in everything, from car mechanics to Latin. Baby wants to be more than just a mechanic like his domineering older brother, so he breaks rank from his peers and takes an aptitude test at school. Honor student Casey begins tutoring Baby, and the misunderstandings they have about each other are slowly stripped away. They quickly become close and learn to trust and love each other. Their relationship provokes a showdown between the Clan and the varsity football team. Grades: 7 and up.

Sutherland, Tui T. *This Must Be Love.*
HarperCollins, 2004.
Setting: New Jersey.
Main Characters: Female, Helena; Female, Hermia; Male, Dimitri; Male, Alex.
　　Helena and Hermia are both in love with boys who do not seem to notice them.

Hermia's love interest Alex has bought tickets for an interactive theater piece in New York City, one of her dreams come true. Her father forbids her to go, so she sneaks out. Dimitri, Helena's love interest, has become infatuated with Hermia, and to win his attentions, Helena tells him where her friend has gone. Many twists and turns lead the girls into their true love's arms in *A Midsummer Night's Dream* ending. E-mails, notes, diaries, poems, and short plays. Grades: 7–10.

Woodson, Jacqueline. *If You Come Softly.*
Putnam, 1998.
Sequel: *Behind You.*
Setting: New York City.
Main Characters: Male, Jeremiah; Female, Elisha; both 15 years old.
    Miah is black and Ellie is white. They meet during their first year at an exclusive New York prep school and fall in love. Miah's father has left his mother for another woman, and Ellie is trying to fight through her feelings about her mother, who twice abandoned her family for extended periods. The teens must deal with the bigotry that they are subject to as a mixed-race couple. Awards: CC. Grades: 7 and up.

MORE SHAKESPEAREAN THEMES

Blackwood, Gary. *The Shakespeare Stealer.*
Puffin, 2002.
Sequel: *Shakespeare's Scribe.*
Setting: 1500s.
Main Character: Male, Widge, 14 year old.
    Widge, a young orphan boy, is ordered by his master to infiltrate Shakespeare's acting troupe in order to steal the script of *Hamlet*, but he discovers instead the meaning of friendship and loyalty. Grades: 5–8.

Cooper, Susan. *King of Shadows.*
Margaret K. McElderry, 1999.
Setting: Globe Theatre, 1599/present day.
Main Character: Male, Nat Field, teen.
    Orphan Nat is chosen as part of an American theater group to perform at the new Globe Theatre in London. Nat's big role will be Puck in *A Midsummer Night's Dream*. However, his debut is pushed 400 years into the past when he is put to bed with a high fever and wakes up in Elizabethan England. Forced to adapt or be discovered, Nat figures out his situation quickly by asking judicious questions. Grades: 5–8.

Draper, Sharon. *Tears of a Tiger.*
Atheneum, 1994.
Series: Hazelwood High Trilogy: *Forged by Fire* (CC; Coretta Scott King); *Darkness Before Dawn.*
Setting: Hazelwood.
Main Character: Male, Andy, 16 year old.
    Andy cannot bear the guilt of being the drunk driver in an accident that killed his best friend. His disintegration builds to inevitable suicide as counselors, coaches, friends, and family all fail him. The story is told through English class assignments,

including poetry; dialogs; police and newspaper reports; and letters. The characters' voices are strong, vivid, and ring true, in a *Macbeth*-themed story. Awards: CC; Genesis (John Steptoe). Grades: 7–12.

Duncan, Lois. **Killing Mr. Griffin.**
Laurel Leaf, 1979.
Setting: Del Norte High School.
Main Characters: Male, Mr. Griffin, adult; Female, Susan; Male, Dave; Male, Mark; Female, Betsy; Male, Jeff; all teenagers.

High school can be tough, and with teachers like Mr. Griffin, it can seem impossible. A student suggests playing a trick on him to scare him, but the plans go wrong and it ends in murder. *Hamlet* theme. Grades: 7 and up.

Katz, Welwyn Wilton. **Come Like Shadows.**
Coteau, 2001.
Setting: Canada, Stratford Theatre, present day.
Main Character: Female, Kincardine O'Neil, 16 years old.

Kinny passionately wants to be an actress. To expose her to the harsh realities of theater life, her mother persuades an old friend, now a famous director, to give Kinny a summer job as an assistant. The play *Macbeth* is said by actors to be cursed, and this production lives up to its reputation. The cast faces deaths, accidents, a fire, and three ancient witches who have been tied up with the play for centuries because of their involvement with the real Macbeth. Grades: 9–12.

Paterson, Katherine. **Bridge to Terabithia.**
HarperCollins, 1977.
Setting: Virginia.
Main Characters: Male, Jesse Oliver Aarons; Female, Leslie Burke; both 10 years old.

Jess is eager to start fifth grade and be the fastest runner at school. But the new girl in class, Leslie Burke, leaves all the boys in the dust, including Jess. Jess and Leslie soon become inseparable. Together, they create an imaginary, secret kingdom in the woods called Terabithia, which can be reached only by swinging across a creek bed on a rope. But one morning a tragic accident changes Jess's life forever. *Hamlet* theme. Awards: Newbery. Grades: 5 and up.

Plummer, Louise. **Unlikely Romance of Kate Bjorkman.**
Laurel Leaf, 1997.
Setting: Minnesota, Christmas season.
Main Character: Female, Kate Bjorkman, 17 years old.

Kate narrates her tale of teen romance in the language and conventions of *The Romance Writer's Handbook*. Spoofing the searing descriptions and pat plots of torrid bodice rippers, this six-foot-tall heroine with glasses thick as Coke bottles and an I.Q. off the charts proves that true love awaits even the gawkiest, most socially inept teen. An *Othello* theme, written in chapters that alternate novel segments with Kate's revision notes. Grades: 7–10.

Pratchett, Terry. **Wyrd Sisters.**
Bantam Doubleday Dell, 2000.

Series: Discworld: includes 34 novels, a number of short stories, and several related books.
Setting: Discworld.
Main Characters: The Three Witches.

Granny Weatherwax is a feisty, powerful, no-nonsense witch who believes in headology. Nanny Ogg is a grandmotherly witch who loves drinking and bawdy songs. Magrat Garlick is a young, idealistic New Age witch, who likes spells to be performed just so, and who falls in love with the court Fool. A fast-paced romp through scenes, themes, and lines from *Macbeth, Hamlet, Julius Caesar, King Lear, As You Like It,* and many more. Grades: YA/A.

Pressler, Mirjam. ***Shylock's Daughter.***
Pan Macmillan, 2001.
Setting: Venice, 1594.
Main Characters: Female, Jessica, 16 years old; Male, Lorenzo, young man; Female, Dalilah, Jessica's servant/friend/sister.

Jessica, the daughter of a Jewish merchant, falls in love with Christian aristocrat Lorenzo in a *Merchant of Venice* story. Grades: 9 and up.

RESOURCES: ADDITIONAL TITLES

DeVos, Gail. 1999. ***New Tales for Old: Folktales as Literary Fictions for Young Adults.*** Englewood, CO: Libraries Unlimited.
Isaac, Megan Lynn. 2000. ***Heirs to Shakespeare: Reinventing the Bard in Young Adult Literature.*** Portsmouth, NH; Boynton/Cook.
Koelling Holly. 2004. ***Classic Connections: Turning Teens on to Great Literature.*** Westport, CT: Libraries Unlimitied.

CHAPTER 19

RELIGION AND SPIRITUALITY

Teens often question their parents' beliefs while searching for their own understanding of "The Big Picture." The titles in the lists in this chapter show the reader that seeking and questioning is a natural part of coming of age in all faiths, whether they explore other religions and return to the faith of their family or adopt a new religion or form their own understanding.

Amish
Christianity
Christmas
Eastern Religions
Islam
Judaism
Last Days/End of the World/Apocalypse
Latter Day Saints/Mormons
Negative Portrayals of Clergy/Church
Spiritual Seekers/ Faith

AMISH

Bender, Carrie. **Birch Hollow Schoolmarm.**
Herald Press, 1999.
Series: Dora's Diary: **Lilac Blossom Time; Beyond Mist Blue Mountains.**
Setting: Pennsylvania.
Main Character: Female, Dora, 16 years old.

Dora is ready to go "rumschpringing" (running around with friends). When her parents forbid her to date Gideon, she sneaks out repeatedly to be with him and then spends much of her time repenting. She prepares for baptism, travels to Minnesota to teach in a one-room school, and falls for upstanding Matthew. Told through a diary, scriptures, sermons, hymns, and prayers with Pennsylvania-German phrases. "Rules for Teachers," from 1872 and 1915, and "Rules for Schoolchildren," dated 1760, are included. Grades: 6–10.

Borntrager, Mary Christner. **Ellie.**
Herald, 1988.

Series: Ellie's People: *Rebecca; Rachel; Daniel; Reuben; Andy; Polly; Sarah; Mandy; Annie.*
Setting: Amish community.
Main Character: Female, Ellie Maust, young woman.

Ellie grows up in the Amish community, seeing the many interesting things that the outside world has, but also all of the things that her own community has. Ellie faces her temptations and her questions, and grows in her faith and in her love for her Amish heritage. Grades: YA/A.

Brunstetter, Wanda E. *The Storekeeper's Daughter.*
Barbour, 2005.
Series: Lancaster's Daughters: *The Quilter's Daughter.*
Setting: Pennsylvania.
Main Character: Female, Naomi Fisher, 20 years old.

Time seems to stand still in Naomi's community, but it cannot hold back tragedy. Helping her widowed father run a store, manage a household, and raise seven children is a daunting task. There is no time to think about courtship or having her own family, though her heart yearns for the attention of Caleb Hoffmeir. Then one afternoon, her baby brother disappears from the yard. Grades: YA/A.

Lewis, Beverly. *The Covenant.*
Bethany House, 2002.
Series: Abram's Daughters: *The Sacrifice; The Prodigal; The Betrayal; The Revelation.*
Setting: Gobbler's Knob, Pennsylvania, 1946.
Main Characters: Female, Sadie Ebersol, 17 years old; Female, Leah Ebersol, 15 years old.

Sadie and her sister, Leah, are exploring the joys of "rumschpringe," the period of relaxed rules and running around that Amish teens enjoy prior to their baptism into the church. Tomboy Leah's first love is Jonas Mast, but her father, Abram, has determined she'll marry Gideon Peachey, whose father's farm adjoins the Ebersols'. Her beautiful sister Sadie's defiance crosses the boundaries, when she becomes involved with and pregnant by Englischer Derek Schwartz. Amish dialect and multiple points of view. Grades: YA/A.

McDaniel, Lurlene. *Angels Watching Over Me.*
Laurel Leaf, 1996.
Sequels: *Lifted Up By Angels; Until Angels Close My Eyes.*
Setting: Indianapolis, Indiana.
Main Characters: Female, Leah Lewis-Hall, 16 years old; Female, Rebekah, 8 years old; Male, Ethan, teenager.

Leah is left alone right before Christmas by her mother, who has just been married for the fifth time. When she is admitted to the hospital for treatment of a broken finger, further tests indicate bone cancer. While in the hospital, she meets Ethan and is drawn to him, despite the difficulties she has understanding his Amish culture, and the mysterious nurse, Gabriella, who may or may not be an angel. Grades: 8–10.

Meyer, Carolyn. *Gideon's People.*
Gulliver, 1996.
Setting: Pennsylvania, 1911.

Main Characters: Isaac Litvak, 12 years old; Gideon Stolzfus, 16 years old.

When Isaac, an Orthodox Jew, is injured on an Amish farm, his peddler father leaves him behind to recuperate with the whispered reminder, "Remember who you are." The Amish family is kind and well-meaning, but their eating habits, language, and religious laws are strange to Isaac. The Amish son, Gideon, resents the rigid tenets of his family's local sect and plans to run away to his uncle's more lenient community. His sister, Annie, fears losing him forever, and she begs Isaac to help her persuade Gideon to stay. Grades: 6–9.

CHRISTIANITY

Carlson, Melody. *Becoming Me by Caitlin O'Conner.*
Multnomah, 2000.
Series: Diary of a Teenage Girl: *Caitlin: It's My Life, by Caitlin O'Connor; Who I Am; On My Own; I Do!; Falling Up.* Kim's Diaries: *Just Ask: Diary of a Teenage Girl; Meant to Be.* Chloe's Diaries: *Sold Out; Road Trip; Face the Music; My Name is Chloe.*
Setting: Present day.
Main Character: Female, Caitlin O'Conner, 16 years old.

Through Caitlin's candid journal entries we see her grapple with such universal teen issues as peer pressure, loyalty, conflict with parents, the longing for a boyfriend, and her own spirituality. Caitlin struggles toward self-discovery and understanding God's plan for her life. Grades: YA.

Carlson, Melody. *Dark Blue: Color Me Lonely.*
Think, 2004.
Series: True Colors: *Deep Green: Color Me Jealous; Torch Red: Color Me Torn; Blade Silver: Color Me Scarred; Pitch Black: Color Me Lost; Burnt Orange: Color Me Wasted; Fool's Gold: Color Me Consumed; Bitter Rose: Color Me Crushed.*
Setting: High school, present day.
Main Character: Female, Kara Hendricks, high school sophomore.

After becoming a cheerleader, Jordan starts to make new, more popular friends, and Kara feels totally burned by her former best friend's icy rejection. These dark blue days are almost more than she can take, until she makes some major choices about who and what she's going to believe in, and if she'll ever trust anybody, including God, ever again. The series includes discussion questions. Grades: YA.

Clinton, Cathryn. *The Calling.*
Candlewick, 2001.
Setting: South Carolina, 1962.
Main Character: Female, Esta Lea Ridley, 13 years old.

A year after she feels God's call, Esta is as surprised as anyone when she lays hands on her grandmother and cures her deafness. Another miraculous healing follows, and soon she is ordained in the family's Beulah Land Healing and Holiness Church, then sent on a healing ministry. She is accompanied by her older sister, Sarah Louise, and newly converted Uncle Peter Earl Jewels, an Elvis lookalike, traveling salesman, and ladies' man, who is their favorite uncle when he's not drunk. Grades: 7 and up.

Heynen, Jim. *Cosmos Coyote and William the Nice.*
Henry Holt, 2000.
Setting: Iowa.
Main Character: Male, Cosmos De Haag, 17 years old.

Cosmos spends his senior year away from home to live with relatives in a religious farming community in Iowa, after he was threatened with six months in "juvie." He leaves behind his rock band, the OughtaBs, and his girlfriend, Salal, for wide-open spaces, cow dung, and Dutch Center Christian Academy. To fit in, he swaps his rebellious persona of Cosmos Coyote for that of William the Nice and meets beautiful and devout Cherlyn Van Dyke, who seems bent on saving him. When a string of thefts occur, all fingers point to Cosmos. Grades: 9 and up.

Lewis, C. S. *The Lion, the Witch and the Wardrobe.*
HarperCollins, 1994.
Sequels, Prequel: The Chronicles of Narnia: *The Magician's Nephew; The Horse and His Boy; Prince Caspian; The Voyage of the Dawn Treader; The Silver Chair; The Last Battle.*
Setting: England, Narnia, 1940.
Main Characters: Male, Peter, teen; Female, Susan, young teen; Male, Edmund, boy; Female, Lucy Pevensie, 8 years old.

Lucy looks into the wardrobe and discovers Narnia and the faun. She and her siblings assist Aslan, the golden lion, to rid Narnia of the White Witch who has cursed the land with eternal winter. A Christian allegory. Grades: 5 and up.

Peretti, Frank. *Hangman's Curse.*
Tommy Nelson, 2001.
Series: Verita's Project: *Nightmare Academy.*
Setting: Baker High School.
Main Characters: Male, Elijah; Male, Elisha; twins; both high school teens.

Elijah, Elisha, and their parents work undercover to seek the truth surrounding mysterious deaths and a legendary school ghost. A Christian series about a family that aids the FBI. Grades: YA.

Wangerin, Walter. *Book of the Dun Cow.*
HarperSanFrancisco, 2003.
Setting: Animal kingdom.
Main Characters: Chauntecleer, a rooster; Mundo Cani, a dog.

Chauntecleer is in charge of a small animal kingdom and is confronted by the evil Coctrice, a half snake/half rooster who is the son of the devil, an evil serpent trapped beneath the surface of the earth, trying to get out to destroy God's creation. The animals come together to confront the evil threat. Grades: YA/A.

CHRISTMAS

Cabot, Meg. *Holiday Princess.*
HarperCollins, 2005.
Series: The Princess Diaries.
Setting: Genovia, Christmas season

Main Character: Female, Mia Thermopolis, 15 years old.

A princess always knows how to celebrate the holidays: Christmas, Hanukkah, Yule, Chinese New Year, Saturnalia . . . to name just a few. Then there's gift giving, the royal Genovian Fabergé advent calendar, hot chocolate with marshmallows, and all those fabulous holiday movies. Grades: YA.

Cabot, Meg. *The Princess Present.*
HarperCollins, 2004.
Series: The Princess Diaries: *Princess in Pink; Project Princess; Princess Diaries; Princess in Love; Princess in the Spotlight; Princess in Training; Princess in Waiting.*
Setting: Genovia, Christmas season
Main Character: Female, Mia Thermopolis, 15 years old.

Every year, Princess Mia spends the holidays in Genovia with Grandmère. This year her boyfriend, Michael, and her best friend, Lilly, are coming to Genovia, too. Lilly has a lot to learn about palace protocol; there's no time to linger under the mistletoe with Michael, and Mia hasn't been able to find him the perfect gift. Grades: YA.

Cooney, Caroline. *What Child Is This?*
Delacorte, 1997.
Setting: Christmas season.
Main Character: Female, Katie, 8 years old.

Katie, an emotionally starved foster child, writes a wish on a paper bell that will be hung on a Christmas tree in a local restaurant. Members of the community can choose a wish and give a gift to a needy child. Katie wishes for a family. Matt, a high school student who lives in the same foster home and works in the restaurant, hangs her bell on the tree. Liz, Matt's classmate, is upset when her uncaring father reads the wish, calls it ridiculous, and tears up the bell. When Matt tells Katie on Christmas Eve that her wish will not come true, the devastated girl runs out into a blizzard. Grades: 5–10.

Cooper, Ilene. *Sam I Am.*
Scholastic, 2004.
Setting: Christmas season.
Main Character: Male, Sam Goodman, 12 years old.

At Christmastime, Sam is trying to figure out what he believes about God, in a family with a Jewish dad and an Episcopalian mom. Meanwhile at school Sam is studying the Holocaust. Grades: 5–7.

Fine, Anne. *The True Story of Christmas.*
Yearling, 2005.
Setting: Christmas Day.
Main Character: Male, Ralph Mountfield, 12 years old.

Ralph, banished to his bed on Christmas Day, details what happens when sixteen relatives descend on his house, and a family feud does them in. It's hard to decide who is the worst of the group: cousin Titania, an egotistical little twit who fancies herself a fairy; great-gran, whose favorite line is, "If I had my own teeth, I'd bite you"; or the twins, who enjoy pelting dinner rolls at the cat. Dark British humor. Grades: 5–7.

McDaniel, Lurlene. *Starry, Starry Night: Three Holiday Stories.*
Laurel Leaf, 2000.
Setting: Christmas season.
Main Characters: Female, Melanie, 15 years old; Female, Brenda; Female, Ellie Matthias; both 16 years old.

Story 1: Even though Melanie is slightly embarrassed about her 42-year-old mother's pregnancy, she finds herself becoming more excited about the baby as time passes. She and her parents are devastated when the baby is born without part of its brain. Story 2: Brenda has a secret crush on a young man who attends a military academy. Her life becomes complicated when she learns that a local cancer patient has a crush on her. Story 3: Ellie is having difficulty with her boyfriend until she befriends a secretive girl who helps her put things into perspective. Grades: 7 and up.

Plummer, Louise. *Unlikely Romance of Kate Bjorkman.*
Laurel Leaf, 1997.
Setting: Minnesota, Christmas season.
Main Character: Female, Kate Bjorkman, 17 years old.

Kate narrates her tale of teen romance in the language and conventions of *The Romance Writer's Handbook.* Spoofing torrid bodice rippers, this six-foot-tall heroine with glasses thick as Coke bottles and an I.Q. off the charts proves that true love awaits even the gawkiest, most socially inept teen. Written in chapters that alternate novel segments with Kate's revision notes. Grades: 7–10.

Scott, Kieran. *Jingle Boy.*
Laurel Leaf, 2005.
Setting: Paramus, New Jersey.
Main Character: Male, Paul Nicholas, teenager.

Paul and his family have the most lit-up house in Paramus every Christmas, and they are devoted to the whole season. Paul is even going to be Santa at the mall, but his new girlfriend dumps him for another Santa, his dad nearly electrocutes himself putting the lights up, and his mom gets fired. Paul joins Holly, his best friend, and a handful of others in an anti-Christmas campaign, which leads to some very questionable activities. Grades: 6–9.

Williams, Carol Lynch. *Christmas in Heaven.*
Putnam, 2000.
Setting: Heaven, Florida.
Main Character: Female, Honey DeLoach, 12 years old.

Honey has lived in Heaven most of her life. Her grandfather, Pop-Pop, is a televangelist, and though Honey worries about not being saved, what she yearns for most is a true friend. Christmas, her sister, Easter, and her movie-star mother, Miriam Season, move to Heaven in an attempt to save Easter from her destructive habits. Christmas and Honey become inseparable friends. Christmas witnesses a truly loving family, and Honey learns to appreciate the simple joys of tree houses, French toast, and parents who care. Easter dies in a car accident, and Honey's brother nearly dies as well. Christmas is forced to leave town, but both girls know that their bond is forever. Grades: 5–8.

Martel, Yann. *Life of Pi.*
Harvest, 2003.
Setting: India, Pacific Ocean.
Main Character: Male, Pi Patel, 16 years old.

The son of an Indian zookeeper, Pi is shipwrecked when his family packs up to move to Canada. Stranded on a life boat with a wounded zebra, a spotted hyena, a seasick orangutan, and a 450-pound Bengal tiger named Richard Parker, Pi survives for 227 days. Grades: 9–12.

Desai Hidier, Tanuja. *Born Confused.*
Push/Scholastic, 2002.
Setting: New Jersey, 2000s.
Main Character: Female, Dimple Lala, 17 years old.

Dimple, an Indian American aspiring photographer, struggles to balance two cultures at home and in the South Asian club scene without falling apart. She sees her hypnotically beautiful, blond, manipulative best friend, Gwyn, taking possession of both her heritage and the boy she likes. Grades: 9 and up.

ISLAM

Budhos, Marina. *Ask Me No Questions.*
Atheneum, 2006.
Setting: New York City/Canada.
Main Characters: Nadira, 14 years old; Aisha, 18 years old.

After September 11, 2001, the immigration authorities crack down on aliens. Nadira, Aisha, and their family must flee New York, where they had been living on an expired visa. Their father is arrested at the Canadian border. Grades: YA.

Clinton, Cathryn. *A Stone in My Hand.*
Candlewick, 2002.
Setting: Gaza Strip, 1988.
Main Character: Female, Malaak Abed Atieh, 11 years old.

A month ago, Malaak's father left their home and never returned. Since his disappearance, Malaak hasn't spoken to anyone except her dove. Every day, she climbs up to her roof and waits for him; she does not know that the bus he was on was a terrorist target. Her mother finally tells her what happened, and she begins to worry about her 12-year-old brother becoming involved with a radical group. Malaak comes out of her shell to try to save him from the growing violence that surrounds them. Grades: 5–8.

Dorros, Arthur. *Under the Sun.*
Harry N. Abrams, 2004.
Setting: Sarajevo, Serbia.
Main Character: Male, Ehmet, 13 years old.

Ehmet and his mother flee Sarajevo to the countryside of Croatia, where his aunt and uncle live. When they are taken away, mother and son flee once again. They dodge sniper bullets, avoid land mines, cross militia lines, smuggle out of a refugee camp, and walk miles with little food or water. When his mother dies, Ehmet is completely alone. Grades: 6–9.

Ellis, Deborah. *The Breadwinner.*
Groundwood, 2001.
Sequel: *Parvana's Journey* (Notable Books for a Global Society).
Setting: Afghanistan.
Main Character: Female, Parvana, 11 years old.

The Taliban have decreed that women must stay inside their homes, unless completely covered by a long, tentlike garment with a veil over the face, and girls can no longer go to school. Parvana accompanies father to the market, where he works as a letter writer and sells family possessions. After he is arrested and taken away, Parvana becomes the breadwinner, dressing as a boy and taking over her father's job. Grades: 5–8.

Hosseini, Khaled. *The Kite Runner.*
Riverhead, 2003.
Setting: Kabul, Afghanistan/United States.
Main Characters: Male, Amir; Male, Hassan; both 12 years old.

Amir, the son of a wealthy businessman in Kabul, and Hassan, the son of Amir's father's servant, were inseparable friends as children. Amir and his father flee to America, but Amir is haunted that he left his friend behind. He returns to his war-torn native land after it comes under Taliban rule, only to learn Hassan has been enslaved by a former childhood bully who has become a prominent Taliban official. Awards: Alex. Grades: YA/A.

Nye, Naomi Shihab. *Habibi.*
Simon Pulse, 1999.
Setting: Israel.
Main Character: Female, Liyana, 14 years old.

Liyana's doctor father, a native Palestinian, decides to move his contemporary Arab American family back to Jerusalem from St. Louis. Arriving in Jerusalem, Liyana and her family are gathered in by their colorful, warm-hearted Palestinian relatives and immersed in a culture where only tourists wear shorts and there is a prohibition against boy/girl relationships. When Liyana falls in love with Omer, a Jewish boy, she challenges family, culture, and tradition. Awards: Notable Books for a Global Society. Grades: 5–9.

Staples, Suzanne Fisher. *Shabanu: Daughter of the Wind.*
Knopf, 1991.
Sequel: *Haveli.*
Setting: Pakistan.
Main Character: Female, Shabanu, 13 years old.

Shabanu, the daughter of a nomad in the Cholistan Desert of present-day Pakistan, is pledged in marriage to an older man, whose money will bring prestige to the family. Now she must either accept the decision, as is the custom, or risk the consequences of defying her father's wishes. Awards: CC. Grades: 8–10.

Staples, Suzanne Fisher. *Under the Persimmon Tree.*
Farrar, Straus & Giroux, 2005.
Setting: Pakistan, 2001.
Main Characters: Female, Najmah, young teen; Female, Nusrat, adult.

When her father and brother are taken by the Taliban and her mother and baby brother are killed in a bombing raid during the Afghan war, Najmah journeys across the border to Peshawar, Pakistan. There, she meets up with an American woman, Nusrat, who has been conducting a school for refugee children while she waits for her husband, Faiz, who has returned to his native country to open medical clinics. Grades: 5–8.

Stine, Catherine. *Refugees.*
Delacorte, 2005.
Setting: 2001.
Main Characters: Female, Dawn, 16 years old; Male, Johar, 15 years old.

Dawn is a runaway from California, headed for New York City. She is resentful of her foster mother, a doctor with the Red Cross, who is helping in a refugee camp near Pakistan. Johar lives in Afghanistan. Many of his relatives are dead, and Johar is left to care for his 3-year-old cousin. The September 11th attack occurs when Dawn arrives in New York. Johar makes it to the refugee camp where Dawn's mother is working. The teens develop an e-mail friendship. Grades: 7 and up.

JUDAISM

Abraham, Pearl. *The Romance Reader.*
Riverhead, 1996.
Setting: Monhegan, New York
Main Character: Female, Rachel, 12 years old.

Rachel, a rabbi's daughter, is expected to follow the traditions of her very Orthodox Hasidic family, but she struggles with her desire to create her own way in life. Grades: YA.

Banks, Lynne Reid. *One More River.*
Morrow, 1995.
Sequel: *Broken Bridge.*
Setting: Israel, 1967.
Main Character: Female, Lesley, 14 years old.

Rich and spoiled, Lesley moves with her family from Canada to an Israeli kibbutz to regain a sense of what it means to be Jewish. At home she was popular, successful at school, and trendily dressed and now she has to start from scratch, including learning a new language, doing manual work, and sharing sleeping quarters with three others. Just across the river Jordan she can see the enemy. Grades: 6–9.

Bat-Ami, Miriam. *Two Suns in the Sky.*
Open Court, 1999.
Setting: Oswego, New York.
Main Character: Female, Chris Cook, 15 years old.

Chris is fascinated by the exotic strangers living the grim refugee camp so close by. She and her friends sneak into the camp, where she meets Adam Bornstein, a Yugoslavian Jew. The two fall passionately in love, in spite of their different languages and religions—and the angry resistance of Chris's father. Their voices, as distinctly different as their cultures, alternate in telling the story of their ill-fated attraction. Awards: Scott O'Dell. Grades: 6–10.

Braff, Joshua. *The Unthinkable Thoughts of Jacob Green.*
Algonquin, 2004.
Setting: New Jersey, 1977.
Main Character: Male, Jacob Green, 11 years old.

Like a child, Jacob's father, Abram, wants what he wants when he wants it and will throw a temper tantrum if he doesn't get it. What Abram wants most of all is the perfect suburban Jewish family: perfectly intelligent, perfectly religious, and perfect at obeying their father. To escape his father's cruel, perverse love, young Jacob shares hilariously unthinkable thoughts, such as the hypothetical bar mitzvah thank-you notes in which Jacob thanks people for Jerusalem stone bookends and the like. He then details his lust for his live-in nanny before signing "Love, Jacob." Grades: YA/A.

Chotjewitz, David. *Daniel Half Human and the Good Nazi.*
Atheneum/ Simon & Schuster, 2004.
Setting: Hamburg, Germany, 1930s
Main Character: Male, Daniel, 13 years old.

Daniel is a member of the Hitler Youth, until he discovers his mother is Jewish and he is thrown out of his school, since he is now considered half human. As tension and racism increase, his best friends begin to pull away. Awards: Notable Books for a Global Society; Batchelder Honor. Grades: 7 and up.

Eisner, Will. *Fagin the Jew.*
Doubleday, 2003.
Setting: London, nineteenth century.
Main Character: Male, Fagin, adult.

Fagin from Charles Dickens' *Oliver Twist* is a scheming but humane criminal. His childhood is marked by emigration from Germany and the early death of his impoverished parents, a doomed romance, and, abroad, as an indentured prisoner. A graphic novel in sepia tones. Grades: YA/A.

Hamill, Pete. *Snow in August.*
Warner, 1998.
Setting: Brooklyn, New York, 1947.
Main Character: Male, Michael Devlin, 11 years old.

Michael, an Irish kid who spends his days reading Captain Marvel and anticipating the arrival of Jackie Robinson, makes the acquaintance of a recently emigrated Orthodox rabbi. In exchange for English lessons and baseball, Rabbi Hirsch teaches him Yiddish and tells him of Jewish life in old Prague and of the mysteries of the Kabbalah. Anti-Semitism soon rears its head in the form of a gang of young Irish toughs out to rule the neighborhood. Grades: YA/A.

Levitin, Sonia. *The Cure.*
HarperTrophy, 2000.
Setting: 1348/2407.
Main Character: Male, Gemm 16884 aka Johannes, 16 years old.

    In the year 2407, societal tranquility is maintained by ample servings of serotonin drinks to the genetically engineered population and by careful monitoring to suppress all expressions of individuality or creativity. When the boy Gemm 16884 somehow feels moved to make music, an extinguished art, he is given a choice between being "recycled" (killed) or sent into virtual reality to experience the bad old days as a cure for his deviant desires. Opting for the latter, he finds himself living as Johannes, the 16-year-old son of a Jewish moneylender in 1348 Strasbourg during the Bubonic Plague. Grades: 5 and up.

Levitin, Sonia. *The Return.*
Atheneum, 1987.
Setting: Ethiopia, 1984–1985.
Main Character: Female, Desta, 12 years old.

    Desta and her family are among the persecuted Jews in Ethiopa. They finally flee the country to a refugee camp in Sudan and attempt the dangerous journey to Israel. Grades: 7–12.

Levitin, Sonia. *The Singing Mountain.*
Simon & Schuster, 1998.
Setting: Israel.
Main Character: Male, Mitch Green, 18 years old.

    Mitch, a suburban Californian bound for UCLA in the fall, is on a summer tour of Israel with his temple's youth group when he meets someone from an Orthodox yeshiva and decides to stay on to study to become Orthodox. Mitch's family is certain he has been brainwashed. Mitch's cousin Carlie, an orphan who is being raised by Mitch's parents, corresponds with Mitch. Grades: 7 and up.

Matas, Carol. *Cross by Day, Mezuzzah at Night.*
Jewish Publication Society of America, 2000.
Setting: Spain, 1492.
Main Character: Female, Isabel de Carvallo, 13 years old.

    Queen Isabel has issued an edict expelling all Jews from Spain. Isabel, named after the Catholic queen, thought she was Catholic. On her thirteenth birthday, her father informs her that they are Marranos, secret Jews. Isabel's older brother has fully accepted Christianity and denies his Jewish heritage, turning in his own family as they try to escape. Grades: 6–8.

Matthue, Roth. *Never Mind the Goldbergs.*
Push, 2005.
Setting: New York City.
Main Character: Female, Hava Aaronson, 17 years old.

    Hava, an observant Jew, is unorthodox in many ways. She has spiked hair, loves punk culture, and her colorful, rebellious language includes four-letter words. Her best friends are her confidant Ian, who is gay and not Jewish, and her platonic soulmate Moishe, who makes offbeat films and practices a kind of countercultural Orthodox Judaism. Hava is offered a lead role in a Hollywood sitcom about a carica-tured American modern Orthodox Jewish family. She is thrust into a world of make-believe and pretense, and tries to sort out what is real and what her religion means to her. Grades: 9 and up.

Meyer, Carolyn. *The Drummers of Jericho.*
Gulliver Books, 1995.
Setting: Jericho.
Main Character: Female, Pazit Trujillo, 14 years old.

Pazit is not getting along with her mother, so she leaves Denver and moves to Jericho, where her father and his new family live. Jericho is not used to Jews, and Pazit calls immediate attention to herself when she joins the marching band and objects to their formation of a cross. Her father calls the ACLU, and Pazit is subjected to taunts and threats. Only one boy, Billy Harper, defends her, at great cost to his own standing with his family and the community. Grades: 6–9.

Miklowitz, Gloria D. *The Enemy Has a Face.*
Eerdmans, 2003.
Setting: Los Angeles, California.
Main Character: Female, Netta, 14 years old.

Newly emigrated from Israel to Los Angeles, Netta assumes that Palestinians are behind every bad thing that happens to Israelis. When her 17-year-old brother is missing, she is certain that they have kidnapped him. While trying to find him, Netta gets to know some Palestinian students and discovers that she has more in common with them than she does with Americans and that it is highly unlikely the Palestin-ians had anything to do with Adam's disappearance. Laith al Salaam befriends her and works especially hard to find her brother. A suspenseful page-turner Grades: 9 and up.

Potok, Chaim. *The Chosen.*
Holt, Rinehart and Winston, New York, 2000.
Setting: Brooklyn, 1944–1948.
Main Characters: Male, Reuvan Malther; Male, Danny Saunders; both teenagers.

Two fathers and two sons pursue the religion they share in the way that is best suited to each. Reuvan is a Modern Orthodox Jew and Danny is the son of a Hasidic rebbe. As the boys grow into young men during the closing of World War II, the Zionist Movement, and the statehood of Israel, they discover in each other a lost spiritual brother. Grades: 7 and up.

Pressler, Mirjam. *Shylock's Daughter.*
Pan Macmillan, 2001.
Setting: Venice, 1594.
Main Character: Female, Dalilah, Jessica's servant/friend/sister, 16 years old.

Jessica, the daughter of a Jewish merchant, falls in love with Christian aristocrat Lorenzo in a *Merchant of Venice* story. Grades: 9 and up.

Rosenberg, Liz. **Heart and Soul.**
Harcourt Paperbacks, 1996.
Setting: Richmond, Virginia.
Main Character: Female, Willie Steinberg, 17 years old.
Willie is a promising cellist and composer who has left her arty school in Philadelphia for a long, hot summer in Virginia with her parents. As Willie looks for inspiration to write a symphony, she becomes depressed because her father is away from home frequently and her mother drinks a lot. When Willie reluctantly helps Malachi, a Jewish classmate, she finds her inspiration. Grades: 7 and up.

Sherman, Eileen Bluestone. **The Violin Players.**
Jewish Publication Society of America, 1998.
Setting: Henryville, Missouri.
Main Character: Female, Melissa Jensen, teenager.
Melissa, a nonpracticing Jew, moves from New York to Missouri with her family and encounters strong anti-Semitism. When Daniel, another Jewish student, is attacked, Melissa stands up for him and then wants to learn about her religion. Grades: 7–10.

LAST DAYS/END OF THE WORLD/ APOCALYPSE

Anthony, Piers. **On A Pale Horse.**
Del Rey, 1983.
Series: Incarnations of Immortality: **And Eternity; Bearing an Hourglass; With a Tangled Skein; Wielding a Red Sword; Being a Green Mother; For Love of Evil.**
Setting: 1980s
Main Character: Male, Zane, young man.
When Zane shot Death, he had to assume his place, speeding over the world, riding his pale horse, and ending the lives of others. The Prince of Evil is forging a trap in which Zane must act to destroy Luna, the woman he loved. Awards: CC. Grades: 6–12.

Brin, David. **Postman.**
Spectra, 1997.
Setting: Post-apocalypse United States.
Main Character: Male, Gordon Krantz, adult.
Gordon survived the Doomwar and spent years crossing a post-apocalypse United States looking for something or someone he could believe in again. He becomes a "Restored United States" postal inspector and he becomes the very thing he's been seeking: a symbol of hope and rebirth for a desperate nation. Grades: YA/A.

King, Stephen. **The Stand.**
Signet, 1991.
Setting: 1980s.
Main Character: Many.
After the Superflu kills 90 percent of the world's population, the survivors

follow instructions given to them in dreams to go west. The Good gather in Denver and the Bad in Las Vegas. Awards: CC. Grades: 9–12.

LaHaye, Tim F. and Jerry B. Jenkins **Taken.**
Tyndale House, 2003.
Series: Kids Left Behind: **Pursued** (books 5–8)**; Hidden** (books 9–12)**; Rescued** (books 13–16).
Setting: Present day.
Main Characters: Male, Judd; Female, Vicki; Male, Lionel; Male, Ryan; all teenagers.
Judd, Vicki, Lionel and Ryan think they know it all. None of them believe the gospel of Jesus Christ, and none believe in God. With Judd running away from his parents, Vicki rebelling against her parents' conversion, Lionel lying about being a Christian, and Ryan skeptical about his friends' faith, the four come together to realize that there is more to life and that God was there all the time. **Taken** includes books 1–4 of the original series. Grades: 5–9.

Niven, Larry, and Jerry Pournelle. **Lucifer's Hammer.**
Del Rey, 1985.
Setting: 1970s.
Main Character: Many characters.
A giant comet has slammed into the earth setting off earthquakes a thousand times larger than can be measured on the Richter scale and tidal waves a thousand feet high. Cities become oceans and oceans become steam as a new Ice Age begins. For the men and women who survived, the struggle has just begun. Grades: YA/A.

Shute, Nevil. **On the Beach.**
Ballantine, 1983.
Setting: Australia.
Main Characters: Male, Dwight Towers, adult; Female, Moira Davidson, young woman.
They are the last generation, the innocent victims of an accidental war, living out their last days, making do with what they have, hoping for a miracle. As the deadly rain moves ever closer, the world as we know it winds toward an inevitable end. Grades: YA/A.

Wyndham, John. **The Day of the Triffids.**
Modern Library, 2003.
Setting: London, 1950s.
Main Characters: Male, Bill Masen; Female, Jo Pleyton.
A comet shower blinds most of the world's population. The few survivors with sight struggle to reconstruct society also fight the triffids, the mobile, flesh-eating plants genetically engineered by the Soviets to produce oil. Grades: YA/A.

Yolen, Jane and Bruce Coville. **Armageddon Summer.**
Harcourt, 1999.
Setting: Massachusetts, 2000.
Main Characters: Male, Jed, 16 years old; Female, Marina, 14 years old.
Reverend Raymond Beelson is gathering 144 Believers on Mount Weeupcut to

pray and await Armageddon will be on July 27, 2000. Jed and Marina have come to the compound out of a sense of responsibility toward their families. Jed is on the mountain to watch over his father who "went a little crazy" after his wife left the family. Marina is a Believer, or so she tries to be, in the hope that somehow her faith will restore harmony to her family. Grades: YA.

LATTER DAY SAINTS/MORMONS

Crowe, Chris. *From the Outside Looking In: Short Stories for LDS Teenagers.*
Bookcraft, 1998.
The feelings of isolation of LDS teens are explored through a variety of voices and plots, with humor, sports, relationships, family, and faith. Short stories by Louise Plummer, Ann Edwards Cannon, Lael Littke, Carol Lynch Williams, Donald Smurthwaite, Kristen Randle, Laura Torres, Paul Pitts, Kristen T. Cram, Jack Weyland, Adrian Robert Gostick, A.P. Bowen, Chris Crowe, Mari Jorgensen, and Alma Yates. Grades: YA.

Heuston, Kimberley Burton. *The Shakeress.*
Front Street, 2002.
Setting: Ohio, 1828 to 1835.
Main Character: Female, Naomi Hull, 13 years old.
Naomi, her sister, and two brothers have been orphaned and sent to live with their Aunt Thankful in Portsmouth, New Hampshire. When her aunt tells Naomi that she is sending her to the mill to work, Naomi decides that she and her siblings should leave and join a Shaker community in Ohio. Naomi begins to wonder about life outside the community and finds a position caring for a large family. Naomi meets Joseph Fairbanks, who is from a wealthy family, and they become engaged. She cannot make the commitment as she is constantly searching for a bigger purpose for her life. She becomes interested in the new Mormon faith. Grades: 5–8.

Johnson, Annabel, and Edgar Johnson. *Wilderness Bride.*
Green Mansion, 2003.
Setting: Salt Lake City, Utah, 1840s.
Main Character: Female, Corey, 15 years old.
When her Mormon father goes off to fight in the Mexican War, he arranges a marriage for Corey to Ethan, a man she never met. Corey, who can swing an ax as well as any man, doesn't know what to think of Ethan, who rebels against the Mormon ways. Corey learns to make her own decisions and follow her heart. Grades: YA.

Parker, Katie. *Just the Way You Are.*
Spring Creek, 2005.
Setting: College, present day.
Main Character: Female, LaNae, 18 years old.
LaNae has a big secret . . . her name isn't really LaNae. She wants to begin college with a new identity, shedding her klutzy old self and appearing as an attractive, self-assured woman. She gets herself into one scrape after another, and Prince Charming

still isn't knocking on her door. If the pressures of freshman college courses weren't enough, she is discovering that life and the people around her don't always conform to her perfect model and no one is what she had expected. Grades: YA.

Randle, Kristen D. *Slumming.*
HarperTempest, 2003.
Setting: High school.
Main Characters: Female, Nikki; Male, Sam; Female, Alicia; all 18 years old.

In the last weeks of their senior year, Nikki, Sam, and Alicia, the only Mormon students in their class, launch a plan for each to befriend a fellow student, someone who seems to need a friend, and then ask that person to the prom. Grades: 9 and up.

NEGATIVE PORTRAYALS OF CLERGY/ CHURCH

Bardi, Abby. *Book of Fred.*
Washington Square, 2002.
Setting: Maryland, 1990s.
Main Characters: Female, Mary Fred; Female, Heather; both 15 years old.

Mary Fred was raised in a fundamentalist community until her parents are jailed for allowing two of their sons to die from untreated illness. She goes to live with Alice, a single-parent librarian who lives with her daughter, Heather, and her brother, Roy. Mary Fred is plunged into Heather's world of TV, pizza, high school, and a family that is disorderly and undisciplined. Grades: YA/A.

Beale, Fleur. *I Am Not Esther.*
Hyperion, 2002.
Setting: New Zealand.
Main Character: Female, Kirby, 14 years old.

Kirby comes home from school to find her mom crying and announcing her intention to leave New Zealand almost immediately to work as a nurse in Africa. Kirby is shipped off to live with an uncle she's never met. He and his family are members of a sect called the Fellowship of the Children of the Faith, and their house has no mirrors, no TV, no radio, no newspapers, and virtually nothing to read but the Bible. Kirby cannot understand why no one will talk about another sister, Miriam, who died just four weeks earlier. Grades: 7–10.

Bennett, James. *Faith Wish.*
Holiday House, 2003.
Setting: Chicago, Illinois.
Main Character: Female, Anne-Marie, 17 years old.

Anne-Marie is a beautiful, privileged, sexually experienced suburban Chicago cheerleader, whose encounter with a charismatic traveling evangelist leads to her religious conversion and later to statutory rape. Anne-Marie signs an academic/ behavioral contract to attend summer school and discovers she is pregnant. She borrows her family's BMW to track down Brother Jackson in Indiana and he takes her to a girls' camp in southern Illinois. Grades: 7 and up.

Crew, Linda. *Brides of Eden: A True Story Imagined.*

HarperCollins, 2001.
Setting: Corvallis, Oregon, 1903.
Main Character: Female, Eva Mae, teenager.

Franz Edmund Creffield, a handsome newcomer with "pale and piercing eyes," sets up his own ministry, and Eva Mae and other girls become obsessed with him and his teachings. Creffield's followers are called to throw their finery into a bonfire and don strange-looking smock dresses. He takes them on an island retreat and then has his way with most of them, telling them that one girl will be chosen to be the "mother of the Second Christ." Desperate relatives have the girls declared insane and sent to asylums for rehabilitation; some girls are slowly cured but then relapse into worshipping Creffield, leading to suicides and murder. Based on a true story. Grades: 7 and up.

Haddix, Margaret Peterson. *Leaving Fishers.*
Simon Pulse, 2004.
Setting: Indianapolis, Indiana.
Main Character: Female, Dorry Stevens, 16 years old.

Dorry moves to Indianapolis and is invited by Angela to join her and her friends for lunch. Through her new friends, she learns about The Fishers of Men, a religious group to which they all belong, and meets Pastor Jim, its charismatic leader. The group invites Dorry to parties and eventually to a retreat where she decides to join the church. Angela, her guide and discipler, not only engages Dorry in Bible study and church activities, but also gives her tasks to discipline her and make her a better Fisher. Dorry's parents worry about the ever-increasing control Angela and the cult has over their daughter's life. Grades: 7–9.

Paulsen, Gary. *The Tent: a Parable in One Sitting.*
Laurel Leaf, 1996.
Setting: Texas.
Main Character: Male, Steven, 14 years old.

Steven's mother has taken off, and he and his father Corey live in an old rented trailer and drive a broken-down truck. Then his father commandeers a tent, steals a Gideon Bible from a hotel room, and hits the back roads of Texas in his new occupation as a preacher. Learning the tricks of the trade as they go, Steven and Corey are soon joined by two drifters, whose act of being miraculously healed by Corey helps to draw larger crowds and bigger offerings. Grades: 6–10.

Peck, Richard. *The Last Safe Place on Earth.*
Laurel Leaf, 2005.
Setting: Walden Woods.
Main Character: Male, Todd, 15 years old.

Todd and his family discover that their secure suburban community is no protection against obsessive, destructive ideas when Todd's little sister is brainwashed into hating and fearing Halloween by an extremist religious group. Grades: 5 and up.

Rylant, Cynthia. *A Fine White Dust.*
Aladdin, 1996.
Setting: North Carolina.

Main Character: Male, Pete, 13 years old.

Pete is swept off his feet by an itinerant revival preacher. His hero worship causes conflicts with his loving but non-religious parents and his best friend, Rufus. The fervor of the church meetings fascinates Pete, and he secretly agrees to leave town with the preacher who he believes can do no wrong. Grades: 5–8.

SPIRITUAL SEEKERS/FAITH

Almond, David. *Skellig.*
Dell Yearling, 1998.
Setting: England, twentieth century.
Main Characters: Male, Michael, 10 years old; Female, Mina, 10 years old.

Michael, upset about his baby sister's illness and the chaos of moving into a dilapidated old house, retreats to the garage where he finds Skellig, a mysterious stranger who is something like a bird and something like an angel. He meets Mina, the girl next door, whose precious blackbird chicks and tawny owls are in her secret attic. Awards: CC; Printz Honor; Carnegie. Grades: 5 and up.

Blume, Judy. *Are You There God? It's Me, Margaret.*
Atheneum/Richard Jackson, 2001.
Setting: New Jersey.
Main Character: Female, Margaret Simon, 11 years old.

Margaret has a very private relationship with God, and it's only after she moves to New Jersey and hangs out with a new friend that she discovers that it might be weird to talk to God without a priest or a rabbi to mediate. Grades: YA.

Fraustino, Lisa Rowe. *Soul Searching: Thirteen Stories about Faith & Belief.*
Simon & Schuster, 2002.

Judaism, Christianity, Islam, Hinduism, Buddhism, Confucianism, Taoism, and even Venezuelan voodoo are represented in these thirteen short stories by Linda Oatman High, Dianne Hess, David Lubar, Uma Krishnaswami, John Slayton, Nancy Flynn, Minfong Ho, William Sleator, Jennifer Armstrong, Shonto Begay, Elsa Marston, Lisa Rowe Fraustino, and Dian Curtis Regan. Grades: 6–10.

Hafer, Todd. *In the Chat Room with God.*
RiverOak, 2002.
Sequel: *Stranger in the Chat Room.*
Setting: Internet chat room.
Main Characters: Male, Blake; Female, Jenn; Female, Kris; Female, Lorri; Male, A.C.; all teens.

Five teens, staying up late, go to a chat room searching for friendship and to rant about life, and are suddenly joined by a mysterious Visitor. Grades: 6–9.

Hautman, Pete. *Godless.*
Simon & Schuster, 2004.
Setting: Water tower, present day.
Main Character: Male, Jason Bock, 15 years old.

Jason, an agnostic leaning toward atheism, resists following in the footsteps of his devoutly Catholic father. Jason and his friend Shin combine their talents to create a new religion, "Chutengodianism," which sanctifies water, the source of all life, as manifested by the Ten-Legged God, the water tower. Shin even begins writing a gospel. Jason soon gathers a handful of followers who follow him on a midnight pilgrimage to the top of the water tower for worship. They hacksaw through the padlock for an impromptu baptism. They are almost trapped inside, and while climbing to the top of the tank, one teen slips and sustains severe injuries, crashing onto a catwalk below. Awards: National Book Award. Grades: 7 and up.

Nolan, Han. **Send Me Down a Miracle.**
Harcourt, 2003.
Setting: Alabama.
Main Character: Female, Charity Pitman, 14 years old.

Charity is attracted to Adrienne Dabney, an artist from New York, who moves into the small Alabama town where she, her sister Grace, and their preacher father live. The artist tries a deprivation experiment in her inherited home, despite the minister's objections. Three weeks later, Adrienne emerges to say that she has seen Jesus sitting in a chair in her living room, and soon a religious turmoil splits the town in half. Charity's father insists that the woman is evil incarnate. Charity believes in the chair and its powers so deeply that she defiantly stands up to her stern, stubborn father when he comes to destroy it. Grades: 6–8.

Nolan, Han. **When We Were Saints.**
Harcourt, 2003.
Setting: New York City.
Main Character: Male, Archie, 14 years old.

Archie takes a road trip pilgrimage with his new friend Clare to the Cloisters Museum in New York, to learn more about God. But Clare has decided she will die there. Archie learns that God does not want us to stand idly by while someone else is hurting, and he calls her parents. He also learns that God wants him to return home to help his grandmother. Grades: 7 and up.

Rylant, Cynthia. **God Went to Beauty School.**
HarperTempest, 2003.

A collection of poems pose the question what would happen if God engaged in the everyday activities of humans—for example, if God took a desk job, or bought a couch at Pottery Barn, or found some fudge in his mailbox. Through these events God finds out what it is like to live like the rest of us. Some conservative readers may feel offended. Grades: 6 and up.

Singer, Marilyn, editor. **I Believe in Water: Twelve Brushes With Religion.**
HarperCollins, 2000.

Teens seek answers in a wide range of beliefs in short stories by Virginia Euwer Wolff, Jacqueline Woodson, Gregory Maguire, Jennifer Armstrong, Marilyn Singer, Kyoko Mori, Jess Mowry, M. E. Kerr, Naomi Shihab Nye, Nancy Springer, Margaret Peterson Haddix, and Joyce Carol Thomas. Grades: 7 and up.

Tolan, Stephanie S. *Ordinary Miracles.*
HarperCollins, 1999.
Prequel: *Save Halloween!*
Setting: Present day.
Main Characters: Male, Mark; Male, Matthew; twins.

Until now, being almost indistinguishable from his brother Matthew hasn't really bothered Mark. When their father asks the boys to deliver the sermon at a midweek prayer service, Mark finds that he's not as excited at the prospect as Matthew is, even though both of them have always assumed that they would be preachers when they grew up. After the service, Mark begins to question whether this career path is what he really wants. The arrival in town of a Nobel Prize–winning scientist who works in genetic engineering ultimately leads Mark to question his faith. Grades: 5 and up.

CHAPTER 20

SCHOOLS/TEACHERS

Teens spend much of their time in class or in school-related activities, and for most teens, school is the center of their social life, where they discover how they fit in. They make friends and enemies and find love and rejection among their peers, and we hope, some will find inspiration and role models in their teachers.

Alternative/Boarding Schools
Bullying/Harassment—Boys
Bullying/Harassment—Girls
Peer Pressure/Conformity
Prom
School Violence
Teachers

ALTERNATIVE/BOARDING SCHOOLS

Atkins, Catherine. *Alt Ed.*
Putnam, 2003.
Setting: Wayne High School.
Main Character: Female, Susan Callaway, 15 years old.

Susan is painfully self-conscious and overweight. She suspects her longtime nemesis, Kale Krasner, is behind the harassing phone calls she's been getting. She makes friends with a fellow outcast, gay Brendan Slater, and they vandalize Kale's pickup truck. They enter a new twelve-week, after-school group designed as an alternative to expulsion. The teens begin to talk in frank, argumentative, and sometimes rude discussions, but with the counselor's guidance, they gradually build respect and understanding for each other. Grades: 8 and up.

Bloor, Edward. *Story Time.*
Harcourt, 2004.
Setting: Whitaker Magnet School, present day.
Main Character: Female, Katie, 13 years old.

Katie and her brilliant Uncle George, a sixth-grader, are mysteriously assigned to Whittaker Magnet School, which focuses entirely on excellence in standardized testing. The regimented students are taught by regimented teachers in the basement of a haunted old library building, and the school is run by a strange family obsessed with its own achievements, whether they are earned or not. Grades: 6–9.

Cormier, Robert. *The Chocolate War.*
Bantam Doubleday Dell, 1986.
Sequel: *Beyond the Chocolate War.*
Setting: Boarding school, 1970s.
Main Character: Male, Jerry Renault, high school freshman.
Jerry refuses to join in the school's annual fund-raising drive to sell chocolates. He arouses the wrath of the school bullies and an instructor. Grades: YA.

Green, John. *Looking for Alaska.*
Dutton, 2005.
Setting: Alabama, present day.
Main Character: Male, Miles Halter, 16 years old.
Miles decides to take charge of his life by going to an Alabama boarding school. He's rechristened "Pudge," and adopted by his roommate Chip and Chip's best friend Alaska. Alaska and Chip teach Miles to drink, smoke, and plot elaborate pranks and Miles fall for Alaska. The chapters are headed by the number of days before and after Alaska's suicide accident. Awards: Printz; Teens Top Ten. Grades: 9 and up.

Knowles, John. *A Separate Peace.*
Scribner's, 2003.
Setting: Devon, New England, pre–WWII.
Main Character: Male, Gene; Male, Phineas; 30 years old reflecting back on their junior year.
Gene and Phineas are roommates and friends at Devon, an exclusive New England prep school, in the summer before World War II. Their complex relationship draws out both the best and worst characteristics of each of them and leads to violence, a confession, and the betrayal of trust. Grades: 9 and up.

Kyi, Tanya Lloyd. *My Time as Caz Hazard.*
Orca Book, 2004.
Setting: Present day.
Main Character: Female, Caz Hallard, teenager.
Punching out her so-called boyfriend for sleeping with another girl seemed like a good idea at the time, but Caz is suspended and sent to a special-education class in a new school. Tests indicate that she is dyslexic, which her super-perfect mother refuses to accept. As her parents' marriage falls apart, Caz is drawn into new exploits with Amanda: shoplifting and teasing Dodie Dunstan, a particularly vulnerable classmate. After Dodie commits suicide, Caz finds herself shocked to her senses. Appealing to reluctant readers. Grades: 8 and up.

Lubar, David. *Hidden Talents.*
Starscape, 2003.
Setting: Edgeview Alternative School, present day.
Main Character: Male, Martin Anderson, 13 years old.
When Martin arrives at an alternative school for misfits and problem students,

he falls in with a group of boys with psychic powers and discovers his own hidden talent. Told in mixed documents. Grades: 6–8.

McDonald, Janet. **Brother Hood.**
Farrar, Straus & Giroux, 2004.
Setting: Edessa Hills, New York, present day.
Main Character: Male, Nate Whitely, 16 years old.
 Nate attends an exclusive boarding school on scholarship while trying to remain loyal to his Harlem roots. So far he gets along equally well in both worlds, with only a quick change from school uniform to do-rag and bomber jacket in the men's room at Grand Central Terminal. Grades: 6–9.

Sittenfeld, Curtis. **Prep.**
Random House, 2005.
Setting: Ault School, Boston, Massachusetts, present day.
Main Character: Female, Lee Fiora, 24 years old reflecting on prep school years in her teens.
 Lee is excited to leave her Indiana home for Ault School. She learns that it's easy to observe her self-assured classmates, but harder to make real friends. Lee discovers on her own how she will impact Ault, and how it will impact her in return. Grades: YA/A.

BULLYING/HARASSMENT—BOYS

Anderson, Matthew. **Burger Wuss.**
Candlewick, 2001.
Setting: Fast-food restaurants, present day.
Main Character: Male, Anthony, 16 years old.
 Hoping to lose his loser image, Anthony plans revenge on Turner, a bully who stole his girlfriend, Diana, which results in a war between two competing fast food restaurants, Burger Queen and O'Dermott's. Grades: 8–10.

Bloor, Edward. **Tangerine.**
Scholastic, April 2001.
Setting: Tangerine County, Florida.
Main Character: Male, Paul, 12 years old.
 Paul lives in the shadow of his nasty football hero brother Erik. He fights for the right to play soccer despite his near blindness and slowly begins to remember the incident that damaged his eyesight. Grades: 6–8.

Brooks, Kevin. **Kissing the Rain.**
Scholastic, 2004.
Setting: Present day.
Main Character: Male, Moo Nelson, 15 years old.
 Moo is shy, overweight, and bullied by his classmates. His life spins out of control after he witnesses a car chase and a fight that results in a murder from his favorite bridge hangout. The stream of consciousness prose leads to an ambiguous ending. Grades: 9–12.

Crutcher, Chris. *Whale Talk.*
Laurel Leaf, 2002.
Setting: Central Washington High School, present day.
Main Character: Male, T J Jones, high school senior, 17 years old.

Intellectually and athletically gifted, adopted and multiracial, TJ shuns organized sports and the jocks at his high school. He finally agrees to form a swimming team and recruits some of the school's misfit students. Grades: 8–12.

Flinn, Alex. *Fade to Black.*
HarperTempest, 2005.
Setting: Northern Florida, 1990s
Main Character: Male, Alex Crusan, 16 years old.

Alex, an HIV-positive, Hispanic teen, is brutalized by an attacker wearing a high school letter jacket and all fingers point to Clinton Cole, a narrow-minded jock and jerk. Daria Bickell, a special-ed student with Down syndrome, is the only witness to the crime. Grades: 8 and up.

Heneghan, James. *Hit Squad.*
Orca, 2003.
Setting: Grandview High School, present day.
Main Character: Female, Birgit Neilsen.

Gorgeous and popular Birgit is tired of the long-standing status quo at school. She organizes a group of misfits to combat the bullying and terrorism that exists. They kidnap Birgit's tormenters, cut their hair, and dump paint on their heads. Their good intentions soon result in tragedy and the death of a fellow student. Appealing to reluctant readers. Grades: 7–10.

Koja, Kathe. *Buddha Boy.*
Puffin, 2004.
Setting: Rucher High School, present day.
Main Character: Male, Justin, sophomore, 15 years old.

Justin is an average kid and a classmate to Michael Martin, who is nicknamed Buddha Boy. Michael's Buddhist teacher renamed him Jinsen. Justin mostly wants to pass through high school unnoticed, doing his work and enjoying his friends. Jinsen is unperturbed by the students who torment him and his attitude intrigues and irritates Justin. Justin is also astonished by Jinsen's artistic abilities. Grades: 7–10.

Lekich, John. *The Losers' Club.*
Ludlow, 2005.
Setting: McLuhan High School, present day.
Main Character: Male, Alex Sherwood, teenager.

Alex is challenged in the Festival of Lights by the school bully. If Alex loses, his Losers' Club must disband. Grades: 9–10.

Mazer, Norma Fox. *Out of Control.*
HarperTrophy, 1994.
Setting: High school, 1990s.

Main Characters: Male, Rollo Wingate, 16 years old; Female, Valerie Michon, teen.

Rollo and his two best friends are the Lethal Threesome. Rollo's friends are school leaders with home problems that fuel their anger and mean-spirited pranks, but Rollo is a follower, thoughtlessly caught up in the excitement. Their horseplay turns into bullying and harassment when they corner Valerie in the hallway. Valerie gets little sympathy from a principal whose first concern is damage control but more girls who have suffered harassment come forward. Valerie decides to write a letter describing her trauma to a local paper. Rollo worries about his behavior and tries to open communication with Valerie. Awards: CC; Grades: 7–12.

McKay, Hilary. *Indigo's Star.*
Margaret K. McElderry, 2004.
Prequel: *Saffy's Angel.*
Setting: England, present day.
Main Character: Male, Indigo Casson, 12 years old.

Just recovered from mononucleosis, Indigo is dreading his return to school where his sensitive, peace-loving nature makes him a target for bullies. Tom, a classmate from America, is living with his English grandmother to avoid dealing with his divorced parents. Tom's arrogance deflects some of the gang's mistreatment away from Indigo, while Indigo sees through Tom's mask and reaches out in friendship. Grades: 5–8.

McNeal, Tom, and Laura McNeal. *Crooked.*
Laurel Leaf, 2002.
Setting: Upstate New York, present day.
Main Characters: Female, Clara Wilson, 14 years old; Male, Amos MacKenzie, 14 years old.

After Amos reports his attackers, the Tripps, to the police, they vow revenge on him and his girlfriend, Clara. The Tripps break into Clara's house and corner her in the attic. Grades: 6–10.

Nodelman, Perry. *Behaving Bradley.*
Simon & Schuster, 1999.
Setting: Roblin High School, Winnipeg, Ontario.
Main Character: Male, Bradley Gold, 16 years old.

Brad works to rewrite the school's code of conduct, believing it will make students treat each other with respect. His efforts are met with abuse from power-hungry teachers, apathy from the students, and he gets beat up by the school bullies—two gorilla girls named Mandy and Candy, who want the code to remain as is. When the new Code is finally approved, Brad discovers that having a Code of Conduct and enforcing it are two very different things. Grades: 8–10.

Philbrick, W. Rodman. *Freak the Mighty.*
Scholastic, 1993.
Setting: Eighth grade.
Main Characters: Male, Max; Male, Kevin "Freak"; both 13 year olds.

Max has a learning disability and Kevin Freak has a physical disability. When

Kevin helps Max with his studies and Max protects Freak from the bullies, they make a powerful team. Grades: 6–9.

Plum-Ucci, Carol. *The Body of Christopher Creed.*
Harcourt, 1999.
Setting: Present day.
Main Character: Male, Torey Adams, 16 years old.
    Chris Creed grew up as the bullies' punching bag. When he disappears, it tears the town apart, affecting even the most normal and happy people. Torey was mentioned in an e-mail to the principal written by Chris and as Torey searches for answers to Chris's disappearance, the town begins to suspect he had something to do with Chris's possible murder. Grades: 8–12.

Wilhelm, Doug. *The Revealers.*
Farrar, Straus & Giroux, 2003.
Setting: Parkland Middle School, present day.
Main Characters: Male, Russell; Male, Elliot; Female, Catalina; all 12 year olds.
    Russell, Elliot, and Catalina create an e-mail forum called The Revealer, where students can relate their experiences of bullying by other kids. As a result, the school's atmosphere improves. Appealing to reluctant readers. Grades: 5–7.

BULLYING/HARASSMENT—GIRLS

Anderson, Laurie Halse. *Speak.*
Farrar, Straus & Giroux, 1999.
Setting: High school, 1990s.
Main Character: Female, Melinda Sordino, 14 years old.
    Melinda won't tell anybody why she broke up an end-of-summer party by calling the cops, and now nobody at school will talk to her. She silently observes the lies and hypocrisies of her school, while she lives in fear of the boy who raped her at the party. Through her work in art class and the support of the compassionate art teacher, Melinda begins to reach out to others and eventually finds her voice to stand up against her attacker. Awards: CC. Grades: 7–10.

Friel, Maeve. *Charlie's Story.*
Peachtree, 1997.
Setting: Dublin, Ireland, 1990s.
Main Character: Female, Charlie Collins, 14 years old.
    Charlie was abandoned by her mother at the age of 4 and lived with her somewhat distracted father in Ireland for ten years. Mercilessly bullied by her cruel classmates, Charlie almost gives up on life. Grades: 6–10.

Goobie, Beth. *The Lottery.*
Orca, 2002.
Setting: Saskatoon, Saskatchewan, Canada, present day.
Main Character: Female, Sal, 15 years old.
    Sal is chosen to be shunned at Saskatoon Collegiate by the secret Shadow Council, to exact personal revenge and demonstrate its power. Grades: 9 and up.

Hopkins, Cathy. *Teen Queens and Has-Beens.*
Simon Pulse, 2004.
Setting: High school, present day.
Main Character: Female, Lia, teenager.

After a game of truth or dare, Lia manages to gain the interest of the school heartthrob Jonno, and alienates teen queen Kaylie, who was after Jonno for herself. Kaylie and her friends then start a campaign of bullying against Lia. Rumors are spread, threats are sent, secrets are exposed, and confidence is undermined. Grades: YA.

Juby, Susan. *Alice, I Think.*
HarperCollins, 2004.
Setting: British Columbia, present day.
Main Character: Female, Alice MacLeod, 15 years old.

Alice has been home-schooled since first grade by her hippie parents and has led a very sheltered life. She begins public high school and old enemies emerge; the odd lives of "normal" teenagers baffle her. Alice's observations about her new environment provide lots of laughs, as she navigates life outside her family's protective embrace. Grades: 7–9.

King, Stephen. *Carrie.*
Pocket, 2002.
Setting: Maine.
Main Character: Female, Carrie, 16 years old.

After enduring years of abuse by her fanatical mother and cruel classmates, Carrie attends the high school prom where she is humiliated for the last time. Grades: YA/A.

Koss, Amy Goldman. *The Girls.*
Puffin, 2002.
Setting: Middle school, present day.
Main Character: Female, Maya, 12 years old.

Maya is shocked and devastated when the other members of her clique decide to ostracize her. She has no clue what she might have done wrong, and neither do Brianna, Renée, or Darcy. Candace is the one who decides who's in and who's not, and, suddenly, Maya's not. The point of view jumps from girl to girl in the clique. Grades: 5–8.

Mac, Carrie. *The Beckoners.*
Orca, 2004.
Setting: Present day.
Main Character: Female, Zoe, 15 years old.

Zoe's mother moves her family to a new town where the school is run by a ruthless gang. Zoe is brutally initiated into the Beckoners, and the situation gets worse as she struggles with her conscience over the Beckoners' cruel attacks on the school loser. Violence, sex, rough language, and out-of-control behavior. Grades: 9 and up.

Tullson, Diane. *Edge.*
Fitzhenry & Whiteside, 2005.
Setting: High school, present day.
Main Character: Female, Marlie, freshman, 14 years old.

Marlie's father, estranged from her family, has taken her younger brother and not contacted her mother. Her longtime childhood friend has dropped her for the popular crowd, and is now friends with a girl who torments Marlie whenever she has the opportunity. Marlie joins a group of outcasts who band together for protection from those who tease and belittle them. Grades: 8–10.

Wishinsky, Frieda. *Queen of the Toilet Bowl.*
Orca, 2005.
Setting: High Road High, present day.
Main Characters: Female, Renata; Female, Karin; both teens.

Renata is a Brazilian immigrant and a gifted singer. Karin, an angry classmate, seems determined to bump her from the school musical when Renata earns the role of Maria Von Trapp. Karin accuses Renata of stealing her watch and tries to embarrass her by posting a picture on the Internet of Renata's mother, a cleaning woman, cleaning a toilet. Appealing to reluctant readers. Grades: 7–9.

PEER PRESSURE/CONFORMITY

Brugman, Alyssa. *Walking Naked.*
Random House, 2004.
Setting: Present day.
Main Character: Female, Megan, 15 years old.

Megan started an exclusive clique in her school. After she spends time in detention with Perdita, the school's freak, Megan begins seeing her clique friends in a different way. Grades: 7–9.

Draper, Sharon. *The Battle of Jericho.*
Simon Pulse, 2004.
Setting: Ohio, present day.
Main Character: Male, Jericho, 16 years old.

When an elite club, The Warriors of Distinction, invites Jericho and his cousin Josh to pledge, the teens look forward to wearing the black silk jacket, going to great parties, and receiving the admiring glances of the other students. The initiation process begins tamely with the new pledges helping with the Christmas toy drive, but as it progresses, Jericho becomes increasingly uncomfortable with what they are asked to do. The pledging then goes tragically wrong. Awards: Coretta Scott King. Grades: 7–10.

Flinn, Alex. *Breaking Point.*
HarperCollins, 2002.
Setting: Gate-Bicknell Christian private school.
Main Character: Male, Paul Richmond, 15 years old.

Paul is bullied and tormented at his expensive school; he is there because his mother works in the guidance office and yearns to be accepted. David Blanco is even worse off: his mom is a cafeteria lady and his father is the janitor. The jocks hound him unmercifully, even killing his dog. When Charlie Good asks for help in the computer lab, Paul is eager to comply, and when Charlie comes for him in the night for a game of mailbox baseball, Paul willingly does the bashing. He is accepted as part of Charlie's group for a price; he has to hack into the school computers to change Charlie's D in biology. Then David kills himself, and the school ignores it, and Paul learns that David had been Charlie's ally *last* year. Grades: 8 and up.

Gallo, Don. *On the Fringe.*
Dial, 2001.
 Inspired by the events at Columbine High School, the authors speculate about the misfit teens who could react so powerfully and violently. Authors include: Jack Gantos, Chris Crutcher, Ron Koertge, Graham Salisbury, Nancy Werlin, Francess Lin Lantz, Angela Johnson, M. E. Kerr, Will Weaver, Alden R. Carter, Joan Bauer. Awards: CC. Grades: 7 and up.

Gardner, Graham. *Inventing Elliot.*
Penguin, 2004.
Setting: Holminster High, present day.
Main Character: Male, Elliot, 14 years old.
 Teased by bullies in his old school, Elliot is determined to reinvent himself at his new high school by donning a cool, unflappable exterior. An elite group of bullies called The Guardians target school losers for punishment in cruel and ritualistic ways. The Guardian leaders recruit Elliot using control tactics adopted from their favorite book, George Orwell's *1984*. He passes the initiation test and he is now required to choose a punisher and a victim. Elliot's outward voice alternates with his inner voice written in italics Grades: 7–9.

Giles, Gail. *Shattering Glass.*
Roaring Brook, 2002.
Setting: High school, 2000s.
Main Character: Male, Thaddeus R. "Young" Steward IV, teenager.
 Rob, the charismatic leader of the senior class, turns the school nerd, Simon Glass, into Prince Charming so his classmates will vote Simon "Class Favorite." Simon appears to go along with the new clothes and haircut, but then he has some ideas of his own. Quotes at the opening of each chapter foretell the disaster to come. A fast-paced page-turning thriller. Grades: 7 and up.

Myracle, Lauren. *Rhymes with Witches.*
Harry N. Abrams, 2005.
Setting: Present day.
Main Character: Female, Jane, freshman.
 When plain Jane is asked to be one of her high school's ultra-elite clique, "The Bitches," she can't believe it. She goes through a secret initiation, and all she needs to do is steal something from a classmate each week and leave the object in the office of the early religion teacher, who is the controlling force behind the group. For that

week, the victim loses popularity while the thief gains popularity. When the clique gangs up on an innocent girl, Camilla, and threaten to harm her, Jane's conscience revives. Grades: 9 and up.

Peretti, Frank. *Hangman's Curse.*
Tommy Nelson, 2001.
Series: Verita's Project: *Nightmare Academy.*
Setting: Baker High School.
Main Characters: Male, Elijah; Male, Elisha; twins.
Elijah and Elisha work undercover with their parents to seek the truth about the mysterious deaths and a legendary ghost at Baker High School. A Christian series about a family who aids the FBI. Grades: YA.

Plum-Ucci, Carol. *What Happened to Lani Garver?*
Harcourt, 2004.
Setting: Hackett Island, present day.
Main Characters: Female, Claire McKenzie, 16 years old; Male, Lani Garver, teenager.
Claire fears her leukemia will return and is comforted by her magical and mysterious androgynous friend, Lani. Lani is threatened by his homophobic class-mates. Grades: 9 and up.

Scott, Kieran. *I Was a Non-Blonde Cheerleader.*
Penguin, 2005.
Setting: Florida.
Main Character: Female, Annisa, teenager.
Annisa is the only brunette in her Florida high school full of glamorous blondes. None of the Barbie-doll clones are interested in Annisa, except to put her down about her looks. Her new best friend is a punk rebel, she is falling for a popular girl's boyfriend, and she accidentally breaks the nose of the captain of the cheerleading team. Grade 7–10.

Shusterman, Neal. *The Shadow Club.*
Bantam Doubleday Dell, 1990.
Sequel: *Shadow Club Rising.*
Setting: High school, present day.
Main Characters: Male, Jared; Female, Cheryl; both 14 years old.
A group of competitive junior high school students, all second best in their areas of talent, form The Shadow Club to pull anonymous practical jokes on their rivals. The pranks, which at first are humiliating but harmless, soon spin out of control until classmate Austin is seriously injured. Grades: 8 and up.

Spinelli, Jerry. *Stargirl.*
Knopf, 2000.
Setting: Arizona, 1990s.
Main Characters: Male, Leo Borlock, 16 years old; Female, Stargirl Caraway, 15 years old.
Stargirl wears pioneer dresses and kimonos to school, strums a ukulele in the cafeteria, laughs when there are no jokes, and dances when there is no music. The

whole school is stunned by her, helpless to resist Stargirl's wide-eyed charm, pure-spirited friendliness, and penchant for celebrating the achievements of others. She is even recruited as a cheerleader. Popularity is fickle, but Stargirl seems impervious to the shunning. Leo is in love with Stargirl and is not so strong. Awards: CC. Grades: 5–9.

Tanzman, Carol M. *The Shadow Place.*
Roaring Brook, 2002.
Setting: Internet chat.
Main Character: Female, Lissa, 14 years old.

For years Lissa has sympathized with Rodney, but the teen's compassion for Rodney competes with her desire to fit in with her friends at school, who ostracize him. Now Rodney appears to be becoming violent and only Lissa knows Rodney well enough to observe the dangerous combination of his rage and his growing obsession with weapons. Includes transcripts of computer chats. Grades: 6–9.

Von Ziegesar, Cecily. *Gossip Girl.*
Little, Brown, 2002.
Series: Gossip Girl: *You Know You Love Me; All I Want is Everything; Because I'm Worth It; I Like It Like That; You're the One That I Want; Nobody Does It Better; Nothing Can Keep Us Together; Only in Your Dreams; Would I Lie to You.*
Setting: Spenford School for Girls and St. Albans for Boys, New York City 2000s.
Main Character: Female, Gossip Girl, 17 years old.

Gossip Girl's Web page opens each chapter with her catty backbiting and exaggerated observations about the in-crowd. The girls talk about boys, sex, clothes, and friends while the boys talk about girls, sex, and parties. Fast pace, sex, alcohol, and raw language. Awards: CC. Grades: 9 and up.

PROM

Anderson, Laurie Halse. *Prom.*
Viking, 2005.
Setting: Pennsylvania, 2000s.
Main Character: Female, Ashley, 18 years old.

When the school's prom money is stolen by the new math teacher, Ashley and her best friend, Nat, decide to make this the best prom ever. Grades: 8 and up.

Bradley, Alex. *24 Girls in 7 Days.*
Dutton, 2005.
Setting: 2000s.
Main Character: Male, Jack Grammar, 17 years old.

When the love of his life rejects Jack's invitation to the senior prom, his friends propose he take out a personal ad in the online school newspaper soliciting a date. Jack agrees to go along with the plan but it is hard to avoid the young ladies who descend on him without warning, as Jack tries to speed-date 24 girls in 7 days. Meanwhile, a mysterious online pen pal gives him dating advice. A humorous adventure, and Jack's dates are real characters. Grades: 7–12.

Dokey, Cameron. *How Not to Spend Your Senior Year.*
Simon Pulse, 2003.
Setting: Beacon High School, Seattle, present day.
Main Character: Female, Jo O'Connor, 17 years old.
Jo and her father are in a witness-protection program, and they have moved again. On her first day at Beacon High she's noticed by Alex Crawford, big man on campus, and is swept into a whirlwind of friends and popularity. She's enjoying herself and considering being Alex's prom date, but she discovers that they have to move again and pretend to die because her father is the key witness in an important trial. Jo goes back to her old school in disguise as Claire Calloway while keeping in contact with Alex as "Jo's ghost." Appealing to reluctant readers. Grades: 9 and up.

Marchetta, Melina. *Saving Francesca.*
Knopf, 2004.
Setting: St. Sebastian School, present day.
Main Character: Female, Francesca, 16 years old.
Francesca is at the beginning of her second term in Year Eleven at an all boys' school that has just started accepting girls. She misses her old friends. Her mother has had a breakdown and can barely move from her bed. Grades: 9 and up.

Sloan, Brian. *A Really Nice Prom Mess.*
Simon & Schuster, 2005.
Setting: High school, 2000s.
Main Character: Male, Cameron Hayes, 17 years old.
Cameron, gay, but not out, reluctantly agrees to go on a double date to the prom with Virginia McKinley, a red-headed bombshell beauty. He would rather be going with his football star boyfriend, Shane Wilson. Shane and Jane are the other half of the double date. By the time Cameron picks up Virginia, she has figured out he is gay and tries to drown her dissatisfaction with alcohol; she throws up into the fish tank at Shane's pre-prom party. Cameron gets caught kissing Shane's date, Shane socks him in the stomach, and Cameron runs off with a Russian waiter/drug dealer to a gay bar. Mature subject matter and language. Grades: 9 and up.

SCHOOL VIOLENCE

Adoff, Jaime. *Names Will Never Hurt Me.*
Dutton, 2004.
Setting: Present day.
Main Characters: Male, Ryan; Male, Kurt; Male, Floater; Female, Tisha.
On the one-year anniversary of a shooting death at their school, four students relate their feelings about school, themselves, and events as they unfold to a TV news crew. A page-turner in free verse. Grades: 8–12.

Carbone, Elisa Lynn. *The Pack.*
Viking, 2003.
Setting: Present day.
Main Character: Female, Becky, 15 years old.
Becky is an overweight misfit at high school and her friend Omar is of mixed-

race parentage. A new student, and Hindu boy, Akhil Vyas, has scars on his body, sits on the classroom floor, and simply walks out when something upsets him. As Becky and Omar get to know Akhil, they are exposed to an older student's neo-Nazi ideas and hatred. They discover that he may be planning a dramatic act of violence at school. Akhil's ethic has been molded on that of a wild wolf pack, and there is wolf lore integrated into the plot. A suspense thriller with a twist that will appeal to reluctant readers. Grades: 6–9.

Huser, Glen. *Stitches.*
Groundwood, 2003.
Setting: Western Canada.
Main Character: Male, Travis, seventh–ninth grade.

Travis lives in a trailer park outside a small prairie town with his aunt, uncle, and a pack of rowdy little cousins. His mother, a country-and-western singer, is on the road a lot; his father is long gone. Travis doesn't mind being poor and having strange relatives, but he knows he's different from his junior high classmates in other ways too. He loves to sew and play with puppets and wants to become a professional puppeteer, which makes him a ripe target for the school thugs. When Travis and friends create a puppet production of *A Midsummer Night's Dream,* anger, jealousy, and prejudice erupt in violence. Grades: 7–10.

Koertge, Ronald. 2001. *The Brimstone Journals.*
Candlewick, 2003.
Setting: Branston High School, 2001.

Short poems written like journal entries profile fifteen struggling students. Grades: 9–12.

Moriarty, Jaclyn. *The Year of Secret Assignments.*
Arthur A. Levine, 2004.
Setting: Ashbury School, Brookfield School, Australia.
Main Characters: Female, Cassie; Female, Emily; Female, Lydia; Male, Matthew; Male, Charlie; Male, Seb; all teenagers.

A tenth-grade English teacher attempts to unite feuding schools, Ashbury and Brookfield, by launching a pen pal project. Best friends Cassie, Emily, and Lydia initiate the correspondence, and are answered by Matthew, Charlie, and Seb. Emily and Lydia are more than pleased with their matches, but quiet Cassie has a frightening experience with Matthew. When Lydia and Emily discover that Matthew has threatened their friend, the Ashbury girls close ranks, and declare an all-out war on the Brookfield boys. Soon, the teens are caught up in everything from car-jacking and lock-picking, to undercover spying and identity theft. Grades: 7 and up.

Myers, Walter Dean. *Shooter.*
HarperTempest, 2004.
Setting: Madison High School, Harrison County, 2000s.
Main Characters: Male, Cameron, 17 years old; Female, Carla, teenager; Male, Len, 15 years old.

Len brought his Kalashnikov rifle, his AR–18, and his Ruger pistol to school and shot and killed football jock Brad Williams, and then himself. Interviews with

Cameron and Carla by the Harrison County School Safety Committee, newspaper reports, a police report, Len's handwritten "die-ary" of his deranged thoughts, and a grim medical examiner's report give different perspectives to the story. Grades: 7–12.

Prose, Francine. *After.*
HarperCollins, 2003.
Setting: Central High School, 2000s.
Main Character: Male, Tom Bishop, 15 years old.
    The ripple effect of a school shooting fifty miles away is shaking up Central High School. Fear and paranoia has authorities changing the rules every day. Students who don't follow the rules are disappearing. Grades: YA.

Shepard, Jim. *Project X: A Novel.*
Knopf, 2004.
Setting: New England, 2000s.
Main Characters: Male, Edwin Hanratty; Male, Roddy "Flake"; both 14 years old.
    Edwin and Flake are beaten up and mocked by bullies, disliked by teachers, and at loggerheads with exasperated parents; they live a nightmare of loneliness and anxiety. Together, the two boys feed each other's wounds, sullen disgruntlement and hatch a plot for vengeance against their classmates. Awards: Alex. Grades: A/YA.

Strasser, Todd. *Give a Boy a Gun.*
Simon & Schuster, Children's, 2000.
Setting: Middletown High School, 1990s.
Main Characters: Male, Gary; Male, Brendan; 15 years old.
    Gary and Brendan hold terrified classmates and teachers hostage during a school dance in a high school gymnasium. In interview quotes from the teens involved, classmates, teachers, and family members, we learn what has led the two boys to the fateful moment. Grades: 8 and up.

TEACHERS

Cappo, Nan. *Cheating Lessons.*
Atheneum, 2002.
Setting: Wickham High School, 2000s.
Main Character: Female, Bernadette Terrell, 17 years old.
    An academic "quiz bowl" challenge pulls together a group of teens to beat the private, wealthy, and elite Pinehurst Academy in a qualifying exam through rigorous tutoring by handsome English teacher Mr. Malory. Bernadette isn't so sure that the numbers add up, and with a little sleuthing it becomes apparent that Mr. Malory has "tweaked" the results. Straight-arrow Bernadette is unsure what to do next. The team members all have strong personal reasons why they need that prize money, and the reputation of the whole school could be at stake. Mystery. Grades: 6–10.

Crutcher, Chris. *Ironman.*
Greenwillow, 1995.
Setting: high school, 1990s.

Main Character: Male, Bo Brewster, senior.

Bo is forced to attend anger-management classes after a series of run-ins with his English teacher/ex-football coach. The group's teacher, Mr. Nak, a Japanese American from Texas, draws Bo into participating in the class, allowing him to learn about himself and his war with his father. Bo spends most of his time outside of school training for a grueling triathlon, but his own father provides his arch rival with an expensive bike, hoping Bo will lose and learn a lesson. Bo's point of view is expressed in letters he writes to Larry King. Awards: CC. Grades: 9 and up.

Duncan, Lois. *Daughters of Eve.*
Laurel Leaf, 1990.
Setting: Modesta High School, 1980s.
Main Characters: Female, Laura Snow; Female, Kelly Johnson; Female, Ruthie Grange; Female, Ann; Female, Bambi; Female, Jane Rheardon; Female, Tammy Carncross; high school teenagers.

Irene Stark, a feminist teacher, manipulates a group of girls to take revenge on offending males. The first male in question is a hateful cad who used overweight, insecure, shy Laura for sex and then cruelly dumped her. The girls shave his head in revenge. But their actions start to get violent under Irene's prodding, and at least one undeserving man is attacked. Grades: YA.

Flake, Sharon. *The Skin I'm In.*
Jump at the Sun/Hyperion, 1998.
Setting: Inner city, 1990s.
Main Character: Female, Maleeka, 13 years old.

Miss Saunders, a new, rich, self-assured teacher comes to Maleeka's depressed inner-city school and gets into kids' faces about both their behavior and their academic potential. Black and bright, Maleeka is so swamped by her immediate problems that Miss Saunders' attention nearly capsize her stability. She seeks solace in writing an extended creative piece in the company of a powerful clique of nasty girls. She learns to respond positively to Miss Saunders. Awards: CC; John Steptoe; Notable Books for a Global Society. Grades: 6–10.

Frank, E. R. *Friction.*
Atheneum/Richard Jackson, 2003.
Setting: Forest Alternative School, present day.
Main Character: Female, Alex, 12 years old.

Simon is Alex's teacher, coach, and friend. He has taught his students with attention toward their intellectual, athletic, and emotional growth. Stacy, a new girl, waltzes into this eighth-grade utopia and the balance of the classroom dynamics tips. She starts rumors about Simon's attraction to Alex, and casts a sticky web of sexual discomfort over the class. Everything Alex sees, feels, and knows becomes laden with ulterior meanings. Grades: 9 and up.

Gaines, Ernest J. *A Lesson Before Dying.*
Knopf, 1997.
Setting: Bayonne, Louisiana, 1940s.
Main Characters: Male, Jefferson, teen; Male, Grant Wiggons, teacher, adult.

Jefferson, a mentally slow, barely literate young man, was an innocent bystander to a shoot-out between a white store owner and two black robbers, but he is convicted of the murder. Jefferson's own attorney claims that executing him would be tantamount to killing a hog, and his incensed godmother, Miss Emma, pleads to Grant to gain access to the jailed Jefferson and help him to face his death by electrocution with dignity. African American characters. Grades: YA/A.

Grimes, Nikki. *Bronx Masquerade.*
Dial, 2002.
Setting: Bronx, New York.
Main Character: High school students.
A high school teacher in the Bronx hosts open-mike poetry readings in his classroom on Fridays. His students find a forum to express their identity issues and forge unexpected connections with one another. Awards: CC; Coretta Scott King; Notable Books for a Global Society. Grades: 7–12.

Hilton, James. *Good-Bye, Mr. Chips.*
Little, Brown, 2004.
Setting: Brookfield School, England.
Main Character: Male, Arthur Chipping, "Mr. Chips."
Mr. Chips is a middle-aged bachelor who falls in love with and marries a young woman whom he met on a mountaineering vacation. They live happily at Brookfield School until her death, only a few years later. Mr. Chips devotes the rest of his life to educating many generations of boys. A classic, originally published in 1934. Grades: YA.

Nelson, R. A. *Teach Me.*
Razorbill, 2005.
Setting: Alabama, 2000s.
Main Characters: Female, Carolina, 17 years old; Male, Mr. Mann, teacher, adult.
Carolina and the language arts teacher, Mr. Mann, begin an affair that ends when he marries someone else right before graduation. Devastated, Carolina confides in her friend, Schuyler, who tries to find out who Mr. Mann is and why he acted as he did while Carolina plots revenge. Grades: 9 and up.

Peck, Richard. *The Teacher's Funeral: A Comedy in Three Parts.*
Dial, 2004.
Setting: Indiana, 1904.
Main Character: Male, Russell, 15 years old.
Russell's summer ends with the unexpected death of old Miss Myrt Arbuckle. Russell and his younger brother are thrilled because just maybe the school board will decide to tear down the one-room schoolhouse, since surely it doesn't pay to hire a new teacher for the six students. To his utter horror, his extremely bossy older sister, Tansy, is hired. Tansy takes to teaching with vigor and manages to circumvent all of the high jinks and calamities that threaten to undermine her authority, including an accidental fire in the privy and a puff adder in her desk drawer. Grades: 6 and up.

Quarles, Heather. *A Door Near Here.*
Laurel Leaf, 2000.
Setting: Present day.
Main Character: Female, Katharine, 15 years old.

The mother of the four Donovan kids has taken to her bed with a bottle, only stumbling out of her room in search of more vodka. Katharine tries to keep her brother and sisters clean and fed and in classes, but things are slipping out of her control. When a kindly teacher begins to ask questions, Katharine panics and lashes out with an accusation that could destroy this concerned man, but is met with an act of forgiveness. Awards: CC. Grades: 7 and up.

Sparks, Beatrice. *Treacherous Love: The Diary of an Anonymous Teenager.*
Avon, 2000.
Setting: 1990s.
Main Character: Female, Jennie, 14 years old.

Jennie's father walked out and her mother seeks solace in pills. Her best friend practically abandons her to be with a boyfriend. It seems like Jennie's only best friend is her diary until she meets Mr. Johnstone, the charismatic substitute math teacher. Mr. J. seems to single her out for special attention and Jennie begins to fantasize about him as her boyfriend. When Mr. J. first reveals his feelings for her, she is thrilled by the relationship that grows outside the classroom walls. Jennie's diary becomes a record of the loneliness, pain, and confusion that develops. Grades: YA.

Whitcher, Susan. *The Fool Reversed.*
Farrar, Straus & Giroux, 2000.
Setting: 1990s.
Main Character: Female, Anna, 15 years old.

Anna loses her virginity to Thorn, an English professor/poet. He manipulates her into also sleeping with his boss and he, in turn, sleeps with her best friend, Pauline. Dylan, a teen friend, disapproves of her adult lover but when he is arrested at a party, Anna asks Thorn to help him. When Anna is almost raped by some reckless teens, Dylan rescues her and a romantic future seems likely. Awards: CC. Grades: 10 and up.

CHAPTER 21

SCIENCE FICTION

Any kind of story, such as adventure, romance, or mystery, can be set in a speculative futuristic setting, with new technology or exciting off-world locations, to become a science fiction story. Authors often use alien settings to create commentaries on our own society or relate their sense of hope or doom for the future of mankind, giving us a warning about the path ahead.

Science Fiction Award
Science Fiction Classics
Aliens
Clones/Genetic Engineering
Computers/Internet/Cyberpunk
Dystopia
Robots/Cyborgs
Science Gone Wrong
Space Travel
Time Travel
Resources: Additional Titles

SCIENCE FICTION AWARD

The Science Fiction and Fantasy Writers of America created the Andre Norton Award to recognize outstanding science fiction and fantasy novels that are written for the young adult market. The award is named in honor of Andre Norton, a Grand Master of the Science Fiction and Fantasy Writers of America and author of more than one hundred novels. The award is an annual honor that will first be given in 2006. Any book published as a young adult science fiction/fantasy novel will be eligible, including graphic novels, with no limit on word length. For more information about the Andre Norton Award: www.sfwa.org/News/nortonaward.htm

SCIENCE FICTION CLASSICS

Asimov, Isaac. *Prelude to Foundation.*
Spectra, 1989.
Series: Foundation: *Forward the Foundation; Foundation; Foundation and*

Empire; Second Foundation; Foundation's Edge; Foundation and Earth.
Setting: Trantor (planet), 12,020 G.E.
Main Character: Male, Hari Seldon, adult.

Emperor Cleon I sits uneasily on the Imperial throne of Trantor, the great multidomed capital of the Galactic Empire. Here, forty billion people have created a civilization of unimaginable technological and cultural complexity. Cleon knows there are those who would see him fall whom he would destroy if he could read the future. Hari has come to Trantor to deliver his paper on psychohistory, his remarkable theory of prediction. Hari possesses the prophetic power, the key to the future that makes him the most wanted man in the Empire. Ties in with Asimov's Robot series in *Robots and Empire.* Grades: YA/A.

Bradbury, Ray. *Fahrenheit 451.*
Simon & Schuster, 2003.
Setting: Earth.
Main Character: Male, Guy Montag, adult.

Guy is a book-burning fireman. His wife spends all day with her television "family," imploring Montag to work harder so that they can afford a fourth TV wall. His next-door neighbor is Clarisse, a young girl thrilled by the ideas in books. When Clarisse disappears mysteriously, Montag starts hiding books in his home. His wife turns him in, and he must answer the call to burn his secret cache of books. Montag flees to avoid arrest and winds up joining an outlaw band of scholars who keep the contents of books in their heads, waiting for the time society will once again need the wisdom of literature. Originally published in 1953. Grades: YA/A.

Burgess, Anthony. *A Clockwork Orange.*
Norton, 1986.
Setting: Future dystopian Britain.
Main Character: Male, Alex, 15 years old.

Teenage gangs dominate the future world of violence, high technology, and total government control. Alex's gang leaves him hanging and he is sentenced to fourteen years. He is given the opportunity for early release if he has a procedure done that will make him nonviolent. Originally published in 1963. Grades: YA/A.

Clarke, Arthur C. *2001: a Space Odyssey.*
Roc, 2000.
Sequel: *2010: The Year We Make Contact; 2061; 3001.*
Setting: Outer space, 2001.
Main Characters: Male, Dave Bowman, adult; HAL, a computer.

A monolith is found buried on the moon and scientists are amazed to discover that it's at least three million years old. After it's unearthed the artifact releases a powerful signal aimed at Saturn. To find the target of the signal, a manned spacecraft, the *Discovery*, is sent to investigate. Its crew is highly trained and they are assisted by a self-aware computer, the ultra-capable HAL 9000. HAL is capable of guilt, neurosis, even murder, and he controls every single one of *Discovery*'s components. Originally published in 1968. Grades: YA/A.

Crichton, Michael. *The Andromeda Strain.*
Avon, 2003.
Setting: Arizona, Nevada.
Main Character: Male, Jeremy Stone, adult.

A Nobel-Prize-winning bacteriologist, Jeremy urges the president to approve an extraterrestrial decontamination facility to sterilize returning astronauts, satellites, and spacecraft that might carry unknown biologic agents. The government builds the top-secret Wildfire Lab in the desert of Nevada. Then the U.S. Army initiates the Scoop satellite program to collect space pathogens for use in biological warfare. When Scoop VII crashes a couple years later in the isolated Arizona town of Piedmont, scientists must find an antidote before the bacteria escapes. Originally published in 1969. Grades: YA/A.

Heinlein, Robert A. *Stranger in a Strange Land.*
ACE Charter, 1995.
Setting: Earth.
Main Character: Male, Valentine Michael Smith.

Earthling Valentine was born and educated on Mars. He comes to Earth with superhuman powers and forms his own Church. Originally published in 1961. Grades: YA/A.

Herbert, Frank. *Dune.*
ACE, 1996.
Series: The Dune Chronicles: *Dune Messiah; Children of Dune; God Emperor of Dune; Dune Heretics; Chapterhouse Dune.*
Setting: Arrakis.
Main Character: Male, Paul Atreides.

The desert planet Arrakis is the sole source of Melange, which is necessary for interstellar travel and grants psychic powers and longevity, so whoever controls it wields great influence. The stewardship of Arrakis is transferred by the Emperor from the Harkonnen Noble House to House Atreides. The Harkonnens don't want to give up their privilege, so they cast Paul Atreides out into the planet's harsh environment to die. There he joins the Fremen, a tribe of desert dwellers who become the basis of the army with which he will reclaim what's rightfully his. Paul might be the end product of a very long-term genetic experiment designed to breed a super human; he might be a messiah. Originally published in 1965 Grades: YA/A.

Orwell, George. *1984.*
Plume, 1983.
Setting: London, 1984.
Main Character: Male, Winston Smith, 39 years old.

London, the largest population center of Airstrip One, is part of the vast political entity Oceania, which is eternally at war with one of two other vast entities: Eurasia and Eastasia. At any moment, depending upon current alignments, all existing records show either that Oceania has always been at war with Eurasia and allied with Eastasia, or that it has always been at war with Eastasia and allied with Eurasia. Winston Smith knows this, because his work at the Ministry of Truth involves the constant "correction" of such records. In a grim city and a terrifying country, where Big Brother is always Watching You and the Thought Police can practically read your mind, Winston is a man in grave danger for the simple reason that his memory still functions. Originally published in 1949. Grades: YA/A.

ALIENS

Bradbury, Ray. *The Martian Chronicles.*
Morrow, 1997.
Setting: Mars, 1999.
   Short stories tell of the many expeditions to investigate Mars. The Martians guard their mysteries well, but they are decimated by the diseases that arrive with the rockets. Earth colonists appear, most with ideas no more lofty than starting a hot-dog stand, and with no respect for the culture they've displaced. Grades: YA/A.

Christopher, John. *The White Mountains.*
Simon Pulse, 2003.
Prequel: *When the Tripods Came.*
Sequels: The Tripods: *The City of Gold and Lead; The Pool of Fire.*
Setting: Earth, 2087.
Main Character: Male, Will Parker, 11 years old.
   Will and his friends flee the Tripods who capture mature humans and make them obedient servants by implanting mind-controlling "Caps" directly onto the human skull. Grades: 5 and up.

Clarke, Arthur C. *Childhood's End.*
Del Rey, 1987.
Setting: Earth.
Main Characters: Male, Stormgren; Female, Jan Rodricks, adults.
   The Overlords, great alien masters, take control of the Earth and bring peace and prosperity under the leadership of Karellen. They have plans to prepare the Earth for its new role in the order of the Universe, but humanity as it is now will not be able to handle what is asked of them. Over the next several generations humans can be evolved and prepared to take their next step, marking the end of humanity's childhood. Explores human potential and destiny. Grades: YA/A.

Gilmore, Kate. *The Exchange Student.*
Houghton Mifflin, 1999.
Setting: Earth, 2094.
Main Character: Female, Daria Wells, 16 years old.
   Nine teens from the planet Chela are sent to Earth to live with host families as part of a cultural exchange. Tall Fen, a Chelan, stays with the Wells family. Daria Wells is a registered zookeeper. Both the Terran and Chelan worlds have experienced environmental disasters. Earth is rebuilding after global warming led to massive extinction of animals. Chela has exterminated creatures through hunting and misuse of resources. Grades: 7–10.

Goodman, Alison. *Singing the Dogstar Blues.*
Viking, 2003.
Setting: University in Australia.
Main Characters: Female, Joss Aaronson, 18 years old; Hermaphrodite alien, Mavkel.

Joss, independent, spirited, and sarcastic, has been expelled from several boarding schools and is close to expulsion from a prestigious university program in time-travel studies. An alien from another planet, Mavkel, is Joss's study partner and roommate. A wicked harmonica player, she is intrigued that Mavkel's species communicates by harmonizing through song. His twin has died and he will, too, if he doesn't find someone with whom to join minds. He chooses Joss. To help him, she needs to find out who her father was, so Joss and Mavkel embark on a dangerous, illegal journey back in time. Grades: 8 and up.

Jones, Diana Wynne. *Dogsbody.*
HarperTrophy, 2001.
Setting: Earth.
Main Character: Dog Star Sirius, immortal.

The great Dog Star Sirius, falsely accused of murder, is on trial for his life. He is sentenced to live out his days as a real dog on Earth. If he can locate the lost Zoi, a weapon of mass destruction belonging to the Luminaries that has fallen to earth and retrieve it in his doggie state, he will be returned to his original star form. Grades: 4–9.

Le Guin, Ursula K. *The Left Hand of Darkness.*
Ace, 2000.
Series: Hainish Cycle: *Rocannon's World; Planet of Exile; City of Illusions; The Dispossessed; The Word for World is Forest; The Telling.*
Setting: Gethen (planet).
Main Character: Male, Genly Ai, adult.

Genly Ai is an emissary from the human galaxy to Winter, a lost, stray world. His mission is to bring the planet back into the fold of an evolving galactic civilization, but to do so he must bridge the gulf between his own culture and prejudices and those that he encounters. Awards: CC; Hugo; Nebula. Grades: YA/A.

Logue, Mary. *Dancing With an Alien.*
Sagebrush, 2003.
Setting: Earth.
Main Characters: Female, Tonia, 17 years old; Male, Branko, alien.

Branko, a visitor from another planet whose entire female population was lost to disease, has been sent to Earth to find a female willing to go back with him. He doesn't anticipate falling in love with Tonia, and he must choose between sacrificing his love for her and watching her become a baby factory, or abandoning her to live her life normally on Earth and possibly seeing his race die. Alternates between Tonia's and Branko's perspectives. Grades: 8–10.

Shusterman, Neal. *Dark Side of Nowhere.*
Starscape, 2002.
Setting: Earth.

Main Character: Male, Jason, 14 years old.

Jason is bored with life in his small town. The school janitor, Grant, presents him with an odd metallic glove that can fire BBs through its fingers. It is actually a training glove for a far more lethal weapon. Jason slowly realizes that he is part of a colony of aliens who maintain human form through DNA obtained from people killed during their failed invasion. Now Grant has reestablished contact with their lost world. The aliens go off to plan another invasion, leaving Grant to assist the young people as they revert to their alien forms and to train them as fighters. But Jason has decided to remain human. Grades: 6–9.

Sleator, William. **Interstellar Pig.**
Dutton, 1984.
Sequel: **Parasite Pig.**
Setting: Seaside.
Main Character: Male, Barney, 16 years old.

Barney's boring seaside vacation suddenly becomes more interesting when he meets the three exotic neighbors who are addicted to a game they call "Interstellar Pig." In the game, rival aliens wage war over an item that allowed their planet to survive and all other planets to die. Barney slowly realizes they are looking for something just like their characters in the game and losing could mean the end of mankind. Tense plot and inventive characters. Awards: CC. Grades: 7–12.

CLONES/GENETIC ENGINEERING

Adlington, L.J. **The Diary of Pelly D.**
Greenwillow, 2005.
Setting: Future colony, off world.
Main Characters: Male, Toni V, 14 years old; Female, Pelly D, 15 years old.

Tony V is part of a crew of drillers excavating the ruins of City 5. While working, he finds a diary hidden in the plaza and begins to read it during his free time. It belongs to a girl named Pelly D, who is pretty, popular, and wealthy. Then everyone is required to be tested for gene ancestry, and she turns out to be Galrezi, one of the undesirable genetic strains that society has turned against. Grades: 7–10.

Bear, Greg. **Darwin's Radio.**
Ballantine, 2000.
Sequel: **Darwin's Children.**
Setting: Centers for Disease Control, 1990s.
Main Characters: Male, Mitch Rafelson; Female, Kaye Lang; Male, Christopher Dicken.

Anthropologist Mitch Rafelson has discovered the mummified remains of a Neanderthal couple and their strangely abnormal newborn child. Kaye Lang, a molecular biologist, has unearthed evidence that junk DNA may have a purpose in the scheme of life. Christopher Dicken, a virus hunter at the National Centers for Infectious Diseases in Atlanta, is in pursuit of Herod's flu, which seems to strike only expectant mothers and their fetuses. The three scientists pool their research and it becomes clear that mankind is about to face a crisis. Awards: Nebula. Grades: YA/A.

Butler, Octavia E. *Wild Seed.*
Aspect, 1999.
Series: Patternist: *Mind of My Mind; Patternmaster.*
Setting: Africa, Colonial America, 1690.
Main Characters: Male, Doro, immortal; Male/Female, Anyanwu.

Doro is an energy being who transfers from one host body to another, killing his hosts in the process. He is afraid of no one until he meets Anyanwu, a shape-shifter who can assume forms of any species, and of either gender. Controversial issues as slavery, race, reproduction, and gender are addressed. Grades: YA/A.

Card, Orson Scott. *Ender's Game.*
Tor, 1992.
Series: Ender Wiggin Saga: *Speaker for the Dead; Xenocide; Children of the Mind; Ender's Shadow; Shadow of the Hegemon; Shadow Puppets.*
Setting: Earth.
Main Characters: Male, Andrew "Ender" Wiggin, 6 years old.

The government breeds child geniuses and trains them as soldiers to build a defense against an alien attack. Ender lives with his parents, his sadistic brother Peter, and the person he loves more than anyone else, his sister Valentine. Peter and Valentine were candidates for the soldier-training program but didn't make the cut. Ender is drafted to the orbiting Battle School for rigorous military training. Awards: CC; Hugo; Nebula. Grades: YA/A.

Crichton, Michael. *Jurassic Park.*
Ballantine, 1991.
Setting: Island near Costa Rica.
Main Characters: Male, Dr. Alan Grant, adult; Female, Ellie Sattler, adult.

Bioengineers clone fifteen species of dinosaurs and establish an island preserve where tourists can view them. A rival genetics firm attempts to steal frozen dinosaur embryos and causes the safety nets devised by the engineers to fail, endangering the first guests in the park. Made into a popular movie. Grades: YA.

Dickinson, Peter. *Eva.*
Laurel Leaf, 1990.
Setting: Dystopian urban world.
Main Character: Female, Eva, 14 years old.

Following a terrible car crash, Eva awakens from a strange dream in a hospital bed. Doctors have pulled her functioning brain from her crushed body and put it into the able body of a chimpanzee. With the aid of a voice synthesizer, she communicates with others and soon adjusts to her new body, because her father is a scientist who has always worked among the chimps. Eva takes on the issue of animal rights, setting up an elaborate scheme to release chimps back into the last of the wild. Grades: 7–10.

Farmer, Nancy. *House of the Scorpion.*
Simon Pulse, 2004.
Setting: Future Mexico.
Main Character: Male, Matteo "Matt" Alacran, 14 years old.

Matt, born to a poor family in a small village in Mexico, is a clone of 142-year-old El Patron, a powerful drug lord. El Patron is ruler of Opium, a country that lies between the United States and Aztlan, formerly Mexico. Its vast poppy fields are tended by eejits, human beings programmed by a computer chip implanted in their brains. Matt becomes aware of what being a clone of one of the most powerful and feared men on earth entails. Awards: Printz; Newbery; National Book Award. Grades: 6–9.

Goobie, Beth. *Flux.*
Orca, 2004.
Sequel: *Fixed.*
Setting: Future dystopia.
Main Character: Female, Nellie, 12 years old.

Nellie is an orphan living in a shack in the Outbacks of a dystopian world. She makes forays into the city for food, and is captured by the Skulls, a predatory male gang. They shave her head, revealing the wormlike scars, reminders of the experiments the Interior has performed on kidnapped Outbacks children. Nellie worships the Goddess Ivana to whom she attributes the phenomenon of flux, which causes her surroundings to shape-shift. Nellie travels between levels of reality by stepping through hidden gates on a quest for the truth about her mother. Traveling between levels creates clonelike, unstable human duplicates. Grades: 6–9.

Haddix, Margaret Peterson. *Double Identity.*
Simon & Schuster, 2005.
Setting: Sanderfield, Illinois.
Main Character: Female, Bethany, 12 years old.

One October evening, Bethany's parents drive her to another state to stay with an aunt she never knew existed. Bethany learns she is the clone of her sister, who was killed twenty years earlier in a tragic automobile accident, and she is being hunted by a man who wants to expose her secret existence for his own benefit. Suspenseful, a quick, engaging read is a good choice for reluctant readers. Grades: 5–8.

Halam, Ann. *Dr. Franklin's Island.*
Laurel Leaf, 2003.
Setting: Tropical island, 2000s.
Main Character: Female, Semirah Garson, 14 years old.

Semirah is among a group of fifty British teen winners of a science contest who are on their way to work with conservationists in Ecuador. A plane crash strands Semirah and two other survivors on a remote island. They finally find the island's inhabitants: the mad scientist Dr. Franklin and his terrified employees. Dr. Franklin can hardly wait to start performing his trans-species genetic-engineering experiments on human subjects, and Miranda and Semirah are to be his first candidates. Grades: 9 and up.

Halam, Ann. *Siberia: a Novel.*
Wendy Lamb, 2005.
Setting: Siberia.
Main Character: Female, Rosita, aka Sloe, 13 years old.

Rosita and her mother live in a camp as political prisoners. Rosita's mother makes nails and secretly at night she creates and harvests animal life with a Lindquist kit. When Rosita excels at school, she is sent away to New Dawn School. She is tricked into betraying her mother and sending her to die, and becomes "Sloe," helping to run a stolen-goods ring in the school. When Sloe is expelled, she returns home to steal the Lindquist kit. Grades: 7 and up.

Halam, Ann. *Taylor Five.*
Wendy Lamb, 2004.
Setting: Borneo.
Main Character: Female, Taylor, 14 years old.
    Taylor is a clone produced by the same company that funds the orangutan reserve where she lives. The reserve is attacked and Taylor escapes with Uncle, a super intelligent orangutan. Fast-moving. Grades: 5–8.

Lasky, Kathryn. *Star Split.*
Hyperion, 2001.
Setting: 3038.
Main Character: Female, Darci Murlowe, 13 years old.
    Darci is a Genhant, or Genetically Enhanced Human, implanted with a 48th chromosome. Darci is fascinated by "Originals," people whose ancestors could not afford to get extra genetic material. Darci runs into a clone of herself, living evidence that her parents must have committed the capital crime of "duplication." Grades: 5–9.

Levitin, Sonia. *Goodness Gene.*
Dutton, 2005.
Setting: Future.
Main Characters: Male twins, Will and Berk, 16 years old.
    Will and Berk believe that they are the sons of Hayli, the Compassionate Director of the Dominion of the Americas. As the founder of The Goodness, a movement to save humanity following nuclear disaster, plague, and environmental collapse, Hayli rules a world in which babies are born in labs, food is manufactured, and the fortunate live under atmosphere-controlling domes and exchange their ration of pleasure stamps to experience everything from travel to sex in carefully controlled situations. Outside the dome there is a growing resistance movement. Grades: 7 and up.

Skurzynski, Gloria. *Virtual War.*
Simon Pulse, 2003.
Series: The Virtual War Chronologs: *The Clones; The Revolt.*
Setting: Domed City, 2080.
Main Character: Male, Corgan, 14 years old.
    Corgan was genetically engineered to be the fastest player on any electronic playing field and he is preparing for the big war: a bloodless, electronic battle against other worlds. On the eve of the battle Corgan decides to break the rules for the first time, questioning if the Council members really know what's best for the Earth. Grades: 5–9.

Sleator, William. **Duplicate.**
Puffin, 1999.
Setting: High school.
Main Character: Male, David, 16 years old.

David needs to be in two places at one time: a family party for his grandmother and a date with Angela. He finds what seems to be the perfect answer to this dilemma, a machine that duplicates organic material. Without considering the possible ramifications, he duplicates himself. Competition between the duplicates is fierce, particularly regarding Angela. The duplicate duplicates himself, and then there are three. Each claims to be the original, and each would like to solve his problems by getting rid of the others. Grades: 6–9.

Werlin, Nancy. **Double Helix.**
Dial, 2004.
Setting: Wyatt Transgenics Lab.
Main Character: Male, Eli Samuels, 18 years old.

Eli, whose mother is losing her long battle with Huntington's disease, is hired at the Wyatt Transgenics Lab. Eli's father is dead set against the job because of a secret he harbors concerning the lab's owner, Dr. Quincy Wyatt, and Eli's mother. Shortly after starting work, Eli meets Kayla Matheson, a beautiful girl who eerily reminds him of a photo of his mother when she was young. Slowly, Eli uncovers the shocking truth about Dr. Wyatt's genetic-engineering experiments and their connection to his parents, Kayla, and himself. Grades: 8 and up.

Westerfeld, Scott. **Uglies.**
Simon Pulse, 2005.
Series: Uglies Trilogy: **Pretties; Specials.**
Setting: Future dystopia.
Main Character: Female, Tally Youngblood, 15–16 years old.

Tally believes that she is ugly until age 16 when she'll undergo an operation that will change her into a pleasure-seeking "pretty." Anticipating this happy transformation, Tally meets Shay, another female ugly, who shares her enjoyment of hoverboarding and risky pranks. Shay urges Tally to defect with her to the Smoke, a distant settlement of simple-living conscientious objectors. Grades: 6 and up.

COMPUTERS/INTERNET/CYBERPUNK

Anderson, M. T. **Feed.**
Candlewick, 2002.
Setting: Future United States.
Main Character: Male, Titus; Female, Violet.

Television and computers are connected directly into the brains of babies, and everyone is an avid and empty-headed consumer. Kids are driven by fashion and shopping and the avid pursuit of silly entertainment; there are constant customized murmurs in their brains of encouragement to buy, buy, buy. Awards: National Book Award. Grades: 9 and up.

Fredericks, Mariah. *Head Games.*
Atheneum, 2004.
Setting: Internet, New York City, present day.
Main Character: Female, Judith, 15 years old.

Judith feels safe role playing as a male online, especially since she was attacked last year walking home. After Irgan, her Internet enemy, forfeits the right to kill her off, Judith drops out of the Game and becomes determined to learn his identity. She discovers the player is Jonathan and he lives in her building. They become close and Jonathan helps Judith overcome her fears through a real-life game. Grades: 7–12.

Gibson, William. *Neuromancer.*
Ace, 1995.
Setting: Future.
Main Character: Male, Case, adult.

Case was the hottest computer cowboy cruising the information superhighway, rustling encoded secrets for anyone with the money to buy his skills. He double-crossed the wrong people, who burned the talent out of his brain, micron by micron. Banished from cyberspace, Case courted death in the high-tech underworld. A shadowy conspiracy offered him a second chance for a price. Awards: Hugo, Nebula. Grades: YA/A.

Noon, Jeff. *Vurt.*
St. Martin's Griffin, 1996.
Sequels: *Pollen; Nymphomation.*
Setting: Manchester, England, twenty-first century.
Main Characters: Male, Scribble; Female, Desdemona, adults.

Vurt is a virtual reality drug. Scribble and his sister Desdemona are addicted. Desdemona gets lost in the Curious Yellow, the ultimate Metavurt, and Scribble tries to rescue her. Grades: YA/A.

Stephenson, Neal. *Snow Crash.*
Spectra, 2000.
Setting: Los Angeles, California/Metaverse.
Main Character: Male, Hiro Protagonist, adult.

Hiro is a hacker, samurai swordsman, and pizza-delivery driver. When his best friend fries his brain on a new designer drug called Snow Crash and his beautiful, brainy ex-girlfriend asks for his help, Hiro rushes to the rescue. Fast-paced. Grades: YA/A.

Womack, Jack. *Random Acts of Senseless Violence.*
Grove, 1995.
Series: Ambient: *Ambient; Terraplane; Heathern; Elvissey; Going, Going, Gone.*
Setting: New York City, twenty-first century.
Main Character: Female, Lola Hart, 12 years old.

Open warfare rages in Brooklyn, smoke from an unspecified toxic disaster fills the sky above Long Island, troops patrol Harlem streets, tuberculosis is rampant, inflation is zooming, and youth gangs rampage through the streets. Nationally, presidents are murdered within months of taking office, and riots are wrecking most of the major cities. This is the world Lola records in the diary she received on her twelfth birthday. Grades: YA/A.

DYSTOPIA

Atwood, Margaret. ***The Handmaid's Tale.***
Anchor, 1998.
Setting: Republic of Gilead.
Main Character: Female, Offred, young woman.

    Offred, a Handmaid, tells how the the Republic of Gilead, formerly the United States, came to be. Far-right ideals have been carried to extremes in the mono-theocratic government. Women are strictly controlled, unable to have jobs or money and assigned to various classes: the chaste, childless Wives; the housekeeping Marthas; and the reproductive Handmaids, who turn their offspring over to the "morally fit" Wives. Grades: YA/A.

Barry, Maxx. ***Jennifer Government.***
Vintage, 2004.
Setting: Australia.
Main Characters: Female, Jennifer Government; Male, Hack Nike; adults.

    American corporations rule the world. Everyone takes his employer's name as a last name and once autonomous nations belong to the United States, and the National Rifle Association is a hot, publicly traded stock. Hack Nike, an employee seeking advancement, signs a multipage contract and then reads it. He's agreed to assassinate kids purchasing Nike's new line of athletic shoes to increase sales. The dreaded government agent Jennifer Government is after him. Grades: YA/A.

Colfer, Eoin. ***Supernaturalist.***
Hyperion. 2004.
Setting: Satellite City.
Main Character: Male, Cosmo Hill, 14 years old.

    Satellite City is in business to make money and orphanages are not exempt. At the Clarissa Frayne Institute for Parentally Challenged Boys, kids are forced to endure product testing and face an average life expectancy of 15. Cosmo knows he's on borrowed time and tries to escape. As he lies dying, a small, hairless blue creature lands on his chest and begins to feed. He is rescued by the Supernaturalists, a motley crew of young people who have dedicated their lives to destroying the Parasites, which appear to feed on the essence of the living. Cosmo joins the group as a Spotter, someone who can actually see the creatures to destroy them. Grades: 9–12.

Huxley, Aldous. ***Brave New World.***
HarperPerennial, 1998.
Setting: twenty-eighth century.
Main Characters: Male, Bernard Marx; Female, Lenina Crowne.

    In the future, humans are conceived and conditioned in hatcheries to fit into one of five castes. Grades: 8 and up.

Lowry, Lois. *The Giver.*
Bantam, 1999.
Sequels: *Gathering Blue; Messenger.*
Setting: Future dystopia.
Main Character: Male, Jonas, 12 years old.

Jonas is given his lifetime assignment at the Ceremony of Twelve. He becomes the Receiver of memories and learns the truth of the society in which he lives where there is no color, pain, or past. Awards: Newbery. Grades: 6–9.

Philbrick, Rodman. *The Last Book in the Universe.*
Blue Sky, 2002.
Setting: Future Earth.
Main Character: Male, Spaz, 14 years old.

Epilepsy prevents Spaz from using the mind probes most people use to blot out reality. He sets out on a quest to save his ill foster sister, crossing forbidden territory and facing frightening gangs. Companions join him: Ryter, a philosophic old man, whose treasure is the book he is writing; Littleface, a young almost speechless child; and Linnea, a genetically improved person. By saving his sister, Spaz learns about himself and his parentage. Grades: 5–8.

Reed, Kit. *Thinner Than Thou.*
Tor, 2004.
Setting: Sylphania Heath Spa.
Main Characters: Male, Reverend Earl, adult; Female, Annie Abercrombie, teenager.

From coast to coast, Reverend Earl's luxury spa, Sylphania, is all the rage where the overweight come for personally supervised weight-loss programs and plenty of preaching on the heavenly state of the Afterfat. Annie, anorexic, is sent to one of the convents where the "proper" ways to eat and think are taught. Awards: Alex. Grades: YA/A.

Shakar, Alex. *The Savage Girl.*
HarperPerennial, 2002.
Setting: Middle City.
Main Character: Female, Ursula Van Urden, 20s.

Ursula comes to MidCity to visit her recently institutionalized sister Ivy, a 21-year-old schizophrenic model who attempted suicide in public. She gets a job with powerful trend-spotting firm, and spends her days in-line skating around town, taking notes on street fashion, trying to see the future trends. She spots a homeless "savage girl" wearing skins and hunting her own food, and Ursula envisions this look sparking a return to nature and becomes the spokesmodel for the savage look. Grades: YA/A.

Stahler, David. *TrueSight.*
Eos, 2004.
Setting: Harmony Station.
Main Character: Male, Jacob, 13 years old.

Harmony Station was established on a distant planet by an association of blind people who have had themselves genetically altered so that their offspring will be blind, too. Jacob is approaching his 13th birthday when he realizes that he can see. Sentenced to surgical blinding after his secret comes out, Jacob flees into an uncertain future. Grades: 5–7.

Weyn, Suzanne. *The Bar Code Tattoo.*
Scholastic, 2004.
Setting: 2025.
Main Character: Female, Kayla, 17 years old.

The thing to do on your 17th birthday is to get a bar code tattoo, which is used for everything from driver's licenses to shopping. Kayla, almost 17, resists because she hates the idea of being labeled. The tattoos begin to drive people to commit suicide, Kayla's father among them, and she soon finds out that the markings contain detailed information, including genetic code. Kayla joins a teen resistance movement and falls for a gorgeous guy, who's a double agent. She discovers she has some psychic ability and has confusing visions of future events. She joins other resisters hiding in the Adirondack Mountains and learns to harness her psychic powers to fight Global–1 and fulfill her visions. Grades: 6 and up.

ROBOTS/CYBORGS

Asimov, Isaac. *I, Robot.*
Spectra, 2004.
Series: Robot: *Caves of Steel; The Naked Sun; The Rest of the Robots; The Robots of Dawn; Robots and Empire.*

Nine short stories of the development of robots based on the Three Laws of Robotics: (1) A robot may not injure a human being or through inaction allow a human being to come to harm. (2) A robot must obey orders given it by human beings except where such orders would conflict with the First Law. (3) A robot must protect its own existence as long as such protection does not conflict with the First or Second Law. Ties in with Asimov's Foundation series. Grades: YA/A.

Bechard, Margaret. *Spacer and Rat.*
Roaring Brook, 2005.
Setting: Freedom Station.
Main Character: Male, Jack, teenager.

Jack and the other Spacers on Freedom Station call the Earthie children abandoned by their parents "rats." Then Jack meets Kit, a rat, and her sentient Bot, Waldo. Jack is drawn into helping them evade the various forces wanting possession of Waldo. Grades: 7–10.

Dick, Philip K. *Do Androids Dream of Electric Sheep?*
Del Rey, 1996.
Setting: 2021.
Main Character: Male, Rick Deckard, adult.

The World War killed millions, driving entire species into extinction and sending mankind off the planet. Those who remained coveted any living creature, and for people who couldn't afford one, companies built incredibly realistic simulacrae: horses, birds, cats, sheep, even humans. Émigrés to Mars received androids so sophisticated it was impossible to tell them from true men or women. The government banned them from Earth, but when androids don't want to be identified, they just blend in. Rick is a bounty hunter whose job is to find androids and retire them. The Blade Runner movie is based on this book Grades: YA/A.

Hoover, Helen. *Orvis.*
Sagebrush, 2003.
Setting: Future Earth.
Main Character: Female, Toby, 12 years old.

Toby and her precocious friend Thaddeus attend school on a future Earth that is sparsely inhabited and largely reverting to wilderness, while the families that have dumped them there pursue their own interests in the space colonies. Toby becomes involved with an obsolete robot, Orvis, destined for the junkyard. When lost with Thaddeus in a wilderness area filled with dangerous animals and human renegades, Orvis is their only hope of survival. Grades: 5–8.

SCIENCE GONE WRONG

Haddix, Margaret Peterson. *Turnabout.*
Aladdin, 2002.
Setting: 2000/2085.
Main Character: Female, Amelia (Melly) Hazelwood, 100 years old in 2000, 15 years old in 2085.

At age 100, Melly and other Riverside nursing home residents were injected with the experimental drug PT–1. The drug was supposed to make them "unage" until they reached a self-determined ideal age, at which point they would get another shot to stop the process. The second shot, however, proved deadly, and the participants of Project Turnabout were doomed to unage until they reached zero. Now teenagers, Melly and her stubborn sidekick Anny Beth need to find parents who can care for them in their approaching infancy. A snooping reporter begins to track Melly, and Melly and Anny Beth must put their search on hold and flee. Grades: 7 and up.

Keyes, Daniel. *Flowers for Algernon.*
Harvest, 2004.
Setting: New York City.
Main Character: Male, Charlie Gordon, adult.

Charlie has an IQ of 68 and can't even beat the laboratory mouse Algernon at solving mazes. Algernon is extra-clever thanks to an experimental brain operation so far tried only on animals. Charlie eagerly volunteers as the first human subject. The effects begin to show and Charlie's reports steadily improve; he records his own progress.. The IQ rise continues, taking him steadily past the human average to genius level and beyond, until he's as intellectually alone as the old Charlie ever was and painfully aware of it. Then Algernon begins to deteriorate. Awards: Hugo; Nebula. Grades: YA/A.

Reeve, Philip. *Mortal Engines.*
HarperCollins, 2003.

Series: The Hungry City Chronicles: *Predator's Gold.*
Setting: London, England.
Main Characters: Male, Tom Natsworthy, 15 years old; Female, Hester Shaw, teen; Male, Thaddeus Valentine, teen; Female, Katherine Valentine, teen.

The Traction City of London is chasing a small town. When it takes over, it processes all reusable materials to create power to run the motorized wheels that enable the city to travel over the land. London's mayor has plans involving the use of the weapon that laid waste to Earth millennia earlier. Tom and his friends endeavor to stop the carnage. Grades: 7–10.

Sleator, William. *House of Stairs.*
Puffin, 1991.
Setting: Labyrinth.
Main Character: Five teens, 16 years old.

As subjects for a psychological experiment on conditioned human response, one by one, five 16-year-old orphans are brought to a strange building with nothing but endless flights of white stairs leading nowhere except back to a strange red machine. The five must learn to love the machine and let it rule their lives for any chance of survival. Grades: YA.

SPACE TRAVEL

Adams, Douglas. *Hitchhiker's Guide to the Galaxy.*
Del Rey, 1995.
Sequels: *Restaurant at the End of the Universe; Life, the Universe and Everything; So Long and Thanks for All the Fish; Mostly Harmless.*
Setting: Outer space.
Main Characters: Male, Arthur Dent, 30 years old; Male, Ford Prefect, alien.

Arthur is rescued by Ford Prefect from Earth moments before a cosmic construction team obliterates the planet to build a freeway. Arthur and Ford travel the galaxy getting into horrible situations and meeting strange characters like the two-headed Zaphod. Grades: YA/A.

Barker, Clive. *Abarat.*
Joanna Cotler, 2002.
Sequels: *Days of Magic; Nights of War.*
Setting: Chickentown, Minnesota/Abarat Islands, 2000s
Main Characters: Female, Candy Quackenbush, 16 years old; Male, John Mischief; Male, Christopher Carrion; Male Rojo Pixler.

Candy hates her life as the daughter of an alcoholic father and a depressed mother. One day, humiliated by her teacher, Candy skips out of school and heads for the prairie, where she stumbles on a derelict lighthouse and a creature with eight heads, John Mischief. Candy begins an adventure to a mysterious archipelago called Abarat, a group of twenty-five islands, each representing a different hour of the day. Grades: 5 and up.

Gerrold, David. *Jumping Off the Planet.*
Tor, 2001.

Series: Starsiders Trilogy: *Bouncing Off the Moon; Leaping To the Stars.*
Setting: Outer space.
Main Character: Male, Charles "Chigger" Dingillian, 13 years old.

Chigger, the middle child, is the human battleground for his divorced parents: a wimpy musician father who kidnaps his boys to give them a chance at a better life off Earth and a newly lesbian mother who chases them into space. Chigger bridges the gap separating his older brother, Weird, and his younger brother, Stinky, as they ride the Beanstalk, a dizzying orbital elevator system running on magnetic induction that lifts humanity from Earth, which it is devouring, to the Moon, the planets and, even the stars. Grades: YA.

Rucker, Rudy. *Frek and the Elixir.*
Tor, 2005.
Setting: The Anvil spaceship, 3003.
Main Character: Male, Frek Huggins, 12 years old.

Frek's pretty much an ordinary kid on an Earth with a collapsed biosphere controlled by NuBioCom. He receives a message that the Anvil, an alien's ship, is coming for him and under his bed. Frek finds a cuttlefish that tells him he's going to save the world. The agents find it, too, and chemically interrogate Frek, ruining his short-term memory. Frek and Wow, his dog, run away and Frek is taken away on the Anvil, traveling the galaxy with the alien, who wants exclusive rights to humanity's "branecast." Awards: VOYA Perfect Ten. Grades: YA/A.

TIME TRAVEL

Browne, N.M. *Warriors of Alavna.*
Bloomsbury USA, 2003.
Sequel: *Warriors of Camlann.*
Setting: Britain.
Main Characters: Male, Dan; Female, Ursula; both 15 years old.

While walking through a yellow mist at the battlefield at Hastings, Dana and Ursula are transported to a world that resembles Roman Britain during 75 A.D. The Combrogi tribesmen are fighting the invading Ravens for their land and their lives, and Combrogi Princess Rhonwen has used magic to summon the teens to help her brother battle the enemy. Grades: 7 and up.

Cooney, Carolyn B. *Both Sides of Time.*
Laurel Leaf, 1997.
Sequels: *Out of Time; Prisoner of Time; For All Time.*
Setting: 1895.
Main Character: Female, Annie Lockwood, 15 years old.

Disturbed by her parents' marital discord and completely taken for granted by Sean, Annie is looking for romance. At a once elegant mansion about to be razed in her hometown, Annie falls 100 years back in time where she encounters the romantic idyll she has yearned for. She and Hiram Stratton Jr. fall in love, but she realizes that the 1890s are not her time and comes back to the present. She then realizes she has to return because a ladies' maid has been wrongfully accused of murder. Grades: 6–10.

Fford, Jasper. *The Eyre Affair.*
Penguin, 2003.
Setting: Swindon, England, 1985.
Main Character: Female, Thursday Next, 35 years old.
 An alternate history of Great Britain, where literature has a prominent place in everyday life. Corner Will-Speak machines quote Shakespeare, *Richard III* is performed with audience participation, and children swap Henry Fielding bubble-gum cards. Special Operative Thursday Next seeks to retrieve the stolen manuscript of Dickens' *Martin Chuzzlewit.* The evil Acheron Hades kidnaps Next's mad-scientist uncle, Mycroft and commandeers Mycroft's invention, the Prose Portal, which enables people to cross into a literary text. He sends a minion into Chuzzlewit to seize and kill a minor character, forever changing the novel. Then the manuscript of *Jane Eyre,* Next's favorite novel, disappears and Jane is spirited out of the book. Next must pursue Hades inside Charlotte Bronte's masterpiece. Grades: YA/A.

Flint, Eric. *1632.*
Baen, 2001.
Series: Ring of Fire: *1633; 1634: The Galileo Affair; 1634: The Ram Rebellion; Ring of Fire.*
Setting: Grantville, West Virginia, 1999; Thuringia, Germany, 1632.
Main Characters: Male, Mike Stearns, adult; Female, Rebecca Abrabanel, adult.
 A six-mile square of West Virginia is tossed back in time and space to Thuringia, Germany in 1632, at the height of the barbaric Thirty Years War. Surrounded by warring armies, Grantville residents turn their new world upside down, beginning the American Revolution a century and a half before its time. A page-turner. Grades: YA/A.

Griffiths, Kimberley. *The Last Snake Runner.*
Knopf, 2002.
Prequel: *Enchanted Runner.*
Setting: New Mexico.
Main Character: Male, Kendall, 14 years old.
 Kendall has rediscovered his Native American roots in New Mexico at the Acoma Pueblo, the ancestral home of his mother's family. He is the last of the Snake Clan, a long line of warriors and mystics responsible for carrying out the yearly ceremonies that appease the gods to bring rain. He is struggling to deal with the death of his mother and cannot accept the woman his father marries and he flees into the desert where he is transported back to 1598. He becomes part of the life of the Acoma people, who live on a mesa and farm the surrounding land. A fast-paced adventure. Grades: 6 –10.

Hautman, Pete. *Mr. Was.*
Simon Pulse, 1998.
Setting: Minnesota.
Main Character: Male, Jack Lund, 13 years old.
 After his alcoholic father murders his mother and then goes out in the yard to hang himself, Jack walks through a door and travels back to 1941, where he befriends Scud, an enterprising young hustler, and his fiancée, Andie. Jack and Andie fall in

love. By the time Scud finds out, he and Jack are in the Marines on Guadalcanal. After a savage fight Scud leaves Jack for dead, goes off to marry Andie, has a daughter (Jack's mother), and makes a fortune with the help of a 1996 stock-market page young Jack brought with him. Alive but disfigured and totally amnesiac, Jack (Mr. Was) spends the next 50 years as a mental patient, beginning to recover only after some illicit acupuncture. Grades: 7–10.

Lasky, Kathryn. ***Blood Secret.***
HarperCollins, 2004.
Setting: New Mexico.
Main Character: Female, Jerry Luna, 14 years old.
    Mute since her mother disappeared from a campground several years before, Jerry has lived in various Catholic Charities homes. Now, she is going to live in New Mexico with her great-great-aunt. Jerry discovers an old trunk in her aunt's basement. The mysterious objects within it seem to call to her, and each time she handles one of them, she is catapulted into the experiences of her ancestors, beginning with Miriam, a Jewish girl living in Seville in 1391 who witnesses the murder of her people and is baptized by force. Jerry, who has been raised Catholic, now realizes that her ancestors were Jews, and she is upset by the religious persecution they endured. Grades: 7 and up.

L'Engle, Madeleine. ***A Wrinkle in Time.***
Farrar, Straus and Giroux, 1962.
Series: The Time Quintet: ***A Wind in the Door; A Swiftly Tilting Planet; Many Waters; An Acceptable Time.***
Setting: Outer space.
Main Characters: Female, Meg Murray, 13 years old; Male, Charles Wallace Murray, 5 years old; Male, Calvin O'Keefe, teenager.
    Everyone in town thinks Meg is volatile and dull-witted and that her younger brother Charles Wallace is dumb. People are also saying that their father has run off and left their brilliant scientist mother. Meg, Charles Wallace, and new friend Calvin embark on a perilous quest through space to find their father via "tesseracts," the wrinkles in time. Awards: CC; Newbery. Grades: 5–7.

Levitin, Sonia. ***The Cure.***
HarperTrophy, 2000.
Setting: 1348/2407.
Main Character: Male, Gemm 16884, aka Johannes, 16 years old.
    In the year 2407, societal tranquility is maintained by ample servings of serotonin drinks to the genetically engineered population and by careful monitoring to suppress all expressions of individuality or creativity. When the boy Gemm 16884 somehow feels moved to make music, an extinguished art, he is given a choice between being "recycled" (killed) or sent into virtual reality to experience the bad old days as a cure for his deviant desires. Opting for the latter, he finds himself living as Johannes, the 16-year-old son of a Jewish moneylender in 1348 Strasbourg during the Bubonic Plague. Grades: 5 and up.

Montes, Marisa. *A Circle of Time.*
Harcourt, 2002.
Setting: California, 1906/1996.
Main Character: Female, Allison Blair, 14 years old.

Allison is struck by a car and almost killed. While in a coma, she is whisked away in time by Becky, who has come to 1996 from 1906 for Allison's help. The book flashes back and forth between the hospital, with Becky in Allison's body and about to undergo brain surgery, and 1906 on a California estate owned by a wealthy Spanish family. There, Allison meets Joshua, who was Becky Thompson's boyfriend before her untimely death. Once she convinces him of her situation, he helps her change history. Grades: 6–10.

Nolan, Han. *If I Should Die Before I Wake.*
Harcourt, 2003.
Setting: Jewish hospital.
Main Character: Female, Hilary Burke, teenager.

Hilary, a young Neo-Nazi, is in a coma after a motorcycle accident. She has been taken to a Jewish hospital and shares a room with elderly Chana, an Auschwitz survivor. Instrumental in the kidnapping of her 13-year-old Jewish neighbor, Hilary hates all Jews and believes one caused her father's death. Through Chana's memories, the girl is transported back to World War II, experiencing for herself the horrors suffered by Polish Jews just trying to survive. Awards: CC. Grades: 7–12.

Paulsen, Gary. *The Transall Saga.*
Laurel Leaf, 1999.
Setting: Desert.
Main Character: Male, Mark, 13 years old.

Mark goes on his first solo desert camping trip. After stepping into a mysterious beam of light, Mark is transported to another world. As Mark tries to find his way back home, he learns to survive in this dangerous jungle. Encountering wild creatures, primitive tribes, and a more advanced and warlike group of humans, Mark is forced to grow up before he can return to his own time. He becomes a slave, a warrior, and falls in love, all before the mystery of exactly where he is becomes clear. Grades: 5–10.

Price, Susan. *The Sterkarm Handshake.*
Eos, 2003.
Sequel: *A Sterkarm Kiss.*
Setting: Great Britain, sixteenth century/twenty-first century.
Main Characters: Female, Andrea Mitchell, young woman; Male, Per, young man.

A British corporation called FUP has built a time machine, planning to mine preindustrialized land for gold and oil and turn it into a resort. But the Sterkarms, one of the warring families inhabiting the Scottish and English border in the sixteenth century, won't cooperate; they keep robbing FUP survey teams. Tensions escalate when FUP's boss, Windsor, kidnaps Per, the only son of a Sterkarm lord. Per and Andrea, an FUP employee sent back in time to live with the Sterkarms, have fallen in love. Both parties question her loyalty, and she faces the impossible task of choosing sides. Grades: 7 and up.

Sleator, William. *The Last Universe.*
Harry N. Abrams, 2005.
Setting: Garden maze.
Main Characters: Female, Susan, 14 years old; Male, Gary, 16 years old.

Susan and her brother Gary live in the house that has belonged to their family for generations. Gary has contracted a disease that has him confined to a wheelchair and traveling to the hospital regularly for transfusions. Susan spends her summer vacation pushing her brother through the garden and the maze that no one has ever seen except from one window in the house created by a great-uncle. Gary is convinced that his illness has somehow triggered a quantum event that is responsible for the bizarre changes he and his sister are finding each day. He also seems to be getting better after each visit to the garden. As the garden begins to change, the pace picks up toward a shocking twist at the end. Grades: 6–10.

Vonnegut, Kurt. *Slaughterhouse Five.*
Laurel, 1991.
Setting: Tralfamadore.
Main Character: Male, Billy Pilgrim "Sacks," young man.

Billy is unstuck in time after he is abducted by aliens from the planet Tralfamadore. He has no control over which period of his life he lands in, so the narrative jumps back and forth in time and place. An antiwar theme has Billy concentrating on his shattering experience as an American prisoner of war who witnesses the firebombing of Dresden. Grades: YA/A.

Wells, H. G. *Time Machine.*
House of Stratus, 2001.
Setting: 802,701 A.D.
Main Characters: Male, Mr. Hillyer; Male, The Time Traveler; Female, Weena, all adults.

The Time Traveler is an inventor who believes that time travel is the fourth dimension, and that he could find a way to travel through time. His colleagues do not believe him, yet they later see the weary man dismount from his time machine. He tells them about his travels to a distant future where the world seemed to be a great paradise where nothing was wrong. He discovers the Eloi who befriend him. They tell him of the horrible night raids where an apelike species will come and hunt them. He decides to go explore the underground world where these creatures live so he may retrieve his time machine and barely escapes alive. Then running from these monsters, he finally gets in his time machine and escapes. He travels to many other time periods where he discovers large and strange creatures roaming the planet, until he finally gets back home. The first time travel story. Grades: YA/A.

Williams, Maiya. *The Golden Hour.*
Harry N. Abrams, 2004.
Setting: Maine/ Paris, France, 1789.
Main Character: Male, Rowan Popplewell, 13 years old.

When Rowan and Nina's father sends them to spend the summer with their deceased mother's aunts in Maine, they explore the secrets surrounding the town and the abandoned Owatannauk resort with their new friends Xanthe and Xavier. The resort comes to life and offers time-travel opportunity during the magical "golden hour," defined as the short period of time between day and night. When Nina disappears, Rowan and the twins assume she went to France and find themselves in 1789 Paris. Grades: 5–8.

Willis, Connie. *Doomsday Book.*
Spectra, 1993.
Setting: Oxfordshire, England, 1348/2048.
Main Character: Female, Kivrin, college student.
 Kivrin, a history student in 2048, is transported to an English village in 1348 on the eve of the onset of the Black Plague. Awards: CC; Hugo; Nebula. Grades: YA/A.

Jones, Diana Wynne. *A Tale of Time City.*
HarperTrophy, 2002.
Setting: London, England, 1939.
Main Character: Female, Vivian Smith, 11 years old.
 When Vivian is evacuated from London in 1939, she expects to end up in the peaceful British countryside. Instead she is kidnapped by two youthful time travelers who mistake her for the "Time Lady" and whisk her off to Time City, an alternative world which exists in time but not in history. Time City observers have reason to believe that the Time Lady, the wife of the founder of Time City, is at large in history and is busily altering it, thereby endangering not only the historical world but Time City itself. If Vivian is to return to her own world and time, it will be necessary for her to help her kidnappers foil the Time Lady first. Grades: 6 and up.

RESOURCES: ADDITIONAL TITLES

Buker, Derek M. 2002. *The Science Fiction and Fantasy Readers' Advisory: The Librarian's Guide to Cyborgs, Aliens and Sorcerers.* Chicago, IL: American Library Association.
Herald, Diana Tixier, and Bonnie Kunzel. 2002. *Strictly Science Fiction: A Guide to Reading Interests.* Greenwood Village, CO: Libraries Unlimited.
Reid, Suzanne. 1998. *Presenting Young Adult Science Fiction.* Twayne United States Authors Series. New York, NY: Twayne/Prentice Hall.

CHAPTER 22

SOCIAL ISSUES

Teens face life and all of its issues at some point, whether through personal experience, through a friend or classmate's experience or more safely, through books and movies. Reading about characters working their way through these issues encourages teens and helps guide them through tough times, giving them a safe preview of the consequences of choices teens may make.

Abuse
Activism/Politics
Censorship
Crime and Detention
Death and Grief
Friendship
Gangs
Homelessness
Racism/Prejudice
Suicide

ABUSE

Amateau, Gigi. ***Claiming Georgia Tate.***
Candlewick, 2005.
Setting: Florida, 1970s.
Main Character: Female, Georgia Tate Jamison, 12 years old.
    Believing her mother is dead, Georgia spent her childhood with her maternal grandparents. Her mostly absent father now demands that she vacation with him and his new wife, Sissy, in Florida. Soon, Georgia calls her grandmother for rescue from her father's sexual advances. The Tates come for her immediately, but neither Georgia nor her grandmother tell anyone else what has happened. Suddenly her grandmother passes away, and Grandfather Tate sends Georgia to stay with her father. Sissy kicks them out, and Georgia is more severely sexually battered in a filthy apartment until Tamika, a transvestite, helps her. Grades: 8 and up.

Jacobson, Jennifer Richard. ***Stained.***
Atheneum/Richard Jackson, 2005.

Setting: Weaver Falls, New Hampshire, 1975.

Main Characters: Female, Jocelyn, 17 years old; Male, Gabe, teen; Male, Benny, teen.

Gabe, Jocelyn's childhood friend, is missing. Jocelyn believes her boyfriend, Benny, and Gabe have been abused by the local Roman Catholic priest. The story alternates between the present (1975) and Jocelyn's childhood. Grades: 9 and up.

Morrison, Toni. *Bluest Eye.*

Knopf, 1993.

Setting: Lorain, Ohio, 1941.

Main Character: Female, Pecola Breedlove, 11 years old.

Pecola's entire family has been given a cloak of ugliness to wear, and they each accepted it without question. Pecola is subjected to most of the ugliness in the world. She's spat upon, ridiculed, and ultimately raped and impregnated by her own father. She yearns to be a white child, possessed of the blondest hair and the bluest eye, the very opposite of what she is. Awards: CC. Grades: 10–12.

Voigt, Cynthia. *When She Hollers.*

Scholastic, 1996.

Setting: One day in Tish's life.

Main Character: Female, Tish, 17 years old.

Tish can no longer endure her stepfather's sexual abuse and threatens him with a knife, saying she will stab him if he ever comes near her again. Tish goes to school, a knife hidden in her Docs, staving off panic until gym class when she can no longer keep the knife a secret. Tish finds someone to help her, but she must determine her course of action. Awards: CC. Grades: 7 and up.

Walker, Alice. *The Color Purple.*

Harcourt, 1992.

Setting: South, 1900–1950.

Main Characters: Female, Celie, 14 to 34 years old; Female, Nettie, younger sister.

Celie is a poor black woman whose letters tell the story of twenty years of her life, beginning at age 14, when she was abused and raped by her father and attempted to protect her sister Nettie from the same fate. Her story continues through her marriage to "Mister," a brutal man who terrorizes her. Celie eventually learns that her abusive husband has been keeping her sister's letters from her. The rage she feels and the love and support of her close friend, Shug, pushes her toward an awakening. For mature readers. Awards: CC; Pulitzer Prize; National Book Award. Grades: 9–12.

Woodson, Jacqueline. *I Hadn't Meant to Tell You This.*

Laurel Leaf, 1995.

Sequel: *Lena.*

Setting: Athens, Ohio.

Main Character: Female, Marie, 13 year old.

Marie lives with her father. Her mother sends arty messages while she travels since leaving the family two years ago. Ignoring the sneers of friends and her father's warnings, Marie befriends white trash Lena, the new girl at school. Lena confides about being molested, and Marie is torn between helping her friend and her promise not to tell anyone. Lena has tried all the textbook solutions, including reporting her father to the authorities, and has learned that outside interference only brings more trouble. Lena and her younger sister decide to run away. Awards: CC. Grades: 7–12.

<hr/>

ACTIVISM/POLITICS

Avi. *Nothing But the Truth: A Documentary Novel.*
Scholastic, 1991.
Setting: High school.
Main Character: Male, Philip Malloy, 14 years old.
    Philip is unable to participate on the track team because of his failing grade in English. Convinced the teacher, Margaret Narwin, dislikes him, he concocts a scheme to get transferred from her homeroom: instead of standing "at respectful, silent attention" during the national anthem, Philip hums. His parents take his side, ignoring the fact that he is breaking a school rule, and concentrate on issues of patriotism. The conflict escalates, and the national news media become involved. Told through conversations, diary entries, letters, school memos, newspaper articles, transcripts. Awards: Newbery Honor. Grades: 6–9.

<hr/>

Barron, T.A. *The Ancient One.*
Philomel, 1992.
Prequel: *Heartlight.*
Setting: Oregon.
Main Character: Female, Kate, 13 years old.
    Kate is visiting her Great-Aunt Melanie and embarks on both a crusade and adventure to save the giant redwoods just discovered near the logging town which is desperate for more trees to provide more income. Going back in time 500 years, Kate battles Gashra, the Wicked One for the trees and fights to get back to her own time to save them. Native American myth and fantasy. Grades: 5–9.

<hr/>

Bauer, Joan. *Hope Was Here.*
Putnam, 2000.
Setting: Rural Mulhoney, Wisconsin.
Main Character: Female, Hope Yancey, 16 years old.
    Hope lives with her diner cook aunt after her mother disappears. When they move to work in the Welcome Stairways diner, they become involved with the diner owner's political campaign to become mayor, in spite of his leukemia. Awards: CC; Newbery Honor. Grades: 7–12.

<hr/>

Bennett, Cherie, and Jeff Gottensfeld. *A Heart Divided.*
Delacorte, 2004.
Setting: Redford, Tennessee.
Main Character: Female, Kate Pride, 16 years old.
    Kate has to leave the comfort of her New Jersey home for the unknown south-ern territories of Redford when her father gets a consulting job in Nashville. The high school proudly waves the Confederate flag, and the team's name is the Rebels. Kate gets involved in a petition to remove the flag and change the name while getting involved with Jackson Redford, the great-great grandson of the Confederate general the town is named for. Grades: 8 and up.

<hr/>

Carvell, Marlene. *Who Will Tell My Brother.*
Hyperion, 2004.
Setting: New York City.
Main Character: Male, Evan Hill, 17 years old.

Evan, an artistic, articulate student embarks on a crusade begun by his older brother to remove the Indian as their high school's mascot in respect for his Mohawk heritage. Intolerance and brutality erupt when long-haired Evan is cornered in the hall by scissors-wielding classmates and when his mother discovers the beloved family dog lying dead atop a paper feather headdress. At graduation, when an Indian mascot banner is displayed, cheers fade as sympathizers join Evan in a silent, seated protest. Told in free verse. Grades: 7 and up.

Hiaasen, Carl. *Hoot.*
Knopf, 2002.
Setting: Coconut Cove, Florida, 2000s.
Main Character: Male, Roy Eberhardt, 13 year old.

Roy's family has moved from Montana to Florida because of his dad's job. Through a strange homeless boy named Mullet Fingers, he learns about a nest of burrowing owls that will be destroyed by the construction of Mother Paula's Pancake House. Ray tries to save the owls. Quirky characters. Grades: 6–9.

Hiaasen, Carl. *Flush.*
Random House, 2005.
Setting: Florida Keys, 2000s.
Main Character: Male, Noah Underwood, teenager.

Noah's dad is arrested for sinking the *Coral Queen*, a casino boat on a Florida Key because, he alleges its owner, Dusty Muleman, has been illegally dumping raw sewage into the local waters. Noah and his sister Abbey try to gather proof to vindicate their father and put the casino out of business. Quirky characters. Grades: 5–8.

Keizer, Garret. *God of Beer.*
HarperCollins, 2002.
Setting: Vermont.
Main Character: Male, Kyle, 17 year old.

Kyle and his friends, "Quaker" Oats, and Diana, form a social protest against drinking. During a party, newcomer Condor gets drunk and sober Diana is killed while driving him home. Grades: 8 and up.

Konigsburg, E.L. *The Outcasts of 19 Schuyler Place.*
Atheneum, 2004.
Setting: 1983.
Main Character: Female, Margaret Rose Kane, 12 years old.

Margaret Rose stood up for herself at Camp Telequa when she told off camp director Mrs. Kaplan. Now that she got sent home from camp, she is spending the summer with her two great-uncles at the house at 19 Schuyler Place, which Margaret adores. Her uncles have been building three clock towers covered in pendants made from broken china, crystal, bottles, jars, and clock parts. After forty years, the city council has declared them to be unsafe. Margaret launches a plan to save the towers. Margaret is the half-sister of Connor, the narrator of *Silent to the Bone.* Grades: 6–9.

Tashjian, Janet. *The Gospel According to Larry.*
Henry Holt, 2001.
Sequel: *Vote for Larry.*
Setting: Internet, present day.
Main Character: Male, Josh, 17 years old.
    Josh is bright, articulate, idealistic, and in love with Beth, the girl next door and his best friend since sixth grade. He pours his energy into a clever Web site, through which his alter ego, Larry, advocates introspection, tolerance, and anti-consumerism. Larry has thousands of fans, including Beth. A media circus surrounds Josh when his identity is revealed. Grades: 8 and up.

Taylor, Theodore. *The Weirdo.*
Harcourt, 1991.
Setting: North Carolina.
Main Characters: Male, Chip Clewt, 17 years old; Female, Samantha Saunders, 16 years old.
    Townsfolk call Chip "Weirdo" since he had been badly burned in an airplane crash and came to live with his artist father in the secluded Powhatan Swamp. Now assisting a graduate student observe and tag bears in the swamp in order to protect them, he has aroused the tempers of local hunters. Samantha, the daughter of one of the opponents of the hunting ban, meets Chip when she follows a prize hunting dog into the swamp. She gradually comes to understand the issues that concern him, and when the graduate student disappears, she and Chip investigate on their own. Awards: Edgars. Grades: 6–9.

Williams, Laura E. *Up a Creek.*
Henry Holt, 2001.
Setting: Louisiana.
Main Character: Female, Starshine Bott, 13 years old.
    Starshine's mom, Miracle, always has a cause, save the whales, save the dolphins, and on and on. This time Miracle is on a crusade to save the trees in the town square from being chopped down for new development. She holes herself up in one of the trees and Starshine wishes she would just come down and be her mom. When Miracle falls from the tree, the mayor immediately begins chopping down the trees. Starshine and her classmates then spring into action and climb the trees. Grades: 5 and up.

Wittlinger, Ellen. *What's in a Name?*
Simon & Schuster, 2000.
Setting: Scrub Harbor.
    During the ongoing debate about which name is best for the town—Scrub Harbor or Folly Bay—goes on, ten teens engage in personal journeys of self-discovery. Awards: CC. Grades: 7 and up.

CENSORSHIP

Atwood, Margaret. *The Handmaid's Tale.*
Anchor, 1998.
Setting: Republic of Gilead.
Main Character: Female, Offred, adult.

In the Republic of Gilead, formerly the United States, far-right ideals have been carried to extremes in the monotheocratic government. Women are strictly controlled, unable to have jobs or money and assigned to various classes: the chaste, childless Wives; the housekeeping Marthas; and the reproductive Handmaids, who turn their offspring over to the "morally fit" Wives. Offred is a Handmaid who tells how the society came to be. Grades: YA/A.

Blume, Judy, editor. *Places I Never Meant to Be: Original Stories by Censored Writers.*
Simon & Schuster, 1999.

Twelve short stories and essays on censorship by authors whose works have been censored or challenged. Authors include: Judy Blume, Joan Bertin, Norma Fox Mazer , Julius Lester, Rachel Vail, Katherine Paterson, Jacqueline Woodson, Harry Mazer, Walter Dean Myers, Susan Beth Pfeffer, David Klass, Paul Zindel, Chris Lynch, Norma Klein. Grades: 7 and up.

Bradbury, Ray. *Fahrenheit 451.*
Simon & Schuster, 2003.
Setting: Earth.
Main Character: Male, Guy Montag, adult.

Guy is a book-burning fireman. His wife spends all day with her television "family," imploring Montag to work harder so that they can afford a fourth TV wall. His next-door neighbor is Clarisse, a young girl thrilled by the ideas in books. When Clarisse disappears mysteriously, Montag starts hiding books in his home. His wife turns him in, and he must answer the call to burn his secret cache of books. Montag flees to avoid arrest and winds up joining an outlaw band of scholars who keep the contents of books in their heads, waiting for the time society will once again need the wisdom of literature. Originally published in 1953. Grades: YA/A.

Crutcher, Chris. *The Sledding Hill.*
Greenwillow, 2005.
Setting: Idaho.
Main Characters: Male, Eddie Proffit; Male, Billy Bartholomew; both 14 year olds.

A dead narrator and an author who writes himself into the story gives this novel about censorship an interesting twist. After Billy dies and is found by his best friend, Eddie, he tries to help Eddie deal with his recent losses and supports him when one of Chris Crutcher's books is challenged at school. A statement against censorship with no profanity, sex, drugs, alcohol, or violence. Grades: 7 and up.

Dunn, Mark. *Ella Minnow Pea.*
Anchor, 2002.
Setting: Nollop, South Carolina.

Main Character: Female, Ella Minnow Pea, young woman.

Ella Minnow Pea is a girl living happily on the island of Nollop. Nollop was named after Nevin Nollop, author of the immortal pangram, "The quick brown fox jumps over the lazy dog." Now Ella acts to save her friends, family, and fellow citizens from the encroaching totalitarianism of the island's Council, which has banned the use of certain letters of the alphabet as they fall from a memorial statue of Nevin Nollop. As the letters progressively drop from the statue they also disappear from the novel. Word lovers will like this one. Grades: YA/A.

Garden, Nancy. *The Year They Burned the Books.*
Farrar, Straus & Giroux, 1999.
Setting: New England.
Main Character: Female, Jamie Crawford, 17 years old.

Jamie is the editor in chief of her small New England high school's paper. She is fairly sure she is gay, and when Tessa Gillespie, a new girl from Boston, shows up wearing a red cape and a star-shaped stud in her nose, Jamie starts falling in love. Fundamentalist Mrs. Buel, a "stealth candidate" during her campaign for a seat on the school committee, leads the committee to set aside the new sex education curriculum, and stages a book burning on Halloween. The liberal faculty adviser to the school paper is put on leave, and Jamie is forbidden to write on controversial subjects in her editorials. Jamie and her staff publish an underground paper. Grades: 7 and up.

Lowry, Lois. *The Giver.*
Bantam, 1999.
Sequels: *Gathering Blue; Messenger.*
Setting: Future dystopia.
Main Character: Male, Jonas, 12 years old.

Jonas is given his lifetime assignment at the Ceremony of Twelve. He becomes the Receiver of memories and learns the truth of the society in which he lives, where there is no color, pain, or past. Awards: Newbery. Grades: 6–9.

Lubar, David. *Wizards of the Game.*
Philomel, 2003.
Setting: Contemporary.
Main Character: Male, Mercer Dickensen, eighth-grader.

Mercer's passion is the fantasy role-playing game Wizards of the Warrior World. When he is asked to help with a fund-raiser to benefit a homeless shelter, he suggests bringing a gaming convention to his school, causing controversy with fundamental Christians in the community. During his visit to the shelter, he meets four genuine wizards who are trapped on Earth and want his help in returning to their own world. Grades: 5–8.

Orwell, George. *1984.*
Plume, 1983.
Setting: London, England, 1984.
Main Character: Male, Winston Smith, 39 years old.

London, the largest population center of Airstrip One, is part of the vast political entity Oceania, which is eternally at war with one of two other vast entities,

Eurasia and Eastasia. At any moment, depending upon current alignments, all existing records show either that Oceania has always been at war with Eurasia and allied with Eastasia, or that it has always been at war with Eastasia and allied with Eurasia. Winston Smith knows this, because his work at the Ministry of Truth involves the constant "correction" of such records. In a grim city and a terrifying country, where Big Brother is always Watching You and the Thought Police can practically read your mind, Winston is a man in grave danger for the simple reason that his memory still functions. Originally published in 1949. Grades: YA/A.

Peck, Richard. *Last Safe Place on Earth.*
Laurel Leaf, 2005.
Setting: Tranquility Lane in Walden Woods.
Main Character: Male, Todd, 15 years old.

Todd and his family discover that their secure suburban community is no protection against obsessive, destructive ideas when Todd's little sister is brainwashed by a fundamentalist sect into hating and fearing Halloween. Grades: 5 and up.

Philbrick, Rodman. *The Last Book in the Universe.*
Blue Sky, 2002.
Setting: Future Earth.
Main Character: Male, Spaz, teenager.

Epilepsy prevents Spaz from using the mind probes most people use to blot out reality. He sets out on a quest to save his ill foster sister, crossing forbidden territory and facing frightening gangs. Companions join him: Ryter, a philosophic old man whose treasure is the book he is writing; Littleface, a young, almost speechless child; and Linnea, a genetically improved person. By saving his sister, Spaz learns about himself and his parentage. Grades: 5–8.

Prose, Francine. *After.*
HarperCollins, February 2003.
Setting: Central High School, 2000s.
Main Character: Male, Tom Bishop, 15 years old.

The ripple effect of a school shooting fifty miles away is shaking up Central High School. Fear and paranoia has authorities changing the rules every day. Students who don't follow the rules are disappearing. Grades: 6–10.

CRIME AND DETENTION

Brooks, Kevin. *Martyn Pig.*
Push, 2003.
Setting: England.
Main Character: Male, Martyn Pig, 15 years old.

Martyn Pig's mother left years ago and his father is an abusive alcoholic. Martyn yells at his drunken father and as he comes at his son with his fist raised, he stumbles, falls, hits his head on the fireplace wall, and dies. Martyn decides not to notify the police and with the help of his friend Alex, he sews him and some rocks into a sleeping bag and pitches him into a quarry. The bleakness is tempered by some tongue-in-cheek and zany humor. Grades: 8 and up.

Cormier, Robert. **The Rag and Bone Shop.**
Delacorte, 2001.
Setting: Monument, Massachusetts.
Main Character: Male, Jason, 12 years old.
    Jason is accused of murdering his young neighbor. An investigator is sent to get a confession whether it is the truth or not. Awards: CC. Grades: 7–12.

Cormier, Robert. **Tenderness.**
Delacorte, 1997.
Setting: 1990s.
Main Characters: Male, Eric Poole, 18 years old; Female, Lori, 15 years old.
    Lori has a crush on Eric who was recently released from a juvenile correctional facility for murdering his mother and stepfather. Eric believes Lori is a witness to his yet undiscovered murders. For mature readers. Awards: CC; VOYA Perfect Ten. Grades: 9–12.

Cormier, Robert. **We All Fall Down.**
Laurel Leaf, 1993.
Setting: Burnside, Wickburg.
Main Character: The Avenger.
    Three teenage boys trash Karen Jerome's suburban home, beat her, and throw her down the stairs; now she lies in a coma. Her sister, Jane, unknowingly falls in love with one of the boys involved. An unseen witness, The Avenger, seeks revenge. Awards: CC. Grades: 8 and up.

Corrigan, Eireann. **Splintering.**
Push, 2005.
Setting: Present day.
Main Characters: Female, Paulie, 15 years old; Male, Jeremy, older brother.
    A stranger high on PCP crashes a family gathering, brandishing a machete. Dad's heart gives out while fending off the intruder, who then hacks his way into the bedroom where Paulie is hiding, calling 911. No one dies, but the aftermath of the attack is told in free verse, alternating points of view between Paulie and her reclusive older brother, Jeremy. Grades: 9–12.

Deuker, Carl. **Runner.**
Houghton Mifflin, 2005.
Setting: Seattle, Washington, 2000s.
Main Character: Male, Chance Taylor.
    Chance's alcoholic Gulf War veteran father is fired from the first steady job he has held in years. Chance has no idea where they'll get the money to pay the mortgage fees for the run-down sailboat they call home. His only pleasure is running by himself along the Seattle waterfront. A marina office employee offers to pay him $250 a week to pick up occasional packages at a tree along his running route, and Chance

accepts the opportunity to pay his bills. As this new job gradually becomes more dangerous and more clearly illegal, Chance's father is able to rise above his personal problems to help his son. Fast-paced and action-packed. Grades: 7 and up.

Ferris, Jean. **Bad.**
Farrar, Straus & Giroux, 2001.
Setting: Girls' rehab center.
Main Character: Female, Dallas, 16 years old.

Dallas used to love "skating" with her rebellious friends—shoplifting, hot-wiring cars, and purse-snatching—but she never expected to be caught with a gun. After being pressured by peers into holding up a convenience store, she is abandoned by her father, who refuses custody, Dallas is confined for six months to a juvenile detention facility for girls. In the rehab she must adjust to shared living quarters, structured schedules, lectures on drugs and sex, and volatile personalities. Grades: 8–11.

Foon, Dennis. **Skud.**
Groundwood, 2004.
Setting: High school.
Main Characters: Male, Brad; Male, Tommy; both 17 years old.

Brad and Tommy suspect Andy of stealing Tommy's girlfriend; they decide to make him pay by beating him up and humiliating him. Shane, a notorious gang member, shows up and claims to be Andy's backup. This unlikely pair forms a tenuous friendship when Shane agrees to help Andy "punk up" for an acting part. Brad runs into trouble on the hockey team and Tommy, an honor student and school hero, is arrested for raping his former girlfriend. Grades: 9 and up.

Hartinger, Brent. **The Last Chance Texaco.**
HarperTempest, 2004.
Setting: Group home.
Main Character: Female, Lucy Pitt, 15 years old.

Lucy's last chance is to make it at Kindle House, a group home where the dedicated counselors try to connect with the kids. If she makes any mistakes, she'll be sent to the prisonlike facility known as Eat-Their-Young Island. With a little romance and a little mystery, this is a realistic portrayal of teens caught in the foster care system. Grades: 7–10.

Hinton, S.E. **Taming the Star Runner.**
Laurel Leaf, 1989.
Setting: Oklahoma.
Main Characters: Male, Travis, 15 years old; Male, Casey, 18 years old.

Released from juvenile hall to cool down at his uncle's Oklahoma horse ranch, Travis looks like a rebel and flies into violent rages, yet he seeks to publish his novel and he loves his cat. He is attracted to Casey, the riding instructor who leases his uncle's barn. Travis ends up a published author. Grades: 7–10.

Hobbs, Will. **The Maze.**
HarperCollins, 1998.
Setting: Canyonlands National Park, Utah.

Main Character: Male, Rick, 14 years old.

Rick is in and out of foster homes, then runs away from a juvenile correctional facility and ends up lost in a wilderness and found by a scientist studying condors who teaches him to hang glide. Awards: CC. Grades: 6–9.

Korman, Gordon. *Son of the Mob.*
Hyperion, 2002.
Setting: New York City, present day.
Main Character: Male, Vince Luca, 17 years old.

Vince refuses to become involved in the family "vending machine business." His father is the Mob boss, his older brother serves as their father's loser lackey, and Mom turns a deaf ear while cooking up a steady storm in the kitchen. Things heat up when Vince falls in love with the daughter of the FBI agent determined to bring down Vince's father. Awards: VOYA Perfect Ten. Grades: 7 and up.

Marsden, John. *Checkers.*
Laurel Leaf, 2000.
Setting: Australia.
Main Character: Female teen.

An unnamed narrator tells how her life spun out of control from media pressure and her father's business scandal. Checkers was her puppy and was murdered by her father. Now in a psychiatric ward, her fellow participants in group therapy include an obsessive-compulsive, a male anorexic, and a girl who thinks she has an animal living in her head. The narrator describes their activities rather than interacts with them. She eventually works up the courage to break her long silence in group, but readers never learn what her diagnosis is. Grades: 7 and up.

Marsden, John. *Letters from the Inside.*
Pan MacMillan, 1992.
Setting: Australia.
Main Characters: Female, Mandy; Female, Tracey; both 16 years old.

Mandy answers Tracey's ad in a magazine, and the girls become pen pals. Their early letters are innocuous, but then there are hints that Tracey is hiding something. She reveals that she is in a maximum security unit of a correctional institution for an unspeakable crime and scared of the brutal truths of young women living together behind bars. Mandy's life seems nearly perfect in comparison. Her complaints about her brother's violent outbursts are easy to ignore, until Mandy's letters stop. For mature readers. Awards: CC. Grades: 8–12.

McNamee, Graham. *Acceleration.*
Wendy Lamb, 2003.
Setting: Toronto, Ontario.
Main Character: Male, Duncan, 17 years old.

Duncan is spending his summer cataloging lost junk in the Toronto Transit Commission's subterranean Lost and Found. He finds a brown leather journal that seems to be the personal history of a serial killer in the making. When local police take no interest, Duncan decides to use its clues to track down the potential killer. Awards: Edgars; VOYA Perfect Ten. Grades: 8–12.

Mikaelsen, Ben. ***Touching Spirit Bear.***
HarperCollins, 2001.
Setting: Alaskan island.
Main character: Male, Cole Matthews, 15 years old.

Angry Cole agrees to accept the sentence given to him by Native American Circle Justice and he is sent to a remote Alaskan Island where he encounters Spirit Bear. Awards: CC. Grades: 6–9.

Myers, Walter Dean. ***Monster.***
HarperCollins, 1999.
Setting: Harlem, New York City.
Main Character: Male, Steve Harmon, 16 years old.

Steve is accused of serving as a lookout for a robbery of a Harlem drugstore. The owner was shot and killed, and now Steve is in prison awaiting trial for murder. Steve, an amateur filmmaker, recounts his experiences in the form of a movie screen-play. Interspersed within the script are diary entries in which Steve describes the nightmarish conditions of his confinement. Awards: CC; Printz; Coretta Scott King Honor; National Book Award Finalist. Grades: 7–10.

Oates, Joyce Carol. ***Freaky Green Eyes.***
HarperTempest, 2003.
Setting: Northwest.
Main Character: Female, Frankie, 15 years old.

Frankie tells of her alter ego Freaky and the events leading up to her mother's disappearance. Resembles the O.J. Simpson story. Haunting and fast-paced. Grades: 9–12.

Pullman, Philip. ***The White Mercedes.***
Random House, 1997.
Setting: Oxford, England.
Main Character: Male, Chris Marshall, 17 years old.

Chris meets and later beds Jenny who has run away from her abusive father. Chris's trusting nature and sense of justice cause the youth to be duped by a vengeful felon into causing Jenny's death because she is mistaken for someone else. For mature readers. Grades: 7 and up.

Sachar, Louis. ***Holes.***
Farrar, Straus & Giroux, 1998.
Setting: Camp Green Lake, Texas.
Main Character: Male, Stanley Yelnats IV.

Stanley is sent to a correctional camp in the desert and has to dig holes because the warden is looking for something. Quirky characters and an ambiguous ending with two story lines that come together. Awards: CC; Newbery. Grades: 6–12.

Shepard, Jim. ***Project X: A Novel.***
Knopf, 2004.
Setting: New England, 2000s.
Main Characters: Male, Edwin Hanratty; Male, Roddy "Flake"; both 14 years old.

Edwin and Flake are beaten up and mocked by bullies, disliked by teachers, and at loggerheads with exasperated parents; they live a nightmare of loneliness and anxiety. Together, the two boys feed each other's wounded, sullen disgruntlement and hatch a plot for vengeance against their classmates. Awards: Alex. Grades: A/YA.

Soto, Gary. *The Afterlife.*
Harcourt, 2003.
Setting: Fresno, California.
Main Character: Male, Chuy, 17 years old.
The book begins with Chuy being knifed in a restroom, where he dies. In afterlife, Chuy is able to accomplish a few things that he wasn't able to in life. He saves a life, punishes a thug, falls in love, and recognizes how much he is loved by family and friends. Grades: 6 and up.

Weber, Lori. *Klepto.*
Lorimer, 2004.
Setting: Present day.
Main Character: Female, Kat, teenager.
After her older sister, Hannah, is sent to a group home for selling drugs and other crimes, Kat reacts by shoplifting. Once her classmates find out, they call her "Kat Burglar," and she soon lives up to her new nickname. Both parents' primary focus is Hannah. Finally, Hannah returns home and Kat manages to avoid her. Then her luck runs out and mall security catches her. It is her sister who picks her up, and Hannah tries to stop Kat from turning her life into a disaster. Grades: 6–9.

Whitney, Kim Ablon. *See You Down the Road.*
Laurel Leaf, 2005.
Setting: Present day.
Main Character: Female, Bridget Daugherty, 16 years old.
Bridget and her family are Travelers, members of a group who live by their own laws and traditions. They believe anyone who isn't a Traveler is fair game for the scams and shoplifting that are the way they earn their living. They teach the skills necessary to be an effective thief to their children. Bridget's parents are worried about her as she wants to keep going to school and leave their lifestyle. Grades: 9 and up.

Wittlinger, Ellen. *The Long Night of Leo and Bree.*
Simon Pulse, 2003.
Setting: Present day.
Main Character: Male, Leo, 18 years old.
On the anniversary of his sister's brutal murder by her boyfriend, Leo escapes from their apartment, frightened and enraged by his mother's drunken ravings and assault. Driving around, he is consumed by anger and despair. When he sees Bree walking alone in her tight skirt and high heels, he concludes that this stranger should be dead, not Michelle. Leo takes her as a hostage and talk is Bree's only weapon. By the time morning rolls around, Leo and Bree have opened their hearts to each other. Grades: 8 and up.

DEATH AND GRIEF

Abelove, Joan. *Saying It Out Loud.*
Puffin, 2001.
Setting: 1990s.
Main Character: Female, Mindy, 16 years old.
　　Mindy judges and rejects her mother and fights with her, but there is always a fond remembrance of a time when they were close. When her mother develops excruciating neck pain, Mindy is annoyed and convinced that her mom is just faking it. Surgery leaves her mother an empty shell, and Mindy is left with all the unfinished business of mother/daughter conflict and love. Grades: 7 and up.

Anderson, Laurie Halse. *Catalyst.*
Viking, 2002.
Setting: 2000s.
Main Character: Female, Kate Malone, 18 years old.
　　Kate has placed all of her eggs in one basket by only applying to her late mother's alma mater, MIT. When MIT sends a rejection, letter, Kate's life begins to unravel. Grades: 8 and up.

Blume, Judy. *Tiger Eyes.*
Laurel Leaf, 1982.
Setting: New Mexico.
Main Character: Female, Davey Wexler, 15 years old.
　　Davey's family has resettled in New Mexico with her aunt and uncle after her father was killed during a holdup of his 7-Eleven store in Atlantic City. Davey has never felt so alone in her life. While climbing in Los Alamos Canyons, Davey meets Wolf, who seems to understand the rage and fear she feels. Awards: CC. Grades: YA.

Brooks, Bruce. *All That Remains.*
Atheneum, 2001.
Setting: 2000s.
　　Three stories about death and the reaction young people have to dealing with the remains of a loved one. Grades: 7 and up.

Bunting, Eve. *A Sudden Silence.*
Fawcett, 1990.
Setting: California.
Main Character: Male, Jesse, teenager.
　　Jesse's deaf younger brother Bryan was killed by a drunk hit-and-run driver. Ashamed of his attraction to Bryan's girlfriend Chloe, Jesse works with her to search for the hit-and-run driver. Money is offered, posters are made, and people are questioned. Finding the drunken driver doesn't bring the expected redemption. Awards: CC. Grades: 9 and up.

Couloumbis, Audrey. *Getting Near to Baby.*
Puffin, 2001.
Setting: One day, sunrise to sunset.
Main Character: Female, Willa Jo Dean, 13 years old.

Willa Jo crawls onto the roof of Aunt Patty's house to watch the sunrise followed by Little Sister and Aunt Patty's pleas and threats to come down. In flash-backs, Willa Jo tells of Baby's death, their mother's grief, and of Little Sister's refusal to talk. Willa Jo and Little Sister were taken to their aunt's house for three weeks; they miss their mother, their baby sister, and are at odds with Aunt Patty. By sunset, the girls are reunited with their mother and reconciled with their aunt. Awards: Newbery Honor. Grades: 6–8.

Coman, Carolyn. *Many Stones.*
Puffin, 2002.
Setting: Washington, D. C., South Africa.
Main Character: Female, Berry Morgan, 16 years old.

Berry's sister, Laura, a volunteer at a school in South Africa, was murdered. Berry is angry and isolated. She collects stones and stacks them on her chest so that she can feel their heft. Berry accompanies her loathed father to South Africa for a memorial service. When she confronts the devastation of a race of people subjected to degradation, imprisonment and torture, her own experiences seem almost trivial by comparison. Awards: Printz Honor; National Book Award. Grades: 7 and up.

Creech, Sharon. *Absolutely Normal Chaos.*
Joanna Cotler, 1995.
Setting: One summer.
Main Character: Female, Mary Lou, 13 years old.

Mary Lou wonders how her visiting cousin, Carl Ray, can be such a silent clod, especially when someone has anonymously given him $5000. Later, when he is in a coma following a car accident, she rereads her journal and wonders how she could have been so unseeing. Her mother forbids her to say "God," "stupid," and "stuff," so she makes a trek to the thesaurus to create some innovative interjections. Grades: 6–9.

Deaver, Julie Reece. *Say Goodnight Gracie.*
HarperTrophy, 1989.
Setting: Chicago, Illinois.
Main Character: Female, Morgan, 17 years old.

Morgan and Jimmy have been inseparable friends since birth. When Jimmy is killed by a drunk driver, Morgan's pain seems unbearable. Morgan narrates the events leading up to the accident and following it. Awards: CC. Grades: 8–10.

Dessen, Sarah *Truth about Forever.*
Viking, 2004.
Setting: Present day.
Main Character: Female, Macy, 16 years old.

Macy avoids mourning her father's death by staying in control: good Grades, perfect boyfriend, always neat and tidy, trying to fake her way to normal. She gets a job at Wish Catering, run by pregnant, forgetful Delia and staffed by her nephews, Bert and Wes, and her neighbors Kristy and Monica. Wes and Macy play an ongoing game of Truth and share everything and fall in love. Awards: Teens Top Ten. Grades: 7 and up.

Goobie, Beth. *Before Wings.*
Orca, 2001.
Setting: Camp Lakeshore, Canada.
Main Character: Female, Adrien Wood, 15 years old.

Adrien barely survived a brain aneurysm two years ago and is haunted, knowing she could die from another one at any time. Issues of life and death completely fill her world at Camp Lakeshore, owned and operated by her Aunt Erin. Adrien bonds with Paul, a teen who is convinced that he has dreamed his own death will be on his next birthday. Adrien seems to be experiencing events in the lives of five girls, a group of campers who died long ago in a tragic accident. Magical realism. Grades: 8 and up.

Green, John. *Looking for Alaska.*
Dutton, 2005.
Setting: Alabama.
Main Character: Male, Miles Halter, 16 years old.

Miles decides to take charge of his life by going to an Alabama boarding school. Once there, he's rechristened "Pudge," and adopted by new roommate Chip and his best friend Alaska. Alaska and Chip teach Miles to drink, smoke, and plot elaborate pranks. The chapters are headed by the number of days before and after Alaska's suicide. Awards: Printz; Teens Top Ten. Grades: 9 and up.

Griffin, Adele. *The Other Shepards.*
Hyperion, 1998.
Setting: New York City, 1990s.
Main Character: Female, Geneva Shepard, 13 years old.

Geneva and her older sister Holland have lived their lives in the shadow of the memory of their three siblings who were tragically killed in a car accident twenty years ago. Geneva suffers from nearly debilitating psychological difficulties. One day, an artist arrives to paint a mural in their home and becomes part therapist, part friend, and part angel. Awards: CC. Grades: 8–12.

Hoffman, Alice. *Green Angel.*
Scholastic, 2003.
Setting: Garden.
Main Character: Female, Green, 15 years old.

Moody, introspective Green stays at home while her parents and younger sister travel to the city to sell their produce. Her disappointment at being left behind causes her to be cold and not say good-bye. Then the city is engulfed in flames, and ashes hover in the atmosphere for a long time. Green is left with her guilt for her sullen behavior and the solitude of her ruined garden. Grades: 8 and up.

Howe, James, editor. *Color of Absence: 12 Stories of Loss and Hope.*
Simon Pulse, 2003.

A dozen young adult authors look at the paradox of loss and hope in all its guises as it touches young lives. Authors include: Annette Curtis Klause, Roderick Townley, Angela Johnson, Norma Fox Mazer, Michael J. Rosen, Virginia Euwer Wolff, C.B. Christiansen, Naomi Shihab Nye, Avi, Walter Dean Myers, Jacqueline Woodson, Chris Lynch, and James Howe. Grades: 7 and up.

Johnson, Maureen. *The Key to the Golden Firebird.*
HarperCollins, 2004.
Setting: Philadelphia, Pennsylvania.
Main Characters: Female, Brooks Gold; Female, May Gold; Female, Palmer Gold.

The Gold sisters try to cope with their father's sudden death from a heart attack, while their mother works overtime to keep them afloat financially. May, the studious, steady middle sister, tries to hold the family together even as she is going to pieces on the inside. She is falling for Pete but is afraid to admit it, so she watches in agony as he dates her coworker at a coffee shop. Palmer, the youngest, begins to have panic attacks. Brooks, the oldest, quits the softball team, gets drunk on a regular basis, and makes plans to have sex with her not-quite-boyfriend. Grades: 7 and up.

Lawrence, Iain. *The Lightkeeper's Daughter.*
Delacorte, 2004.
Setting: Lizzie Island, British Columbia.
Main Character: Female, Elizabeth McCrae, aka Squid, 17 years old.

When Squid returns to her childhood home on remote Lizzie Island, where her father serves as lightkeeper, she has a three-year-old daughter and memories of her brother, Alastair, who drowned when his kayak overturned. The events surrounding his death gradually come to light, through his journal entries, scraps of remembered conversations, and an alternating narrative between Squid and her parents. For mature readers. Grades: 10 and up.

Rylant, Cynthia. *Missing May.*
Scholastic, 1992.
Setting: West Virginia.
Main Character: Female, Summer, 12 years old.

Summer is grieving after her foster mother's sudden death, but also witnesses the grief of Ob, her foster father. Summer realizes that she may not be reason enough for him to go on living, until Summer and Ob take a short car trip that transforms their lives. Awards: Newbery. Grades: 6 and up.

Saenz, Benjamin Alire. *Sammy and Juliana in Hollywood.*
Cinco Puntas Pr., 2004.
Setting: Late 1960s, Las Cruces, New Mexico, Mexican American barrio.
Main Character: Male, Sammy Santos, 17 years old.

Sammy comes to grips with the death of Juliana, his first love, and the increasingly complex demands and needs of his remaining friends, as well as of his family and neighbors. Among Sammy's friends are two boys who meet first with violence and then banishment from the community when they are caught together in a romantic moment. Grades: 9 and up.

Woodson, Jacqueline. *Behind You.*
Putnam, 2004.
Prequel: *If You Come Softly.*
Setting: New York City.
Main Character: Male, Jeremiah Roselind, 15 years old.

Jeremiah, shot dead by New York City police in a case of mistaken identity, is

THE TEEN READER'S ADVISOR

back here telling the story from the great beyond. Jeremiah's is not the only voice, as his friends and relatives also reveal their sorrow. Grades: 8–10.

Woodson, Jacqueline. ***Miracle's Boys.***
Putnam, 2000.
Setting: Harlem, New York City, 2000s.
Main Characters: Male, Ty'ree; Male, Charlie; Male, Lafayette; all teenagers.
   Ty'ree, Charlie, and Lafayette are trying to cope with the death of their parents. Ty'ree, the oldest brother, accepts responsibility for keeping the family together. Charlie, the middle brother, who has just been released from a juvenile correctional facility, comes home angry. Lafayette, the youngest, fears he will be separated from his siblings. Awards: CC; Coretta Scott King. Grades: 7–10.

FRIENDSHIP

Brashares, Ann. ***The Sisterhood of the Traveling Pants.***
Delacorte, 2001.
Sequels: ***The Second Summer of the Sisterhood; Girls in Pants: The Third Summer of the Sisterhood.***
Setting: Washington D.C., Greece, Mexico.
Main Characters: Female, Lena; Female, Bridget; Female, Carmen; Female, Tibby; all 15 years old.
   A pair of jeans with magical qualities from a thrift shop bond four friends together when they spend their first summer apart. Grades: 7–12.

Crutcher, Chris. ***Staying Fat for Sarah Byrnes.***
Greenwillow, 1993.
Setting: High school/Child and Adolescent Psychiatric Unit.
Main Characters: Male, Eric Calhoune; Female, Sarah Byrnes; both 17 years old.
   A social outcast in junior high, overweight Eric found a kindred spirit in Sarah Byrnes, whose face and hands were hideously disfigured in a childhood accident. Now a senior and considerably slimmed down through competitive swimming, Eric is still devoted to his friend. When Sarah abruptly stops talking and is committed to a mental ward, Eric is compelled to take action to help her. He risks their friendship by breaking his vow of secrecy and enlisting others' aid. Awards: CC. Grades: 7 and up.

Danziger, Paula, and Ann Martin. ***P. S. Longer Letter Later.***
Scholastic, 1998.
Sequel: ***Snail Mail No More.***
Setting: Ohio.
Main Character: Female, Tara*Starr; Female, Elizabeth; both 12 years old.
   Best friends Tara and Elizabeth stay in contact through letters after Tara moves to another state. Elizabeth is the shy quiet one and Tara streaks her hair purple. Their letters record the chaotic changes that happen in their lives. Grades: 5–8.

Dessen, Sarah. ***Keeping the Moon.***
Viking, 1999.
Setting: Colby, North Carolina.

Main Character: Female, Colie, 15 years old.

Because her aerobics-star mother is taking her famous weight-loss program to Europe, Colie spends the summer with her unusual Aunt Mira. Colie has recently dropped 45 pounds, but she has not succeeded in shedding her negative self-image. Colie feels hopeless until she accepts a job in a restaurant, where two fellow waitresses, both past their high school angst, share their beauty, and life-management secrets with her. Awards: CC. Grades: 7 and up.

Dessen, Sarah. *Someone Like You.*
Viking, 1998.
Setting: Suburbia, 1990s.
Main Characters: Female, Halley; Female, Scarlett; both 16 years old.

Halley and Scarlett have been best friends since grade school. Growing up like sisters, they've shared everything except a bedroom. Then boys step into their lives. Scarlett's boyfriend Michael dies in a motorcycle accident and she's left carrying his child. Halley's close relationship with her psychologist mother is fractured as her friendship with secretive, irresponsible Macon Faulkner deepens into romance. Awards: CC. Grades: 7 and up.

Fredericks, Mariah. *The True Meaning of Cleavage.*
Atheneum, 2003.
Setting: Eldrige High School, 2000s.
Main Characters: Female, Jess, freshman; Female, Sari; both 14 years old.

Best friends since seventh grade, Jess and Sari are inseparable until their freshman year of high school. Sari becomes obsessed with a senior boy and Jess wonders if their friendship will survive. Grades: 7–9.

Kerr, M. E. *Dinky Hocker Shoots Smack!*
HarperCollins, 1972.
Setting: Brooklyn, New York City.
Main Character: Male, Tucker Woolf, 15 years old.

When his family moves to Brooklyn, Tucker brings home a stray cat, but his father is allergic. An unusual overweight girl, Dinky Hocker, gives his cat a home and introduces him to her cousin and a friend. Their parents have their own politics and problems that distract them from their children. The quirky characters and realistic relationships make this a winner. Grades: 7–12.

Koertge, Ron. *Stoner and Spaz.*
Candlewick, 2002.
Setting: Los Angeles, California.
Main Characters: Female, Colleen Minou, teenager; Male, Ben Bancroft, 16 years old.

Colleen is a hard-core stoner, and Ben is a movie-addicted preppie who suffers from cerebral palsy. Together, they form a most unlikely couple. For once, Ben is actually more interested in his real life than a movie. Colleen takes him clubbing, lights his first joint, even challenges him to direct his own movie. But when Ben, in turn, dares her to stay straight, Colleen admits that, despite his devotion, she still needs the drugs to "smooth out the edges." Grades: 8 and up.

Oates, Joyce Carol. *Big Mouth and Ugly Girl.*
HarperCollins, May 2002.
Setting: Rocky River High School, New York City, 2000s.
Main Characters: Female, Ursula Riggs; Male, Matt Donaghy; both 16 years old.

When Matt is falsely accused of threatening to blow up his high school and his friends turn against him, Ursula comes to his aid. They become friends, then romantically involved. Grades: 8 and up.

Peters, Julie Ann. *Define "Normal".*
Little, Brown, 2000.
Setting: Middle school, 1990s.
Main Character: Female, Antonia, 13 years old.

When she agrees to meet with Jasmine as a peer counselor at their middle school, Antonia never dreams that this girl with the black lipstick and pierced eyebrow will end up becoming a good friend and helping her deal with the serious problems she faces at home. Antonia and Jazz learn to look beyond the outside to find common feelings and frustrations on the inside. Awards: CC. Grades: 7–10.

GANGS

Coburn, Jake. *Prep.*
Dutton, 2003.
Setting: Manhattan, New York City, present day.
Main Character: Male, Nick, teenager.

A one-time tag-artist, Nick tries to figure out who he really is while coming to terms with the death of a friend amid the violence of wealthy New York City prep school hoods. With too much money, too little family, and too few morals, these young men beat and cut one another for fun, territory, or girls, and to gain reputation, power, and control. Reveals the darker side of growing up rich, including drugs, easy sex, and drinking. Raw gang slang. Grades: 9–12.

Draper, Sharon. *Romiette and Julio.*
Atheneum, 1999.
Setting: Cincinnati, Ohio, 1990s.
Main Characters: Female, Romiette Capelle; Male, Julio Montague; both 16 years old.

After falling in love on the Internet, African American Romiette and Latino Julio discover that they attend the same high school. They must deal with their parents' prejudices and with the threats of a local gang called The Family, whose members object to interracial dating. Awards: CC. Grades: 7–12.

Ewing, Lynne. *Drive-By.*
HarperCollins, 1998.
Setting: Los Angeles, 1990s.
Main Character: Male, Tito, 12 years old.

Tito thought Jimmy was joking around that night in front of the library. But when the gang car speeds away and Jimmy lays motionless on the ground, Tito realizes that his brother is dead. He later learns that Jimmy had been skimming money from his "deliveries" and hiding it from his gang and now that he is gone, the gang members begin a destructive search of Tito's house for the stolen cash. Grades: 5–8.

Herrera, Juan Felipe. *CrashBoomLove: A Novel in Verse.*
University of New Mexico Press, 1999.
Setting: Fowlerville, California, 1990s.
Main Character: Male, Cesar Garcia, 16 years old.
  Cesar doesn't fit in at his new school or at home with his broken family. He wants to crash into everything and gets involved in petty crimes, some violence, and drugs, but he is always searching for something more. A page-turner narrative poem. Awards: CC. Grades: 8 and up.

Hinton, S. E. *Outsiders.*
Viking, 1978.
Setting: 1960s.
Main Character: Male, Ponyboy Curtis, 14 years old.
  Ponyboy can count on his brothers and his friends. And trouble with the Socs, a vicious gang of rich kids whose idea of good time is beating up "greasers" like Ponyboy. One terrible night his friend Johnny kills a Soc. The murder gets under Ponyboy's skin, causing his world to crumble and teaching him that pain feels the same whether a Soc or a greaser. Grades: YA.

Hinton, S. E. *That Was Then, This Is Now.*
Puffin, 1998.
Setting: 1970s.
Main Characters: Male, Mark; Male, Bryon; both 16 years old.
  Mark and Bryon have been like brothers since childhood, but now, as their involvement with girls, gangs, and drugs increases, their relationship seems to gradually disintegrate. Grades: YA.

Martinez, Victor. *Parrot in the Oven: Mi Vida.*
HarperColins, 1996.
Setting: California.
Main Character: Male, Manny, 14 years old.
  Manny relates his coming-of-age experiences as a member of a poor Mexican American family in which the alcoholic father only adds to everyone's struggle. Awards: CC; Pura Belpré. Grades: 7–12.

McDonald, Janet. *Brother Hood.*
Farrar, Straus & Giroux, 2004.
Setting: New York City, present day.
Main Character: Male, Nate Whitely, 16 years old.
  Nate attends an exclusive boarding school on scholarship while trying to remain loyal to his Harlem roots. He gets along equally well in both worlds, with only a quick change from school uniform to do-rag and bomber jacket in the men's room at Grand Central Terminal. Grades: 6–9.

Myers, Walter Dean. *Beast.*
Scholastic, 2003.
Setting: Harlem, New York City.
Main Characters: Male, Anthony "Spoon" Witherspoon; Female, Gabi; both 16 years old.

Anthony leaves Harlem, and his girl, Gabi, to spend his senior year at Wallingford Academy, with the hope that he will get into an Ivy League college. While he adjusts to prep school life, Gabi's life comes undone. Her mother is dying, her younger brother may be running with a gang, and her blind grandfather has come to stay. When Spoon comes home for Christmas, Gabi is addicted to heroin. Awards: Notable Books for a Global Society. Grades: 8 and up.

Myers, Walter Dean. *Scorpions.*
HarperCollins, 1988.
Setting: Harlem, New York City.
Main Character: Male, Jamal, 13 years old.

Jamal, who is pressured to become leader of the Scorpions gang, worries about school, family, and the rough kids on the street. When a fellow gang member gives him a gun, Jamal suddenly gains a new level of respect from his enemies. Awards: CC; Newbery Honor. Grades: 6–9.

Randle, Kristen D. *Breaking Rank.*
HarperCollins, 1999.
Setting: High school, 1990s.
Main Characters: Male, Thomas, aka Baby; Female, Casey Willardson; both 17 years old.

Baby is a member of a nontraditional gang called the Clan. The Clan disavows participation in school, doesn't believe in drugs or violence, and advocates self-education. The older members tutor younger apprentices in everything from car mechanics to Latin. Baby wants to be more than just a mechanic like his domineering older brother, so he breaks rank from his peers and takes an aptitude test at school. Honor student Casey begins tutoring Baby and the misunderstandings they have about each other are slowly stripped away. They quickly become close and learn to trust and love each other. Their relationship provokes a showdown between the Clan and the varsity football team. Grades: 7 and up.

Soto, Gary. *Petty Crimes.*
Harcourt, 1998.
Setting: Central Valley, California.

Ten short stories rich in simile and metaphor and sprinkled with Spanish words about Mexican American teens. Awards: CC. Grades: 5 and up.

HOMELESSNESS

Brooks, Martha. *Being with Henry.*
DK Children, 2000.
Setting: Canada.
Main Character: Male, Laker, 16 years old.

Laker and his mother have always had a close relationship, but things change after she remarries. When his stepfather verbally abuses her, Laker attacks him and is thrown out of the house. Alone and with no resources, Laker takes off to another town. When his money runs out and he can't get a job since he has no address, he begins to beg. An elderly man, Henry, invites him to stay at his home and do yard work. Laker accepts his offer, and an uneasy friendship develops. When Henry's health begins to fail, Laker realizes how important the old man has become to him and that he cannot go back home even after he and his mother reconcile. Laker keeps a dream journal. Grades: 7 and up.

Flinn, Alex. *Nothing to Lose.*
HarperTempest, 2004.
Setting: Miami, Florida.
Main Character: Male, Michael Daye, 16 years old.

Michael ran away with a traveling carnival to escape his unbearable home life a year ago and when he returns to Miami, his mother is going on trial for the murder of his abusive stepfather. Alternating present day and last year chapters. Grades: 9–12.

Frost, Helen. *Keesha's House.*
Farrar, Straus and Giroux, 2003.
Setting: Joe's house, 2000s.
Main Characters: Joe, adult; Keesha, teenager.

The house is really Joe's, left to him by his aunt that took him in when he was twelve years old. Now he helps other kids, including Keesha, whose mother has died and father gets drunk and mean. Keesha tells her friends who need help about the house. The sestinas and sonnets tell the circumstances that brings the teens to the house. Awards: Printz Honor. Grades: 9–12.

Gaiman, Neil. *Neverwhere.*
Avon, 1998.
Setting: London, England, Underground.
Main Character: Male, Richard Mayhew, adult.

After helping a wounded girl named Door, Richard, a bumbling young business-man, is trapped in an alternate dimension, known as London Below, or the Under-ground. Once he steps into it, his normal life no longer exists. The only chance of getting his old life back is to accompany Door on a dangerous mission across the Underground. Includes detailed maps on the endpapers. Grades: YA/A.

Strasser, Todd. *Can't Get There From Here.*
Simon & Schuster, 2004.
Setting: New York City.
Main Character: Female, Maybe, teenager.

Maybe is tired of being hungry and seeing the other homeless teens dying one by one. She takes the youngest, Tears, with her and turns to Anthony, a librarian, for help. Grades: 7 and up.

Whelan, Gloria. *Homeless Bird.*
HarperCollins, 2000.
Setting: India.

Main Character: Female, Koly, 13 years old.

Koly feels apprehensive about leaving home to live in a distant village with her in-laws and husband, none of whom she has met. It is worse than she could have feared: the groom, Hari, is a sickly child, and his parents have wanted only a dowry in order to pay for a trip to Benares so Hari might bathe in the holy waters of the Ganges. Koly is soon widowed and abandoned in the holy city of Vrindavan by her cruel mother-in-law. She is saved from a dismal fate by her love of beauty, her talent for embroidery and the philanthropy of others. Awards: CC; National Book Award; Notable Books for a Global Society. Grades: 6–9.

RACISM/PREJUDICE

Curtis, Christopher Paul. *The Watsons Go to Birmingham—1963.*
Delacorte, 1995.
Setting: Alabama, 1963.
Main Character: Male, Kenny Watson, 9 years old.

The Watsons leave Flint, Michigan, to visit relatives in Birmingham, Alabama, just in time for the historical church bombing. Awards: CC; Newbery; Coretta Scott King. Grades: 6–10.

Davis, Ossie. *Just Like Martin.*
Puffin, 1995.
Setting: 1963.
Main Character: Male, Isaac Stone, 14 years old.

Isaac admires Martin Luther King, Jr. and wants to go to the civil rights march in Washington. D.C. Since his mother has just died, his father worried that something will happen to him. His father is also bitter from the Korean War and disagrees with King's nonviolent methods. Grades: 7–9.

Hamilton, Virginia. *White Romance.*
Harcourt, 1989.
Setting: Colonel Glenn High, 1980s.
Main Character: Female, Talley Barbour, teenager.

Talley's formerly all-black high school has been converted to an integrated magnet school for the entire district which means an influx of white students. The culture shock is immediate and prolonged. Add to the mix drugs, heavy metal rock, and Talley's struggles to establish her own values. Awards: CC. Grades: 8–10.

Hesse, Karen. *Witness.*
Scholastic, 2001.
Setting: Vermont, 1920s.

Eleven townspeople, young and old, of various races and creeds, express their views about the Ku Klux Klan coming to town. The story is divided into five acts in free verse. Grades: 6 and up.

Lee, Harper. *To Kill a Mockingbird.*
Warner, 1988.

Setting: Maycomb, Alabama, Depression era.
Main Character: Female, Scout Finch, 8 years old.

A young black man is arrested for raping a white woman and his defense lawyer is Atticus Finch. His daughter, Scout, tells the story of life in Maycomb and about the trial. Awards: CC; Pulitzer Prize. Grades: 8–12.

Martin, Nora. *Perfect Snow.*
Bloomsbury USA, 2002.
Setting: Montana.
Main Character: Male, Ben Campbell, 17 years old.

Ben is a brawler, a trailer-park kid who rails against RETCH (rich enough to cheat) kids. At the same time, he feels empowered by the escalating acts of violence he commits as a new member of Guardians of the Identity, a group exposing racial, ethnic, and gender/identity intolerance. Ben meets Eden and begins to see the error of his ways. Grades: 8 and up.

Meyer, Carolyn. *White Lilacs.*
Gulliver, 1993.
Setting: Dillon, Texas, 1920s.
Main Character: Female, Rose Lee Jefferson, 12 years old.

Rose Lee's favorite place is the garden tended by her beloved grandfather who has planted a profusion of colorful flowers around his home. Happily surrounded by her hardworking, loving family, the girl is shocked when she overhears the casual plan to move her entire black community to the sewer flats, so that a park can be built in the middle of town. Reactions from her neighbors range from quiet resignation and prayer to calls for strikes and a return to Africa. Some whites respond with threats of violence. Based on a real incident. Awards: CC. Grades: 7–10.

Sebestyen, Ouida. *Words by Heart.*
Dell, 1997.
Setting: Southwest, 1910.
Main Character: Female, Lena, 12 years old.

Lena can recite the scriptures by heart. Hoping to make her adored Papa proud of her and to make her white classmates notice her "Magic Mind," not her black skin, Lena vows to win the Bible-quoting contest. But winning does not bring Lena what she expected. Instead of honor, violence and death erupt and strike the one she loves most dearly. Awards: CC. Grades: 6–9.

Woodson, Jacqueline. *If You Come Softly.*
Putnam Juvenile, 1998.
Sequel: *Behind You.*
Setting: New York City.
Main Characters: Male, Jeremiah; Female, Elisha; both 15 years old.

Miah is black and Ellie is white. They meet during their first year at an exclusive New York prep school and fall in love. Both teens are also dealing with difficult family situations. Miah's father has left his mother for another woman, and Ellie is trying to fight through her feelings about her mother, who twice abandoned her family for extended periods. The teenagers must also deal with the subtle and not-so-subtle bigotry that they are subject to as a mixed-race couple. Awards: CC. Grades: 7 and up.

Wright, Richard. *Native Son.*
Buccaneer, 1997.
Setting: Chicago, Illinois, 1940s.
Main Character: Male, Bigger Thomas, 40 years old.

Bigger Thomas accidentally kills the daughter of his wealthy white employer. He tries to frame the young woman's fiancé for the crime and attempts to extort ransom from the victim's family, but his guilt is discovered, and he is forced into hiding. After a terrifying manhunt, he is arrested and brought to trial. Though his fate is certain, he finds that his crimes have given meaning and energy to his previously aimless life, and he goes to his execution unrepentant. Extremely violent language and situations. Awards: CC. Grades: 10–12.

SUICIDE

Dewey, Jennifer. *Borderlands.*
Marshall Cavendish, 2002.
Setting: Psychiatric hospital.
Main Character: Female, Jamie, 17 years old.

Jamie's attempt to take her own life has brought her to a mental institution, where her friendship with Adam is a first step toward recovery. Adam is in a body cast as a result of jumping from a three-story building. They exchange their stories and learn to care about each other, although their fates will be as different as their diagnoses. Grades: 8 and up.

Green, John. *Looking for Alaska.*
Dutton, 2005.
Setting: Alabama.
Main Character: Male, Miles Halter, 16 years old.

Miles decides to take charge of his life by going to an Alabama boarding school. Once there, he's rechristened "Pudge" and adopted by new roommate Chip and best friend Alaska. She and Chip teach Miles to drink, smoke, and plot elaborate pranks. The chapters are headed by the number of days before and after Alaska's suicide. Awards: Teens Top Ten. Grades: 9 and up.

Lynch, Chris. *Freewill.*
HarperCollins, 2001.
Setting: Vocational school.
Main Character: Male, Will, 17 years old.

Will is disconnected from his reality due to the deaths of his parents, which may have been a murder suicide. The narrator is another voice in Will's mind. When there are two more possible suicides, Will begins to sink into oblivion. Awards: CC; Printz Honor. Grades: 8–12.

Mahy, Margaret. *24 Hours.*
Margaret K. McElderry, 2000.
Setting: New Zealand.
Main Character: Male, Ellis, 17 years old.

Ellis, an aspiring actor who has just graduated from prep school, runs into Jackie, an old public school friend, who leads him on a 24-hour escapade, ending up in the Land-of-Smiles, a run-down former motel and gathering place for aging activists, tattoo artists, hairdressers, and other fringe characters. Ellis develops a crush on Leona, the middle of three sisters who preside over the hotel. The experience helps Ellis deal with his best friend's recent suicide. Grades: 8 and up.

Mayfield, Sue. *Drowning Anna.*
Hyperion, 2002.
Setting: Northern England.
Main Character: Female, Anna Goldsmith, 13 years old.

Beautiful and an ace student, Anna is praised by her teachers, given a violin solo, and assigned to play center in hockey, displacing Hayley Parkin, who is her first and seemingly devoted friend. What Anna doesn't know is that Hayley is an adept manipulator and all of her classmates live in fear of her. When Melanie Blackwood, who really wants to be Anna's friend, gradually gives in to Hayley's pressure, Anna begins to cut herself. Anna is comatose through most of the book and speaks mostly through her diary entries and letters. Grades: 7–10.

Miller, Mary Beth. *Aimee.*
Dutton, 2002.
Setting: 2000s.
Main Character: Female, Zoe, 17 years old.

Zoe is angry. Having recently been acquitted of assisting her best friend's suicide, she is seeing a court-appointed psychiatrist who has suggested she write the journal that forms this book. The entries slip backward and forward in time and Zoe has complaints about 99 percent of her life. Her parents have moved to another town and seem to be hoping that she will get over Aimee's death. Forbidden to communicate with her hometown friends, Zoe feels hung out to dry. Grades: 9 and up.

Mori, Kyoko. *Shizuko's Daughter.*
Fawcett, 1994.
Setting: Japan.
Main Character: Female, Yuki, 12 years old.

Shizuko kills herself to escape a soured marriage, leaving her husband free to marry his mistress of eight years, and having vague ideas about making her daughter's life better. Her daughter Yuki now faces a bleak world with a stepmother who tries to eradicate all traces of Shizuko and curtail the girl's visits to her mother's family. Yuki must cope with the loss of her mother and piece together some meaning for her death and ultimately for her life. Grades: 7 and up.

Peck, Richard. *Remembering the Good Times.*
Laurel Leaf, 1986.
Setting: 1980s.

Main Characters: Male, Buck Mendenhall; Male, Trav Kirby; Female, Kate Lucas; all 16 years old.

Buck, Trav, and Kate are inseparable friends during junior and senior high school, until Trav hangs himself at age sixteen. Parents and school boards accuse each other of irresponsibility in the matter, while Buck's father and Kate's great-grandmother come forward to bring teen suicide into the open. Grades: 7 and up.

Plath, Sylvia. *The Bell Jar.*
HarperPerennial, 2000.
Setting: New York City, 1950s.
Main Character: Female, Esther Greenwood, young adult.

A gifted young woman suffers a mental breakdown during a summer internship as a junior editor at a magazine. The real Plath committed suicide in 1963 and left behind this honest tale of a woman's descent into insanity. Grades: YA.

CHAPTER 23

SPORTS

Many issues are addressed in a sports novel, including family relationships, friendships, racism, violence, drug abuse, and much more. While sports novels often appeal mostly to boys, there is a list of titles with female main characters who are participating in a wide variety of sports, which will appeal to girl readers.

Baseball/Softball
Basketball
Boxing and Wrestling
Football
Girls in Sports
Hockey, Skiing, Skating
Miscellaneous Sports
Running/Track
Soccer
Swimming
Resources: Additional Titles

BASEBALL/SOFTBALL

Bennett, James W. *Plunking Reggie Jackson.*
Simon & Schuster, 2001.
Setting: Contemporary.
Main Character: Male, Coley Burke, 18 years old.
 Coley is a baseball star courted by the major league scouts and has his choice of college scholarships for his pitching arm. His sexy, red-headed girlfriend Bree is secretive about her family and Coley has his own family troubles with a father who criticizes every detail of Coley's pitching and compares Coley to his dead older brother. Now Coley is flunking English, he's injured his ankle and can't play, and then Bree gets pregnant. If Coley can't fix his problems, his career is over before it begins. A sports novel with a bit of sex thrown in. Grades: 7 and up.

Chabon, Michael. *Summerland.*
Miramax, 2002.
Setting: Clam Island, Washington, 2000s.

Main Character: Male, Ethan Field, 11 years old.

Ethan is a less than mediocre Little League baseball player, but he is recruited by a mystical baseball scout and guided to interconnected worlds, where he must win a series of games against fantastical creatures. Harry Potter fans will like the adventure and magical fantasy aspect of the story, while there is plenty of baseball for sports fans. Awards: Mythopoeic. Grades: 5–12.

Crutcher, Chris. *The Crazy Horse Electric Game.*
Greenwillow,1987.
Setting: Montana, California.
Main Character: Male, Willie Weaver, 17 years old.

Willie, a star pitcher, leads his team against the powerful squad from Crazy Horse Electric for the Eastern Montana American Legion baseball championship. When Willie suffers a head injury in a water-skiing accident, he is unable to accept the loss of his athletic skills, the pity of others, and his parents' troubled marriage. Willie runs away and ends up in the inner city of Oakland, California. Willie's story has a lot going on: the crib death of his sister, parents' divorce, drugs, sexual feelings, gang violence, mental handicaps, physical handicaps, prostitution, child beating, and more. Awards: CC. Grades: 8–12.

Deuker, Carl. *High Heat.*
HarperTrophy, 2005.
Setting: Seattle, Washington.
Main Character: Male, Shane Hunter, 15 years old.

After his dad is arrested for money laundering and commits suicide, Shane, his mother, and his younger sister are forced to move into subsidized housing. Shane is soon arrested for stealing beer from a convenience store. As part of his probation, he helps repair a local baseball diamond, where he meets the coach of his school's baseball team. Shane tries out for the team, and becomes a relief pitcher. Soon Shane faces the team from his old school. Angry, he pitches a fastball directly at Reese Robertson's head. Grades: 7–12.

Johnson, Scott. *Safe at Second.*
Puffin, 2001.
Setting: Edgeville High.
Main Character: Male, Todd Bannister, 17 years old.

Todd's pitching has the attention of scouts, agents, and recruiters and the admiration of his classmates. Then he is hit in the face by a line drive and loses an eye. His attempt to come back is unsuccessful as he can no longer control his pitches and he becomes angry and bitter. His best friend, Paulie Lockwood tells Todd's story. Grades: 7–12.

Mosher, Howard Frank. *Waiting for Teddy Williams.*
Houghton Mifflin, 2004.
Setting: Kingdom Common, Vermont.
Main Character: Male, Ethan "E.A." Allen, 8 years old.

Ethan's greatest desire is to play major league baseball. He is being raised by his mother and grandmother; his father absent. E.A. encounters fascinating and often comic characters, heroes and villains who abuse their power in his small community. When his father, a promising player in his youth, returns, E.A. begins to work towards his dream . . . the day he plays at Fenway Park. Grades: YA/A.

Powell, Randy. *Dean Duffy.*
Farrar, Straus & Giroux, 2003.
Setting: 1990s.
Main Character: Male, Dean, 18 years old.

When he was 15, Dean pitched for the world championship Little League team, and as a freshman he hit a game-winning grand slam. Then his arm gave out and he moved to first base and had a two-year batting slump. Losing hope for a college scholarship, he now wonders what his future holds since graduation. A longtime mentor arranges a trial scholarship at a small college for him, but Dean is hesitant because he fears failure. An accident and the support of friends help Dean when he has to make his decision whether to go. Grades: 7–12.

Ritter, John H. *The Boy Who Saved Baseball.*
Philomel, 2003.
Setting: Dillontown, California.
Main Character: Male, Tom Gallagher, 12 years old.

Doc Altenheimer, an 87-year-old apple rancher, is ready to sell his 320 acres of prime real estate that makes up a good part of Dillontown and its baseball field to a developer. He proposes that the decision should ride on a baseball game between the local residents and the summer camp team down the road. Tom works to get a team together and ready to save his town. Grades: 5–8.

Ritter, John H. *Over the Wall.*
Philomel, 2000.
Setting: New York City.
Main Character: Male, Tyler Waltern, 13 years old.

Tyler is spending the summer with his aunt, uncle, and cousins, where he can play serious baseball and avoid his father, a troubled recluse since the accidental death of Tyler's sister nine years earlier. Tyler's explosive temper and combative disposition is attracting the wrong kind of attention from his coaches. One coach, a Vietnam veteran, and Tyler's cousin helps him sort out his feelings about his grandfather's death in the war. The "wall" represents the wall in a baseball field, the Vietnam Wall, and the wall Tyler's father has built between himself and the rest of the world. Grades: 6–9.

Weaver, Will. *Striking Out: A Billy Baggs Novel.*
Sagebrush, 1999.
Sequels: *Farm Team: A Billy Baggs Novel; Hard Ball: A Billy Baggs Novel.*
Setting: Minnesota.
Main Character: Male, Billy Baggs, 13 years old.

Billy's older brother died in a tractor accident. Five years later, Billy is still wrestling with guilt over his death. Playing summer baseball offers Billy and his family some hope. Grades: 8–12.

BASKETBALL

Bee, Clair, et al. ***Backboard Fever.***
Broadman & Holman, 1999.
Series: Chip Hilton Sports Series (24 titles).
Setting: State College, 1950s.
Main Character: Male, William "Chip" Hilton, college student, 19 years old.
    An injury prevents Chip from joining the college basketball team. He serves as a replacement coach for the high school and participates in an important basket shooting tournament. Christian sports fiction by a Hall of Fame football coach. Grades: YA.

Bennett, James. ***The Squared Circle.***
Scholastic, 2002.
Setting: Southern Illinois University, contemporary.
Main Character: Male, Sonny Youngblood, college freshman, 19 years old.
    Sonny is an All-American basketball player in his freshman year at Southern Illinois University on a scholarship. As the pressures of college life build, repressed memories return, and the NCAA investigates his recruitment, Sonny begins to question who he really is and seeks to reclaim the person he once was. For mature readers. Grades: 9–12.

Brooks, Bruce. ***The Moves Make the Man.***
HarperCollins, 1984.
Setting: North Carolina.
Main Character: Male, Jerome Foworthy, 12 years old.
    Jerome, the Jayfox to his friends, thinks he can handle anything. He handled growing up without a father, being the first black kid in school, and he sure can handle a basketball. Then Jerome meets Bix Rivers, mysterious and moody, but a great athlete. So Jerome decides to teach Bix his game. He can tell that Bix has the talent. All he's got to do is learn the right moves. Awards: CC; Newbery Honor. Grades: 7–12.

De La Pena, Matt. ***Ball Don't Lie.***
Random House/Delacorte, 2005.
Setting: Los Angeles, California, contemporary.
Main Character: Male, Sticky, 17 years old.
    Sticky, an abused foster kid, sometimes homeless, with obsessive compulsive disorder, can sure play basketball. His skill has gained respect from his mostly black peers. He gets a girlfriend named Anh-thu, and Sticky sees basketball as his way out of his dead-end life. He makes a bad decision that leads him to confront dark secrets. Street lingo, basketball jargon, and trash talk, with basketball action. Grades: 9 and up.

Deuker, Carl. ***Night Hoops.***
HarperTrophy, 2001.
Setting: Contemporary.
Main Character: Male, Nick Abbott, 15 years old.
    Nick is trying to deal with his parent's divorce. He wants to be a star player on his high school basketball team. Nick learns how to control the tempo of a game as a

point guard. His disturbed and angry teammate and neighbor, Trent Dawson, practices every night on Nick's backyard court. Nick and Trent become a dominating duo on the court. Grades: 8–10.

Deuker, Carl. *On the Devil's Court.*
Avon, 1991.
Setting: Seattle, Washington.
Main Character: Male, Joe Faust, 17 years old.

Joe and his family move to Seattle and Joe is enrolled in a private academic school, when Joe had hoped to experience public school and competitive basketball. He unleashes his frustrations in an abandoned gym and shoots a series of perfect shots. Joe vows, "Give me a full season, give me twenty-four games of this power, and my soul is yours." He becomes a superstar this season and his studies of Dr. Faustus in English class lead him to fear he has made an irrevocable pact with the devil. Exciting sports action, literary references, and analogies. Awards: CC. Grades: 8–12.

Feinstein, John. *Last Shot: A Final Four Mystery.*
Knopf, 2005.
Setting: New Orleans, Louisiana.
Main Characters: Male, Steven Thomas; Female, Susan Carol Anderson; both 13 years old.

Stevie and Susan Carol are the winners of the U.S. Basketball Writer's Association 14-and-under writing contest. Their prize is a trip, with press credentials and reporting responsibilities, to the men's Final Four basketball tournament in New Orleans. While exploring the Superdome, they overhear Minnesota State University's star player, Chip Graber, blackmailed to deliberately lose the final game against Duke. Stevie and Susan Carol become determined to save Chip and to expose the scandal. Famous basketball personalities make cameos in this sports mystery. Grades: 6–10.

Klass, David. *Danger Zone.*
Sagebrush, 1999.
Setting: Los Angeles, California/Rome, Italy.
Main Character: Male, Jimmy Doyle, 16 years old.

Jimmy, a standout guard from Minnesota, is one of ten players selected to represent the USA in an international tournament to be held in Rome. Team practices are in Los Angeles where Jimmy's thrown together with ethnic and culturally diverse teammates. He immediately clashes with team star and South-Central L.A. native Augustus LeMay, who feels Jimmy is on the team only because he is white. In Rome, the American team is verbally abused by a group of skinhead fans from Germany, which escalates into a physical confrontation, and later a death threat against the American squad. Lots of hoop action and racial tension. Grades: 7–12.

Lupica, Mike. *Travel Team.*
Philomel, 2004.
Setting: Present day.
Main Character: Male, Danny Walker, 12 years old.

Danny is a basketball fanatic. He is smart, talented, fast, and dedicated, but short. He fails to make the seventh-grade travel team to follow in the footsteps of his legendary father, Richie Walker, who led his own team to win the nationals but whose career was tragically ended by a car accident. Danny did not make the squad because of Richie's childhood nemesis, Mr. Ross, who is determined to build a winning team. Danny has a strained relationship with his father, but he and the others cut from the travel team form their own squad. Richie, battling alcoholism, coaches them to face their arch rivals. Grades: 5–8.

Myers, Walter Dean. *Hoops.*
Laurel Leaf, 1983.
Setting: Harlem, New York City.
Main Character: Male, Lonnie Jackson, 17 years old.
  Lonnie practices with his team for a citywide basketball Tournament of Champions. His coach, Cal, knows Lonnie has what it takes to be a pro basketball player. Cal had been a professional player but had to quit because of a scandal, and is now being pressured by heavy bettors to bench Lonnie so the team will lose. Grades: 7–12.

Myers, Walter Dean. *Slam!*
Scholastic, 1998.
Setting: Harlem, New York City.
Main Character: Male, Greg "Slam" Harris, 17 years old.
  Greg transfers to a magnet school for the arts, a more academically challenging, mostly white school. After being the hot-shot star of his Harlem high school team, he has to learn to fit in and be a team player at his new school. The basketball court is the only place Greg feels in control. He's failing his classes, his grandmother is dying, his father is out of work and hitting the bottle again, and his oldest friend appears to be dealing crack. Good hoop action! Appealing to reluctant readers. Awards: CC; Coretta Scott King. Grades: 8–12.

Soto, Gary. *Taking Sides.*
Harcourt, 2003.
Setting: San Francisco suburb, California.
Main Character: Male, Lincoln Mendoza, 14 years old.
  Lincoln and his mother have just moved from a San Francisco barrio to a wealthy, predominantly white suburb. He misses his Hispanic friends and his old neighborhood. He's made the basketball team, but the coach dislikes him for no good reason. A big game between his new school and the old one is coming up and Lincoln cannot decide which team he wants to win. Appealing to reluctant readers. Grades: 5–7.

Strohm, Craig. *Comeback.*
Pelican, 2001.
Setting: Empire High School.
Main Character: Male, Coach Peterson, adult.
  Coach Peterson, a high school teacher and girls' basketball coach, is haunted by the disappearance of his son at a shopping mall. His guilt and not knowing what really happened has shadowed everything in his life. Now, a college basketball player comes to his attention because there's something so familiar about his laugh and

expression in his eyes. Coach Peterson has to find out if the player could be his missing son. Grades: YA.

Sweeney, Joyce. *Players.*
Marshall Cavendish, 2005.
Setting: Miami, Florida.
Main Character: Male, Corey Brennan, 18 years old.

Corey hopes to lead his Catholic high school basketball team to win the Miami all-city trophy. When the season starts Corey discovers a transfer student, Noah Travers, will stop at nothing to make the starting squad. Noah's ambition leads him to blackmail, tampering with a player's medications, and planting a gun in a teammate's locker. Corey tricks him into admitting his crimes. Fast-paced. Grades: 8–12.

Volponi, Paul. *Black and White.*
Viking, 2005.
Setting: Queens, New York, 2000s.
Main Characters: Male, Marcus Brown; Male, Eddie Russo; both 17 years old.

Marcus, an African American, and Eddie, who is white, are best friends on and off the court. They risk scholarship offers from New York City colleges for more spending money. They turn to armed robbery, and during the third robbery, they shoot and wound their victim. In alternating chapters, they each tell their own stories as they wait for the police to find and arrest them; they receive different treatment because of their racial differences. Grades: 9–12.

Wallace, Rich. *Playing Without the Ball.*
Knopf, 2000.
Setting: Pennsylvania.
Main Character: Male, Jay McLeod, 17 years old.

Jay is on his own, living in an apartment over a bar while he finishes his senior year of high school. His mom left when he was nine and his dad left last year to live his own life. Jay has an evening job downstairs in the kitchen and he has time for lots of basketball, and the freedom to check out girls. Jay joins a YMCA church league and leads his team to a championship game. Grades: 9 and up.

BOXING AND WRESTLING

Benjamin, E. M. J. *Takedown.*
John F. Blair, 1999.
Setting: High school.
Main Character: Male, Jake Chapman, 17 years old.

Jake, a star high school wrestler with a legitimate shot at winning the state championship, is diagnosed with epilepsy. A feminist English teacher has unfairly kept Jake out of the National Honor Society. The one girl on the wrestling team comes late to practice and frequently skips it altogether, but she is not disciplined because the coach fears a lawsuit. Jake's own mother sacrifices the welfare of her family for the sake of her career. Heavy on the negative female characters. Grades: 9 and up.

Cadnum, Max. *Redhanded.*
Viking, 2000.
Setting: San Francisco Bay Area, California.
Main Character: Male, Steven, teenager.

Boxing is the most important thing to Steven and winning an upcoming Golden Gloves West Coast tournament may be the ticket to get everything he wants. The entry fee is hefty and he doesn't have the money. His parents are separated and he lost his dishwashing job. He lets his friend Raymond and street-smart Chad lead him into crime. When they plan to rob a liquor store, Chad grabs a woman and shoots her, and Steven uses his boxing skills to bring Chad down. Grades: 7 and up.

Conifer, Dave. *Throwback.*
iUniverse, 2004.
Setting: New Jersey.
Main Character: Male, Ben Pietrak, 19 years old.

Although Ben is now in college, he still regrets the way his high school wrestling career ended. He convinces himself he needs to go back to high school to experience a varsity season. Once there, he sees other missed opportunities and meets Judy, a student whom he would never have had anything to do with the first time in high school. He seeks wrestling vindication at the New Jersey Wrestling Championships. Grades: YA.

Davis, Terry. *Vision Quest.*
Delacorte, 2005.
Setting: High school.
Main Character: Male, Louden Swain, 18 years old.

Louden is a high school wrestler whose life has been defined by his family, his school, his friends, and his sport. When his family breaks up, he realizes that he must go on a vision quest, a Plains Indian tradition, to find his place in the world. He chooses as his quest to drop two weight classes in order to challenge Shute, a fearsome wrestler from another school. Grades: 7–12.

Karr, Kathleen. *The Boxer.*
Farrar, Straus & Giroux, 2004.
Setting: Manhattan, late nineteenth century.
Main Character: Male, Johnny, 15 years old.

Johnny is desperately looking for work to support his fatherless family. There are sweatshops where many of the immigrants work for little pay. Jimmy sees a sign in a bar window asking for young men to try their fighting skills to win a five-dollar prize. Jimmy is arrested during his first fight, but he meets former lightweight champion Michael O'Shaunnessey in jail. O'Shaunnessey recognizes Johnny's raw talent and begins training him as a serious boxer. When he gets out, Johnny is winning fights, working regularly in the New York Athletic Club, and saving money for a new home for his family in Brooklyn. Johnny's winning concentration is shaken when his alcoholic father returns. Grades: 6–10.

Lipsyte, Robert. *The Contender.*
HarperTrophy, 1987.

Sequels: *The Brave; The Chief.*
Setting: Harlem, New York City.
Main Character: Male, Alfred, 17 years old.

Alfred's a high school dropout working at a grocery store. His best friend is drifting behind a haze of drugs and violence, and now some street punks are harassing him for something he didn't do. Alfred wants to be a champion, on the streets and in his own life. He gathers up the courage to visit Donatelli's Gym, the neighborhood's boxing club, where Mr. Donatelli tells him it is the climbing that makes the man. Grades: YA.

Lynch, Chris. *Shadow Boxer.*
HarperTrophy, 1995.
Setting: Boston.
Main Character: Male, George, 14 years old.

After their father dies from a boxing injury, George struggles with the increasingly difficult responsibility of guiding and protecting his younger brother, who wants to box like his father. Grades: 7–12.

Martino, Alfred C. *Pinned.*
Harcourt, 2005.
Setting: New Jersey.
Main Characters: Male, Ivan Korske; Male, Bobby Zane; both 17 years old.

Alternating story lines follow two talented high school wrestlers who meet in the finals of the 129-pound division of the New Jersey State Wrestling Championship. Bobby comes from an affluent family and school with a winning wrestling tradition and a first-class coach, but his parents' breakup and his pregnant girlfriend add more stress to his already stressed body. Ivan's mother recently died, and he chafes under the thumb of his old-school Polish papa. His unspoken anger makes him an outcast even on his own team, yet a wrestling scholarship could take him far away from his depressing blue-collar town. Raw language. Grades: 8–12.

Wallace, Rich. *Wrestling Sturbridge.*
Knopf, 1996.
Setting: Sturbridge, Pennsylvania.
Main Character: Male, Ben, 17 years old.

Ben doesn't want to be like his father and get a job at the cinder-block plant after graduating. He hopes to become a state wrestling champion and win an athletic scholarship. His friend Al reigns supreme in their weight class, and Ben is relegated to being Al's practice partner and a benchwarmer during tournaments. Kim, a Puerto Rican track enthusiast transplanted from New Jersey, won't put up with Ben's self-pity, and pushes him to try his best. Awards: CC. Grades: 7–12.

FOOTBALL

Bee, Clair. *Freshman Quarterback.*
Broadman & Holman, 1999.
Series: Chip Hilton sports series (24 titles).
Setting: State University, 1950s.

Main Character: Male, William "Chip" Hilton, 19 years old.

As a member of the freshman football team at State University, Chip Hilton encounters cliques, rivalries, and a conspiracy by the Booster Association to favor some players over others. Christian sports novel. Grades: YA.

Cheripko, Jan. *Imitate the Tiger.*
Boyds Mills, 1998.
Setting: Valley View High School.
Main Character: Male, Chris Serbo, 17 years old.

Chris is an outside linebacker for the Valley View High School Dragons and an alcoholic. His mother died when he was a child, and his father is also an alcoholic. Each chapter begins with an account telling what's going on in the present as Chris works through the Alcoholics Anonymous Twelve Steps and, after football season is over, tries to finish high school at a rehab. Each chapter continues with Chris's story of his championship season with the Dragons and the downward spiral his personal life took due to his drinking. Grades: 8–12.

Cochran, Thomas. *Roughnecks.*
Harcourt, 1999.
Setting: Oil Camp, Louisiana.
Main Character: Male, Travis Cody, senior.

Travis is preparing for the final game of his high school career against his school's chief rival. His whole town is crazy for football, cheering on the Roughnecks as Travis concentrates on regaining his confidence and evening the score when he confronts archrival Jericho Grooms. Grades: 7 and up.

Coy, John. *Crackback.*
Scholastic, 2005.
Setting: Present day.
Main Character: Male, Miles, 15 years old.

Regardless of his efforts or his talents, Miles can't seem to satisfy his coach. He winds up on the bench where he meets, and likes, the second-string players who have lives outside of football, something that has never occurred to Miles or his father. He refuses to take steroids, even though his teammates do. The family secret that drives his father, the interesting girl who shows him that the world is a big place, and the intense, sometimes unbelievable coach who teaches him that you can't please some people, no matter what, give Miles a new, perhaps healthier, perspective. Great football action. Grades: 7 and up.

Crutcher, Chris. *Running Loose.*
Greenwillow, 1983.
Setting: Idaho.
Main Character: Male, Louie Banks, 17 years old.

Louie has a car, a starting spot on the team, good friends, and a dream girl. Everything changes when he's kicked off the football team for taking a stand against the coach and his girlfriend is killed in a car accident. Crutcher's first novel. Awards: CC. Grades: YA.

Dygard, Thomas J. *Backfield Package.*
HarperCollins, 1992.
Setting: Hillcrest High, Indiana.
Main Character: Male, Joe, 17 years old.
    Four teammates and close friends make up the offensive backfield for their high school football team and decide early in the season that they will continue their football careers together as a "package" at a small state college. Joe, the quarterback, begins receiving interest from a major college, and he realizes that the future holds greater possibilities for him than for his teammates. Joe is torn between loyalty to his friends and his desire to succeed. Grades: 6–10.

Jenkins, A.M. *Damage.*
HarperCollins, 2001.
Setting: Parkersville.
Main Character: Male, Austin Reid, 17 years old.
    Austin, the star of the football team, is depressed and suicidal but afraid to tell anyone he needs help. He refers to himself in the second-person voice, illustrating how disconnected and distant he feels. Awards: CC. Grades: 7–12.

Klass, David. *Home of the Braves.*
HarperTempest, 2004.
Setting: Lawndale High School, New Jersey suburb.
Main Character: Male, Joe Brickman, 18 years old.
    Joe, captain of the soccer and wrestling teams, wants to ask Kristine, his best friend since childhood, out on a date. Antonio, a Brazilian soccer star, arrives as a transfer student, threatening to take over the soccer team and Kristine. Antonio scoffs at the school's social order and violence erupts. The school administration responds with a zero-tolerance policy complete with bars on the windows, metal detectors, video monitors, and police in the halls. Grades: 9 and up.

Lee, Marie G. *Necessary Roughness.*
HarperTrophy, 1998.
Setting: Minnesota.
Main Character: Male, Chan, 16 years old.
    Chan and his twin sister, Young, move from Los Angeles to a small town in Minnesota with their parents, who immigrated to the United States from Korea when the twins were small. The only Asians in town, the twins enter their junior year facing bigotry and prejudice. Chan finds refuge on the football team, and the twins begin to adjust to the new school and town. Then Young is killed in a car accident. Grades: 7–10.

Powell, Randy. *Three Clams and an Oyster.*
Farrar, Straus & Giroux, 2002.
Setting: High school, 2000s.
Main Characters: Male, Flint McCallister; Male, Dwight Deshutis; Male, Rick Beaterson; all 16 years old.
    Flint, Dwight, and Rick's four-man flag football team, Three Clams and an Oyster, is short one player. Cade Savage, their fourth, would rather party than practice. They

know they have to get serious if they want to go to Nationals, so they're soon scrambling to find a replacement before the September deadline. They have to decide among Thor Hupf, who's a great player but a total stoner, or Tim Goon, who, despite his silk shirts and bad hair, owns a ski cabin that he might invite the Clams to, or pretty jock Rachel Summerfield, whose natural talent for flag football almost outweighs the fact that she doesn't shave her legs. Grades: 8 and up.

Walters, Eric. *Juice.*
Orca, 2005.
Setting: High school.
Main Character: Male, Moose, teenager.
    Moose is an excellent football player, a good kid, and a good leader. He deals with a new coach who is determined to win at all costs. The players are offered steroids, and they have to make decisions. Appealing to reluctant readers. Grades: 6–9.

GIRLS IN SPORTS

Coleman, Evelyn. *Born in Sin.*
Atheneum/Richard Jackson, 2001.
Setting: Georgia.
Main Character: Female, Keisha, 14 years old.
    Keisha is enraged when her high school guidance counselor thwarts her efforts to get into Avery's fast-track pre-med program and instead places her in a summer program for at-risk kids. Through the program, Keisha learns to deal with her own racial prejudice, makes her first real friends, and discovers that she has a natural talent for swimming. Grades: 9 and up.

Fitzgerald, Dawn. *Getting in the Game.*
Roaring Brook, 2005.
Setting: Ohio, 2000s.
Main Character: Female, Joanna Giordano, 13 years old.
    Jo prefers ice hockey to figure skating, and is determined to make her middle school team. Despite opposition from the other athletes (all male), the coach, the school principal, the father of her friend Ben—also trying out for the team—and many of the other seventh-grade girls, she perseveres and makes the cut. Ben also makes it, but his desire to fit in with the other boys leads him to turn away from Jo. She also has to deal with her parents' separation, caused largely by her father's inability to control his temper, and her grandfather's progressive Alzheimer's symptoms. Grades: 5–7.

Gutman, Dan. *The Million Dollar Kick.*
Hyperion, 2003.
Setting: Middle school.
Main Character: Female, Whisper, 13 years old.
    Whisper can't stand soccer; her younger sister is the family sports star. But it is Whisper who is chosen for a contest promotion to kick a goal past the town's leading professional soccer star in front of a whole stadium full of soccer fanatics. The prize is one million dollars, but Whisper suspects that no one believes she can do it and

feels the humiliation isn't worth it. But Jesse, a computer nerd, who has created a laptop simulation that could help her succeed, believes she can do it. Grades: 5–8.

Koss, Amy Goldman. *Strike Two.*
Dial, 2001.
Setting: 2000s.
Main Character: Female, Gwen, young teenager.
　　Gwen is excited to play summer softball with her best friend and cousin, Jess, for the *Press Gazette*, the city's newspaper, where their fathers work. A strike at the *Gazette* divides their families, as Gwen's dad is labor and Jess's dad is management. At first they are hopeful the strike won't last long, and Gwen is happy to have her dad home. As the strike continues, tensions build between families, disrupting friendships and the softball season. Grades: 4–7.

Macy, Sue. *Girls Got Game: Sports Stories and Poems.*
Henry Holt, 2001.
Setting: 2000s.
　　Nine American women authors were invited to contribute original short stories about girls playing sports: Virginia Euwer Wolff, Jacqueline Woodson, Lucy Jane Bledsoe, Pat Connolly. Christa Champion, Sue Macy write about baseball, softball, basketball, soccer, stickball, football, tetherball, swimming, and horseback riding. Grades: 6–9.

Mackel, Kathy. *MadCat.*
HarperCollins, 2005.
Setting: New Hampshire.
Main Character: Female, Madelyn "Mad Cat" Catherine, 12 years old.
　　Mad Cat is the catcher for the Sting, an all-girls fast-pitch softball team. The team has always enjoyed playing and played well. The board of directors and parents reorganize it in order to compete nationally. Some of the new team members used to be rivals and have replaced friends. The mood of the team changes, and the games become more cutthroat than fun. Parents are now telling the coach who plays, and the girls fight. After a bad experience at the national championships, several girls reassess their priorities. Grades: 5–8.

Nitz, Kristin. *Defending Irene.*
Peachtree, 2004.
Setting: Merano, Italy.
Main Character: Female, Irene Benenati, 13 years old.
　　Irene is living in Merano, Italy with her family for one year, where there are no girls' soccer teams. Irene plays on the boys' team but feels like an outsider. She eventually earns the support of her classmates and teammates. Chapter headings consist of Italian words, pronunciations, and definitions. Grades: 5–7.

Rallison, Janette. *Life, Love, and the Pursuit of Free Throws.*
Walker, 2004.
Setting: Present day.
Main Character: Female, Cami, 14 years old.

Cami wants to become the MVP of her basketball team so she can run drills with Rebecca Lobo, former star of the WNBA. No matter how hard she tries, her best friend Josie is better. Basketball comes naturally to Josie but she is preoccupied with Ethan, even though he never pays any attention to her. Ethan notices and begins to telephone Cami. Josie feels betrayed and angry. Grades: 6–9.

Roberts, Kristi. *My 13th Season.*
Henry Holt, 2005.
Setting: Oregon.
Main Character: Female, Fran Cullers, 13 years old.
Star baseball player Fran is not welcome on the boys' team in her new town. Her father isn't much help or support in his grief over her mother's recent death. The coach is removed from the team for his abuse toward Fran, but she falls into a slump. She decides to give up the game. Her friend Steven comes to get Fran for an important game. Her dad rallies and coaches the team and Fran regains her old form. Grades: 5–8.

Spinelli, Jerry. *There's a Girl in My Hammerlock.*
Aladdin, 1993.
Setting: Suburban junior high school.
Main Character: Female, Maisie Potter, 13 years old.
When Maisie starts noticing Eric Delong, she quits girls' field hockey to try out for cheerleading. When she doesn't make the squad, she tries out for wrestling and makes the team. It is an all boys' team, and Eric Delong is one of the boys on the team. Maisie surprises everyone with her endurance and skill. Grades: 5–8.

Wolff, Virginia Euwer. *Bat 6.*
Scholastic, 1998.
Setting: Oregon, May 28, 1949.
Main Characters: Female, Shazam; Female, Aki, 11 years old.
The members of two rival girls baseball teams begin the traditional annual game between them, but are interrupted when Shazam violently attacks Aki, a Japanese American. Twenty-one points of view. Awards: CC; Radical Reads. Grades: 5–8.

MISCELLANEOUS SPORTS

Bo, Ben. *The Edge.*
First Avenue Editions, 2002.
Setting: Glacier National Park, Canada.
Main Character: Male, Declan, teenager.
Declan passes the initiation challenge into the Urban Xtreme Team. The skater gang's graffiti is all over town. When Jaz, the group's leader accidentally sets a warehouse fire, Declan is the only survivor. He is sentenced to an experimental rehabilitation program at a ski lodge at Canada's Glacier National Park, where the wise Big Foot, elderly great-grandson of a great Indian chief, will teach him to channel his restless spirit. Declan's talent at skateboarding makes him a natural to learn snowboarding. He is attracted to his tutor Manu, the daughter of the lodge owner,

and then is drawn into a duel with Mad Dog, the local snowboarding champion. Nonstop action. Grades: 5–8.

Crutcher, Chris. *Athletic Shorts.*
HarperTempest, 2002.
   Six short sports stories take on racism, homophobia, sexism, and parents with characters from *The Crazy Horse Electric Game, Stotan!,* and *Running Loose* in small towns in Montana and Idaho. Awards: CC. Grades: 7 and up.

Crutcher, Chris. *Ironman.*
Greenwillow, 1995.
Setting: High school, 1990s.
Main Character: Male, Bo Brewster, 17 years old.
   Bo is forced to attend anger-management classes after a series of run-ins with his English teacher/ex-football coach. The group's teacher, Mr. Nak, a Japanese American from Texas, draws Bo into participating in the class, allowing him to learn about himself and his war with his father. Bo spends most of his time outside of school training for a grueling triathlon, but his own father provides his archrival with an expensive bike, hoping Bo will lose and learn a lesson. Bo's point of view is expressed in letters he writes to Larry King. Awards: CC. Grades: 9 and up.

Deuker, Carl. *Runner.*
Houghton Mifflin, 2005.
Setting: Seattle, Washington, 2000s.
Main Character: Male, Chance Taylor, 17 years old.
   Chance's alcoholic Gulf War veteran father is fired from the first steady job he has held in years. Chance has no idea where they'll get the money to pay the mortgage fees for the run-down sailboat they call home. His only pleasure is running by himself along the Seattle waterfront. A marina office employee offers to pay him $250 a week to pick up occasional packages at a tree along his running route, Chance accepts this opportunity to pay his bills. As this new job gradually becomes more dangerous and clearly more illegal, Chance's father is able to rise above his personal problems to help his son. Fast-paced and action-packed. Grades: 7 and up.

Gallo, Don. *Ultimate Sports.*
Laurel Leaf, 1997.
   An anthology of original sports short stories with girl and boy characters from Thomas Dygard, Robert Lipsyte, Virginia Euwer Wolff, David Klass. Chris Crutcher, T. Ernesto Bethancourt, Carl Deuker, Norma Fox Mazer, Harry Mazer, Tessa Duder, and Chris Lynch on basketball, football, track, cross-country, sailing, scuba diving, boxing, wrestling, racquet ball, triathalon. Grades: 8 and up.

Hughes, Pat. *Open Ice.*
Wendy Lamb, 2005.
Setting: Connecticut.
Main Character: Male, Nick Taglio, 16 years old.
   Hockey is the framework of Nick's life. His friends are all players, his hot new girlfriend is a huge fan, and his hopes for college hang on earning an athletic scholar-

ship. After his fourth concussion, his doctor, coach, and family decide he must stop playing. His schoolwork, family relationship, and his love life falls apart. Sex, obscenities, and pot smoking. Grades: 9 and up.

Lynch, Chris. *Iceman.*
HarperTrophy, 1995.
Setting: 1990s.
Main Character: Male, Eric, 14 years old.

Eric's need for an emotional connection with his family creates a burning anger that comes out on the ice in mean hitman tactics encouraged by his father. His fanatically religious mother and slacker brother Duane are unaware of his feelings, both trying to pull him into their ways of thinking. The only peace he finds is with a recluse who works in a mortuary. Eric becomes the skilled skater, sharpshooter, and team player he always wanted to be and abandons his notion of pursing a career in mortuary science, opting instead to deal with the living. Raw language. Awards: BBYA. Grades: 8 and up.

Peck, Robert Newton. *Horse Thief.*
HarperCollins, 2002.
Setting: Chickalookee, Florida, 1938.
Main Character: Male, Tullis Yoder, 17 years old.

Tullis takes care of the horses that perform in the Big Bubb Stampede Rodeo until the day he fills in as a bull rider. His first ride ends with the loss of two fingers. Dr. Agnolia Platt repairs his hand. When the star of the show, Big Bubb, is killed in an attempt at bulldogging, the owner of the show decides to close down and sell all of the livestock. Tullis enlists the help of Doc and her jailbird father, Hitch, to steal the horses in order to save them from the slaughterhouse. Grades: 7 and up.

Powell, Randy. *Tribute to Another Dead Rock Star.*
Farrar, Straus & Giroux, 1999.
Setting: Seattle, Washington.
Main Character: Male, Grady Grennan, 15 years old.

Grady is invited to speak at a tribute to his dead rock-star mother in Seattle, staying with his father and his new family. For a tribute to his mother, a dead rock star, 15-year-old Grady returns to Seattle, where he faces his mixed feelings for his retarded younger half-brother Louie while pondering his own future. A moving and memorable story told in an alternating sarcastic and self-reflective narrative. Awards: CC. Grades: 8–11.

RUNNING/TRACK

Crutcher, Chris. *Chinese Handcuffs.*
Greenwillow, 1989.
Setting: 1980s.
Main Character: Male, Dillon Hemingway, 18 years old.

Dillon is a brilliant student and athlete. His older brother, Preston, who lost his legs in a motorcycle accident, blows his head away in front of Dillon. Dillon writes long letters to his dead brother. He tells him about Stacy, who was Preston's girl and the mother of their child but who may secretly love Dillon. He also tells about Jennifer, a star basketball player, whose father sexually abused her and whose stepfather also abuses her. Awards: CC. Grades: 9–12.

Powell, Randy. *Run If You Dare.*
Farrar, Straus & Giroux, 2006.
Setting: Seattle, Washington.
Main Character: Male, Gardner Dickinson, 14 years old.

Gardner is comfortable being laid back, never finishing anything, while his friends and his sister Lacey have long-term goals. His dad gets laid off and can't seem to motivate himself to find another job and Gardner begins to suspect that his inability to concentrate may be hereditary. Lacey agrees Gardner and his father have a problem focusing and following through. Gardner wants to to prove Lacey wrong and takes up running. He sticks with it, even when he wants to quit, while his father slips into depression. Grades: 8 and up.

Voigt, Cynthia. *Runner.*
Scholastic, 1994.
Setting: 1960s.
Main Character: Male, "Bullet" Tillerman, teenager.

Track star Bullet has to decide if he will stay on the family farm or go to war. His father drove out his older siblings and made impossible demands on Bullet. His mother no longer resisted his father's ways. When a black student joins the track team, Bullet begins to question his prejudices. Grades: 7 and up.

Wallace, Rich. *Losing is Not an Option.*
Laurel Leaf, 2005.
Setting: Pennsylvania.
Main Character: Male, Ron, 12 to 18 years old.

Nine interrelated stories follow Ron from junior high to his senior year in high school. Most of the stories revolve around Ron's involvement in sports, but also his complicated family situation and relationship with girls. The sports action is gritty and well described. Grades: 8 and up.

SOCCER

Bloor, Edward. *Tangerine.*
Harcourt, 1997.
Setting: Tangerine County, Florida.
Main Character: Male, Paul, 12 years old.

In spite of thick glasses, Paul is determined to play soccer on the school team. His father is obsessed with his older brother Erik's football career and doesn't see how dangerous Erik is, as Paul does. No one is able to face the truth about how Paul lost his vision. Awards: CC. Grades: 6–8.

Murrow, Liza Ketchum. *Twelve Days in August.*
Backinprint.com, 2004.
Setting: Vermont.

Main Character: Male, Todd O'Conner, 16 years old.

Todd's summer has been carefree with his girlfriend Kai and a year of varsity soccer to look forward to. Alex and his beautiful twin, Rita, move to their town. Todd is attracted to Rita, and Alex turns out to be a star soccer player. Another teammate, Randy, gets nervous about his own position and decides to blackball Alex and tells everyone he is a "fag." Todd and the rest of the team join in. Eventually, Todd believes Alex really is gay and avoids him. Todd then discovers a favorite uncle is gay and rethinks his prejudices. Grades: 7 and up.

Wallace, Rich. **Shots on Goal.**
Laurel Leaf, 2005.
Setting: Pennsylvania.
Main Character: Male, Bones, 15 years old.

Bones and Joey have always been close friends. They focus on soccer, hang out by the Turkey Hill convenience store, and watch girls. Suddenly things are different; it starts over a girl but quickly escalates into every part of their relationship, from soccer to their part-time jobs. The tension spreads to the rest of the team, causing problems between teammates and making the coach furious. Appealing to reluctant readers. Grades: 5–10.

SWIMMING

Crutcher, Chris. **Staying Fat for Sarah Byrnes.**
Greenwillow, 1993.
Setting: High school/Child and Adolescent Psychiatric Unit.
Main Characters: Male, Eric Calhoune; Female, Sarah Byrnes; both 17 years old.

Eric, an overweight outcast in junior high, found a friend in Sarah, her face and hands disfigured from burns in a mysterious childhood accident. Eric slims down quite a bit through competitive swimming in high school but remains devoted to Sarah. Sarah stops talking and is committed to a mental ward. Eric wants to help her, so he risks their friendship by breaking his vow of secrecy. Awards: CC. Grades: 7 and up.

Crutcher, Chris. **Stotan.**
HarperTempest, 2003.
Setting: Frost High School, Spokane, Washington.
Main Character: Male, Walker Dupree, adult.

The high school swim coach offers Stotan Week for his team. The grueling four-hour-a-day workout is a test of physical and emotional stamina. Four swimmers accept the challenge: Walker, the captain of the team; Lionel, an orphan; Nortie, who has an abusive father; and Jeff, who has a terminal illness. Through the challenge, the team finds strength together to face life and death. Awards: CC. Grades: 9 and up.

Crutcher, Chris. **Whale Talk.**
Greenwillow, 2001.
Setting: Cutter High School.
Main Character: Male, T. J. Jones, 17 years old.

Multiracial and adopted, T.J. is a natural athlete but steers away from organized sports. During his senior year, his favorite teacher, Mr. Simet, convinces him to form a school swim team. By choosing the school outcasts for his team, the Cutter All Night Mermen, T.J. gets revenge on the jock establishment. His team's dedication to swimming and each other helps them overcome many obstacles. Awards: CC; BBYA. Grades: 8–12.

RESOURCES: ADDITIONAL TITLES

Crowe, Chris. 2003. *More Than a Game: Sports Literature for Young Adults.* Lanham, MD: Scarecrow Press.

REFERENCES

Amazon. Available: www.amazon.com. Available: March 2006.

American Library Association. "Banned Books Week." Available: www.ala.org/bbooks. November 2005.

American Library Association. "Best Books for Young Adults." Available: www.ala.org/yalsa/booklists/bbya. March 2006.

American Library Association. "The Michael L. Printz Award for Excellence in Young Adult Literature." Available: www.ala.org/yalsa/printz. March 2006.

American Library Association. "Popular Paperbacks." Available: www.ala.org/yalsa/booklists/poppaper. March 2006.

American Library Association. "Welcome to the Newbery Medal Home Page!" Available: www.ala.org/alsc/newbery.html. March 2006.

Benedetti, Angelina. 2001. "Leading the Horse to Water: Keeping Young People Reading in the Information Age." In: *The Reader's Advisor's Companion* Englewood, Colo.: Libraries Unlimited.

Bodart, Joni Richards. 2002. *Radical Reads: 101 YA Novels on the Edge.* Lanham, Md.: Scarecrow Press.

Booth, Heather. "RA for YA: Tailoring the Readers Advisory Interview to the Needs of Young Adult Patrons." *Public Libraries* 1/1/2005, vol. 44 no. 1, pg. 33.

Chelton, Mary K., and David G. Hartwell. "Readers' Advising of the Young SF, Fantasy, and Horror Reader." *Reference & Users Services Quarterly* 1/1/2002, vol. 42, no. 2, pg. 133.

Chelton, Mary K. "Readers Advisory 101." *Library Journal* 11/1/03, pp. 38–39.

Donelson, L. Kenneth, and Alleen Pace Nilsen. 2003. *Literature for Today's Young Adults,* seventh edition. Boston: Pearson Education.

George, Jane, Michelle McGraw, and Sarah Nagle. "Readers Advisory Training in the North Star State." *Public Libraries* 1/1/2005. vol. 44, no. 1. p. 29.

Hastings, Dr. Wally. "Young Adult Literature." Available: www.northern.edu/hastingw/YAintro.html. Accessed: November 2005.

Herald, Diana Tixier. 1997. *Teen Genreflecting.* Englewood, Colo.: Libraries Unlimited.

Herald, Diana Tixier. 2005. *Teen Genreflecting: A Guide to Reading Interests,* second edition. Englewood, Colo.: Libraries Unlimited.

Hoffert, Barbara. "Taking Back Readers' Advisory." *Library Journal* 9/1/2003, vol. 128, issue 14.

Jones, Patrick, Michele Gorman, and Tricia Suellentrop. 2004. *Connecting Young Adults and Libraries,* third edition. New York: Neal-Schuman.

Jones, Patrick. 2002. *New Directions for Library Services to Young Adults.* Chicago: American Library Association.

Jones, Patrick, Patricia Taylor, and Kirsten Edwards. 2004. *Core Collection for Young Adults.* New York: Neal-Schuman.

Libretto, Ellen V., and Catherine Barr. 2002. *High/Low Handbook,* fourth edition. Westport, Conn: Libraries Unlimited.

McCook, Kathleen de La Pena, and Gary O. Rolstad. 1993. *Developing Reader's Advisory Services: Concepts and Commitments.* New York: Neal-Schuman.

Nilsen, Alleen Pace, and Kenneth L. Donelson. *Literature for Today's Young Adults.* New York: Longman.

Nottingham, Janet. "Doing It Right: A Reader's Advisory Program." *Reference & Users Services Quarterly* 7/1/2002, vol. 41, no. 4, p. 335.

Outlaw, Keddy Ann. "Self-Service Readers Advisory." *Public Libraries* 1/1/2005, p. 9.

Picker, Lauren. "Girls' Night Out Gets Smart." *Newsweek* 3/21/2005, p. 54.

Reilly, Rob, "Building an Online Reader's Advisory and Getting Good Reads." *Multimedia Schools,* 9/2003, vol. 10, issue 4.

Ross, Catherine Sheldrick, and Mary K. Chelton. "Reader's Advisory: Matching Mood and Material." *Library Journal,* 2/1/2001, vol. 126, issue 2.

Saricks, Joyce G., and Nancy Brown. 1997. *Readers Advisory Service in the Public Library,* second edition. Chicago: American Library Association.

Scarecrow Press. VOYA. Available: www.VOYA.com. Accessed: March 2006.

Shearer, Kenneth D., and Robert Burgin, eds. 2001. T*he Readers' Advisor's Companion.* Englewood, Colo.: Libraries Unlimited.

Smith, Duncan. "Talking with Readers: A Competency Based Approach to Readers' Advisory Service." *Reference & Users Service Quarterly* 1/1/2000, vol. 40, no. 2, p. 135.

Walter, Virginia A., and Elaine Meyers. 2003. *Teens & Libraries: Getting It Right.* Chicago, Ill.: American Library Association.

YALSA-BK electronic discussion list. Available: www.ala.org/ala/yalsa/electronicresourcesb/websitesmailing.htm

AUTHOR INDEX

N

TITLE INDEX

(Note: Non-italicized entries are series titles.)

D

F

I

P

X

Y

Z

ABOUT THE AUTHOR

RoseMary Honnold is the Young Adult Services Coordinator at the Coshocton Public Library in Coshocton, Ohio.

In addition to being an amateur painter, Honnold finds that reading, writing, programming, presenting workshops, and working full-time keeps her busy, while her grandchildren, Caleb, Evelyn, and Wesley, keep her priorities in order.

She is the author of *Serving Seniors: A How-To-Do-It Manual for Librarians, 101+ Teen Programs that Work,* and *More Teen Programs that Work. The Teen Reader's Advisor* is her fourth book.